MONGOLIA

• Tun-huang

MANCHURIA

Peking
(Peiching)

GREAT WALL

Tientsin

NORTH KOREA

Sea
of
Japan

HOKKAIDO

HONSAU

Tokyo

Yokohama

SOUTH
KOREA

Izumo

Seoul

Nara

Ise

Kyoto

SHIKOKU

JAPAN

Yellow
Sea

Huang Ho
(Yellow river)

T'ung Kuan

Loyang

Hankow
(Hank'ou)

Nanking

Shanghai

CHINA

Ch'ang
Chiang
(Yangtze)

KYUSHU

Taipeh
(T'aipei)

TAIWAN

Hsun Chiang

Canton

NATIONALIST
CHINA

PACIFIC OCEAN

NORTH
VIET NAM

Hanoi

Hongkong

Haiphong

HAI-NAN

LUZON

PHILIPPINES

LAOS

Mekong

THAILAND
(SIAM)

Bangkok

SOUTH
VIET NAM

Angkor
Vat

CAMBODIA

Saigon

Gulf of
Siam

IRRAWADDY River

BURMA

ngoon

South China Sea

Philippine
Sea

MINDINAO

BRUNEI

N. BORNEO

SARAWAK

MALAYA

SUMATRA

Singapore

BORNEO

Jakarta
(Djakarta)

INDONESIA

Bandung

Borobodur

JAVA

TIMOR

Harvin

Paths of Faith

Paths of Faith

Fourth Edition

John A. Hutchison

McGraw-Hill, Inc.
New York   St. Louis   San Francisco   Auckland   Bogotá
Caracas   Hamburg   Lisbon   London   Madrid   Mexico   Milan
Montreal   New Delhi   Paris   San Juan   São Paulo   Singapore
Sydney   Tokyo   Toronto

This book was set in Garamond by the College Composition Unit
in cooperation with Monotype Composition Company.
The editors were Cynthia Ward and David Dunham;
the designer was Amy Becker; the cover illustrator was Marc Yankus;
the production supervisor was Janelle S. Travers.
R. R. Donnelley & Sons Company was printer and binder.

Paths of Faith

1 2 3 4 5 6 7 8 9 0 DOC DOC 9 5 4 3 2 1 0

ISBN 0-07-031543-4

Library of Congress Cataloging-in-Publication Data

Hutchison, John Alexander, (date).
    Paths of faith / John A. Hutchison.—4th ed.
        p.   cm.
    Includes bibliographical references.
    ISBN 0-07-031543-4
        1. Religions.   2. Religion, Primitive.   I. Title.
BL80.2.H78   1991
291—dc20   90-35525

About the Author

John A. Hutchison is Danforth Professor of Philosophy of Religion, Emeritus, at the Claremont Graduate School. He was educated at Lafayette College, Union Theological Seminary (New York), and Columbia University. He holds a Ph.D. from Columbia and has taught at the College of Wooster, Williams College, Columbia University, and the Claremont Colleges.

Among his publications are *Faith, Reason, and Existence, Language and Faith,* and *The Two Cities*. He is a member of Phi Beta Kappa, the American Academy of Religion, the American Philosophical Association, and other professional societies.

Contents

16   *The Reformation and Protestantism*   *512*

17   *Modern Criticism of Religion*   *545*

18   *Traditional Faiths and the Human Future*   *573*

Letter to the Reader

Any book is quite literally an essay in communication between author and reader, and this fourth edition of *Paths of Faith* is no exception. Why a new edition? This question has been before me as I have worked on the book before you.

Originally I sought to write a book that would be a reliable and adequate guide for the general reader and beginning student of the world's religions. This is still my basic objective. Since 1969, when the first edition appeared, I have continued to study and teach in this field, correcting errors, filling in gaps in my knowledge, seeking more adequate formulations of this wide and varied subject matter. I remain grateful to the many colleagues and students who have helped me in this never-ending quest.

As to specific changes in the new edition, Chapter 2 now has a needed section on ancient Egyptian religion. I have substantially reworked the "Issues and Questions" sections at the end of each chapter, since many readers have found them useful aids to discussion and reflection. I have also continued to pursue fair-minded exposition by combing out misleading expressions and errors of fact. I wish here specifically to thank the critics who have assisted me in this process, and to invite all the readers of this fourth edition to join in the corporate process of critical study and reasonable evaluation of humanity's faiths and philosophies.

I wish especially to call the reader's attention to the Glossary which begins on page 596. Some readers did not know that it existed; others have said it is a useful tool.

Fundamentally, history of religions is a variety of the species history. I have sought to write adequate and accurate history. However, it is necessary to add immediately that there is no such thing as uninterpreted history. The ideal of naked fact altogether divested of interpretative context is a will-o'-the-wisp. To the contrary, fact and interpretation are inseparable aspects of all historical study, but they are distinguishable elements within the total inquiry. I have sought to keep this distinction clearly before myself and my readers; and I hope that they will be able to read my pages with a view toward forming their own reasoned interpretations.

Courses in the history of religions are so well established in American universities and colleges that they need no special advocacy here. Yet the textbooks for such courses suffer from a number of defects. Perhaps the commonest fault is the gap—which has increased in recent decades—between textbooks on the one hand, and on the other hand ongoing scholarship in this field. My effort has been to put the beginning student in touch with contemporary scholarly study and research.

Another defect in textbooks on religions of the world, though by no means limited to this subject matter, is special pleading for a particular viewpoint. I can only say that in the pages that follow I have earnestly pursued fair-minded and critical exposition of all the faiths studied. What is even more important, my own deepest commitment here is not to my own conclusions, but rather to the whole ongoing process of study. This implies once more an open invitation to every reader to join the cooperative process of inquiry, making contributions and criticizing and correcting the mistakes of other contributors.

Paths of Faith is based on the assumption that the religions of humanity represent a form of experience sufficiently important and pervasive to warrant their study as a part of any education which claims the name *liberal*. Along with politics, art, economics, and science, religion is a basic and recurring aspect of human life. In every human culture of which reliable knowledge exists, there is evidence of religious behavior of some sort. Hence it follows that its study makes a claim on humane or liberal education.

Incidentally, this approach to religion as a pervasive aspect of human experience seems to me a good starting point for study in an age when religious opinion is divided among believers, nonbelievers, and also the many equally honest and thoughtful people who cannot place themselves in either of the first two camps. Whatever else and whatever more religion may, or may not be, it is a pervasive and recurring form of human experience. Let critical inquiry begin at this point.

It is a fact of some importance that ours is an age of unprecedented religious illiteracy. This is particularly true of the American academic community. While religion, along with sex and politics, continues as a perennial subject for discussion, it is also true that in such discussion a shocking lack of ordinary factual knowledge is often shown. People who would feel disgraced to be ignorant of science, art, or politics show no compunction about harboring the grossest and crudest misconceptions in the field of religion. This book is written as a modest contribution toward combating this contemporary religious illiteracy. Let rebels continue to rebel, but let them at least know what they are rebelling against. Let believers continue to believe, but let them at least give critical attention to what they believe. Both groups owe it to themselves to be acquainted with the range and variety of humanity's religious attitudes, practices, and beliefs.

Obviously, these are ambitious goals. Taken as a whole they constitute a large order for any book to fill; and readers will have to make their own judgment as to whether I have even come close. Yet I must add that to have attempted less would have been to concede failure before the task began.

Adequately understood, the title *Paths of Faith* expresses the main emphases of my approach to the subject matter. The word *path* (or any of its numerous translations) is a recurring metaphor in the literature of the world's religions. China has its *tao*; the Japanese have the analogous term *michi.* Buddhists speak of their faith as the *path of the Buddha,* and Muslims characterize Islam as the *straight path.* In both the Old Testament and the New Testament, this same metaphor is used extensively. According to the New Testament Book of Acts, Christians called themselves the *people of the way.* Thus people have envisaged their religions as paths through the mortal woods.

As it is used in my title, I have understood *path* to mean a cluster of life values which provides persons and cultures with a convincing and illuminating answer to the fundamental human question: "Why live?" These values are expressed symbolically in each of the world's faiths. Each distinct cluster of such values and symbols constitutes a path to be walked. People set their feet on it and make their way toward a destination. In effect, their path defines their journey of life. Such I believe to be the historic function of the world's faiths. The religions of humanity are so many paths of life.

What is the meaning of the word *faith* as used in the title? A half century ago, Paul Tillich coined the phrase *ultimate concern* as a definition of faith. Understood as Tillich expounded and qualified it, the definition is, I believe, still valid, useful, and sufficiently general for our purposes. By the word *concern* Tillich sought to designate the active or volitional area of human experience. Interests, loyalties, allegiances, and values have all been proposed as synonyms. However characterized, this region of human experience provides the human raw material from which all religions are made.

My own preference is for the term *value* because it establishes a connection—validly, as it seems to me—with the current interest in values among social scientists and also with the philosophic discipline known as *value theory,* or *axiology.* Faith or religious experience is, accordingly, experience of ultimate valuation.

Faith defined or interpreted as ultimate concern or valuation still remains ambiguous. It will clarify our usage of the word to point out three facets of meaning. (1) Faith in its most general and basic sense is experience of ultimate concern or valuation as just defined. As such, it is a general religious phenomenon, embracing all the world's religions. Indeed, it may be argued that this experience is universal. Not only all religions but all human beings experience faith in this sense of the word. They do so, it may be added, whether they are conscious of the experience or not. (2) People seek to express faith in the first sense through the expressive-directive symbols of some historic community—Christian, Buddhist, Marxist, or other. Hence in the second sense we speak of *Buddhist faith, Christian faith,* or even of *Marxist faith.* In this second sense, *faith* is a label designating a distinctive way of expressing faith in the first and most general sense. (3) The word *faith* is used in still a third sense as a set of statements or propositions which endeavor to set forth the content of the first two meanings of the term. The third meaning might be characterized as propositional faith, or "belief." Its function is to analyze or explore the meaning of the experience. However, this analysis often takes place amid divided and conflicting views, with attack of one position and defense of another. As a consequence, some communities of faith demand of their adherents an unquestioning acceptance of a particular set of such propositions, thus fastening upon faith the meaning of unreasoning belief, beyond or against reason or evidence.

The word *paths* also points to the irreducible plurality of faiths in the world. Some of these faiths show large and impressive similarities with one another. Yet invariably there are differences as well. In the apparently irreducible plurality of faiths, each faith is addressed "to whom it may concern." This also implies that the student of religion must normally expect to find adherents of the various religions in a state of ultimate concern, directed to different, and often mutually incompatible objects. Such objects range from Yahweh to brahman, heaven, nirvana, the "one," and many, many more. Yet whatever the particular understanding of the religious object, the concern is ultimate. That is to say, people really believe their faiths, rather than live in that state of mingled accommodation, questioning, and sentimentality which often characterizes the modern liberal attitude toward the historic faiths.

Considering the title *Paths of Faith,* perhaps the reader has already asked "Why *faith,* rather than *religion*?" This issue will be before us recurrently throughout our study. Here it must suffice to observe that virtually every one of the faiths discussed denies for one reason or another that it is a religion. In contemporary Western study, many theologians and historians of religion join in questioning or rejecting the term *religion* as radically distorting the forms of experience that it seeks to communicate. Yet problematic as it is, I do not think we can entirely dispense with it. Therefore I have sought in Chapter 1 to give it careful and guarded definition.

Still further caution is necessary concerning the term *religion.* If it is to be used at all, it must be used descriptively and not with either affirmative or negative valuation. Many readers will approach this book either "for religion" or "against religion." Both parties must be prepared for discussion which seeks to explore what the phenomenon is, apart from these affections and disaffections. In the popular culture of America today, it is fashionable to be "for" religion, whatever that may mean. In the academic subculture of contemporary America, it is almost as fashionable to be "against" religion, whatever that may mean. For the present task of critical understanding, few popular issues have muddied the waters of discussion more than these. Such attitudes place urgent items on the agenda of study.

The faiths described in my book may be characterized as adventures of the human spirit, or more specifically as explorations of the humanity of human beings. Like all processes of exploration they involve risk and experiment. Sometimes experiments end in negative results, explorations come to a dead end, and adventures end in disaster. The reader must be prepared to see such results in humanity's religious history. Yet the history of human faiths shows great fulfillments as well. There have been, and still are, great paths through the woods of human existence, leading to great fulfillments or, as the religions often say, to salvation. Whatever the readers' views of the humanization and dehumanization of our life—which is to say, of those lifelong and agelong processes which make for the essential humanness of our kind, and those opposite processes which threaten or deny this humanness—they find much to learn concerning both from the paths of faith described in this book.

Yet there is another possible interpretation for our subject matter, more frankly religious than the humanism of the preceding paragraph. We have already mentioned some of the many symbols for the religious object, or object of ultimate concern—Yahweh, brahman, heaven, the "one," and even humanity. In their respective ways they symbolize the transcendent—namely that which is in some way beyond the common world of nature and society and which demands of us human beings our responsive service, in return for which it promises us well-being or fulfillment.

From our human side of this divine-human transaction, it is an observable fact that human nature seeks inexorably to serve something bigger and better than ourselves. In Milton's *Paradise Lost* it was Satan who boasted, "I will not serve," and ended in most abject service. For the rest of us, the issue is not *whether* to serve, but *what* or *whom* to serve, what the terms and quality of our service will be, and also the status in existence of the object of our service.

All the symbolic objects of the world's faiths come to us claiming validity or truth. To be sure, not all these claims can be true, for some disagree radically with each other; and it is at least logically possible that all may be false or invalid. In any case, no subject on the contemporary study of religion is more important—and more truly interesting—than the critical appraisal of these claims to truth. We shall return to these issues in the last chapter, Chapter 18. Meanwhile let the reader work at their formulation as our study proceeds, so that his or her conclusions can emerge at the end of the study.

I especially wish to thank critical readers of the manuscript: David Johnson, Indiana State University; Ted Solomon, Iowa State University; Bradley Starr, California State University, Fullerton; and Wesley Vesey, Mt. Union College. All have helped to produce a better book. For the remaining defects I accept sole responsibility.

I also wish to make personal acknowledgment to a great many people who have rendered valuable help in the writing of this book: to David Polk, who composed the glossary for the first edition; to my wife, who labored long over the text and endured the author's long preoccupation; to many secretaries, who deciphered my handwriting and produced a readable manuscript; and to students past and present, whose questions and discussions have stimulated and clarified my study of the world's faiths.

JOHN A. HUTCHISON

Paths of Faith

1

On Being Students of Religion

HUMANKIND: THE RELIGIOUS ANIMAL

Humankind is the religious animal, or in other words religious experience of some sort is both common and peculiar to the human species. Attempts to show religious behavior in some animal species have collapsed, and it is now generally conceded that only the human species exhibits religious behavior. Further, within humankind all cultures or societies of which reliable knowledge exists show some kind of religious behavior. To be sure, these kinds or forms often differ vastly from the familiar forms of our society. Also, in some societies such as the modern West, there are individuals who in varying degrees question or reject these forms. Yet for the overwhelming majority of human beings in history, religious experience of some sort has been a common and fundamental fact of life. The human being is, once more, *homo religiosus*, the religious animal. At least this has been true throughout the past and present; what the future may hold remains to be seen. This assertion is made as a factual statement; whether religion is good or evil, valid or invalid, awaits our critical study and appraisal.

Granting this conclusion, it is a promising clue to seek the source of religious experience in those features of the human situation which are unique to this species. This suggestion goes counter to the thought of much modern social science, which has placed emphasis on the continuities of humankind with other forms of life, and indeed with inorganic nature. Is not humanity only a single twig on the great tree of life? Is not the human body made of the same matter and subject to the same laws as inorganic nature? Surely, one must understand and accept the full force of these continuities before legitimately proceeding to consider any unique or distinctive features of the human species.

Yet that there are unique features of *Homo sapiens* is undeniable. For example, simple tools are present in some animal species, but tools are elaborated with an utterly new complexity in human technology. Hence humanity is *Homo faber*, the maker. Again, animals signal to each other in many ways, yet only in the human species is there evidence that signals are formally organized

1

in syntax and grammar. Thus animal signals are transformed into human language. As Ernst Cassirer has persuasively argued, humanity is *animal symbolicum*.[1]* Still again, learning and training are important features of life for many animal species, yet between animal training and human education there is a difference of kind as well as degree. The former develops new means or instrumentalities, while the latter is concerned with ends or goals of life as well as means. To cite just one more unique trait among the very many possibilities, human beings alone among living species appear to be aware of their own death and to face it as a conscious problem. From this awareness spring such diverse forms of human behavior as funerary customs and the erection of monuments to oneself or others. Thus, too, while almost unknown to other species, suicide is a human problem of very considerable magnitude.

All these and doubtless many more differences between humanity and our nearest animal relatives may be seen to be rooted in a single fact, namely, a new quality of human consciousness. Human beings share with many animal species awareness of objects. However, in humankind alone awareness is turned not only outward upon the objective environment but inward upon the self. Indeed, it is precisely when awareness is turned inward that the human self is born. In the words of G. H. Mead, the self may be defined as that form of reality which can be an object to itself.[2]

This reflexive turn of consciousness in human beings generates self-consciousness, and with it also self-transcendence (from the Latin *transscendere*, "to go beyond"). By self-transcendence is thus meant the capacity of the human self forever to push beyond itself. This new power of the imagination creates what may be termed an *Archimedean point* above or beyond human experience (the ancient Greek scientist Archimedes said, with reference to the lever, "Give me where to stand, and I will move the earth"). The concept of transcendence will be of basic importance throughout our study of the world's religions. All religions possess symbolic forms for transcendence and either explicitly or implicitly make claims for the validity of these forms.

The reader who wishes to verify this new emergent form of human awareness can perform a simple experiment. In imagination, stand clear of yourself and look at yourself. Then stand clear of this new viewpoint. A moment's reflection will suffice to show that you can continue this inward journey indefinitely. This is what is meant by self-transcendence.

Yet it must immediately be added that human beings who exhibit this Archimedean point beyond the self and the world are also creatures of nature, subject to the same physical and biological laws and necessities as their humblest animal relatives. The unique aspect of human experience is then precisely the structure of combined freedom and necessity or dependence. Indeed some philosophers and theologians have defined human beings as "structures of dependent freedom" or "freedom and finitude."[3]

---

*This note and the others which follow throughout the book will be found at the end of each chapter.

Two representations of self-transcendence. At left, the closed eyes of the Buddha symbolize inwardness; the dot, circle, or "divine eye" is a sign of spiritual insight. At right, the open eye simultaneously represents the human eye and the eye of God, symbolizing their union. (Left, Amida Buddha, The Metropolitan Museum of Art, Rogers Fund; right, René Magritte, *The False Mirror,* 1928. Oil on canvas, 21¼ x 31⅞. Collection, The Museum of Modern Art, New York, Purchase.)

Whatever one's precise formulation, it is this configuration which generates the perennial religious questions: "Who am I?" "Why am I alive?" "Whence?" "Whither?" In the pages which follow, religion will be interpreted as the functioning answer which people give to these and similar questions. As we shall soon see, such answers are normally given in symbolic form.

At the emergent human level, life becomes open and free; the guidance or determination by physical and biological laws, causes, and needs, while still necessary elements in experience, are no longer sufficient for either the explanation or guidance of human life. Rather, a conscious relation to the wider human world, including the world of ideal possibilities, becomes a fundamental "need"—the religious need—of humankind. It is precisely the function of what the next section will call *ultimate values* to meet this unique and pervasive human need. These values or value systems provide for persons and cultures an answer to the question: "Why live?" Religious experience may thus be characterized as life valuation, or life orientation.

This function of total life valuation has been expressed metaphorically as the activity of plotting and then walking a "path of life." Charles Morris's book entitled *Paths of Life*[4] is devoted to the interpretation of the world's religions as alternative ways of life or different systems of life orientation or life valuation. Each of these paths is expressed in symbols which are distinctively its own. Conversely, it is this function of life orientation which imparts religious significance to a symbol or a symbol system. *Hence a religion may appropriately be defined as a holy or sacred symbol system.*

The great religions are often spoken of as paths or ways of life. For example, the New Testament Christians spoke of themselves as people of *the way* before the label *Christian* was used. Buddhists speak of the *path of the Buddha.* In Chinese, the word *tao* means "way," "path," or "street" in a literal as well as a metaphorical sense. The Japanese word is *michi*. Muslims speak of their religion as the *straight path*. The title of this book expresses a basic feature of the world's religions: they are truly *paths of faith*.

In a notable recent essay, Robert Bellah has sought to carry the concept of human freedom through the history of the world's religions, finding increasing degrees and understandings of freedom in different ages of religious history.[5] The religions of prehistoric and folk societies show a relation of human beings to nature different from the relation of animal species to nature. The high gods of the ancient world show a new degree of freedom or transcendence. The modern world shows still a further degree of freedom. As we shall see in the course of our study, each of the many faiths of humanity involves its own degree and its own distinctive interpretation of human freedom.

TOWARD A WORKING DEFINITION OF RELIGION

The study of the world's religions may be likened to a journey into new and strange lands. As we begin this journey, let us pause briefly to consider its nature and meaning, our equipment and means of travel, and the kinds of response we can expect to the varied scenes before us. In other words, what does it mean to be students of religion in the twentieth century? What is the relation between the viewpoint of the critical observer or student, on the one hand, and that of the religious participant, on the other? Even more fundamentally, what is religion? How shall we define our subject matter?

Formal definitions of religion are as numerous, as various, and often as mutually conflicting as there are students of religion. Often such definitions illustrate the oriental parable of the blind men describing the elephant, each taking hold of a part of the beast and defining the whole in terms of this part. Like the elephant, religion is a large and complex phenomenon. In this connection, some historians of religion question or reject the word *religion* as a distortion of the form of experience which it seeks to communicate. Several of the world's major languages lack any word which can adequately be translated as "religion." The common noun *religion* imputes a unity or homogeneity of experience that many observers believe does not exist. In a notable discussion, *The Meaning and End of Religion*, Wilfred Cantwell Smith recommends the abolition of the term *religion* and a substitution of *the faith of individual persons*, which is then expressed in those concrete traditions or communities of faith which others call the *religions of mankind*.[6] Critical readers of Smith have pointed out that *faith* is as ambiguous a term as *religion*.

Acknowledging the force of these and other difficulties with the word *religion*, it still appears impossible to dispense with it completely. At least, it is necessary as a provisional term to get the process of study under way. Then, at appropriate stages, qualifications will be introduced to guard against some of its misleading implications. Such at least will be the procedure of this book.

It is convenient at this point to begin not with the noun or substantive *religion*, but with the adjective *religious*, as in *religious experience*, which Paul Tillich characterized in a memorable but highly controversial phrase as *ultimate concern*.[7] Tillich chose *concern* as a neutral and descriptive word to designate the affective or motivational aspect of human experience.

Concerns are what move people to action. R. B. Perry has used the more colorless term *interest* for this same aspect of experience.[8] Other writers employ various terms, such as *values, allegiances*, and *loyalties*.

The preference of the author of this book is for *value*. Hence *religious experience* is definable as experience of *ultimate valuation*. There are important distinctions among these words; yet whatever terms and interpretation the reader may choose, the crucial assertion is that this area of human experience provides the raw material out of which religions are constituted. Religious experience and religions are made of—are constituted by—human interest or value. Keep this assertion in mind as you make your way through the world's faiths, testing it on the factual data there to be encountered.

What is the meaning of the adjective *ultimate* in the phrase *ultimate concern*? Tillich suggested *unconditional, absolute*, and *unqualified* as synonyms.[9] It is well to note that these are adjectives modifying *concern*. In other words, the primary meaning of the terms *ultimate* or *absolute* is a quality of human experience rather than an object or a substantive reality. The latter meaning, if it is to be affirmed at all, must be approached through the former.

The structure of interests, concerns, or values which constitutes a human self shows many levels or strata. The idea of ultimate concern or ultimate value implies that if we dig deep enough we will come upon an underlying value or interest which constitutes the final ground of validation or justification for a person's whole life, giving meaning and orientation to all other interests, providing a functioning answer to the question: "Why am I living?" Of experiences of this kind, religions are made. Such at least is the thesis or hypothesis of this book.

CHARACTERISTICS OF ULTIMATE VALUATION

PRIMACY

Ultimate concerns or values possess several identifying characteristics. The first is that an ultimate concern has priority in the system of concerns which constitutes a personality or a culture. From this it follows that an ultimate concern has the function of giving meaning, purpose, and direction to human life. An ultimate concern is one to which in a crisis a person willingly sacrifices every other value, including life itself. Historically it may be observed that such concerns or values tend to take on religious significance, whether officially labeled *religious* or not. For example, one thinks of family loyalty or of patriotism as values which tend to take on such religious quality—sometimes implicitly, but sometimes explicitly, as patriotism in Shintoism or family allegiance in Confucianism.

Again, an ultimate value is not derived from or dependent upon other values. Rather it is the case that from it, a person derives other values. Hence etymologically it is more accurate to speak of *primary* than of *ultimate* values. To employ a mathematical metaphor, a primary value, or an ultimate concern, provides the coordinate system or frame of reference for all other values.

Questions of many sorts are raised by this approach to religion as ultimate valuation. Are there in fact such values? Is it not rather the case that human beings devote themselves at one moment to one concern, at the next moment to another? Accordingly, is not the relation between the different values of a person or a culture simply one of mutual accommodation rather than hierarchical organization under a single supreme value? Is not the problem of human value simply the juggler's problem of keeping several balls in the air without dropping any of them?

The answers to these critical questions must, of course, be factual answers—that is to say, conclusions based on the actual, detailed observation of human personality and culture. At this point in our study, let us take ultimate value as an initial hypothesis to be tested on the facts. Meanwhile it may be observed that the state of commitment to many values or value systems is strikingly similar to the religious phenomenon of polytheism. One writer has even proposed the hypothesis of "momentary gods."[10] Yet against a purely polytheistic faith or value system it may fairly be urged that human personality needs some functioning unity or integration if it is to continue at all. Such a unity, like the hub of a wheel which holds the spokes together, is provided by what we have here termed an *ultimate concern* or *value*.

Ultimate or religious concerns are thus unifying concerns for both persons and cultures. Perhaps too it may be observed that the fact which is decisive against a pure polytheism of values is the kind of human situation which demands unconditional decision and allegiance. Such all-or-nothing decisions, where one's whole life and life's meaning are at stake, presuppose unity. Such, for example, is the decision for or against a totalitarian political system, or for or against human freedom. In these situations one chooses or decides, as the Bible suggests, with *all* one's heart, soul, mind, and strength.[11]

Another suggestion for understanding the religious aspect of human experience is to imagine a straight line along which are placed a person's concerns or values. At one end are placed immediate or momentary concerns, or those which have in the literal or etymological sense a superficial quality. At the other end are ultimate concerns or values. As one moves along this line from the superficial to the serious concerns, one observes the increasing emergence of religious quality. Also, if the latter end of the line represents what has been called *ultimate concern*, then one may perhaps call the interests near this end *penultimate*, or possessing an "almost religious" quality.[12]

PERVASIVENESS

A second trait of ultimate values, as the term is used here, is that such interests or values are spread over the totality of experience. Some interests or values are limited to a part of experience, while others claim dominance over all human existence. The most obvious illustration is the contrast between political allegiance as construed by free and by totalitarian societies. In the former case, political concern is one partial human interest among others. Exactly the opposite is the case in totalitarianism, as indicated by this word itself. Members of the Communist party, for example, agree to guide *all* their activities by the directives of the party. It is precisely the unlimited, unrestricted, or total quality suggested by *all* which gives to communism and to other forms of totalitarianism their often-observed but little-understood religious character. Religious concerns are by nature total, all-embracing concerns, demanding not less than all that we have and are.

HOLINESS

A third observable feature of ultimate concerns is their emotive or affective accompaniment: namely, the holy. Like *religion*, the terms *holy* and *sacred* are commonly used with many and varying meanings. Here it is convenient to begin with Rudolph Otto's approach to the holy as a unique emotion.[13] By analogy with the Latin derivatives *omen* and *ominous*, Otto coined the adjective *numinous*, from the Latin noun *numen*, meaning "divinity," "god," or "spirit."

For Otto the holy is a unique affection, for the good reason that it is the human response to transcendence, or in theistic terms, to God. He assumes both the object and the response to be unique. Like any unique entity, Otto's holy is, logically speaking, indefinable. Nevertheless, it is possible to point to any unique object and say that it is *like* this or that other object of experience. In this way, Otto says that the experience of the holy is like the experience of fear, wonder, awe, or mystery. As the study of this book unfolds, readers will be able to see for themselves how infinitely various are the forms of the holy. In this variety, perhaps the highest expression of the holy is the quality of reverence. Chapter 2 will return to the holy and consider some of its concrete manifestations.

Here the most significant way of pointing to the holy is to indicate its relation to ultimate concern or valuation. The holy is the affective accompaniment of ultimate concern and commitment. Wherever people commit themselves unconditionally, there this accompanying affection emerges in their lives. Conversely, wherever we come upon this emotion, we have reason to believe that ultimate concern is occurring. Some writers distinguish between the sacred and the holy, asserting that the holy is an emotive response and the sacred a volitional or valuational response.[14] In this usage of terms, *sacred values* may be characterized as ultimate values plus their unique affective quality of holiness. Such, at least, is the hypothesis of this book.

This relation between ultimate concern and holiness is extremely useful to students of religion. It may be likened to the relation between atmospheric temperature and the height of the mercury column in a thermometer, in that the presence or absence of the holy in human experience is an accurate indicator of ultimate or religious concern. If this emotion is absent, the student may assume that living religious experience is absent. Wherever it does occur, even in response to such officially nonreligious symbols as a nation's flag, ultimate or religious concern may be presumed to be present.

The holy designates not only the source but also the common feature of humankind's diverse faiths. This latter fact provides a decisive clue for definition. Among well-nigh innumerable definitions of religion, perhaps the least inadequate and least misleading is in terms of human experiences which exhibit the quality of the holy. *A religion may thus be defined as an existent system of holy forms.* These forms are patterns or structures of human attitudes, beliefs, or practices; they are organized, structured ways of thinking, feeling, or doing. Sometimes they are individual forms of experience; sometimes they are social. Most often they are a mixture of both. In the wide world, and in the long course of history, these systems or structures of holy forms have exhibited enormous variety. Yet their common and defining feature is their embodiment of the holy. Systems which exhibit this quality are religions, while systems which lack this feature are thereby rendered nonreligious in character. The reader will note that this definition does not commit us either negatively or affirmatively concerning the truth or validity of religion generally or of any particular religion.

SYMBOLIC EXPRESSION

A fourth feature of religious experience has to do with its expression and communication. Here a distinction must be made between the participant and the observer, or between the religious adherent and the student of religion. While it is legitimate for the student or observer to speak of *religious experience*, or *ultimate concern*, this is seldom the language of the participant or adherent. People rarely say, "Let us have a religious experience," or "Let us be ultimately concerned." Rather, religious experience takes place in a context of powerful symbolic objects and words. These objects elicit the participants' religious responses. How natural, then, for them to assume that the holy or sacred actually dwells in these symbolic objects, for it is these objects which mediate their experience of the holy. Conversely, it is the function of eliciting ultimate concern which constitutes these objects as symbols. It is precisely at this point of symbolic expression that the adjective *religious* becomes the noun *religion*.

In the history of religions, how infinitely various are these symbolic objects or forms! No object or event is too bizarre or too commonplace to have been treated somewhere, sometime, as a holy symbol. Rocks, trees, mountains, rivers, caves, and territories—these are only a few of the holy symbols of the world's religions. Similarly, commonplace actions like eating, drinking, and dancing (and doing nothing)—as well as particular persons, groups, seasons, and times—have all served as symbolic vehicles of holiness or ultimate valuation for some individual or community.

The distinctive function of these religious symbols and symbol systems is, once again, to provide individuals and groups with convincing answers to the questions "Why live?" and "How live?"—or, in other words, to enable them to plot their path of life.

CULT AND CULTURE

A fifth trait of religious experience is its double aspect both as *celebrated* and as *lived*. On the one hand, ultimate concern may be *said* or celebrated in ritual and myth; on the other hand, it may also be *lived out*. The latter aspect sets important problems for the whole structure of both personality and culture. In respect to personality, ultimate concern means those convictions which give unity and meaning to a person's life. Such presumably is the basic function of religion in individual life. In respect to culture, ultimate concern signifies the convictions which create and sustain the life of a culture and which also make it a shared life or community. So it is that culture is "lived faith" or "lived religion."[15] Ultimate concern is in this respect another name for those convictions which create and sustain the common life of a people. Hence, as Tillich has said, no great work of culture can hide its religious foundation.[16] That is to say, it is an expression of ultimate concern, or valuation.

APPROACH TO THE STUDY OF RELIGION

Human beings not only *have* religion, but they also seek to *understand* this form of experience. Hence we turn from the question "What is religion?" to the question "How do we study it?" What is the proper attitude of the student of religion toward the subject? How does this attitude differ from that of the religious participant or adherent? With what tools and methods does the project of study proceed?

There are many ways of study, each with its own merits and limits and potential contributions to the goals of understanding. Yet underlying all the methods are certain general issues and problems, one of which is the tension between commitment and objectivity and the closely related tension between the attitude of the religious adherent or participant and that of the student of religion. As previously noted, the former attitude is one of ultimate concern. Is there not a head-on conflict between this attitude of passionate attachment on the one hand, and, on the other hand, the detached and fair-minded objectivity which is required of the student of religion? That there is a genuine tension here is undoubtedly true, but it is by no means unique to the area of religious experience. Rather, it holds true for all areas of experience where significant forms of human value are involved. It is true, for example, of politics and of art. Can a person be a student of politics and at the same time an active member of a political party? Or in the case of art, is it possible to behold and enjoy art, to take in the meaning of a work of art, and also to engage in critical analysis and dissection of it?

This book is written with the conviction that in all such cases, the tensions between objectivity and commitment, between the attitudes of participant and observer, while they are real facts of life, can be creative and not destructive for both parties. In the case of religion, a faith can be the better for the searching, critical scrutiny of reason; and on the other hand, without religious participation the study of religion would soon wither and die. Unless there be religious practice, students of religion will soon find themselves unemployed! They will have nothing to study.

Even more immediately, the viewpoints of participant and observer are both integrally involved as aspects of all good study. Here as in other fields of liberal learning, students must identify with their subject matter, at least to the degree necessary to establish its existence and significance. But then they must step outside and look in critical detachment at this same subject matter. From this point onward, the work of understanding alternates, as in a kind of leapfrog game, between the attitudes of attachment and detachment.

These comments will impinge differently upon different people. For religious adherents who seek to be students of their own faith, it will doubtless be difficult to step outside and look with critical detachment at values to which they are unconditionally committed. Yet the adherent may be reminded that an unthinking faith is a curious offering to the creator of the human intellect. Speaking more affirmatively, the many fair-minded and reasonable people who adhere to any of the world's great faiths testify to the real possibility of a faith which is critically, reasonably held.

For those who claim no religious adherence or who seek to study a religion different from their own, the problem will be a very different one—seeking by imaginative sympathy to identify with the subject. Such students must strive to reproduce in some measure by imagination or empathy the viewpoint which adherents possess by virtue of their real participation. Doubtless this is very difficult, and no one achieves it perfectly. Yet some such act is necessary if significant study is to get under way at all.

Once it is under way, what are the characteristics of good study? Here follow in summary form three maxims for the study of religion in all its manifold varieties. The first is that *students of religion ought to seek the facts as objectively, as fully, and as freely as is humanly possible.*

To state it negatively, students of any subject ought not to hide, suppress, or distort facts. Rather, they will seek facts as freely and fully as they are able, and will invite other inquirers to do likewise. This maxim is particularly necessary in the study of religion, in order to dispel deep-rooted prejudices. The charge is often made that the putative or supposed study of religion is simply a massive structure of rationalization after the fact. Against all such charges and insinuations, the best possible defense is the actual day-to-day practice of openness to fact, of intellectual freedom in the presence of facts.

In this connection it may be asked: What is a fact? To answer very briefly, a fact is whatever the human mind *finds* and does not *make, discovers* and does not *invent*, in its encounter with the world. Facts are data—both literally and etymologically, "things given." Facts are thus pieces of reality. Beyond this general remark, what the pertinent facts are is an issue to be settled within each discipline.

It is a commonplace of discussion that there are no naked facts, denuded of all interpretation. To use a metaphor, facts do not grow like berries on a bush, waiting to be picked. They are more like nuggets buried deep in the ground waiting to be dug out, polished, and exhibited to the world. It must also be observed that whenever we exhibit them, we do so in an interpretive context. Hence, the second maxim is to *seek those explanations or interpretations which best illuminate the factual data, and form judgments on the basis of factual evidence.* Students should seek explanations which really explain; among the various alternative explanations in any given situation, they should choose that which explains most adequately. It will sometimes be difficult to apply this rule to specific situations, but at least it provides us with the common goal of explanation or understanding.

A third general maxim for students of religion is to *distinguish between fact and value, or between factual judgments and value judgments.* Factual judgments assert that something *is* or *is so*, while value judgments assert that in some way something is good or valuable, or that in some way it *ought* to be or to exist. In actual human experience, fact and value are seldom or never separated. Values are built into factual situations, and conversely factual situations impinge upon human beings in ways which are good or evil, valuable or the opposite. Yet for purposes of study, while fact and value are inseparable, it is sometimes important to distinguish between them, or more strictly, to distinguish factual judgments from value judgment.

A fundamental contrast among the methods for the study of religion is based upon the distinction between fact and value. As we have noted, all religions and religious experiences make claims of transcendent value and validity. Some methods of study systematically suspend judgment on these claims, proceeding to study religion as an observable and factual human phenomenon. Other methods of study deliberately assume normative or value-oriented stances. The former approach is illustrated by the history and social sciences of religion, the latter by theology and philosophy.

Religions, we conclude, may validly be viewed as expressive symbol systems whose proper function is to illuminate and to guide or direct the course of human existence, both socially and individually. If this assertion at first appears radical, let the reader reflect upon the oft-repeated assertion by many traditions that religious faith consists of "truth to live by."

It may be asserted that other uses or purposes are sometimes added, or indeed sometimes usurp, this primary function. Marxist critics argue that religions are often used to justify oppressive political systems. At the opposite extreme, we may sometimes observe religious contemplation in words or in art, as an end in itself, often as an esthetic value or good. While all this appears factually and observably true, we argue that religious experience itself asserts or claims for itself the distinctive function which we have described here.

ACADEMIC FORMS OF STUDY

THEOLOGY

Theology is probably the oldest form of the study of religion. Both the word and the idea are Greek in origin, going back to Aristotle, Plato, or perhaps even Socrates, for whom theology was the "ology" dealing with "theos." *Ology* derives from the Greek word *logos*, whose meanings range from "speech" to "study," "inquiry," or "rational structure" which may be apprehended by human speech or mind. Hence the proper aim of any inquiry or study is to set forth the *logos* of the subject matter. *Theos* in Greek means "god," "deity," or "things pertaining to deity." Theology was thus for the Greeks rational inquiry into things pertaining to the gods.

In this wide and generic sense, theological study has probably accompanied religious experience from its earliest human occurrences to the present moment. This is so for the good reason that the same human self which commits itself in ultimate concern is also a mind seeking critical understanding of its own commitments and those of other people as well. In this sense every person is perforce his or her own theologian. So conceived, theological study combines factual and value judgments in comprehensive synthesis.

During the Christian ages of the West, theology acquired a more limited meaning, coming to mean in effect the internal effort of the Christian faith at self-understanding. As a corollary, it has often been asserted that participation in theological study is limited to adherents of Christian faith, for surely only a Christian can truly understand the faith! However, in more modern times this attempt of theology to understand "from within" has given theology an exceedingly bad name. Hostile critics ask if it is not thus simply a vast enterprise of justifying a previously held position. Are not theologians committed in advance to rationalizing some of the most provincial and prejudicial viewpoints of the medieval past? How, then, can they claim the intellectual freedom so essential to fair-minded, objective study? No candid observer would deny that theology has often deserved this bad reputation. On the other hand, these vices are by no means limited to theology, and at its best theological study is as rigorous, as critical, as free and fair-minded as any other intellectual discipline.

In recent decades many American colleges and universities have established departments of religion, or, as they are often labeled, *departments of religious studies*. The difference between theology and religious studies is hard to state in any generally acceptable or applicable form. The latter label is in part a concession to academic prejudice against theology. However, *religious studies* claims a wider scope than traditional theology and also asserts or clearly implies freedom and fair-mindedness among many different religious viewpoints. Nevertheless, the label *religious studies* does not escape a serious ambiguity. Does the adjective *religious* designate a religious (pious?) quality of study, or does it simply denote the subject matter? The courses embraced by religious studies range over the whole field of academic study of religion.

PHILOSOPHY

Philosophy is in some of its manifold aspects concerned with the study of religion. In ancient Greece, which is the historical source of western philosophy, critical reflection upon religious mythology was a primary source of philosophical reflection or study. Similar relations will be observed in the history of both India and China. Since Kant (1724–1804) and Hegel (1770–1831), *philosophy of religion* has been the customary label for a philosophic approach to religious issues and problems. Contemporary philosophy, particularly in the West, has not infrequently been scornful or hostile toward religion. Nevertheless, the philosophic exposition and appraisal of religious issues continues to be a major context and method for the study of religion. Sometimes in the contemporary situation the label *philosophical theology* is applied to this form of study. Whatever the label, this kind of thought impinges upon the subject of this book in two ways. In several of the religious traditions to be studied, the emergence of philosophical thinking will be observed as an important part of the tradition. In addition to this, students will wish to make their own philosophical judgments concerning the subject matter. Philosophical thinking is thus both a part of the subject matter to be studied and also an aspect of our study of it.

Many questions come to mind concerning the nature of philosophy and its relation to religion. Where does philosophy stand relative to the distinction between factual study and value-oriented, or normative, study? What indeed is the relation of philosophy to religion? On these and similar questions there exist vast disagreements among contemporary philosophers and theologians. Here it must suffice to observe that we shall follow the traditional view of philosophy as a form of study which seeks to embrace fact and value in a synoptic unity of all reality. Philosophic thinking about religion, or anything else, has, the author believes, an indefeasibly normative character.

What then is the present relation of philosophy to theology, to religious studies, and to the practice of religion? These are questions that will be with us throughout our study. Here a few general comments must suffice. Much philosophizing, some good and some of questionable quality, occurs in departments of theology and religious studies. Courses labeled *philosophy of religion* sometimes occur in the religious studies department, sometimes in philosophy. More generally and more fundamentally, it is important that philosophic criticism and appraisal be applied to religious ideas and experience, whatever the auspices.

As to the relation between philosophy and religious practice, both are human activities claiming a reference to *all* human experience. The crucial difference lies in their respective attitudes. As we have seen, the characteristic attitude of religion is that of concern and commitment, while that of philosophy is one of critical inquiry. The philosophic attitude is one of asking questions, while that of religion is one of answering questions. Hence it will not be surprising to find that many of the recurring questions of philosophy are precisely the abiding assurances of religion, e.g., the existence of God, the nature of the human self or soul, the end or goal of human life.

HISTORY

From ancient times history has constituted an important method and instrumentality for the study of religion. Once more, both the word and the discipline are Greek in origin. Greek and Roman historians often dealt with religious beliefs and practices as aspects of their historical studies. In the ancient Greco-Roman world, the Stoics were preeminent for their interest in the diverse religious phenomena of their world.

When in early modern times, following the Middle Ages of Europe, historical study began again, it placed great emphasis on a critical evaluation of the sources from which historians derive their data. Modern historical study and writing have shown a very great many emphases and varieties. Among these has been a noteworthy concern with the history of religions. Applied to western religions, this study has emphasized free and critical study of biblical and Christian sources. However, history of religions has since the nineteenth century also sought to embrace all religions of humanity in its scope. It has been particularly concerned with the critical reconstruction (as well as the communication to occidental readers) of essential aspects of the various oriental faiths. Thus, it also has produced a persistent interest in the comparative study of the world's religions. With many changes of emphasis, these historical forms of study continue to the present moment. It is an important part of the task of this book to put the student in touch with the main conclusions of these historical forms of study.

How does historical study stand with respect to the distinction between fact and value? Clearly many kinds of valuation impinge upon the minds of historians, influencing their study in innumerable ways, from their selection of data to be studied to their concluding appraisals. Yet despite all these influences, history is in its central aims a form of factual study, which seeks the factual reconstruction of this or that part of the human past. The final test of historical study is adequacy as to facts. Such tests and aims stand in contrast to the systematic evaluations of the philosopher and theologian. Similarly factual in method and aim are the social sciences, described below.

SOCIAL SCIENCES

In modern times scientific methods of study have been extended to include human beings and society, producing bodies of knowledge variously labeled: e.g., *social sciences* and, more recently, *behavioral sciences*. These are large, various, and important enterprises, and they are pertinent to us as they bear upon the study of religion.

At least three of the social sciences have done notable work in the study of religion, namely, psychology, sociology, and anthropology. All three of these disciplines laid their scientific foundations in the nineteenth century. The first psychology laboratory was established in Leipzig under Wilhelm Wundt in 1879; and Wundt's student Tichner established the first American department of psychology at Cornell University. Among the American pioneers of psychology was

William James (1842–1910), whose interests ranged widely over both psychology and philosophy. James was one of the first and surely one of the greatest psychologists of religion. His book *The Varieties of Religious Experience* (the Gifford lectures of 1901–1902) has remained a classic in this field. James worked from the manuscript collections of E. D. Starbuck, which embraced all sorts of religious experiences, and deliberately emphasized extreme, bizarre, and pathological forms. In his psychology of religion, James sought to develop inductively from factual data the categories and generalizations essential for scientific understanding of religion. He was joined in this enterprise by such diverse workers as J. H. Leuba and J. B. Pratt. Despite some continuing interest along these lines, it must be added that in recent decades psychological interest in religion has shifted to other approaches and tasks.

Much recent experimental psychology, especially of the behaviorist school, has been either scornful or indifferent toward religion. Meanwhile other schools—e.g., that including Gordon Allport and centering on the psychology of personality, as well as those influenced by psychoanalysis—have continued a lively though critical interest in religious phenomena. This interest has operated at both a theoretical and a practical or clinical level, and has often provided fresh critical perspectives on religion and religious experience.

Sociology derived not only its name and many of its basic categories but also a critical concern with religion from Auguste Comte (1798–1857) and his "positive" philosophy. It has been concerned with religious belief and behavior as aspects of the society and social groups which it aims to study. Pioneering work in this area was done by Max Weber (1863–1920), who in his book *The Protestant Ethic* discussed a close relation between the ethics of Calvinistic Protestantism and the rise of capitalism. Weber turned the same categories of social analysis on the religions of ancient India and China and on ancient Judaism. His influence has continued in such contemporary sociologists as Talcott Parsons.

Anthropology is, as the etymology of the word implies, the "science of man"—that is, of human beings. Cultural anthropology has tended to be the comparative study of human beings in different cultures. Dating from Darwin's *Descent of Man* (1871) and E. B. Tylor's *Primitive Culture* (1875), it has maintained a special interest in primitive or preliterate cultures. The geneticism and evolutionism which characterized nineteenth-century anthropology have been largely replaced in the twentieth century by an interest in varieties of human culture and cultural patterns and in the human function performed by a society's many structures and processes. Chapter 2 includes a discussion of some of the current findings of the anthropology of religion.

THREE TYPES OF RELIGION

We have already noted the way in which the adjective religious becomes the noun or substantive religion. A religion comes into being when religious experience finds expression in a distinctive system of expressive symbols. These symbols, or free images, include those representing the human self, society, and environing nature; but most basic of all is some expressive symbol or metaphorical image for transcendent Reality. Such symbolic forms for transcendence range from the one God of monotheistic religions and the many gods of polytheistic religions, to Brahman of philosophic Hinduism, to Confucianism's Heaven, or even to Marxism's Humanity.

As we cast our glance over all of humanity's faiths and value systems, two observations come readily to mind. First, all of these many faiths or value systems claim explicitly or implicitly to be the human response to transcendence or, in Judeo-Christian terms, to God. The critical appraisal of this claim is an important aspect of all theological and philosophical study. Meanwhile, let us characterize religion in its most general meaning as consisting of our human responses to transcendence.

The second observation is that, focusing attention upon the symbolic object of ultimate concern or transcendence in its relation to the common world of nature and society, three possibilities emerge. First, this object—or these objects—is or are asserted to be *within* this common world. Second, this symbolic object may be asserted to exist *beyond* this world; or third, it may be asserted to be both *within* and *beyond* the common world. From these three relations emerge three distinct types of religion which may appropriately be labeled as (1) cosmic, (2) acosmic, and (3) historical.[17]

COSMIC RELIGION

The first type usually has a plurality of religious objects or gods; in other words, it is polytheistic. Its many deities are located within the common world of nature and society and are more or less personified statements of the human relation to this world or to specific aspects of it. This type of religion has often been accurately characterized as *nature-culture religion*. It has also been termed *cosmic religion*.[18] The limiting case for this type of religion takes the universe or world itself as divine. Something like this apparently was the view of the philosopher Aristotle. Chapter 17 will present the faith of Spinoza, who achieved his own highly distinctive formulation of this view.

Prehistoric and folk religions are clearly of this first type, as will be seen in Chapter 2. So are ancient Mesopotamian and Greek religions. China's classical faith is of this type. Among the world's living religions, Shinto in Japan, to be discussed in Chapter 9, most clearly exemplifies the nature-culture religion. It may also be asserted that whatever people formally profess, the actual functioning faith of most people in human history is of this type. This is often so even when people formally profess different types of faith, such as those of the second and third types.

ACOSMIC RELIGION

The second type of religion locates the religious object beyond the common secular world of nature and society. Here, in contrast to the first type, the religious object is usually conceived as singular rather than plural. It is *one* rather than *many*. Sometimes it is understood as deity, but sometimes not. In either case this type of religion represents the achievement by the human mind of what we have called an *Archimedean point* outside the world. Sometimes this type of religion is labeled *transcendent monism*. It may also be labeled *acosmic religion*. The clearest historical illustrations are Jainism and philosophic Hinduism. Popular Hinduism doubtless continues as a religion of the first rather than the second type.

HISTORICAL RELIGION

The third type of religion finds the religious object both beyond and within the common world. With the second type, it shares a transcendent point beyond the common world; yet with the first type it asserts the reality and goodness of the world of nature and culture. These features taken together generate what has been called a *linear view* of history, in contrast to the cyclic view of the first two types. Hence this third type is often labeled *historical religion*. The fundamental concern of this type of religion with one God makes appropriate the label *monotheism*, though we shall need to add important qualifications to this term in the course of our study. The historical or monotheistic religions of human history are Judaism, Christianity, Islam, Zoroastrianism, and possibly Sikhism.

MIXED TYPES

As subsequent chapters of this book will show, many further important distinguishing features cluster around defining characteristics of the three types. Yet historical study also reveals many mixed types. Human history, it seems, tends to blur the sharp outlines of typological distinctions. At least one living religion, Sikhism, began as a deliberate attempt to mix a religion of the second type, Hinduism, with one of the third type, Islam. Much interest in Sikhism derives from this fact, as we shall see in Chapter 7.

The differences implied by the threefold classification of religions by no means preclude the possibility of similarities of many sorts extending across the boundaries of the types. To use a musical metaphor, it may be said that there are three main keys in which religions are composed, but in these keys a great many themes and images recur. Some of these recurring features of the world's faiths are discussed in the next section of this chapter.

DISTRIBUTION OF THE TYPES

The geographical source regions and distribution of the three types of religion are also subjects of interest. Religions of the first type are scattered widely over the face of the earth, embracing all prehistoric and primitive religions, as well as the religions of archaic civilizations from Greece and Mesopotamia to China.

South Asia, or the subcontinent of India, seems to be the leading source region of religions of the second type, though such possible exceptions as ancient Taoism in China and Neoplatonism in Rome come readily to mind. The map in the front cover of this book shows the main distribution of religions of this type. The source region of monotheistic religions is the ancient Near East, extending from Iran westward, which may be seen on the map inside the back cover. However, the present distribution of these religions of the third type tends to be global—the historical relation of Christianity to the West notwithstanding. There are communities of Jews, Christians, and Muslims on every continent of the earth.

SOME PROBLEMS OF TRUTH AND VALUE

It is probably the case that all religious experience makes some claim, either explicit or implicit, to be true or valid. Just by existing or being, it claims the right to be, hence to justified existence. Often religions do not tell us specifically or in detail what their truth claims mean or what they do and do not imply.

Among the many meanings of religious truth or validity which we will encounter in the course of our study, some religions claim transcendent truth, meaning divine or absolute truth. Indeed some religions have at times pushed this claim a step even further, making claims to exclusive truth. As we shall see later, in Chapters 14 to 16, such claims have sometimes been made by theologians of Christianity and Islam. In a word, these assertions are that Christianity or Islam is the divine truth about human life and destiny, and that all other religions are basically false or invalid. As a contradictory opposite in this argument, there have been skeptical and anticlerical thinkers who summarily reject all religious truth-claims. In their view, any and all religious truth-claims are either false or meaningless. We shall meet such thinkers and their arguments in the course of our study and especially in Chapter 17.

At this point in our study we propose a more modest and tentative approach to these issues. Let us, provisionally at least, look away from issues of transcendent truth and value, focusing our attention upon religion as a phenomenon of human experience and history.

In order to set forth this view, let us first recall what previous sections of this chapter have asserted to be the distinctive function of religion, namely, to illuminate and guide the course of human existence, or as we have alternatively formulated this function, to answer the question, Why am I (or are we) alive?

Truth in its ordinary meaning has been summarily defined as the "adequacy of thought to things" or of statement to referent or object. In these common terms, the truth of a religion may be judged in terms of the adequacy with which it fulfills the function of illuminating and guiding the course of human existence, or in other words the adequacy of its answer to the existential question, Why live? Adequacy means satisfaction of the widest field of facts which human beings encounter in ordinary daily existence.

As this concept of truth is applied to the world's religions, we encounter many controversial issues. For one thing, "wholesale" assertions that one religion is true and all others are false give way to "retail" assertions of truth or falsity. Here the Buddhist parable of the blind men and the elephant provides a useful model. Each such blind person characterizes the beast in terms of the part available for his or her touch or hearing. No one such observer has a view of the whole elephant. So it is for our present approach to the truth or falsity of the world's religious traditions! We may also add that as our present definition of truth is applied in detail, it yields the concept of many different degrees of adequacy.

Turning from issues of truth to the related but distinguishable concept of value, we recall once again that some traditional religions have made absolute and exclusive claims. Here we introduce a more modest and pragmatic approach by a distinction between what we shall call "high religion" and "low religion."

In order to formulate this contrast we recall that all of humanity's faiths centrally contain some symbolic form for transcendent Reality, or the object of ultimate concern. Two possibilities exist for our human relation to this object, in whatever symbolic form. First, this symbol may be used as an expression and projection of human egotism, either individual or collective. In this formulation, religion becomes a pious facade for attitudes or interests which are basically and truly self-regarding or self-centered. Such configurations of egotism constitute what we have called "low religion."

We note in passing that two of the great atheists of modern times, Karl Marx and Sigmund Freud, understood (or misunderstood) all religion as expressions or products of human egotism, and hence summarily rejected it. In other words, they regarded all religion as what we have called "low religion."

The second possibility, "high religion," occurs when the human ego, both individual and collective, is actually or existentially placed under the criticism and judgment of some symbol for transcendent Reality. Out of this encounter emerges a new or renewed self, and with it the possibility for creative response, or for "high religion."

In contrast to the view that a particular tradition, e.g., Christianity, Islam, Buddhism, or other, is true or valid, and all others are false, the clear implication of our present distinction is that there are both high religion and low religion in most or all of humanity's traditions.

MYSTICS AND MYSTICISM

The words mystic, mysticism, and their various derivatives present issues of such pervasive importance to the study of religion that some introductory comments are demanded. What is mysticism? Who or what is a mystic? These questions are answered in so many different and often conflicting ways that we must at least begin the process of definition and clarification.

Webster's Dictionary defines mysticism as "the experience of mystical union or direct communion with ultimate reality reported by the mystics," and adds concerning the process of cognition involved, "immediate intuition, insight or illumination in a sense different from ordinary sense perception and ratiocination." The Oxford English Dictionary presents a similar definition, appending as a historical reference, "pertaining to the branch of theology which relates to the direct communion of the soul with God." As a fringe benefit these definitions exclude those popular uses which interpret "mystic" or "mystical" as polar opposites of "rational."

To begin etymologically, the word mystic and its derivatives, and indeed such related terms as mystery, stem from the Greek verb *muein*, meaning to close the eyes or mouth, that is, to be or remain silent. The original reference was to initiation rites into any of the secret religious communities known to us as Greek mystery religions. However, in the philosophic-religious tradition from Plato to Plotinus, this mystical silence acquired a new meaning, namely, human silence in the presence of God or ultimate Reality. This understanding in turn soon found application to analogous relations in many other religious traditions. Thus indeed we find mystics in all the major religions of the world.

Recent and current religious thought has been massively influenced by the approach to mysticism and mystical experience of William James's *Varieties of Religious Experience* (1903). James listed five traits of mystical experience, namely, ineffability, immediacy, noetic quality, passivity, and transcendency. However, James's application and discussion of the concept of mystical experience was so broad that all living religious experience might properly be termed mystical, thus depriving it of distinctive meaning.

Encountering mystics in all of the world's traditions, we also find them using the concrete symbolic forms of their own traditions. Thus Hindu mystics see visions of Shiva or indeed of Brahman, Islamic mystics see (or hear) Allah, Platonic mystics have mystical union with the One of Plotinus's philosophy, Catholic Christian mystics see visions of the Blessed Virgin, and so on through all of the traditions. But what is it that sets mystics apart from the other adherents of any given tradition?

The summary answer to this question is that the mystic has a strong sense of immediacy, or of the intuitive quality of the religious experience. For most human beings religious experience occurs through the mediation of church, of Holy Scripture, of human reason, or indeed of some social group. By contrast, the experience of the mystic has an urgent sense of immediacy or the direct experience of the object. Often, though by no means always, this immediacy is expressed metaphorically through the sense of sight or seeing. The mystic directly *sees* God, Brahman, or some other symbolic form for ultimate Reality. Often too this direct experience of seeing is a preface for mystical union in which all finite experience is transcended. I became *one* with God. Among the metaphors for this mystical union is the drop of water returning to the sea, the spark returning to the fire, or the river flowing to the ocean. We shall presently encounter significant illustrations of all of these metaphorical expressions for mystical experience.

We shall, however, also encounter a different metaphor. In contrast to seeing, then being absorbed (or reabsorbed) in ultimate Reality, some traditions speak of *hearing* and *doing* the divine will. These traditions use for mystical experience the social metaphors of love or friendship, thus creating what we may call the mysticism of *communion* in contrast to the mysticism of *union*. The difference between these two contrasting metaphors is that while the mysticism of union culminates in the complete transcending of all finite reality, in the mysticism of communion, the self and Reality are at one with each other; the two parties maintain their own finite reality.

We shall find both types of mystic and mysticism in most of the world's religions, though differently related to each other. As we shall presently see, in Hinduism and Buddhism the mysticism of union is dominant, and the mysticism of communion is ancillary. However, in the monotheistic religions, Judaism, Christianity, and Islam, the mysticism of communion is dominant, and the mysticism of union, when it occurs, is a minority form. We shall pursue these issues as our study proceeds.

ISSUES AND QUESTIONS

At the end of each of the chapters of this book we shall list some of the main issues and questions raised by the chapter. These questions and issues seek to provoke individual reflection on the main topics of the chapter, but they also aim to locate and indicate issues of current religious study and thought. Thus the reader is invited to participate in this ongoing corporate discussion and reflection.

Among the basic issues involved in this first chapter are those dealing with methods and approaches to religious study. We have already noted several traditional and current forms of study, as well as the relation of study to religious practice. By means of a metaphor, let us sharpen a basic contrast in the forms of study. In this metaphor let us compare religious experience to a telephone conversation. Two approaches to the critical study of this telephone conversation are possible. First, the observer may eliminate from consideration any and all reference to the party at the other end of the telephone line. Thus our study is limited to careful and comprehensive consideration of the party at this end of the line. The student will observe that the person involved in the telephone call believes that a conversation is actually taking place, but the student will make no judgment either positive or negative concerning the validity of that assumption. Once more, the student is limited in this approach to careful observation and study of the party at *this* end of the telephone line. By contrast the second approach to study removes this limitation, and makes judgments, either affirmative or negative, concerning the party at the further end of the telephone line.

Applied to the critical study of religion the first approach includes history of religion and such social sciences as psychology, sociology, and anthropology, all of which properly limit their study to religion as an aspect of human experience. The term *phenomenology of religion* is sometimes applied to this approach.

By contrast the second approach, including both traditional theology and philosophy, is centrally involved with judgments concerning the party at the other end of the telephone line. In our present study we shall be mainly involved with religion as an aspect of human history and experience. However, from time to time we shall also be inevitably drawn to the second or philosophical-theological forms of study. This issue is broached early in our study, for the reason that it is important for us to be aware which form of study is going on at any given moment.

A second cluster of issues centers in the definition of religion, especially in its further implications for the nature of our subject matter. We have noted that many definitions of religion differ and clash with each other. We have offered a tentative working definition for the student's critical appraisal. What may come as a surprise to many beginning students is the fact that virtually every one of the world's great religious traditions has at one time or another denied that it is a religion, saying in effect: others have religion, but I or we have something better, called faith, vision, etc.

The term religion is moreover a modern western word having no precise parallels in other times or places. For example, biblical scholars have long observed that there is no word in biblical Hebrew or Greek which is accurately translatable as religion. The same is true for the Sanskrit of India as well as for classical Chinese or Japanese.

Even in the historical development of the English language the word religion has undergone significant change, as may be seen from the definitions offered in the *Oxford English Dictionary* or *Webster's International*. It is indeed a significant project to compare these definitions, then to write one's own working definition, and to test it on the whole subject matter which follows in this book.

Still a third cluster of issues centers in the nature and significance of the object of ultimate concern or valuation. People nurtured in the Judeo-Christian tradition tend to assert that this object consists simply and plainly of different understandings of God. This viewpoint radically underestimates the variety of outlooks we shall encounter in the course of our study. Looking over the wide range of symbolic forms for transcendent Reality, it is important to see their irreducible diversity or indeed their multi-versity! As we have argued, the human contents of these religions consists of some distinctive configuration of basic values, which in turn elicits its own equally distinctive symbolic forms.

If views of transcendent Reality vary widely, this is equally true of the correlative views of the human condition—of the human self and its ways of fulfillment and frustration. The highest fulfillment or realization of human life is often called salvation, and contrariwise that which opposes salvation is sin or evil. In this generalized sense of both of these words, what we shall find in the world's religions are many diverse ways of sin and salvation.

A fourth issue has to do with the indefeasibly personal character of religious thinking. In many areas of experience, thinking or reasoning is largely impersonal; and in those areas the authority of the expert tends to dominate. Thus, for example, if I wish to know the answer to a scientific question, I ask a qualified scientist. Similarly in medical counsel much the same authority of the expert prevails. In the different field of law this is also dominantly the case.

However, in other areas of human experience a different relation prevails. So, for example, no one can be born or can die for me. Indeed no expert can eat my dinner and have it nourish me. Some forms of experience thus appear irreducibly personal or individual. Clearly this is the case for religious experience. No one can have religious faith for me. Here experience and thought must finally be my own. The same is true for the closely related experience of making a moral decision.

In all such fields the authority of the expert or professional (if indeed these are the correct words) is radically different from such fields as science, medicine, or law. Here the role of the teacher is more like that of a guide who can lead others over a long and arduous mountain trail which presumably the teacher has walked, but along which each individual person must make his or her own way.

A fifth cluster of issues emerges from the immediate or intuitive character of the expressive symbols in which the great religions speak their distinctive messages to humanity. Like all free images these occur in what the philosopher Whitehead has called "the mode of presentational immediacy." The images or symbols of religion share this quality of immediacy with the images which are the elements of artistic experience.

Out of this common feature is born the historic relation of the world's religions to the arts. As one philosopher has observed, religion is the fruitful mother of the arts. We shall have occasion to observe this maternal relation as we proceed. Conversely stated, art in one medium or another constitutes the first or primary language of religion.

While this relation applies most directly to the mythopoeic words in which the religions speak their messages, it has a comparable application to the other arts, ranging from music and dance to painting, sculpture, and even architecture.

This relation has implications for the study of this book. For the beginning student of a religion the distinctive forms of art of that religion constitute an important door of entry to understanding. This is true for the sound reason that in their various and distinctive ways the arts embody and express the basic values of the religious traditions which give them birth. Thus we shall frequently find ourselves using the art of a religion as a way to understand that religion.

NOTES

1. E. Cassirer, *An Essay on Man*, Yale, New Haven, Conn., 1944, p. 26.
2. G. H. Mead, *Mind, Self, and Society*, University of Chicago Press, Chicago, 1932, p. 240.
3. H. R. Niebuhr, *The Meaning of Revelation*, Macmillan, New York, p. 62f, and *The Protestant Era*, University of Chicago Press, Chicago, 1948.
4. C. W. Morris, *Paths of Life*, Harper, New York, 1942.
5. R. Bellah, "Religious Evolution," quoted from W. Lessa and E. Vogt, *Reader in Comparative Religion*, 3d ed., Harper & Row, New York, 1972, p. 326.
6. W. C. Smith, *The Meaning and End of Religion*, Macmillan, New York, 1963.
7. See inter alia Paul Tillich, *The Protestant Era*, University of Chicago Press, Chicago, 1948, and *Systematic Theology I*, University of Chicago Press, Chicago, 1951.
8. R. B. Perry, *General Theory of Value*, Longmans, London, 1926, p. 115f.
9. P. Tillich, passim.
10. E. Cassirer, *Language and Myth*, Dover, New York, 1946, p. 22f.
11. Mark 12:30.
12. *Penultimate* is a term I first encountered in an unpublished paper by Thomas O'Dea of the University of California, Santa Barbara.
13. R. Otto, *The Idea of the Holy*, Oxford University Press, London, 1923.
14. J. Oman, "The Sphere of Religion," in Joseph Needham (ed.) *Science, Religion and Reality*, Macmillan, New York, 1925.
15. T. S. Eliot, *Notes on the Definition of Culture*, Harcourt, Brace & World, New York, 1949, p. 30.
16. P. Tillich, *The Protestant Era*, p. 8.
17. J. Hutchison, *Language and Faith*, Westminster Press, Philadelphia, 1963, p. 248f.
18. W. Eliade, *Cosmos and History*, Harper, New York, 1953.

BIBLIOGRAPHY

Bergson, H.: *The Two Sources of Morality and Religion*, University of Notre Dame, Notre Dame, Ind., 1977.

Betts, J. D. (ed.): *Phenomenology of Religion*, Harper & Row, New York, 1969.

Burtt, E. A.: *Man Seeks the Divine*, Harper & Row, New York, 1964.

Carmody, D.: *Women and World Religions*, Prentice-Hall, Englewood Cliffs, N.J., 1989.

Cassirer, E.: *An Essay on Man*, Yale, New Haven, Conn., 1962.

———: *Language and Myth*, Dover, New York, 1946.

Dawson, C. H.: *Religion and Culture*, AMS Press, New York, 1981.

Eliade, M.: *Patterns in Comparative Religion*, New American Library, New York, 1987.

———: *Cosmos and History*, Garland, New York, 1985.

——— (ed.): *Encyclopedia of Religion*, 16 vols., Macmillan, New York, 1986.

Frankfort, H., et al.: *Before Philosophy*, Penguin, Baltimore, 1949.

Hocking, W. E.: *Living Relgions and a World Faith*, AMS Press, New York, 1976.

Huxley, A.: *The Perennial Philosophy*, Harper & Row, New York, 1970.

James, W.: *The Varieties of Religious Experience*, Macmillan, New York, 1985.

Jayne, J.: *The Origin of Consciousness and the Breakdown of the Bicameral Mind*, Houghton Mifflin, Boston, 1976.

King, W. L.: *Introduction to Religion*, Harper, New York, 1954.

Langer, S.: *Philosophy in a New Key*, Harvard, Cambridge, Mass., 1957.

Lessa, W., and E. Vogt: *Reader in Comparative Religion*, Harper & Row, New York, 1979.

McNeil, W. H.: *The Rise of the West*, University of Chicago, Chicago, 1970.

Moore, G. F.: *Birth and Growth of Religion*, A. R. Allenson, Geneva, Ala., 1929.

Morris, C.: *Paths of Life*, University of Chicago, Chicago, 1973.

Needham, J. (ed.): *Science, Religion and Reality*, Macmillan, New York, 1925.

Noss, J. B.: *Man's Religions*, Macmillan, New York, 1984.

Otto, R.: *The Idea of the Holy*, Oxford, London, 1950.

Parrinder, G.: *Worship in the World's Religions*, Littlefield, Totowa, N.J., 1976.

Redfield, R.: *The Primitive World and Its Transformations*, Cornell University, Ithaca, N.Y., 1957.

Smart, N.: *The World Religions*, Prentice-Hall, Englewood Cliffs, N.J., 1988.

————: *The Long Search*, Little, Brown, Boston, 1977.

————: *Worldviews*, Scribner, New York, 1983.

Smith, W. C.: *The Meaning and End of Religion*, Harper & Row, New York, 1978.

Streng, F.: *Understanding Religious Life*, Wadsworth, Belmont, Calif., 1985.

Tillich, P.: *The Protestant Era*, University of Chicago, Chicago, 1957.

————: *Theology of Culture*, Oxford, New York, 1959.

Van der Leeuw, G.: *Religion in Essence and Manifestation*, Princeton, Princeton, N.J., 1986.

Wach, J.: *Sociology of Religion*, Chicago University Press, Chicago, 1944.

Whitehead, A. N.: *Religion in the Making*, New American Library, New York, 1974.

Zaehner, R.: *A Concise Encyclopedia of Living Faiths*, Beacon Press, Boston, Mass., 1967.

————: *Concordant Discord*, Clarendon Press, Oxford, 1970.

2

Religion in Various Cultures

Before proceeding to the main subject of this book, namely, the world's great living religions, it will be useful for purposes of critical perspective to glance briefly at a sampling of other religions, past and present. More precisely, in the light of Chapter 1's definition and description of religious experience and religions, this chapter will explore religious phenomena in a variety of different historical and social contexts. We shall glance briefly at a few salient aspects of six religions. The first three are preliterate and precivilized, and the second three are religions of ancient civilizations. The first three are (1) prehistoric, (2) African traditional, and (3) Native American religions; the second three are the religions of ancient (4) Egypt, (5) Mesopotamia, and (6) Greece.

The terms preliterate and precivilized must be understood as descriptive and historical, not as evaluative. Nineteenth-century social scientists called such societies and religions "primitive," thus presupposing a negative value judgment. A recent attempt to overcome this negative valuation is the distinction between folk societies and civilizations, the former being small and simple enough for social life to proceed on a face-to-face basis.[1] However, as we shall presently see, many African and Native American societies are too large and too complex for this designation.

The term preliterate refers to the absence of a written language, and as we shall soon see, this is one of several distinctions between precivilized and civilized cultures. Humankind's historic breakthrough to civilization occurred in what has recently been called the ancient "urban revolution."[2] This historic change to city-centered society occurred ca. 4000 to 3000 BCE in several of the great river valleys of the Eurasian continent from Greece or Egypt in the west through Mesopotamia and India to China in the east. Attention may be called to our use of BCE and CE instead of the traditional convention of B.C. (Before Christ) and A.D. (Anno Domini). We use BCE (Before the Common Era) and CE (Common Era) as religiously neutral, and hence appropriate to our religiously pluralistic contemporary world. One archeologist, V. Gordon Childe, has listed nine clearly observable features which distinguish the new city-state civilizations from previous human societies.[3] These features are as follows:

1. The size of the settlement is greatly increased.
2. There is an increase in the amount and importance of tribute and taxation.
3. As a direct result of the increase in wealth, there are large public works.
4. Writing emerges as an essential social function, probably first in business transactions.
5. Related to writing are the beginnings of mathematics and science.
6. There is greatly increased differentiation of economic activities and structures.
7. Metalworking becomes an important activity, for both war and peace.
8. A privileged class makes its appearance.
9. The state emerges as a distinct social structure and function.

Attention may be called to the realism of this list, including war and taxes as it does among the distinguishing features of civilization. Truly this distinction between civilized and precivilized society is one of historic fact and not of value! A further implication of this list is that many human cultures, including many African and American Indian societies, possess some but not all of these features—an essential fact to hold in mind as we consider these religions.

PREHISTORIC RELIGION

The scientific study of human origins and prehistory is barely a century old, but it has already gone through several stages of development, with no end in sight. It began in the nineteenth century with concepts of evolutionary development stimulated by the monumental work of Charles Darwin. If the human species had evolved biologically, as Darwin so effectively argued, could not the model or concept of evolution be applied to the study and explanation of every aspect of human culture, including religion?

Nineteenth-century evolutionists in anthropology asserted in succession a variety of theories to explain the origin and development of religion. A notable example was E. B. Tylor's proposal that religion began in animism or belief in spirits (as explanatory hypotheses for many problematic events) and developed through progressive stages of polytheism to monotheism.[4]

More recent anthropologists and historians of religion have abandoned evolutionary forms of explanation, asserting to the contrary that we simply do not know how, when, or under what circumstances religion began. Contemporary anthropologists have turned from genetic explanations to what is often termed *functionalism*, or explanation of the various aspects of human culture in terms of use or function rather than genesis.

The beginnings of this shift from genesis to function may be detected in E. Durkheim's *Elementary Forms of the Religious Life*.[5] Even though Durkheim still sought to understand religion by examining the simple preliterate forms (in particular, the religion of the Arunta tribe of Australia), he nonetheless found the real source of religion in the relation of the human individual to society or humanity. The full implications of functionalism in anthropology of religion may be seen in such twentieth-century anthropologists as B. Malinowski and C. Kluckhohn.[6]

Other social-scientific theories concerning the source of religions have ranged widely—from J. G. Frazer's hypothesis that humankind first sought to control powers of the spiritual world with magic, but when magic failed, sought by religion to appease these powers; to Freud's theory that God is in reality a repressed infantile father image.[7] In Chapter 1 an alternative hypothesis was outlined briefly: that the source of religions lies in the distinctive combination of freedom and dependence which characterizes the emergent human situation.

But let us turn from theoretical speculation to paleontology and human prehistory for factual evidence concerning prehistoric religion. First we take note of recent work in this field, which has pushed human origins back to some 2 million years ago, with Africa as the location where humankind began. From this African source region, the human species spread out over Europe and Asia during the following 500,000 to 1 million years. From Asia the human race made its way over the Aleutian or Bering land bridge to the Americas as recently as 50,000 to 25,000 years ago.

Paleontologists and anthropologists continue to scrutinize extant human remains from different parts of the world, observing, analyzing, and hypothesizing even as the digging continues. The admittedly meager bits of factual data or evidence are extended by carefully controlled inferences drawn from several related sciences. The result is that today we possess a fuller and more accurate picture of the human prehistoric past that has ever before existed.

The chronology that emerges from this reconstruction of the human past begins with the Paleolithic, or Old Stone Age, which coincides approximately with the Pleistocene geological era and extends from approximately 2 million years ago to 10,000 BCE. According to recent and current systems of classification, this was followed by the Mesolithic, or Middle Stone Age, from ca. 10,000 to ca. 5000–3500 BCE, which in turn was followed by the Neolithic, or New Stone Age, whose more developed culture shows such features as agriculture and domestication of animals. Neolithic times were followed in several regions of the world by the civilized societies of the bronze age (ca. 2000–800 BCE).[8] (Variations in these dates result from differences among students of human prehistory and also from different developments in different parts of the world.)

The oldest human remains discovered to date which yield positive evidence of religious behavior are those of "Peking man" and "Java man," both from a period estimated to be 400,000 to 500,000 years ago. The discoveries of "Java man" began in 1892 and extended through the 1930s, producing a number of skulls and other human remains. Meanwhile, in 1927, a cave near Choukoutien, 40 miles from Peking, China, turned up skulls and other skeletal remains of some forty human beings. These remains show positive evidence of fire, tools, language, cooking, and food gathering. Holes in the skulls and the fractures of other bones have also yielded the conclusion that "Peking man" was a ritual cannibal. One expert speaks of "Peking man" as having genuine human sensibility and being devoted to the dead by means of a cult of skulls which made the dead present to the living.

Other somewhat later Paleolithic remains from many parts of the world provide several additional and independent lines of evidence for prehistoric cultures' concern with death. Near the Bavarian village of Noerdlingen was found embedded in red ocher a cluster of some twenty-seven skulls, all facing westward.[9] Many other discoveries show the same red color which, as the color of blood, is inferred to have been a magic instrumentality to preserve or reestablish life. At Le Moustier in France the skeleton of a Neanderthal youth was discovered under fragments of animal bones, lying face down with forearm under the head and surrounded by stone tools and weapons.[10] These are only samples of the extensive evidence from widely separated regions of the world. From this evidence the student of religion may conclude that Paleolithic people were aware of death and responded to its mystery and its threat in the only ways they could conceive.

Birth and the related phenomena of sex constituted another realm of mystery for prehistoric people, as may be seen from the so-called Venus figures, small female statues from all parts of the world whose exaggerated and sometimes voluptuous lines suggest fertility, sex, and pregnancy. It has been argued that these figures functioned as magical charms to guarantee successful pregnancy and safe birth. Scholarly controversy continues as to their precise significance, though there seems to be general agreement that they symbolize some sort of magical-religious concern with the origin of life in an age long before the emergence of the earth mother as a goddess.

This interest found other expressions in Paleolithic times—for example, in the fertility dance depicted in the rock shelter near Lerida, Spain. In this fresco a group of nine women, narrow-waisted and wearing skirts, is shown dancing around a smaller, naked male figure. Similar fertility dances and other rituals recur in folk religions throughout the world. A modern echo from the prehis-

Willendorf Venus. (American Museum of Natural History, New York.)

At left: "The Sorcerer," a cave painting from Les Trois Frères, France; at right: a wall painting in a prehistoric rock shelter. (American Museum of Natural History, New York.)

toric tradition may be heard in such continuing ceremonies as dancing around the maypole.

Of comparable significance to birth, sex, and death was the relation of Paleolithic humanity to environing nature. Most immediately this involved the food supply, without which our prehistoric ancestors would speedily have starved. As has been said, nature was their "living larder."[11] In the absence of agriculture and domestication of animals, Paleolithic people were predators upon nature. But they were also dependent upon nature in other ways as well. They were ever at the mercy of larger, stronger animal species. From summer's heat to winter's cold, and from flood to drought, dependence upon nature was inexorably driven home.

Many of these concerns became the subject of magical-religious ritual, embodied in Paleolithic cave art. In various regions, notably southern France and Spain, painting and sculpture from later Paleolithic times have been discovered deep within nearly inaccessible, dark caves. Cave paintings originated as an aspect of magical-religious ritual whose themes ranged from fertility and sex to hunting. One such painting depicts a dying bison with missiles being hurled at it. Another particularly notable painting from the same region has been called "The Sorcerer." It shows a figure with human face and feet but with stag's antlers, ears of a wolf, claws of a lion, and tail of a horse. Whether this figure was a human shaman who guaranteed good hunting, or whether some less obvious unity of human and animal life was intended, is not clear. In either case, the human relation to animal species was in some way being celebrated.

The Neolithic age was marked by the most radical and far-reaching change in all human prehistory: the agricultural revolution. From being hunters and nomads, the human species became farmers. From being food gatherers, they changed into food growers and cultivators.

Obviously so vast a change was a process and not an event—indeed a process which took place over long periods of time and also in widely separated parts of the earth. One aspect of this process was the domestication of plants and the saving and cultivation of seed. Another was the domestication of animals. Still another was the invention of the plow. Other aspects and implications of the agricultural revolution range from life in fixed habitation, in contrast to previous nomadism, to such new arts as weaving, brewing, and the manufacture of pottery.

The religious implications of the agricultural revolution were equally significant and numerous. The new agricultural way of life underscored and emphasized aspects of animal magic and mysticism in such figures as the bull, who was destined for a long and varied career in the history of human religions.

There is also much factual evidence that human imagination was grasping at larger features of environing nature. Sun, moon, and stars were engraved on tools and weapons. The cycle of the seasons in earth and heaven was noted. The deliberate arrangement of ritual stones, sometimes of vast size and weight, as at Stonehenge in England and at Carnac in Brittany, argues some sort of religious relation to wider aspects of heaven and earth. Such sites as these were also religious sanctuaries or temples, possibly the first such in history.

The sky or heaven became an expression of ultimate mystery and of the power upon which human life is dependent. For many peoples the gods were asserted to live "up there." The metaphor of height for deity or transcendence was destined to retain its symbolic power for a very long time—perhaps until those modern times when people turned telescopes upon the heavens, or, even more recently, when they began to fly through the sky. How far back into prehistory the symbol of height may be pushed is an open question. Yet if the theories of Wilhelm Schmidt and Andrew Lang are correct, a high god is one of humankind's most ancient memories.[12] The agricultural revolution invested sky or heaven with new and poignant meanings.

Among the other new aspects of religion in Neolithic times were new gods and goddesses as well as new priestly functions and functionaries. Among the new deities, the earth mother, known by many names in different parts of the world, was particularly important. Often she was married to Father Heaven or Sky, and the copulation of this divine pair was asserted as the source of fertility alike in agriculture and human life. Around these deities were woven innumerable patterns of myth and ritual.

Despite the changes of the Neolithic age, prehistoric religion remained what in Chapter 1 was labeled as the *nature-culture*, or *cosmic*, type, in which the meaning of human life is sought and found in relation to nature and society. Within this context of the cosmos, the adventure of humanity began.

AFRICAN TRADITIONAL RELIGION

The label *African traditional religion* designates those religions (specifically excepting Christianity and Islam) which are local to Africa; and our first assertion must be that African traditional religion is a subject as vast and as various as the African continent itself. From north to south, Africa extends across the Sahara Desert through the rain forests and rivers of the central region to the plains and mountains of the south, a distance of almost 5,000 miles. From east to west, at its widest point, this distance is almost as great, extending from the shores of the South Atlantic some 4,500 miles to the Red Sea and the Indian Ocean. John Mbiti states that black Africa comprises more than 1,000 tribes or peoples, each with its own language and culture, including religion.[13] These black African cultures or societies vary enormously in size, ranging from a few hundred people to groups like the Dinka of southern Sudan, whom Lienhardt estimates at nine hundred thousand people.[14] Variations in time are probably as great as those in space.

In terms of the distinction between folk societies and civilizations drawn earlier in this chapter, the African societies show some but not all of the nine features of civilization. Many, though by no means all, show highly developed social classes and distinctions of economic and political function. However, there is a general absence of written languages—a fact which poses massive obstacles to historical study. In terms of the threefold classification of Chapter 1, African religions are of the first, or cosmic, type.

RECURRING THEMES OF AFRICAN TRADITIONAL RELIGION

Here we cannot do more than sample a few of the persistently recurring themes of African traditional religions, citing some illustrations drawn from different regions of the continent. We shall employ this same approach for the other religions which follow in this chapter.

First, the most important and basic theme will be the images or symbolic forms for transcendence or deity, together with the myths and rituals by which Africans and others relate themselves to such "higher powers." A second theme will be the ways in which the stages of individual life from birth to death are hallowed or infused with religious meaning and also related to society, by what A. Van Gennep felicitously called "rites of passage" or the ritual celebration of the stages on life's way.[15] A third theme will be some of the religious figures or roles, such as priests, prophets, sacred kings, and medicine men. In each society, let it be added, these diverse elements are parts of a cultural whole which is that people's way or path of life.

TRANSCEN-DENCE   Transcendence or divinity (the latter is the term used by Lienhardt in his classic study of the Dinka entitled *Divinity and Experience*) is known to Africa by many names and in many ways and symbolic forms. However, behind and beyond all the names and symbols, and overarching their infinite diversity, is the image of supreme being, unitary or single in nature. True, African religions show a veritably infinite plurality of powers or spirits, but all are under a supreme being or god.

The earlier view of European and American observers that African traditional religion presents a picture of "primitive polytheism" is wide of the mark. To the contrary, African religions assert that beyond and over the vast plurality of spirits and powers is a single unique divinity. E. B. Idowu characterizes this situation as "diffused monotheism."[16]

The words of Evans-Pritchard for the Nuer tribe of Sudan have a general application.

> A theistic religion need not be either monotheistic or polytheistic. It may be both. It is a question of the level or situation of thought rather than exclusive types of thought. On one level Nuer religion may be regarded as monotheistic, at another level as polytheistic, and it can also be regarded at other levels as polytheistic or fetishistic. These conceptions of spiritual activity are not incompatible. They are rather different ways of thinking of the numinous at different levels of sequence.[17]

Different African peoples have different ways of picturing or symbolizing the one god or supreme being. Often, though by no means always, he is conceived as dwelling in the sky. The Nuer word for "spirit" is *kwoth*; and "god" is *kwoth nhial*, or "spirit dwelling in the sky."[18] He is conceived to have existed for a very long time ("the everlasting one in the forest").[19] The supreme being is beneficent ("He is good, for he has never withdrawn from us the good things, which he gave us").[20] God is holy ("the pure king who is without blemish").[21] Divinity is thought of as father, or in some cases as mother, and human beings are the offspring of divinity. In some symbolic forms, order and structure are emphasized, and in others, images of vitality and dynamism predominate.

If at the highest level of supreme being African religion is monotheistic, it is at the lower levels of more familiar powers luxuriantly polytheistic. And we must add that the daily life of African people involves closer relation with these powers than with supreme being. The Ashanti of Ghana have a pantheon of such spirits or powers (their word is *abosom*)[22] who are intermediaries and messengers of God and guardians of the people. In this populous pantheon there are divinities representing war, smallpox, harvest, health and healing, weather, cattle, and different clans.

Mbiti cites the Yoruba as having some 1,700 such divinities (*orisa*), each with its own appropriate function, including a heavenly chief of staff (*orisa-nia*).[23] Another member of this pantheon, not insignificantly, is an omniscient linguist! Among the Dinka, according to Lienhardt, a prominent divinity is Dang, who is said to be a son of heaven and earth and ancestor of the Dinka.[24] However, he is also closely associated with the storm, and his name is used for rain. Lightning is called his club, and both rain and human birth are manifestations of Dang. Among the Ibo the earth mother Ala is second only to Chukwu, who is "Father Heaven" and creator.[25] Ala is the spirit of fertility in both earth and human life. Temples to Ala are scattered over Ibo country. Since the land is sacred to Ala, selling real estate is highly unpopular and was in earlier times impossible. Evans-Pritchard speaks generally of "Spirits of the Above," and "Spirits of the Below." While all are under supreme being, they are all active and influential in human life.

Myth and ritual are ways of sacred story and symbolic action by which people seek good relations with transcendence. A persistent thread in the intricate fabric of African myth and ritual is stories of creation or beginnings. Parrinder tells of the Dogon people of Mali and Upper Volta who say that God (*Amma*) first created sun and moon, then threw the earth as a lump of clay into space, where it flattened out.[26] Amma then united sexually with earth to produce first a mischief-making jackal and thereafter other creatures. The jackal appears as the local version of the widely recurring trickster divinity.

Yoruba myth from Nigeria says that *Ol Orun*, "owner of the sky," lived with other gods above the waste of earth.[27] He called his agent *Orishan'a* ("great god") and gave him a snail shell filled with earth, a pigeon, and a hen. The hen assisted by scattering earth until the existent world was formed. The original place of solid ground was If'e, sacred city of the Yoruba. Orishan'a created human beings out of clay, but needed the high god Ol Orun to breathe life into them.

Varied opinions are expressed concerning how near or far divinity is above the human world. Along the Ivory Coast the story is told that God was once so near to human beings that they grew too familiar and he withdrew to distant heavens.[28] In earlier times children wiped their hands on the sky and women broke off pieces to put into the soup, and so the sky drew apart. The Dinka say that people used to climb a rope joining earth to sky, but divinity was offended by women and sent a blue bird to cut the rope. The neighboring Nuer say that people used to climb this rope; however, now that the rope is cut, people cannot be rejuvenated.

This wooden mask from the Baoule tribe of the Ivory Coast represents the Creator god. All its lines direct the eye to its mouth, from which the universe and deities are said to have come. (Marc and Evelyne Bernheim/Woodfin Camp & Associates.)

These and innumerable other myths along with accompanying rituals constitute the staple religious practice of African peoples. Parrinder notes that supreme being, while generally assumed, nevertheless yields to specific powers and spirits as the effective foci of both belief and practice. He also adds that the African practice of worship is not "regular or usual" but "occasional" in character.

From the nature and function of the spirits or powers, it may be seen that African religion is intensely experiential, being constituted of the homely stuff of daily life. This quality is underscored by a notable passage from Lienhardt's *Divinity and Experience*:

> To the Dinka the Powers are known by personal encounter, as living agents influencing their lives for good and evil....Europeans may perhaps concede an objective reality of the order to the Dinka Divinity where it resembles "God" of the universal religions, but no European actually encounters Deng, Garang or the

other Powers as the Dinka claim to do. For analysis then the Powers [and logically all equally including Divinity] must be regarded as representatives of realities.[29]

Lienhardt speaks of the powerful and luminous images by which these realities are mediated to people in personal encounter. While to western observers many of the Dinka images seem bizarre to the point of sheer subjective fantasy, the basic and general fact (which will be with us throughout our whole study of the world's religions) is that religious faith comes to human beings through the filter of such powerful, luminous images.

A further and even more pervasive manifestation of power or transcendence lies in the images of the holy and of taboo. To be sure, God and the spirits are all holy, but holiness also has other wider, less personal, and less specific manifestations. As was noted in Chapter 1, the holy is in its simplest sense a unique emotion or affection, like a combination of awe, fear, wonder, and mystery, which indwells the symbolic forms and objects of religion. Here we must add that in African traditional religion it finds infinitely many and diverse embodiments.

Denuded of ethical and spiritual significance, the holy becomes taboo, so that its embodiments are forbidden. It becomes the power which the magician seeks to manipulate for weal or woe. Among its infinitely various embodiments

A dancer from a South African tribe in ceremonial costume and mask. (Hubertus Kanus/Rapho-Photo Researchers.)

are fetishes and charms, witches and sacred kings, priests, women in childbirth, ghosts, corpses, and many, many more. In Africa as elsewhere the holy in its higher ranges becomes the sentiment of reverence. But whatever its quality, the occurrence of the holy may be said to function as a sign indicating human encounter with transcendence.

STAGES ON LIFE'S WAY

The second recurring theme of African religions is the ritual by which the course of individual life from birth to death is sanctified and is also related to the common life of society. Such *rites of passage* occur widely throughout the world; hence it is no surprise to find them fully exemplified among African societies. Here, four main rites of passage will be discussed briefly: (1) birth; (2) coming of age, or initiation; (3) marriage; and (4) death.

Birth

Children are accounted a great good in African societies, and childlessness is an equal and opposite evil. Indeed so important are children that in some African societies a marriage is not secure until there is a child. Along with offspring, sex and family life are widely regarded as gifts of deity.

The naming ceremony is a time of general rejoicing and of momentous significance alike for child and family. Here, as elsewhere in the world, names are fraught with great power. Often they are taken from gods or spirits, thus laying hold upon this power or relation to the god for the benefit of the new child.

In a variety of rites the mother and child are first set apart, then drawn back into the community, thus illustrating the pattern which Victor Turner and other anthropologists have delineated for rites of transition or passage. Sometimes the umbilical cord is made into a charm to be worn by the child. Elsewhere it is buried under a tree which is henceforth the child's tree. Often too the father offers sacrifice and prayer to celebrate successful birth. The birth of twins or triplets is an extraordinary event, frequently viewed with superstitious fear. Some African societies expose or kill such children, or even kill the mother.[30]

Initiation

The coming of age of all boys and girls, and their assumption of full and responsible membership in society, is set in ritual context. A frequent feature of puberty rites is circumcision for boys and an operation of excising a portion of the clitoris for girls.[31] Among the Ibo, adolescent girls were at times sent to "fattening houses" and fed heartily, since obesity was accounted erotically attractive.[32] Among the Poro and Sande tribes of Sierra Leone and Guinea, secret societies of adults have the responsibility of initiating boys and girls into the tribal traditions. These societies meet in a sacred grove where the clan founder is said to be buried, there to instruct the boys in tribal rites and the girls in their female responsibilities.[33]

Marriage

That marriage is vested with a social significance in Africa is attested by the intricate network of rules regulating the whole process of choosing a partner, of sustaining the relation, and if necessary of breaking it in divorce. Parental ar-

Circumcision celebration. (Nancy Durrell McKenna/Photo Researchers.)

rangement of marriage is customary, and betrothal is celebrated by an exchange of gifts between the families. Dowries are a frequent rule in Africa. The wedding ceremony is celebrated in ritual that is often both extensive and expensive. Polygamy is common though by no means universal. Divorce customs vary, though divorce occurs most often for reasons of sterility or barrenness. While sex is set within an intricate network of regulations, it generally carries an affirmative valuation and indeed often takes on symbolic significance as an expression of the will to live.

Death As in all human societies, death is for African societies a matter of deeply serious—indeed fearful—concern. This concern finds expression in ritual. There is general belief among African religions in a life beyond death. Ceremonies seek to prepare the corpse for its journey into a new world and also seek to help society and the survivors cope with their grief and loss. Death is generally regarded as an enemy, and it is sometimes asserted to be a penalty for the misdeeds of the dead or those close to them. Reincarnation is a frequent belief, although often the dead are feared and their return is regarded as a threat to the living.

RELIGIOUS African traditional religion shows an instructive variety of specialized religious
ROLES roles, ranging from prophets, shamans, or oracles through sacred kings to the traditional medicine man. In a variety of symbol systems and by a variety of

techniques throughout Africa, shamans or prophets foresee the future and offer advice and guidance. The most frequent device is a chance event such as the tossing of dice, nuts, or shells, plus interpretation by the prophet. As Noel King has observed, an element of shrewd advice is usually added to this mixture. Notable among instrumentalities or devices is the poison oracle, in which poison is administered to an animal (formerly, it is said, to human subjects) with one answer if the animal survives and the other if it dies. Whatever the means and medium, oracles still exert great influence on both individual and social conduct throughout Africa. Parrinder observes that in times of social stress, resort to oracles increases proportionally to felt anxiety.[34]

Closely related to, but distinguishable from, oracles or prophets are magicians. Like prophets, they invoke occult powers, but they do so with the intention of control or manipulation. Magical charms or amulets are of great frequency, and practitioners of magical arts are in great demand. Harmful or black magic is much feared; and wherever it is detected, its practitioners are punished and their power is nullified by forms of white magic. The latter, whose function is to help people, is applied especially to problems of health and disease. The medicine man is a traditional figure who supplements magic with a variety of folk medical remedies.

In sharp contrast to both the prophet and the magician is the figure of the priest, whose field is the established ritual forms which relate human life to transcendence and in which the central values of the society find expression. Hence priests are important and generally respected social functionaries. In some cases they are set apart from secular society for their sacred duties; in other cases the priestly function is an avocation for individuals whose vocation is within secular society. Priestly ritual often deals with such practical matters as crops, weather, and the keeping of temples and other sacred places. Often the functions are political: the validation or ratification of society's power system. Indeed in some African societies priest and king are the same person.

The sacred king is an important and frequent figure in African society. Noel King lists the names and achievements of several recent sacred kings, such as Muteesa I of Buganda (d. 1884) and Kabalego of Bimyoro (d. 1923).[35] This traditional sacredness of African rulers seems to have rubbed off on some contemporary African political leaders. In this, as in other respects, the customs of centuries cannot be undone by a decade or two of modernization and westernization.

THE FUTURE OF AFRICAN TRADITIONAL RELIGION

What the future holds for African traditional religion is today a vast question mark. The impact of modern science and technology and the rapid and radical social change which follow in their wake render much of traditional religion problematic. Also, other faiths and philosophies as divergent as Islam, Christianity, and Marxism pose new issues for traditional religions. Will Africa's traditional religions be able to cope with these new situations? One possibility already illustrated in fact is a combination of traditional religion with these other faiths. Two instances of this combination can be cited. Simon Kimbangu, educated in a British Baptist mission, began in 1921 to preach a black African Christianity. He died in jail in 1950, and his followers revere him as a black Christ. Isaiah Shembe, Zulu visionary and prophet, founded the Ama Nazaretha church in 1911. He became for his followers a messiah, or—as they claim today—king of the Nazarenes and prophet to the Zulus. His movement continues in vigorous life as what has been labeled a *Zulu Zion*.

In the ambiguous present situation, one fact is clear: African people as individuals and as societies will continue to need the kind of guidance which in the past they have derived from their traditional religions.

NATIVE AMERICAN RELIGION

American Indian religion, like African religion, takes a position on the border territory between precivilized and civilized cultures and religions, possessing some but not all of Childe's nine features of civilization. As in Africa there is a general absence of writing. Yet many of the American Indian societies have been far too large and too differentiated for classification as folk societies. For example, the Kwakiutls of the northwest possessed a society with elaborated economic and political structures and functions. The same might also be said of the Iroquois of the northeast. As might be expected for so vast an area as North America, there are extensive regional variations.

A distinction with implications for every aspect of culture is that between tribes which are hunters and gatherers, on the one hand, and the food cultivators or farmers, on the other. Not only do the latter celebrate the cycle of the agricultural year in ways unknown to the former, but as one writer points out, even their myths of creation differ sharply. For the hunter-gatherers there are stories of a transformer or trickster who set things in motion, while for the farmers the creator is not a person but a "Power in the Sky."[36]

One important issue is the persistence among white Americans of stereotypes of American Indian people, a caricatured picture which mixes in equal amounts ignorance, hostility, and sentimentality. In such a situation our first duty for factual study is to listen and look with an open mind.

In sharp contrast to Africa, where—according to present theory—the human species began, humankind has only recently come to the American continents, crossing the Aleutian land bridge, as it then existed, sometime between 25,000 and 50,000 years ago and then fanning out to populate both North and South America.[37] Radioactive carbon dating and other contemporary instrumentalities give evidence of human habitation of North America over this period of time.

RECURRING THEMES

Like African religion, American Indian religion presents a picture of great diversity. Hence here too we shall have to content ourselves by sketching a few persistently recurring themes with illustrations. As with Africa, these themes will be (1) images and forms of transcendence, along with human responses in myth and ritual, (2) some milestones in the course of individual life, and (3) some special religious roles such as shaman and priest. Reasons of space also force a limitation to Indians north of the Rio Grande. Here again, as in the case of African religion, we note these elements as parts of an integral whole which is a people's way or path of life. Indeed, for American Indian religions, this integral whole constitutes an excellent expression of an ordered, harmonious cosmos. These religions are emphatically of the first, or cosmic, type.

TRANSCEN- Images and forms of the transcendent begin with what Ruth Underhill calls the
DENCE *supernatural.*[38] In *Red Man's Religion* she argues that this is a more adequate category for Indian religious experience than either "god" or "spirit," citing many instances where such Indian words as *wakan, orenda*, and *manitu* refer to a power, good or evil, which like a mysterious kind of spiritual electricity flows through unusual persons, events, or objects, rendering them holy or sacred, hence not to be dealt with in ordinary secular ways. Hence the supernatural is the source of both magic and religion. Historians of religion have often used the Melanesian term *mana* as a label for this power and its effects.

While, as Underhill clearly shows, holy power often assumes this pervasive and impersonal form, it also assumes personal shapes and images. Indeed these same words, *wakan, orenda*, and *manitu*, often designate deities or spirits. As in Africa, American Indian religion has the idea of a single high god as presence in the background of human life. He (or she) is great spirit or even at times first cause or power. *Wakan Taka* is sometimes translated as "Great Spirit," but also alternatively as "Great Mystery." More anthropomorphically, the high god is "Man Above."[39] The Zuni even say that the creator, Awonawilona, thought himself into being, thus illustrating the philosophically sophisticated conception of self-subsistence or self-existence.[40]

Paul Radin, in an article entitled "Monotheism among American Indians," contrasts two aspects or images of the high god: the supreme deity, just and rational but remote, on the one hand, and on the other hand, the transformer (or trickster, as he is sometimes portrayed), who is not always just or fair, but who actively intervenes in human life.[41] For example, for the Crow of Montana, the sun is the supreme deity, but the transformer and trickster is Coyote, whose activities are sometimes capricious but always important. A variation of the transformer or trickster is the myth of the "earth diver" which recurs in different forms in Indian and other cultures. According to this account, an animal spirit (sometimes, plausibly, Beaver) dived into the primeval waters and brought up a piece of earth from which the world or cosmos takes its origin.

The "personalizing of power" produces not only the high god but also a vast throng of gods and spirits who are influential in the Indian world for good and evil. The Navajo speak of Mother Earth and Father Sky.[42] Of these "nature persons" many are the animals upon whom the hunting tribes are dependent for life and livelihood. Often hunters ask permission of the animal spirit to kill their prey. Sometimes there are myths and rituals concerning the owner, leader, or mother of the animals who can assume either human or animal form, and who sets conditions for human hunters.

In this populous pantheon Thunderbird plays various roles. Among the Kwakiutl he has been the divine friend who helped to build their first house, who appears on the chief's totem pole, and who promises to watch over the tribe. On the central plains his great voice signaled the coming of spring, and he is also pitted in myth against the evil water monster.[43]

Indian pantheons include evil as well as good spirits. For example, the Ojibwa told of Windigo, a gruesome cannibal who ate a man and spewed him out as also a cannibal. The Kawkiutl told of a fearful female spirit who pursued travelers and haunted the forests.

More amiable are the kachina figures, dancers, and dolls of the southwest—the last, well-known to visitors and tourists. In their original meaning the kachinas were spirits of ancestors, animals, plants, and other "nature persons," which is to say important personal forces of the living natural and social environment of the Indians. The Kachina cult, which is at least 600 years old, features festival dancing in which the dancers wearing kachina masks lose their own identity and take on that of the spirit or god.[44]

The integral relation of myth and ritual as responses to the supernatural finds many illustrations among American Indians. Many myths of the cosmos deal with images of the center and the four directions, with such correlative ceremonies as smoking the sacred tobacco and blowing the smoke successively in the four directions, thus ritually relating human life to the cosmos. Indian designs and diagrams show this same relation of center to the directions, often also illustrating the ever-recurrent relation of microcosm to macrocosm. A further corollary of such cosmological myth and ritual is the sacredness, and hence the inalienability, of the land.

The four-directions theme figures prominently in the Shalako ceremony of the Zuni. This midwinter ceremony, as reported in a notable essay by Edmund Wilson, features masked figures representing the tribal gods, who dance, sing, and speak, coming in council to bless the community. Wilson concludes of the Zuni that this ceremony guarantees their favor with the gods. "The whole complicated society of the Zuni depends on this dance."[45]

Equally important but different in meaning is the Sun Dance ceremony of the plains Indians of the United States and Canada. Its origin and history are uncertain; earlier forms of this ceremony featured dancers who skewered their chest muscles and attached the skewer by a thong to a pole of a tipi, which then they circled in continuous dance. Hence the sun dance was, among other things, a way in which young braves demonstrated their indifference to pain. This dance, outlawed by the Canadian and United States governments in this early cruel form, has been revived as a festive occasion in which the dance persists, to quote Ruth Underhill, as a ritual "for the general welfare."[46]

Still different in both inception and significance was the Ghost Dance of 1870 and 1890. The Ghost Dance movement began at a time when, in the face of the westward movement of white people, the situation of the Indians ap-

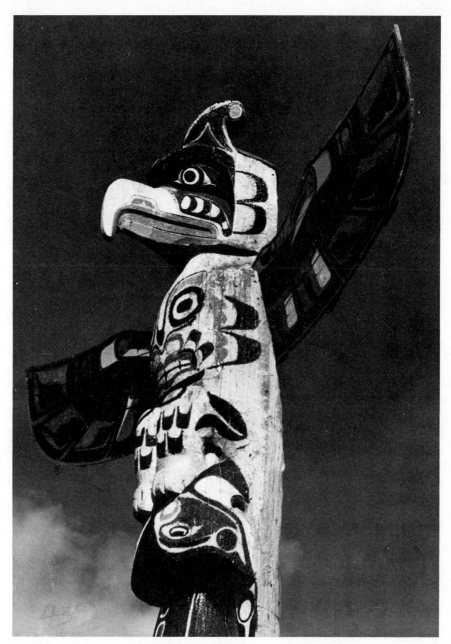

This totem pole of the Kwakiuti Indians, with Thunderbird perched on Whale, is a mortuary pole at a burial ground. (Paolo Koch/Photo Researchers.)

Pottery water vessel from Acoma Pueblo, New Mexico. (Fine Arts Museum of San Francisco at the M. H. de Young Museum.)

peared desperate. It began with a Paiute charismatic leader named Jack Wilson (whose Indian name was Wowoka), who declared that if Indians would join in his dance the whites would recede, the lands would be restored to the Indians, the Indian ancestors would return, and a great new and good age would dawn.[47] The ceremony lasted five nights and was characterized by ecstatic dancing and hypnotic states. The first outbreak of the movement in 1870 was limited largely to California Indians, but in 1890 it broke out again and gained followers throughout the western states. A grim climax was achieved at Wounded Knee, South Dakota, in December 1890, where hundreds of Indians wearing ghost shirts, which they believed would protect them against the whites' bullets, were massacred by United States soldiers.

Similar in its origin in the desperate situation of the Indians but different in form and function is the Peyote cult. This centers in the sacramental eating of

Ghost dance shirt of Sioux Indians, South Dakota. (The Museum of the American Indian.)

peyote, a hallucinogenic Mexican cactus plant. With accompanying prayer, song, and ceremony, peyote is eaten and results in states of religious exaltation. The Peyote cult is actually an Indian variant of Christianity in which, as an adherent expressed the matter to an observer, "the white man talks about Jesus; we talk to Jesus."[48] Many anthropological observers regard the Peyote cult as more of an escape than a solution for American Indians.

STAGES ON LIFE'S WAY   From birth to death, American Indian religion has sanctified and socialized the milestones of individual life.

Birth   Social concern has often anticipated birth with prenatal care. In one ritual of American Indians, the umbilical cord of the newborn is dried and hung on the child's cradle and later carried on the child's belt. The naming ceremony is frequently a notable social occasion alike for the child and for family and community.

Initiation   One of the most important and widely recurring features of American Indian religion has been the vision quest for adolescent boys, and sometimes for girls as well. Many tribes have sent their young people into the wilderness to fast and endure hardship and solitude, all in quest of a vision. When finally the vision comes, it is received as a supernatural visitation. The effect upon the human recipient is to make him or her a devotee of the visitant spirit or power. The psychological impact of the experience is to provide the young person with a new and stable integration of character, and a clear direction for his or her relation to society. Once received, the vision becomes one's possession for life. There are even stories of attempts to sell this possession to others!

Marriage

Marriage among American Indians is set within intricate networks of social relations. There is no single pattern, and matrilineal and matrilocal customs have been not infrequent. There are occasional records of polygamy. Among the Arapahos, a girl could set the flap of the family tipi to indicate her interest in a possible partner. The marriage ceremony itself is generally simple, the couple sharing a meal and a fur robe for bed. Divorce has usually been possible.

Related to marital customs has been the widespread Indian belief in what Underhill terms "womanpower."[49] This is the Indian belief that embodied in women is a mysterious numinous power for good or evil. This is illustrated by attitudes toward menstruation, many tribes segregating women in menstrual lodges during their monthly period. Childbirth has followed a similar pattern of separation. The custom of *couvade*, in which the husband ironically takes to bed when his wife gives birth, has been practiced by some tribes.

Death

The general Indian attitude toward death has been one of fear and avoidance. Contact with the corpse leads to separation or isolation from other people. There is a variety of beliefs in survival of some sort. There are also mourning customs, some both expensive and extensive. The souls of the dead are viewed ambivalently, being told in one funeral ritual, "You are gone now. Go."[50]

RELIGIOUS ROLES

Of the special religious roles, those of medicine man, shaman, and priest have been particularly notable. At times they have overlapped. The medicine man, like his counterpart in other traditional religious systems around the world, has been a healer, using both supernatural power and folk remedies. Another somewhat different kind of charismatic religious figure is illustrated by the succession of popular leaders, such as Wowoka of the Ghost Dance movement. Many writers use the terms *messiah* and *messianic* to characterize their roles, for they have sought to lead their people out of present misery to a good age of the future. Some have been hostile to white people; others counsel coexistence. Among the best known of such prophets or messiahs were Handsome Lake, an Iroquois leader of the early nineteenth century; John Smohalla of the mid-nineteenth century in the northwest; John Slocum of the same region in the 1880s; and, as already mentioned, Jack Wilson or Wowoka of the Ghost Dance movement.[51] The American Indian movement provides contemporary illustrations of aspirants for this kind of leadership and power.

In contrast to such charismatic prophets, whose credibility depended upon a vision of some sort, are the priests who lead in established ritual and for whom no vision is deemed necessary. By established rite and myth they lead their people into the presence of the supernatural. In some situations the two roles of priest and prophet are separated; in other situations they overlap.

Priests play particularly significant roles in the rituals of farming Indians of the southwest.

THE FUTURE OF NATIVE AMERICAN RELIGION

In the present revival of interest in the life and culture of American Indians has come a renewed interest in their traditional religion, on the part of both observers and participants. Amid current claims and counterclaims, how much of this renewed interest will endure and how much will pass yet remains to be seen.

EGYPTIAN RELIGION

Ancient Egypt is one of humanity's oldest civilizations, the date for its historical or civilized beginning now being reckoned as 3110 BCE. Egypt is also one of the longest continuous civilized traditions in the world, extending from its beginning to Alexander the Great's conquest of Egypt in 332 BCE. This history is conventionally chronicled by modern historians in some thirty dynasties which are grouped into three Kingdoms, Old, Middle, and New. The Old Kingdom comprised dynasties 1 to 6, and was followed by an intermediate period of breakdown in central authority consisting of dynasties 7 to 11. The Middle Kingdom consisted of dynasty 12. This was followed by a second intermediate period of dynasties 13 to 17, which were noteworthy for the rule of Egypt by foreign invaders called the Hyksos. The New Kingdom consisted of dynasties 18 to 30.[52]

Many of the distinctive features of this ancient civilization such as pyramids, mummies, and scarabs are still securely lodged in humanity's memory, testifying as they do to the fact of long endurance through time. Even more memorable was the Egyptian conception of the pharaoh as god-king—an idea destined to be repeated many times in subsequent human history.

Geographically Egypt was—and still is—the Nile Valley, as it has been vividly characterized, that "green gash of life" bounded on both sides by brown desert.[53] Never more than a few miles wide, the Nile Valley extends, and the river flows, from south to north for 900 miles, from its source in modern Lake Nasser to the wide delta from which its waters empty into the Mediterranean Sea.

While ancient Egyptian history and archeology possess rich resources in texts and artifacts, great ambiguity in their interpretation as well as large gaps in the record still persist. It is also true that the Egyptians never achieved the systematic task of ordering either their records, or more basically the myths and rituals of their common life. The pantheon of their many gods and goddesses also remained similarly unordered and chaotic.

From prehistoric times come a great number of local sites in the Nile Valley, each with its own local deities. Often when one city conquered another, its god was likewise victorious. At times these deities were conjoined, as, for example, Amon-Re. Many of these divine figures were animals or animal-headed. Several such prehistoric deities persisted into historical times. Among them were Hathor, the cow, and Horus, the hawk. Thoth, the god of learning, wore the head of an ibis, and Anubis, the guardian of the cemetery, had a jackal's head.

Prominent among the enduring themes of Egyptian religion was the sun as the source of both light and life or vitality. Many gods presided over different aspects of the sun. Thus the rising sun was Kheprer. Re or Ra was the noontide sun, as well as the dominant deity of several dynasties and city states. Atun presided over the declining or evening sun. Yet further the sun was also Horus, the high-flying falcon.

Perhaps most unusual of all was the identification of the sun with the scarab or dung beetle. Modern interpreters have speculated that the Egyptians observed the dung beetle emerging from its source, and misunderstood it as self-generating, or *sui generis*. From this mistaken interpretation it was only a single step further to view the scarab as a symbol, like the sun, for life or vitality.

A distinctly different and also temporary variation on the sun as deity took place in the eighteenth dynasty with the accession to the throne of Amenhotep IV (1372–1354 BCE).[54] This pharaoh changed his name to Ikhnaton or Akhnaton, and redirected Egyptian religion to a new sun god named Aton. Rejecting polytheism, Akhnaton proclaimed Aton as the sole object of worship and service. He moved his capital to the new city of Akhetaton (the modern tel el Amarna), apparently in order to break the power of the priesthood of the old god, Amon. He pushed to the extreme of defacing all monuments on which Amon's name appeared.

However, this new solar monotheism of Aton did not outlive Akhnaton's life. With his successor Tutankamon, the influence of the priests of Amon returned, and the old cult resumed its sway.

Another distinctive and persistent configuration of myth and ritual centered in the god Osiris and his wife, or sister, Isis. Dating from prehistoric time Osiris was said to have been the originator of agriculture and other useful arts. According to one cycle of myths, Osiris was treacherously slain by his evil brother Set, who cut his body into fourteen pieces and spread the pieces throughout Egypt. Thereupon Isis sought and found the scattered body and buried the pieces in places which then became sacred shrines.

According to still another version of the myth, Osiris's body was placed in a coffin which floated down the Nile and out to sea. It was recovered off the Syrian coast and brought back to Egypt by Isis. Meanwhile Horus, the son of Osiris and Isis, killed the villain Set and became king and judge of the underworld.

The worship of Osiris became one of the great cults of ancient Egypt, persisting until Roman times. Variously identified with the waters of the Nile, and the moon and sun as well as the seasonal cycle of agricultural life, Osiris was commonly represented as swathed in grave clothes, though wearing the crown of upper Egypt and also carrying a whip and crook.

Still another related configuration of elements in Egyptian religion centered in death and life after death. Among the earliest and surely the largest monuments to this aspect of Egyptian religion are the pyramids. The pyramids were royal tombs. In their developed form they date from the fourth to the sixth dynasties of the Old Kingdom. The best known and greatest of the pyramids is that at Gizeh, built by Khufu or Cheops of the fourth dynasty (2680–2565 BCE).

In the dry climate of upper Egypt mummies survive from prehistoric times. By the time of the New Kingdom the art of mummification reached its highest point. The process was based upon the belief that the body was necessary for survival to the next life. The internal organs including the brain were removed by the embalmer, and the body cavity was filled with myrrh, then sewn together and wrapped in linen.

All of this was related to the double concepts of the soul as *ba* and *ka*. The former was conceived as the animating spirit, seated in the heart or abdomen and flying away from the body at death. However, the *ba* loved its body and sought to return at the next life.

By contrast the *ka* consisted of the mental aspects of personality. It was thought to be the source of motives and intentions, and was symbolized by two arms outstretched. It was this soul which took up residence in the statue of the deceased which was placed in the tomb.

In such ways the Egyptians envisioned the life of the spirit, both here and hereafter. Conceptions of the next world were similarly concrete and vivid. The

Sphinx and pyramids of Cairo. (George Daniell/Photo Researchers.)

needs of the *ba* were met by jars of water and food placed in the tomb. The *ka* was provided with chair, bed, and other equipment. Placed in the tomb as a guidebook for the soul's journey were chapters of the *Book of the Dead*, or, as it has been more accurately translated, *The Book of the Going Forth by Day*.[55] This "book" consisted of a variety of spells, incantations, and prayers.

A persistent and recurrent myth depicted the soul's entry into Osiris's court. The person's heart would then be weighed in a scales against a feather. Persons of hearts thus proved "light" were assured of passage to a blessed realm in the land of the sun. Boats were often provided for this passage. The dead were at times thought to become stars or to be merged with the sun and sun-god. In such ways the Egyptians envisaged themselves and their destiny in life and in life beyond death.

MESOPOTAMIAN RELIGION

Mesopotamia (this Greek word means "between the rivers," i.e., the Tigris and Euphrates) has been both the cradle and the tomb of many civilizations during its more than six millennia of history and prehistory. The "fertile crescent," of which Mesopotamia is a part, is a crescent-shaped band of habitable land bordering the Arabian desert. Beginning from Mesopotamia, it extends northwestward to Syria, then bends southward along the Syrian and Israeli coast to the border of Egypt. This region has been inhabited from the stone ages to the present, and throughout its history it has been the scene of ever-recurring wars and struggles for possession. It has also been important as a source region for religions. At least three living religions began here: Judaism, Christianity, and Islam. Another, Zoroastrianism, began in adjacent Iran.

In a notable study of ancient mideastern civilizations entitled *Before Philosophy* the authors propose as a basic metaphor for Mesopotamia, "the cosmos as state."[56] For Mesopotamia, gods, human beings, and the many and various objects of nature are citizens together of this cosmic state. While authority is located in the gods or "higher powers," it is extended homogeneously over the entire cosmos. Citizens of this state are also related to each other in I-thou or person-person terms, and their lives are ruled and guided by the characteristic myths and rituals of Mesopotamian religion.

Mesopotamia is also one of the primary source regions of the ancient urban revolution, or the breakthrough from folk society to civilized city-states. The first known civilized inhabitants of Mesopotamia were Sumerians, a people associated with Sumer, which was one of the several city-states that sprang into being ca. 4000 BCE. The new social form was, in part at least, a result of new irrigated forms of agriculture. Apparently unrelated to other known languages, Sumerian used an alphabet of wedge-shaped cuneiform characters.

In addition to Sumer, there were other city-states, such as Kish, Lagash, and Ur—Ur being the one from which, many centuries later (ca. 2000 BCE), Abraham is said to have migrated along the fertile crescent, first to Syria then to Israel.[57]

These Sumerian city-states possessed a new and significant religious organization. Each city had its own god, whose representatives, i.e., the local priests, not only cared for the temple and presided at festivals but also were managers of local agriculture. Indeed, according to one hypothesis, writing was first invented in Mesopotamia as a device for recording agricultural and commercial transactions. These Sumerian city-states maintained a stable way of life for several hundred years, before their conquest by a Semitic people whose Mesopotamian base was the city of Akkad. The newcomers spoke a Semitic tongue, Akkadian. Under King Sargon I of Akkad they conquered and held extensive sections of Mesopotamia. However, in another few centuries the cycle of rise and fall of empires carried the new conquerors to downfall. Then another turn of the same wheel brought still another Semitic dynasty to power.

The most important king of this new dynasty was Hammurabi (1728–1686 BCE), famous for his code of laws. As Moses received the Ten Commandments from the Lord, so Hammurabi received his code from Shamash, the Babylonian sun god. These two ancient law codes are similar in their avowal of the *lex talionis*, or "law of equal vengeance," prescribing an eye for an eye and a tooth for a tooth. Soon after Hammurabi's time, Babylon fell to another invading group, the Kassites, whose brief triumph gave way in turn to the Assyrians, then the Chaldeans, and after them the Persians.

Throughout these vast and violent changes, the Mesopotamian religion maintained remarkable stability. Its populous pantheon of gods and goddesses dating from early Sumerian times gained some new names and new functions, and the basic myths were altered from time to time to fit new situations and new needs, yet the overarching fact was continuity.

Mesopotamian seal showing sacred tree flanked by priests. (Pierport Morgan Library, New York.)

Most of the many deities of ancient Mesopotamia were expressions of some natural or social force or object, or a combination of these. The social forces were those of the urban or city-state civilization. The gods were transcendental rulers modeled after their earthly counterparts, and the council of the gods was also drawn from earthly models. It is not too much to say that Mesopotamian religion was a kind of transcendental reflection of the order of social life.

The gods also continued to be the rulers of nature, the persistent and encompassing environment of society. For example, Anu was the god of heaven and also chief deity of Erech. In some early pantheons he was also the ruler of the gods. Enlil, god of the air, ruled at Nippur. Sin was a moon goddess who ruled at Ur. Shamash was the sun god of Lachish. Ea, or Enki, was a water god whose home was Eridu. Nintud, later to become Ishtar, was the mother goddess of Kish. These and other deities were said to gather in a celestial council, like the councils of leading men of a city. These deities also were regarded as the superior citizens of the cosmic state whose other members included human beings on earth and even objects of nature as well. In this cosmic state the principle of continuity, described in Chapter 1, prevailed among all elements of the whole. From the highest deity down through humankind to the humblest object of nature, all were members together of a single homogeneous and ordered society.

In many documents the Mesopotamian pantheon featured divine couples, each god being paired with a goddess. Thus familial (and also extrafamilial) relations were assumed as matters of fact for the gods. Often in Mesopotamia and elsewhere in the ancient world, these assumptions produced erotic forms of ritual. The ritual marriage of god and goddess was widely believed to induce the fertility of the earth which brought forth each year's crop. In emulation of god and goddess, erotic rituals with priests or priestesses of the gods were customary religious practices. Temple prostitution was frequent in ancient Mesopotamia.

Probably the most prominent and important later arrival in the Mesopotamian pantheon was Marduk of Babylon. His rise coincided with that of the city of Babylon under the second Semitic dynasty in the late centuries of the third millennium. That Marduk was a war god constituted a religious recognition of the historic fact that war was becoming an increasing preoccupation of the Babylonian servants of the gods. Marduk was also a god of the light of the heaven and of the city of Babylon. The ancient Sumerian creation story was probably altered by Marduk's priests to give their god a central place in its dramatic liturgy. Again we note the impact of the urban revolution on Babylonia's religious thought and practice.

Beside Marduk was Ishtar, the great mother goddess. She was wife and mother of Tammuz, god of the spring, and she presided over fertility in nature and human beings. The planet Venus was sacred to her, and her annual descent to the underworld and return to earth marked the seasonal cycle of the year.

Ishtar was one of the great deities of the ancient Near East. We shall meet her repeatedly elsewhere under other names.

The lively imagination of Mesopotamia produced a luxuriant variety of myths and other literature, among which were two of the great documents of the world's religious literature, the creation story (often called by its first two words, *Enuma Elish*, meaning "when on high") and the Gilgamesh epic. The Babylonian creation story is significant both in itself and for its similarities to and contrasts with the biblical creation story and stories of origin in other religions. The present text is a seventh-century BCE version from the library of the Assyrian king Ashurbanipal, but the original may be traced back to the early part of the second millennium BCE.

The Babylonian story begins with the original divine pair, the god Apsu and the goddess Tiamat, the former a deity of fresh water and the latter of the salt sea. From these two are derived the host of gods and goddesses who inhabit the regions on high. The dramatic conflict which forms the plot of the Enuma Elish begins when Apsu is disturbed by the noise of his children. He and his mate resolve to destroy their offspring. However, the god Ea acts first, killing his father, Apsu. Gathering allies, Tiamat resolves upon revenge. The opposing gods, gathering for council of war, find a leader in Marduk, who accepts the role of mortal combat with Tiamat, but only on condition that he be accorded chief place among the gods.

The combat between Marduk and Tiamat forms the highly dramatic climax of the story. Tiamat draws into her service many of the monsters of the deep. She covers herself magically with a protective red paste which recalls the red color of prehistoric art and religion. But Marduk is equal to the situation. When Tiamat opens her mouth, he drives in his sword so that she cannot close it. Then he slits Tiamat apart, placing the one half over humankind as the heavens above and the other half under foot as the earth. The outlines of cosmogonic myth are clearly present in this episode, interpreting heaven and earth in terms of Tiamat's body.

Having begun the task of fixing the definite outlines and forms of the cosmos, Marduk continues the work of creation by making humanity. He does so, speaking words similar to those in Genesis:

> Marduk opened his mouth and unto Ea he spoke
> That which he conceived in his heart he made known unto him:
> "My blood will I take and bone will I fashion
> I shall create man who shall inherit the earth."[58]

From humanity Marduk proceeds to complete the work of creating the world, culminating in the city of Babylon. The creation story comes to dramatic completion with the recitation of the fifty names of Marduk. This and other features of the story make clear its ritual use as a part of the Babylonian New Year's day celebration. The recitation of the myth was conceived as an essential feature

in sustaining the orderly cosmos of which Babylon and its way of life constituted the center. The Babylonian creation story is an excellent illustration of the
first, or cosmic, type of myth, in contrast to the historical, or third, type as illustrated by Genesis in the Bible.

The Gilgamesh epic differs from the Enuma Elish in that its characters are
more human than divine. Gilgamesh, the hero, is like many of the Greek heroes, part god and part human. He is ruler of the city-state of Uruk. The plot of
the epic consists of his futile, tragic pursuit of a medicine of immortality. Here
is history's first story of a human being against death. Seeking an answer to the
problem of mortality, Gilgamesh sets out toward a western land guarded by a
divine monster named Humbaba. His friend and travel companion, Enkidu, of-
fends Ishtar and is condemned to die. In his wanderings Gilgamesh comes to
an ancient ancestor, Utnapishtim, who tells him a flood story which is at several
significant points identical with the biblical story. Both stories tell of a universal
deluge from which a few people and animals escape by means of an ark. The
main difference between the Hebrew and Babylonian stories is the monotheism
of the former and the polytheism of the latter. Utnapishtim also gives Gilgamesh
an herb of immortality, which Gilgamesh carelessly leaves on the shore of the
pool while he bathes, only to have it swallowed by a serpent. The conclusion
apparently is that human beings have no alternative but to endure their mortality, to continue to live in the face of the death which is human fate.

Magic, which is by no means absent from the two great epics, was also a
pervasive element in Babylonian popular religion. The people were provided
with spells or incantations for every occasion of life, there were priests to administer the spells, and there were innumerable gods, godlings, and demons
who effectively carried them out.

The orders and corporations of priests constituted an important class of
Babylonian society. Many of the temples in which these priests worshiped,
lived, and worked have been uncovered by modern archeology. The temple
compound, consisting of numerous buildings for worship as well as schools,
libraries, and buildings for the numerous other activities of the priests, centered in a *ziggurat*, which was a pyramid-shaped structure with a shrine at the
top. Similar to other religious edifices, ranging from the pyramids of Egypt to
the stupas of India or pagodas of the Buddhist world, the ziggurat appears to
have symbolized the earth mountain. The Akkadian word *ziggurat* means
"mountaintop" or "pinnacle." At the summit was an *axis mundi*, or "axis of the
world." The ziggurat was probably a remote ancestor of the church steeple.

In their temple compounds, the Babylonian priests not only prayed, recited their endless spells, and made oracular forecasts of the future, but pursued lore and scholarship which led them to the beginnings of astronomy.
Their knowledge was passed on to their students in the first known schools of
history.[59] These priests also carried on extensive business and commercial activities.

Like many other chapters of the human past, ancient Mesopotamia was destined to be surpassed and left in oblivion to await the spades of modern arche-

ology. Mesopotamia lacked the adventurous mind of Greece or the adventurous faith of Israel. Yet within this Mesopotamian cosmos—and others like it in many other regions of the world—the journey of civilized humanity began. From these ancient sources, humanity took its beginning.

GREEK RELIGION

In contrast to Mesopotamia, important elements of ancient Greece still live today. Twentieth-century western languages, arts, philosophy, science, and politics all still bear living and powerful Greek influence. While no one worships Zeus, Apollo, or Dionysus, these gods too live on in many aspects of contemporary religious and cultural life.

Modern historical and archeological study is radically revising our understanding of the origins and early days of Greece and Greek religion. Before the city-states of the Hellenic age, indeed before the earlier Homeric age, lies a long period of migrations and movements of peoples which historians are only beginning to understand. Perhaps as early as the twentieth century BCE invaders swept into Greece from the north, subjugating the so-called Helladic peoples. *Aryan* or *Indo-European* is a label which identifies the speech of these invaders as one of a family of languages extending from Sanskrit in India to Greek, Latin, and modern European languages. The first civilization of which there is detailed and reliable knowledge is that of the Minoans of Crete (ca. 2200–1100 BCE) and the related bronze age Aegeans of the mainland and the Greek archipelago. Around 1400 BCE disaster overtook Knossus on Crete. Perhaps it was an earthquake, perhaps a new wave of invaders, but Crete never regained its previous glory. However, Minoan influence spread to the mainland in the form of Mycenaean civilization. The Homeric age may be understood as a later stage of

Three deities from Mycenae. (National Archeological Museum, Athens, Greece.)

this culture. Again, however, invasion from the north, this time from the Dorians, was the spur to change. It overthrew Mycenaean culture but at the same time dispersed Mycenaean influence to the western shores of Asia Minor. From the new combination of elements emerged the city-state civilization of Greece's golden age.

Greek history from this period onward is better known to us. Among the Greek city-states Athens led the heroic resistance to Persia, and thereby gained both glory and the leadership of the Greek world. The great age of Athens lasted approximately from the time of the Persian wars (490–480 BCE) until the Peloponnesian War (430–404 BCE). The fratricidal strife of the latter war sealed the doom not only of the great age of Athens but of the Greek city-states. The next century saw the rise of Philip of Macedon and his son, Alexander, whose far-flung conquests marked the historic transformation from Hellenic to Hellenistic Greece. The Hellenic age was the great creative period of Greek thought and life; the Hellenistic age was the later period (usually dated from the death of Alexander, 321 BCE) in which Greek language, literature, and thought were spread over the whole Mediterranean world. Greek culture combined with Roman power to produce a more or less unified civilization which endured for eight centuries, until Rome fell. Then, out of the Dark Ages, a new civilization called the *West* or *Christendom* came into being.

Gilbert Murray has called attention to the historical changes and developments of Greek religion in his book *Five Stages of Greek Religion*.[60] While much of Murray's analysis has been changed and corrected by more recent scholarship, his five stages remain useful as an outline for historical development. We shall use them for this purpose.

STAGE 1: PRE-HOMERIC (BEFORE 700 BCE)

The first stage was the early pre-Homeric period during which successive waves of invaders swept into Greece from the north, mixing their own religious beliefs and practices with those of previous inhabitants. It was an age of local gods, who often were envisaged not as definite persons but as holy powers, and before whom (or which) people bowed in primitive and fearful awe, appeasing by sacrifice and celebrating in a wide variety of folk festivals. These holy powers provide significant illustration of the definition of religion given in Chapter 1 and elaborated in the section on folk religion in this chapter. Many of these gods or powers were *chthonic*, or derived from the earth and dwelling in the earth rather than in the sky. Murray reconstructs this very ancient period of Greek religion by inference from later Athenian folk festivals such as the Diasia, which was devoted to Zeus Meilichus, or Zeus of Placation; the Thesmophoria, devoted to Demeter and Persephone; and the Anthesteria, devoted to placating the spirits of the dead. Some of the gods of the later Homeric times go back to this early period, but their characters and functions differed from those of subsequent ages. Zeus was Father Sky, but he also assumed many local roles and functions in different regions. At Dodona he gave oracles through a sacred oak tree. In other places he was a fertility deity, a quality preserved in his later philanderings. He was the guardian of several city-states. He was also the god of clouds, rainmaking, and the thunderbolt.

At this period Zeus was not yet married to Hera, who in some regions appears to have been a cow goddess. In the Peloponnesus she was a maiden who made love with the hero Hercules. Some myths connected her with Jason and his quest for the golden fleece. Hera's subsequent marriage to Zeus has been interpreted by Jane Harrison as a mythical expression of the subjugation of indigenous peoples by northern invaders.[61] Thereafter Hera became the jealous wife and Zeus the henpecked and philandering husband. Somewhat ironically, the Greeks came to regard the marriage of Zeus and Hera as the archetypal holy union. Hera became the patron of married women, affording divine protection of marriage and family.

Apollo also had a pre-Homeric history. In early times he was a god of shepherds and farmers, playing his lyre for rural and pastoral followers. He was also an archer whose arrows brought deadly illness. He was probably not Greek in origin, for as late as the *Iliad* he sided not with the Greeks but with the Trojans. Apollo killed a python on the slopes of Mount Parnassus and became the patron deity of Delphi, most famous of Greek oracles. Thereafter he became the god of revelation whose priestesses foretold the future and spoke his words in trance to human seekers. Much later he became also a sun god.

There were many other deities as well. Artemis was a virginal goddess of wild nature and a protector of animals as well as lover of children. Poseidon was probably a horse deity before he became ruler of the sea. Athena was a warrior maiden and owl goddess who came to be patron and protector of Athens. Demeter was Mother Earth, and so presided over agricultural fertility, husbandry, and the seasonal cycle. She was also the mother of the maiden Persephone. There was Dionysus, god of wine and ecstatic rites. There were innumerable local heroes who after death hovered in protection over their local regions. In these and innumerable other divine figures, what the Greeks added to the recurring theme of nature-culture gods was their own sharp and sensitive perception. As a result their gods came in time to be extremely interesting and vivid people.

From this earliest period Greek religion involved rites or ceremonies which formed integral parts of the common life of family, clan, and state. Families had their own gods and ritual forms, as did clans and states, in which participation was as much a civic duty as a religious practice. The cult of the dead united the living with the departed members of the group. Offerings of food and wine were presented at graves. Animal sacrifice, with an accompanying sacrificial meal, was the most frequent ceremony. Divination also played a part in Greek religion from earliest days. In addition to innumerable local oracles throughout Greece, there was the great oracle at Delphi, which gave a semblance of unity to Greek religion and to the Greek people. In order to participate in religious ceremonies, it was necessary to be ritually pure; hence purification rites abounded. Some of these very ancient rituals continued to exist throughout Greek history at the foundation of Greece's many-layered religious structure. Greek people continued in these various ways to act out the values that gave meaning to individual and common life.

STAGE 2: FROM HOMER TO GREEK TRAGEDY (CA. 700–400BCE)

In Gilbert Murray's second stage of Greek religion the gods came to live their immortal lives on Mount Olympus in the divine household presided over by Zeus. While they differed from humankind in not having to die, like human beings they were subject to the impersonal law of fate, or *moira*. Such at least was the view of Homer, who more than any other person was responsible for the organization of the Olympian pantheon in the form which is familiar and traditional in Greece and the West. Current scholarship dates Homer before 700BCE.

The Homeric pantheon was a characteristically Greek achievement in order and humanism. Few religious traditions of humankind have achieved a genuine and widely accepted order for their pantheons. The Babylonians had only minimal success, and the experience of other peoples will be noted as our study proceeds. As noted above, Homer's Olympian deities often represented new characters and functions attached to early pre-Homeric deities. What emerged in the Olympian pantheon were gods and goddesses who were interesting and vividly etched personalities in their amours, their squabbles, and their other activities—as interesting and human as people who created and listened to the Homeric epics.

Yet this achievement was purchased at a price. The Olympian deities still maintained relations to various aspects of nature, as Zeus to his thunderbolt, Apollo to the sun, and Artemis to wild nature. But now a gulf was fixed between nature and the gods. The old, primitive awe and mystery were gone or greatly reduced. Likewise, Homer's reinterpretation of traditional mythical themes often replaced the earlier emotions with a characteristically Greek sense of esthetic measure and beauty. It is also probable, as Murray argues, that the Olympian pantheon was the expression of a new conquering people who cast out old rites and myths as they completed their work of conquest. In any case, it is a historic fact that the Olympian pantheon gave to Greece, divided into many city-states and regions, the unity of a common tradition and a common civic faith. Society equally with nature found expression in Greek religion.

The sturdy Boetian farmer-poet Hesiod (ca. 750 BCE), as well as Homer, left his imprint on Greek religion. Arranging the innumerable multitude of deities in a family tree, beginning with the origin of the world, Hesiod showed how they formed parts of the orderly cosmos which arose out of the original chaos.[62] From chaos came gods and goddesses as well as elements of the cosmic order, and frequently the two are identical. Hesiod's *Theogony* has been significantly contrasted with the Babylonian Enuma Elish.[63] Where the Enuma

Elish expresses a static world, Hesiod's depiction of the world is full of dynamic tensions, pushing onward to new developments. Where the Enuma Elish is a story of order emerging from chaos, the *Theogony* also depicts conflicts among divine authorities. Also, Hesiod's myth is well on the way to becoming philosophy. His gods and goddesses are thinly veiled personifications of metaphysical entities.

As many writers have pointed out, the Olympian gods ignored a crucial human need. This missing element, namely, a strong sense of individual participation and destiny, was provided by the mystery religions. The word *mystery* is from a Greek verb meaning literally "to put one's hand over the mouth," i.e., to be silent. The Greek mystery cults in all their variety seem to have involved certain common elements: (1) preparatory purification such as ritual bathing, (2) instruction in knowledge given behind closed doors and held as the secret possession of members, (3) a secret and solemn beholding of sacred symbolic objects which are closely related to this knowledge, (4) narration or dramatic enactment of a sacred story, and (5) a crowning or wreathing of initiates as full members of the brotherhood, with the promise of a blessed immortality hereafter.

There were three main traditions of mystery religions in ancient Greece—Eleusinian, Dionysian, and Orphic—all dating from the sixth century BCE or before, and lasting for most or all of Greece's long history. The first took its name from the seaside town of Eleusis where its ritual was enacted and to which its sacred processions made their way. The Eleusinian mysteries combined the myth and ritual of Demeter and Persephone with that of Dionysus, and they assured adherents of a "better lot," that is, immortality hereafter. The Dionysian mysteries involved their members in more violent rites. Intoxication with wine being regarded as possession by Dionysus. Was he not god of wine? Often, too, an animal—a kid or bull—was torn apart while still alive, and its blood was drunk and its flesh eaten by maddened worshippers in a rite called *omophagia*. For these reasons the Dionysiac rites maintained throughout Greek history their reputation for wildness and fury, and Dionysus remained a god apart, largely unrelated to the Olympian pantheon.

Orpheus, the traditional founder of the Orphic rites, was himself said to have been the victim of the Dionysiac rite. The Orphic mysteries, as they spread over the Greek world, took the opposite path of asceticism. By following Orphic rules of purity—wearing white garments and abstaining from meat eating, from sexual indulgence, and from other pollutions—one might avoid hell and secure a blessed portion in the hereafter. Orphic influences were strong upon such other groups in Greece as the Pythagorean brotherhood of mathematicians and philosophers, and Plato and his followers. In their forms of thought and worship, the mysteries exerted great influence upon western religion and philosophy. For ancient Greek people they expressed dimensions of life lacking in Olympian religion.

Another distinctively Greek development which took place during Murray's second stage of Greek religion was the emergence of tragic drama. Modern, secular theater goers often forget the religious origin of drama, even when they view modern presentations of Greek tragedy. In ancient Greece, tragic drama grew out of religious ritual and maintained a relation to Greek religion. Indeed it must be viewed as a distinctively Greek religious development—in its time, a new and boldly original development of Greek religion.

The idea of tragedy was a probing of the issues of human fate under the gods; and the tragic dramatists all asserted, with their individual emphases and accents, that when human beings overreach themselves in pride (*hybris*), they are overtaken by doom (*nemesis*) acting in accordance with the law of fate (*moira*). The Greek tragic heroes and heroines are great men and women whose inexorable doom is brought about by a fatal flaw in their nature. While human fate is inevitably tragic, people who meet and undergo this fate achieve their own dignity. The Greek tragedians were humanists in the highest sense.

Extant works of Greek tragedy are from three writers, Aeschylus (d. 455 BCE), Sophocles (d. 406 BCE), and Euripides (d. 406 BCE), each of whom developed and modified the central theme of tragedy in his own way. For example, at the end of Aeschylus's three plays making up the *Oresteia*, Orestes is acquitted by the Athenian court (of which Athena is judge) of the murder of his mother. At the end of Sophocles's cycle of three plays on the life of Oedipus and his family, King Oedipus accepts his tragic fate with more inner peace than he had experienced at any previous time of his restless life.

Not only human fate but also the relations of human beings to deity and to divine justice are explored by the tragedians. The chorus in Aeschylus's *Oresteia* declares:

> Sing sorrow sorrow; but good win out in the end.[64]

Yet the same dramatist in *Prometheus Bound* represents Zeus as the cruel tyrant who keeps Prometheus chained to a rock in never-ending agony, and Prometheus's attitude toward his tormentor is one of mortal defiance toward an immortal power which is cruel and antihuman in quality.

Of all the tragedians, it was Euripides who raised the problem of evil in sharpest form. Euripides's character, Hippolytus, cries out in words like those of the biblical Job:

> Ah pain pain pain
> O unrighteous curse
> Thou Zeus does thou see me? Yet it is I.
> The proud and pure, the server of god
> The white and shining in sanctity
> To a visible death, to an open sod
> I walk my ways
> And all the labor of saintly days
> Lost, lost without meaning.[65]

In the view of many students of Greek tragedy, Euripides's seeking, probing mind pushes him beyond the other tragic dramatists in the direction of some new form of faith, intimated but never fully articulated.

STAGE 3: PHILOSOPHY (400–300 BCE)

Murray classifies as the third stage of Greek religion "the great schools of the fourth century," that is, the philosophic schools such as the Platonists, Aristotelians, Cynics, Stoics, and Epicureans.[66] Behind these schools lay several centuries of philosophic history of which they were the culmination. Like tragic drama, Greek philosophy must be viewed as a distinctive emergent from Greek religion. Alone among the peoples of the ancient Near East, the Greeks made the journey from myth to philosophy and set western philosophy on its own distinctive path.[67]

Hesiod's *Theogony* has been noted as myth on the verge of transformation into philosophy. Greek philosophy began with Thales (ca. 500 BCE) and his view that the underlying substance of all things was water. Thales apparently made the decisive step from saying that Poseidon was god to asserting that water was the underlying metaphysical substance. In contrast to Thales, Anaximander argued that the substance underlying all things was the "boundless"; and Anaximenes maintained that it was air.[68] Still other proposals were made and developed, but underlying all the specific assertions and systems was philosophy's concern with the nature of being as such. It was the ancient Greek way of thinking and expressing the unique sort of all-inclusive totality, which in Chapter 1 was identified as the distinctive feature of philosophical thinking. To this concern the name *metaphysics* or *ontology* has traditionally been given in western philosophy.

Early in Greek philosophy there emerged a critical concern with Greek religion and an attempt at philosophic reconstruction of religion. Xenophanes wrote a philosophic poem critically attacking anthropomorphic views of the gods.[69] Other philosophers such as Pythagoras and his followers sought philosophic constructions, or reconstructions, of religion.

A new, more extensive and intensive criticism of tradition, not only in religion, but in ethics and politics as well, emerged with the Sophists of the fifth century. The Sophists, literally the "wise ones," were also the first professional teachers of Greek history. They were interested not so much in metaphysical views of the universe as in systematic criticism of popularly held views. As a consequence, the Sophists were viewed with suspicion by traditionally minded Greek people. The views of different Sophist philosophers varied widely, though they tended to skepticism toward traditional metaphysics and religion. Some of them attacked traditional Greek religion as both unreasonable and immoral.

Sophist criticism set the context for Socrates (d. 399 BCE), who was both Sophist and supreme anti-Sophist. Socrates must be viewed as an important figure in Greek religion as well as in philosophy. He used arguments and ideas similar to those of the Sophists, and like the Sophists was devoted to unremitting criticism of traditional religion. Moreover, he sought to push the process of criticism to its conclusion, which he viewed as the emergence of necessary general definitions in logic and general norms of action in ethics. This task of making a new beginning Socrates apparently viewed as his calling, or vocation, and he attributed its source to the promptings of his god (or *daimon*). Socrates viewed his philosophic task of criticism as a mission to be "a gadfly to Athens."[70]

Plato (d. 347 BCE) continued the criticism begun by Socrates and the Sophists, charging traditional Greek religion again with irrationality and immorality. Yet in the *Republic* and dialogs of Plato the reader finds not only criticism, but also the clear outlines of a reconstructed religion. Plato offers a view of reality in which the unchanging realm of Platonic ideas lies beyond the realm of changing appearances. In this unchanging realm are the archetypal ideas which are exemplified in the forms of the objects of experience. Over all the ideas, like the sun above the world, shines the idea of the good. The realm of ideas constituted for Plato a timeless dwelling place for the souls of good men and for gods. It was a kind of city of God, of which it is said:

> In heaven…there is laid up a pattern of it, methinks, which he who desires may behold, and beholding may set his own house in order. But whether such an one exists or ever will exist in fact is no matter; for he will live after the manner of that city, having nothing to do with any other.[71]

Plato did not designate the idea of the good as divine or God, but in later ages, the theologians of three of the world's religions (Christianity, Judaism, and Islam) used Plato's philosophy as a theological vehicle for expression of their monotheistic faiths. In one of his later works, the *Timaeus*, Plato sketched his view of a divine artisan or demiurge.[72]

Plato's philosophy also set forth a view of human nature as intellectual or spiritual, and hence not limited to the body. Among the numerous other religious suggestions in Plato's philosophy is his view of Scorates as the idealized figure in whom philosophy was incarnated. In the *Symposium*, Socrates appears as the hero of a new kind of philosophical religious orientation.[73] Plato's account of the trial and death of Socrates sufficed to place the figure of Socrates at the source of the western tradition of philosophy and indeed of all humane knowledge.

Plato's student Aristotle (d. 322 BCE) gave a different direction to philosophy. He was the son of a physician and himself a scientist of wide and varied interests which found expression in his philosophic writings. As a consequence, his writings do not show religious themes or qualities comparable to those of Plato. Yet Aristotle's writings as well as Plato's were destined many centuries later to be used by Muslim, Jewish, and Christian theologians for their own purposes.

In addition to Platonists and Aristotelians, the schools of philosophy of which Murray writes as the third stage of Greek religion included Cynics, Stoics, Epicureans, and others too numerous and too unimportant for mention. These schools were a significant feature of the Hellenistic, or Greco-Roman, world and had considerable influence on that world. Each school had its own body of philosophic teachings received from its founder and carried on in the tradition and community of the school. Each had its list of worthies who had advanced the teachings. These teachings ran the full range of philosophical reflection from metaphysics through epistemology and logic to ethics. The Platonists held to the doctrine of ideas and the spiritual nature of reality. They also produced a wide range of epistemological and ethical doctrines. The Epicureans held to their idea of atoms and the void, and to a hedonistic ethic. All this, they said, resulted in a quieting of needless fears and in a peaceful mind. The Cynics held a view of nature which led them to scorn society and its conventions. While the Stoics maintained an interest in the full range of ideas from metaphysics through logic to ethics, they placed primary emphasis upon their distinctive ethical teachings. Stoic ethics made a clear and sharp cut between reason on the one hand and emotion on the other, maintaining that human beings should guide their lives by reason and not by passion. The good is the rational, argued the Stoics, and they did not doubt that human reason sufficed for the purpose of rational guidance. They also made a fundamental distinction between goals which are under human control and those which are not. As regards the latter, human beings are called simply to endure what cannot be altered while cultivating the inward and self-sufficient life of reason.

These philosophic schools had many of the traits of religious communities. They maintained attitudes of respect amounting to reverence for their founders—even the Epicureans termed their founder, Epicurus, a savior. In effect they were communities of disciples. All of them maintained an attitude of religious veneration for the figure of Socrates. They also maintained a common life not unlike that in monastic orders of many of the world's religions. In short, they functioned religiously for many people throughout the Greco-Roman world; so doing, they formed the environment and the main competition in that world for both Judaism and Christianity.

STAGE 4: "FAILURE OF NERVE" (300BCE—400CE)

Murray's last two stages are not clearly defined historical periods but rather two aspects of the later Hellenistic world. Both clearly reflect Murray's bias against religion and for what he regarded as humanistic philosophy. Murray characterized the fourth stage of Greek religion, in a celebrated and controversial phrase, as a "failure of nerve," seeking to embrace within this characterization a wide variety of religious phenomena ranging from a notable revival of mystery cults to a great influx of oriental cults such as Manichaeism and Mithraism, a greatly enhanced popularity of astrology, and a widely shared mood of fatalism.[74] Whereas the great schools of the third stage preserved a faith in human beings and in reason, the newer faiths surrendered this tenet for a belief in some transhuman deity who was alleged to be revealed supernaturally to humans. Murray included the rise of Christianity among the symptoms of failure of nerve, for Christianity found the meaning of life in the service of God rather than in the fulfillment of human life. In this judgment, Murray's preference for Stoicism over Christianity becomes apparent, for Stoicism is a faith centering in the fulfillment of humankind rather than primarily in the service of God. From this viewpoint, Christians' service of the one transcendent God has seemed to many a form of escapism and a failure of nerve.

STAGE 5: NEOPLATONIC MYSTICISM (300bce–400ce)

The final stage of Greek religion, according to Murray, occurred in late antiquity and centered on such figures as the philosopher Plotinus (d. 270 CE), whose *Enneads* sought a systematic statement of Plato's philosophy, culminating in a description of a mystical experience of the "One."[75] The teachings of Plotinus constituted still another philosophical-religious school which attracted wide allegiance throughout the Greco-Roman world. Neoplatonism, as Plotinus's system of thought came to be called, was also destined for a long and notable career in the western world as a vehicle of mystical religion. Plotinus taught the supreme reality of the One, with various grades of being emanating in concentric circles from this center and returning to it. The congeniality of this system to what was termed in Chapter 1 as the *mysticism of absorption*, or *ontological union*, has been apparent to many great mystics of the western world.

Among the ancient adherents of this Platonic or Neoplatonic view of reality was the fourth-century Roman emperor Julian the Apostate (332–362 CE), who sought to oppose the growing power and influence of Christianity. Julian sought, in vain as it turned out, to return his people to the old gods and to the old way of life which they bequeathed to their followers. From this time onward, Greek influences were exerted through the Christian movement which Julian sought to combat. As we shall see in Chapter 13, the Christian movement constituted a synthesis of Greek and Hebraic sources.

The late Dean Inge once characterized the Christian church as the last great achievement of Hellenistic culture. It was also the first great work of western culture, but that is a matter which must await discussion in later chapters. Meanwhile it may be observed here that Greek influence has been strong in western religion as in all other aspects of western culture.

ISSUES AND QUESTIONS

This chapter's six samples of religious phenomena show several features which will prove significant for our whole study. First, we note that in all six, religion appears as a force pervading all of society. This contrasts sharply with the modern western concept of religion as an optional concern for individuals interested in such things. At this point in our study, let us simply be prepared for both of these attitudes, at different times and places in human history.

Second, let us note that with a single possible exception (namely, the Platonic tradition in Greek religion culminating in Plotinus) all of these religions are of the first, or cosmic, type. This characterization carries several implications. For example, the many gods or "higher powers" of polytheism recur throughout these examples. Also, be it noted that the one God of historical monotheism, our third type of religion, nowhere appears. This poses an issue to which we shall return for fuller exposition later, notably in Chapter 11. Concerning the many gods of polytheism, they appear as more or less personified formulations of natural or social phenomena or concerns.

A further implication of these religions as of the first or cosmic type is that their outlook is almost entirely limited to a single culture. In a word, these are culture religions and not universal religions. Universal religions are those which contain a vision of universal humanity. We shall explore this concept further as we meet universal religions in the course of our study.

Third, let us note that the actual configurations of value which constitute the human content or substance of these six religions vary across a wide range. Thus, for example, Mesopotamian religion differs from Egyptian religion. There are enormous differences within the varieties of African and Native American religion. However, we must also observe that these differences in the content of value achieve a new level and significance in Greek religion.

Such Greek phenomena as Homer's *Iliad* and *Odyssey* or emergence of Greek tragic drama constitute a new and creative level of esthetic value as the human content of Greek religion. While modern western students tend to forget this fact, Greek art was essentially and explicitly religious in character. For example, tragic drama was a Dionysian celebration, at which the priest of Dionysius occupied a ritual seat during the performance. With qualifications the same may be said for the distinctively intellectual values which formed the content of Greek philosophy.

The emergence of philosophy in ancient Greece poses several significant issues for our study. First we note the historical fact that Greek philosophy arose in the questioning of Greek religion. While there were important secularizing trends as in the Sophists, Greek philosophy retained a religious context or ethos throughout its long history.

Another fact of considerable significance for our study is the emergence of philosophical thinking in other cultures. For many people of the twentieth-century West, the Greek origin and substance of philosophy is the whole story. Let us not deny or underestimate the Greek heritage of western philosophy. Indeed, the very word philosophy is Greek, originating in Socrates's assertion in Plato's *Apology* that while he was not wise, he was nevertheless a seeker and lover of wisdom. Yet, important as this Greek heritage is, we must be prepared in subsequent chapters, especially those dealing with India and China, to meet similar forms of thought for which the word philosophy is appropriate.

As a fifth and final issue, we may observe in the ancient Mediterranean world the existence of secularizing trends or tendencies. By this we mean interests as values which move away from the quality of ultimacy or holiness which characterize religious experience. Such concerns may be graphically represented by a circle with religious or ultimate values as radial lines pointing inward toward the center, and secular or secularizing concerns as radii pointed outward toward the circumference. Thus, for example, in ancient Greece we may observe the movement from Homer to Hesiod as a secularizing trend. So too, the development of philosophical thinking from Thales to the Sophists is a journey in secularization. Let us be prepared to meet such trends or tendencies in other times and places. However, let us also be prepared for trends or tendencies which move in an opposite, or *sacralizing*, direction.

NOTES

1. See inter alia, R. Redfield, *The Primitive World and Its Transformation*, Cornell University Press, Ithaca, 1953.
2. V. Gordon Childe, *Man Makes Himself*, New American Library, New York, 1951, passim.
3. Redfield, op. cit.
4. E. B. Tylor, *Primitive Culture*, Henry Holt, New York, 1889.
5. E. Durkheim, *Elementary Forms of the Religious Life*, Free Press, New York, 1965.
6. See inter alia, B. Malinowski, "Magic, Science, and Religion," in J. Needham (ed.), *Science, Religion, and Reality*, Macmillan, New York, 1925.
7. S. Freud, *The Future of an Illusion*, Anchor Books, Garden City, N.Y., 1957.
8. J. Maringer, *The Gods of Prehistoric Man*, Weidenfeld and Nicolson, London, 1960, p. 10f.
9. E. O. James, *History of Religion*, Harper, New York, 1957, p. 17.
10. Ibid., p. 20.
11. Ibid., p. 149.
12. W. Schmidt, *The Origin and Growth of Religion*, Methuen, London, 1931. A. Lang, *The Making of Religion*, Longmans, London, 1931.
13. J. Mbiti, *African Religions and Philosophies*, Anchor Books, Garden City, N.Y., 1970, p. 1.
14. G. Lienhardt, *Divinity and Experience*, Clarendon Press, Oxford, 1971, p. 1.
15. A. Van Gennep, *The Rites of Passage*, University of Chicago, Chicago, 1960.
16. E. B. Idowu, *African Traditional Religion*, Orbis, Maryknoll, N.Y., 1978, p. 168f.
17. E. E. Evans-Pritchard, *Nuer Religion*, Clarendon, Oxford, 1956, p. 216.
18. Ibid., p. 14.
19. Mbiti, op. cit., p. 39.
20. Ibid., p. 47.
21. Ibid., p. 49.
22. Ibid., p. 98.
23. Ibid., p. 99.
24. Lienhardt, op. cit., p. 52f.
25. G. Parrinder, *Religion in Africa*, Praeger, New York, 1969, p. 53.
26. Ibid., p. 29.
27. Ibid., p. 30.
28. Ibid., p. 31f.
29. Lienhardt, op. cit., p. 147.
30. Mbiti, op. cit., p. 152.
31. Ibid., p. 160f.
32. Parrinder, op. cit., p. 80.
33. Ibid., pp. 80–81.
34. Ibid., p. 66.
35. N. King, *Religions of Africa*, Harper & Row, New York, 1970, p. 48f.
36. R. Underhill, *Red Man's Religion*, University of Chicago, Chicago, 1965, p. 38.
37. National Geographic Society (ed.), *The World of the American Indian*, Washington, D.C., 1974, p. 29f.
38. Underhill, op. cit., p. 21f.
39. C. Starkloff, *The People of the Center*, Seabury, New York, 1974, p. 32.
40. Underhill, op. cit., p. 32.

41. D. and B. Tedlock (eds.), *Teachings from the American Earth*, Liveright, New York, 1975, p. 224f.
42. National Geographic Society, op. cit., p. 16.
43. Underhill, op. cit., pp. 45–46.
44. National Geographic Society, op. cit., p. 177.
45. Quoted from W. Lessa and E. Vogt (eds.), *Reader in Comparative Religion*, Harper & Row, New York, 1972, p. 372f.
46. Underhill, op. cit., chap. 14.
47. Lessa and Vogt, op. cit., p. 512f.
48. Ibid., p. 516f.
49. Underhill, op. cit., chap. 6.
50. Ibid., p. 64f.
51. *Encyclopedia of Religion*, ed. M. Eliade, Macmillan, Chicago, 1987, vol. 5, p. 37f.
52. H. Frankfort et al, *Before Philosophy*, Penguin, Baltimore, 1948, p. 39.
53. Ibid., p. 40.
54. *Encyclopedia of Religion*, vol. 1, p. 169.
55. Ibid., vol. 5, p. 56.
56. H. Frankfort, op. cit., chap. 5, p. 137f.
57. See the Bible, Genesis 12:1.
58. H. Frankfort, op. cit.
59. I. Mendelsohn (ed.), *Religions of the Ancient Near East*, Liberal Arts, New York, 1955, p. 17.
60. G. Murray, *Five Stages of Greek Religion*, Columbia University Press, New York, 1925.
61. Jane Harrison, *Mythology*, Marshall Jones, Boston, 1924, p. 94.
62. Hesiod, *Theology*, N. O. Brown (trans.), *Liberal Arts*, 1953.
63. Ibid., p. 77f.
64. Aeschylus, *Oresteia*, University of Chicago, Chicago, 1953.
65. Euripedes, *Hippolytus*, Bradley Head, London, 1949.
66. Murray, op. cit., p. 108.
67. Frankfort, op. cit., p. 248f.
68. M. C. Nahm, *Selections from Early Greek Philosophy*, Appleton Century, New York, 1947, p. 66f.
69. Ibid., p. 109.
70. Plato, *Apology*, in B. Jowett, *The Dialogues of Plato*, vol. II, Tudor, New York, n.d., p. 120.
71. Ibid, vol. II, p. 377.
72. Ibid, vol. IV, p. 363f.
73. Ibid, vol. III, p. 293f.
74. Murray, op. cit., p. 153.
75. Ibid., p. 17.

BIBLIOGRAPHY

Albright, W. F.: *From the Stone Age to Christianity*, Johns Hopkins, Baltimore, 1957.
Angus, S.: *Religious Quests of the Greco-Roman World*, Biblo and Tannen, Cheshire, Conn., 1967.
Benedict, R.: *Patterns of Culture*, Houghton Mifflin, Boston, 1989.
Breasted, H.: *Development of Religion and Thought in Ancient Egypt*, University of Pennsylvania, Philadelphia, 1972.
Caillois, R., *Man and the Sacred*, Greenwood Press, Westport, Conn., 1980.
Capps, W. (ed.): *Seeing with a Native Eye*, Harper & Row, New York, 1976.
Carmody, D.: *The Oldest God: Archaic Religion Yesterday and Today*, Abingdon Press, Nashville, Tenn., 1981.
Childe, V. G.: *Man Makes Himself*, New American Library, New York, 1983.
Durkheim, E.: *Elementary Forms of the Religious Life,* Free Press, New York, 1965.

Eliade, M.: *Cosmos and History*, Garland, New York, 1985.

Evans-Pritchard, E. E.: *Nuer Religion*, Clarendon Press, Oxford, 1956.

————: *Theories of Primitive Religion*, Oxford, New York, 1965.

Ferm, V. T. A. (ed.): *Forgotten Religions*, Books for Libraries Press, Freeport, N.Y., 1970.

Feuerbach, L.: *The Essence of Christianity*, Harper & Row, New York, 1967.

Frankfort, H., et al.: *Before Philosophy*, Penguin, Baltimore, 1949.

Frazer, J. G.: *The Golden Bough*, Macmillan, New York, 1985.

Freud, S.: *The Future of an Illusion*, Norton, New York, 1975.

Gill, S.: *Beyond "the Primitive,"* Prentice-Hall, Englewood Cliffs, N.J., 1982.

Grant, F. (ed.): *Hellenistic Religions,* Bobbs-Merrill Co., New York, 1953.

Harrison, J.: *Prolegomena to the Study of Greek Religion*, Ayer Co., Salem, N.H., 1976.

Idowu, E. B.: *African Traditional Religion*, Orbis, Maryknoll, N.Y., 1973.

James, E. O.: *Prehistoric Religion*, Harper, New York, 1957.

King, N.: *African Cosmos*, Wadsworth, Belmont, Calif., 1986.

————: *Religions of Africa*, Harper & Row, New York, 1970.

Lessa, W., and E. Vogt (eds.): *Reader in Comparative Religion*, Harper & Row, New York 1979.

Lienhardt, G.: *Divinity and Experience*, Clarendon Press, Oxford, 1961.

Malinowski, B.: *Magic, Science and Religion*, Doubleday, Garden City, N.Y., 1965.

————: *The Foundations of Faith and Morals*, Folcroft LIbrary Editions, Folcroft, Pa., 1974.

Marrett, R. R.: *The Threshold of Religion*, Oxford, 1936.

Mbiti, J.: *African Religion and Philosophy*, Heinemann Educational Books, Portsmouth, N.H., 1969.

————: *Introduction to African Religion*, Heinemann Educational Books, Portsmouth, N.H., 1975.

Mendelsohn, I. (ed.): *Religions of the Ancient Near East*, Liberal Arts, New York, 1955.

Murray, G.: *Five Stages of Greek Religion*, AMS Press, New York, 1978.

National Geographic Society: *The World of the American Indian*, Washington, D.C., 1974.

Nilsson, M.: *Greek Popular Religion*, University of Pennsylvania, Philadelphia, 1972.

Parrinder, G.: *Religion in Africa,* Praeger, New York, 1969.

Radin, P.: *Primitive Religion,* Viking, New York, 1937.

Ray, B.: *African Religions: Symbol, Ritual and Community*, Prentice-Hall, Englewood Cliffs, N.J., 1976.

Redfield, R.: *The Primitive World and Its Transformations*, Cornell University, Ithaca, N.Y., 1957.

Schmidt, W.: *The Origin and Growth of Religion*, Cooper Square, Totowa, N.J., 1972.

Starkloff, Carl: *The People of the Center*, Seabury, New York, 1974.

Taylor, J. V.: *The Primal Vision*, SCM Press, London, 1963.

Tedlock, D., and B. Tedlock (eds.): *Teachings from the American Earth*, Liveright, New York, 1976.

Tylor, E. B.: *Primitive Culture*, Henry Holt, New York, 1889.

Underhill, R.: *Red Man's Religion*, University of Chicago, Chicago, 1972.

Van Gennep, A.: *The Rites of Passage*, University of Chicago, Chicago, 1961.

Vlahos, Olivia: *New World Beginnings*, Fawcett, New York, 1970.

3

The Beginnings of Indian Religion

As we embark for our passage to India most of the familiar landmarks of western religion and culture must either be left behind or be subjected to fundamental redefinition in the new situation. Even such terms as Hindu, Hinduism, and indeed the basic word and concept religion are problematic. The English term "Hinduism" is recent, being first used in 1829.[1] "Hindu" is older, deriving from the Sanskrit word *sindhu* meaning "river" and referring to the river and region now known to us as the Indus. From this Sanskrit source are derived this whole cluster of words, Indus, Hindu, Hindi, and indeed India, the traditional Indian term for this last being *Bharata*.

Central to our study is the fact that there is no Sanskrit term accurately translatable as "religion." The Sanskrit and Hindi word *dharma* has been coopted for this use, but its original meaning was "righteous law."

We shall not be able completely to avoid some of these vexing and problematic words, since we must use them for the purpose of getting the process of study under way. However, these linguistic observations may serve to put us on guard against the characteristic western vice of reading western meanings into Indian words, ideas, and practices—and also, in subsequent chapters, those of other Asian peoples. Stated more affirmatively, our aim is to listen while the Indian tradition speaks for itself through the ideas, images, and persons as well as the events, documents, and artifacts to be discussed in this chapter and Chapters 4 to 7.

One specific and substantive difference in terminology must also be noted. Some writers used the word Hinduism for the total complex of Indian religion, while others give it various more restricted extensions. This volume follows the latter course. Thus we shall call the religious phenomena covered in this chapter early Indian or Vedic religion. The term Hinduism will be reserved for the phenomena to be discussed in Chapter 6, that is, the central religious tradition of India which assumed definitive shape in the last centuries BCE, becoming the dominant pattern of Indian religion in the millennium 1–1000 CE and continuing to the present day.

We shall approach the Indian religious tradition historically. This approach is somewhat ironical, because ancient India was little concerned with history.[2] Our contemporary account, fragmentary as it is, of "the wonder that was India"[3] has been reconstructed only very recently, and with tools of historical study constructed largely by modern western scholars. Yet to the twentieth-century western student, and hence to most readers of this book, the historical approach will be most illuminating.

The history of Indian religion may fruitfully be compared to a landscape as it is seen by geologists. As geologists make their way over a countryside, noting the strata of rocks, the hills, the valleys, and innumerable other features of the landscape, using them all as data from which to reconstruct the geological history of the region, so students of religion must approach India. Chapters 3 to 7 are concerned in one way or another with the complex landscape of Indian religious history. As geologists speak of successive layers or strata of rock laid down during long geological ages, so we can speak of successive strata of religion laid down during Indian history. At least six such layers or strata can be identified and distinguished.

1. The oldest layer is the religion of the Indus Valley peoples of the third and early second millennium BCE.
2. The second is that of the Aryan invaders who poured into India through the northwest passes about the middle of the second millennium, subjugating previous inhabitants, quarreling among themselves, singing their songs and performing their sacrifices, leaving the Vedas as their one monument.
3. The third is the philosophic religion of the Upanishads, dating from the end of the second millennium to the middle of the first.
4. The fourth consists of the religious thought, documents, and movements stemming from men like Buddha and Mahavira, who lived in what has been called the axis age, or axis time, i.e., the seventh and sixth centuries BCE. Some modern scholars call this period in India the *age of the great heresies*.[4]
5. The fifth consists of Indian responses to these "heresies," notably in the Bhagavad Gita and the Code of Manu.
6. The sixth and most recent consists of the practices and attitudes originated in the centuries which the West calls CE and which are sometimes labeled *Hinduism*, or *popular Hinduism*. This designation is somewhat misleading, since this religious complex contains elements, like vedic *mantras*, or prayers, that go back to the ancient vedic past. Yet the analogy of a geological landscape can be helpful here, for sometimes the most ancient rocks lie on the surface of the ground as outcroppings alongside newer features from many different ages. So it is with the Indian religious landscape. Hinduism reached back and claimed ancient vedic materials.

In this chapter we deal with the three most ancient strata of Indian religion. Chapters 4 and 5 will deal, respectively, with Mahavira and Buddha; Chapter 6 with Hinduism; and Chapter 7 with the newest Indian religion, Sikhism.

INDUS VALLEY CIVILIZATION AND RELIGION

Remnants of the most ancient known stratum of Indian civilization and religion are visible to the twentieth century as a series of mounds in northwest India, notably at Harappa and Mohenjo-daro in the Indus Valley. There is sufficient similarity in these and other remains to posit a single civilization over the whole region of northwest India. Archeological excavation of these sites began only in the present century, and much more digging and interpretation remain to be done before anything like an adequate account of these ancient people is possible. For example, despite reports to the contrary their language remains to date undeciphered.

Present evidence points to an archaic urban or city-state culture not unlike that of Mesopotamia and of the other great river valleys of the ancient world. Despite these similarities, there is little reason to conclude that the Indus Valley civilization was greatly influenced from Mesopotamia. According to most authorities, this civilization seems to have flourished from approximately 2500 to 1500 BCE, though some historians argue for a later date.[5] Apparently an intense social conservatism dominated these people, for in their millennium or so of existence their pattern of life appears to have changed only very slightly. Remains of houses indicate a structure of social classes ranging from working people to an opulent merchant class whose plumbing excelled anything else prior to Rome. Their public buildings included a fortified citadel and a large public bath. The cities were laid out on a grid pattern. Technology was of a relatively advanced sort, producing, for example, a highly efficient saw. Crops included wheat, barley, peas, and cotton. There is also evidence of several of the main species of domestic animals.[6]

Among the archeological findings are female figurines, presumably fertility images of the kind which are widely distributed over the world of antiquity. There are also sculptured figures of the Mother Goddess, who apparently was a favorite deity and whose icons adorned the homes of the people. She was similar to the Venus figures mentioned in Chapter 2; she has reappeared many times and under many names in subsequent Indian history.

These and other figures testify to a well-developed interest in sculpture and other arts as well. The representation of animals was remarkably lifelike. As in other cultures and in subsequent Indian religion, these people apparently regarded some animals as holy. Particularly noteworthy are icons of the bull in profile, often depicted with a single horn. The cow, so generally revered in later Indian religion, is nowhere depicted in Harappa and Mohenjo-daro.

Noteworthy also in this culture is the so-called horned god, depicted on seals, usually in the seated posture of yogic meditation well known to later Indian holy men. His body is nude except for necklaces, and on some of the seals he is surrounded by four wild animals. His face has a fierce aspect, which has led to the suggestion that he is meant to be superhuman. Protuberances on the sides of his head have led to the suggestion of some modern students that these were second and third faces. One authority has boldly termed the horned god

Dancing girl of Mohenjo-Daro done in copper. (National Museum of New Delhi.)

Proto-Shiva, and the name has gained wide acceptance. In any event, this figure has much in common with the later Indian god Shiva.[7]

Phallic worship may be inferred to have been an important element of Indus Valley religion; at least there were many cone-shaped objects similar to the lingam of later Indian religion. Some observers have inferred that these objects were related to a cult of Proto-Shiva, as the lingam later became the symbol of Shiva. Some have seen the horned god with an erect phallus, but others have argued that the object is a waistband tassle. It has also been suggested that certain large ring-shaped stones were female sex symbols related to the Mother Goddess, as was the *yoni* of later Indian religion.

In Harappa, a cemetery with fifty-seven graves was discovered in 1947. The dead were buried in extended posture with pottery and personal ornaments—a notable difference from the general practice of cremation in later Indian history. Many other supposed features of Indus Valley religion, ranging from sacred trees to sacred ablution rituals, suggested by the large public baths at Mohenjo-daro, have been advanced by different investigators. In the absence of

Indus Valley seal of the horned god. (National Museum of New Delhi.)

deciphered written record, however, the whole scene remains to date vague and speculative.

The Indus Valley civilization apparently came to a violent end at approximately the middle of the second millennium BCE. Harappa and Mohenjo-daro were defended throughout their history by citadels, but toward the end of their existence there is evidence of greatly increased fortifications and other military activity. There is also other concurrent evidence of violent destruction of many villages in the region. One recent archeological expedition reports finding a group of huddled skeletons, strongly suggesting the final sack of the city. While the evidence is by no means conclusive, it is persistently suggested that the destroyers of the Indus Valley civilization were the Aryan invaders, to whom we must turn attention in the next section.

As we do so, let us note a bold speculative hypothesis, proposed first by Heinrich Zimmer, of a continuous tradition of distinctive ideas and attitudes stemming from pre-Aryan India and maintaining its identity against the more powerful, dominant Aryan tradition throughout the long course of Indian history.[8] Zimmer and others explain many characteristic features of Indian religion and culture in terms of the interaction of these two traditions. In Zimmer's formulation of the hypothesis, the Vedic thought and values brought to India by the Aryan invaders are dominantly monist and idealist in outlook, meaning that reality is conceived in unitive terms and that the human self or mind is regarded as a part of this great unity. By contrast, the thought and values of the pre-Aryan peoples show an outlook which is dualist or even pluralist, meaning that reality has an irreducible diversity. Also in contrast to Aryan idealism, the pre-Aryan outlook is realist, that is, one's self and mind are considered to be in some way independent of the reality they envisage. Scholars continue to question and argue different aspects of Zimmer's hypothesis. The pages which follow will raise some of these critical questions. Nevertheless, the hypothesis is valuable as a way of focusing attention upon significant aspects of Indian religious history and suggesting new questions to put to the factual data.

THE VEDIC ARYANS AND THEIR RELIGION

Around the middle of the second millennium BCE, a wave of invaders broke through the mountain passes from central Asia and fought their way into northwest India. In later centuries they moved eastward as far as the plain of the Ganges. The invaders called themselves *Aryans*, a word meaning "lords" or "nobles." Linguistic evidence links them with other groups who swept off the central Eurasian plain at about this time and established themselves in such different lands as Iran, Greece, Rome, and Germany. The Sanskrit language of the Aryan Indians is closely related to Iranian, Greek, Latin, and German, and is generally recognized as the oldest of the Indo-European, or Indo-Aryan, language group.

The literature of the Aryans, which constitutes the sole body of evidence from which to construct our picture of their life and faith, consists of the four collections of hymns called *Vedas*, and certain closely related documents called *Brahmanas, Aranyakas*, and *Upanishads*. Of the Vedas, the most important is the Rig Veda, which consists of 1,028 hymns or poems composed by a great many seers, or *rishis*, most of them anonymous, during the period of approximately 1500 to 1000 BCE, for use in the religious ritual of the Aryans. Originally composed for oral recital, these hymns were not written down until the fifteenth and sixteenth centuries CE. Scholarly discussion of the date of the Vedas still goes on. One extreme Indian estimate pushes the date back to 6000 BCE and asserts that they were the work of a people then inhabiting an arctic region, who only later undertook the long migration to India. Western scholars tend to hold to a period in the second half of the second millennium BCE as the most likely period of origin. For example, W. Norman Brown feels that the Rig Veda was complete by the year 1000 BCE.[9]

Of the other three Vedas, the Sama Veda is an arrangement for ritual purposes of certain verses of the Rig Veda. The Yajur Veda, later than the Rig Veda, contains sacrificial formulas in prose and verse to be chanted by the priest. The Atharva Veda consists of magical spells and incantations in verse that cover a wide variety of situations, ranging from conceiving a child to preventing conception, and from winning in gambling to confounding one's enemies and averting many assorted kinds of ill fortune.

In the Indian tradition, the massive Brahmanas are regarded as appendices to the Vedas. The Aranyakas (or "forest books") are in turn appendices to the Brahmanas, and the Upanishads bear a similar relation to the Aranyakas. All these writings were included by those who later established Hindu orthodoxy within the category of Veda or vedic literature. The poems are Veda Samhita, and other elements are, respectively, Veda Brahmana, Veda Aranyaka, and Veda Upanishad. As vedic, these documents constitute the most sacred writing in Indian religion. They are *shruti*, meaning "that which is heard," since the inspired seers were supposed to hear the sacred words which they recited or composed. Writings which are shruti are to be distinguished from writings which are *smriti*, literally "that which is remembered," a category which embraces traditional Indian religious classics such as the Bhagavad Gita, the Laws of Manu, and the two epics.

Between the lines of the Vedas lies the story of the Aryan invasion of India, as well as that of the exploits and the priestly life of these invaders. Their enemies, called the *Dasas*, are described as dark-skinned and ill-favored, yet rich in cattle and dwelling in fortified places that have been conquered by the Aryans. The Vedas refer to this conquest as well as to internecine warfare among the Aryan tribes.

The Aryans lived by a mixed pastoral and agricultural economy. The Vedas contain many references to cattle, thus providing a beginning for the devotion accorded in subsequent ages in India to the cow. There are also references to other domestic animals, such as sheep, goats, and horses, and to stock breeding. Horses and chariots constituted the basis for the Aryan victory over the previous inhabitants.

Aryan society did not involve, at least for some centuries, either writing or cities. Political organization centered in a chief, called a *raja* (or *rajah*), who was head of the larger family. Marriage was apparently monogamous and permanent. Priestly tasks were not involved in the chief's functions. The rajah's political power was limited by a council of leading men, of the sort common in ancient societies.

Like most traditional cultures, Aryan society had four main classes: warriors or nobles, priests, workers and a middle class, and serfs. This division is particularly important in India, for it developed subsequently into the caste system. In this traditional Indian system the priestly, or Brahman, caste struggled to achieve and then maintain a position of primacy, subordinating the noble class as well as the others.

The Aryans were a simple, warlike people, singing, gambling, brawling, and generally loving life. Their religious ceremonies and their gods were of a piece with their life. The sacrificial ritual which was the central feature of their religion was performed in the open air and was conceived as a means of securing the favor of their gods, who were thought to descend and join the human participants in the ceremonies, sitting on straw mats set out for them in the sacrificial enclosure. Though the gods were invisible, humans knew them through their effects. They knew the demons in a similar way, and took precautions to avert the effects of their pranks and misdeeds. Both deities and demons were expressions of natural and social forces.

The vedic gods have often been compared with the Olympian Greek pantheon, several deities being similar in both name and function. For example, the vedic sky god, Varuna, resembled the Greek Uranus, and the vedic Dyaus Pitar was like the Greek Father Zeus. Yet there were differences as well. The vedic Indians never successfully ordered or organized their gods into a pantheon as did the Olympian Greeks; and despite their similarity, these vedic gods were never as clear, as sharply defined, or as interesting as persons as their Greek relatives. Furthermore, as Zimmer has pointed out, ancient India, unlike Greece, never underwent a period of religious skepticism. Rather, the gods were "homogenized" by philosophical speculation into a single metaphysical substance. The many vedic gods and goddesses became in the course of time manifestations of a single supreme deity or principle—a distinctive Indian development of the greatest significance for its whole religious tradition.

Among the vedic deities was Dyaus Pitar, or Father Heaven, to whom there are numerous references, but not a single hymn, in the Rig Veda. Apparently he was already in eclipse even in early vedic times. As Father Heaven, he was often linked with the goddess Prithivi, or Mother Earth, thus illustrating a recurring pattern of devotion to two fundamental aspects of the natural environment. Vedic deities were often classified into three groups—of the sky, air, and earth.[10]

Clearly the most important and characteristic deity of the Aryans was the hard-fighting, hard-drinking god Indra, to whom some 250 hymns of the Rig Veda were dedicated. He was probably the son of Father Sky and Mother Earth and was both war god and storm god. In more recent times, Indra has receded to the position of a minor rain deity. In ancient times, however, he led the Aryan warriors into battle, drinking large drafts of the potent soma to enable him to fight and win over all foes. His wife, Indrani, was less well known, but many of his attendants, lesser spirits of the storm called *maruts*, shouted and sang martial songs as they accompanied their leader into battle. A luxuriant mythology celebrated Indra, rider of the storm and Aryan champion.

Probably the most important single myth of the Rig Veda centers in Indra's slaying of the demon of cosmic waters, Vritra, thus releasing the cosmic waters and setting the stage for the emergence of the cosmic order. This battle was the climax of the agelong struggle between two kinds of forces. Vritra was the champion of the demons of restraint, bondage, and nonbeing, while Indra was the leader of the forces of light, life, and being. Immediately after he was born, Indra's aid was sought for this crucial battle. He accepted on the condition that he should be king of the gods. Then he took three great drafts of soma, which gave him overpowering strength and vast size. By means of these newly acquired powers, he split apart heaven and earth, so that he might occupy the intervening space. For the battle with Vritra, he was armed by Tvashtar, blacksmith of the gods, with the weapon of lightning.

After a fierce struggle Indra conquered and slew Vritra, bursting his belly and thus releasing the seven cosmic waters or rivers. These waters were pregnant with the sun, whose light and heat were essential to sustain life. Soon the earth too was spread out and stabilized, and the sky attached at the four corners of earth. Over this whole order Indra reigned as supreme ruler. In the course of events, human beings were fashioned as servants of the gods. Though Vritra, chief of demons, has been slain, the demons still exist in the dark underworld, from which they sally forth to tempt and mislead humans. So the age-old battle between good and evil, between being and nonbeing (*sat* and *asat*) continues.[11] (As an example of dualism, which plays a basic role in vedic thought, this myth poses important negative evidence for Zimmer's hypothesis.) This Indra myth bears important similarity to ancient Mesopotamia's mythical narrative of Marduk, as described in Chapter 2.

Comparable in importance to Indra, but very different in nature, was the sky god Varuna. The heavens constituted his primary domain and the sun was his eye, but he came in time to preside over the days and seasons, and so, with the help of Rita, to preside over the order and law of the universe. Rita was conceived either as cosmic law or as a more or less definite personification of it. It was only a step from cosmic order to moral order, or righteousness. Varuna took that step. In many hymns he appeared as the revealer of sin, the judge of truth to whom were addressed human prayers for forgiveness. Varuna sent his agents to all parts of the world, receiving reports of the deeds of human beings. Not even the secrets of the individual heart were hidden from Varuna; wherever two people planned together, there Varuna stood, judging their plans. Like Yahweh in the Bible he punished sin and rewarded righteousness. Before him, humans bowed in penitence and humility. An attendant of Varuna watched as humans were brought at their life's end either to the "house of clay" or to the "place of blessing."

Another god of heaven, Surya, appears to have been primarily the shining sun. He prolonged life and drove away both disease and evil dreams. He was the priestly figure who declared human beings righteous in the presence of the gods. One of India's most famous and splendid ancient temples is that of Surya of Konarak. There were still other deities of the sun and solar functions. Savitar has been since vedic times the stimulator, to whom is still addressed the Gayatri, perhaps the best-known and most important prayer in Hindu devotional practice (Rig Veda III.62.10): "We meditate upon that adorable effulgence of the resplendent vivifier, Savitar, may he stimulate our intellects." The Asuras were the "bright ones" whose chariot bore the sun. Ushas, the dawn, was a beautiful woman, sometimes said to be Surya's wife.

Agni the fire god (note the similarity to the Latin *ignis*) was the fire of sun and thunderstorm as well as of hearth and altar. As god of sacrificial fire, it was Agni who carried to the gods the sacrifices consumed by the fire. Some said there were many Agnis. It is hard at times to see when there is personification and when Agni is simply sacred or deified fire. The connection of fire with altar and sacrifice gave Agni a relation to priestly ritual—as priests increased in importance, so did Agni. For many he was the priest of the gods.

Two deities important in later Indian religion, Vishnu and Shiva, occupied only a minor place in the vedic pantheon. To Vishnu only five vedic hymns were addressed. He did not come into his own until later times. Like Vishnu, Shiva was a minor vedic deity, and his early name was Rudra. At least the equa-

Wheel of the sun chariot at Konarak temple. (Archeological Survey of India.)

tion of Rudra and Shiva is widely accepted among students of the Vedas. His later name, Shiva, means "the shining one," or "auspicious one." In the vedic period Rudra was primarily a storm god. He also shot arrows of plague and disaster, but he could bring healing as well. He dwelt in remote mountains and visited human beings according to his wishes.

Among the many other vedic deities were Tvashtar, the heavenly blacksmith, like Hephaestus in Greece; Vayu, the wind; Yama, lord of the dead; and Soma, lord of the potent drink which found its way into vedic ceremonies, producing visions and feelings of exaltation. Sometimes Soma is personified; sometimes it appears to be simply the holy or deified object itself. During vedic times, these and innumerable other gods and half-gods dwelt in the sky, in the air, or on the earth around human beings, influencing them for weal or woe.

The most important ritual of vedic religion was sacrifice (*yajna*). Doubtless many attitudes and ideas played a part in the sacrificial cultus. Awe and wonder were important, but so was the desire to gain the favor of gods. As we have seen, the gods were thought to descend and fraternize with the humans who sacrificed to them. Yet perhaps the most important element in sacrifice was the concept of restoring and maintaining right relations with the cosmos, and of maintaining the stability of the cosmos. There were no temples in vedic times; rituals took place in the open air. Offerings were of milk, ghee (clarified butter), or grain, and of animals. There is no reason to believe that at first the priests were more important than in any other ancient society. Yet as masters of the sacred formula which rendered the sacrifice effective, the priests possessed an incalculably valuable monopoly which in the course of time established for the Brahman caste the dominant position in Indian society. Many of the priestly elements in Indian religion were already visible in vedic times. Already there was an elaborate division of labor among four types of priests: the *adhvaryu*, or altar builder and often master of ceremonies; the *hotar*, who invoked the gods; the *agnidh*, who kindled the fire; and the *brahman*, who offered the central *brahma*, or prayer.

Already in the Vedas we meet the sacred syllable *Om*, or *Aum*. As with many another sacred word, the origins of *Aum* are buried in antiquity. However, in the course of later times its three letters came to symbolize the three major Vedas, and also the three major deities, Vishnu, Shiva, and Brahma. More philosophically, it was understood to body forth into sound the fundamental reality of the universe. Obviously such a potent sound could exert mystical power upon the minds of those who meditated upon it.[12]

The later part of the vedic period brought notable changes. Place names in the later hymns of the Vedas change, and one infers that the Aryans were moving eastward along the Ganges. Also the power of the kings or chiefs grew at the expense of the earlier tribal assemblies, and around the kings gathered courts and courtiers. Priestly power also grew apace, and with it the ritual of sacrifice took on endless elaboration. A new sacrifice, the *ashvamedha*, or horse sacrifice, appears in later vedic ritual. In this ceremony a consecrated horse was set free to roam at will for a year, followed by a chosen band of warriors. Tribes on

An ancient Vedic fire ritual is performed by Brahmin priests to inaugurate a place of worship within a home. (William Carter/Photo Researchers.)

whose land the horse wandered were forced to do homage or fight. At the year's end, the horse, if not captured, was brought back home and sacrificed. Despite its great expense, it was the ambition of every aspiring monarch to perform this fertility ritual. The final climactic ceremony involved the slaughter of over one hundred horses. The whole practice was said to guarantee heaven to those who completed it. A. L. Basham comments that it bedeviled Indian politics for a millennium. There were also other royal consecrations, and there was *vajapeya*, which was a sort of rejuvenation ceremony designed to restore the vital energies of a middle-aged monarch.[13]

Several new developments in later vedic thought are intimated in the vedic texts. There were tendencies toward ritualism, toward monotheism, toward skepticism, and toward philosophic monism. As already noted and as will be seen in the image of cosmic sacrifice, some vedic seers pushed in the direction of increasing ritual domination. Other seers, however, took up the idea of deity and pushed in the direction of a single supreme god. There were even some skeptics among these ancient poets who questioned the whole system. Most important of these movements, at least in the light of subsequent development, was the trend toward philosophic monism.

The ritual tendency is intimated by the name *Brahmanaspati* (or *Brhaspati*), which occurs with increasing frequency in later portions of the Rig Veda. The Sanskrit root *brh* denotes the holy prayer or devotional utterance which was a central feature of vedic sacrifice, and the whole name, *Brahmanaspati*, has been rendered as "lord of the ritual." Here was a kind of deification of the sacrifice, probably set up by priests as a supreme principle in deliberate rivalry to Indra. Such was the increasing power of the priests!

Tendencies of a more theistic sort were expressed in *Prajapati* (literally "lord of creatures") and *Vishvakarman* (literally "maker or doer of all"), though the nature and implications of these tendencies may only be guessed. At least it can be inferred that the Indian mind was casting about in search of new forms. Skeptical tendencies are apparent in many of the hymns which raise questions or cast doubt on the power of virtue of Indra and other deities. There is a hymn addressed to *Ka* (literally the interrogative pronoun "Who?") in which the author presses home his questionings regarding the traditional deities. There are even some straightforward personifications, such as *Kala* ("Time") and *Skambha* ("Frame," or "Cosmic Pillar"), suggested for membership in the vedic pantheon.

The two most important hymns of the later vedic writings are X.90 and X.129 of the Rig Veda, the so-called Hymn to Purusha and Hymn to Creation, respectively, *Purusha* is the Sanskrit term for "person" (though one translator has rendered it as "male," which is one of its meanings); the hymn turns upon the relation of microcosm and macrocosm. Purush is represented as the cosmic person, and then to compound the metaphor the cosmic person is treated as both priest and sacrifice in the cosmic, or universal, sacrifice. Yet the interest of this hymn is not simply hieratic but cosmogonic as well, for from Purusha are derived the seasons of the year, the four Vedas, and the three-storied Indian universe. If this imagery is too compact and complex for the imagination of western readers, its influence on Indian imagination—and Indian practice—can hardly be overestimated, for this notable hymn contains the first reference in Indian history to the four castes, Brahman, Kshatriya, Vaishya, and Shudra, deriving respectively from the head, shoulders, abdomen, and feet of the cosmic person.

Equally important as a harbinger of things to come was Rig Veda X.129:

CREATION

Non-being then existed not nor being:
There was no air, nor sky that is beyond it.
What was concealed? Wherein? In whose protection?
And was then deep unfathomable water?
Death then existed not nor life immortal;
Of neither night nor day was a token.
By its own inherent force the one breathed windless;
No other thing than that beyond existed.
Darkness was at first by darkness hidden;
Without distinctive marks this all was water.
That which, becoming by the void was covered,
That one thing by force of heat that came into being.
Desire entered the one in the beginning:
It was of earliest seed of thought the product.
The sages searching in the hearts with wisdom,
Found out the bond of being in non-being.
Their ray extended light across the darkness:
But was the one above or was it under?
Creative force was there, and fertile power:
Below energy, above was impulse.
Who knows for certain? Who shall declare it?
Whence was it born, and whence came this creation?
The gods were born after this world's creation:
Then who can know from whence it has arisen?
None knoweth whence creation has arisen;
And whence he has or has not produced it:
He who surveys it in the highest heaven,
He only knows, or haply he may not know.[14]

"That one," or "that one thing" (in the Sanskrit language *tadekam*, the neuter third-person singular demonstrative pronoun joined to the neuter form of *one*), is here boldly taken to designate the original reality from which all other entities derive their existence. This is even true of the gods, who, we are assured, were "born after this world's creation." In the imagery of this remarkable philosophic poem, out of darkness and water, which constituted the original chaos, first emerged "that one thing," and from this primal reality all the various phenomena of the universe have derived successively, by means of desire. Of equal importance are the dualistic references to nonexistence and existence (asat and sat), and to death and immortality. Here is the dualism of the Indian myth, and monism is represented as being prior and dominant to it. Of equal significance in this ancient Indian account of the origins of things is the spirit of skeptical inquiry in which the anonymous poet wrote. The last lines are the record of his bold, skeptical questioning.

Another feature of the later vedic age was the body of literature called *Brahmanas*. It is impossible to assign a definite date for these documents; estimates range from 1000 to 300 BCE. It is even harder for the modern western reader to make sense of these vast, rambling documents, apparently so totally lacking in order or coherence. They were probably guidebooks or textbooks for Brahman priests. There are occasional hints of philosophic meaning, jumbled together with esoteric meanings, word magic, and what often seems sheer verbiage. A. B. Keith remarks that "they are works in which the imagination of successive generations of priests has been allowed to run riot."[15] A twentieth-century Hindu scholar speaks of the "extreme conservatism and the stagnant ritualism of these documents."[16]

Yet some patterns of meaning and order are detectable. For one thing, the rise to prominence of the Brahman priesthood and its innumerable sacrifices as well as its priestly caste status all appear here. The image of cosmic sacrifice of Rig Veda X.90 was apparently an intimation of things to come, for it was elaborated in great and intricate detail in the Brahmanas. In successive metaphors the Shatapatha Brahmana treats the universe as a vast fire altar and as a sacred, sacrificial horse. One particularly poignant and characteristic statement of this Brahmana asserts that the sun would not rise if the Brahman priest did not correctly perform the daily sacrifice! To this, we must hastily add that this imputed relation between ritual and reality is by no means unique to India. In Chapter 2, we saw that the Babylonian New Year's festival was regarded as necessary to sustain the structure of the cosmos. However, only in India has priestly power gained dominance so completely and for so long a time. Although a long succession of rebels, from Buddha to Gandhi, have arisen to speak against one or another aspect of caste, none of them has succeeded in breaking the hold of this massively sacred custom on the mind and practice of India. What the reader sees in the Brahmanas is the sacred power of priests asserting its domination over the whole of life.

Other tendencies are also visible. Vishnu, whom we have seen in earlier vedic times as a minor deity, now rises to prominence as god of the sacrifices. Shiva's identification with the vedic Rudra here becomes a fact. Also in the Brahmanas one catches occasional glimpses of notable philosophic ideas such as that of the self-existent brahman of which all other gods and all realities are transitory manifestations. These ideas demanded further expression and development. In the course of time they formed the content of a new stratum of Indian religion, namely, the Upanishads.

PHILOSOPHIC VISION OF THE UPANISHADS

BACKGROUND

Priestly ritual was not the only nascent tendency of the later vedic period. In addition to the Brahmanas, there were other documents: the Aranyakas, and the Upanishads. The Aranyakas ("forest books") are the record of men who drew away from civilized society to the forests, there to meditate, to practice asceticism, and to seek salvation. Their thought found expression in the Upanishads. The word *upanishad* means to "sit down before"—i.e., at the feet of a teacher—and the image is that of teacher and students sitting apart in the forests, discussing the great themes of human existence. *Upanishad* also clearly implies the esoteric nature of the teaching, limited to a closed circle of teachers and students, not for general public consumption. As these ancient Indian teachers and students discussed, meditated, and practiced asceticism, a new perspective, that of philosophic vision, opened before them. Hence the Upanishads constituted a new stratum of religion in ancient India.

The figure of the ascetic who seeks salvation by the practice of austerities is present in the earliest vedic documents. These records tell of several kinds of holy men, including "the silent ones" who left civilized life for the forests, as well as others who traveled from village to village, teaching and demonstrating their ways. In all cases, the ascetic was believed to possess a special kind of power, often plainly magical, and his influence was based on this widespread belief.[17] Yet in the Upanishads his austerities and meditation were transformed into something new.

As already observed, in ancient India, unlike ancient Greece, the coming of philosophy brought no head-on collision of priest and philosopher. The viewpoint of the Upanishads did involve a devaluation of priestly ritual, and at least one Upanishad characterizes sacrifices as uncertain or leaky vessels to salvation.[18] Presumably, philosophic speculation or contemplation was a better path to salvation. Unlike the Sophists of ancient Greece, these ancient Indian philosophers did not attack the popular religion. Instead, they did something far more characteristic of Indian thought: they treated both vedic deities and Brahmanic ritual as symbolic manifestations—both to be transcended—of a supreme philosophic principle.

Some 108 Upanishads are said to exist, but of this number only a dozen or so are truly important. Among them are the Brihad Aranyaka, the Chandogya, the Katha, the Isha, the Kena, the Mandukya, the Mundaka, the Shvetasvatara, the Taittiriya, and the Aitareya.[19] The earlier Upanishads such as the Brihad Aranyaka and the Chandogya are in prose, while later ones are in verse. They vary in length from the very short Kena and Mandukya to the long and rambling Brihad Aranyaka. Most of them contain dialog of some sort. Many persons, including even some women and members of different castes, participate in the dialog. While a few of the characters are historical persons, as for instance the philosophically minded King Janaka of Videha, traditional father-in-law of Rama of the Ramayana, most are either fictional or unknown to us.

RECURRING THEMES

Clearly no unified system of philosophic doctrine emerges from these ancient dialogs; indeed the ideas which are proposed often clash with each other. Western readers have compared them to Plato's dialogs. In both there is questioning and argument which constitute a kind of drama of ideas, sometimes resulting in solution or agreement, but sometimes not. The reader encounters in both Plato and the Upanishads several recurring themes of great importance. These themes of the Upanishads became in many cases the systems of later Indian philosophy. Here we shall sketch and illustrate nine such recurring themes, though others will occur even to the casual reader of the Upanishads.

BRAHMAN   The first and perhaps dominant theme of the Upanishads is the "absolute reality" which we have already met in "that one thing" of Hymn X.129 of the Rig Veda. This idea is by no means a unique achievement of these ancient Indian explorers of the mind's life. Rather, the conception of a self-subsistent reality beyond the common objects of everyday life, yet pervading them and giving them whatever reality they possess, recurs in many times and places and under many names. We shall meet it in many of the world's faiths as our study proceeds. Indian thought called it *brahman*, which is derived from the mantras or sacred words of the sacrifices, but which came to mean for the philosophers of the Upanishads "the supreme reality." Brahman as supreme reality is to be distinguished from the Brahman priesthood, and from the four-faced deity Brahma. If the word *God* be shorn of its personal, Judeo-Christian meanings and assigned an impersonal or transpersonal sense, then *brahman* might possibly be translated as "God."

The limited, finite character of all the objects of everyday life, not to speak of one's own self, point toward a supreme, or absolute, reality, which does not change or pass away but simply and supremely *is*. It is that which supremely or absolutely *exists*, in its own power, not dependent on other existing things. Indeed, the *via negativa* so popular in the philosophic thought of India consists of stripping away all qualifying predicates from this verb *to be*, or *to exist*, until one comes at last to the idea of being as such, or supreme being. As the Brihad Aranyaka Upanishad puts the matter, the supreme reality is *neti, neti*, "not this, not this." It lies at the end of the road of philosophic abstraction when we have stripped away from the verb *to be* every last predicate adjective and predicate nominative and are left simply with naked being. Here again is tadekam, that one thing, of Rig Veda X.129.

There are other paths which lead to the same goal, among them the path of religious devotion. So, for example, the devotee in the Brihad Aranyaka Upanishad is admonished to utter the prayer: "From the unreal lead me to the real, from darkness lead me to light, from death lead me to immortality."[20] Here one sees the same struggle of the forces of unreality, darkness, and death against reality, light, and immortality which characterized Rig Veda X.129; but here as there, the single divine principle of reality, light, and immortality wins out.

Here is the way the Mundaka Upanishad puts this same fundamental matter:

> Two kinds of knowledge are to known, as indeed, the knowers of Brahman declare—the higher as well as the lower.
> Of these, the lower is the Rig Veda, the Yajur Veda, the Sama Veda, the Atharva Veda…
> And the higher is that by which the Undecaying is apprehended.
> That which is ungraspable, without family, without caste, without sight or hearing, without hands or feet, eternal, all-pervading, omnipresent, exceedingly subtle, that is the Undecaying which the wise perceive as the source of beings.
> As a spider sends forth and draws in (its thread), as herbs grow on the earth, as the hair (grows) on the head and the body of a living person, so from the Imperishable arises here the universe.[21]

To cite just one more expression of this theme from the innumerable possibilities, the Chandogya Upanishad says this:

> In the beginning, my dear, this was Being alone, one only without a second.
> Some people say "in the beginning this was non-being alone, one only; without a second. From that non-being, being was produced."
> But how, indeed, my dear, could it be thus? said he, how could being be produced from non-being? On the contrary, my dear, in the beginning this was being alone, one only, without a second.
> It thought, May I be many, may I grow forth….[22]

While many, if not most, references to this supreme reality suggest an impersonal or transpersonal being, others, like the following from the Shvetasvatara, clearly reflect a personal, or theistic, concept:

> The Lord supports all this which is a combination of the mutable and immutable, the manifest and the unmanifest. And the soul, not being the Lord is bound because of his being an enjoyer. By knowing God (the soul) is freed from all fetters.[23]

This and other similar passages depicting the path to brahman in personal terms developed in the course of time into the distinctive way of *bhakti*, or devotional theism, which contrasts sharply with the way of *jnana*, or philosophic vision.

ATMAN The supreme reality which lies beyond all the specific objects of the universe as a world spirit may also be sought in the depths of the human self. Here it is not brahman but *atman*, which is the Sanskrit word for "self," or "soul." Yet the term appears to mean to the philosophic seers of the Upanishads not any particular self or any particular aspect of the experience of selfhood but rather the experience of selfhood in its widest, deepest, and most general significance.

Again, one may approach the true nature of the atman best by stripping away one by one all the predicates which make any self particular—make it this self rather than that self. At the bottom of this deep well of the self lies the universal self, or atman. To the exploration of the atman are devoted many passages of the Upanishads.

Like brahman, the atman is to be approached by a process of negation (neti, neti). Atman is not easily known, for the good reason that it lies beyond every normal waking act or attitude. Serious seekers of the self must by means of ascetic discipline detach themselves from the pursuits of the world and from an interest in their own existence. Gradually as they tread this path of detachment and introspection the atman opens before them.

In the metaphor of the Katha Upanishad, the self is compared to chariot and charioteer:

> Know the Self as the lord of the chariot and the body as, verily, the chariot, know the intellect as the charioteer and the mind as, verily, the reins. The senses, they say, are the horses; the objects of sense the paths (they range over); (the self) associated with the body, the senses and the mind—wise men declare—is the enjoyer....
>
> He who has no understanding, whose mind is always unrestrained, his senses are out of control, as wicked horses are for a charioteer.
>
> He, however, who has no understanding, who has no control over his mind (and is) ever impure, reaches not that goal but comes back into mundane life.
>
> He, however, who has understanding, who has control over his mind and (is) ever pure, reaches the goal from which he is not born again....
>
> Beyond the senses are the objects of the sense, and beyond the objects is the mind; beyond the mind is the understanding and beyond the understanding is the great self.[24]

TAT TVAM ASI   The climactic and characteristic declaration of the Upanishads is the identity of atman and brahman, or in the words of the Chandogya Upanishad, *tat tvam asi.*[25] In other words, there is a complete identity between the absolute or universal reality underlying the objective world and that which everyone may find at the foundation of his or her subjecthood. These are two paths to the same supreme reality. Of this reality each human soul is a broken fragment. Hence a person's highest destiny is to realize this fact and so to realize the great identity or unity which is fulfillment, salvation, and blessedness. The Chandogya Upanishad puts it this way in dialog between father and son:

> These rivers, my dear, flow the eastern toward the east, the western toward the west. They go just from sea to sea. They become the sea itself. Just as these rivers while there do not know "I am this one," "I am that one." In the same manner, my dear, all these creatures even though they have come forth from Being do not know that "we have come forth from Being." Whatever they are in this world, tiger or lion or wolf or boar or worm or fly or gnat or mosquito that they become.
>
> That which is the subtle essence, this whole world has for its self. That is the true. That is the self. That art thou, Shvetaketu....[26]

This same dialog pursues the theme by means of two other metaphors, that of the seed of the nyagrodha tree and that of salt dissolved in water. In both cases the illustrations arrive at the conclusion "that art thou," meaning that the human self is one with universal reality. As the salt pervades the water in which it is dissolved, or as the whole tree is implicitly given in its smallest seed, even so the self and reality, or the atman and brahman, are ultimately equivalent to each other.

No more important or characteristic words than these are spoken throughout the Upanishads. These ideas echo and reecho through many of the most important systems of Indian philosophy. The path to salvation by emancipation from all finite things ends in absorption in the absolute reality. This way was discovered and explored by the philosophic seers of the Upanishads; it was destined to be trodden by Indian seekers and pilgrims from that day to this. Thinkers and seers of many schools and sects devoted themselves to making explicit some of the implications of the Upanishadic vision. Some of these further implications or corollaries were developed by the Upanishads themselves.

STAGES OF CONSCIOUS-NESS

Among the corollaries is the idea of stages of consciousness. First is ordinary waking consciousness, which is the lowest rung on the ladder to salvation. Next above it is dreaming consciousness, and above that dreamless sleep. Above dreamless sleep, however, lies a fourth and nameless form of consciousness recognizable only to those who have experienced it, to whom it is understood as that absorption of the individual in absolute reality which constitutes salvation. From the Upanishads onward, Indian religious and philosophic thought has never ceased to explore the nature of consciousness with a view to understanding and achieving this fourth state. So it is that these early insights of the Upanishads led onward in the course of time to such detailed systems as Yoga.

The Mandukya Upanishad, whose twelve brief verses are descriptions of the four stages, characterizes the fourth state thus: "The fourth is that which has no elements, which cannot be spoken of, into which the world is resolved, benign, non-dual. Thus the syllable *aum* is the very self. He who knows it thus enters the self with his self."[27]

For the Upanishads the experience of absorption in brahman-atman constituted salvation, or *moksha*. Most of India's philosophers and seers have had their own version of salvation as emancipation. As we shall see in coming chapters, the founders of Jainism and Buddhism had their own distinctive interpretations. In this ancient argument of the schools, the authors of the Upanishads spoke of it as the great identity, tat tvam asi, and as the top of the ladder of ascent through the four stages of consciousness.

JNANA OR SAVING KNOWLEDGE

This same salvation is also characterized as the highest and truest form of knowledge; conversely, perdition is characterized as a state of ignorance, or the absence of this supreme knowledge. To be sure, this is not ordinary secular knowledge, nor is it simply intellectual knowing of this or that metaphysical proposition. Rather it may be characterized as a living awareness on the part of the whole mind, or self, of the great identity of atman and brahman. In this supreme awareness, mind is not so much conscious of this identity as actually absorbed in it. In this unique form of awareness everything is unified and transcended.

This unique knowledge has its own distinctive moral prerequisites. A person who still clings to finite life, or to any of the concerns pertaining to mortal existence, will be unable to rise to the higher state. The discipline of asceticism is necessary to break the fetters which bind the self to the lower world. Then by the discipline of meditation the mind may be directed to its true object, the supreme reality. Awareness of this true object also contains the implication that all else is illusory and delusory appearance. All sense experience and all objects of finite reality are only relatively true, for they are the products of the illusion maker. The veil of illusion must be torn away if the real is to be found. Such, said the seers of the Upanishads, is the saving knowledge which is the proper aim or goal of human life.

DESTINY BE-
YOND DEATH

Closely related to this supreme experience was the question of what lay beyond death. Many of the Upanishads allude to this perennial question, but the Katha is devoted specifically to it. The boy Nachiketas was about to be sacrificed by his father and asked Yama, the lord of the underworld, to grant him three boons. The first was that his father should be pacified; the second, that the fire sacrifice be named for him; but the third was that he be told what lies beyond death. Yama was reluctant, but Nachiketas was persistent. So Yama was led to set forth the view of human destiny beyond death as absorption in the absolute reality. This blessed destiny was asserted to go beyond both extinction and continued finite existence in some supramundane realm. From this viewpoint, finite existence was regarded as a form of bondage which humans must transcend if they are truly to be saved. Only those who have risen beyond all finite desires for survival or extinction are truly saved. The Katha Upanishad puts the matter thus:

> The knowing self is never born; nor does he die at any time. He sprang from nothing and nothing sprang from him. He is unborn, eternal, abiding and primeval. He is not slain when the body is slain.
> If the slayer thinks that he slays or if the slain think [sic] that he is slain, both of them do not understand. He neither slays nor is he slain.
> Smaller than the small, greater than the great, the self is set in the heart of every creature. The unstriving man beholds Him, freed from sorrow.
> Through the tranquility of the mind and the senses [he sees] the greatness of the self.[28]

COSMOGONY

We have already noted some of the cosmological and cosmogonic suggestions of the Vedas and Brahmanas, that is, suggestions concerning how the world began and what it is made of. Rig Veda X.129 derived the world from chaos and desire. Ever and again the Upanishads suggest that all things derive from brahman. A wide variety of other suggestions are strewn throughout the Upanishads. Among teachings which subsequent generations considered orthodox, creation was ascribed to Purusha, the cosmic person who felt loneliness and need for companionship and so took a wife. This primordial couple procreated the whole phenomenal universe. Somewhat similar to this imagery is the idea of creation from a primordial cosmic egg. The Brihad Aranyaka says it was a golden egg.

Other, less orthodox minds put forward less traditional cosmogonic suggestions. Some said the world began as water; others, that the universe began as fire, wind, or ether; still others put forward fate, or time, or chance as the ruling principle of all things; some skeptically questioned the possibility of any knowledge of these matters. Materialists also appeared on the scene, tracing all things to a source in matter. We shall have occasion in Chapters 4, 5, and 6 to sketch in more detail some of the systems of thought which had their origin in this seminal period of Indian religious and philosophic history.

KARMA-
SAMSARA
One theme is delineated in the Upanishads which overlaps both cosmology and ethics and has very great importance for the future of Indian thought and life; it is *karma-samsara*. Karma is the law of the deed; it occurs in many religious traditions as the perception that moral deeds carry their consequences, or "as you sow, so will you reap." Ancient Indian thought asserted this insight to be an inexorable law and joined it to belief in transmigration (samsara). The result was the traditional Indian view that evil deeds have consequences through many incarnations. One Upanishad puts the matter in the following words:

> If you thus indicate the greatness of this self then there is that other, different one also called self, who, affected by the bright or dark fruits of action, enters a good or evil womb, so that his course is downward or upward and he wanders about, affected by the pairs [of opposites like pleasure and pain].[29]

The Chandogya Upanishad asserts karma-samsara in specific detail:

> Those whose conduct here has been good will quickly attain a good birth [literally, "womb"], the birth of a Brahman, the birth of a Kshatriya or the birth of a Vaisya. But those whose conduct here has been evil, will quickly attain an evil birth, the birth of a dog, the birth of a hog or the birth of a candala [outcast].[30]

Compared with this grim prospect, it was small wonder that emancipation from all finite existence seemed a joyful prospect!

ETHICS
While the main concern of the Upanishads was with salvation, or blessedness, nevertheless morality was dealt with as an important aspect of the journey to salvation. Thus, for example, indulgence of material or sensual desire is evil, as is attachment to the things of the world. Conversely, sacrifice, study, and charity

are great goods; so too are discipline, austerity, and celibacy. These qualities are good because they lead the soul upward on the path to salvation.

The Maitri Upanishad has this to say concerning the body and its needs:

> In this foul-smelling, unsubstantial body, a conglomerate of bone, skin, muscle, marrow, flesh, semen, blood, mucus, tears, rheum, feces, urine, wind, bile, and phlegm, what is the good of the enjoyment of desires? In this body which is afflicted with desire, anger, covetousness, delusion, fear, despondency, envy, separation from what is desired, union with the undesired, hunger, thirst, old age, death, disease, sorrow, and the like, what is the good of the enjoyment of desires?...But, indeed, what of these?...Among other things, there is the drying up of great oceans, the falling away of mountain peaks, the deviation of the fixed pole-star, the cutting of the wind-ropes [that hold the stars in their places], the submergence of the earth, the departure of the gods from their station. In such a world as this, what is the good of enjoyment of desires? For he who had fed on them is seen to return [to this world] repeatedly. Be pleased, therefore, to deliver me. In this world [cycle of existence] I am like a frog in a waterless well. Revered Sir, you are our way [of deliverance], you are our way.[31]

In a notable passage, the Brihad Aranyaka Upanishad moves through a long list of goods such as husband, wife, sons, wealth, love of the gods, and the like, asserting that they are not dear for their own sake but for love of self (or atman). The conclusion is an ethic which harmonizes many human goods under an ideal detachment, concluding in these words:

> Verily, not for the sake of all is all dear but all is dear for the sake of the Self. Verily, O Maitreyi, it is the Self that should be seen, heard of, reflected on and meditated upon. Verily, by the seeing of, by the hearing of, by the thinking of, by the understanding of the Self, all this is known.[32]

The ethical spirit of the Upanishads is admirably summed up in a notable passage of the Brihad Aranyaka (which incidentally is echoed in T. S. Eliot's poem "What the Thunder Said," from *The Wasteland*):

> The threefold offspring of Prajapati, gods, men and demons, lived with their father Prajapati as students of sacred knowledge. Having completed their studentship the gods said, "Please tell [instruct] us, sir." To them then, he uttered the syllable *da* [and asked] "Have you understood?" They [said] "We have understood, you said to us 'damyata,' 'control yourselves.' " He said, "Yes, you have understood."
> Then the men said to him, "Please tell [instruct] us, sir." To them he uttered the same syllable *da* [and asked] "Have you understood?" They said, "We have understood. You said to us 'give.' " He said, "Yes, you have understood."
> Then the demons said to him, "Please tell [instruct] us, sir." To them he uttered the same syllable *da* [and asked] "Have you understood?" They said, "We have understood, you said to us, 'dayadhvam,' 'be compassionate.' " One should practice this same triad, self-control, giving and compassion.[33]

ISSUES AND QUESTIONS

Glancing back over this chapter and over the centuries of Indian religious history which it chronicles, we lift up for discussion several questions and issues. First we note the gods of the Vedic hymns, some of whom live on to this day as objects of devotion in India. With due qualifications, these Vedic gods appear similar to the deities of other traditions of the first or cosmic type around the world and throughout history. They symbolize distinctive objects or values of nature and society.

Clearly the most important development of this chapter is the movement from this typically cosmic and traditional perspective to such concepts as "That One Thing" of Rig Veda 10:129 or Brahman of the Upanishads. Here we see human imagination achieving what may appropriately be called an Archimedean point (Archimedes was the Greek who said, "Give me a point outside the world and I will lift the world.") above or beyond all the particular realities of nature and society. The implications of this achievement will become clearer in the next three chapters.

Correlative with this change in viewpoint is the movement from the mythopoeic language of the Vedic hymns to the philosophic words and vision which begin to emerge in the Upanishads. We shall see this development continue in the next three chapters culminating in the six orthodox Hindu philosophies of Chapter 6. The central tradition of Indian philosophy is Vedanta, and the primary sources of Vedanta are the Upanishads and Book X of the Rig Veda.

As we observe the beginning of Indian philosophy we must note a basic difference between the Indian and Greek beginnings of philosophy. This is the presence in Greece and the absence in India of a radical and at times acerbic criticism of traditional religion. As a consequence of this absence, the typical Indian philosopher continued to be a holy man. This has been by no means always or necessarily true of western philosophy, ancient or modern.

A third main issue, closely related to the preceding, is the presence in Vedic literature of two distinguishable and contrasting configurations of religious thought and devotion. Let us call them *transpersonal monism* and *devotional theism*. The former, which is clearly the major pattern, is precisely the vision of Brahman as the transcendent Reality of our previous paragraphs. The metaphorical images of this vision are the drops of water returning to the sea, sparks in a central fire, or rivers running to the still and waveless ocean.

In sharp contrast, the religious configuration which we have called devotional theism employs for supreme Reality social metaphors such as love or friendship, or human allegiance to a social superior. This pattern occurs in the Vedas as the personal allegiance of people to any of the many Vedic gods. As we shall see in Chapter 6, it finds climactic expression in the *Bhagavad Gita* and the tradition of religious devotion stemming from this source. We shall also find these two patterns in varying combinations in other religious traditions throughout our study.

There is still a further aspect of Vedic literature which recurs throughout Indian history and has emerged in explicit form in the nineteenth and twentieth centuries. This is the assertion of the literal inerrancy and infallibility of the Vedas. Having made an initial acquaintance with the Vedas, we shall return to this topic too in Chapter 6.

Notes

1. W. C. Smith, *The Meaning and End of Religion*, Macmillan, New York, 1963, p. 63. See also "Hinduism" in *Oxford English Dictionary*, vol.5, p. 293.
2. W. H. Moreland and A. C. Chatterjee, *A Short History of India*, Longmans, New York, 1957, pp. 34–35.
3. A. L. Basham, *The Wonder That Was India*, Grove Press, New York, 1959.
4. G. F. Moore, *History of Religions*, I, Scribner, New York, 1948, p. 279f.
5. B. Allchin and R. Allchin, *The Birth of Indian Civilization*, Penguin, Baltimore, 1968.
6. Basham, op. cit., pp. 14–28.
7. J. Marshall et al. *Mohenjo-daro and the Indus Civilization*, Oxford University Press, London, 1931; quoted from Basham, op. cit., p. 23.
8. Heinrich Zimmer, *Philosophies of India*, Meridian Books, New York, 1957, pp. 59–60.
9. W. Norman Brown, *Man in the Universe: Some Continuities in Indian Thought*, Oxford and IBH Publishing Co., Calcutta, 1966, p. 7.
10. Arthur B. Keith, *The Religion and Philosophy of the Vedas and the Upanishads*, vol. 1, Harvard, Cambridge, Mass., 1925, chap. 8.
11. Brown, op. cit., pp. 21–23.
12. Zimmer, op. cit., pp. 372–378.
13. Basham, op. cit., p. 42.
14. A. A. MacDonell, *A Vedic Reader for Students*, Oxford University Press, London, 1917, pp. 207–211.
15. Keith, op. cit., vol. 2, p. 440.
16. Kenneth W. Morgan (ed.), *The Religion of the Hindus*, Ronald, New York, 1953, p. 440.
17. Basham, op. cit., p. 42.
18. Mundaka Upanishad I.2.7, in S. Radhakrishnan, *The Principal Upanishads*, Harper, New York, 1953, p. 676.
19. Robert E. Hume, *The Thirteen Principal Upanishads*, Oxford University Press, New York, 1923.
20. Radhakrishnan, op. cit., p. 162.
21. Ibid., pp. 672–673.
22. Ibid., p. 447.
23. Ibid., pp. 714–715.
24. Ibid., pp. 623–625.
25. Ibid., pp. 457–459.
26. Ibid., pp. 460–461.
27. Ibid., p. 701.
28. Ibid., pp. 616–617.
29. Ibid., p. 805.
30. Ibid., p. 433.
31. Ibid., pp. 796–797.
32. Ibid., p. 197.
33. Ibid., pp. 289–290.

BIBLIOGRAPHY

Allchin, B., and R. Allchin: *The Rise of Civilization in India and Pakistan*, Cambridge, New York, 1982.

Basham, A. L.: *The Wonder That Was India*, Grove Press, New York, 1959.

Brown, W. N.: *Man in the Universe*, University of California, Berkeley, 1960.

Danielou, A: *Hindu Polytheism*, Bollingen Series, Pantheon Books, New York, 1964.

Dasgupta, S. N.: *Indian Idealism*, Cambridge, New York, 1933.

Deussen, P.: *Philosophy of the Upanishads*, Dover, New York, 1966.

Dimmitt, C. (ed): *Classical Hindu Mythology*, Temple University Press, Philadelphia, 1978.

Eliot, Sir Charles: *Hinduism and Buddhism*, Routledge, London, 1954.

Embree, A., and S. Hay (eds.): *Sources of Indian Tradition*, Columbia, New York, 1988.

Griffith, R. T. H.: *The Hymns of the Rig Veda*, South Asia Books, Columbia, Mo., 1987.

Hopkins, T.: *The Hindu Religious Tradition*, Wadsworth, Belmont, Calif., 1971.

Hume, R.: *The Thirteen Principal Upanishads*, Oxford, New York, 1923.

Keith, A. B.: *The Religion and Philosophy of the Vedas and the Upanishads*, Orient Book Distributors, Livingston, N.J., 1976.

Klostermaier, K.: *A Survey of Hinduism*, State University of New York, Albany, N.Y., 1988.

Marshall, J. (ed.): *Mohenjo-daro and Indus Civilization*, Oxford, London, 1931.

Morgan, K. (ed.): *The Religion of the Hindus*, Ronald, New York, 1953.

O'Flaherty, W. D.: *Hindu Myths*, Penguin, Baltimore, 1975.

————: *The Origins of Evil in Hindu Mythology*, University of California, Berkeley, 1976.

Pannikar, R.: *The Vedic Experience*, Auromere, Pomona, Calif., 1983.

Piggott, S.: *Prehistoric India*, Cassell, London, 1962.

Potter, K.: *Guide to Indian Philosophy*, G. Hall & Co., Boston, 1988.

Radhakrishnan, S.: *History of Indian Philosophy*, G. Allen, London, 1929–1931.

————: *The Principal Upanishads*, Harper, New York, 1953.

————, and C. Moore (eds.): *Source Book in Indian Philosophy*, Princeton, Princeton, N.J., 1957.

Renou, L.: *Religions of Ancient India*, Oxford University Press, London, 1953.

Smart, N.: *Doctrine and Argument in Indian Philosophy*, G. Allen, London, 1964.

Zaehner, R. C.: *Hinduism*, Oxford, London, 1962.

———— (trans.): *Hindu Scriptures*, Biblio Distribution Center, Totowa, N.J., 1978.

Zimmer, H.: *Philosophies of India*, Princeton, Princeton, N.J., 1969.

4

Mahavira and Jainism

THE AXIS AGE IN ANCIENT INDIA

This chapter begins with the period of human history which Karl Jaspers has called the *Axis Age* or *Axis Time*, that is, approximately the seventh and sixth centuries BCE, when in several different regions of the world there were significant new beginnings, new stirrings of life.[1] The Axis Age was marked by the emergence of several historic individuals and new movements stemming from them, in regions as far separated as Greece and India, or Israel and China. The first philosophers of Greece, the prophets of Israel, and such Chinese figures as Lao-tzu and Confucius were individuals of the Axis Age. So too were Buddha, Mahavira, and other Indians. It was an age whose importance to the history of religions can hardly be overstated.

The twentieth-century student can only guess as to the causal factors of this ancient age of genius. The urban revolution, sketched in Chapter 2, had produced a kind of traditional civilization which had held sway for over two millennia. During this time people had been held within the close embrace of traditional society. Now individual persons began to chafe at these bonds and in various ways asserted their individuality. It was a time of ferment and change around the world. What technical and social factors spurred the change can only be surmised. Perhaps new forms of commerce contributed, for business people have often been revolutionary figures in history—sometimes in spite of themselves. Whatever the causes, out of the Axis Age emerged new individuality, new ideas, and new directions for humanity.

In a word, during the Axis Age the human self made its appearance on the stage of history. The self may critically be characterized as a new way of response by human organism to the objective world. While firmly based in the biological structure of the organism, the self is by no means identical with the organism. For it shows a range of individuality and freedom which is radically new. Once in existence, the self and its distinctive combination of freedom and dependence have continued unendingly to undergo historical development and change in different times, places, and cultures.

In India the Axis Age has been called "the age of the great heresies."[2] This is a somewhat anachronistic designation, since Buddhism and Jainism which came into existence at this time were not formally declared heretical until centuries later. Then they were declared heresies for two reasons: they did not acknowledge the sacred authority of the Vedas, and they rejected that touchstone of Hindu orthodoxy, caste.

In India the Axis Age was a time of world-weariness and restiveness, when not only Buddha and Mahavira, but a great many other people as well, shook the dust of society from their feet and sought the solitude of the forest, there to practice asceticism, to meditate, and, significantly, to think new thoughts about human nature and human destiny.

India's Axis Time produced a wide range of teachers, each with a group of followers and a body of distinctive teaching about the proper conduct of life, the goal of life, and the kind of fulfillment or blessedness this goal would bring. Among these teachers, Nataputta Vardhamana (the founder of Jainism), Buddha, and the anonymous seers of the Upanishads are outstanding and have left enduring marks on Indian thought and life. Others were more like Makkali Goshala, founder of the Ajivikas sect, which exerted significant influence for a millennium in India until it finally died out in the fourteenth century. While well known in India, the Ajivikas are little known in the West.[3]

The historical sources testify to many other notable figures, some known, but many unknown to us. For example, the Buddhist Digha Nikaya lists no fewer than six different teachers who offered themselves as instructors to Buddha during his seven-year search for salvation.[4] One was Purana Kassapa, an antinomian who taught that the moral or immoral quality of a person's life had no influence on his or her *karma*. The second was Goshala, founder of the Ajivikas sect already mentioned, whose tenets included a rigid fatalism and an equally rigid atheism. A third teacher was Ajita Kesakambala, a materialist who railed against India's already heavily sacral religious tradition. A fourth, Pakuda Kacchayana, was an atomist and apparently the forerunner of other philosophers of this sort in later Indian history. The fifth was none other than Nataputta Vardhamana, a rigid and extreme ascetic, founder of Jainism. The sixth was a man named Sanjaya Belatthiputta, whose teachings centered in philosophic skepticism.

Other historical sources mention still other teachers, such as Kapila, the founder of the Sankhya philosophy, and Gautama, the founder of the Nyaya philosophy. Undoubtedly there were still others whose names and ideas have perished but who participated in this ancient age of intellectual ferment and wide-ranging speculation.

Despite the great diversity of doctrines, some patterns of similarity do emerge. All these ancient teachers (except the materialists and skeptics) acknowledged the emancipation from mortality, or from finitude, as the chief goal of human beings. This goal, as we saw in Chapter 3, was called *moksha* in the Sanskrit language of ancient India and is variously interpreted by these teachers. It pointed to a realm of blessedness or salvation beyond all the limitations of the human, relative world. Many of these systems provided their own distinctive paths of meditation and of ascetic practice leading to this goal. Most of them also accepted the idea of karma, which was the law of the deed ("as you sow, so will you reap"), and applied it with ironclad rigor to all human life; many of them, like the philosophic seers of the Upanishads, extended its application to many incarnations, past and future.

Among these ancient teachers, Nataputta Vardhamana, known also as Mahavira, stands out for the extreme rigor of his ascetic practice and the clear, bold outlines of his philosophy. Also, he was, along with Buddha, the first of a long line of Indian rebels against caste. Above all he was the founder of the religious community and tradition of Jainism.

JAINISM: A STUDY IN EXTREMES

Heinrich Zimmer places Mahavira and Jainism as first among those traditions of philosophy, art, and religion which go back to the ancient pre-Aryan past of India, citing as evidence the realism and dualism of this philosophy in contrast to the monistic idealism of the Aryan tradition, and pointing also to Jainism's own insistent tradition of a long line of twenty-four *tirthankaras*, or "fordfinders," of whom Mahavira was the last.[5] By *fordfinder* Jains have meant a great man who has discovered a way across the stream of mortal misery to the farther shore of salvation. The images of the ford and the fordfinder are strong not only in Jainism but also in Buddhism and throughout other Indian faiths. Once the ford has been discovered, other lesser mortals may make their passage through it to the farther shore. Jainism has always insisted that each individual person must do this alone, without the help of any god or savior. Hence Jainism honors Mahavira and the long line of twenty-three tirthankaras before him, but resolutely refuses to deify them. Particularly notable for Jainism is the probably historical figure of Parshva, who is honored as the twenty-third fordfinder and who lived ca. 872–772 BCE.[6]

Jain thought and practice present themselves to students of the world's religions as a study in extremes. Jainism is extreme even within its Indian environment in its atheism, its asceticism, and its devotion to *ahimsa*, the ethic of noninjury. Western students of the world's religions are sometimes puzzled by the attitudes of indifference and negation toward God which are to be found among the oriental faiths.

Jainism goes beyond indifferentism and agnosticism to an explicit and unqualified denial that any deity either created or rules the world. True, it concedes the existence of higher powers or gods, but it asserts that these powers, like human beings and other creatures, are prisoners within this evil universe with little or no chance of escape. The term "transpolytheistic atheism" has been proposed as accurately descriptive. Making the necessary adjustments from modern western culture to that of ancient India, let us simply say atheism. Jainism was not alone in its rejection of any deity as creator or ruler of the world. Goshala of the Ajivakas apparently joined in this denial. Modern students can only speculate as to what led these Indian teachers to such dogmatic rejection of the traditional gods of their people. Two possibilities appear in the sources. First, they regarded the gods as unnecessary, for humans could achieve salvation through their own power and without neurotic dependence on powers beyond themselves. Second, the gods seemed even at this early stage of history to be an irrational principle of explanation. Consider the naturalism of the following bold declaration from the Jaina Sutras:

> A monk or nun should not say: The god of the sky! the god of the thunderstorm! the god of the lightning! the god who begins to rain! the god who ceases to rain! may rain fall or may it not fall! may the crops grow or may they not grow! may the night wane or may it not wane! may the sun rise or may it not rise! may the king conquer or may he not conquer!
>
> But knowing the nature of things he should say: The air...a cloud has gathered or come down; the cloud has rained.[7]

Asceticism (*tapas*) is of widespread occurrence in humankind's faiths and nowhere more frequent or intensive than in India. Yet here again, Jain theory and practice stand out as extreme. Two general patterns of motivation lead to asceticism. On the one hand it is a kind of spiritual athleticism; the Greek word *askesis* originally denoted the training which athletes underwent in preparation for the games. On the other hand, some forms of asceticism posit a dualism of matter and spirit and then seek to rescue the human spirit from its prison house of flesh. In fact, both of these interpretations converge in Jain thought, and as a consequence Jain practice is more extreme than any other on earth. Some of the greatest Jain heroes or saints are recorded with approbation as having ended their lives by fasting to death. The Jain monk traditionally has worn a piece of cheesecloth over his mouth to prevent swallowing and thereby destroying insects, and has carried a small broom to sweep living things from his path.

In these practices there is a convergence of asceticism and noninjury to living beings. The latter may be said to be based upon the idea of the unity of all life and the feeling of reverence for life. Again, most of humanity's faiths have taught these precepts in some qualified form, but only Jainism has carried this tenet to the extreme of absolute noninjury to *all* living beings. Indeed some Jain source documents find souls imprisoned in such inorganic things as fire and stones. The Jain doctrine of ahimsa has influenced Hindu tradition and was acknowledged by Gandhi as an influence on his own ethical thinking. Yet Jainism's own extremes of practice are vividly summarized in a paragraph by Heinrich Zimmer:

> Non-violence (ahimsa) is thus carried to an extreme. The Jaina sect survives as a sort of extremely fundamentalist vestige in a civilization that has gone through many changes since the remote age when this universal piety and universal science of the world of nature and of escape from it came into existence. Even Jaina lay folk

must be watchful lest they cause unnecessary inconvenience to their fellow beings. They must, for example, not drink water after dark; for some small insect may be swallowed. They must not eat meat of any kind, or kill bugs that fly about and annoy; credit may be gained, indeed, by allowing the bugs to settle and have their fill. All of which has led to the following bizarre popular custom, which may be observed even today in the metropolitan streets of Bombay. Two men come along carrying between them a light cot or bed alive with bedbugs. They stop before the door of a Jaina household, and cry: "Who will feed the bugs? Who will feed the bugs?" If some devout lady tosses a coin from a window, one of the criers places himself carefully in the bed and offers himself as a living grazing ground to his fellow beings. Whereby the lady of the house gains the credit, and the hero of the cot the coin.[8]

Historically Jainism is notable among India's religions for the vigor and vitality of its community and consequently for the tenacity with which it has resisted the absorptive powers of Hinduism and maintained its own existence. It remains today a small but vital community of some 2,600,000 people, almost all of them in India.[9] However, like some other minority groups it has made contributions to Indian culture out of all proportion to its numerical strength. Indian ethics, philosophy, literature, architecture, and sculpture all show significant Jain influence. The observer of Indian religion gets the impression that the Jain community is still very much alive. One reason among others for that vitality is that this community owes its origin to a personal founder, or—as the Jains would correct us—to twenty-four founders. Here apparently history is the lengthened shadow of several great men. Among them was Mahavira, the last fordfinder, founder of the Jain community and tradition and discoverer of the Jain path.

LIFE OF THE FOUNDER

Jain tradition places Mahavira at the end of a succession of twenty-four saviors, or fordfinders, extending back to the very ancient pre-Aryan past of India. While evidence for the full historicity of this view is less than compelling, it fits with what is known of Indian history, and it does point instructively to the diversity of Indian religious thought and faith.

Whatever his antecedents, Mahavira appears as an older contemporary of Buddha and a participant in India's Axis Age. While there is no unanimous agreement concerning his dates, 540–468 BCE is widely accepted.[10] Mahavira and Buddha shared a common geographical origin in northeast India, a common cultural heritage as well as many similarities of both biography and thought.

It is thus impossible to discern the outlines of a real human life amid the formal and stylized recollections which constitute the story of the founder according to the Jaina Sutras and other Jain source documents.[11] A summary of this traditional material runs somewhat as follows. Nataputta was born to noble parents in northeastern India in the region of Magadha, or modern Bihar. As a noble, he was reared in courtly luxury and destined apparently to succeed to his father's throne, but his heart was with a band of ascetics of the order of Parshva who inhabited a park outside his town. As a filial and obedient son, he could not join them—yet. At length, and by divine prearrangement, his parents died. One source says they met death by the approved Jain method of self-starvation.

Nataputta was now free to join the monks and to set out on the ascetic path to salvation. A retinue of servants carried him to the park on an expensive litter. There he abandoned his ornaments and finery, threw off his clothes, plucked out his hair in five handfuls, and took the vow to live a life of complete detachment from all worldly things, saying: "I shall for twelve years neglect my body and abandon care of it. I shall with equanimity bear, undergo and suffer all calamities arising from divine powers, men or animals."[12]

The *Venerable One*, as his followers called him, observed two basic rules on this rigorous quest for salvation by emancipation: (1) asceticism, conceived as a way of liberating the soul from the contamination of matter, and (2) noninjury to all living things. His asceticism was of the strictest sort. Refusing shelter, he became literally the "houseless one," exposing his body to wind and rain, to summer's heat and winter's cold. Even the temporary refuge of sleep was scornfully minimized, for after brief moments of sleep he would wake him-

Jain fordfinder Gomatesvara, from a cave temple at Ellora. (Courtesy of E. Eilefson.)

self again to endure (one is tempted to say, masochistically to *enjoy*) the misery of consciousness. His body went altogether uncleansed and unclothed. He maintained the strictest detachment from human society, refusing even to answer when other people addressed him. Villagers set their dogs on him, threw dust on him, even lit a fire under him and drove nails through his ears, but through all these innumerable miseries he remained steadfastly imperturbable.

Just as scrupulously he avoided injury to any and all living things. As will soon be seen, ahimsa is an essential feature of Jain philosophy; it is based presumably on the founder's precept and practice. He distinguished between living beings (*jivas*) and nonliving beings (*ajivas*) in order to avoid all possible harm to living things. Here too his way was absolute, uncompromising. Carrying a small broom, he swept insects from his path. He strained his drinking water with a piece of cloth to avoid swallowing living things. Thus did Vardhamana establish a kind of world's record for his practice of tapas and ahimsa.

At the end of this hard, twelve-year journey was the experience of emancipation. Giving precise details of time and place, the Jain source describes this climactic experience: "In a squatting position with joined heels exposing himself to the heat of the sun with the knees high and the head low in deep meditation in the midst of abstract meditation he reached *nirvana*, the complete and full, the unobstructed, unimpeded, infinite and supreme, best knowledge and intuition called *kevala*."[13] Thus he became Jina ("conqueror"), Mahavira ("great hero"), and the twenty-fourth tirthankara, the titles by which he has been known among his followers ever since. Jain tradition has understood the nature of this crucial and definitive experience as a final breaking of the fetters which bound Vardhamana to the world of mortal misery. To employ Jainism's other root metaphor, in this experience he made his way across the ford to the farther shore of emancipation and salvation. In Jain metaphor and idea, the liberating experience, far from being one of absorption, was rather one of total isolation or separation.

His achievement of emancipation impelled Mahavira to set forth on a thirty-year period of teaching and preaching in which he proclaimed to others his way of salvation by ascetic detachment. He also gathered followers about himself and sent them forth in their turn to teach the way of salvation. Mahavira died at the age of seventy-two and is now, according to his followers, in a state of bliss called *isatpragbhara*, a place at the top of the Jain universe and beyond the grim cycle of death and rebirth. In contrast to the Hindu Advaita Vedanta tradition, but in common with several other Indian traditions, Jainism teaches the continuance of individual selves in this state.

JAIN PERSONS, TEXTS, AND EVENTS

The state of Jain source documents precludes anything like a continuous and critical history. However, a few persons and events stand out as worthy of note.

Jains claim King Bimbisara of Magadha (modern Bihar), and a contemporary of Mahavira, as sympathetic to their teaching and community. They claim as one of their own, King Chandragupta Maurya of the third century BCE, asserting that in old age he left his throne to become a Jain monk, and died by the approved Jain way of fasting.

The Jain community divided between the Shvetambaras (Whiteclad) and Digambaras (Skyclad, hence nude) in 79 CE, each group going its separate way. In the centuries which followed, each produced its own body of literature devoted to many topics, ranging from cosmology to ethics or poetry, and of widely varying degrees of sacredness. The seventeenth century CE produced a dissenting group, the Sthanakvadins, who rejected all icons or images in their temples and worship.

Among Shvetambaras Hemachandra (1088–1172) was a celebrated leader. A minister to a local Gujarat king, he used his position to spread Jain teaching and also to sponsor Jain temple building and other arts. Still another notable name is that of Hiravijaya, who represented Jain teaching in the discussion of many religions at the court of Akbar (1555–1605 CE). Even more recent is the nineteenth-century Jain poet, Raychandrabhi Mehta, whose influence was acknowledged in the social thought of Mohandas Gandhi.

The Jains have exerted an influence on Indian arts out of all proportion to their numbers. At least one of the caves among the thirty-odd cave temples at Ellora is Jain. The temples at Mount Abu in Rajasthan are Jain. A unique Jain monument is the statue of Gommata (or Bahi Bala, "strong arm") at Belgola in Mysore, South India. Erected in 980 CE, this 60-foot statue depicts the Jain hero, Gommata, the son of Rshaba, the first fordfinder. The human figure stands erect with hands at the side in the conventional Jain posture of meditation. Close observation shows vines growing around his legs—so long has he stood thus! The massive statue also follows the traditional Jain concept of great size, depicting virtue in the course of historic cycles.

JAIN PHILOSOPHY

The system of thought which has formed the core of Jainism might be accurately characterized as a philosophy of salvation. It is a cluster of general ideas about human life and the world which, if believed and acted upon, will guide a person's footsteps along the hard, steep path out of the world's misery to emancipation and salvation. Such at least is the claim of Jainism. How much of this thought goes back to the founder and how much consists of later accretion is impossible to say. Yet Mahavira emerges from the records of Jain history as a bold and original philosophic mind arguing his case amid the schools and discussions of his time.

Notice has already been taken of Zimmer's hypothesis that Jainism belongs in a tradition of ideas and attitudes going back to India's ancient, pre-Aryan past. A part of Zimmer's evidence is the realist and pluralist outlook of Jain philoso-

Jain monks place offerings at the foot of the statue of Gommata at Belgola. (Alex Webb/Magnum.)

phy, in contrast to the monistic idealism of the Upanishads and the Vedantist tradition. This realism and pluralism, Zimmer argues, represents the philosophic outlook of the pre-Aryan, Dravidian peoples. In Chapters 5 and 6 we shall encounter several other systems which fit into this pattern and tradition, including Buddhism and the Nyaya, Vaishesika, Yoga, and Sankhya philosophic systems of Hinduism.

THE PATH TO SALVATION

If Jainism is a philosophy of salvation, *from* what and *to* what is a person saved? The Jain view is that people are to be freed *from* bondage or attachment to this world of complete misery, and *to* the blessedness called *kevala* or *kaivalya*, meaning, as has been noted, isolation or separation. This means a release from bonds, which is the Jain version of the common Indian idea of emancipation from mortal enslavement. It is completed in a transcendental realm of bliss called *isatpragbhara*, at the top of the universe. It entails continued individual existence rather than absorption, though this tenet is not greatly emphasized in Jain teaching and is unknown to many Jains.

The world out of which human beings seek salvation is a thoroughly miserable, wretched place, inhabited by an infinite number of souls, most of whom have no hope of rescue from the hell which is existence. Jainism has a fivefold classification of living beings according to their number of senses. Thus human beings, gods, and demons, which have five senses, are classified together. A second class contains creatures of four senses—touch, taste, smell, and sight. The three-sense creatures includes such small organisms as fleas, ants, and moths. Two-sense creatures include worms, leeches, and shellfish. The one-sense beings are a vast class including vegetable bodies ranging from trees to turnips, earth bodies which include stones, clay, and jewels, water bodies, fire bodies, and wind bodies. Indeed, it is hard to think of any existing entity which is excluded from this comprehensive classification of putative living forms. Thus the Jain claim appears to be that the whole universe is alive. One writer speaks of this view as *hylozoism.*[14] Every object contains a soul which is imprisoned in wretchedness within its body, groaning in misery, vainly seeking escape. This cosmic misery is regarded as the inexorable working of the iron law of karma.

> Thus say all perfect souls and blessed ones, whether past, present, or to come—thus they speak, thus they declare, thus they proclaim: All things breathing, all things existing, all things living, all beings whatever, should not be slain or treated with violence, or insulted, or tortured, or driven away.
>
> This is the pure unchanging eternal law, which the wise ones who know the world have proclaimed, among the earnest and the not earnest, among the loyal and the not-loyal, among those who have given up punishing others and those who have not done so, among those who are weak and those who are not, among those who delight in worldly ties and those who do not. This is the truth. So it is. Thus it is declared in this religion.
>
> When he adopts this Law a man should never conceal or reject it. When he understands the Law he should grow indifferent to what he sees, and not act for worldly motives....
>
> What is here declared has been seen, heard, approved, and understood. Those who give way and indulge in pleasure will be born again and again. The heedless are outside [the hope of salvation]. But if you are mindful, day and night steadfastly striving, always with ready vision, in the end you will conquer.[15]

Jainism says that the world has no beginning and no end, holding this tenet in common with Buddhism and other oriental philosophies. The world exists eternally as a kind of permanent cosmic receptacle for the misery of its creatures. For humans alone there is a possibility of salvation. The state of humanity is a kind of escape hatch from the world. One Jain religious poem bids its readers:

> After tossing on the ocean of being, of which birth and death are waves,
> You have come to man's estate.
> Avoid the things of sense and pluck the fruit of human birth.[16]

The "fruit of human birth" refers to the salvation that is possible to human beings alone.

Jainism is thus first of all an ascetic way of life; and, as we have seen, the manner in which emancipation may be achieved is by the practice of tapas and ahimsa. A Jain Sutra expresses the ideal way of life in these words:

If another insult him, a monk should not lose his temper,
For that is mere childishness—a monk should never be angry.
If he hears words harsh and cruel, vulgar and painful,
He should silently disregard them, and not take them to heart.
Even if beaten he should not be angry, or even think sinfully,
But should know that patience is best, and follow the Law.
If someone should strike a monk, restrained and subdued,
He should think, "[It might be worse—] I haven't lost my life!"...
If on his daily begging round he receives no alms he should not be grieved,
But think, "I have nothing today, but I may get something tomorrow!"...
When a restrained ascetic, though inured to hardship,
Lies naked on the rough grass, his body will be irritated,

And in full sunlight the pain will be immeasurable,
But still, though hurt by the grass, he should not wear clothes.
When his limbs are running with sweat, and grimed with dust and dirt
In the heat of summer, the wise monk will not lament his lost comfort.
He must bear it all to wear out his karma, and follow the noble, the supreme Law.
Until his body breaks up, he should bear the filth upon it.[17]

To ascetic practices the Jain monk seeks to add fortitude.

Oh man, refrain from evil, for life must come to an end.
Only men foolish and uncontrolled are plunged in the habit of pleasure.
Live in striving and self-control, for hard to cross are paths full of insects.
Follow the rule that the Heroes have surely proclaimed.
Heroes detached and strenuous, subduing anger and fear,
Will never kill living beings, but cease from sin and are happy.
"Not I alone am the sufferer—all things in the universe suffer!"
Thus should man think and be patient, not giving way to his passions.
As old plaster flakes from a wall, a monk should make thin his body by fasting,
And he should injure nothing. This is the Law taught by the Sage.[18]

The monk articulates his ascetic way of life in the traditional five great vows. In the Jaina Sutra each vow has its own detailed fivefold application, spelling out its application to all possible circumstances. In summary fashion the vow is as follows:

I renounce all killing of living beings whether subtle or gross, whether movable or immovable. Nor shall I myself kill living beings (nor cause others to do it, nor consent to it). As long as I live, I confess and blame, repent and exempt myself of these sins in the thrice threefold way in mind, speech and body....

I renounce all vices of lying speech [arising] from anger or greed, fear or mirth. I shall neither myself speak nor cause others to speak lies nor consent to the speaking of lies by others....

I renounce all taking of anything not given either in a village or a town or a wood, either of little or much, of small or great, of living or lifeless things....

I renounce all sexual pleasures, either with gods or men or animals. I shall not give way to sensuality....

> I renounce all attachments, whether little or much, small or great, living or lifeless; neither shall I myself form such attachments nor cause others to do so, nor consent to their doing so....[19]

For lay adherents of Jainism there are twelve vows, notably less severe than those of the monk: (1) never knowingly to take the life of a sentient being, (2) never to lie, (3) never to steal, (4) never to be unchaste, (5) to check greed, (6) to avoid temptations, (7) to limit the number of things in daily use, (8) to guard against all avoidable evil, (9) to keep stated periods of meditation, (10) to observe periods of self-denial, (11) to spend occasional periods as a monk, and (12) to give alms.[20] For the devout Jain layperson, ahimsa involves a strict vegetarian diet, extending even to a prohibition on eating eggs.

Whether practiced by monks or the laity, the Jain ethic has been accurately characterized as a kind of higher egoism. In the conduct of life and the pursuit of salvation, it is everyone for himself, or herself. True, Jains observe the rule of ahimsa, but they do it, as Jains say, to reduce their own karma, to wipe the stain of karmic matter off the soul, or—to use Jainism's other root metaphor—to break the fetters which bind the soul to the material universe.

ATHEISM

In this way of life and salvation there is no help from any savior or god, for—as previously noted—Jainism dogmatically rejects the existence of any god as creator or ruler of the world. To be sure, there may be gods or superior beings in the universe, but, as we have seen, they are fellow prisoners along with humans and other living beings, and subject to the same iron law of karma. Once more, what Jain atheism denies is that God either made the world or rules it. Jain thought argues this conclusion with great conviction and by means of arguments which in the West have usually been associated with Humean skepticism. It is asked: "If God created the world, where was he before creation?" It is asked whether any single being could have the skill to make the world, or whether or not God used raw material to fabricate the world. If so, this is independent of God; if not, whence comes this stuff of which things are made? Moreover, if God created the world out of love for human things, why did he not make the creation wholly blissful? Indeed, the fact of evil leads us to the conclusion that God commits great sin in killing the children he has made. The conclusion of these lines of thought is that the very idea of a creator and lord is self-contradictory, that the universe itself is uncreated and indestructible, enduring by the compulsion and necessity of its own nature. Let us see this view in Jainism's own words:

> Some foolish men declare that Creator made the world.
> The doctrine that the world was created is ill-advised, and should be rejected.
>
> If God created the world, where was he before creation?
> If you say he was transcendent then, and needed no support, where is he now?
>
> No single being had the skill to make this world—

For how can an immaterial god create that which is material?

How could God have made the world without any raw material?
If you say he made this first, and then the world, you are faced with an endless
regression.

If you declare that this raw material arose naturally you fall into another fallacy,
For the whole universe might thus have been its own creator, and have arisen
equally naturally.

If God created the world by an act of his own will, without any raw material,
Then it is just his will and nothing else—and who will believe this silly stuff?

If he is every perfect and complete, how could the will to create have arisen in him?
If, on the other hand, he is not perfect, he could no more create the universe
than a potter could.

If he is formless, actionless, and all-embracing, how could he have created the world?
Such a soul, devoid of all modality, would have no desire to create anything.

If he is perfect, he does not strive for the three aims of man,
So what advantage would he gain by creating the universe?

If you say that he created to no purpose, because it was his nature to do so, then
God is pointless.
If he created in some kind of sport, it was the sport of a foolish child, leading to
trouble.

If he created because of the karma of embodied beings [acquired in a previous
creation]
He is not the Almighty Lord, but subordinate to something else....

If out of love for loving things and need of them he made the world,
Why did he not make creation wholly blissful, free from misfortune?

If he were transcendent he would not create, for he would be free;
Nor if involved in transmigration, for then he would not be almighty.

Thus the doctrine that the world was created by God
Makes no sense at all.

And God commits great sin in slaying children whom he himself created.
If you say that he slays only to destroy evil beings, why did he create such beings
in the first place?[21]

The idea of a nontheistic religion is so foreign to the western mind that the
question inevitably arises: "Is this a religion, and if so in what sense?" One answer is that, in the terms of the hypothesis stated in Chapter 1, it is an existing
system of holy forms. It is also a path to salvation. Indeed, Jainism is a highly
distinctive and an extremely difficult path of faith and life.

DUALISM OF MIND AND MATTER

Jain metaphysics is characterized by a fundamental dualism of mind and matter,
or as Jains put it, of jivas and ajivas. This duality extends metaphysically to the
entire universe, but it also goes through the heart of each human being, divid-

ing the person into a soul and a body which imprisons the soul. Life is enmeshed in nonlife. From the prison house it is barely possible that one's soul, or life monad, may be liberated by tapas and ahimsa.

PLURALISM AND KARMIC MATTER

Beyond its basic matter-spirit dualism, Jain metaphysics is realist and monadic, or atomistic, in character. That is to say, reality is asserted to be made up of many irreducible units independent of each other and of the human minds which know them. As one Jain document says, "There are many souls, just as there are many pots and other things."[22] In contrast to the monism of Aryan philosophy, Jain thought asserts many kinds of living and nonliving beings, of spirit and matter. Against the monism of Aryan thought, Jainism maintains an irreducible pluralism, not only of souls but also of elements in the universe beyond humans. In addition to souls, the universe is composed of matter, space, dharma and adharma (good and evil), and time.[23]

We have already noted Jainism's acceptance of the traditional Indian idea of karma-samsara. Jain metaphysics added a novel theory concerning the way in which this grim and endless process takes place. It teaches that in general karma is due to a mixing of jivas, or soul, with ajivas, or matter, and that karma may be stopped by cleansing the matter from one's soul. In the course of time Jainism elaborated a theory of special kinds of matter, called *karmic matter*, which clings to the soul like barnacles to a ship, causing karma and bondage. Over 148 kinds of karmic matter, each causing its own distinctive kind of bondage, have been listed by Jain thinkers.[24]

Jainism also elaborated an ingenious theory of the way in which karmic matter stains the soul, or life monad, in a variety of different colors. Different colors of karmic matter are thought to correspond with different types of persons. At the bottom of the scale is black, the color of merciless and cruel persons. Next above are dark-blue characters, who are roguish and venial. Gray typifies the reckless and thoughtless soul. Fiery red is the color of prudent, honest, and devout persons. Yellow is the color of compassionate character. White souls are disinterested and impartial and thus the best of all karmic types. Yet the highest aim is to cleanse all the stain of karmic matter from the soul in order to facilitate release from bondage. Also, as we have seen, karma has its cosmic as well as its individual results; as souls go on transmigrating eternally, they generate the vast cosmic cycles of history.

CYCLIC VIEW OF HISTORY

No less fantastic than these psychological speculations is the Jain view of history, which is also characteristically pessimistic. It centers attention on the wheel of time (*kalacakra*), which is of enormous size and is unceasing in its cyclic motion. The wheel is said to have twelve spokes; while six of them are turned toward the world of human beings, there is improvement, but while the other six are turned, there is degeneration and evil. A single twelfth-turn of the wheel is called a *palyopama* and is estimated by Jains to take as many years as would be needed to fill a container 4 miles high and 4 miles in circumference with fine, tightly packed human hair, if a single hair is added every 100 years. Truly, the Jains seem intent upon outdoing other competing faiths in their description of the human predicament!

Somewhat more comprehensible to human imagination are the effects of evolution and devolution on the human body and the duration of human life. In the supremely good periods of history, human bodies are 6 miles tall and human beings live for three palyopamas. However, as the wheel of time turns to its negative phase, bodies reduce gradually to a mere 18 inches and life span shrinks to sixteen years.

The coming of Jain saviors, or fordfinders, is also related to this cyclic movement of history. The world was good enough to get along without saviors until the third period in the downward course, when the first savior arose. During the third and fourth periods came the succession of twenty-four saviors. Mahavira arrived just before the close of the fourth period. The world is now regarded as too evil to permit the coming of another savior, and it will remain so for another 80,000 years. Only then will the upward course of history permit human beings to achieve salvation.[25]

DOCTRINE OF MANY-SIDEDNESS

A further and final aspect of Jain philosophy which has often baffled western students is its subtle logic and epistemology, featuring the doctrines of "viewpoints" (*nayavada*) and of "perhaps," or "conditional predication" (*syadavada*), which taken together are the doctrine of "many-sidedness" (*anekantavada*).[26] Considered as a whole this aspect of Jain thought constitutes a recognition that the world is more complex than simple black-and-white distinctions allow. Also, human limitations resulting from karma condition make relative human knowledge of their world.

The doctrine of perhaps entails a sevenfold view of predication, beginning with simple affirmation, simple negation, a qualified combination of the two, and a recognition that the truth or falsehood may be unknown to us, the last three of the seven forms being odd combinations of these first four forms.

The doctrine of many-sidedness is a recognition of the thoroughly conditioned and relative aspects of all human thought and speech. It may be illustrated by the Indian parable of the blind men describing the elephant. The attempts of the blind men at truth reflect their specific, limited situations, which in turn are the result of karma. While all their efforts contain some truth, none is the whole or final truth. In short, it is argued that humans here on earth know in part and imperfectly. Only when they have achieved kaivalya does their knowledge attain perfection.

Here then, in summary, is the philosophy which is offered as a road map for the hard, ascetic Jain path to salvation, or emancipation. It is a path which leads through that vast and dismal swamp which is the world and in which innumerable wretched and suffering creatures are mired forever. Yet to human beings is given the hope—slender though it be—of escape. It is an escape by each individual's power of knowledge and self-mastery. This path can be plotted only by means of correct knowledge—namely, that of Jain philosophy, by which each person must then resolutely live. For the few who successfully traverse this difficult path, salvation lies at the end.

THE JAIN COMMUNITY

As the student turns from Jain philosophy and teaching to the community and tradition of people who profess to live by it, many questions and tensions arise. How can people derive guidance and orientation from such unworldly doctrines? What is the source of the persistent vitality of the Jain community? Part of the answer to the latter question lies in the fact that the Jains have always been a small minority group, which here as elsewhere in human history has maintained its vigor by swimming against the stream. Another significant fact is the middle-class character of the Jain community.

Early in their history the Jains were barred by their view of ahimsa from the traditional pursuit of agriculture. It is somewhat ironical, perhaps, that they turned to trade, commerce, and banking, where they have prospered. The discipline of their faith prepared them for the discipline of the marketplace. While their white-clad monks and nuns have stood at the spiritual center of their community, the practical affairs of the community have been in the capable hands of lay-people. The Jains are governed by popularly elected regional councils in which the laity predominates.

The Jain community devotes itself to manifold activities of education and philanthropy directed to its own members and also to the larger Indian society. Jain schools provide both secular and religious instruction for children of adherents. Monastic institutions are well supported. Jains also support such various enterprises as rest houses for pilgrims, orphanages for children, and even, in devotion to ahimsa, hospitals for sick and defective animals. All these activities testify to the extent and quality of lay participation.

Jain worship centers in its temples and assembly halls. For the Sthanakvadins, assembly halls having no images are the meeting places where Jain teaching is expounded, and devotions, both individual and corporate, are performed. The temples of the Digambaras and Shvetambaras are in many ways similar to those of Hindus. The central object is an icon of a Jain savior, which is daily bathed, garlanded, and cared for like a Hindu god. However, the attending priest is careful to inform the visitor that this is no deity but a discoverer of the path. As in the Hindu temple, much (though not all) of the worship is by individuals. Jain temples are notable throughout India for their spotless cleanliness as well as for the rich ornamentation of their furnishings.

Jain devotion also includes periodic fasts and other ascetic practices and pilgrimages to famous places. Parasnath in the region of Calcutta is celebrated

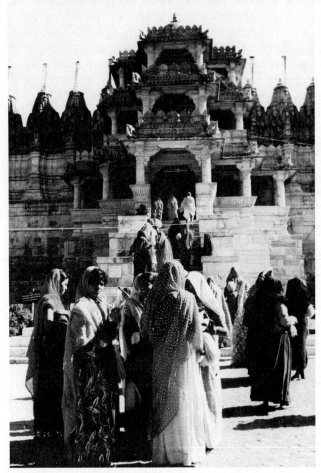

Worshippers entering a Jain temple in Ranakpur. (Marc Bernheim/ Woodfin Camp & Associates.)

as the burial place of Parshva, the twenty-third fordfinder. At Shatrunjaya there is a veritable city of temples—863 of them—to Rishabha, the first in line of succession; and at Girnar there are temples to Nemi, the twenty-second. Pilgrims throng to many such places.

Jains have made distinctive contributions to Indian art. For example, at Ellora there are several Jain cave temples along with those of Buddhist and Hindu inspiration and origin. The observer soon develops an eye for the distinctive style of Jainism. Probably the most notable feature is the standing posture for the ascetic saint. Unlike their Buddhist and Hindu counterparts, Jain ascetics do not sit in the lotus posture but stand erect in all their nudity, with hands at sides and looking straight ahead. Apparently Jain ascetics were not

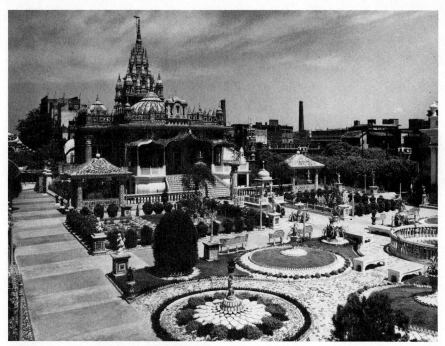

Jain temple in Calcutta. (Nat Norman/Photo Researchers.)

even permitted the comfort of a sitting posture, but rather stood in complete immobility and passivity as they meditated. The abstraction of these Jain figures constitutes a powerful artistic expression of Jain detachment from the world. The most famous such Jain figure, the Gomatesvara at Sravana Belgola in south India, is more than 56 feet high. The sculptor has depicted vines growing around the legs—so long has the ascetic saint stood in contemplation. The Gomatesvara is a notable center for Jain pilgrimages and devotions.

Jains carry on an active campaign of writing and pamphleteering to explain their faith to the outsider. While they seek converts, their efforts to date have not been notably successful. Their apologetic literature recommends fasting in terms of its benefits to health. Even the strict Jain vegetarian diet, which includes a prohibition on the eating of eggs, need not involve a protein deficiency! Jain monks and nuns are extolled as athletes of the spiritual life. The Jain philosophy is advocated as an adequate way of understanding the existing world and as a guide to the breaking of fetters along the upward path to emancipation.

The Jain shopkeeper or professional may not be a monk or a nun, but such people can participate in the activities of the community. They can keep their own lay vows—such as to observe periodic fasts—and they can go on pilgrimages. They can honor Mahavira and other fordfinders as the great conquerors; then, setting their own feet on the Jain path, they can hope that someday they too will be conquerors.

Jain hero, Lord Gomatesvara at Belgola, Mysore. (Courtesy of Leonard Dart.)

ISSUES AND QUESTIONS

For western students of religion, probably the most striking feature of the Jain tradition is its explicit atheism or rejection of any belief in a divine creator or lord. However, it must be added that this impression derives at least in part from the Judeo-Christian tradition which associates religion with belief in God, and atheism with irreligion. In this study we have urged the more historically correct viewpoint that there are many symbolic forms for transcendence, of which the monotheistic God is only one. Let us also add that looking over the whole field of the world's religions, the concepts of God and religion vary independently of each other. It is possible to have a religion without God, as in Jainism, and also it is possible to have a philosophically conceived God with little or no religious response.

Beyond its atheism there are other extreme features of Jainism. One such is Jain pessimism regarding human life and the environing creation. In the course of our study we shall encounter several faiths which take a negative view of these matters (as, for example, the biblical image and concept of the Fall of humanity), but in many ways the Jain view seems to win the world championship in this competition. As we have seen, the whole creation is asserted as irredeemably evil, the one exception being a few selected human beings. To accentuate this tale of woe, Jain thought adds two closely related concepts, the notion of the world as a beginningless and endless series of cycles and unimaginably vast sequences of time.

Another example of Jain extremism is its interpretation of the sanctity or holiness of life. Many religions make their own presentation of this basic and recurring theme. Often too this concept is a way of asserting the solidarity of all life. The common Indian concept of karma, extending as it does to all three traditions, Jain, Buddhist, and Hindu, underscores this affirmation. Yet of the three the Jain interpretation surpasses the other two in asserting the sanctity of every least and last living thing.

If we ask why Jainism went to such extremes no single or easy answers are forthcoming. One partial answer lies in Jainism's status as a vital and vigorous minority community in Indian history. Swimming against the mainstream as the Jains have done, their tenets often find expression in extreme ways.

Jain philosophy likewise raises questions to which there is no easy or ready answer. As we have seen, Jain philosophy consists of a highly distinctive metaphysical system. This much can be understood in terms of its ancient Indian context. This was the way all or most ancient Indians pursued philosophy. However, viewed more closely, the Jain philosophy appears as a patchwork of striking and valid insights, such as its concept of many perspectives, or syadrada, mixed with long passages of rigid traditionalism. Like members of some other traditional religions, most recent and current Jain philosophers seem more concerned to defend their traditional system than to do fresh philosophical thinking.

NOTES

1. Karl Jaspers, *The Origin and Goal of History*, Routledge, London, 1953, pp. 51f.
2. George F. Moore, *History of Religions*, vol. 1, Scribner, New York, 1948, chap. 12.
3. A. L. Basham, *The Wonder That Was India*, Grove Press, New York, 1959, pp. 294f.
4. Digha Nikaya 1.47f, as quoted in William T. de Bary (ed.), *Sources of Indian Tradition*, Columbia, New York, 1958, pp. 41–43.
5. Heinrich Zimmer, *Philosophies of India*, Meridian Books, New York, 1957, pp. 181f.
6. Ibid., p. 183.
7. Jaina Sutras, H. Jacobi (trans.), *Sacred Books of the East*, vol. 12, Oxford University Press, London, 1884, p. 152.
8. Zimmer, op. cit., p. 279.
9. W. Norman Brown, *India, Pakistan, Ceylon*, rev. ed., University of Pennsylvania Press, Philadelphia, 1951, p. 93.

10. Basham, op. cit., p. 288.
11. Jaina Sutras, op. cit.
12. Ibid., p. 200.
13. Ibid., p. 201.
14. de Bary, op. cit., p. 49.
15. Ibid., pp. 61–62.
16. Ibid., p. 91.
17. Ibid., pp. 64–65.
18. Ibid., p. 64.
19. Jaina Sutras, op. cit., pp. 202–210.
20. John B. Noss, *Man's Religions*, Macmillan, New York, 1963, p. 163.
21. de Bary, op. cit., pp. 79–80.
22. Ibid., p. 82.
23. Ibid., p. 76.
24. Zimmer, op. cit., pp. 248–252.
25. W. Norman Brown, *Man in the Universe*, Oxford and IBH Publishing Company, Calcutta, 1966, p. 76f.
26. See inter alia de Bary, op. cit., pp. 74–75; Sarvepalli Radhakrishnan and Charles A. Moore (eds.), *Source Book in Indian Philosophy*, Princeton, Princeton, N.J., 1957, p. 261.

BIBLIOGRAPHY

Barodia, V. C.: *History and Literature of Jainism*, Bombay, 1907.
Basham, A. L.: *The Wonder That Was India*, Grove Press, New York, 1959.
————: *History and Doctrines of the Ajivikas*, South Asia Books, Columbia, Mo., 1981.
Bist, U.: *Jaina Theories of Reality and Knowledge*, South Asia Books, Columbia, Mo., 1985.
Brown, W. N.: *Man in the Universe*, University of California, Berkeley, 1966.
Buhler, J. G.: *On the Indian Sect of the Jains*, Luzac, London, 1903.
Caillat, C.: *Jain Cosmology*, Crown, New York, 1982.
Chatterjee, A.: *A Comprehensive History of Jainism*, South Asia Books, Columbia, Mo., 1978.
Dasgupta, S.: *History of Indian Philosophy*, Cambridge, New York, 1922–1935.
Embree, A., and S. Hay (eds.): *Sources of Indian Tradition*, Columbia, New York, 1988.
Hiriyanna, S.: *Essentials of Indian Philosophy*, Unwin Hyman, Inc., Winchester, Mass., 1978.
Jaina Sutras, H. Jacobi (trans.): *Sacred Books of the East*, vol. 12, Oxford, London, 1884.
Jaini, J.: *Outlines of Jainism*, Hyperion Press, Westport, Conn., 1988.
Jaini, P.: *The Jain Path of Purification*, University of California, Berkeley, 1979.
Pratt, J. B.: *India and Its Faiths*, Houghton Mifflin, Boston, 1915.
Radhakrishnan, S.: *History of Indian Philosophy*, G. Allen, London, 1929–1931.
———— (ed.): *History of Philosophy, Eastern and Western*, G. Allen, London, 1952.
————, and Moore (eds.): *Source Book in Indian Philosophy*, Princeton, Princeton, N.J., 1957.
Renou, L.: *Religions of Ancient India*, Oxford, London, 1957.
Schubring, W.: *The Doctrine of the Jainas*, Orient Book Distributors, Livingston, N.J., 1978.
Smart, N.: *Doctrine and Argument in Indian Philosophy*, G. Allen, London, 1964.
Stevenson, S.: *The Heart of Jainism*, Oxford, London, 1916.
Zimmer, H.: *The Art of Indian Asia*, Bollingen Series, Princeton, Princeton, N.J., 1982.
————: *Philosophies of India*, Princeton, Princeton, N.J., 1969.

5

Buddha and Early Buddhism

Buddha belongs along with Mahavira to the Axis Age of Indian history. There are striking similarities in the biographies and teachings of these two men. They were born and lived in the same northeastern region of India. Both were nobles born to rule; both renounced the throne for the austere life of the religious ascetic, seeking and then finding emancipation. Both were rebels against hardening caste lines and increasing Brahman domination of Indian religion and life, with the result that later ages of Hinduism judged both men heretics. Indeed, so similar are their biographies that some observers have concluded Buddha and Mahavira were the same man.

But there are important differences too. While both Mahavira and Buddha were boldly original philosophic minds, their philosophies differ fundamentally. While both founded ascetic, monastic movements, Jainism is as we saw in the last chapter a path of extreme asceticism, while Buddhism in deliberate contrast and opposition has described itself as a middle way to emancipation. For this as well as other reasons, these two religions have developed historically in profoundly different ways. The Jains have remained a small community of less than 3 million adherents, all within India, while Buddhism claims some 500 million followers. It has interacted significantly with most of the great civilizations of Asia, it has adherents in all parts of the world, and it constitutes one of the world's universal religions.

For many western students, the comparison of Buddhism and Christianity has provided an initial focus for study. Both are personally founded religions, and in both cases the founders have been regarded as saviors.[1] In both cases there has been considerable pious concern with the founder's life. There are stories of preexistence, of miraculous birth and supernatural guidance for both Buddha and Christ. Both Buddhism and Christianity have generated whole systems of highly distinctive philosophy or theology.

Both the similarities and differences are epitomized in the respective founders' names and titles, that is, Jesus Christ and Gautama Buddha. The names Jesus and Gautama designate, as proper names characteristically do, specific historical persons. The respective titles, namely, Christ and Buddha, ex-

115

press the significance of these religious founders for their followers. In Chapters 11 to 13 we shall see that *Christos* is the Greek translation of the original Hebrew term *Messiah* meaning God's *Anointed One*, and we shall there explore the significance of this title. The title Buddha is usually translated as *The Enlightened One* but is more accurately rendered as *The Awakened One*. In this chapter we shall see from what sleep to what awakened state Gautama arose to become the Buddha.

Among the many significant differences between Christ and Buddha for their respective followers is the uniqueness of the single figure of Christ in Christian thought and devotion, and by contrast the virtually endless replication of Buddha figures in Buddhism. One implication of this basic difference is the modern Christian concern expressed in the title of Albert Schweitzer's book, *The Quest for the Historical Jesus*.[3] There is in traditional Buddhist thought little or no quest for the historical Buddha. Buddhism has been content with traditional recollection of its founder's life, on the one hand, and on the other hand, the pure concept or idea of the Awakened One multiplied endlessly in the world of delusory appearance.

THE FOUNDER'S LIFE

As was the case with Mahavira, the primary source documents on Buddha provide us at best with a few highly stylized and traditional recollections of the founder's life. The first reaction of the modern western reader is that here is little or nothing of genuine biography. Yet this apparently is what the Buddha has meant to the people who told these stories in the first place and who have passed them on ever since. The stories constitute a kind of traditional portrait painted by many artists over long periods of time.

Yet in wrestling with these problems, the modern, critically minded student of Buddhism begins to see in these recollections of the Buddha an unusually forceful mind and personality. While it is admittedly impossible to discern or reconstruct fully the life of the historical Buddha, it is possible to see beneath the many layers of tradition the seismic impact of a uniquely great man's mind and life. That Buddhism is a personally founded religion is a fact of the greatest importance. A summary of the traditional material relating to Buddha's life follows here.

Buddha was born to noble parents in the region of Magadha of northeast India, in the foothills of the Himalaya Mountains, in what is now the state of Bihar. The dates 560–480 BCE for his life must be understood as approximate or probable only. Traditional Buddhist stories of many preexistent lives of the Buddha have been gathered into the Jataka tales, some 550 of which exist. Buddhist tradition also recounts stories of Buddha's miraculous birth.[2] In a dream his mother saw a heavenly white elephant with a lotus flower in his trunk, who approached and entered her side.[3] The next day the dream was interpreted by the astrologers, who said that she had conceived a son who would be either universal teacher or universal emperor. The baby was named Siddhartha (meaning "wish fulfilling"). Seven days after his birth, his mother died, leaving him in the care of her sister.

Brahman astrologers prophesied that the child would see what Buddhism has called the *four passing sights*, which would wake him to the grim facts of human misery. Accordingly, his father took every possible precaution to shelter him from the world. He was reared in luxury and destined to succeed to his father's throne. He married his cousin, Yashodhara, whose hand he won in a contest of feats of strength. She bore him a son named Rahula (meaning "fetter"). Even then, apparently, he desired detachment.

Prince Siddhartha was not inwardly happy with his princely life. His unhappiness came to climactic expression when he was twenty-nine years old. Despite paternal protectiveness, he saw the four passing sights, namely, an old man, a sick man, a dead man, and a monk. The first three expressed to the future Buddha the misery of human existence, and the fourth symbolized emancipation from it. Siddhartha's mind was made up. Indifferent to his father's redoubled efforts to distract him by means of parties and dancing girls, he roused a faithful servant and rode off into the night. Putting the city far behind him, he dismounted, stripped off his fine clothes, cut off his hair, and assumed the meager garments of a wandering ascetic. Thus occurred what Buddhist tradition has called the *great renunciation* or the *great retirement*.[4] Thus also began Buddha's seven-year quest for salvation.

As noted in Chapter 4, Buddhist scriptures tell of no fewer than six teachers who during this time sought to instruct Gautama in their ways. One of them represented Jain teaching and in some sources is identified as Mahavira himself. But his way did not bring salvation to the seeking Siddhartha. Other teachers instructed him in Brahman speculation and Yoga discipline, still others in different philosophic systems popular at the time. But alas, none of those ways communicated salvation to the princely ascetic.

Influenced by fellow ascetics, he embarked upon the way of extreme asceticism. One day, worn out by hunger, he fainted. His fellow ascetics believed he was dead. As he recovered consciousness, he concluded that this way too was futile. He secured a little food by begging, and his body regained some of its strength. The other ascetics turned in disdain from this backslider. Yet Siddhartha was actually on the threshold of the great discovery which would make him the "enlightened one," or the Buddha.

In the numerous and sometimes variant accounts of the Buddha's enlightenment or awakening, it is impossible in any precise way to distinguish historic facts from pious tradition and mythological elaboration.[5] Hence we shall summarize the earliest traditional accounts, leaving the readers to draw their own conclusions.

Siddhartha was now thirty-five years old and had followed successively many paths that had failed to lead him to his goal. Could there be another way? Seated one day under a pipal tree on the outskirts of Gaya in the realm of King Bimbisara of Magadha, he vowed to remain until his quest was achieved, until

The great departure and Buddha's temptation. (Metropolitan Museum of Art, Fletcher Fund, 1928.)

he had solved the problem of mortal misery. For forty-nine days he sat beneath the tree, known ever since as the *bo*, or "wisdom," tree.

One account says that, rejecting extreme austerities, he took a small amount of simple food. Was this perhaps his recognition that a healthy body was necessary for spiritual search and achievement? At any rate, other ascetics turned away in disgust at this defection. There are also accounts of a last futile assault by Mara the Tempter, who sent his three daughters, Discontent, Delight, and Desire, to seduce the future Buddha.

Successfully resisting the last assault, he moved inward and upward through the four stages of meditation, the first detaching him from sense objects, the second moving from discursive to intuitive thinking, the third moving past vitality to blissful peace, and the fourth going beyond such opposites as pleasure and pain to the goal of pure awareness.

According to some traditional accounts the Buddha-to-be also made his way through the six superknowledges and the three cognitions. A traditional list of the former is: (1)magic powers, (2) the divine ear, (3) knowing other minds, (4) memory of past incarnations, (5) the divine eye, and (6) extinction of sensual desire and of ignorance. The three cognitions are (1) of one's previous existences, (2) of the whole world of death and rebirth, and (3) of the happy consequences of good deeds and the miserable consequences of evil deeds in the round of life. Achievement of the sixth superknowledge and the third cognition yielded the four noble truths: (1) the truth of suffering, (2) the source of suffering, (3) the cessation of suffering, and (4) the noble eightfold path to this goal. The meditating Siddhartha was now the Buddha—in traditional etymology, the "enlightened one," but in more accurate etymology, the "awakened one." He had achieved his goal!

Involved in this climactic experience, according to Buddhist tradition, was also the discovery of the law called, in Sanskrit, *pratitya samutpada*, and variously translated as the law of "dependent arising," "dependent origination," or more simply, "the twelve preconditions," i.e., of mortal existence.[6] However translated, this principle, which was discovered and disclosed by the Buddha, asserts a twelvefold chain of causation at the end of which is the world of mortal misery. Conversely, by breaking its first link—ignorance (*avidya*)—the Buddha broke successively the whole chain. The twelve links of the chain of preconditions are (1) ignorance, (2) dispositions, (3) consciousness, (4) name and form, (5) the six sense fields, (6) contact, (7) feeling, (8) craving, (9) appropriation, (10) becoming, (11) birth, and (12) aging and dying. The metaphor of chain as well as the necessities of exposition make this principle sound linear. Buddhists insist, however, that a circle would be a more accurate image or symbol. Some accounts of the Buddha's meditation and awakening assert that he began with the twelfth link of the chain and worked backward to the first. In any case, his climactic experience and thought under the bo tree broke the chain and solved the problem of mortal misery.

If we ask again what was the content of the experience which made Siddhartha Gautama the Buddha, tradition, which may indeed go back to the Buddha himself, summarizes it in the form of the four noble (or Aryan) truths and the noble (Aryan) eightfold path. The former resemble a physician's terse diagnosis and prescription or therapy for a disease—the disease being human misery.[7] The first two truths are diagnosis, and the third and fourth are therapy. The first asserts that existence is misery (*duhkha*), and the second, that misery is rooted in ignorant craving (*trishna*). The third asserts that misery may be abolished by abolishing ignorant craving, and the fourth asserts that this may be done by the noble eightfold path. Thus, as one Buddhist writer puts the matter, Buddha had found the sovereign remedy for all the major ills of humankind.[8]

The noble eightfold path is understood as the middle way to nirvana, being the mean between the two extremes of Jain asceticism on the one hand and worldliness on the other. This eightfold path consists of (1) right understanding, (2) right-mindedness, (3) right speech, (4) right action, (5) right livelihood, (6) right effort, (7) right meditation, and (8) right emancipation. The first two steps have to do with understanding and the attitude of the human mind toward the Buddhist way; they are called the *higher wisdom*. The next three taken together constitute the *ethical disciplines* and have to do with the moral quality of Buddhist life. The final three steps are called the *mental disciplines* because, based upon the previous ones, they prepare, direct, and then move the seeking mind onward to the achievement of its goal, nirvana.

The significance of this experience of awakening in the life of Buddha and all who reproduce it in their lives is once and for all to break the iron chain of karma-samsara, or the fated cycle of rebirths. Mahavira had spoken analogously of the stoppage of karma; Buddha and his followers spoke of breaking the chain of cause and effect which holds human beings in bondage to delusion. Buddhists believe that Buddha's great insight opened up a new chapter in the history of human spiritual life. Once this path to salvation had been discovered and opened up by Buddha, other persons might also walk it.

To western ears Buddha's goal of nirvana sounds extremely negative. Etymologically it means "blowing out" (of the flame of passion). Does it not then clearly imply extinction or the desire for a quiet death? Buddhists reply that this is by no means the case. Buddha himself expressly denied that nirvana meant annihilation. What is extinguished is only the ignorant cravings which produce misery. What is left is bliss beyond the comprehension of all save those who know it by direct experience. Words serve here only to indicate the path which people must walk; they are meaningful only to those who set their feet on the path to nirvana.

Buddhist tradition tells of Buddha's subsequent meditation for another seven weeks during which he went through a period of doubt as to whether this new wisdom should be proclaimed to humanity. The question at issue was whether, having experienced nirvana, he should immediately seek its full realization (a state which Buddhists call *parinirvana* and believe he achieved at death) or whether out of compassion for suffering humanity he should tell others the good news of deliverance from misery. The latter course won out, and the Buddha embarked upon what turned out to be a forty-five-year mission.

He preached first to his five former fellow ascetics in the Deer Park near Banaras, thus setting in motion the wheel of the *dharma*. As he approached, the ascetics resolved to show scornful indifference to one who had defected from their austere way, but Buddha's attitude of victorious calm and peace won first their attention, then their respect, and finally their adherence. The Buddha's sermon was an exposition of the four noble truths and the noble eightfold path. The conversion of these men marked the beginning of the *Sangha*, or Buddhist monastic order. Some days later fifty-three more converts were added, and Buddha sent them out in all directions to teach the new way to deliverance.

At Rajagaha, King Bimbisara and many of his royal court became lay followers and supporters of the order. There, too, Buddha received his two chief disciples, Shariputta and Moggallana, together with a large group of their friends. Each new monk took the vow which has become traditional throughout the Buddhist world: "I take refuge in the Buddha, the Dharma and the Sangha." Members of the order were bound together by a common discipline and by their saffron robes, but most of all by their common allegiance to Buddha. The discipline is summarized in the traditional ten precepts:

Deer Park sermon. (Government of Andhra Home.)

1. I take the vow not to destroy life.
2. I take the vow not to steal.
3. I take the vow to abstain from impurity.
4. I take the vow not to lie.
5. I take the vow to abstain from intoxicating drinks, which hinder progress and virtue.
6. I take the vow not to eat at forbidden times.
7. I take the vow to abstain from dancing, singing, music, and stage plays.
8. I take the vow not to use garlands, scents, unguents, or ornaments.
9. I take the vow not to use a high or broad bed.
10. I take the vow not to receive gold or silver.[9]

Lay followers are committed to the first five of these ten precepts. Abstention from "impurity" means for monks strict celibacy, but for the laity it means abstention from extramarital sex relations.

Returning home, Buddha converted his royal father, his wife and son, and other members of the court, including his jealous cousin Devadatta. Despite formal conversion, Devadatta's heart remained full of jealousy and evil. In many stories of the Buddha, Devadatta appears as the villain. In one tale he set loose a mad elephant in Buddha's path, but the beast was so impressed by Buddha's gentleness that it bowed calmly at his feet.

The Sangha was, in the words of one Buddhist writer, a democracy, "the earliest monastic institution governed by perfect democratic principles which continues to the present day."[10] Its brotherhood ignored barriers of caste and class; Buddha's son Rahula was a member, but so was the former court barber Upali and the former noble Ananda. Each new monk was placed under the tutelage of an older member of the order. There were fortnightly public confessions of shortcomings.

Buddha's practice was to gather his monks for intensive instruction during the four months of the rainy season. During the balance of the year, they traveled through the towns and countryside of north India, teaching Buddha's message of deliverance from misery.

The earliest Buddhist records are ambivalent concerning miracles of Buddha and his monks. There are many stories of wonders attributed to Buddha, yet he is also recorded as sternly forbidding his monks to perform miracles. There are innumerable stories of the Buddha's beneficent power; for example, once he converted a notorious bandit, and another time he achieved an armistice between two armies drawn up for battle. There are also many stories of philosophic controversy between Buddha and other teachers and schools, notably the Jains.

The consistent image of the Buddha contained in these stories is that of an irenic and compassionate spirit, a sharp and highly original philosophic mind, and above all, a man dedicated in single-minded fidelity to his own emancipation and that of his fellow beings. So passed years of teaching, preaching, and organization. The brotherhood grew. It gained lay followers who provided material support for the monks. Buddha's influence spread throughout northern India. The earliest Buddhist sources also show a clear beginning for the idea of Buddha as a celestial or divine figure.

The Buddha's death, or parinirvana, occurred at the age of eighty on a journey with a group of monks to the obscure village of Kusinara. Details vary according to different accounts. According to one, he took his midday meal at the home of Chunda, a blacksmith, and was afflicted with mortal illness. In his illness he lay down between two sal trees and died, surrounded by devoted followers. Buddhist tradition attributes to both Buddha and his followers prescience of his impending death. His last words were: "And now, O priests, I take my leave of you; all the constituents of being are transitory; work out your salvation with diligence."[11]

BUDDHA'S TEACHINGS

We have already considered some of Buddha's teaching in sketching his life, for it is a notable fact that his teaching and his life were inextricably interwoven. As we have seen, the core of his message to humanity was his insight into the nature of mortal misery and its cure. Misery (duhkha) is rooted in ignorant craving or the delusory itching will to be, to get, and to have. Ignorance (avidya) of the true state of reality leads to craving, which in turn attributes reality to transitory and unreal things. If this root of ignorant craving is cut, the whole vast tree of misery will wither and die. What is left is not extinction—though it will seem so to those ignorant minds still held fast in their bondage to the world. Rather it is the bliss of nirvana, which despite its negative etymology is not in actuality negative, but superaffirmative (noting the parallels between Latin and Sanskrit, Coomaraswamy has coined the term "despirated" for Nirvana, as the negative of "aspirated"). Such, at least, is the testimony of Buddha's followers.[12]

Buddha wanted just enough philosophy to serve as a vehicle for this vision of emancipation—and not one sentence more. Whatever was useless for his purpose was effectively pruned away. When his disciples asked him whether the world is eternal or not, whether there is a substantial soul independent of the body or not, whether this soul exists after death, and whether there are gods or not—questions, be it noted, which others have regarded as of religious significance—he replied that these were questions "which do not edify."[13] In the philosophical style of the twentieth century they are meaningless questions.[14] What was meaningful to the Buddha was misery and its cure—that and only that.

In the historical context of his time, this must be read as a rejection of traditional Brahman metaphysics with its fantastic speculations concerning gods, future lives, immortal souls, and substantial realities. Buddha's rejection of all this bears striking analogy to modern philosophic positivism and its rejection of metaphysics. To be sure, the twentieth-century western reader may observe residual metaphysics to a great extent in Buddha's teaching, such as the teaching of karma-samsara. Yet to Buddha those doctrines were apparently not matters for speculation; they were directly experienced. The fact that this assertion seems incredible to the modern reader simply serves to underscore the chasm which yawns between people of different times, places, and cultures.

Buddha likewise rejected Indian bhakti, or devotion to a god, as an unhealthy dependence on external realities. Rather, each person must climb the ladder of salvation for himself or herself; all must use their own resources of perception and strength for the achievement of nirvana. In fact, no other resources are available. As has been remarked, this is "the strictest sort of humanism in religion."[15] Here indeed was a bold and original philosophical mind.

As a part of the ancient Indian tradition, Buddha accepted the ideas of karma and samsara, but he gave to these traditional ideas his own original and distinctive interpretation. Most important, he parted company from the hardening lines of Indian orthodoxy in his teaching that a person of any caste can experience an awakening of heart so complete as to destroy karma and thus effectively, at one stroke, eliminate future rebirth. Negatively stated, it is those who have not conquered ignorant craving who still live on in the ceaseless treadmill of rebirth, or samsara. Stated affirmatively, enlightenment and emancipation may come for a person of any caste who will meet the hard but simple conditions.

Buddha's philosophical outlook sought to provide a supporting context for this vision of deliverance from misery. The basic categories were *anatta* and *anicca*, or the ideas of (1) no substantial soul and (2) no substantial realities in the world. The concept of anatta, no-ego or no-soul, denies the existence of a substantial self or soul and asserts the apparent self or soul to be a temporary configuration of five components (called *skandha* in Sanskrit and *kandha* in Pali), which are (1) body, (2) feelings, (3) perceptions, (4) states of mind, and (5) awareness. These elements are asserted to enter into combination at the individual's birth and to separate at death. This analysis of the human self is the foundation of Buddhist psychology. Incidentally, it shows striking similarity to modern western behaviorist views of the self.

Buddha denied substantial reality not only to the human self, but to the external world and all the things or objects in it. The idea of anicca asserts the transitory, impermanent nature of all things in the universe. There are no substances, no abiding entities; as Heraclitus asserted in ancient Greece, all is flux. Buddha would agree with the Christian hymn writer: "Change and decay in all around I see." As has been said, the Buddhist universe knows no being, but only becoming.

Buddha bequeathed to his followers a lofty and distinctive system of moral ideals, whose central and characteristic feature is a tension between detachment and compassion. This tension is rooted apparently in the experience of the founder, who having achieved nirvana was confronted by the alternatives of immediate and final entrance into nirvana or of delaying this consummation in order compassionately to communicate this message of deliverance to suffering humanity. He was, in short, confronted by the choice between detachment and compassion, and his solution was to seek a balance in tension between these goals.

For both Buddha and his followers, the tension between detachment and compassion must be judged creative rather than destructive. The two ideas support each other. It is by the breaking of the fetters which fasten a person to misery that one can achieve compassion. Negatively, it is the bondage to craving which leads to cruel action and prevents compassion. Knowledge (vidya) is the insight which overcomes attachment and self-centeredness, making possible both individual fulfillment and compassion for fellow human beings. It is the balance between these two elements which distinguishes Buddhist morality from that of Jainism, imparting to Buddhism the notes of moderation and even quiet joy, lacking in Jainism.

Both detachment and compassion have specific applications in Buddhist ethics. How many of these teachings may be traced back to the historical Buddha it is impossible to say. As expressions of detachment, Buddhism lists the "three intoxications," the "five hindrances," and the "ten fetters." The three intoxications, or defilements, are, in one formulation, evil attitudes, evil thoughts, and evil actions.[16] The five hindrances are (1) sensual desires, (2) hatred, (3) sloth, (4) restlessness and worry, and (5) doubts.[17] One version of the ten fetters is as follows: (1) delusion of self, (2) doubt, (3) dependence on works, (4) sensuality, (5) hatred, ill-feeling, (6) love of life on earth, (7) desire for life in heaven, (8) pride, (9) self-righteousness, and (10) ignorance.[18]

Detachment points to the transmoral goal of nirvana. In nirvana there is no individual existence, and hence there are no moral relations. So it is that the ideal of detachment generates in Buddhist social attitudes a tendency toward passivity and withdrawal. In this spirit the Buddha encouraged his followers to "wander alone like a rhinoceros."[19] This attitude is also illustrated by the well-known Buddhist parable of Kisa Gotami, a poor mother whose only child, a baby son, died. Refusing to give up, she went from place to place and from teacher to teacher seeking medicine to bring the dead son back to life. She came at length to the Buddha, who told her to go around the city until she found some grains of mustard seed from a house in which no one had ever died. She sought in vain from house to house until in a moment of insight the Buddha's lesson became clear to her.

> Thought she: In the entire city this alone must be the way! This the Buddha, full of compassion for the welfare of mankind, must have seen! Overcome with emotion, she went outside of the city, carried her son to the burning-ground, and holding him in her arms, said: "Dear little son, I thought that you alone had been overtaken by this thing which men call death. But you are not the only one death has overtaken. This is a law common to all mankind."[20]

Yet Buddhism from the first included the cultivation of love for fellow human beings as well as detachment, though in early Buddhism the former was clearly subordinated to the latter. Buddhism's compassion was founded upon the archetypal example of Buddha's own sympathy for suffering humanity. The root ideas are those of compassion (*karuna*, literally "feeling with others") and of friendliness or loving-kindness (Pali *metta* and Sanskrit *maitri* mean "friend"). By these moral ideals the whole human family is bound together in its interdependence of misery and also need and aspiration for well-being or health. So it is that Buddhism follows its founder in being "a religion of infinite compassion."[21] Says the Metta Sutta:

> As a mother, even at the risk of her own life, protects and loves her child, her only child, so let a man cultivate love without measure toward all beings. Let him cultivate love without measure toward the whole world, above, below, and around, unstinted, unmixed with any feeling of differing or opposing interests. Let a man remain steadfastly in this state of mind all the while he is awake, whether he be standing, walking, sitting, or lying down. This state of mind is the best in the world.[22]

This ideal is given more specific social application in the following passage from the Sutta Nipata:

Husbands should respect their wives, and comply as far as possible with their requests. They should not commit adultery. They should give their wives full charge of the home, and supply them with fine clothes and jewellery [sic] as far as their means permit. Wives should be thorough in their duties, gentle and kind to the whole household, chaste, and careful in housekeeping, and should carry out their work with skill and enthusiasm.

A man should be generous to his friends, speak kindly of them, act in their interest in every way possible, treat them as his equals, and keep his word to them. They in turn should watch over his interests and property, take care of him when he is "off his guard" (i.e., intoxicated, infatuated, or otherwise liable to commit rash and careless actions), stand by him and help him in time of trouble, and respect other members of his family.

Employers should treat their servants and workpeople decently. They should not be given tasks beyond their strength. They should receive adequate food and wages, be cared for in time of sickness and infirmity, and be given regular holidays and bonuses in times of prosperity. They should rise early and go to bed late in the service of their master, be content with their wages, work thoroughly, and maintain their master's reputation.[23]

The spirit of Buddha's ethics is well summarized in some well-known lines from the Dhammapada:

All that we are is the result of what we have thought: it is founded on our
    thoughts, it is made up of our thoughts. If a man speaks or acts with a pure
    thought happiness follows him, like a shadow that never leaves him.
"He abused me, he beat me, he defeated me, he robbed me"—in those who
    harbor such thoughts hatred will never cease.
"He abused me, he beat me, he defeated me, he robbed me"—in those who do
    not harbor such thoughts hatred will cease.
For hatred does not cease by hatred at any time; hatred ceases by love—this is an
    old rule.
The world does not know that we must all come to an end here; but those who
    know it, their quarrels cease at once.[24]

THE FORMATIVE CENTURIES OF INDIAN BUDDHISM

Buddhist tradition asserts that there was a great assembly of 500 Buddhist monks at Rajagaha in 480 BCE, the first of a long succession of such councils, comparable to the ecumenical councils of Christianity. Tradition claims that these monks recited the Pali canon of scripture called the *Tipitaka* (the Sanskrit *tripitaka*, meaning "three baskets"), thus fixing or codifying this document. The same Buddhist tradition goes on to say that the Tipitaka was transmitted by oral tradition until the fourth council, when it was put into writing. The Tipitaka, or Tripitaka, consists of three main parts, the Vinaya Pitaka (obedience or discipline basket), consisting of rules for the Sangha; the Sutta Pitaka, consisting of expositions of the Buddhist way of life; and the Abhidhamma Pitaka (metaphysical or philosophical basket), consisting of philosophical treatises. According to one Buddhist source, this last part of the Pali scriptures was not formally adopted until the third council.

The second great council was held a century later, in 380 BCE, at Vesali. It witnessed the first signs of a split destined to widen in the course of time between what were to become Theravada and Mahayana forms of Buddhism. This council was also marked by disputes over monastic discipline, some monks asking for relaxation of rules forbidding gold and silver, liquor, beds, and meals after midday. They also asked for private rather than public confession of shortcomings.

A third council was convened ca. 240 BCE at Paliputra under the sponsorship of King Ashoka. Led by this great king, it was a milestone in the history of Buddhism, transforming it from an Indian movement to a universal religion.

Ashoka, the third king of the Maurya dynasty, was the grandson of the founder, Chandragupta Maurya, who had carved out a kingdom in northwest India as Alexander the Great's armies withdrew. Ashoka began as king of Magadha but achieved by conquest an empire which embraced most, if not all, of the vast Indian subcontinent. He came closer to the political unification of India than any other ruler until the arrival of the British in the seventeenth and eighteenth centuries CE.

Ashoka's conquests included what he subsequently came to regard as a particularly bloody victory over the kingdom of Kalinga on the Bay of Bengal. Apparently the carnage pricked his conscience. In penitence he renounced his warlike ways and reformed the extravagant practices of his luxurious court. The royal hunt was abolished, and the allowance of meat for the court was reduced to two peacocks and an antelope daily. These actions as well as Ashoka's establishment of hospitals for people and animals expressed his avowal of the traditional Indian idea of noninjury, or ahimsa. Significantly, it did not entail complete pacifism.

Ashoka's activities are recorded on the rock edicts and pillar inscriptions by which he communicated his deeds and reforms to the people of his far-flung realm.[25] These records constitute (except for Harappa and Mohenjo-daro) the oldest extant historical monuments of Indian civilization. They also reveal Ashoka's intensely interesting personality. He was apparently much concerned with religion in general and with all the varieties of religion within his realm. His rock edicts proclaim religious freedom and toleration for all the numerous sects of his realm in a manner which is unique in ancient history.

Although a Buddhist adherent and patron, Ashoka's religion was that of a layperson, emphasizing moral practice and social service. His records mention planting fruit trees along the roads of his realm, digging wells, and setting up rest houses. To ensure the morals of his subjects, he established a new class of officials, the "officers of righteousness," whose duties included inspection and supervision of the conduct of his subjects. For Ashoka religion seems to have meant moral conduct in this life and heaven in the next. Significantly, his records speak of *svarga*, the Sanskrit word for "heaven," rather than of nirvana.

Ashoka's relation to Buddhism was momentously important. Some authorities believe that he actually entered the Buddhist order, though this is far from certain. What is more probable is that he conceived and called the Council of Paliputra. He did not hesitate to prescribe reading for the Buddhist order; he also ordered unworthy monks to be unfrocked. He erected shrines at Buddha's birthplace and place of enlightenment and encouraged pilgrimages to these and other sacred places.

From Ashoka's time onward, Indian Buddhism assumed more of the distinctive features of a religious movement than previously, including temples, rituals, and many other institutional appurtenances of a religion. These in turn led to some of the great and characteristic forms of Indian Buddhist art such as the *stupa* and the *chaitya*. The latter is a kind of chapel or temple built to celebrate some holy place and often housing a relic of the Buddha. Not infrequently, as in the case of Karla, such chaityas were carved out of live rock. In many cases a chaitya was accompanied by a *vihara*, or monks' living quarters. The stupa is basically an earth mound built over a relic of the Buddha, to be visited and circumambulated by the faithful. Among the greatest works of Indian art are the stupas at Sanchi.

Ashoka seems to have conceived of Buddhism as a universal faith rather than as simply an Indian movement. He sent missionaries to many distant places. Most notably, he sent his son (some accounts say his brother) Mahinda to Ceylon. Whatever Mahinda's relation to Ashoka, Ceylonese Buddhism, with its manifold implications for the culture of that land, dates from this time.

Ashoka's period was crucial for the division between Theravada (or Hinayana) and Mahayana as the two major historical forms of Buddhism. The former is the Buddhism of Ceylon, or Sri Lanka, and southeast Asia, and the latter is the Buddhism of China, Korea, and Japan and, in its own distinctive way, Tibet.

The terms Mahayana and Hinayana were coined by Indian Mahayana adherents. These words mean, respectively, "the great vehicle" and "the small vehicle," or as Zimmer has suggestively rendered them, the great and the small ferryboats, whose function is to carry people across the stream of mortal misery to the bliss of the farther shore.[26] Adherents of Hinayana regard this word as a negative valuation and prefer the name Theravada, which means "the way or teaching of the elders." By this term they also assert their claim to the Buddha and his disciples.

The separation between Theravada and Mahayana did not come simply or quickly. One of the first breaks, occurring in the second century A.N. (after nirvana) or the third century BCE, was that between *Mahasanghikas* (Great Assemblyites) and the *Sthaviras* (elders, in Pali, Thera). This first split seems to have focused on the agelong issue of the lay persons' relation to the monks. Documents of the time list a great number of other sectarian groups based upon differing tenets or beliefs. One such group were the *Vibhajyavadins* (distinctionists). Another group, splitting away from the Vibhajyavadins, first applied the name *Theravada* to themselves. In the following centuries this name was extended to cover all of southeast Asian Buddhism.

In India at least one great Buddhist monument celebrated this early period of Buddhism, namely, the stupas at Sanchi near Bhopal in central India. Like the pyramids of Egypt and the ziggurats of Mesopotamia the stupas of India were earth mounds celebrating the relation of microcosm to macrocosm. As early Buddhists, the stupas at Sanchi did not depict the figure of the Buddha, rather representing his life by the three symbols of bodhi tree, footsteps, and empty chair.

In the next section we shall characterize the Theravada tradition, and in the following section the development of Indian Mahayana.

THE WAY OF THE ELDERS

Theravada claims to stand in direct succession from Buddha and his disciples. This succession is embodied in the great councils, the first three of which have been described. A fourth, the Council of Matale, was held in Ceylon in 25 BCE. There the Tipitaka, previously transmitted orally, was committed to writing.

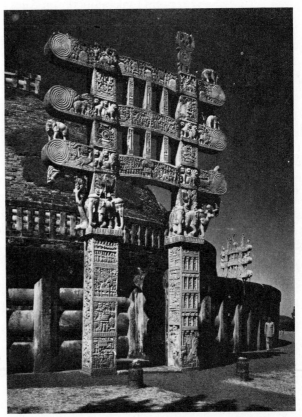

East gate of Great Stupa at Sanchi. (Archeological Survey of India.)

There was another council in northwest India under King Kanishka in the first century CE, but its authority is not recognized by Theravada Buddhists. The fifth great Theravada council was held in 1891 in Mandalay, Burma, and the sixth in 1956. Both of the latter grew out of modern reassertions of Buddhist vitality.

The Pali canon fixed at Matale consists, as we have seen, of the "three baskets," or Tipitaka, each of which has several main subdivisions, as follows:

1. The Basket of Discipline (Vinaya Pitaka): This contains five main divisions, all devoted to monastic discipline.
2. The Basket of Discourses (Sutta Pitaka): This contains narrative and didactic material, notable among which are Jataka and Dhammapada.
3. The Basket of Ultimate Things (Abhidhamma Pitaka): This contains seven books of Theravada philosophy.[27]

It is significant to note that the Pali scriptures were preserved in Sri Lanka while they were lost in India. As a consequence the great fifth-century Indian Buddhist scholar Buddhaghosa came to Sri Lanka in order to retranslate them from Sinhalese to Pali and take them back to India.

Sri Lankan Buddhism dates from the third century BCE when King Ashoka's son (or brother) Mahinda, together with six companions, came to Sri Lanka as missionaries. Mahinda proclaimed the *dhamma* (the Pali term for the Sanskrit *dharma*) with such eloquence that King Tissa and his court embraced the new faith. Monasteries were founded, and stupas and temples were erected. Nuns were brought from India to found an order for women. Tradition says that they brought a sprig of the original bo tree from Bodhgaya, which still lives and grows at the monastery at Anuradhapuna. Buddha's collarbone and other relics are said to have been brought to Sri Lanka at this time. Later, in 310 CE, the tooth relic was brought from India and given a place of honor in the Temple of the Tooth in Kandy.

Buddhist fortunes in Sri Lanka have ebbed and flowed with the changing centuries. Social disorders, invasions, and religious decline brought Buddhism to the point of extinction around 1000 CE. However, a devout king imported a new order of monks from Burma. Later, during the Dutch domination of Sri Lanka in the eighteenth century, still another new order was introduced from Thailand. British rule in the eighteenth and nineteenth centuries brought increased Christian missionary activities, but this stimulated new life and thought in Sri Lankan Buddhism, which continues to the present day. Theravada Buddhism continues as the national faith of Sri Lanka.

From Sri Lanka, Buddhism found its way to the lands of southeast Asia. Tradition tells many tales, but reliable history concerning the origins of Burmese Buddhism is meager or lacking. Buddhist legend tells the story of two merchants named Tapassu and Bhallika who gave the Buddha his first meal after his enlightenment and who, having been converted by the Buddha, went on to Burma to lay the foundations of Buddhism in that country. Another legend says that the Buddha gave them a few hairs from his head, which are now properly enshrined in the celebrated Shwedagon Pagoda of Rangoon. Still another story asserts that two missionaries of King Ashoka first brought Buddhism to Burma. It is said, presumably with better basis, that the fifth-century missionary-scholar Buddhaghosa visited Burma and planted the seeds of Burmese Buddhism.

What can be historically established is that under the eleventh-century king Anawrahta, who first unified Burma, Buddhism enjoyed a golden age. Ever since this time Buddhism has been the established religion of Burma. It has had its ups and downs, but it has never been seriously challenged as Burma's major faith.

Similar tales are told concerning Thailand, where Buddhism has been the established religion since the fourteenth century. This has meant governmental support and often also a large measure of governmental control for the 165,000 monks in 20,000 Thai monasteries.

From Sri Lanka, Burma, and Thailand, Buddhism made its way to Cambodia, Laos, and Vietnam, and from there to Indonesia. Since these cultures were greatly influenced by India, their Buddhism shows extensive Hindu mixtures. Nor indeed was their Buddhism purely Theravada; there were important mixtures of Mahayana as well.

In Theravada lands the center of Buddhism remains the brotherhood of Buddhist monks. In these lands Buddhism is essentially a monastic brotherhood surrounded and supported by lay followers and radiating its influence into the surrounding society. The characteristic institutional structure for Theravada is the monastic complex called in Thai language the *wat* (and in Burmese *phongyi chaung*).[28] Within the complex the chief building is the *bot*, which is a hall for worship or meditation as well as teaching and preaching. Here the most prominent feature is the image of the Buddha seated high above the altar and surrounded by images of Buddha's disciples. On the altar are candlesticks, incense burners, and other equipment for ritual. Also there is likely to be a bouquet of flowers brought as homage to the Buddha. In some prominent place in the meditation hall is a raised seat for the teachers or preachers who dispense instruction and inspiration to members of the order and at times to the public.[29] Other parts of the monastic complex include living quarters for the members, as well as a number of stupas, or *dagobas*, and pagodas, whose graceful towers tapering upward give the whole structure its characteristic appearance.

Notable among southeast Asian Buddhist monuments are those of Angkor in Cambodia near the Thai border. The Angkor Wat was begun by King Suryavarman II (1113–1150), and constructed over a period of three centuries. Different stages in this process show the Hindu cult of Vishnu and Krishna, while others celebrate Theravada and Mahayana Buddhism as well as the divinity of the king. In 1177, Angkor was sacked by invading armies and fell into ruin. In the following century a new king erected Angkor Thom, celebrating both Buddha and his own divine kingship. Repeatedly overrun by invaders and overgrown by jungle, Angkor was rediscovered in the nineteenth and twentieth centuries by French colonists.

Another monument of southeast Asian Buddhism is the great stupa of Borobudur in central Java. Dating from the eighth and early ninth centuries CE, it was built by local monarchs. As a vast earth mound, it is square at the base, depicting the four main cosmic directions. It rises in successive terraced levels, expressing in Buddhist symbolism the ascent of the human spirit to nirvana. Significantly the icons of the intermediate levels contrast with the empty summit, symbolizing nirvana.

Authorities disagree as to the origin of the pagoda, but the most probable guess is that it began as the stupa or relic mound, such as that at Sanchi, India, and that the multiform roof began as a series of parasols placed over a relic. Whatever their beginning, pagodas are characteristic features of the southeast Asian landscape—and also, as we shall see, of China and Japan.

Although the pagoda retains its function as a relic shrine, it has also gathered to itself other functions. It is the center of ritual and public festivals of many sorts. The Perahera festival at Kandy in Sri Lanka features music, dancing, and processions in which relics are taken from the pagoda and returned to it. Sri Lanka also has a New Year's festival (similar to the Hindu Holi) in which cars or floats bearing images of the Buddha are paraded about the streets. The Buddha is also honored by exhibitions of national dance. As in India, people splash each other with colored water.

The most important popular festival of Theravada Buddhism is Wesak, usually observed during the full moon of May and celebrating the birth, enlightenment, and parinirvana of the Buddha. Houses and streets are decorated, and gifts are given to monks and to the poor.

Theravada Buddhism has struck deep roots in these cultures, influencing art, ethics, politics, and indeed, all aspects of the common life. In Thailand and Burma it has been customary for young men to spend at least a few weeks in study and meditation in a monastery before assuming the duties of citizenship. Others may go to the monastery for periods of meditation or instruction. Buddhist religious practices of many sorts, ranging from retreats and pilgrimages to marriages and funeral ceremonies and to public holidays or festival days are established features of the society.

What is Theravada's view of the Buddha, whose images line the meditation halls of monasteries and dot the landscape of southeast Asia? Buddha is honored and reverenced by his Theravada followers as the great discoverer of the path to salvation. Yet, having discovered and walked it, Buddha is now in nirvana, beyond the reach of human adoration or petition. Hence, while Theravada religious followers honor and reverence him and even meditate before his image, they do not, properly speaking, worship him or pray to him. The flowers on his altar, as well as the many Buddha images, are ways of paying homage to the discoverer of the path which leads from mortal misery to the blessedness of *nibbana* (the Pali version of *nirvana*).

Theravada lagged far behind Mahayana in its speculation about Buddha and other Buddha figures. Yet the beginnings of such speculation are present in Pali sources. They affirm the Buddha's preexistence and his descent to earth

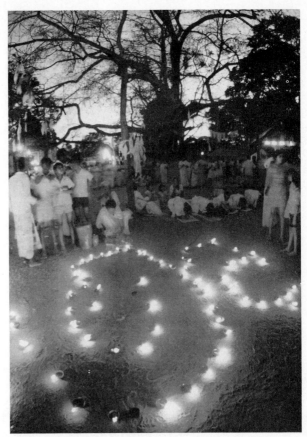

Wesak festival, Sri Lanka. (Joe Viesti/Viesti Associates.)

from the *tushita* heaven in order to bring enlightenment to humankind. They also affirm the existence of other buddhas in the making. Gautama himself was a bodhisattva in a long series of transmigrations before achieving his final birth and enlightenment. While Gautama Buddha clearly continues to occupy the central place, Theravada Buddhism finds place in its devotion for *Metteya* (Sanskrit, *Maitreya*), now a bodhisattva and, more specifically, the buddha of the next age. In Pali sources there are a few allusions to other bodhisattvas, ranging from six to twenty-four in number. They are said to be candidates for buddhahood, or enlightenment, who delay their entrance into nibbana in order to help suffering fellow creatures. As will presently be clear, the bodhisattva figure assumed other different and greatly expanded meanings in Mahayana Buddhism.

Theravada philosophy—if this term be permitted—has consisted largely of reflection upon the main themes of Buddha's thought, such as the nature of misery and of deliverance to nibbana, the transitory, unsubstantial character of self and world, and the nature and transmission of *kamma* (Sanskrit, *karma*). Beyond these limits it has, in obedience to Buddha, refused to venture.

Theravada thought has made much of the silence of the Buddha in response to questions whose answers would have taken him into speculative answers which do not edify. Buddha's silence may be taken as his rejection of the Indian speculative philosophy of his time. Such thought contributed nothing to the way out of misery to deliverance.[30] Buddha would, presumably, agree with the modern philosophic formulation: "What we cannot speak about we must pass over in silence."[31]

Yet despite themselves, Theravada Buddhists did in their way speak concerning these matters; they elaborated Buddha's doctrines of anatta and anicca, as a kind of philosophic explication and guide for the Buddha's way to salvation. One celebrated Theravada source compares the human self to a chariot which is composed of wheels, frame, reins, spokes, etc. When the chariot is dismantled—one is tempted to say dissolved—into these component parts, nothing of the chariot remains. So, analogously, the human self is analyzed into the five kandhas, or components.[32] They come together in a temporary configuration to constitute the self which appears, but they separate at death and nothing remains. Hence, death signifies the end of a temporary phenomenon.

This view of selfhood raised significant questions for personal identity. Is the adult really the same person as the infant of many years ago? Buddhist thought replied with the metaphor of a light which burns continuously through the night.[33] Further, the continuity of the body provides a pragmatic unity of self.

This uncompromising denial of a substantial self seemed to leave the issue of rebirth dangling. How can there be rebirth if nothing transmigrates? Again, Buddhist thought used the metaphor of a light—this time the light passed from one lamp to another. The lamps might crumble and disappear, but the light continues. Even so does kamma pass from one transitory configuration of selfhood to another.[34] Despite the absence of substantial existence, Theravada thought managed to say a great deal concerning kamma. As there are different kinds of seeds, so there are many kinds of kamma, some good, some bad, each producing its own kind of character and behavior. Other refinements and elaborations of the idea arose in the course of time.[35]

More affirmatively, Theravada Buddhist thinkers formulated the noble eightfold path as stages of development for the self, or apparent self, passing through the realms of morality, concentration, and wisdom.[36] In this process, Theravada has changed the traditional order of the eightfold path, beginning with right speech, right action, and right livelihood. From these a person goes on to wisdom, preparatory to meditation and thence to the goal of emancipation. Theravadins also emphasize that this is a journey of the soul undertaken and carried out through a person's own strength. No gods are available for help or guidance on this journey.

Theravada ethics continued the tension between the goal of individual emancipation and compassionate love for humankind. The latter is by no means lacking. There is an attitude of quiet friendliness, if not of overt generosity in Theravada virtue:

> This a man should do who knows what is good for him,
> Who understands the meaning of the Place of Peace—
> He should be able, upright, truly straight,
> Kindly of speech, mild, and without conceit.
>
> He should be well content, soon satisfied,
> Having few wants and simple tastes,
> With composed senses, discreet,
> Not arrogant or grasping....
>
> In his deeds there should be no meanness
> For which the wise might blame him.
> May all be happy and safe!
> May all beings gain inner joy—[37]

As previously noted, this Buddhist love can sometimes become the virtue that returns good for evil. Yet in Theravada, Buddhist compassion continues to be fundamentally the impartial goodwill of those who have delivered their own souls from craving and wish to show others how they may do the same.

While its goal has remained a clearly transsocial and transmoral salvation, Theravada ethics has generated significant moral teachings and social values. It continued the hostility to caste. So, for example, the Sutta Nipata says,

> No brahman is such by birth.
> No outcaste is such by birth.
> An outcaste is such by his deeds.
> A brahman is such by his deeds.[38]

It has continued to hold up the fivefold rule for laypersons: (1) Do not take life; (2) do not take what is not yours; (3) do not act basely in sexual matters; (4) do not tell falsehoods; and (5) do not drink spirits.[39] For the Buddhist laity rule 1 as traditionally interpreted has meant that they cannot be butchers, though they can eat meat provided by non-Buddhist butchers. While not strictly pacifist in its teaching, Buddhism has been among the most peaceful and peace-loving of the world's religions. It has been remarkably successful in promoting abstinence from alcohol.

Despite its somewhat nonpolitical nature, Buddhism has discouraged the pretensions of kings to divine or semidivine status. Like other Indian faiths and philosophies of its time, Buddhism sees the historical origin and development of the human world within a vast and pulsating universe in which periods of growth and decay, of improvement and degeneration, seem to follow each other in an endless succession of ages. As for the recent past and present, the times are becoming worse, as is evidenced in the increase of immorality and in people's shorter life spans. They will continue to worsen until a climax of evil is reached. Then the wheel will turn again.

Yet Theravada teaches that human destiny and blessedness lie beyond all the ups and downs of the world of ceaseless becoming. In this world, which is without beginning or end, people live and labor as prisoners until they reach the state of nibbana, where sorrow and illusion exist no longer. To lay bare the great illusion is the work of human beings. "To contemplate life without being enmeshed in worldly things and then to go forth into higher spiritual life is the path of the Buddha and his Theravada followers. To be united with what is real and permanent—that is, to attain nibbana—is the goal of that path."[40]

THE GREAT VEHICLE

While Theravada was developing and spreading over southeast Asia, Mahayana, the Great Vehicle, was assuming its distinctive forms and moving toward domination in India. This process extended over several centuries during which these two main forms of Buddhism lived and meditated together and argued with each other.

As it emerged, Mahayana showed four distinctive features. First, in addition to the Pali scriptures which it held in common with Theravada, Mahayana added the new sutra literature in Sanskrit. Second it added new forms of devotion to the Buddha as well as a vast number of new Buddhist savior figures. Third, it produced new and distinctive forms of philosophic speculation.

Fourth, underlying all three of these features was a new mode of interpretation called *upaya* or "skillful means." By this concept was meant skill in relating the Buddha's teaching to the capacity of the receiver. Occurring in many of the Mahayana sutras, upaya is found in especially concentrated form in the *Saddharma Pundarika*, the Lotus Sutra.[41]

For example, in this document the Buddha speaks to a father whose sons are trapped in a burning house unable to leave. The father tells them of three carts or chariots which await them outside. They make their exit to find only one cart. Buddha and his disciple, Shariputra, agree that the father's deception was indeed a skillful means in motivating his sons to leave the burning house. Again, the teaching of the Buddha is likened to rain which falls on each plot of ground in ways specially calculated to induce growth. Again, in a Buddhist version of the prodigal son parable, a father describes home only very gradually to his wandering son, thus facilitating the son's return home.

In a summary word, upaya was the interpretive instrument by which Mahayana Buddhists were able to mediate between the Buddha's teaching, on the one hand, and on the other hand, the life of the world with which Mahayana sought to interact. Meanwhile we can gain insight into the meaning of the Great Vehicle by following Heinrich Zimmer's elaboration of the parable of a big ferryboat crossing an Indian river.

"The gist of Buddhism can be grasped more readily and adequately by fathoming the main metaphors through which it appeals to our intuition than by a systematic study of the complicated superstructure, and the fine details of the developed teachings. For example, one need only think for a moment about the actual, everyday experience of the process of crossing a river in a ferryboat, to come to the simple idea that inspires and underlies all of the various rationalized systematizations of the doctrine. To enter the Buddhist vehicle—the boat of the discipline—means to begin to cross the river of life, from the shore of the common-sense experience of non-enlightenment, the shore of spiritual ignorance (avidyā), desire (kāma), and death (māra), to the yonder bank of transcendental wisdom (vidyā) which is liberation (moksa) from the general bondage. Let us consider, briefly, the actual stages involved in any crossing of a river by ferry, and see if we can experience the passage as a kind of initiation-by-analog into the purport of the stages of the Buddhist pilgrim's progress to his goal.

"Standing on the nearer bank, this side the stream, waiting for the boat to put in, one is a part of its life, sharing in its dangers and opportunities and whatever may come to pass on it. One feels the warmth or coolness of its breezes, hears the rustle of its trees, experiences the character of its people, and knows that the earth is underfoot. Meanwhile the other bank, the far bank, is beyond reach—a mere optical image across the broad, flowing waters that divide us from its unknown world of forms. We have really no idea what it will be like to stand in that distant land. How this same scenery of the river and its two shorelines will appear from the other side we cannot imagine. How much of these houses will be visible among the trees? What prospects up and down the river will unfold? Everything over here, so tangible and real to us at present—these real, solid objects, these tangible forms—will be no more than remote, visual patches, inconsequential optical effects, without power to touch us, either to help or to harm. This solid earth itself will be a visual, horizontal line beheld from afar, one detail of an extensive scenic view, beyond our experience, and of no more force for us than a mirage.

"The ferryboat arrives; and as it comes to the landing we regard it with a feeling of interest. It brings with it something of the air of that yonder land which will soon be our destination. Yet when we are entering it we still feel like members of the world from which we are departing, and there is still that feeling of unreality about our destination. When we lift our eyes from the boat and boatman, the far bank is still only a remote image, no more substantial than it was before."[42]

The historical development of Mahayana in India took place under the beneficent influence of a group of monarchs whom Zimmer has called "the great Buddhist kings."[43] We have already noted the career of King Ashoka and his decisive impact upon Buddhism. Shortly after his death, the Maurya dynasty and empire disintegrated and disappeared. But other, lesser kings arose to take his place as royal patrons of Buddhism, principally in northwest India. From the few shreds of archeological evidence, they are labeled Greco-Bactrian, since their remains, from coins to sculptured likenesses of Buddha, show possible Greek influence, and since they lived and reigned in the region of Bactria. One of these Greco-Bactrian kings, perhaps the greatest, King Milinda (125–95 BCE), whose Greek name was Menander, is known to us through a notable document, *The Conversations of King Milinda*, which reports the king's serious questions concerning Buddhist thought, addressed to his guide and tutor, the monk Nagasena. Many aspects of these conversations are more sympathetic to Theravada ideas than to Mahayana; clearly there was no unanimity among these royal patrons of Buddhism. Another such Buddhist king was Kanishka (79–123 CE) of Kushana. From these and presumably similar royal adherents and patrons of the faith, one sees in development a relation of faith to culture somewhat different from that of Theravada. There is in the case of Mahayana a notably greater affirmation of the varied life of human culture. Increasingly this affirmation was extended to all aspects of the culture.

Other differences also emerged, including a different attitude toward Buddha. As early as Ashoka we note in some Buddhist documents an attitude of personal devotion toward the Lord Buddha which is similar to bhakti in Hinduism. From this root grew several new and significant developments. One was the development of great new Buddhist arts. Early Buddhism had been reluctant to make sculptured or painted likenesses of the Buddha. At Sanchi, whose devotion was Theravada, there was a careful avoidance of any likeness of the Buddha. This reticence was overcome by Mahayana. In northwest India from the first century of the Common Era onward, a great new tradition of sculpture celebrated the main events of Buddha's life, and the different aspects of his many-sided personality and message. The sculptors who created this art owed a debt to Greek sculpture, but they developed their own new and highly distinctive style. Similarly in the early centuries of the Common Era, fresco paintings such as those which adorn the walls of the monastic caves at Ajanta celebrated new Mahayana devotion to Buddha and to such new Buddha figures as Amitabha.

As we have seen, a central and determining feature of Mahayana was its new sutra literature. While its adherents claimed it to be the revealed word of the Buddha, to the critical reader it shows many significant new religious and philosophical features.

One such feature of Mahayana is what may be called *the path of the bodhisattva*. Both the term and the idea antedated Mahayana. The word *bodhisattva* means "body or being of enlightenment or wisdom," and we have already noted in Theravada the presence of such figures as Maitreya, the buddha of the next age. In both Theravada and Mahayana the proliferation of buddha figures who come from heaven to earth seems to be rooted in the conviction of Buddha's transmundane nature and significance or, in other words, the conviction that he is greater than a mere human being—in western terms, divine.

In Mahayana the bodhisattva path was based upon the assumption that every person is a potential buddha. The path to buddhahood may be extremely hard and eons long, but laypeople and monks alike may set their feet upon it. The motives are aspiration for enlightenment and compassion for humankind.

Standing Buddha. (Archeological Survey of India.)

The characteristic bodhisattva vow promised not to enter full buddhahood until all others are saved.

The six perfections to which the bodhisattva is committed are (1) giving, (2) morality, (3) patience, (4) vigor or zeal, (5) meditation, and (6) wisdom. The last, called in Sanskrit *prajna paramita* ("the wisdom of the further shore"), is a necessary ingredient of all the others, defining the spirit in which they are to be sought, namely, without ulterior motivation and without attachment to the unreal world. Mahayana Sutras assert that prajna, or wisdom, is a subtle and difficult perfection to achieve. Wisdom is also personified as a goddess who is asserted to be the mother of all the buddhas.

To the perfections Mahayana added the theory of *bhumis*, or stages on the way to becoming a buddha. In different formulations the number and order of stages varies, but they all begin with the bodhisattva's first thought of enlightenment and culminate in the final achievement of buddhahood. The intervening time might be eons or *kalpas* long; it involves such requirements as declaring one's vows in the presence of a buddha, thus necessitating waiting until a buddha arrives in the world. Yet perhaps the most significant feature of the bodhisattva ideal is its implication of universal compassion and salvation. Compassionately the bodhisattva seeks the salvation of all, and in the end all will be saved. Truly Buddhism is a religion of infinite compassion and universal salvation!

For mortals who are about to set their feet on the bodhisattva path, there is encouragement in the contemplation (and the grace!) of heavenly bodhisattvas or *mahasattvas* ("great beings"). These savior gods and goddesses are both more numerous and more significant in Mahayana than in Theravada. Some sound Christlike in their expression of suffering love, as the following passage illustrates:

> I take upon myself...the deeds of all beings, even of those in the hells, in other words, in the realms of punishment....I take their suffering upon me,...I bear it, I do not draw back from it, I do not tremble at it,...I have no fear of it,...I do not lose heart....I must bear the burden of all beings, for I have vowed to save all things living, to bring them safe through the forest of birth, age, disease, death and rebirth, I think not of my own salvation, but strive to bestow on all beings the royalty of supreme wisdom. So I take upon myself all the sorrow of all beings. I resolve to bear every torment in every purgatory of the universe. For it is better that I alone suffer than the multitude of living beings. I give myself in exchange. I redeem the universe from the forest of purgatory, from the womb of flesh, from the realm of death. I agree to suffer as a ransom for all beings, for the sake of all beings. Truly I will not abandon them. For I have resolved to gain wisdom for the sake of all that lives, to save the world.[44]

Of the virtually innumerable celestial bodhisattvas, there is space here for only the briefest mention of the most important and widely known. Maitreya, the buddha of the next age, has been mentioned in the section on Theravada. He was historically the earliest bodhisattva to gain a following, and his human followers include both Mahayanists and Theravadins. He appears frequently in the Buddhist sculpture of Gandhara and of central Asia. Maitreya became Mi-lo-fu in China.

Probably the most important celestial bodhisattva is *Avalokiteshvara* or *Lord Avalokita* (the word means "descender to the world"), who was an early attendant of other buddha figures and only later achieved independent status. He is said to grant boons to those in distress or trouble, and to save his devotees from lust, hostility, and folly. He is symbolized in art as a bejeweled layperson with a high crown, and was later represented with eleven heads and many arms. In China Avalokita changed sex, often becoming the goddess Kuan Yin, deity of mercy. In Japan she is known as Kwannon.

Of comparable importance is *Manjusri* (the name means "sweet glory"), also known as *Manjughosa* ("sweet voice"). He is the patron of wisdom, whose

Bottisatva Maitreya. (Archeological
Survey of India.)

sharp sword cuts through ignorance and illusion and whose ever-present book
depicts the bodhisattvas' perfection. Followers say that very long ago and very
far away he began the bodhisattva path as a devout king. Now, even though he
has completed the path, he stays in the samsara world until all are saved. In
China Manjusri became Wen-yu.

In addition to the bodhisattvas on the way to buddhahood, there are the
buddhas who have completed the journey and are now in nirvana. Of these
there are two kinds, first *manushi* buddhas, or those who began their journey
from a human base, and *dhyani* (or meditation) buddhas, who began from
some other part of the universe. Of the first, in addition to Gautama
Shakyamuni are two supposed predecessors, Dipankara and Kashyapa. Sometimes included in this list is Maitreya, the buddha of the next age, but since he
has not yet achieved buddhahood, he is still a bodhisattva.

Among important and widely worshipped dhyani buddhas is *Amitabha*
("endless light"), also known as *Amitayus* ("endless life"). He is known as
Omito in China and Amida in Japan; in both countries he is the blessed "lord of
sukhavati," the pure land or heaven of devotional Buddhism. His devotees con-

fidently proclaim that if human beings will meditate on Amida with a faith-filled heart, Amida will meet them and guide them to the pure land.

Another dhyani buddha, *Samantabhadra* ("universal sage"), has been associated with the teaching and practice of the Lotus Sutra. He watches over its devotees, protecting those who keep its teaching and admonishing those who forget. In China his name is Pu-hien. *Vairocana* ("illuminator") was, as his name indicates, related to the sun. He achieved a separate identity in later Mahayana and played a significant role in tantric Buddhism. Still later in Japan he came to be identified with the Shinto sun goddess Amaterasu. *Kshitigarbha* ("womb of earth"), who is Ti Tsang in China and Jizo in Japan, is the judge of the lower regions and delivers people from the sufferings of the samsara world. *Vajrapani* ("thunderhand") is the stern foe of evil; he bears the weapon of the thunderbolt in his hand.

The proliferation of buddha figures in Mahayana inevitably suggests a contrast to Christianity, which though it has multiplied saints and angels, has steadfastly maintained the uniqueness of its one Christ.[45] Yet if the solution was different, the root issue was similar. For in the case of both Christianity and Buddhism, the source of these developments was a conviction which we have labeled as the *celestial significance of the founder*. Believers were convinced that Jesus and Gautama were more than merely human. It was this conviction which generated in early Christianity such doctrines as the incarnation and the trinity. Holding a similar conviction in the very different intellectual and spiritual climate of ancient India, Buddhists multiplied buddha figures as has been indicated.

They also conceived and elaborated the *trikaya* ("three bodies") doctrine, which has been compared to the Christian trinity. Indian Mahayanists asserted a *dharmakaya* ("body of reality"), which included all the meditation buddhas of our preceding paragraphs. In addition there was a *nirmana kaya* ("body of appearance or manifestation"), which included those whom we have called *manushi buddhas*. Such "bodies of appearance" contrast with the Christian claim that Christ was "truly human" or fully incarnated as a human being. From a Christian viewpoint Buddhism is a gnostic or docetic religion, while Buddhists might reply that Christianity is still bogged down in the unreal world of matter!

Later Mahayana philosophers added to the dharmakaya and nirmanakaya a third body, *sambhogakaya* ("body of bliss"), thus constituting a kind of buddhist "trinity." Again, while there is numerical similarity, there are radically different valuations in these Buddhist and Christian doctrines.

Mahayana Buddhism brought into being not only new forms and objects of devotion but new philosophies as well. These Buddhist philosophers believed that they were really fulfilling Buddha's philosophic intention, and they did not hesitate to attribute their words to him. However, to modern critical students of Buddhism, their speculative ideas go far beyond the words and thoughts of Buddha's teaching.

Among the new Mahayana philosophies the most influential and most original was the Madhyamika (central way) of Nagarjuna (150–250 CE). This philosophy was "central" in two ways. First it maintained a middle position among Buddhist philosophies, and second it espoused a middle way for Buddhism among the religious options of the time.

Concerning Nagarjuna's life few factual details are known. He was apparently a south Indian who as an itinerant teacher-scholar became at length the court philosopher of a north Indian ruler. He wandered too amid the faiths and philosophies of his time, at last coming to rest in Mahayana Buddhism. The Buddhist philosophy which he constructed was destined to influence the Buddhism of China and Japan as well as India, and also such subsequent Hindu philosophies as Vedanta. His was one of the great philosophic systems of world history.

Nagarjuna's philosophic method began by showing that all opposing philosophic views are riddled with self-contradiction, and hence lack true being. Pushing this double-edged argument a step further he asserted a similar conclusion for the whole vast world of appearance, in Buddhist terms, the samsara world. It too is riddled by self-contradiction, hence lacks substantive being (*svabhava*).

Thus all is *shunya*, argued Nagarjuna. Nagarjuna and his philosophy is sometimes called *Shunyavada* (the Way of Emptiness). Shunya is the Sanskrit word for zero in the number series, and is variously translated as "void" or "empty." For Nagarjuna this meant they have only relative being. One translator has rendered Shunyavada as "universal relativity."[46]

It is important to note that for Nagarjuna none of these terms such as emptiness or relativity carried a negative meaning, such as relativism or nihilism frequently imply in English. Indeed to the contrary, they open the way to supreme affirmation!

This can be seen in Nagarjuna's Buddhist motivation. As we have noted, Buddha had argued in the concepts of anatta and anicca that neither the self nor the external world possesses substantive existence. Truly perceived, both are transitory and delusive appearance which must be overcome if a human being is to be saved or liberated.

Nagarjuna's concept of shunya may be understood as an attempt to guard and explicate Buddha's view of self and world, and to fulfill Buddha's intention. In this task Nagarjuna did not shrink from declaring that both Buddha and nirvana are shunya, or empty. Thus they are not objects to which one should become attached. Consistently maintained, shunya is asserted in order to free human beings from all enslaving attachment to the samsara world, and thus to direct us to the enlightenment and liberation of nirvana.

To nirvana one is, in Buddha's terms, awakened. Nagarjuna further argued that nirvana and samsara are not two separate realms or regions. Rather it is the case that there is only one world which may be seen from two different viewpoints or perspectives. When the world is viewed from the perspective of everyday unsaved humanity it is samsara; while viewed from the perspective of awakening or enlightenment, it is nirvana. Hence also there are two kinds of truth or knowledge, namely, everyday truth and higher or transcendent truth. From Nagarjuna onward, Buddhist philosophy has been committed to this doctrine of a lower and higher truth and to coping with some of the issues involved in these assertions.

Nagarjuna's role in the history of classical Indian philosophy has been likened to that of Immanuel Kant in modern European philosophy. All preceding European philosophers were drawn into the all-devouring criticism of Kant; and out of Kant's critical philosophy issued the various philosophic idealisms of the nineteenth century. Analogously in ancient India, preceding philosophies found their way into Nagarjuna's criticism and out of this criticism issued the diverse forms of philosophic idealism of both Buddhist and Hindu traditions.

Two of the former were the *Yogacara* (practice of yoga) and *Vijnanavada* (way of consciousness) of the fourth century CE figures Asanga and Vasubhanda. The foundational idea of these philosophers was the concept of *alayavijnana* (receptacle consciousness) which is the primal reality from which are derived successively everything else in heaven and earth. From this primal being all else emanates!

This absolute cosmic consciousness was a positive rendering of Nagarjuna's shunya or void. It was also labeled as tathata (suchness), and in relation to Buddha as *abhidharnakaya* (Original Being).

From this transcendent source Buddhist philosophic idealism drew out, successively and in order, all the various objects and forms of the world of appearance. These Buddhist philosophies listed eight stages for the derivation of the world from its source: (1) receptacle or absolute consciousness, (2) mind consciousness, (3) consciousness of touch, (4) consciousness of sight, (5) consciousness of hearing, (6) consciousness of smell, (7) consciousness of taste, (8) sense-center consciousness.[47]

Like philosophic idealism of other times and places, in this Buddhist idealism all things partake of the nature of mind.

THE THUNDERBOLT VEHICLE

It is important to realize that during the centuries of Buddhism's power in India there was never a clear or sharp separation between Buddhism and Hinduism. These two faiths—as they have seemed to later generations—overlapped and mingled together in many ways. Fa Hsien, Chinese traveler and student of Buddhism, early in the fifth century observed that Buddhist monks joined in many Hindu processions and rituals.

During these centuries of Indian Buddhist influence, there grew up in both Buddhist and Hindu communities a new way called *Vajrayana* (meaning "the way of the thunderbolt"), or *Tantrayana* (*tantra* meaning a book or manual, i.e., of spells and directions for ritual). In addition to tantras, this way featured *mantras*, or sacred verses, and also *yantras*, or *mandalas*. These last were complex diagrams, enclosed in circles and designed to aid meditation. The mandala was thought to be a microcosm of the macrocosm or world, meditation on which would guide a person along a path to the center or supreme reality.

The origins and chronology of Tantrism are obscure. By the fifth century the new way was in evidence, and two centuries later the Chinese visitor Hsüan Tsang comments on its continued incidence. Whether of the Buddhist or Hindu variety, Tantrism consisted of a new combination of several elements. Magic had seldom been wholly absent from the quest for salvation in India (or elsewhere, for that matter), and in Tantrism it attached itself to the formulas or manuals (tantras), to the diagrams or pictures (yantras), and to the sacred words (mantras). Among the powerful mantras, *Om mani padme hum* was believed to possess a peculiar and unique efficacy. *Om* or *aum* is the mystic syllable we have observed in Indian religion from the time of the Vedas onward. The whole sentence is translated "the jewel is in the lotus," and in tantra the reference is doubtless erotic or sexual. Allied with the sacred words and diagrams were the mystical and magical postures of Yoga. An even more potent ingredient in the new mixture was witchcraft.[48]

Tantric ritual involved partaking of the five forbidden M's, in the fashion of a black mass. These five prohibited things were *madya* (wine), *mamsa* (meat), *matsya* (fish), *mudra* (parched grain), and *maithuna* (sexual intercourse), all partaken of as a sacrament of forbidden things.[49]

The sexual, and more broadly the antinomian, character of the secret tantric rites and beliefs illustrates a pattern which recurs throughout the world's religions. The sexual rites, here as elsewhere, were thought to reproduce in human life a cosmic pattern. These tantric practices might also be characterized as ways of catharsis by indulgence. The devotee went through this experience of passion, sexual or of other sorts, with eyes fixed on the farther shore of emancipation. As one tantric source says:

> The mystics, pure of mind dally with lovely girls
> Infatuated with the poisonous flame of passion
> That they may be free from desire…
> The mystic duly dwells
> On the manifold merits of his divinity
> He delights in thoughts of passion
> And by enjoyment of passions set free.[50]

While tantra began with overtly sexual rituals, in the course of time these beliefs and practices achieved a sublimated and symbolic significance. Important in this process was the symbol and figure called *Shakti*. Of ancient Indian origin was the belief that each deity possessed an inner source of power, called by this name and feminine in character. It was only a step to deify this power as a female deity. In tantric Buddhism this led to the emergence of *taras*, or divine consorts for the buddhas. In both Hindu and Buddhist tantric groups this concern with male and female principles in myth and ritual has been expressed sometimes in sublimated and sometimes in unsublimated forms, known in Indian terms as Right-hand and Left-hand Shaktism, respectively.

From their tantric source, these symbols and images have exerted an en-

Shri-yantra of tantric Buddhism.

during influence, both powerful and pervasive, on Indian art and religion, and indeed on the Indian imagination in all its aspects.

Tantrism was only one of several signs of decline in Indian Buddhism. Hsüan Tsang, Chinese visitor to seventh-century India, commented on Buddhism's waning vitality. Hindu devotees, particularly in southern India, mounted an increasing opposition to the way of the Buddha. Shankara's writings from the early ninth century are studded with passages strongly hostile to Buddhism. Yet the grand strategy of Hinduism was not to oppose but to absorb—or to reabsorb. And in the end it proved effective. Buddha became for many devout Indians an avatar of Vishnu.

Despite these shreds of evidence, the well-nigh total decline of Indian Buddhism remains an enigma. Apparently it lost the original vitality which carried it to every part of India and then sent its missionaries forth to every corner of

Asia. Another factor was a vigorous new assertion of Hindu devotion. As a result of these—and doubtless other factors of which the modern student is ignorant—Buddhism virtually perished in the land of its birth.

The final blow to Indian Buddhism was struck in successive waves by invading Muslims beginning with the eleventh century. The servants of Allah smashed the monasteries and slaughtered the "shaven-headed brahmans," as they called Buddhist monks. Although Buddhism had a firm base in lands beyond the mountains and beyond the sea, it was virtually extinguished in the land of its birth.

Only within the past century have Indians sought to reclaim their Buddhist heritage. King Ashoka's pillar now appears on the Indian flag, and contemporary Indian writers speak proudly of "Hindu-Buddhist civilization." But this is another and more recent story, to which we will return in a different context.

TIBETAN BUDDHISM

Buddhism found its way to Tibet in the reign of King Songstan-Gampo, who came to the throne in 632 CE. As a social reformer he sought for his people the benefits of both Indian and Chinese civilizations. His two wives—one Indian and one Chinese—were both Buddhist; he therefore sent to both India and China for Buddhist books, teachers, and ideas. He sought to introduce Buddhism to his people along with other benefits of civilization.

The indigenous religion of Tibet, called *Bonism* (or *Pönism* in some translations), was a kind of polydemonism devoted to placating the spirits of that bleak and austere land. It featured animal sacrifice and sometimes human sacrifice, and other ritual offerings to the spirits. Magic words and magic dances were all part of a pattern of averting the damage that evil or capricious spirits could bring to people.[51]

For many years there was dispute between the pro-Buddhists and those who supported the old ways. The coming of the Indian masters Shantarakshita and Padmasambhava, the latter a master of Tantrism, led to the founding of the Tibetan Buddhist Sangha and its first monastery. Shantarakshita was a typical celibate scholar monk, while Padmasambhava was a wonder-working guru bound neither to celibacy nor to monastic regimen; Tibetan Buddhism has through the centuries interacted between these two models.

The ninth and tenth centuries saw the translation of Buddhist scriptures from Sanskrit into Tibetan as well as the involvement of Buddhism in the sordid politics of the country. There were also successive waves of anti-Buddhist persecution.

The Indian scholar and tantric master Atisha (982–1054) came to Tibet in 1042, imparting tantric instruction and initiation and also founding a monastery and an order of monks. He was followed by Marpa (1012–1077) and Milarepa (1040–1123), who became the first and second patriarchs of the Kargyüpa sect. Milarepa is both a popular saint and the greatest poet of Tibet. His poetry has been translated into English.[52]

The forms of Buddhism which took shape in Tibet have been in many ways distinctive and different from those of other countries. The title *lama* (literally, "one who is superior") was applied both to leading monks and at times to outstanding householder yogins. The monastic orders dwelt in thick-walled monasteries designed for protection against Tibet's bleak climate. However, they also became veritable fortresses held by powerful hereditary abbots who exercised temporal as well as spiritual power. Within these walls tantric beliefs and practices often supplanted monastic celibacy and more traditional forms of meditation. As is the case with monastic movements and orders in all faiths and all parts of the world, worldliness and reform have alternated in Tibetan Buddhism. Atisha, Marpa, and Milarepa were reformers.

At the popular level, Tibetan Buddhism has concerned itself with sacred formulas, such as "Om mani padme hum," and with sacred devices, such as *thangkas* (the Tibetan word for mandalas) and the prayer wheel. The latter is a cylinder revolving on its axis and containing a sacred formula or prayer which is addressed to the buddhas in each revolution. Some Tibetans have had their prayer wheels turned by water power, and there are even reports of prayer wheels powered by electricity.

At a higher religious level Buddhism interacted with Tibetan culture to produce distinctive forms of thought and devotion. The basic text is the *Bardo Thötröl*, translated into English as the "Tibetan Book of the Dead." Tibetan tradition attributes it to Padma Sambhava, and asserts that after writing it, he buried it so that future generations might recover this buried treasure and live by it.

To western students this book and its distinctive way or path of life presupposes the main cluster of ideas we have seen in Mahayana and Vajrayana Buddhism. There is the supreme goal of liberation or enlightenment, there is the ever-present fact of karma-samsara or transmigration, there are the hosts of buddhas and bodhisattvas with the tantric pairing of male and female deities, and there is the guidance of sacred words, mandalas, and ceremonies.

Yet the Book of the Dead is distinctively Tibetan. Initially it appears to the western reader as a guidebook for the transmigrating soul as it leaves this life at death in an experience of intense luminosity and wanders in an intermediate region, then moves toward the next incarnation. In its journey through supermundane regions it travels through strange realms and sees strange sights, such as hungry ghosts, jealous gods, animals, etc.

Yet by clear implication this book is a guide for the living as well as the dying, and it has long had this function for Tibetan people. Its regions of the universe are in effect possibilities of existence for readers with ears to hear and eyes to see.

An event which Tibetan Buddhists recall with pride was the appointment by Chinese Emperor Kublai Khan of the grand abbot of Tibetan Buddhism as *kuo-shih*, "instructor of the nation," i.e., all of China. Kublai Kahn was an interested inquirer into many faiths, but he apparently concluded that Lamaism was best adapted to the needs of the people. This abbot, Phakpa by name, was also

Tibetan with prayer wheel and beads. (Keith Gunnar/Photo Researchers.)

given by Kublai Khan supreme authority over all Tibet, making him the first lama to be sovereign ruler of the country.[53]

Still another significant wave of monastic reform swept over Tibetan Buddhism in the fourteenth century, under the great monk and reformer Tsong-kha-pa. From this reform Tibetan Buddhism emerged in substantially the form it held until 1959. There are three main orders of monks. The largest is the Gelukpa school, often called by westerners the *Yellow Hat* sect, founded by Atisha, reformed by Tsong-kha-pa, and ruled by the Dalai Lama. Next in size is the *Old Translation* school, which goes back to Padma Sambhava. The third in size is the Kagyupa school founded by Marpa and called the *Red Hat* school. The grand lama of the Yellow Hat monastery at Lhasa acquired the name *Dalai Lama* in the sixteenth century. In response to a request from a Mongol chieftain, the lama journeyed to Mongolia to revise and revive Buddhism. The grateful chieftain gave him the title *dalai*, meaning "the sea," that is, measureless and profound.

Until his flight to India in 1959, the Dalai Lama was the temporal as well as the spiritual leader of his people. He is conceived to be an incarnation of Avalokita, whereas the Panchen Lama, abbot of the Tashilumpo monastery, second in the hierarchy, is regarded as an incarnation of Amitabha. It is worth noting that the latter abbot and order have throughout modern Tibetan history been sympathetic to China, while the Dalai Lama has, by contrast, looked to India. For some years after the Chinese conquest, the Panchen Lama was maintained by the conquerors as a puppet ruler and leader of Tibet, but recent reports indicate that he too seems to have disappeared from Tibet.

Tsong's fourteenth-century reform of Tibetan monasticism led to the strict imposition of celibacy, thus ending hereditary monastic rule and creating the problem of succession. The problem was solved by the Tibetans with the world-famous theory of the reincarnation of the head lamas in their successors. The present Dalai Lama is the fourteenth in succession. A Tibetan account of his selection tells of signs and miracles perceived by a Tibetan governmental official called the *state oracle* indicating the location of the Dalai Lama's new birthplace.[54] Other visions and oracles were perceived, and in response a searching mission disguised as ordinary pilgrims set out for the distant Amdo Province of China. Finding the supernaturally indicated house, they came to the boy, who was said to greet the travelers with recognition. He also identified belongings of the previous, recently deceased lama. Securing permission from the lad's parents, the embassy took him back to Lhasa and with pomp and ceremony installed him as Dalai Lama.

Tibetan Buddhism as well as traditional Tibetan life came to a sudden and violent end with the invasions by the communist Chinese in 1950 and 1959. For many centuries Tibet had been claimed by both India and China. Since the fall of the Manchu dynasty in China, Tibet has asserted its autonomy, and both India and China have recognized it. However, in 1950, the Chinese invaded the land and placed a puppet government in power, thus forcibly securing Chinese hegemony. The Tibetans remained restive and rose in hopeless rebellion in 1959

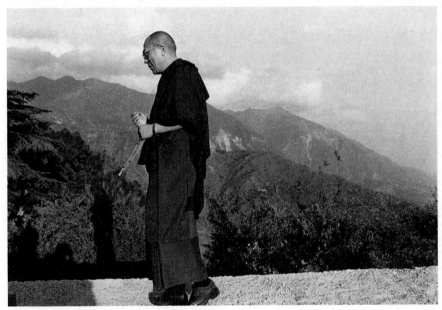

The Dalai Lama on the grounds of his residence in exile in the Himalayan hill town of Dharamsala, Northern India. (Raghu Rai/Magnum.)

under the leadership of the Dalai Lama. Chinese arms promptly and ruthlessly destroyed the opposition. The Dalai Lama and some of his followers made good their escape to India, where they remain today as refugees. A United Nations investigation condemned the Chinese action as genocide but was unable to do anything about it.

Since 1959 some Tibetans, especially lamas and gurus, have made their way to Europe and America, where they now live in exile. They continue to practice their faith in a kind of dispersion which for students of religion suggests a parallel to the great dispersion of Jews from Israel. Some continue actively to teach their distinctive form of Buddhism and have gained a following of Europeans and Americans.

At this point we must temporarily terminate our study of the way of the Buddha, promising to resume it later in other contexts. So far we have seen its rise and fall in India and its rise in Tibet. As lengthy as this chapter has been, however, it is only a beginning. We shall resume the study of Buddhism in Chapter 8 on Chinese religion and Chapter 9 on Japanese religion.

Issues and Questions

Among the many issues and questions raised by this chapter, none is more important both for Buddhism and for human history than to observe what began as a reform movement in sixth century BCE India well on its way to becoming a universal religion. Several aspects of this transformation may be noted. First it is a historical fact that many of humanity's religions began as attempts to reform or reshape some previous tradition. Second, let us note the concept of a universal religion in its contrast to culture religions. The latter has its entire being within the bounds of a single culture, its gods or higher power expressing the basic values of that culture, and having no reference beyond those bounds. In sharpest contrast, a universal religion transcends the bounds of any single culture and articulates a vision of universal humanity. We shall see several such universal religions in the course of our study, and we shall also see the significance of this concept for humanity's twentieth-century situation.

In the case of early Buddhism, it is interesting to see several steps in the course of this transformation, beginning with the vision of the Buddha, but including also such factors as the intervention of King Ashoka and the rise of the great Mahayana philosophies. Crucial in this development is the interaction of Buddhist faith with more than one culture. We have already seen its interaction with the different cultures of southeast Asia and of Tibet. However, still before us for consideration in Chapters 8 and 9 is Buddhist interaction with the cultures of east Asia.

Crucial in the emergence of a universal religion is a set of basic and general concepts for the human self, and for what we may call in general terms sin and salvation, that is, for human evil and human fulfillment. Such concepts pull the mind loose from its tight embrace with a single culture and open it to the general concept of humanity and humanity's issues.

We have noted Buddhism's relational concept of the self as part of its protest against the substantive concepts of the self of other Indian philosophies of the time. However, Buddhism pushed onward with a distinctive view of what is basically wrong with the self and how it may be set right or fulfilled. What is wrong is embodied in the concept of avidya, or the false and delusive view, that the present world of nature and society is both real and significant. This disease may be cured (for as we have seen, Buddha employed the medical language of his time) by the integral vision of nirvana, which may be described as that state of well-being or bliss which transcends all finite existence. To glimpse this supreme good, and then to live in its light constitutes for Buddhism human fulfillment.

This Buddhist vision shows both similarities and differences from the biblical vision of Judaism and Christianity which we shall study later, in Chapters 11 to 13. For these religions, evil is not avidya but sin which may be described as some violation of or wrong relation to God's will. A similar contrast is visible between Buddhist nirvana and Judeo-Christian heaven or kingdom of God. The latter is asserted to consist not in transcending all finite existence but rather in the full communion of the self with other selves and with God. If these contrasts appear at first as remote and abstract, let it be remembered that beliefs about the "hereafter" often decisively influence values for the "herein."

As we have already noted, there is also both similarity and contrast in the way in which Buddhists and Christians view their respective founders. Both

Buddha and Christ are revered as in some general sense saviors. Yet detailed analysis shows sharp difference.

As previously noted, the multitudinous replication of Buddha figures contrasts with the singularity of Christ in Christian faith and life. Christianity also teaches in the doctrine of the Incarnation that in Christ God took on human flesh, becoming "fully human." Buddhism significantly makes no such assertion concerning the Buddha. In the *trikaya* doctrine of the Mahayana, Buddha is manifested to the samsara world, but that is all. In part this difference derives from the sharp differences between the Buddhist conception of the samsara world on the one hand and the biblical doctrine of the world as God's creation.

In one very important respect there is significant similarity between Buddhism and Christianity, namely, in the moral values of Buddhist compassion (*karuna*) and Christian ethical love (*agapé*). While there are many important and suggestive differences in these concepts, there is an underlying similarity in their basic appeal to overcome human egotism in a generous concern for other human beings. In today's world this is sufficient basis for common social action on urgent social problems.

Notes

1. B. H. Streeter, *The Buddha and the Christ*, Macmillan, London, 1932; Masutani, *Buddhism and Christianity: A Comparative Study*, Young East Association, Tokyo, 1954.
2. A. Schweitzer, *The Quest of the Historical Jesus*, Black, New York, 1920.
3. A. L. Basham, *The Wonder That Was India*, Grove Press, New York, 1959, p. 257.
4. Warren, op. cit., pp. 60–67.
5. For different interpretations of Buddha's enlightenment, see Warren, op. cit., p. 67f; Basham, op. cit., p. 358; Kenneth Morgan (ed.), *The Path of the Buddha*, Ronald, New York, 1950, p. 8f; Richard Robinson, *The Buddhist Religion*, Dickenson, Belmont, Calif., 1970, p. 17f.
6. Robinson, op. cit.
7. Morgan, op. cit., p. 8.
8. Ibid., p. 3f.
9. T. W. Rhys Davids, *Buddhism*, SPCK, London, 1903, p. 160.
10. Morgan, op. cit., p. 35.
11. Warren, op. cit., p. 109.
12. H. Zimmer, *Philosophies of India*, Meridian Books, New York, 1957, p. 473.
13. Warren, op. cit., p. 101.
14. Ninian Smart, *Doctrine and Argument in Indian Philosophy*, G. Allen, London, 1964, p. 34f.
15. J. B. Noss, *Man's Religions*, 2d ed., Macmillan, New York, 1956, p. 167.
16. Ibid., p. 107.
17. Ibid., pp. 109–110.
18. Davids, op. cit., pp. 109–110.
19. Sutta Nipata, V. Fausboll (trans.), *Sacred Books of the East*, Oxford University Press, London, 1881, p. 6f.
20. Clarence Hamilton (ed.), *Buddhism, A Religion of Infinite Compassion*, Liberal Arts, New York, 1952, p. 99.
21. Ibid., title.
22. Metta Sutta, quoted from Morgan, op. cit., p. 94.
23. Basham, op. cit., p. 286.
24. Hamilton, op. cit., p. 65.

25. Ibid., pp. 100–103.
26. Zimmer, op. cit., p. 474.
27. Morgan, op. cit., pp. 68–70.
28. J. B. Pratt, *The Pilgrimage of Buddhism*, Macmillan, New York, 1928, p. 129.
29. Morgan, op. cit., p. 75.
30. T. R. V. Murti, *The Central Philosophy of Busshism*, G. Allen, London, 1955, p. 35.
31. L. Wittgenstein, *Tractatus Logico Philosophicus*, Humanities Press, New York, 1961, p. 151.
32. W. T. de Bary (ed.), *Sources of Indian Tradition*, Columbia, New York, 1958, pp. 106–108.
33. Ibid., pp. 108–109.
34. Ibid., p. 109.
35. Morgan, op. cit., p. 86.
36. Ibid., pp. 104–107.
37. de Bary, op. cit., p. 120.
38. Ibid., p. 143.
39. Ibid., p. 138.
40. Morgan, op. cit., pp. 100–101.
41. Zimmer, op. cit., pp. 474–476.
42. Ibid., p. 488.
43. Basham, op. cit., p. 275.
44. Alice Getty, *The Gods of Northern Buddhism*, Oxford University Press, London, 1928.
45. For discussion of these issues in early Christian thought, see H. Bettenson, *Documents of the Christian Church*, Oxford University Press, Fairlawn, N.J., 1947.
46. S. Radhakrishnan and C. Moore (eds.), *Source Book in Indian Philosophy*, Princeton, Princeton, N.J., 1957, p. 340.
47. Ibid., p. 328f.
48. Robinson, op. cit., p. 64f.
49. Zimmer, op. cit., p. 572.
50. de Bary, op. cit., pp. 198–199.
51. Morgan, op. cit., p. 238.
52. G. C. Chang, *The Hundred Thousand Songs of Milarepa*, University Books, New Hyde Park, N.Y., 1962.
53. Morgan, op. cit., p. 248.
54. Ibid., p. 257.

BIBLIOGRAPHY

Beyer, S. (ed.): *The Buddhist Experience: Sources and Interpretations*, Wadsworth, Belmont, Calif., 1974.

——: *The Cult of Tara*, University of California, Berkeley, 1974.

Blofield, J.: *The Tantric Mysticism of Tibet*, Shambala, Boston, 1987.

Conze, E.: *Buddhist Thought in India*, University of Michigan, Ann Arbor, 1967.

——: *Buddhist Scriptures*, Penguin, Baltimore, 1959.

Dayal, H.: *The Bodhisattva Doctrine in Buddhist Literature*, Orient Book Distributors, Livingston, N.J., 1975.

Evans-Wentz, W. V.: *The Tibetan Book of the Great Liberation*, Oxford, New York, 1968.

——: *Tibetan Yoga and Secret Doctrines*, Oxford, New York, 1967.

Freemantle, F., and C. Trungpa: *The Tibetan Book of the Dead*, Shambhala, Boston, 1988.

Getty, A.: *The Gods of Northern Buddhism*, Dover, New York, 1988.

Guenther, H.: *The Life and Teachings of Naropa*, Shambhala, Boston, 1986.

Hopkins, J.: *Tantra in Tibet*, George Allen and Unwin, London, 1978.

Kalupahana, D.: *Buddhist Philosophy*, University of Hawaii, Honolulu, 1976.

King, W.: *Buddhism and Christianity*, Westminster, Philadelphia, 1962.

————: *A Thousand Lives Away*, Oxford, London, 1962.

Ling, T.: *The Buddha, Buddhist Civilization in India and Ceylon*, Scribner, New York, 1973.

Morgan, K. (ed.): *The Path of the Buddha*, Ronald, New York, 1950.

Murti, T. R. V.: *The Central Philosophy of Buddhism*, G. Allen, London, 1955.

Overmyer, B.: *Folk Buddhist Religions*, Harvard, Cambridge, Mass., 1976.

Pardue, P.: *Buddhism*, Macmillan, New York, 1968.

Prebisch, C.: *American Buddhism*, Wadsworth, Belmont, Calif., 1979.

————: *Buddhist Monastic Discipline*, Pennsylvania State University, University Park, 1975.

Robinson, R.: *The Buddhist Religion*, Wadsworth, Belmont, Calif., 1982.

Smart, N.: *Doctrine and Argument in Indian Philosophy*, G. Allen, London, 1964.

Streng, F.: *Emptiness: A Study in Religious Meaning*, Abingdon, Nashville, Tenn., 1967.

Thomas, E. J.: *The Life of Buddha as Legend and History*, Routledge & Kegan Paul, London, 1927.

Warren, H. (trans.): *Buddhism in Translations*, South Asia Books, Columbia, Mo., 1987.

6

Hinduism

WHAT IS HINDUISM?

The problems of terminology with which we have wrestled in preceding chapters become acute in the present chapter, for several reasons. *Hinduism* is, as previously noted, a modern western term, dating from the early nineteenth century. While the word *Hindu* is of older and wider occurrence in India, its origin is a mispronunciation of Sindh. What this means is that few of the people included within the popular designations of Hindu or Hinduism have themselves used these labels. Some recent Indian writing has proposed the alternative term *Sanatana Dharma*, meaning "eternal teaching or religion," but this presents even more formidable problems.[1]

Another issue is raised by the extension of the terms *Hindu* and *Hinduism*. Just how much of the vast accumulation of religious phenomena in Indian history is to be embraced by these terms, and on what basis are the inclusions and exclusions to be made? Mention has already been made of the fact that Jainism and Buddhism are usually regarded as heretical and therefore excluded. Yet there are no formal authorities recognized by all or most adherents of the Hindu faith; Hinduism has no pope and no bishops to rule on such matters. The sole effective authority seems to be the long-time operation of public opinion. The student has no alternative but to regard as within the bounds of this faith what its adherents have so regarded.

Another kind of issue is raised by the contention that Hinduism is, for one reason or another, not a religion. The claim is sometimes made that it lacks one or more of the necessary features of a religion; or it is alleged that this is not simply a religion but a total way of life. Neither of these strictures need delay us long. In Chapter 1 we guarded against the first by defining religion as a system of holy forms. Clearly Hinduism is such a system, though it is profoundly different from other such systems, particularly those of the West, and must be understood on its own terms. Indeed, the term *dharma* as a synonym for Hindu religion will not be seriously misleading.

Chapter 1 should also have prepared us for the contention that Hinduism is a total way of life or that its effects are spread widely throughout traditional Indian culture. As students of the world's religions see the varieties of relations between faith and culture in the long course of history, they will not be greatly

156

surprised at the fact that this central Indian religious tradition bears a unique and significant relation to virtually the whole of Indian society.

In Chapter 3 we likened Indian religious history to a geological landscape. This chapter brings us to its most recent strata. An analogy with geology, with its concept of outcroppings, can help us here. Just as very ancient layers of rock lie exposed on the surface of the earth as outcroppings alongside more recent strata, so in India's religious landscape one may hear a Brahman priest chanting a vedic mantra and see nearby a shrine or temple of more recent origin or see a procession devoted to some twentieth-century saint or holy happening. The leaders of Hinduism claim to be the inheritors of the whole vedic tradition, as described in Chapter 3; the only question which the student of religion would wish to raise is whether they are the sole legatees of this tradition. It is even possible to observe in contemporary Hinduism the influence of pre-Aryan Dravidian elements in such phenomena as the continuing vitality of the god Shiva. Not even Buddha and Mahavira can be excluded from these influences, for the historical development of Hinduism must be understood as among other things a reaction to these faiths. In order to absorb (or reabsorb) Buddhism, Hinduism incorporated into itself Buddhist elements. The Lord Buddha elicited a response of personal devotion from his followers—as many another religious founder before and since. One notable Hindu response was a new accent and emphasis on bhakti, or devotional religion. Hence, it has often been said of one group of devotees that they literally sang Buddhism out of south India.

During the crucial millennium of Hinduism's historical development (roughly from 500 BCE to 500 CE), a great many different historical causes and conditions influenced emerging Hinduism. Caste lines hardened and castes proliferated, with the result that caste came to express in a massively conservative fashion the interdependence of life within Indian society. *Bhakti marga*, or personal devotion, developed as a way of faith of enormously wider social appeal than the more aristocratic and austere ways of ritual words (*karma marga*) and knowledge (*jnana marga*). These *margas* (roads or paths) are all affirmed as acceptable ways to salvation. In these and other ways Hinduism came more and more to be an inclusive expression of the Indian community and tradition.

The main forms of belief, practice, and, not least of all, feeling which have constituted Hinduism were in existence before the end of the first millennium in the Common Era. Nevertheless, Hinduism continued to serve as the Indian faith during two important succeeding periods—and to be significantly influenced by this historic function. First was the approximately 750 years of Muslim domination (999–1757), and second was the 250 years of European domination (1757–1947).

Mahmud of Ghaznin broke into India in 999 CE, beginning over two decades of raids and depredations and three-quarters of a millennium of Muslim rule, during which the relation between Islam and Hinduism was a centrally important issue, both religiously and politically. At first Islam was a hostile faith of alien conquerors who in the service of Allah smashed Hindu temples and massacred Hindu people. In later periods Islam put down its own roots in Indian soil, but the problem of its relation to Hinduism has never achieved a solution satisfactory to either religion. Muslims sought to convert Hindus; Hinduism sought to absorb Islam. Neither succeeded. One Indian reformer, Nanak, troubled at the ill will between Islam and Hinduism, sought to transcend these differences; it is ironic that he succeeded in founding still another religion, Sikhism, which fought both Islam and Hinduism. (Sikhism is the subject of Chapter 7.) Meanwhile, during the Muslim centuries, Hinduism was greatly strengthened in its historic role as India's faith.

The eighteenth and nineteenth centuries brought the European West in force to India and thus confronted Hinduism with a new challenge. Would India desert its ancestral faith for western Christianity or for a modern, secular, nonreligious path of life? Indian answers to this question have, as usual, varied over a wide spectrum, yet the dominant answer today has linked Hinduism closely with emerging Indian nationalism. Yet to this it must be added that the voices of nationalism in Hindu faith have never completely drowned out those which seek to speak a Hindu message to all humankind.

Throughout its long history Hinduism has had few if any institutional forms which extended to all its vast and various community of adherents, who now number between 500 and 600 million people.[2] Its unity is the unity and historical continuity of Indian culture. In its infinite variety of rites, attitudes, beliefs, and practices, only two appear to be common to all Hindus: (1) acknowledgment of the validity of the Vedas and (2) the practice of caste. Even for these two recurring features, important qualifications will prove necessary.

SOURCES OF HINDUISM

To what documents and other sources will students look for the history of Hinduism? First they will recognize that Hinduism was the inheritor of much that had gone before, specifically of the Vedas and the whole vedic tradition—though, one hastens to add, molded and interpreted in terms of later tradition. After the close of the vedic period, other documents emerged to give expression and distinctive shape to developing Hinduism. For Hindus they were, and still are, smriti and not shruti (literally "remembered" and not "heard"), that is, religious classics and not canonical scripture. Nonetheless their authority is very great, and in some cases they are more frequently read than the canonical Vedas. Among these classical documents, none has been more influential in the development and maintenance of religious practice than the Code of Manu (ca. 200 BCE). The later Yajnavalkya Code (ca. 200 CE) has wielded similar influence. They illustrate the type of literature known to Indians as *dharma shastra*, or manuals for moral guidance.

India's two great epics, the Mahabharata and the Ramayana, have been fruitful sources of religious images and ideas as well as tales of divine and human heroes and heroines in their never-ending adventures and misadventures.

The *Mahabharata*, traditionally attributed to the sage Vyasa, is the story in Sanskrit poetry of the great Bharata War. (The Bharatas were one of the principal tribes of the ancient Aryan invasion.) Consisting of over 100,000 stanzas, the *Mahabharata* is the world's longest poem. Stripped of its many interpolations, it tells the ancient and heroic tale of internecine struggle and war in the Bharata tribe. The throne of the Kurus, or Kauravas (a leading group among the Bharatas), fell to Dhrtarashtra, who was blind and was therefore barred from the throne. Hence it went to his younger brother, Pandu, who as the result of a curse renounced the throne for an ascetic's life. By default the crown reverted to Dhrtarashtra. When Pandu died, the heirs apparent were his five sons, Yudhishthira, Bhima, Arjuna, Nakula, and Sahadeva. However, the sons of the reigning Dhrtarashtra conspired against the true heirs.

The five sons of Pandu wandered forth for a time as disguised *brahmacarins*. While they were wandering, Arjuna won as his wife Draupadi, who then subsequently became the common wife of all five brothers. Also dur-

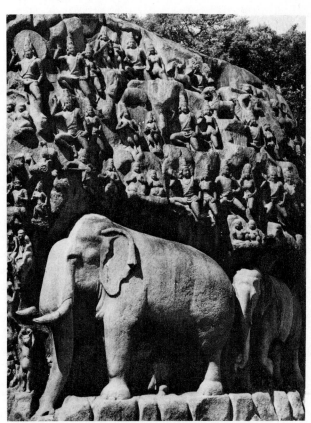

Arjuna's penance, from the epic Mahabharata, as depicted at Mahabalipuram. (Government of India Tourist Office.)

ing the course of their wandering, they met their divine friend and helper, Krishna. Finally Dhrtarashtra recalled Pandu's sons and prepared to renounce his throne. His own sons, however, continued to connive to deny the succession to the sons of Pandu. Duryodhana enticed Yudhishthira into a gambling match in which, with the help of a magician, he won not only the kingdom but also the brothers and their joint wife. A compromise settlement of this gambling debt was achieved according to which the five Pandavas (sons of Pandu) went into exile for thirteen years, after which they would return and receive the kingdom.

As this time approached, they sent word to Duryodhana demanding their kingdom. Receiving no answer, they began to prepare for the inevitable and climactic battle. All the kings and warriors of India and of kingdoms as far away as Greece and China lined up on one side or the other. The two armies met on the plain of Kurukshetra, traditionally located on the broad plain north of Delhi. There for eighteen days the great battle raged, until at the end no one on either side was left alive except the five Pandava brothers and their divine helper, Krishna. Yudhishthira finally received his kingdom, and with his brothers and their wife lived peacefully and gloriously. At the close of the poem, Yudhishthira renounced his throne in favor of Arjuna's grandson, and the five brothers and wife set out for the Himalayas where they climbed up to the city of the gods.

The Ramayana, shorter than the Mahabharata, is attributed to the sage Valmiki. It tells the story of the trials and tribulations of the righteous Prince Rama and his equally virtuous wife Sita. Rama was cheated of his succession to the throne and retired to the forest with his wife, who was then abducted and carried off to Sri Lanka by the demon king Ravana. She was rescued by her husband, who was assisted by the monkey god Hanuman and his army of valiant monkeys. Finally Rama was restored to this throne, where with Sita he reigned happily. There is a final book of the Ramayana in which Rama, knowing fully his wife's innocence while she had been a prisoner in Sri Lanka, nonetheless yields to popular rumor and opinion and divorces her. Thus the Ramayana is given a somewhat tragic ending. Modern scholars are divided in their view of this ending, some holding that it formed no part of the original poem but was added later. However this may be, Rama and Sita have lived on in Indian imagination as the ideal king and queen and the ideal husband and wife.

Not only have the epics served as sources for countless religious images and themes; they have, particularly in their more popular versions, served as vehicles of popular devotion and feeling for countless generations of Indians. They illustrate the fact that Indian literature lacks a precise line separating the sacred and the secular realms of life and thought.

Probably the most influential single document in Indian religious history is the Bhagavad Gita. Many scholars believe that it was originally one of many interpolations in the Mahabharata, but for many centuries it has been an independent document and has been the classical source of bhakti, though it is by no means the first or only source. Dating from as early as the third century BCE, it begins as a conversation between the Pandu warrior Arjuna and his charioteer, who turns out to be the god Krishna, and who also turns out to dominate the conversation with his expositions of traditional Hindu faith culminating in bhakti marga, or way of devotion. Some western scholars trained in text criticism have found evidence of multiple authorship in the Bhagavad Gita's inclusion of several distinguishable viewpoints. Many scholars find in it an attempt to combine monistic Aryan thought with the dualistic viewpoint of Sankhya philosophy. The Gita's repeated listing of virtues which are distinctively Buddhist suggests that the author was deliberately incorporating Buddhist elements in this statement of Hindu faith. Other commentators point to its attempt to affirm and combine the viewpoint of action with that of devotion. It may be characterized as the document into which flowed the whole previous tradition and out of which emerged virtually the whole subsequent Hindu tradition. The influence of the Gita is in important measure due to this inclusive and synoptic viewpoint. We shall return later in this chapter to an analysis of the Gita.

Still another kind of document functioned as a Hindu source, namely, the Puranas (or "ancient tales"). Eighteen Puranas exist, of which the best known are the Bhagavata, Vayu, Vishnu, and Agni. They do not antedate the Gupta period of Indian history (300–500 CE); their content is a miscellany of tales, teaching, and other matters. Traditionally a Purana dealt with five topics: (1) creation of the universe, (2) re-creation of the universe after its periodic destruction, (3) genealopgy of gods and sages, (4) ages of the world and their rulers, and (5) genealogies of kings. While the Puranas are clearly not as great as many of the earlier works of Indian religion, their importance as sources of popular piety is very great.

To this list of source documents, it is important to add the qualification that significant aspects of Hinduism will elude us if we limit our study solely to literary sources, for Hinduism is above all a tradition of innumerable people, past and present, whose behavior has no significant relation to written sources. Their actual practices in the great cities and countless villages of India are the all-important source for the study of Hinduism. This is the importance of what is termed *popular Hinduism*.

FOUR ENDS OF HUMAN LIFE

As has been repeatedly observed, the chief end of human life in Hinduism is moksha, conceived as emancipation from all those fetters, hindrances, and delusions which taken together constitute human experience and personality. Yet with Hinduism's inclination toward inclusiveness, it is not surprising that in the course of history other goals were added to form the traditional tetrad. It is Hinduism's claim to offer something to everyone and every condition and stage of human life. The four ends of human life help to make good this claim; together they provide scope and expression for all the varied capacities of a person's life. The traditional four ends of human life (*purushartha*) are duty or righteousness (dharma), material success (artha), love or pleasure (kama), and emancipation (moksha).

DHARMA

The first aim, dharma (from *dhr*, meaning "to sustain"), is the moral law and order which sustain the world, society, and the individual. Construed as a human virtue, *dharma* is best translated as "righteousness or duty." It is moral virtue, held and pursued in the religious context of Hinduism.

Dharma is a pervasive goal of Hinduism, and all humans are exhorted to pursue it. Hindu literature and philosophy are devoted to the study of the science of dharma. For example, the hero of the Ramayana is said to be a veritable incarnation of dharma,[3] and the hero of the Mahabharata proclaims dharma as its content and message: "With uplifted arms I cry, none heeds; from dharma, material gain and pleasure flow; then why is not dharma pursued? Neither for the sake of pleasure, nor out of fear or avarice, no, not even for the sake of one's life should one give up dharma; dharma stands alone for all time; pleasure and pain are transitory."[4]

The content of dharma varies with an individual's position in society and station in life. As traditionally interpreted, dharma appears to lack the assumption of human equality so basic to western morality and ethics. While it assumes the unity of life and the universality of duty, it is duty construed within the context of inequality of different persons and classes (castes) and different stages of life. For the young man, for example, dharma implies the duties of the student; for a mature man, those of the householder; and for an older man, possibly those of *sadhu* and *sannyasin*. It always includes observance of caste and of the religious ritual appropriate to one's position in life. The continuing and constant element in dharma may perhaps be described as harmonious but unequal order, first of the individual person, then of society, and finally of the universe, as these fields of experience are envisioned by Hinduism. Here truly is a morality of "my station and its duties."

One aspect of traditional dharma which is particularly noteworthy in the twentieth century is that which prescribes subordination of women. The Code of Manu declares (IX, 3), "a woman is never fit for independence," explaining that her father protects her in childhood, her husband in youth, and her sons in old age. The same code asserts (V, 154), "Though destitute of virtue or seeking pleasure (elsewhere) or devoid of good qualities (yet) a husband must be constantly worshipped as a god by a faithful wife." Centuries of Indian women have submitted to this harsh rule, though it is fair to add that today it is increasingly questioned by Indians as well as by western observers.

ARTHA

Artha means material gain or advantage, but in many instances this idea is extended to include the necessary means or instrumentalities supporting any human activity. Notably it includes the instrumentality of politics and statecraft. Traditional Indian literature is studded with references to artha, but Kautilya's Artha Shastra (usually translated as "treatise on material gain"), since it first came to light in 1905, has been taken as the classic statement of artha.[5] While it contains discussion of economic goods, it also includes many sections devoted to political problems.[6] The latter deal with the acquiring and maintaining of political power, in ways that read like Machiavelli's book *The Prince*. Kautilya, the putative author of this document, is said to have been foreign minister of Chandragupta Maurya, grandfather of King Ashoka and founder of the Maurya dynasty.

The Artha Shastra lists three ends of human life, dharma, kama, and artha, but argues that the last is most important for the reason that on this foundation alone the other two can be realized.[7] The Artha Shastra and the subjects it treats are particularly important as a corrective for popular western views of the Hindu mind as devoted solely to unworldly or superworldly goods. Here are a writer and a tradition within emerging Hinduism bidding us to pursue worldly goods with open-eyed realism. In Zimmer's formulation, here is a "philosophy of time" rather than of eternity. The third end, kama, is also of time rather than of eternity.

KAMA

Kama is a protean thing, ranging from sexuality to the enjoyment of art.[8] *Kama* is the name of the Indian god of love. Like the Greek word *eros* it functions as both a proper and a common noun; and also like its Greek analogue, it embraces wide ranges of meaning. The Kama Sutra of Vatsyayana is a gentlemen's guide to sexual behavior and related topics.[9] This meaning of *kama* points to a significant strand of Indian tradition which may be characterized as a candid affirmation of sex as a human good. This attitude is also illustrated by erotic sculpture and painting such as those which adorn the temples at Konarak and Khajuraho.[10] Yet the main Indian tradition in sex morality, as illustrated by the Code of Manu and other dharma shastras, can only be characterized as conservative, indeed, austere to the point of asceticism. The reconciliation of these conflicting attitudes is no easier than of the many other dualities and diversities of Indian thought and life.

Kama includes not only overt sexuality but also what may perhaps be termed *sublimated sexuality* in art and culture. In this guise the pursuit of pleasure as the goal of life includes all the refinements of esthetic experience and speculation as these occur in the various arts.[11] Again, it is not easy to reconcile this affirmation of pleasure with an overall view of life in which pleasure is regarded as a hindrance to emancipation or a fetter binding humans to this passing world of flesh and matter. The Indians have not been unaware of these inner tensions among the four goals, and they have made many suggestions for harmonizing them. One suggestion takes the line that each end has its own proper time and place.[12] Another suggestion has been that both artha and kama exist in relation to dharma; if dharma be pursued, artha and kama will be added. Sometimes Indians have been enjoined to pursue artha and kama in ways conformable to dharma.[13]

MOKSHA

In any case the final and supreme goal remains moksha, or emancipation. The supremacy of moksha has been asserted by Hinduism in a variety of ways. The main image for this superworldly goal is that of absorption in brahman, in which all finite and mortal conditions of life are overcome and transcended. Indian thought from the Axis Age onward (including both Buddhist and Jain philosophies) has interpreted human freedom as emancipation and asserted it as humanity's supreme goal. (The sole exception, Carvaka, or materialism, will be discussed later in this chapter.) The preoccupation of all these systems of thought and faith with the problem of time and the freeing of humans from the "noose of time" may be cited as a specific illustration. Philosophic interpretations may vary, but they are variations on the theme of human emancipation. While emancipation is regarded as a form of contemplative knowledge in which one sees, or sees through, the delusory character of mortal life, this knowledge has usually been achieved or at least accompanied by ascetic practices.

In addition to the achievement of moksha by saint or sannyasin, and to its envisagement by philosophers and seers, traditional Indian society has also placed its highest social valuation upon those individuals who are said to have achieved this supreme goal of emancipation. Ordinary people, toiling amid the hindrances and illusions of this world, may not enjoy or immediately anticipate this fulfillment for themselves, but they can acclaim those pioneers of the spirit who have done so. Sympathetically they can share in the achievement of others.

Hindu practice: three paths to salvation

The same Hindu tendency to inclusiveness which brought into being the four ends of human life has also created the three *yogas* ("ways") or *margas* ("roads"). These roads of life may be characterized as configurations of thought, practice, and feeling designed to achieve emancipation for those who walk them. Which road a person chooses is a matter of temperament, tradition, individual aptitude, or social status. It is also important to note that the three paths are by no means mutually exclusive; the religious life of many devout Hindus is a combination of all three. The three paths are (1) personal devotion (bhakti), (2) works (karma), and (3) knowledge (jnana).

BHAKTI MARGA

The way of personal devotion is actually older and of wider occurrence than its classic statement in the Bhagavad Gita. The idea of a personal relation to a divine lord is at least intimated in several of the Upanishads and is clearly delineated in the Shvetasvatara Upanishad. It is as widely diffused as the idea and emotion of love in religious experience. Bhakti has a base, moreover, not only in vedic tradition and in human nature, but also in Indian society. The practice of bhakti is more widely possible than the other two ways. The way of ritual works requires leisure time available only to an aristocrat, and the way of knowledge calls for both a guru, or teacher, and the intellectual capacity to respond to the guru's teachings. However, workers or tradespeople going about their daily tasks are able to cherish and cultivate a love for a chosen lord.

From the Gita has stemmed a long tradition of devotional feeling, writing, and activity which continues to the present day. Yet the Gita itself is still widely read; it remains the prime source of bhakti.

The Bhagavad Gita is a Sanskrit poem of eighteen chapters or sections. As we have seen, it begins as a conversation between a Pandu warrior, Arjuna, and the Lord Krishna, who is an avatar, or incarnation, of Vishnu. Yet from the time of the Gita to the present, Krishna has been a deity in his own right. The portrait of Krishna in the Gita is accordingly an intrinsically important theme in Indian religion. The conversation moves from Arjuna's pacifism to the three paths of salvation, each of which is described and affirmed as in some sense valid. Yet bhakti is asserted as supreme.

In the Gita's synoptic affirmation of all the options in every choice, some scholars have seen evidence for multiple authorship. Not only are all three margas affirmed, but there is acceptance and a fusion of two main philosophical viewpoints, of Sankhya-Yoga on the one hand and of Vedanta on the other. (These philosophic viewpoints will be sketched in the next section of this chapter.) Again, as we have seen, the Gita seeks to incorporate Buddhist values in its Hindu synthesis. Likewise all the gods are affirmed, though under the supreme lordship of Krishna. In this disposition to embrace every alternative the Gita appears typically Indian.

The conversation between Arjuna and his charioteer which opens the poem takes place on the field where Kurus and Pandavas are drawn up for impending battle. Arjuna expresses dismay at the prospect of war's carnage and destruction as well as its evil social consequences (including the mixing of castes). He ends on the pacifist note that he prefers being killed to killing. Krishna's answer is that the real self, or atman, is essentially immortal, and that therefore both killing and being killed are illusory experiences. Both the words and the sentiments recall the Katha Upanishad.

> Some say this Atman
> Is slain, and others
> Call It the slayer:
> They know nothing.
> How can It slay
> Or who shall slay It?
>
> Know this Atman
> Unborn, undying,
> Never ceasing,
> Never beginning,
> Deathless, birthless,
> Unchanging for ever.

> How can It die
> The death of the body?
>
> Knowing It birthless,
> Knowing It deathless,
> Knowing It endless,
> For ever unchanging,
> Dream not you do
> The deed of the killer,
> Dream not the power
> Is yours to command it.[14]

In response, Krishna bids Arjuna to fight as a member of the noble or Kshatriya caste, whose divinely appointed duty is to fight. As the conversation continues, Krishna sketches two paths to salvation. One is the path of yogic meditation in which the human soul turns away from action to contemplation, leading to total emancipation from finite existence; the other path is that of action, but without concern for the fruits of action. As the argument continues, Krishna ranges widely over the main themes of Indian religion and philosophy. As the discussion turns from human beings to God or Brahman in Chapter VI, the author makes a crucial distinction between lower Brahman and higher Brahman, identifying the former with prakriti, or nature, and the latter with Krishna, conceived even more clearly as a personal lord or savior. As the latter theme is developed, the monism of the Upanishads and vedanta is depicted as a stage onward toward the way to the personal relation to Lord Krishna, thus deliberately reversing the order of vedantist monism. What is often called *Indian theism* begins clearly to emerge as an alternative religious option.

This view rises to dominance in Chapters XI and XII, which constitute the climax of the Gita. In XI Arjuna asks Krishna for a direct vision of himself. Krishna responds by endowing Arjuna with a supernatural eye. Then follows the dazzling theophany of Krishna's universal forms. Arjuna exclaims:

> Ah my God I see all gods within your body;
> Each in his degree the multitude of creatures,
> See Lord Brahma throned upon the lotus;
> See all sages and the holy serpent.
> Universal form, I see you without limit,
> Infinite of arms, eyes, mouths and bellies
> See and find no end, midst or beginning.

The self-disclosure or revelation of Lord or God to the human devotee is a theistic form or relation, similar to many such experiences depicted in the Judeo-Christian Bible or in the Qur'an. Similar too is the response of faith and love on the part of the human recipient. There is in all this one marked difference from the Judeo-Christian God. The monotheistic religions depict God solely in ethically good forms. In sharp contrast, Krishna's universal forms combine good and evil in mixed and frightening combination, as Chapter XI of the

Gita clearly shows. The Gita is characteristically Indian in its affirmation equally of creative and destructive processes of the universe.

As a personal lord, Krishna claims Arjuna's loving devotion. While all three of the margas or paths to salvation are affirmed as valid in the Gita, it is the way of devotion or bhakti which the Gita proclaims as supreme. Arjuna puts the central and crucial question:

> Some worship you with steadfast love. Others
> worship God the unmanifest and changeless.
> Which kind of devotee has the greater
> understanding of yoga?[15]

Lord Krishna answers:

> Those whose minds are fixed on me in steadfast love, worshipping me with absolute faith. I consider them to have the greater understanding of yoga.
>
> As for those others, the devotees of God the unmanifest, undefinable and changeless, they worship that which is omnipresent, constant, eternal, beyond thought's compass, never to be moved. They hold all the senses in check. They are tranquil-minded, and devoted to the welfare of humanity. They see the Atman in every creature. They also will certainly come to me.
>
> But the devotees of the unmanifest have a harder task, because the unmanifest is very difficult for embodied souls to realize.

> Quickly I come
> To those who offer me
> Every action,
> Worship me only,
> Their dearest delight,
> With devotion undaunted.

> Because they love me
> These are my bondsmen
> And I shall save them
> From mortal sorrow
> And all the waves
> Of Life's deathly ocean.

> Be absorbed in me,
> Lodge your mind in me:
> Thus you shall dwell in me,
> Do not doubt it,
> Here and hereafter.[16]

From bhakti is derived a high code of ethics which draws into its pattern many threads from traditional Indian thought, ranging from the unity of all life to the spiritual conquest of desire or pleasure, or to the ideal of imperturbability. All these are held together by the unifying insight of bhakti. Krishna declares to Arjuna:

A man should not hate any living creature. Let him be friendly and compassionate to all. He must free himself from the delusion of 'I' and 'mine.' He must accept pleasure and pain with equal tranquillity. He must be forgiving, ever-contented, self-controlled, united constantly with me in his meditation. His resolve must be unshakable. He must be dedicated to me in intellect and in mind. Such a devotee is dear to me.

He neither molests his fellow man, nor allows himself to become disturbed by the world. He is no longer swayed by joy and envy, anxiety and fear. Therefore he is dear to me.

He is pure, and independent of the body's desire. He is able to deal with the unexpected: prepared for anything, unperturbed by anything. He is neither vain nor anxious about the results of his actions. Such a devotee is dear to me.

He does not desire or rejoice in what is pleasant. He does not dread what is unpleasant, or grieve over it. He remains unmoved by good and evil fortune. Such a devotee is dear to me.[17]

Not only has the Gita been India's most widely read and cherished religious classic, but from it has stemmed a continuing tradition of devotional poets, singers, and mystics who have kept the bhakti marga alive to the present day. To this company belong the *alvars* (poet-devotees of Vishnu) and the *nayanars* (poet-devotees of Shiva) as well as India's greatest modern poet, Rabindranath Tagore.[18]

KARMA MARGA

The way of works, or karma marga, is ancient, aristocratic, conservative, and for its adherents all-encompassing. Karma means both ritual and moral deeds, for Hinduism draws no sharp distinction between the two. One shades imperceptibly into the other. However, the primary emphasis is on ritual deeds. The most ancient sources of this way are the Vedas and the Brahmanas, but it is elaborated in precise detail in the dharma shastras, notably the Code of Manu. The way of works provides an appropriate ritual for every event of human life, from cradle to the grave, and for every significant occasion of human society. To those who fulfill its requirements it promises salvation.

Here, as elsewhere in the infinite diversity of Hinduism, there are at least a few recurring patterns. Among these are the five daily obligations, the offerings to the gods, to the seers, to the forefathers, to lower animals, and to humanity. The first is met by the performance of prescribed sacrifices. The offering to the seers consists of devotional reading and study of the Vedas. The offerings to animals and to humanity consist of giving food and alms.[19]

The offering to the forefathers consists of the shraddha rites. These are sacrifices of water and food to one's father and other ancestors. For a year after the father's death these rites are required every month; thereafter, once a year. The offering of cooked rice balls covered with sesame and honey together with cereals and seasonal fruits is believed to restore the body of the deceased. It is deemed a great violation of filial piety not to perform shraddha rites. A major motive for marrying and having children is to have one's shraddha rites fully and correctly performed. Indian stories tell of confirmed celibates who married for this purpose.[20]

The life of an individual human being is invested with religious significance from the cradle to the grave by means of appropriate sacraments or symbolic ceremonies. One source lists forty such sacraments.[21] Of this number, particular importance is placed upon four or five which mark milestones in the course of an individual life. The first is a birth ceremony performed by the newborn infant's father, in which vedic prayers are repeated and the infant's tongue is rubbed with clarified butter and honey.[22] While there are ceremonies related to the naming of the child, to the first haircut, and to the study of the Veda, the next major sacrament is that which celebrates a boy's coming of age in things religious. This age varies between eight and twenty-four years according to caste and other circumstances.[23] At this time members of the upper two castes receive their symbolic caste threads. The marriage ceremony is next in the course of an individual's life. The final sacrament is performed at death, and consists of the cremation of the body on a funeral pyre with appropriate mantras and expiation rites. Whenever possible, this sacrament takes place on the bank of a sacred river such as the Ganges.[24]

Beyond these common ritual activities, Hinduism entails wide varieties of religious practice, ranging from temple rituals to pilgrimages to sacred places

A Hindu bridegroom is blessed by his aunt during the wedding ceremony as relatives and friends look on. (Arvind Garg/Photo Researchers.)

and attitudes of reverential respect to the various kinds of holy men. A few of these practices will be described later in this chapter.

The Code of Manu and the various other source documents for the karma marga deal in detail with the obligation of moral as well as ritual actions. One primary duty is that of caste. The four main castes with their various duties and prohibitions are described in detail, and the massive authority of Indian religion is placed squarely behind the system.[25] Traditional Hindu defense of the caste system usually takes the form of asserting that caste is an expression of the interdependent character of human life and society, arguing that without caste Indian society might not have survived at all.[26]

The Code of Manu also deals with the status and duties of women. While a woman is by no means without rights, it is repeatedly asserted that she must remain throughout her life dependent upon men—first her father, then her husband. For a "woman is never fit for independence"; and "husband must be constantly worshipped as a god by a faithful wife."[27] These and innumerable other teachings are asserted as the content of dharma, or righteousness. The goal of a righteous life pursued with the guidance of the Code of Manu is the attainment of salvation. All three paths have this same destination.

JNANA MARGA

Jnana marga seeks salvation by philosophic knowledge. This is of course not knowledge in any ordinary secular sense. It is not knowledge which may be found between the covers of a book, but rather a contemplative intellectual vision of the sort first achieved by the seers of the Upanishads. Saving knowledge, or jnana, is the direct experience of this vision of the one supreme reality, together with the forms of study and the discipline of life which support and sustain it.

As saving knowledge consists of the vision of all-embracing unity, so the opposite of knowledge, avidya, consists of the delusion of separate, individual existence. The human individual may be compared to a single wave on the ocean, which during its momentary existence may proudly assert its separateness from every other wave and from all else in the world. However, in the next moment the ocean reaches out and draws this wave back to itself. So indeed for human beings the highest truth and greatest blessedness is to be emancipated from the delusion of separate, finite existence, and to be absorbed in supreme being.

FOUR STAGES OF LIFE   To walk this path to salvation is the work of a lifetime and requires not only hard study, but ascetic discipline of life. While the idea of the four stages of life, or *ashramas*, is by no means limited to jnana marga, they do find explicit exemplification here. (1) The first stage is that of the student of religion in which under the guidance of a guru a young man devotes himself to the study of the Vedas and vedic tradition. (2) Upon completion of study, the young man takes a wife and enters upon the life of a householder. Here he must play out fully and faithfully the role of husband, father, and citizen. He must do so even though he realizes that this social way of life involves him in all sorts of stains, compromises, and injury to living beings. He will also perform faithfully all the appropriate rituals. Yet even in the midst of the world his heart is fixed on the distant goal of emancipation. (3) When his family has been reared and his skin is wrinkled and his hair white with age, the man is free to embark upon the third stage, a hermit's life. Then, detaching himself successively from all worldly objects, he seeks the fourth and final stage. His wife may accompany him up to this final stage, but presently seeing him liberated from all worldly bonds, she will depart, leaving him to meditate alone on the goal that lies before him. (4) The fourth stage is that of the sannyasin, who has achieved, in mind and heart at least, the final emancipation from mortality and union with, or absorption in, ultimate reality. While the final and complete absorption can only take place at death, the sannyasin is one who by following the jnana marga has achieved a direct experience of absorption in the trancelike state of *samadhi*. He is then *jivan mukti*; he has achieved emancipation while still living.

HINDU PHILOSOPHY: SIX VIEWPOINTS

Related to the jnana marga as specific applications and interpretations of its basic outlook are the six orthodox systems, or *darshanas*. Indian tradition has listed six philosophies as orthodox by their acknowledgment of the Vedas, and three as heretical, namely, Buddhism, Jainism, and Carvaka (India's indigenous tradition of materialism). Of the three unorthodox or heretical philosophies, Buddhist and Jain thought share some though not all of the assumptions of the orthodox systems; but the Carvaka tradition is significant for its virtually complete rejection of the orthodox traditions.

Like philosophic materialism in the West from Lucretius onward, the major motivation of Carvaka seems to have been anticlerical and antireligious. In a tradition as sacral and often as extreme as that of India, such a critical tradition is at least understandable. Like many of its western counterparts, this Indian tradition found in philosophic materialism a vehicle for its fundamental and often radical criticism of religion. The Carvaka philosophy is named for its supposed founder. But his dates and indeed his existence are matters of inconclusive argument. The Carvaka Sutra has been lost. The tenets of this philosophy have to be reconstructed from orthodox writings which describe it in order to refute it. Yet the existence of many orthodox refutations and polemics against Carvaka philosophy argue a continuing tradition. People do not attack nonexistent philosophies.

Beyond its notes of ridicule and contempt for all persons and actions relating to things religious, the philosophy mounted its attack, like many forms of western materialism (and as the student will see in Chapter 8, Chinese forms as well), by means of a combination of materialism, empiricism, skepticism, and an ethic of egoism and hedonism. In existing documents, there is little subtlety in blending these diverse and sometimes conflicting elements. At least a few twentieth-century Indian philosophers have sought to establish a continuity between this traditional philosophy and the dialectical materialism of Marxism.

Indians have termed the six orthodox systems *darshanas* (from the Sanskrit verb *drsh*, meaning "to see," hence "viewpoints"). As one sees them in Indian history, they may also be characterized as different strands of tradition. In some areas they are mutually exclusive or incompatible, yet more often they overlap each other. All of them aim at the goal of emancipation, each offering its own interpretation of the knowledge necessary for this purpose. In this respect they might be considered as road maps for the journey to salvation. Not all of these viewpoints are equally alive today. Most recent and contemporary Indian philosophers tend to be followers of the sixth, or Vedanta, tradition and system, though in their varying formulations many have woven into their philosophies strands from one or more of the other traditions. Conversely, Vedantism may be said to have largely absorbed the other ways. The six are, however, discussed separately below.

INDIAN LOGIC The Nyaya philosophy is said to have begun with an ancient figure named Gautama, who was possibly a contemporary of the founder of Buddhism. He was nicknamed Aksapada (literally "footeyed," thus at least possibly one who spoke or lectured with his eyes fixed on his own feet). He was the traditional author of the Nyaya Sutra. However, the oldest authentic documents of this school are from the third century BCE. Like other Indian philosophies, Nyaya seeks salvation by knowledge. However, Nyaya is distinctive in its concern with the problems of logic, semantics, and epistemology. *Nyaya* means "inference," and its adherents have been concerned to study and list the valid forms of inference, as well as the general conditions of knowing. Knowing, in turn, exists to facilitate emancipation. Nyaya recognizes four sources of true knowledge: (1) perception, (2) inference, (3) analogy, and (4) credible testimony. Inference is subdivided into inference from cause to effect, from effect to cause, and from perception to abstract principle. Three kinds of causes are recognized: (1) material, e.g., the wood of which this desk is made, (2) formal, e.g., the carpenter's blueprints, and (3) effective, or efficient, e.g., the carpenter's tools and activities.[28] Nyaya developed its own theory of the syllogism, as well as its interpretation of proof and doubt. It has a realist view of the relation of knowing to its objects, and hence illustrates Zimmer's hypothesis of a way which goes back in origin to India's ancient pre-Aryan past. It is also avowedly theistic in outlook. Both Nyaya and the closely related Vaisheshika seek to establish the existence of deity by arguments from the design of the universe to a divine designer, and from the fact of motion to a prime mover. Yet all its manifold distinctions and activities are aimed at the liberation of the soul.

ATOMISM Vaisheshika philosophy not only is similar at many points to Nyaya, but has also been traditionally closely linked to it. Its originator was a seer of the third century BCE, named Kanada. Like Nyaya, Vaisheshika has a realist view of knowledge; the object of knowing is regarded as independent of the mind of the knowing process. It is also pluralist in outlook; *Vaisheshika* means "particular," and refers to the belief that the world contains an irreducible plurality of real entities or atoms. Vaisheshika also contains what is probably history's oldest statement of an atomic system. Like Nyaya it aims at salvation as a result of true knowledge. The content of this saving knowledge consists of an awareness of the separateness of the human soul from all material existence. In this respect, Vaisheshika is often characterized as a matter-spirit dualism, like that of Jain philosophy and also of Sankhya-Yoga.

DISTINCTION- The Sankhya school is traditionally traced back to Kapila, a shadowy figure of
ISM the seventh century BCE, though its earliest reliable documents come from the third century of the Common Era. Like Vaisheshika, Sankhya seeks emancipation through knowledge of the separateness of the human soul from matter. The soul is inherently spiritual in nature, and salvation consists of an adequate realization of this fact. *Sankhya* means "distinction," that is, the capacity to distinguish spirit from matter. Originally Sankhya was nontheistic or atheistic. It had no god to effect or assist this realization; rather, each person must achieve it independently. Bondage, on the other hand, was asserted to consist of a confusion, in fact as well as in ideas, of mind and matter. Actually, the soul as such can never be anything except free; but human awareness of freedom is obscured and overlaid by matter, thus producing a state of ignorance which constitutes human bondage.

Surrounding this central core of teaching in Sankhya is a body of distinctive metaphysics and an equally distinctive and closely related psychology. This metaphysical system posits two basic elements of the universe, *purusha* (mind) and *prakriti* (matter). The interrelations of purusha and prakriti produce a kind of cosmic process which some western students have likened to evolution. However, it is a cosmic process which repeats itself in undulating fashion, age after age, producing recurring cycles of evolution and devolution.

From this cosmic system and process are derived, by means of the various combinations of purusha and prakriti, the different types of individual human beings. Human souls differ in their combination of the three *gunas*, namely, intellect (*sattva*), active power or passion (*rajas*), and inertia (*tamas*). Taken together in distinctive combinations, the three gunas define a personality. Yet Sankhya regards them all as hindrances or impairments, that is, hindrances to emancipation. Hence it follows that personality, in the western sense of that word, consists of a bundle of such hindrances or impairments, which bind human beings to the world. Accordingly it is the purpose of Sankhya to provide liberation from personality.[29]

In these three preceding darshanas, and in Yoga as well, we can observe the similarity of a realist and pluralist outlook. We will recall that this is also a feature of the heretical Jain philosophy. Again, in this connection attention is called to Zimmer's thesis that this outlook was originally part of the very ancient pre-Aryan past of India, in sharp contrast to the monistic idealism of the Aryan invaders which is to be seen in the sixth and last darshana, Vedantism.

YOGA Yoga philosophy has traditionally been linked to Sankhya. In the view of some students, Sankhya provided the philosophy and Yoga the exercises and regimen for a single system or tradition. However, Yoga philosophy came in the course of time to have a lord, an element which was originally lacking in Sankhya. The whole path of Yoga was then defined as a form of devotion or dedication to the lord. Some scholars hold that originally Yoga was as nontheistic as Sankhya. Among the many traditions of Yoga, the raja-yoga of Patanjali, developed during the second century of the present era, is perhaps the best known. Hatha-yoga is distinguished for its emphasis on physical exercises and control of the body.

Philosophically the two systems differ in terminology but agree in the basic feature of attributing human bondage to matter and in seeking liberation by separating or distinguishing mind from matter. Yoga holds the human ego to be immersed in ignorance and affliction. From this bondage humans can be emancipated by a realization of their spiritual nature. However, what is distinctive in Yoga is the way in which this realization is achieved, namely, by an eightfold series of steps, demanding full participation of both body and mind. This eightfold way might be likened to an eight-rung ladder, at the top of which stands salvation. To ascend these eight steps to salvation, the student of Yoga must have a guru who, through intimate personal relation, will impart the real meaning of the way of Yoga. While different traditions of Yoga differ at specific points and in their particular emphases, all would agree on these eight steps.

1. *Yama*. Restraint or self-control. Abstention from theft, falsehood, violence, etc.
2. *Niyama*. Observance or self-culture. Study, purity, austerity, etc.
3. *Asana*. Posture, body control. In hatha-yoga this step expands into many exercises aimed toward self-liberation.
4. *Pranayama*. Breath control. In many formulations this step assumes the identity of breath and self or soul.
5. *Pratyahara*. Restraint of the senses and withdrawal from external sensation.
6. *Dharana*. Concentration of attention by fixing upon a particular object.
7. *Dhyana*. Meditation or contemplation which stabilizes the mind by concentrating on this object.
8. *Samadhi*. Emancipation by successively transcending all objects and thus achieving pure consciousness.[30]

The similarity of Yoga to Buddhist meditation testifies to their common Indian origin. It is also strikingly similar to mystical disciplines in many of the world's traditions, which have also constructed their ladders to eternal blessedness. Often, too, these have been eight-rung ladders.

EXEGESIS Purva Mimamsa originated with Jaimini (fourth century BCE) and is unique
(PURVA among the orthodox viewpoints for its deliberate rejection of speculative meta-
MIMAMSA) physics and for its passionate belief in the absolute literal validity of the Vedas. *Mimamsa* means "interpretation," or as one writer has rendered it,

"exegesis."[31] So completely true are the Vedas that there is no need for any deity to guarantee or establish their validity. Hence Purva Mimamsa is nontheistic or atheistic. In Western terms, this system might be characterized as atheistic fundamentalism.

The validity of the Vedas is explicated by a distinctive and subtle theory of verbal meaning. Words, this theory argues, are the outward expression of eternal, timelessly valid ideas. These Platonic ideas and their verbal expressions are altogether independent of the human processes of speaking and thinking by which they are apprehended and expressed. Hence it is not truth but error or falsehood that requires explanation. So, at least, argues Purva Mimamsa.

In keeping with its characteristic literalism, Purva Mimamsa alone among the orthodox ways believes in a literal heaven inhabited by literal individual selves, thus rejecting the idea of unitive absorption so important to other orthodox systems. It believes this because the Vedas say so. In recent times Purva Mimamsa has made common cause with such organizations as Arya Samaj, which are devoted to the superiority of the Vedas and the India culture which has flowed from them, thus becoming in effect a religious expression of cultural nationalism.

VEDANTA

The sixth and historically most important orthodox system is Vedanta, which means "end of the Vedas," that is, both culmination and termination of Vedic thought and devotion. The primary source of Vedanta is the unitive strain of thought of the Upanishads, but it derives also more directly from the *Brahma Sutras* (also called *Vedanta Sutras*) of the third century BCE figure, Badarayana. In pithy aphoristic statements (the word "sutra" means thread), Badarayana summarized the unitive vision of the Upanishads. The great *acharyas*, or teachers of Hinduism, following in this tradition expounded their systems as commentaries on the *Brahma Sutras*. The best-known and greatest figure of this tradition is Shankara. While there is no unanimity concerning his dates, 788–820 CE are widely accepted. He was a many-sided genius whose brief life left its imprint on many aspects of Indian culture. A devotee of Shiva and poet and scholar as well as philosopher, he was also a vigorous opponent of Buddhism. His rendition of many Vedic texts is still accepted as standard. He was also a reformer of Hindu monasticism. His system is called Advaita Vedanta (*dva* means "two" and *a* is a negative prefix; hence *advaita* means etymologically and philosophically "nondualistic").

Many of the writings attributed to Shankara are undoubtedly spurious. However, his *Crest Jewel of Discrimination* (in Sanskrit *Vivekachudamani*) is a poem summarizing his philosophical and mystical vision. So too is his *Selfknowledge* (in Sanskrit *Atmabodhi*), though the western reader of this work soon discovers that the title misleads, for it refers not to discursive knowledge of one's individual self, but rather to intuitive or mystical knowledge of the absolute or transcendental Self.

The key to Shankara's philosophy is the sole and supreme reality of Brahman or Absolute Being, beside which all else is *maya* or delusory appearance.

To be sure, many other things seem real enough from the viewpoint of everyday life. The trouble—or more specifically the illusion—lies precisely in this viewpoint. Seen from the distinctive viewpoint of eternity, we recognize the world for what it really is, namely, maya or delusory appearance. Shankara's philosophy is the most forthright expression in Indian thought, or indeed in all the world's religions, of this transcendent One or Absolute Being.

Shankara's philosophic method is explicit and clear, being based upon two equal and opposite movements of the mind, namely, first, superimposition (*adhayaropa*) and second, discrimination (*viveka*). The first means literally the assertion or attribution of a predicate to a subject. However, for Shankara it carries the additional meaning of attaching a false and delusive predicate to the subject of Being or Reality, which is to say, Brahman. This word also connoted the flattering language of eulogy which poets addressed to kings or lovers to their mistresses. For Shankara's philosophy such predication is false and must be stripped away.

The opposite process of stripping away false predicates is the task of discrimination, at the end of which lies the crest jewel of wisdom. The source of this central metaphor is the widely recurring story of the jewel for which a person seeks over all the world, only to find it has been in his own heart all the time. In a summary word, for Shankara's thought the crest jewel is the great identity of Atman and Brahman.

In his commentary on the Vedanta Sutras, Shankara begins with the individual self, or empirical ego, then in the depths of this self seeks and finds the Atman or Universal Self. From there it is only a single step further to assert the identity of Atman and Brahman.

Apart from this supreme reality there is only maya or the delusion of finite appearance. Yet fully articulated, there are no less than four degrees of unreality and reality. In ascending order there are two degrees of maya and two of Brahman. Least real and most delusive is the realm of subjective images, shadows and the like. One level above this, but still maya, is the ordinary world of things and people.

Above maya are two forms of Brahman, namely, *saguna* Brahman, or Brahman with qualities or predicates, and highest of all *nirguna*, or quality-less Brahman. At the level of saguna Brahman occurs in Shankara's thought the service or devotion of a deity, whether Shiva or some other. Shankara himself was a devotee of Shiva and wrote devotional poetry to his chosen lord (*ishvara*). However, Shankara regarded this level as only a concession to human finitude. Above all such concessions and illusions is the ultimate truth of nirguna Brahman.

Correlated with these degrees of being or reality is Shankara's concept of two kinds or degrees of truth or knowledge, namely, common or everyday truth and transcendent truth. Seen from the former viewpoint the world appears real. Rather it is only from the viewpoint of supreme or transcendent truth that a person sees and knows the true nature of Brahman and maya.

From this philosophic and religious vision follows a distinctive and characteristic ethic of calm and peaceful human relations above all the strident desires and drives of egotism. However, above and beyond the whole ethical region of human life lies a supraethical or transmoral realm of passionless peace.

While Advaita Vedanta has constituted the central tradition of Indian philosophy, its stark monism has never gone unchallenged. Three centuries later, Ramanuja (ca. 1137 CE) argued for a greater degree of reality for the persons and objects of common experience. After Ramanuja, Madva (d. 1296 CE) pushed even further in this direction. In our century, Sarvapelli Radhakrishnan modernized Advaita Vedanta by greatly reducing the world-denying character of Shankara's maya.

POPULAR HINDUISM

All religions seem to show different faces to intellectuals and nonintellectuals, and so it is not surprising to find this true in Hinduism. Yet in Hinduism this distinction is more important than in many other religions, for a great measure of Hinduism's tenacious vitality lies in its hold upon the hearts of India's masses. Hence we must now ask what religion means to ordinary people in India as they go about the business of life in the countryside, the villages, and the cities. In this connection it is well to bear in mind the fact that India's population is still at least 75 percent rural.

As often is the case with large generalizations, some advance qualifications are in order. First, in a country as large as India, regionalism is a fact of life; we will, therefore, not be surprised to find significant variants in Indian popular religion. Particularly important is the difference between north and south India. Second, life changes even in as massively traditional and conservative a society as India. Some traditional patterns of caste are being eroded. These evidences of erosion are strikingly visible in the cities.

The religious practices of ordinary people throughout India present a picture of infinite variety. There probably is an altar or shrine in the home (or in wealthy homes a room set apart as a chapel) where *puja*, or devotion, is performed by members of the family. In wealthier families there may be a Brahmin priest who functions as a domestic chaplain. As individuals venture forth into the community, they may perform puja before roadside shrines to this or that god. They pause to place a bouquet of flowers before a Shiva shrine with its lingam and yoni or to pour a libation of water or repeat a prayer before the symbol of some other god. They toss coins to holy mendicants or perhaps join a religious procession or enter the temple of some particular lord to do their devotions amid the buzzing confusion of other worshipers and then go their way. The options that open before the individual are unlimited in number and variety.

An individual may join with others or go alone on pilgrimage to some famous temple or other holy place. An example of the latter is Hardwar in north India, where the holy Ganges River flows out of the mountains onto the plains. Pilgrims gather from all parts of India seeking purification from their sins by immersion in the icy waters. It may be the great cave of Shiva at Amarnath in

Roadside shrine in India. (Anne Sager/Photo Researchers.)

Kashmir, where pilgrims gather by the thousands every August to worship at a frozen spring which forms a lingam of ice. Or it may be the sea at Cape Comorin, the southern tip of India, or the Magh Mela celebration at Allahabad in January, when hundreds of thousands of pilgrims crowd their way onto the beach and into the cold water where the Ganges and Jumna Rivers flow together.[32] All Hinduism's holy cities, Ayodhya, Dwarka, Mathura, Hardwar, Banaras, Kanchipuram, and Ujjain, are celebrated places of pilgrimage.

The Ganges is the most holy of India's many rivers, and its most holy place is at Banaras. To Banaras people come from all parts of India to wash away their sins in the sacred waters of Mother Ganga. Not only do pilgrims return home purified from past sins, but if they die in this holy city, their feet need only be immersed in the river's water for them to be assured of happiness hereafter. Thousands of pilgrims bottle some of the water to take home to friends or neighbors. For the faithful, Ganges water is a veritable medicine for all ills.

India has other sacred places to which pilgrims may go to rekindle their faith or to acquire spiritual merit. There are innumerable hills and valleys, rocks, rivers, and caves sacred to some deity or sanctified by some reference in sacred scripture or legend. They dot the landscape from the Himalayas to Cape Comorin. Their faded and tattered yellow banners announce to the passerby that they are holy places where people pause to say a prayer, to do obeisance to higher—or in some cases lower—powers.

Times, days, and seasons are sacred in India. Probably no other religion or nation has so many holidays. Lord Krishna's birthday in September is celebrated in all parts of India. Likewise national in scope is Holi, which comes in late winter or early spring. It was originally devoted to Kama, the god of love, though now he has no apparent relation to it.[33] It is a kind of Hindu saturnalia, a time of universal merrymaking and license. Respectable citizens forget caste restrictions, scattering red powder over their neighbors, squirting them with red-colored water, and playing all kinds of practical jokes. The autumn festival to Durga is a notable holiday throughout north India. In some parts of Maharashtra the September festival to Ganesh or Ganpati takes on the proportions of contemporary western Christmas, with floats, parades, colored lights, and processions.

Indian piety has other kinds of attachments too, notably to sacred cows and to sacred men of various kinds. Reverence for cows, or *cow protection* as it is commonly called, is a widely occurring pattern. In many states of India it is forbidden on pain of capital punishment to kill cows. The sacredness of cows is

Holi festival. (Lindsay Hebbard/Woodfin Camp & Associates.)

historically rooted in their actual importance to the ancient Aryans and in the resulting references to cows in India's ancient and sacred writings. To most devout Hindus it appears sufficient to know that this is a part of their tradition.

This strict taboo has many consequences: it reinforces the traditional Indian vegetarian diet; it means that old and decrepit cattle cannot be dispatched; it means that the tanner's occupation is the lowest form of human life; it means continuing Hindu agitation against what is called *cow slaughter*, that is, any killing of cows. Affection and respect for cows are shown by adorning them with flower garlands and anointing their hoofs with oil. It does not extend to such rational proposals as the development by scientific genetics of a better strain of cows. Cow dung and cow urine are sacred substances; a holy man may mat his hair with the former and anoint his body with the latter. In recent history Hindu reverence for cows has played a part in Hindu-Muslim tension. Hindu sensibilities are outraged by the fact that Muslims eat beef and also by the fact that most Indian butchers seem to be Muslims. No less a person than Gandhi has defended cow protection as a valuable and sacred symbol of the unity of life and of humans' relation to the whole animal world.[34]

Human beings of many different sorts are sacred in Hinduism. First and most obvious in this category are members of the Brahmin caste. In recent times there has been an erosion of the caste system, especially in the urban centers, but in the countless villages of India the Brahmins continue to claim and to receive the traditional reverential respect. The four main castes are subdivided into hundreds and even thousands of subcastes, which function in ways ranging from holy labor unions to exclusive clubs.

There are other kinds of holy men too. The sadhu and sannyasin are widely believed to be the repositories of spiritual and sometimes magic power, sometimes transcending the limitations of caste. The extremes of this pattern are well known even to people who know little or nothing else about India. Indian holy men recline on beds of spikes, skewer themselves with knives and swords, look into the sun until their eyes are blinded, sit in strange postures until their limbs are atrophied, and do countless other strange deeds to show their self-mastery. Yet such strange and masochistic extremes ought not to obscure the goal of Indian religion, to emancipate the spirit from the flesh, from time, and from mortal bondage of all sorts. It is this goal which gives religious significance to the activities of the sadhus. There are also countless holy men of humbler calling, whose holiness consists of the practice and the aphoristic teaching of traditional piety.

Indian popular religion shows a variety of gods equal to that of its religious practices. One Hindu scholar has written that in India the one supreme being is known in many ways and worshiped in many forms.[35] For India's masses these ways and forms are frankly polytheistic. Ancient efforts to order India's populous pantheon fixed the number of deities at thirty-three, eleven each in heaven, air, and earth. But later attempts increased the number to 33 crores, a crore being 10 million. So it is that deity may be conceived as one or as 330 million, according to one's viewpoint. Critically minded Hindus like to say that deity is one, but that the supreme one is manifested in many forms.

A few deities stand out as particularly important. There is the mother goddess, known by many names and in many guises, some to be listed below. There is Ganesha the elephant, Nandi the bull, and Hanuman the monkey, and there is Kama, the god of love. As we have already observed, Krishna is a great god in his own right. So too are Rama and Sita. Yet preeminent among India's innumerable deities is the Hindu *trimurti*, or trinity, consisting of Brahma, Shiva, and Vishnu. This trinity is often interpreted as nature or the universe in its three roles as creator, destroyer, and preserver.

Brahma, the creator, is not to be confused with Brahman, which is absolute reality. Brahma, while he has fewer than half a dozen temples and no contemporary cult of devotees, is important in both religion and art. Religiously, he stands in the background as the creator who set the world in motion. In art he is represented with four faces and often is depicted riding on a white swan or goose. His wife is named Sarasvati and is the patron of wisdom. In the guise of Prajapati, Brahma is said to have been born of the primal golden egg and in turn to have been the agent in creating the rest of the universe. The ordered structure of both nature and society derive from Brahma.

Shiva, the auspicious one, is also known to his devotees as Mahadeva, the great god; and he surely is one of India's great gods. Descended from Rudra, the Dionysus of the vedic pantheon, Shiva has retained many of Rudra's destroying and terrifying aspects. He is the expression of the vitality and dynamism of both nature and human nature, in both its destructive and its creative aspects. Hence Shiva has both a terrifying and a gracious aspect. Innumerable groups of Shiva devotees have existed and do exist in all parts of India, including an enormous variety of people and religious attitudes, ranging in the past and present from asceticism to overt eroticism, from ascetics to bandits and prostitutes.

Around Shiva has grown up a luxuriant mythology. A well-known shrine, the eighth-century Elephanta cave temple on an island in Bombay harbor, displays the central lingam surrounded by nine massive pieces of sculpture depicting varying aspects of his many-sided life and activities. These are: (1) Shiva Nataraja, lord of the dance, (2) Shiva killing the demon of darkness, (3) marriage of Shiva and Parvati, (4) Shiva as the source of the three rivers, Ganga, Jumna, and Sarasvati, (5) the Trimurti or three-form deity, Shiva, Brahma, and Vishnu, (6) Shiva as androgyne, that is, half male and half female, (7) Shiva and Parvati quarreling, (8) Mount Kailasa shaken by the demon, Ravana, but stabilized by Shiva, and (9) Shivayoga, or lord of ascetics. The Shiva temple at Chidambaram in south India is sacred to the first of these roles, Shiva Nataraja. The figure of Shiva surrounded by a ring of fire, standing on the dwarf of world illusion and dancing the end of one world epoch and the beginning of the next, is among the most familiar and popular figures in Indian art and religion.

Shiva has both wives and attendants, or *vehicles*. This last term is a technical word employed by Hinduism, meaning "carrier" or "that on or in which the

Three faces of deity, at Elephanta cave temple, Bombay.
(Government of India Tourist Office.)

deity rides." All major deities have such vehicles. In Shiva's case the principal vehicle is the bull, Nandi, who is frequently depicted in sculpture in front of Shiva temples. Shiva also has numerous consorts or wives. There is Kali, the black goddess, fierce and unapproachable, adorned with a necklace of skulls, and with four arms to flail her victims to pieces before she devours them. Yet Kali also has a kindly aspect; to her devotees she appears as the kindly mother. There is Parvati, gracious and kind; and Uma, the goddess of light. Among the incarnations of Parvati is Meenakshi, to whom the famous south Indian temple at Madurai is devoted. But there is also Durga, or Thaga, the fierce patroness of a cult of robbers and killers known as Thugs. For many centuries prior to their forcible suppression in the nineteenth century the Thugs served their goddess by making the waylaying and killing of travelers a fine art as well as a holy vocation.[36]

By means of these wives Shaivism has maintained a close relation to Shaktism, or the cult of the female. *Shakti* is a word of many meanings, ranging

Shiva, lord of the dance. (Metropolitan Museum of Art, purchase 1946,
Hicks Brisbane Dick Fund.)

from the more or less personified idea of a god's power or energy to the
mother goddess, and to a wife or consort of a god. In popular religion the word
seems to embrace all or many of these varieties of meaning. In short, *Shakti*
means "female power" and is exemplified by Durga, Kali, the goddesses
Lakshmi (wife of Vishnu), Sarasvati (wife of Brahma), and many more as well. As
Kali, the mother goddess is a fierce fighter against demons, yet she is also depicted as a dispenser of grace. As Lakshmi, she is the giver of good fortune; in
this form she is depicted sitting on a lotus or being bathed by two attending
elephants. As Sarasvati, the mother goddess is both the personification of the
Sarasvati River and the patron of learning and wisdom.

Shaktism as the cult of female energy embraces a wide range of Hindu
phenomena. *Right-handed Shaktism* might be termed the *cult of sublimated
eroticism*, whose characteristic emotions range from kindness and gentleness to
esthetic appreciation. To such attitudes and ways of life the mother goddess has
inspired many Indians. *Left-handed Shaktism*, as it has traditionally been called,

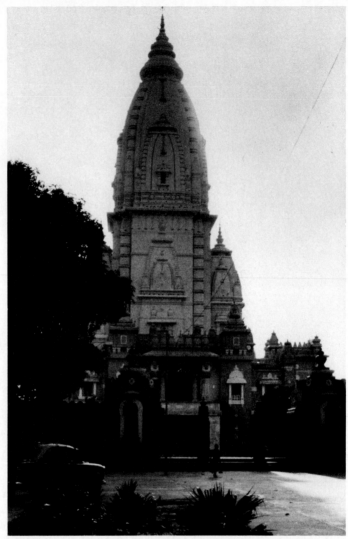

Shiva temple at Banaras Hindu University. (Courtesy of Leonard Dart.)

has been the *cult of unsublimated eroticism,* whose orgiastic forms of worship have been a matter of record in India for many centuries. These Hindu practices have sometimes made common cause with Buddhist forms of tantrism, as described in Chapter 5. The central thought apparently was the same: catharsis by holy indulgence. In this case the ritual had the additional dimension of serving the goddess who epitomized the female spirit.

Vishnu, who has rivaled Shiva in the number of devotees and the luxuriance of the mythology surrounding him, is also an expression of vital forces in nature and human nature. But it is vitality in kindlier ways and forms of expression than Shiva's. Vishnu is a god of love in several meanings of that many-faceted word. He is a lover of righteousness and a dispenser of divine grace to the aspiring human soul. But he also loves his wife Lakshmi as well as the innumerable maidens who gather admiringly around him. Vishnu's vehicle is the bird god Garuda. Vishnu has many great temples and groups of devotees in all parts of India.

A notable feature of the worship and mythology of Vishnu has to do with his many incarnations, or avatars. The word *avatara* means "descent," in this case that of the blessed Lord into the world of humans and animals. Literally innumerable avatars are claimed and celebrated by Vishnu's followers. Yet myth and ritual have concentrated attention upon ten main ones, nine of which have occurred, with the tenth being expected in the near future. In some formulations each avatar defines a new age, the whole list thus constituting a Hindu view of history. The divinities and heroes composing the list were adopted by Vaishnavism at different times, though all were incorporated by the eleventh century. The total list and the mythology of each avatar vary in different formulations. In one formulation they are as follows:

1. The Fish (*Matsya*). The world being overwhelmed by a disastrous deluge, Vishnu took the form of a fish who saved Manu (the Hindu Noah), carrying him and his family to high ground in a ship fastened to his head. He also saved the Vedas from the flood. The Fish incarnation has never been widely popular.
2. The Tortoise (*Kurma*). In the flood many treasures were lost, including the ambrosia by which the gods renewed their youth. Vishnu transformed himself into a great tortoise and dived into the depths of the ocean. The gods placed Mount Mandara on his back and, turning a mythical serpent around the mountain, churned the ocean by pulling the serpent. From this churning emerged the ambrosia as well as many other treasures, including the goddess Lakshmi.
3. The Boar (*Varaha*). The earth was cast into the ocean by an evil demon. Vishnu took the form of a boar who killed the demon and raised the earth to its former position by means of his tusk. The cult of the boar was popular in some parts of India during the Gupta period.
4. The Man-Lion (*Narasimha*). A demon, having obtained a promise from Brahma that he could not be killed by day or night, by human or beast, persecuted gods and humans, including his own pious son. Vishnu turned himself into a man-lion (thus neither man nor beast), burst from a pillar in the palace at sunset (when it was neither day nor night), and slew the villainous demon.
5. The Dwarf (*Vamana*). Still another demon, named Bali, gained power over the world of gods and humans. Vishnu changed himself into a dwarf and asked the demon for as much of the world as he could cover in a stride. When the boon was granted he changed himself into a giant, taking two strides over heaven and earth and leaving only the underworld to the demon and his followers.
6. Rama with the Axe (*Parashurama*). Vishnu took the form of a Brahman named Rama (not to be confused with the hero of the Ramayana) whose

father was robbed by an evil king. Killing the evil king, the enraged Brahman warrior turned upon the whole Kshatriya caste whom he wiped out twenty-one times in succession.

7. Rama, hero of the Ramayana. Vishnu transformed himself into the hero of this epic in order to save the world from the oppressions of the demon king Ravana. In this avatar Vishnu combined the virtues of faithful husband, brave leader, and beneficent king. This avatar and the next one are clearly the most important for Vaishnavate devotion.

8. Krishna, the god-hero of the Mahabharata. Throughout this epic Krishna appears as the friend and advisor of the Pandava warriors. Alongside the epic and supplementing it, a rich mythology grew up, celebrating Krishna, as both a warrior hero and a pastoral flutist calling women and girls to dance with him in the moonlight. In this manner, it was added in pious commentary, the voice of god calls human beings to leave earthly things for the joys of divine love!

9. Buddha, founder of Buddhism. According to Hindu theology Krishna became Buddha in order to delude the wicked, leading them to deny the Vedas and insure their damnation.

10. Kalkin, the avatar yet to come, will be a warrior mounted on a white horse with a flaming sword. He will judge the wicked, reward the virtuous, and restore the ideal age.[37]

This sketch of a few significant themes and patterns in popular religion has barely hinted at Hinduism's inexhaustible store of religious rites, myths, and movements. Yet enough has been said to classify popular Hinduism as predominantly a religion of the first, or nature-culture, type. Its gods and goddesses are expressions of one or another aspect of the world of nature and society. Its myths and rites celebrate diverse aspects and values of the same world.

Yet there is much evidence that the faith of many of India's sages, seers, and philosophers is that of the second type, transcendent monism, devoted to a blessedness which is yonder or elsewhere. It is also true that these same seers and sadhus are the culture heroes of the people of India. In other traditions more concerned with consistency, this relationship might cause embarrassment, tension, or conflict. Yet all that it appears to mean in India is that Hinduism enjoys the best of both worlds.

MODERN AND CONTEMPORARY MOVEMENTS

The cluster of elements in Indian religion to which we have given the label *Hinduism* assumed its distinctive shape before the coming of Islam to India around the year 1000. For the approximately three-quarters of a millennium during which Islam was the faith of India's rulers, Hinduism maintained itself by the simple but effective strategy of resisting conversion and continuing to exist. There was some marginal interaction between Islam and Hinduism, particularly

Krishna overcoming snake demon Kaliya. (Metropolitan Museum of Art, Rogers Fund, 1927.)

in the regions of India where adherents of the two faiths met and mingled. Yet the large historic fact is that Hinduism and Islam continued as living faiths of many millions of Indians, with the fateful result of conflict and, in the twentieth century, partition of the nation into India and Pakistan.

The coming of the West in modern times confronted Hinduism with many new challenges and issues. The Portuguese arrived first, landing on the Malabar coast in 1498. Their explorers were soon joined by Jesuit missionaries. The British and French were present in force by the seventeenth century. In mid-eighteenth century the English won out in the struggle for domination. In 1757 an army under Clive defeated the French at the Battle of Plassey, thus gaining control of the crucial region of Bengal. From this base the English moved out until they ruled all of India.

By the early decades of the nineteenth century Christian missionaries, both Protestant and Catholic, were in India in force. This century was to see several significant Indian responses to Christianity, ranging from liberal receptiveness to extreme nationalistic rejection. Hindu religion was a central component of all these responses. Taken together they constitute a great revival of Hinduism, the effects of which are still being felt.

The first response was illustrated by Ram Mohun Roy (1772–1833), founder of the Brahmo Samaj, reformer of Hinduism, and often called the *father of modern India*.[38] A Brahmin educated in traditional Sanskrit learning and a devout Hindu, Roy entered the employ of the British and soon rose as high as an Indian could in the Bengal civil service. Of independent income by the age of forty-two, he went to live in Calcutta and characteristically threw himself into a great number of humanitarian and religious causes. He founded and edited newspapers in English, Bengali, and Persian, he started schools, and he led successful campaigns against such traditional evils as *sati*, or widow burning. He also argued the case of Hinduism against Christian missionaries so effectively that he converted to Unitarianism the Scottish missionary with whom he was translating the New Testament into Bengali.

In 1828 he founded the Brahmo Samaj (Society of God), for the reformed or purified worship of God and for the pursuit of humanitarian morality. Roy was convinced that the conception of deity as one and spiritual in nature was a common element of all high religions, including both Hinduism and Christianity. Hence no pictures, no images, and no animal sacrifices were used in religious sacrifices of the Brahmo Samaj. Its members met for congregational worship of the one God—a novel practice in Hinduism.

Roy remained a faithful Hindu, wearing his Brahman caste thread to his death. Yet he was a liberal who sought to learn from all religions, incorporating their elements of strength into his reformed version of Hinduism. He was particularly attracted to the humanitarian ethic which he saw in Christianity, but felt that this could be separated from Christian dogma and grafted onto Hinduism. From this viewpoint he mounted a vigorous counterattack against the Christian missionaries, maintaining Hinduism as in no way inferior to Christianity.

The Brahmo Samaj attracted to its membership some of the outstanding Indians of the time, among them Dwarkanath Tagore and his son Debendranath Tagore, and the fiery young Keshub Chunder Sen. The society fell into inactivity following Roy's death in 1833. It was revived by Tagore in 1843. But it was split in 1865 over differences between Debendranath Tagore and Keshub Chunder Sen. Tagore was more devotional than activist in spirit and vastly more conservative than Sen, who attacked the caste system root and branch. Sen also disagreed with Tagore in his incorporation of extensive elements of Christian faith. Sen and Tagore split the Brahmo Samaj into two competing fragments. Sen's followers subsequently deserted him, forming still another group, while he came to view his organization as what he termed a "new dispensation," claiming to build upon a Christian foundation but going beyond historic Christianity. These three groups continue a nominal existence in present-day India.

A different and decisively negative response to the West as well as to Christianity may be seen in the life and ideas of Swami Dayananda Sarasvati (1824–1883), founder in 1876 of the Arya Samaj.[39] Born a Brahman in the state of Gujarat, he rebelled against family and religious tradition as a youth, running away from home at the age of nineteen. He spent fifteen years as a wandering ascetic, coming at length to view the four Vedas as absolute and final truth. He spent the rest of his life proclaiming this message in all parts of India, arguing the validity of the Vedas against all comers. His conviction that the Vedas were for all Indians, and not just for Brahmans, brought upon him the wrath of orthodox Hindus. As a result of his own strong and controversial views, numerous attempts were made on his life, one of which finally succeeded. In 1876 in Bombay he founded the Arya Samaj as an expression of his militant faith in the Vedas. His ideas made contact with the Purva Mimamsa philosophy of Jaimini, which in the nineteenth and twentieth centuries became a powerful vehicle of Hindu nationalism. Like Dayananda, his followers see the Vedas as the source of all human truth. They assert that firearms and electricity were predicted in the Vedas and that whatever is valid in modern science and democracy is actually of vedic origin. Such was—and is—Dayananda's acerbic way of expressing total rejection of Christianity and the West.

Still a different response found expression in Sri Ramakrishna (1836–1886) and his follower Swami Vivekananda (1863–1902). Ramakrishna, though a Brahmin, was a child of the Indian countryside and its simple traditional piety. But he was a mystic and a saint in whom India's ancient religious tradition came to new and compelling life. Installed as a priest in a temple at Dakshineswar near Calcutta, he became at once a devotee of Kali. He also became a religious seeker who tried over a twelve-year period the novel experiment of being a Christian, a Muslim, and a Hindu, in short, seeking to embody in his own agonized life the forms of spirituality of all the world's religions. At length he came home to his own reformed, revitalized interpretation of Hinduism.

He attracted as students and disciples many of the leading men, especially young men, of India. His disciples transcribed his aphoristic teachings, published later as the *Gospel of Ramakrishna*.[40] It expresses the world as he saw it, permeated by the presence of the divine. Among his disciples was a young Indian lawyer who, when he first visited Ramakrishna, was about to sail to England for further legal study. He abruptly changed his plans and underwent a twelve-year discipleship, at the end of which he became Swami Vivekananda, apostle to the world of his master Ramakrishna's message. In 1893 Vivekananda attended the First World Parliament of Religions, held in conjunction with the Chicago World's Fair. His eloquence and his message made an immediate and forceful impression on his hearers. From Chicago he set out on four years of lecturing in America and England, as a kind of Hindu missionary to the West. Returning home, he founded the Ramakrishna mission and with characteristic energy set about the task of reform and regeneration of India. He died at the age of thirty-nine, but his influence has continued and spread in India and throughout the world through the Ramakrishna mission. Gandhi has acknowledged the influence on his own life of Vivekananda's zeal to serve India's downtrodden masses.[41]

As the nineteenth century wore on, the thinking and idealism of India's leaders became increasingly political in nature. The Indian National Congress was founded in 1885, and until India's independence in 1947 it served as a focus for Indian political leadership. The movement had begun with a moderate liberalism, in the spirit of Ram Mohun Roy. However, increasingly extreme views forced their way to the front. In the thinking of many of these Indians there was a close relation between Indian nationalism in politics and Hinduism in religion. For example, B. C. Chatterjee (b. 1838) edited anti-British magazines and wrote devotional poetry to the mother goddess, who now appeared in the guise of Mother India.[42] B. K. Tilak (1856–1920), imprisoned by the British for inciting India's masses to violence, wrote books entitled *The Mystic Import of the Bhagavad Gita* and *The Arctic Home of the Vedas*. He also reformed and reshaped Hindu festivals and other ritual to serve as a vehicle for his anti-British political views.

The career of Aurobindo Ghose (1872–1950) led from education to political agitation and prison, but soon thereafter to a career of religious meditation and philosophic writing. After an English education and posts in Indian higher education, he threw himself into Bengal politics, associating himself with the extreme nationalist group in the Indian National Congress of 1907. He was jailed by the British for suspected participation in a bombing plot. A mystical experience in jail led him after his release to withdraw from politics to an ashram at Pondicherry, to spend the rest of his life in religious exercises and philosophic writing through which he produced some striking new accents in Indian thought and faith.[43]

A different relation of India to the West found expression in the philosophy and the life of Sarvapelli Radhakrishnan (1888–1975). Defending the Hindu philosophic and religious tradition against Christian aggression, he espoused an interpretation of Vedanta as philosophic idealism which gave parallel expression to philosophic and religious formulations. What all the various religions say in their concrete images, philosophy, in the tradition of Shankara's advaita Vedanta, expresses more fully and adequately. Radhakrishnan's exposition of Shankara's philosophy is also marked by a notable softening of the world negations of maya. Hence he has been called a modernist in this tradition. Radhakrishnan's career was also characterized by notable dedication to affairs of the world. He was chancellor of several Indian universities, professor at Oxford University, Indian Ambassador to Russia, and both vice-president and president of India.

The twentieth century brought to the forefront of leadership in Indian political society and Hindu faith the great figures of Mohandas Gandhi (1869–1948) and Rabindranath Tagore (1861–1941). Gandhi stands as contemporary India's greatest political leader and the architect of the free Indian nation. He was reared in Gujarat as a member of the Vaishya, or merchant caste. Particularly important was the influence of his devout mother and Jain friends of the family. Gandhi studied law in England and then, after a brief return to India, spent twenty years in South Africa as the leader of the Indian minority. During that time his basic convictions and methods were being formed and tested, notably that of *satyagraha* (literally "truth force") or, as he expressed it, "the force which is born of truth and love."[44] Returning to India in 1915 he soon became the unchallenged leader of the Indian National Congress. His leadership during three decades led to Indian independence.

Called a saint in politics, Gandhi replied that he was a politician trying to become a saint.[45] Religiously his great significance was his ability to reach back into Indian tradition for apparently dead ideas and to give them fresh and vital application in contemporary Indian life. Such were satyagraha and *swadeshi* (loyalty to one's own land or tradition), both major political weapons in Gandhi's arsenal. Gandhi's independent conscience led him to protest the inhuman custom of outcasting, as well as the bloody rioting between Muslims and Hindus which accompanied independence and partition between India and Pakistan. The latter position led to his death, for he was assassinated while at prayer by a fanatical Hindu nationalist, N. V. Godse, who felt he had made too many concessions to Muslims. Clearly the Hindu faith as well as the Indian nation owes an inestimable debt to the quickening influence of Gandhi's thought and life.

In many ways the great figure of Gandhi overshadowed that of the poet and mystic Rabindranath Tagore. Son and grandson of men prominent in the nineteenth century, Rabindranath Tagore grew up as a Bengali Brahman. He was given an excellent education by his father. As a youth he turned to the writing of mystical and devotional poetry in the classic, bhakti tradition. He translated his own poems from Bengali to English, publishing in 1912 the volume *Gitanjali* ("Song Offerings").[46] A year later he was awarded the Nobel Prize for literature, an event which made him a world figure as well as a hero to fellow Indians. In the years which followed, he lectured widely in America and Europe, dwelling on the twin evils of the West, as he saw them, nationalism and militarism. To these twin manifestations of western materialism, he opposed India's spiritual heritage.

Gandhi Memorial at Delhi. (Courtesy of Leonard Dart.)

In India he came under increasing attack for his continuing criticism of Indian nationalism. In 1921 he and Gandhi disagreed on this issue. Tagore had previously hailed Gandhi as India's "frail man of spirit," an embodiment of Indian virtue against the vices of the West.[47] But as Gandhi moved toward such forms of Indian nationalism as swadeshi, Tagore raised his voice in criticism. He remained to his death a cosmopolitan and an internationalist. In this he believed that he had spoken not only for Asia against the nationalist West, but for India's religious heritage as well.

Gandhi's friend and protégé, Jawaharlal Nehru, never shared Gandhi's devout religious faith. His autobiography reveals an agnostic and a secular mind.[48] Nehru's leadership, among other important factors, led to an independent Indian government which is ostensibly completely secular in nature. Such a neutral political arena is in effect a new experience for Hinduism. Other aspects of contemporary Indian society, notably the introduction of science and technology with their inevitable concomitant of urbanization, continue to drive in the same direction, to a secular society. A coalition of secular forces and Gandhi's religiously based idealism led to the 1948 law of the Indian national government abolishing untouchability and forbidding its practice in any form. While social practice falls somewhat short of legal enactment, this is an important statement of social purpose and direction.

Hinduism in present-day India shows many facets and diverse tendencies. Political and military events, including partition and continuing friction with Pakistan, as well as the Chinese attack of 1963, have notably increased Indian nationalism and with it the nineteenth-century alliance between nationalism and various forms of Hindu religion. This alliance continues its existence in several organizations and minority political parties such as the Mahasabha, the Rashtriya Swayamsevak Sangh, the Jan Sangh, and the Ram Rajya Parishad. Gandhi's moral ideals lived on in the saintly Vinoba Bhave (b. 1895) and his program of *bhudan*, the voluntary giving of land by wealthy landowners to landless peasants.[49] Conceived as a nonviolent, Gandhi-type alternative to communism, it has had some slight influence in India's rural life. Still other Indians turn hopefully to a secularism which sees in religion only a combination of outmoded superstition with social reaction. Meanwhile India's masses continue in their traditional ways of piety and faith, oblivious to twentieth-century winds of doctrine. As we observe their ways of worship, we are impressed with the fact that however uncritical, extreme, and sometimes repugnant these ways may seem, they do constitute a living, functioning part of individual and social life in present-day India.

ISSUES AND QUESTIONS

In the veritable jungle of religious phenomena which is Hinduism, it is difficult to perceive many patterns of coherent order. This difficulty is increased by the realization, as we have already noted, that no single voice speaks authoritatively for all Hindus, or concerning the meaning of what is or is not Hinduism. Rather it is the case that what secular thought calls public opinion—indeed public opinion at the grassroots of India's five to six hundred million Hindus—is ultimately decisive concerning what is and is not Hinduism.

Nevertheless two significant configurations may be observed in Hinduism, and both of them center in questions. The first question is whether Hinduism is a universal religion or rather a religion of Indian culture. Traditionally many Hindus have claimed India to be literally sacred soil, from which it is prohibited to emigrate. For example, Gandhi's mother opposed his going to England to study law. However, as we have seen, Indian nationalism later found other forms of expression in Gandhi's political credo and activity.

An opposite view is to be seen not only in Tagore, as we have noted, but also in the philosophy of Radhakrishnan, who proclaimed Hinduism as a universal religion with a message for all humanity. In our present age of extremism, when waves of fundamentalism sweep over many traditional religions, Hinduism has not lacked its right-wing extremists, as, for example, Gandhi's assassin.

Another significant configuration in both traditional and contemporary Hindu thought and devotion is the contrast which we have labeled transpersonal monism and devotional theism. Historically the former finds classic expression in Vedanta, and the latter in the Bhagavad Gita and the tradition which flows from it. Among contemporary figures with due qualifications, Aurobindo and Radhakrishnan illustrate the former viewpoint and Gandhi's life epitomizes the latter. Yet it must be added immediately that the contrast is never simple or total. Radhakrishnan and Aurobindo were involved in action, and Gandhi conceded the validity of moksha.

If we look to the moral values which are in traditional religion, the overall record of Hinduism is one of tolerance. There is little bigotry and persecution in Hindu history. The traditional posture of Hinduism has been to absorb or assimilate dissenting views and people rather than to anathematize and kill. Hindu tolerance is put to its extreme test in Hindu-Muslim relations, the tragic counterexample of Hindu tolerance being the mass killings which accompanied the 1948 partition of India.

Gandhi stands as the great example of Hindu social action. Indeed of all the great figures of Hindu history—of which he is surely one—he stands alone in asserting the primacy of moral values in society. By contrast the central tradition of Hinduism, while counseling a life of goodwill and calm integrity, nonetheless asserts that the highest fulfillment of human life lies in a contemplative and passionless state which is literally beyond good and evil.

NOTES

1. Swami B. K. Tirtha, *Sanatana Dharma*, Bhayatriya Vidhya Bhavan, Bombay, 1964.
2. *Encyclopedia of Religion*, ed. Eliade, New York, Macmillan, 1987, Vol. 6, p. 336.

3. William de Bary (ed.), *Sources of Indian Tradition*, Columbia, New York, 1958, p. 212.

4. Ibid., p. 212.

5. Ibid., p. 237.

6. Ibid.

7. Ibid., p. 236.

8. Ibid., pp. 258–259.

9. Ibid., pp. 259–261.

10. See inter alia Heinrich Zimmer, *The Art of Indian Asia*, Bollingen Series, Pantheon Books, New York, 1955, for illustrations of Khajuraho (vol. 2, plates 348–375).

11. de Bary, op. cit., pp. 261–275.

12. Ibid., p. 266.

13. Ibid., p. 212.

14. *The Song of God: Bhagavad-Gita*, Swami Prabhavananda and Christopher Isherwood (trans.), Mentor Books, New York, 1954, p. 37.

15. Ibid., p. 97.

16. Ibid., p. 97f.

17. Ibid., p. 99.

18. Rabindranath Tagore, *Gitanjali*, Macmillan, London, 1916.

19. Kenneth W. Morgan (ed.), *The Religion of the Hindus*, Ronald, New York, 1953, p. 139.

20. Ibid., p. 139.

21. de Bary, op. cit., p. 235.

22. Morgan, op. cit., p. 51.

23. Ibid., p. 182.

24. Ibid., p. 183.

25. Sarvepalli Radhakrishnan and Charles A. Moore (eds.), *Source Book in Indian Philosophy*, Princeton, Princeton, N.J., 1957, p. 172.

26. Morgan, op. cit., pp. 147–148.

27. Radhakrishnan and Moore, op. cit., p. 172.

28. See Heinrich Zimmer, *Philosophies of India*, Meridian Books, New York, 1957, pp. 610–612. See also Radhakrishnan and Moore, op. cit., pp. 356–385.

29. Zimmer, op. cit., pp. 280–330.

30. Ibid., pp. 433–436.

31. Ninian Smart, *Doctrine and Argument in Indian Philosophy*, G. Allen, London, 1964, p. 236.

32. James B. Pratt, *India and Its Faiths*, Houghton Mifflin, Boston, 1915, pp. 37–42.

33. A. L. Basham, *The Wonder That Was India*, Grove Press, New York, 1959, p. 207.

34. W. Norman Brown, *Man in the Universe*, Oxford and IBH Publishing Co., Calcutta, 1966, p. 58.

35. Morgan, op. cit., p. 51.

36. See John Masters, *The Deceivers*, Penguin Books, New York, 1955, for a work of fiction depicting the practices of the Thugs.

37. Basham, op. cit., pp. 302–307.

38. de Bary, op. cit., p. 571.

39. Ibid., p. 628.

40. Ibid., p. 638f.

41. Ibid., p. 646f.

42. Ibid., p. 707f.

43. Ibid., p. 725f.

44. Ibid., p. 801.

45. Ibid., p. 802. See also Mohandas K. Gandhi, *An Autobiography: The Story of My Experiments with Truth*, Beacon Press, Boston, 1957, p. 35.

46. Tagore, op. cit.

47. de Bary, op. cit., p. 790.

48. Ibid., p. 893. See also Jawaharlal Nehru, *An Autobiography*, Bodley Head, London, 1936.

49. de Bary, op. cit., p. 924f.

BIBLIOGRAPHY

Basham, A. L.: *The Wonder That Was India*, Grove Press, New York, 1959.

Bharat, A.: *The Tantric Tradition*, Rider, New York, 1965.

Brown, W. N.: *Man in the Universe*, University of California, Berkeley, 1960.

Danielou, A.: *Hindu Polytheism*, Bollingen Series, Pantheon Books, New York, 1964.

Dasgupta, S. N.: *History of Indian Philosophy*, Cambridge, New York, 1922–1935.

———: *Indian Idealism*, Cambridge, New York, 1933.

Dimmitt, C. (ed.): *Classical Hindu Mythology*, Temple University, Philadelphia, 1978.

Dimock, E., and D. Levertov: *In Praise of Krishna*, University of Chicago, 1981.

Eliade, M.: *Yoga, Immortality and Freedom*, Princeton, Princeton, N.J., 1970.

Embree, A., and S. Hay (eds.): *Sources of Indian Tradition*, Columbia, New York, 1988.

Gonda, J.: *Vishnuism and Sivaism*, International Publications Service, New York, 1976.

Hart, G. L.: *The Poems of Ancient Tamil*, University of California, Berkeley, 1975.

Hiltebeitel, A.: *The Ritual of the Battle, Krishna in the Mahabharata*, Cornell University, Ithaca, New York, 1976.

Hiriyanna, M.: *Outlines of Indian Philosophy*, Unwin Hyman, Inc., Winchester, Mass., 1978.

Hopkins, T.: *The Hindu Religious Tradition*, Wadsworth Press, Belmont, Calif., 1971.

Kinsley, D.: *The Sword and the Flute*, University of California, Berkeley, 1975.

Mitchell, G.: *The Hindu Temple*, Harper & Row, New York, 1978.

Morgan, K. (ed.): *The Religion of the Hindus*, Ronald, New York, 1953.

Mueller, F. Max: *The Six Systems of Hinduism*, AMS Press, New York, 1976.

Naravane, V.: *Modern Indian Thought*, Asia Publishing, New York, 1964.

O'Flaherty, W. D.: *Hindu Myths*, Penguin, Baltimore, 1975.

———: *The Origins of Evil in Hindu Mythology*, University of California, Berkeley, 1976.

Potter, K.: *Presuppositions of India's Philosophies*, Prentice-Hall, Englewood Cliffs, N.J., 1963.

Radhakrishnan, S.: *History of Indian Philosophy*, G. Allen, London, 1929–1931.

———, and C. Moore (eds.): *Source Book in Indian Philosophy*, Princeton, Princeton, N.J., 1957.

Renou, L.: *Hinduism*, Washington Square, New York, 1963.

———: *Religions of Ancient India*, Oxford, London, 1953.

Smart N.: *Doctrine and Argument in Indian Philosophy*, G. Allen, London, 1964.

Whitehead, H.: *Village Gods of South India*, Garland Publishing Co., New York, 1980.

Zaehner, R. (trans.): *The Bhagavad Gita*, Oxford, London, 1969.

———: *Hinduism*, Oxford, London, 1962.

———(trans.): *Hindu Scriptures*, Biblio Distribution Center, Totowa, N.J., 1978.

Zimmer, H.: *The Art of Indian Asia*, Bollingen Series, Princeton, Princeton, N.J., 1982.

———: *Myth and Symbol in Indian Art and Civilization*, Princeton, Princeton, N.J., 1971.

———: *Philosophies of India*, Princeton, Princeton, N.J., 1969.

7

Sikhism

Centered in the Punjab but scattered throughout India and overseas, the Sikh community is estimated at 9 to 10 million adherents.[1] Sikhism is India's newest religion, having come into being during the sixteenth and seventeenth centuries of the Common Era. It continues to engender in its people a strong and lively sense of community and tradition. A prominent Sikh writer characterized it as the only wholly Indian religion and as the mature fruition of both Hindu and Muslim thought and devotion.[2]

Like so many "isms" in religion the term *Sikhism* may easily mislead. The word *Sikh* in the Punjabi language means disciple or student. As we shall soon see, in the present case it originally meant students or disciples of the *guru* or teacher, the first such teacher being Nanak, the traditional founder of this religion. The present reference of the term is to the community and tradition of the Sikh people of India and overseas.

The Sikhs present the student of religion with a formidable list of significant issues. First and most prominent is the fact that Sikhism is an example of a syncretism which has actually worked, producing a vital and vigorous religious faith. Most examples in history of syncretism, or the mixing of religions, have not produced vigorous or vital faith. However, this mixing of Hindu and Islamic elements in Sikhism has produced a faith which is still very much alive after more than four centuries. In the last section of this chapter we shall return to the question of why this example of syncretic mixing has worked where others have failed.

Second, as the newest of the world's religions, Sikhism began in the full light of history. Hence it may well shed light on the conditions essential for the birth of a religion. Third, the Sikh faith began as a peaceful protest against the intolerance and divisiveness of Hindu-Muslim relations. Yet within a century the Sikhs had become a military theocracy with a strong continuing martial tradition, amounting at times to a tradition of holy war. The history of religions exhibits many ironies, but here certainly is one of the sharpest ironies of all! Finally, the sociology of the continuing Sikh community in India shows many interesting features. The Sikhs are not only outstanding soldiers, but also are visible in the larger Indian society as mechanics, taxi drivers, and athletes of distinction. Their turbans, beards, and other marks are the visible signs of a vigorous minority group.

Portraits of Sikh warriors. (Museum of Fine Arts, Boston.)

THE FOUNDER'S LIFE

Nanak (1469–1539) was born in the village of Talwandi some 40 miles from Lahore, and his life and influence are inextricably bound up with the Punjab. Nanak's life must be understood against the background of the history of this northwest Indian region. For several centuries this had been an area where Hindu and Muslim met and mingled—and also fought and killed each other. It is not by chance that Nanak raised his voice in protest against religious conflict.

Other currents of religious thought and feeling had their impact on Nanak. The bhakti tradition of Hinduism produced a succession of devotional poets and saints who went about the countryside singing their songs of faith. Muslim mystics, called sufis, sang similar songs and praised Allah in similar ways of devotion. To an ordinary person like Nanak, these devotional traditions must have seemed indistinguishable. Often their followers worshipped at the same shrines and marched and sang in the same processions.

Many of these saints of the Hindu and Muslim traditions raised their voices on common issues. They spoke against religious conflict and empty ceremonialism and for human brotherhood. The Hindu bhakti saints protested the evils of caste. Notable among these figures were the fifteenth-century Ramanand and his better-known disciple Kabir (1440–1518), who described himself as "a child of Rama and Allah" and devoted himself to the reconciliation of Hindu and Muslim.[3] Kabir was born a Muslim but found no difficulty in worshiping with Hindus and others. He seems to have believed in one God, the supreme reality, beside whom all else was illusion. More important, he believed that each person must find his or her way to God with the guidance of a guru as well as by meditation and singing hymns of praise and love. Over five hundred of Kabir's hymns have been incorporated into the Sikh Bible, the *Adi Granth;* and a small sect of Kabir's followers, the Kabir panthis, still exists. There is no evidence that Kabir and Nanak ever met, but Kabir's influence on his younger contemporary was strong. Both men owed much to a common tradition of devotional religion. This tradition of devotion influenced the development of Sikhism in many ways, not least of all in the Sikh emphasis on a personal teacher, or guru.

Nanak's parents were Hindus, and his father was a village accountant and farmer. His schoolmaster was a Muslim. Nanak was a dreamy and meditative child, and marriage at the age of twelve failed to turn his mind toward more worldly concerns. His wife came to live with him at the age of nineteen, and two sons were born to them. His father sought to settle Nanak into a stable occupation, but he failed as cowherd and as tradesman.

Leaving wife and children with his parents, he found his way to the district capital, Sultanpur, where he had better success as manager of a state store. He was joined there by a Muslim friend and musician, Mardana, and the two organized a group for the singing of hymns, which soon became a group of religious seekers.

The great crisis in Nanak's life occurred one day as he was bathing in the river before going to his daily work. The Sikh account of it is that God gave him a cup of nectar to drink and spoke to him in the following words:

> Nanak, I am with thee. Through thee will my name be magnified. Whosoever follows thee, him will I save. Go into the world to pray and teach mankind how to pray. Be not sullied by the ways of the world. Let your life be one of praise of the Word, charity, ablution, service, and prayer. Nanak, I give thee my pledge. Let this be thy life's mission.[4]

In response to the divine summons, Nanak uttered the words which introduce the Japji, the morning prayer which is repeated silently each morning by every devout Sikh to this day:

There is one God.
He is the supreme truth.
He, the creator,

Is without fear and without hate.
He, the omnipresent,
Pervades the universe.
He is not born,
Nor does He die to be born again.
By His grace shalt thou worship Him.
Before Time itself
There was truth.
When time began to run its course
He was the truth.
Even now, He is the truth.
Evermore shall truth prevail.[5]

The divine voice spoke again, saying to Nanak, "Thou art the Guru, the Supreme Guru of God." At this time Nanak is said by his followers also to have received the robe of honor from the God who spoke to him. Meanwhile he was reported missing, and it was presumed that he had drowned in the river. On the fourth day he returned home and gave away all his possessions except a loincloth. From the gathering crowds he turned away in silence. Then he went with his friend Mardana and joined a group of mendicants. The next day he arose and spoke, saying only: "There is no Hindu and no Mussalman."

Mural depicting the life of Nanak. (Silverstone/Magnum.)

According to Khushwant Singh, this crucial experience took place in 1499, during Nanak's thirtieth year.[6] As a result of these experiences Nanak was ready to set out, accompanied by Mardana, to proclaim the truth he had received.

There is no reliable knowledge concerning the journeys of Nanak and his friend Mardana, though it is generally agreed that they traveled widely throughout India, making their way as far as Assam in the east, Sri Lanka in the south, and Tibet on the north. Wherever he went, Nanak preached and sang his message of God the True Name who sought the salvation of everyone and the peaceful brotherhood of humankind. In order to dramatize the unity of Hindu and Muslim, Nanak devised and wore a ridiculously mixed costume, combining a Muslim mango-colored jacket with a white Hindu safa and dervish's hat, with Hindu caste marks on his brow. Mardana was the constant companion of Nanak's journeys, accompanying his songs on a small stringed instrument. Wherever he went, Nanak labored to found communities of Sikhs, or disciples. He had his greatest success in his native Punjab, where first one and then several such communities sprang up and flourished.

Later in life Nanak took Mardana and set out on the traditional Muslim pilgrimage to Mecca. They wore the garb of Muslim pilgrims and carried the customary carpet for prayer and cup for ablution. Sikh tradition tells a tale of what happened to Nanak on the way:

> He was staying in a mosque and fell asleep with his feet toward the Ka'ba—an act considered of grave disrespect to the house of God. When the mullah came to say his prayers, he shook Nanak rudely and said: "O servant of God, thou has put thy feet toward Ka'ba the house of God; why has thou done such a thing?" Nanak replied: "Then turn my feet toward some direction where there is no God nor the Ka'ba."[7]

During the last fifteen years of his life Nanak settled down in the Punjab village of Kartarpur as guru of his community. He was teacher, preacher, and leader. He required a strict routine of his followers, each day beginning with a bath in cold water before daybreak, followed by worship. The day was then free for secular affairs until the evening prayers.

The death of his friend Mardana reminded him of his own advancing years. Knowing that his end was near, he chose as his successor a devoted follower named Lehna, to whom he gave the name Angad (meaning "of my own limb"). For the choice of succession, he passed over his own sons, who had not obeyed him. Nanak died in 1539, and his followers tell the following story about his demise:

> Said the Mussalmans, "we will bury him"; the Hindus, "we will cremate him"; Nanak said: "You place flowers on either side, Hindus on my right, Muslims on my left. Those whose flowers remain fresh tomorrow will have their way." He asked them to pray. When the prayer was over, Baba pulled the sheet over him and went to eternal sleep. Next morning when they raised the sheet, they found nothing. The flowers of both communities were fresh. The Hindus took theirs; the Muslims took those that they had placed.[8]

In death as in life, Nanak proclaimed his gospel of the oneness of all humans under the one God.

NANAK'S TEACHINGS

The source of Sikh teaching is the holy book called the Adi Granth, which is a remarkable collection of the writings of Nanak, of the gurus who followed him, of Kabir, and of numerous other Sikh, Hindu, and Muslim religious teachers. The compilation of these writings was begun by the fifth guru, Arjan, and the Adi Granth was given its position of unique holiness by the tenth guru, Gobind Singh, who declared that after him there would be no more gurus, but that the Granth would serve this function for the Sikh community. It has since been revered as a sacred or even divine book. It is not only the Sikh source book, but the center of its devotion and worship.

While the teachings of the Granth are by no means limited to those of Nanak, his writings do occupy a central place in it. His fundamental teaching was "God the True Name." Several motives may be detected in this formulation. The designation *True Name* was in part his effort to transcend such limiting and partisan names as Shiva, Rama, or Allah, though at times he did not hesitate to use these and other names. There were, furthermore, devotional traditions in

Worshippers in a Sikh temple in Old Delhi, India, reading from the Adi Granth. (Hiroji Kubota/ Magnum.)

both Islam and Hinduism which concentrated the devotee's attention on the names of God.

One student of Sikhism comments that Nanak's metaphors for deity are those natural to Hinduism, citing the line, "He Himself is the Relisher; He Himself is the relish."[9] Other traditional Hindu metaphors might be added, such as that of the formless one pervading all things. However, Nanak's poems also feature such clearly monotheistic metaphors as *sovereign, creator*, and *lord*. There are also a great many terms, such as *love*, sometimes clearly erotic love, which were common to both sufi and bhakti traditions.

To this, one must add that while the student of religion with an eye for the differences between faiths of the monistic and the monotheistic types can easily distinguish these different kinds of metaphors in the writings of Nanak and his followers, nevertheless, despite this volume's hypothesis of three types of religion, these metaphors appear to lie side by side with no suggestion of inner disharmony or conflict.

These differences are even clearer as we turn to the discussion of God's relation to the world, where Nanak spoke alternately of both maya and creation. For example, he wrote the following:

Maya, the mythical goddess,
Sprang from the One, and her womb brought forth
Three acceptable disciples of the One:
Brahma, Vishnu and Shiva.[10]

Nanak's view of maya seems to have been that of the deceptive force of illusion pervading all things other than the one. Yet alongside such references, and indeed much more frequently, the reader finds references to the world as the work and creation of the sovereign monotheistic Lord of all.

Again there are references to predestination, yet Khushwant Singh is probably correct in asserting that Nanak's view was that human freedom under God conquers fate and predestination.[11] Here, in short, is the teaching of monotheistic freedom. Yet Nanak also clearly taught the Hindu doctrine of karma-samsara, asserting that evil conduct led to the bondage of continued rebirths, while obedience led to liberation.

One prominent teaching of Nanak derived from both Hindu and Muslim sources, that of the need for a guru who sustains a personal relation to his students or disciples. As we have seen, the word *sikh* means "disciple." The Sikh gurus have also been charismatic leaders of their people in war and politics. Sikhism has imparted its own distinctive definition to the word *guru*. Nanak rejected many of the Hindu forms by which God is mediated to humans, but he underscored the need for a guru. The guidance of a guru is both necessary and sufficient to lead humans to God:

O Man, repeat God's name and praises;
But how shalt thou obtain this pleasure without the guru?
It is the guru who uniteth man with God.[12]

This was a tenet which was destined to grow in importance with the historical development of Sikhism.

In his doctrine of humanity Nanak managed to combine a view of human dignity and fulfillment with a strong sense of sin, folly, and evil. "Numberless are the ways of folly and vice," said Nanak.[13] His writings also trace evil to human pride, in ways sounding strangely similar to Christian descriptions of sin.

Nanak's ethical and social teachings enunciated several of his lifelong convictions. First and most notably, he never tired of criticizing empty ceremonialism in religion, as well as religious forms such as caste which he believed to conflict with human morality or righteousness. The story is told of Nanak that when on the banks of the Ganges he saw Hindus throwing water to the rising sun as an offering to their dead ancestors, he turned and began to throw water in the opposite direction. Asked what he was doing, he replied that he was watering his fields at home in the Punjab. For, he said, if these people could send water to heaven surely he could send it to his home village![14] Religion, he never ceased to say, consists not of things like this, but of deeds of kindness and goodness. At times Nanak used the traditional Indian word *ahimsa* for this moral quality.

One notable respect in which Nanak broke with Hindu moral values was his rejection of asceticism. He remained within the world and bade his followers to do likewise. Indeed, the ascetic way of his own son, Sri Chand, was doubtless a reason for the son's being passed over when a successor to Nanak was being chosen. Sri Chand's followers were destined to create differences of opinion in the Sikh fellowship. However, while Nanak commanded his followers to live within the world, he prescribed an austere and disciplined way of personal righteousness for them. While within the world, it was nevertheless at first a distinctly quietistic or passive way of life. However, this heritage which Nanak bequeathed to his followers was destined within two centuries to be transformed into an activist, fighting faith.

THE GREAT TRANSFORMATION OF SIKHISM UNDER THE GURUS

Nanak was succeeded in order by nine gurus, making ten in all, as follows:[15]

1. Nanak, 1469–1539
2. Angad, 1504–1552
3. Amar Das, 1479–1574
4. Ram Das, 1534–1581
5. Arjan, 1563–1606
6. Har Govind, 1595–1644
7. Har Rai, 1630–1661
8. Har K'ishan, 1656–1664
9. Tegh Bahadur, 1621–1675
10. Gobind Singh, 1666–1708

2nd .
Angad .

The great transformation of Sikhism came not suddenly, but gradually, step by step, in the Sikh community under these leaders.

The second guru devised a new script and began the compilation of Sikh writings. He also emphasized physical fitness, making drill and competitive games a part of the community life. Amar Das, the third guru, made the *langar*, or the communal meal, an integral part of Sikhism. In this, the human equality and casteless aspect of the community were emphasized. Visitors were required to accept the guru's hospitality by eating with his disciples. Among Amar Das's visitors was the Moghul emperor Akbar, who was himself much interested in religious reform. Amar Das also pursued such reforms as prohibition of *purdah* and sati, that is, of the veiling and seclusion of women and of the self-immolation of widows on their husband's funeral pyres. The fourth guru, Ram Das, began the change of Sikh ethics from quietism to activism, teaching, "If anyone treat you ill, bear it. If you bear it three times, God Himself will fight for you the fourth time."[16] The same guru, Ram Das, was notable for beginning both the famous Golden Temple at Amritsar and the city around the temple. He also sent missionaries to many parts of India. His son, the fifth guru, Arjan, proved to be one of the greatest and most energetic of the ten leaders. He completed the temple and also the tank of Amritsar, making bathing a sacred ritual. He compiled the Adi Granth and installed it in the temple. He was himself a poet of high ability.

The death of Akbar and the accession of Jahangir to the Moghul throne brought bad times to Arjan and his Sikh community. Jahangir did not share Akbar's religious tolerance and sought an excuse to suppress the Sikhs. Arjan was implicated—just how deeply, and how serious the plot, historians disagree—in a plot to overthrow Jahangir and was summoned to Lahore, where he was imprisoned and tortured to death.[17] Arjan's dying injunction to his son, who became the sixth guru, Har Govind, was to "sit fully armed on the throne and maintain an army to the best of his ability."[18] From this point may be dated the beginning of the gradual emergence of the fighting Sikh theocracy.

The young Har Govind, only eleven years of age at the time, took the seat of his father, girded with two swords, and began to gather soldiers, horses, and arms for the defense of his community. He carried on intermittent warfare against both Jahangir and his successor, Shah Jahan. No match for the Moghul armies in the open field, the Sikhs took to the hills and perfected the tactics of guerrilla warfare. Har Govind's leadership increased the solidarity as well as the military confidence and resolution of his people. Surrounded by increasingly hostile Muslims, the Sikhs increased in their own nationalism. Har Govind also increased the far-flung missionary activities of the Sikh community and provided efficient administration for its increasing numbers of adherents.

These trends continued during the terms of the seventh and eighth gurus. The ninth guru, Tegh Bahadur, like the fifth, was a martyr for his faith. He was a victim of the Muslim fanaticism of the Moghul emperor Aurangzeb. The final step in the transformation of Sikhism to a fighting theocracy occurred under Bahadur's son, Guru Gobind, or as he came to be known, Gobind Singh, meaning "Gobind the lion." A talented writer of verse, a courageous soldier and leader, and above all else a man who believed that he acted under divine authority, Gobind Singh provided leadership—military, religious, and social—for his people until his assassination by a Muslim fanatic in 1708.

Gobind took a decisive step for himself and for the Sikhs when in 1699 he instituted the Khalsa, or the Community of the Pure, by a new ritual called the *baptism of the sword*. The ceremony began after the morning worship when the guru appeared before the congregation, drew his sword, and demanded five men for sacrifice. After some hesitation, one volunteer offered himself. He was taken into a tent, and a little later the guru reappeared with his sword dripping blood and asked for another victim, and so on to the number of five. Only then did the guru produce the five goats he had sacrificed and gather the five men about him for a new ritual of initiation, or baptismal ceremony.[19] Mixing sugar in plain water and stirring it with a dagger to the recitation of his own martial hymns, he made each of the five drink from the single bowl. Since they had come from different Hindu castes, this signified their initiation into the casteless community of the Khalsa. Their Hindu names were changed to the family name of Singh (from the Sanskrit *simha*, meaning "lion"), and they professed the martial creed of the Khalsa. Five symbols were prescribed: (1) unshorn hair and beard (*kes*), (2) comb (*kangha*) to keep the hair tidy, (3) knee-length breeches (*kach*, from which "khaki" is derived), (4) a steel bracelet (*kara*) on the right wrist, and (5) the saber (*kirpan*). Four rules were prescribed: (1) not to cut any hair of the body, (2) not to smoke or chew tobacco or drink alcohol, (3) not to eat meat of any animal slaughtered by the customary Muslim bleeding to death, (4) not to molest Muslim women or to have sexual relations with any women except a lawful wife. Having initiated the five Khalsa, Gobind asked them in turn to baptize him, to symbolize their equality with him in the new brotherhood.[20]

So began the new disciplined order of fighting Sikhs. Gobind threw membership in this austere new brotherhood open to all who wished to join and so gathered about himself a band of free and fearless fighting men. In the years that followed, there was ample opportunity to test their mettle in actual combat, for Gobind and his followers spent their lives in continual conflict with the Moghuls and other regional rulers. Thus the transformation from quietist sect to a fighting theocracy was completed.

The rest of Gobind's life was spent in mortal and tragic combat. In 1704, after three years of siege, his headquarters at Anandpur fell to the armies of Aurangzeb. His mother and his two youngest sons were among the victims. Gobind escaped to fight again at Chamkaur, where again his forces were surrounded and finally were destroyed. In this siege his two remaining sons as well as many devoted followers perished. When his fortunes were at low ebb, he was summoned to Delhi by Aurangzeb, but he replied by penning his famous *Zafar Namah*, or "victorious epistle," in which he hurled defiance at the emperor and assured him that one day the Khalsa would take vengeance upon him.

Gobind escaped through the siege lines and made his way to the Deccan, where later he joined with Aurangzeb's successor, Bahadur Shah, who had ex-

Assembly of Sikhs. (Museum of Fine Arts, Boston.)

pressed interest in him and his cause. He spent the rest of his life with Bahadur Shah and was assassinated at Nanded by a Muslim fanatic. As the place of Gobind's death, Nanded has become a Sikh pilgrimage spot.

The years which followed Gobind's death continued the violence of Sikh history. Not even the Golden Temple, which housed the Adi Granth, was exempt, for within the following century it was destroyed and rebuilt several times. Following Gobind's demise, the Sikhs rallied around a follower who sought to be Gobind's successor, Banda Singh Bahadur, but they fell away when he sought to assume the mantle of the guru. He was executed in Delhi in 1716. During the greater part of the eighteenth century Sikh military power was divided among confederacies called *misls*.

Unity and domination came to the Sikh community again early in the nineteenth century under the leadership of one of the most colorful and romantic figures in Sikh history, Ranjit Singh. Ranjit was a brave soldier and a military leader of great ability. He was also a shrewd politician, who succeeded in carving out and maintaining a kingdom which included virtually the whole of the Punjab.

Ranjit's kingdom did not long outlive his death, which occurred in 1839. During his last years his most formidable opponents turned out to be not native rulers but the British, who were intent upon pushing their hegemony into northwest India. British diplomacy and arms checked Ranjit's expansion, and after his death British arms brought the Sikhs within British India. Two wars, in 1845–1846 and 1848–1849, brought Sikh recognition of British power. The Sikhs became valuable allies of the British, who put Sikh military propensities to work throughout their empire. In the Indian mutiny of 1857, the Sikhs remained loyal to the British, for in the Muslim and Hindu leaders of the mutiny they saw enemies rather than allies. Sikh soldiers and constabulary were important to British dominion in Asia through the nineteenth century and up to the First World War. However, British policies in the Punjab following that war turned support to alienation and hostility.

With the British to the Punjab came Christian missionaries. One notable Sikh response in the second half of the nineteenth century was the Singh Sabha (or assembly), which carried on an active campaign of education and propaganda in defense of the Sikh faith. Khalsa College was organized in 1892, followed by the Khalsa Tract Society and a weekly newspaper called *Khalsa Samachar*. In the present century many of these activities have been taken over by other organizations.

The largest single issue in recent Sikh history has been the independence and partition of India. The 1947 line of division between India and Pakistan went through the middle of the Sikh homeland, and Sikhs found themselves in the middle of the disastrous and bloody riots which accompanied partition. For the Sikh community these events can only be described as an unmitigated disaster. Almost two and a half million Sikhs abandoned homes, lands, and temples, fleeing as refugees from Pakistan to India. In many cases they virtually exchanged places with landless Muslim peasants from Punjab.

With independence has come a secular Indian state in which traditional privileges enjoyed by some religious communities have been abolished. Sikhs have often found this to their disadvantage. One result has been a continuing agitation for a Punjab state in which there would be a Sikh majority. This was granted by the Indian government in 1966 with the division of Punjab into Punjab and Haryana. However, agitation has continued for more satisfactory conditions for this new Sikh state.

THE SIKH COMMUNITY TODAY

Whatever one's estimate of Sikh teaching, it is undeniable that the Sikhs have continued as a hardy and vital community. They have defended their faith and themselves heroically and often against great odds. Sikhs today are bound together by this tradition. Like the Jains and the Parsees, the Sikhs are today a vigorous and visible minority within the wider Indian society. In contrast to the Jains and Parsees, the Sikhs are not predominantly of the middle class. Rather they are farmers, mechanics, taxi drivers, and soldiers.

Most of their number continue in the traditional occupation of agriculture in their northwest Indian homeland, and they are some of India's best farmers. Within the past century, migration to the cities, often spurred by famine in the Punjab, has increased the numbers of Sikhs in the cities of India and indeed throughout Asia, where their beards, turbans, and names make them a highly visible social minority. Government service and politics have claimed some of them. To themselves and to other Indians they are people of action.

The Sikh community is a culture centering in a faith whose home is the Sikh temple, or *gurdwara* (literally "gate of the guru"). The most famous is the Golden Temple of Amritsar, which houses the Adi Granth and continues as a popular pilgrimage place for Sikhs throughout India. Destroyed and rebuilt many times during the stormy history of the Sikhs, it maintains its original design and function. It is of the Moghul style of architecture, and if it lacks the artistic distinction of the Taj Mahal, it continues to be a living house of faith for millions. Its worship service, as in all Sikh gurdwaras, is open to all who will observe the minimal conditions of covering their heads and baring and washing their feet.

Other celebrated gurdwaras are at Tam Taran near Amritsar, at Nanak's birthplace, at Anandpur where Gobind Singh lived, and at Nanded in Maharashtra, where he died. Yet probably more important are the local gurdwaras in the innumerable cities and towns of India. The central object of any gurdwara is the Granth, and it is sometimes charged that this holy book is treated like a Hindu deity, being aroused and reverenced in the morning and put to bed at night. Sikh defenders deny this charge, asserting that the Granth is the source and guide but not the object of faith. Sikh worshipers upon entering the gurdwara go up a gangway leading to the Granth and there leave an offering and make an obeisance. Then, without turning their backs on the Granth, they

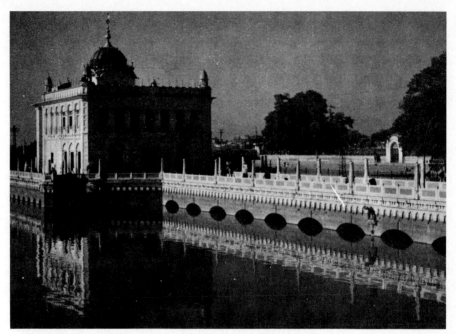

Golden Temple of Amritsar. (Government of India Tourist Office.)

retrace their steps. Reading from the Granth is the central act of worship both in the temple and in the home. Often it is read through continuously for periods of from two to seven days. Other aspects of Sikh worship include daily prayers, public and private, and the singing of hymns.

Sikhs share many of the festivals of Hinduism, but they have added some of their own, mainly related to celebrated figures and events in their history. In many of these ceremonies the Granth is taken out of the temple and is marched around the city in procession, often accompanied by musicians and singers. A notable feature of many Sikh holidays is the *guru ka langar*, or "kitchen of the guru," which is a mass meal at which all participants, sometimes numbering many thousands, eat together.

The life of the individual is guided by ceremonies at such milestones as birth, coming of age, marriage, and death. Most of these emphasize membership in the Sikh community. The death ceremony is notable for its strict prohibition of unrestrained lamentation. Sikhs customarily practice cremation.

Pilgrimages are prominent among other religious observances of Sikhs. Yet probably for most members of this faith, the paramount religious facts are membership in the community and the duties of an active social life. Sikhism is an ethical and social religion.

Like other religions of the modern world Sikhism has faced problems of attrition due to secularization. In recent times increasing numbers of its adherents have cut their hair, shaved their beards, and in varying degrees broken with the traditional prohibition on the use of tobacco and alcohol. Even more fundamental has been an increasing neglect of prayer and worship. One study of a small Sikh village in the Punjab found only a small minority who prayed daily and even fewer who observed the formal morning and evening prayers.[21] In some quarters, education has eroded Sikh piety, with the result that pious Sikhs have taken a dim view of education.

ISSUES AND QUESTIONS

Is Sikhism a religion? This is to say, is it a distinct religion, or is it rather a religious movement within the larger unity of Indian religion or Hinduism? Apparently this is a real question, for many lists of the world's religions do not include Sikhism as a separate item. However, we have included it in our list of religions, and this for several reasons. Speaking generally, a *prima facie* case can be made for any group which claims itself to be a distinct religious community and tradition. Surely the Sikhs qualify on this basis. Second it seems reasonable to consider as a religion any group whose symbolic forms or images exhibit distinctive existence. Again the Sikhs qualify.

True, the founder of Sikhism did not consciously intend to found a new religion, but this is true also of several other religious founders as well, including both Buddhism and Christianity. Rather is it the case with the Sikhs and others that history thrusts distinct existence upon a particular community.

Let us return to the issue of the Sikhs as an instance of syncretism which has worked. This is to say, it has produced a vital and vigorous faith. By syncretism we mean a mixing together of elements drawn from different religious traditions. (This word derives from "Cretans," and in ancient Greece they were a disunified group often at war with each other; hence their unity was highly improbable.) It is useful to distinguish two kinds or degrees of syncretism, first *peripheral* and second *central*. The first means the kind of peripheral or marginal and largely unintentional meeting and mingling which occurs whenever two religions or philosophies coexist. The impact of Stoicism and Platonism on early Christianity would be cases in point. By contrast the second or central syncretism refers to deliberate mixing of central elements of two distinguishable religious traditions or communities.

Examples range from Akbar's *Divine Faith* to theosophy or to Bahaism. Some examples such as the Ramakrishna movement in nineteenth-century India appear to be on the borderline between the two types. On this disputed issue, perhaps it is the part of discretion, if not of conviction, to observe each instance of syncretism to see whether, as with the Sikhs, the mixture produces a community of vital faith or on the other hand it produces a general lessening or diminution of conviction or faith.

Another puzzling aspect of Sikh history, as we have seen, is their transformation from a peaceful, even passive, community to a military theocracy in less than a century's time. The history of human religion abounds in ironics, but surely this is the sharpest irony of all! Surely too it does not yield to any easy explanation. Perhaps the most that can be said is that the Moghul rulers of India presented the Sikhs with a hard choice, namely, submit or fight. Faced with these options the Sikhs chose to fight, and in this course became experts in guerrilla warfare. Clearly theirs is not the only martial tradition in human history which invoked religious sanctions. Others come to mind from Roman Stoicism to state Shinto in recent Japan. In India the lesser-known Gurkhas show attitudes similar to the Sikhs. The Sikhs, then, take their place among several other religions as a martial tradition and indeed at times even a tradition of holy war.

Finally, what can be said in general explanation or understanding of the Sikh community? We suggest that here is a classic example of a minority community which derives strength and vitality from its minority status, growing strong by swimming against the stream. We shall find other examples of this phenomenon.

Like many other religions, Sikhism has been riven by sectarian divisions. A close relation of church to state has long been a traditional tenet. Since India's independence this has generated demands for autonomy or even separate nationhood for the state of Punjab. In 1984 a group of Sikh extremists occupied the Golden Temple at Amritsar in order to dramatize their demands. In desperation Indian prime minister Indira Gandhi ordered the army to expel them. As a tragic consequence, Mrs. Gandhi was assassinated by a member of her own Sikh guard.

NOTES

1. *The New Encyclopaedia Britannica*, Encyclopaedia Britannica, Inc., Chicago, 1974, vol. 27, p. 294.
2. Khushwant Singh, *The Sikhs Today*, Orient Longmans, Calcutta, 1964, p. xiii.
3. Khushwant Singh, *History of the Sikhs*, vol. 1, Princeton, Princeton, N.J., 1963, p. 24. See also William T. de Bary (ed.), *Sources of Indian Tradition*, Columbia, New York, 1958, p. 532.
4. K. Singh, *History of the Sikhs*, p. 31.
5. Ibid., p. 32.
6. Ibid., p. 36.
7. Ibid.
8. Ibid., p. 37.
9. de Bary, op. cit., p. 533.
10. *Selections from the Sacred Writings of the Sikhs*, Trilochan Singh et al. (trans.), G. Allen, London, 1960, p. 46.
11. K. Singh, *History of the Sikhs*, p. 45.
12. de Bary, op. cit., p. 537.
13. Ibid.
14. K. Singh, *The Sikhs Today*, p. 5.
15. *Selections from the Sacred Writings of the Sikhs*, p. 17.
16. M. A. MacAuliffe, *The Sikh Religion*, as quoted in J. B. Noss, *Man's Religions*, 2d ed., Macmillan, New York, 1956, p. 283.
17. de Bary, op. cit., p. 541.

18. K. Singh, *The Sikhs*, G. Allen, London, 1953, p. 27f.
19. Ibid., p. 29.
20. Ibid.
21. John C. Archer, *The Sikhs in Relation to Hindus, Moslems, Christians and Ahmadiyyas*, Princeton, Princeton, N.J., 1946, p. 291.

BIBLIOGRAPHY

The Adi Granth, or Holy Scriptures of the Sikhs, Ernst Trumpp (trans.), Trubner, London, 1877.

Archer, J. C.: *The Sikhs*, Princeton, Princeton, N.J., 1947.

Brown, W. N.: *Man in the Universe*, University of California, Berkeley, 1960.

Cole, W., and P. Sambhi: *Sikhism*, State Mutual Book and Periodical Service, Ltd., New York, 1985.

Embree, A., and S. Hay (eds.): *Sources of Indian Tradition*, Columbia, New York, 1988.

Field, Dorothy: *The Religion of the Sikhs*, J. Murray, London, 1911.

Gupta, H. R.: *History of the Sikhs*, Dawson, London, 1950.

Harbans Singh: *The Heritage of the Sikhs*, South Asia Books, Columbia, Mo., 1983.

Khushwant Singh: *A History of the Sikhs*, Princeton, Princeton, N.J., 1984.

Loehlin, C. H.: *The Sikhs and Their Book*, Lucknow Publishing, Lucknow, India, 1945.

———: *The Sikhs and Their Scriptures*, Lucknow Publishing, Lucknow, India, 1958.

MacAuliffe, M.: *The Sikh Religion*, Coronet Books, Philadelphia, Pa., 1963.

McLeod, W. H.: *The Evolution of the Sikh Community*, Oxford, New York, 1976.

———: *Guru Nanak and the Sikh Religion*, Oxford, London, 1968.

———: *Sikhism*, State Mutual Book and Periodical Service, Ltd., New York, 1985.

Selections from the Sacred Writings of the Sikhs, Trilochan Singh et al. (trans.), G. Allen, London, 1960.

8

Chinese Religion

The transition from India to China presents one of the most massive contrasts in all the history of religion. India's reaching for an absolute reality beyond the common world of nature and society, with the accompanying alienation of humans from this world, stands in polar opposition to China's staunchly this-worldly attitude. The Chinese perception of particular realities contrasts with India's fondness for abstract speculation. In short, while the dominant attitude of the Indian tradition is acosmic, that of China is cosmic; in terms of our typology of religions, India's is type 2 while China's is type 1.

In contrast to the heavily sacral quality of Indian culture, where holiness seems to suffuse and permeate everything, Chinese culture, past and present, seems secular. There are holy or sacred objects in the Chinese tradition, but they have, as it were, a low-voltage holiness. In contrast to the widespread supernaturalism or transcendentalism of India, China presents a strong indigenous tradition of naturalism. *Naturalism* may be defined as the attitude which asserts that nature is all of reality and denies the existence of anything beyond. Along with this naturalism the Chinese tradition developed a vigorous criticism of popular religious forms (and religious abuses) for which there is all too little parallel in India.

In the Chinese tradition the great continuities are nature and society; taken together they constitute the universe, or cosmos, which forms the enduring context of human life. For most people in the Chinese tradition it is unthinkable even to conceive of human life or anything else outside of this context. As one Chinese scholar has remarked, from the Chinese viewpoint the biblical creation story, with its transcendent deity who brings the world into being from nothingness, is meaningless, because in the Chinese view the universe has always existed and literally is all that is or exists.[1] In a word, the world or cosmos just *is*. The basic Chinese symbols for the principal aspects of this cosmic reality are Heaven, Earth, the Central Kingdom, and Man.* W. T. Chan has underscored the

---

*In this book we follow the rule of inclusive language. However, for this instance, in classical Chinese context, "Man" understood as a symbolic form appears irreplaceable, and also historically accurate. The Chinese character *jen* 人 translates as a "person," and *jen* 仁 (literally "two persons") translates as "humanity" or "humanness." However, traditional Chinese culture was massively male-dominated. Hence we have retained "Man" as a symbolic form, to translate *jen* 仁, which is the Chinese ideal of humanity and humanness.

213

last term, asserting that "the one word which sums up the Chinese tradition is humanism."[2]

The great figures of ancient China, notably Confucius and Lao tzu, were of the Axis Age, and hence strong persons. As human selves they also showed what was called in Chapter 1 *ultimate concern* or *valuation*. What is unique about Confucius and the tradition to which he gave definitive expression is that the object of ultimate concern was Chinese society itself. In other words, the distinctive religious response (which following Tillich we have called *ultimate concern*) is in Confucius reflected back to society itself. Although this attitude was generated in very ancient times, it became explicit and conscious in the life and thought of Confucius.

As we begin to study Chinese religion, we must consider the question that arises in the study of virtually every religious tradition considered in this book: "Is this religion?" Many scholars have denied that the Chinese tradition is religious or, specifically, that Confucianism is religion. Y. L. Fung has written that whereas western people are religious in outlook, the Chinese are philosophical.[3] At least a part of this controversy is a quibble over words. If *religion* is defined in western monotheistic terms, then clearly the word has little or no reference to China. Indeed, there is no word in the Chinese language accurately translatable as "religion." In modern times the Chinese character *chiao* has been co-opted for the purpose, but the original meaning of this term is "teaching." However, if religion is defined more generally, as proposed in Chapter 1, as an existent system of holy forms, then clearly the Chinese tradition does show observable phenomena which fit this definition. Heaven, Earth, the Central Kingdom, and Man constitute such a system of holy forms—withal a distinctively Chinese system.

CHINESE BEGINNINGS

China stands as perhaps the oldest continuous civilized tradition in the world. (The only serious competition is India.) In the sixth century BCE, when our study of its religion begins, China was already an old society in which people looked back to the "good old days" of an ancient past. The Chou dynasty had come to power in 1120 BCE, but back of the Chou lay the Shang, which had reigned from 1800 to 1120 BCE, and back of the Shang lay the prehistoric Hsia dynasty with its sage kings, Yao and Shun.

The Chou dynasty has destined to last until 221 BCE, when it was forcibly displaced by the Ch'in. (The word *Ch'in* is from the far western province of Ch'in, whose duke became the famous First Emperor, Shih Huang-ti, 221–210 BCE, founder of the Ch'in dynasty. From *Ch'in* is derived the western word *China*. The Chinese do not use this name, speaking rather of themselves as the people of the Central Kingdom, *Chung Kuo*.* Our story begins in the declining period of the Chou dynasty, often called the *warring states* period (ca. 600–250 BCE), which was an age of feudal disintegration immediately preceding the rise of the Ch'in.

The Ch'in dynasty lasted only from 221 to 207 BCE, yet during this time it built the Great Wall, as well as canals and roads and much else. More than any single achievement, the Ch'in unified China for the first time. Yet this unity was bought at the price of the cruel tyranny which brought about the downfall of the dynasty. An example of this tyranny was the famous, or infamous, "burning of the books." Many traditionally minded scholars had resisted Ch'in efforts at unification. Their resistance was based upon their ancient classical texts. It was broken by a summary governmental order to turn over all books for destruction, on pain of death.

*There are two different systems for transliterating Chinese characters into English, first the nineteenth-century Wade-Giles system and second *Pinyin*, devised by the Chinese in the 1950s. They differ greatly from each other. Consider the following illustrations: Wade-Giles *Peking*, Pinyin *Beijing*; Wade-Giles *Tao*, Pinyin *Dao*; Wade-Giles *ch'in*, Pinyin *qin*; Wade-Giles *chou*, Pinyin *zhou*. Despite the superior accuracy of Pinyin, this book necessarily retains Wade-Giles, largely for reasons of the English alphabet. To change to Pinyin would cut off the student from the whole body of English translations of Chinese works in Wade-Giles which are classified alphabetically in our libraries.

Kneeling man, bronze. Late Chou dynasty, c. sixth- to third-century BCE. (Minneapolis Institute of Arts, Pillsbury Collection.)

The great achievement of the Ch'in dynasty was the idea of a Chinese empire and of the bureaucracy necessary to carry the idea into effect. The Ch'in was succeeded by the classical dynasty of ancient China, the Han. With an interregnum from 9 to 23 CE dividing the Han into "earlier" and "later," this dynasty lasted from 202 to 220 CE. It was ancient China's classical age, a time of greatest importance and achievement in all aspects of culture, including religion. During the Han dynasty Confucianism achieved the role of the established faith or philosophy, which endured until 1911 CE.

THE CLASSIC TEXTS

As we begin the study of Confucius, Lao tzu, and the other Chou teachers and schools, we find them presupposing a set of classical books or texts whose ideas and images served even in those ancient times as traditional premises of thought and the norms of action. The customary word *classic* (the Chinese term is *ching*) designates the reverential respect and authority accorded these books from the ancient period onward. One list of classics includes thirteen books; the better-known list of classics includes five books.[4] The latter is as follows:

1. The *Shih ching*, or "Classic of Songs," was also known as the "Book of Poetry." It consisted of 305 songs or poems dating from the tenth to the seventh century BCE. Many were simple love poems, others were ritual hymns, and still others had political or social significance. All testified to the importance of poetry to the Chinese even at this early time. The ability to compose and even to recite poetry remained the mark of an educated person in China. It has been claimed that Confucius edited the Shih ching, though this is far from certain.
2. The *Shu ching*, or "Classic of Documents," was known also as the "Book of History." It consisted of chronicles, speeches, and other similar matters from the early Chou period, though extensive sections have been shown to consist of later forgeries added to the text.
3. The *I ching*, or "Classic of Changes," was a diviner's handbook of uncertain and mixed age which came into existence by gradual accretion. Parts of it go back to the early Chou period. It was built around eight trigrams, or combinations of three horizontal lines, broken or unbroken, which served as a basis for foretelling the future. The I ching, with its trigrams and hexagrams (composed of two trigrams), served the purpose not only of divination but, later, of Chinese cosmology and cosmogony as well. Out of these materials developed a highly distinctive Chinese folk philosophy that envisaged the universe as a single, vast relational system.
4. The *Ch'un ch'iu*, or "Spring and Autumn Annals," was a chronological record of important events in the state of Lu from 722 to 481 BCE. The chronology is factual, and it has often been asserted that Confucius either wrote or edited this document.

5. The *Li chi*, or "Record of Rites," was a second-century compilation of earlier materials dealing with ceremonies. These rites constituted a key element in the Confucian view of social order.

A thousand years after the end of the Chou period, four shorter texts, the Four Books, were officially added to the Five Classics. These were (1) the "Analects," or "Sayings of Confucius," (2) the "Mencius Book," (3) the "Great Learning," and (4) the "Doctine of the Mean." The last two were selected chapters from the Li chi. The Four Books together with the Five Classics constituted the authoritative sources of the Chinese tradition. What is even more important, we have here in the process of writing, reading, and then honoring a body of writings a clue to the nature of the Chinese tradition. The Chinese are a people who have looked to ancient writings interpreted by scholars or sages for the answers to life's questions.

RECURRING THEMES AND IMAGES

Pervading these classical writings and the culture which the writings informed and guided is a series of themes and images which, taken together, shed valuable light on the religious viewpoint and outlook of ancient China. The following summary makes no claim to completeness, but it will serve to put the reader in touch with the basic Chinese attitude which speaks through these texts.

HEAVEN

The Chinese universe consisted, as noted, of Heaven and Earth, and in the middle of the flat disk of Earth, the Central Kingdom. Heaven was the vault of the sky, but it was also the source of human destiny and in an impersonal way also the object of natural piety. In the very early days of the Shang dynasty people spoke of *Shang-ti* (meaning "lord on high"). But during the Chou dynasty *T'ien* became the customary term and idea, possibly at least as a result of the thought of Confucius. At least one translation of the "Sayings of Confucius" has translated *T'ien* into English as "Sky."[5] Yet perhaps the term *heaven* as used in the somewhat impersonal phrases "heaven knows" or "thank heaven" is a more adequate rendering. One Chou dynasty school of philosophy argued that Heaven had a personal nature, but Confucius and the other schools held it to be impersonal.

From very ancient times onward, the emperor, acting as the representative of his people, performed prescribed sacrifices to Heaven, on the days of the summer and winter solstice. At the spring and autumn equinox he performed similar sacrifices to Earth. Other, similar ceremonies to Earth were also performed in state capitals and local villages throughout China. In this manner was

Chinese landscape *Streams and Mountains without End.* (Cleveland Museum of Art, Gift of Hanna Fund.)

celebrated the dependence of Man on Heaven and Earth, and Man's place in this cosmic scheme of things.

TAO

Pervading the classical documents is the term *Tao*, meaning "way" or "path." While western students may despair of a truly adequate translation, nevertheless "cosmic way" comes close. Tao is the ongoing dynamic way of the universe, as well as its preordained rational structure. Hence to follow the Tao is to follow the path of the cosmos, which leads to self-realization, and to diverge from the Tao is to lose one's way. While one group of Chinese thinkers, the Taoists, developed their own highly distinctive views on the Tao, they had no monopoly on either term or idea, both of which pervaded ancient Chinese thought.

YIN AND YANG

The components of the Tao were the dual-energy modes, *yin* and *yang*, which in different combinations came together to constitute all things in nature and society. Yang was the active, male principle, and yin the passive, female principle. Thus, for example, Heaven was yang, the Earth yin. The sun was yang, and the moon was yin. Yang was bright and yin dark; hence the bright sunlit side of a hill was yang, while the dark, shadowed side was yin. Yin and yang were embodied in different combinations in the trigrams of the I ching, the unbroken line being yang and the broken line yin. Two trigrams combined to form one hexagram. All possible combinations produced sixty-four hexagrams which together represent the universe. Combined with the traditional Chinese five agents, or elements—metal, wood, water, fire, and earth—yin-yang speculation produced a kind of protoscientific investigation of nature not unlike alchemy. Historical and human events were also analyzed by court astrologers in terms of yin and yang and the five agents, using the I ching as their guide; and the future was forecast in these terms.

THE MANDATE OF HEAVEN

The mandate of Heaven (*T'ien ming*) was ancient China's way of imparting divine sanction to the ruler. The idea recurs in the Shu ching, and with Confucius it became a fundamental category of political thought and practice. The mandate of Heaven meant that the emperor ruled with the sanction of Heaven, that he was veritably the son of Heaven. It imposed special responsibilities and requirements on China's ruler, for it was asserted that if the emperor did not properly perform the rituals, or if he were an evil person, the mandate would be withdrawn. It was a matter of controversy just how or when the mandate might be given or withdrawn. Mo tze, for example, taught the right of rebellion against a ruler who no longer sought his people's well-being. Realistic and cynical thinkers pointed out that any ruler who maintained himself in power seemed to have Heaven's mandate. Others argued that if China and Chinese people suffered misfortune, it was a sign that the mandate had been withdrawn. However interpreted, the mandate was a powerful force for social unity under the emperor.

FAMILY REVERENCE

The underlying social unit throughout Chinese history has been the family. Indeed, by extension, what was the Central Kingdom but a great family under the son of Heaven? The solidarity of the family was guaranteed by reverential respect for one's father and for seniors in general. This reverence, or *hsaio*, was not limited to living persons, but extended to the family ancestors, to whom prayers and sacrifices were regularly offered and who were visibly present in tablets over the family altar. Similarly, on important occasions of life one consulted one's ancestors (that is, visited their graves for reflection and meditation) on the decision to be made.

Indeed the most important rituals of family reverence and solidarity were funerals, which traditionally in China were momentous—and expensive—affairs. In very ancient times members of the nobility were buried with weapons, furnishings, and animal and human attendants. Such human sacrifices continued until late Chou times, when they were supplanted by pottery and subsequently paper substitutes. Even in relatively recent times the manufacture of paper money and paper images for funerals has been a major industry.

Family loyalty has been a massive stabilizing and conserving force throughout Chinese history. The "way of the fathers" has been a powerful sanction for ethics as well as a device for hallowing all tradition or custom. In all this, the scholars, highly honored as they have been, have had the function of advising rulers and society on the ways of the past and the present.

SPIRITS

Much of the substance of the previous five themes has permeated Chinese society to its grass roots. Yet in China the popular level of religion had homelier ingredients as well. The worship of Heaven was present—in the background. The worship of Earth, often in the form of local fertility gods, was closer at hand. So too were the innumerable spirits, good, evil, and capricious, with which the world was populated. The popular religion of most societies is marked by animism; that of China was notably so. The spirits were classified as good spirits, or *shen*, and evil spirits, or *kwei*. Natural phenomena, from mountains and rivers to animals, both real and imaginary, were conceived as dwelling places of these spirits. Chinese people went to great lengths to keep the goodwill of the shen and to avert evil at the hands of the kwei. Sacrifices, incanta-

Temple of Heaven, Peking. (Bruno Barbey/Magnum.)

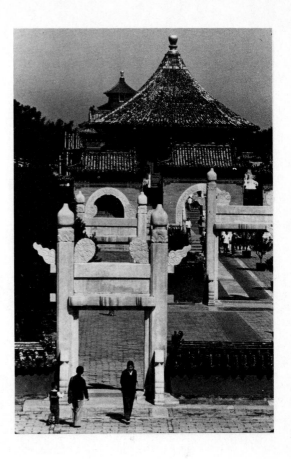

tions, bonfires, torches, and firecrackers were only a few of the means of averting supernatural evil and securing good. This popular preoccupation with spirits had as one of its consequences a haughty condescension on the part of the intellectuals, who were led to look down upon popular religion with mingled detachment and scorn.

CHOU SCHOOLS OF PHILOSOPHY

According to the great Han historians, there was a notable flowering of philosophy during the declining period of the Chou dynasty, extending, they asserted in typical hyperbole, to as many as "a hundred schools." The primary meaning of philosophy for them was ethics, though several of them included significant teachings in epistemology, logic, and philosophy of religion. The Chinese term used by modern philosophers, *che hsüeh*, literally "wisdom study," is modern and probably influenced by the West. Confucius used the term *che*, "wisdom." These ancient schools of philosophy were in effect bodies of teaching concerning the conduct of life. The term for schools, *chia*, actually meant "family" or "household." Disciples gathered in communities around leading teachers, and in traditions stemming from these teachers. Of the putative hundred schools or traditions, six turn out to be historically significant, and of the six, one, Confucianism, has had altogether central significance in Chinese history. The pages which follow will consider the six Chou schools in turn, beginning with Confucianism.

CONFUCIUS, THE FIRST TEACHER

The main source for the life and teachings of Confucius is the "Analects," or "Sayings," which was written not by Master K'ung himself, but by immediate disciples. (The title "Analects" is a Latin rendering of the Chinese title *Lun yü*. Like the name *Confucius*, the Latin title, "Analects," comes from the sixteenth- and seventeenth-century Jesuit missionaries to China. The Chinese know Confucius as *K'ung fu tzu*, Master of the K'ung family, or familiarly as *Ch'ung ni*.) The "Sayings" are organized in twenty chapters, consisting in all of 479 aphoristic sayings. There is also a biography of Confucius by the Han historian Ssuma Ch'ien (d. 80 BCE). Fragments of teaching and recollections of the master's life are contained in the "Great Learning" and the "Doctrine of the Mean." There are also widespread traditions concerning Confucius scattered throughout ancient Chinese history and folklore; needless to say, all such materials must be critically sifted.

Confucius's traditional dates, 551–479 BCE, are doubtless not far wrong. He was born in the province of Lu at the base of the Shantung Peninsula. His ancestors are said to have been aristocratic refugees who had fled from Sun to Lu during a revolution, perhaps that which toppled the Shang dynasty and put the Chou in power. The twentieth-century scholar, Hu Shih, has advanced the thesis that Confucius was a *Ju*, or court intellectual of an ancient traditional type which had gone out of fashion and which, argues Hu Shih, Confucius succeeded in reviving in his own time.[6]

Confucius's father died shortly after his birth, leaving the family in straitened circumstances. Nonetheless, his mother secured for her son a typical aristocratic liberal education. Apparently Confucius achieved all-round excellence as a student, his studies ranging from archery, chariot driving, and the like, through lute playing, to historical and literary scholarship, which together constituted the ideal of the educated gentleman. As a young man he held minor governmental posts. The death of his mother caused him great grief. Confucius mourned the prescribed twenty-seven months, but even after this time, when he took up the lute, his grief prevented him from singing.

He opened a school which became the model of Chinese education. Its curriculum consisted of the traditional six disciplines: history, poetry, government, propriety, music, and divination. While the sons of many wealthy families were his students, Confucius was proud to say that no student was ever turned away for lack of money. The school was oriented toward government as an application of ethics to society. Its graduates have been estimated at three thousand, of whom seventy-two became close personal disciples of Confucius.

Tradition (not verified by the "Sayings") asserts that he took public office at the age of fifty, rising through various posts to that of prime minister in the state of Lu, only to be framed by less righteous officials. Losing face, he resigned. However this may be, there is better historical evidence for a thirteen-year period of wandering beginning in his mid-fifties. Accompanied by three close disciples Confucius went from state to state, seeking a ruler wise enough to accept him as advisor. He could find none. During these years he was sustained by a very genuine sense of calling and mission. Beset by mobs and harried by police and other officials, he declared, "Heaven begat the power (*te*) that is in me. What have I to fear…?"[7] The motivation and form of Confucius's mission were his obedience to the mandate of Heaven; its content was the application of morality to politics in order to restore the ancient and good order of the early Chou dynasty. This harmonious way of life seemed utterly lost in the disorder and violence of his lifetime. Confucius believed fervently that he was born to restore this original, virtuous, archaic order.

Apparently through a former student who was an official of Lu, and thus politically more successful than his teacher, Confucius was invited home to Lu in 484 BCE. He spent his last years in the scholarship he greatly loved, perhaps editing some of the classics, and died in 479 BCE at the age of seventy-two. He died in apparent disillusionment, yet great success for his teachings lay in the history yet to come. Master K'ung was destined to live on in the impact of his teachings on China.

CONFUCIAN THEMES

The teachings of Confucius often seem flat and unexciting to the modern western student, lacking the intellectual appeal of Socrates and the radical faith and love of Jesus. They seem blandly conservative, a complacent rationalization of the status quo. To the ancient Chinese student they held both relevance and power, expressing as they did the essential meaning of humanity set in the context of the Chinese cosmos. In the fabric of Confucius's teachings, eight recurring themes will be pointed out as main threads.

Li

First and perhaps most basic is *li*, hard to translate precisely, and variously rendered as "propriety," "courtesy," "rites and ceremonies," and "decorum." Actually it means, or can mean, all these things. Perhaps "good form" is as accurate a translation as can be achieved. It begins with those good forms which constitute decorum or etiquette, and it continues without any discontinuity through morality to the nature of the universe. For in contrast to the West, classical Chinese thought saw no discontinuity between these two aspects of social relations. Nor indeed does the matter end there. The Li chi quotes Confucius as asserting that li:

> . . . is the principle by which the ancient kings enbodied the laws of heaven, and regulated the expressions of human nature. Therefore he who has attained li lives and he who has lost it dies. . . . Li is based on heaven, patterned on earth, deals with the worship of the spirits and is extended to the rites and ceremonies of funerals, sacrifices to ancestors, archery, carriage driving, capping, marriage, and court audience or exchange of diplomatic visits. Therefore the sage shows the people this principle of a rationalized social order and through it everything becomes right in the family, the state and the world.[8]

There is a good order or harmony of the universe in which humans participate by their practice of li. Conversely, the pervasive and harmonious order of the universe finds illustration and application in human life in a person's practice of good form.

Hsiao It has already been noted that respect for one's father in particular and for elders in general constitutes a basic virtue of the Chinese tradition. Confucius gave eloquent expression and wholehearted assent to filial piety (hsia) even to the extent of defending and concealing a father's crime from the government.

> The Duke of She observed to Confucius: "Among us there was an upright man called Kung who was so upright that when his father appropriated a sheep, he bore witness against him." Confucius said the upright men among us are not like that. A father will screen his son and a son his father—yet uprightness is to be found in that.[9]

At its best, filial piety consisted of an inward respect or reverence for one's parents. It was generalized to include elders of all sorts, and indeed all that was ancient or archaic.

> Tzu Yu asked about filial piety. Confucius said: "Nowadays a filial son is just a man who keeps his parents in food. But even dogs or horses are given food. If there is no feeling of reverence, wherein lies the difference?"[10]

A significant application of the virtue of filial piety to Chinese society lay in the traditional five great relations. In the Li chi's formulation, they are as follows:

1. Kindness in the father, filial piety in the son
2. Gentility in the elder brother, humility and respect in the younger
3. Righteous behavior in the husband, obedience in the wife
4. Humane consideration in elders, deference in juniors
5. Benevolence in rulers, loyalty in ministers and subjects[11]

It will be noted that none of these relations is symmetrical, or in other words, none is a relation between equals. Confucius's ethic is that of a well-ordered feudal hierarchy, where goodness consists in finding one's station and doing its duties.

Jen   The humane quality of Confucius's ethic is exemplified by the quality called *jen* in Chinese and variously translated as "humanity" or "human-heartedness." The Chinese character consists of the radicals for "man" and "two."

> Fan Ch'ih asked about humanity. Confucius said: "Love men."[12]...Again, Confucius said: "Without humanity a man cannot long endure adversity, nor can he long enjoy prosperity; the wise find it beneficial."[13]

Jen required properly conceived responses to all the many human situations of social life. Someone inquired: "What do you think of requiting injury with kindness?" Confucius said: "How will you then requite kindness? Requite injury with justice, and kindness with kindness."[14]

In general, jen provided the moral foundation for Confucius's humanistic ideal, which included also excellence of many sorts.

Shu   Jen is fulfilled or realized in the closely related quality of *shu*, which is perhaps best translated as "reciprocity."

> Tzu Kung asked: "Is there any one word that can serve as a principle for the conduct of life?" Confucius said: "Perhaps the word 'reciprocity': Do not do to others what you would not want others to do to you."[15]

Western teachers should not be confused by the negative formulation, which is largely the result of Chinese polite convention which seeks not to intrude upon the privacy of another person. The moral sentiment is remarkably similar to that of the "golden rule" of Christianity.

Yi   Jen and shu are applied to specific social relations by means of *i* or *yi*, usually translated as "duty," "obligation," or "righteousness." It is by means of yi that the individual is related to other individuals in the precisely ordered society of ancient China. Yi is the form of social relations, while jen and shu are the human values communicated by this form. While other later thinkers such as Mencius developed this idea, the germ of it is present in Confucius's teachings.

Chih   Still a further basic value of the good life, according to Confucius, is *chih*, or knowledge. While chih included book learning and scholarship, it did not stop there, but extended both to artistic taste and to insight into the good life which constitutes wisdom. The wise person, for Confucius, was one who could take the materials of human nature and shape them into humane patterns. "Confucius said by nature men are pretty much alike; it is learning and practice that set them apart."[16]

For a summary one cannot do better than to quote Confucius's first students and disciples: "There were four things that Confucius was determined to eradicate: a biased mind, arbitrary judgments, obstinacy and egotism."[17] Or again, "Confucius said: Having heard the Way (Tao) in the morning, one may die content in the evening."[18]

Cheng Ming Confucius found a social application of knowledge in the virtue which he called *cheng ming*, usually translated as "rectification of names." It means a kind of semantic honesty in social relations, and especially in political relations. Kings and their subjects should say what they mean and mean what they say. Indeed they should *do* and *be* what they say. The "Sayings" put the matter this way:

> Duke Ching of Ch'i asked Confucius about government. Confucius replied: "Let the prince be the prince, the minister be minister, the father, father, and the son, son."
>
> "Excellent," replied the duke. "Indeed if the prince is not prince the minister not minister the father not father and the son not son, then with all the grain in my possession shall I ever get to eat any?"[19]

He meant apparently that the country would be ruined.

Chün tzu All these values are summed up and embodied in the man whom Confucius called *chün* tzu, variously translated as "magnanimous man," "great man," or "man at his best." It was this man who would put the Confucian teachings into practice and thereby achieve human fulfillment. In many respects this ideal man was similar to the magnanimous man of Aristotle's ethics in ancient Greece. Both ideal men were well-educated, wise, socially conscious aristocrats, whose greatest enjoyment lay in the goods of the mind, but who were willing to assume the tasks of political leadership in their community. Magnanimous man in ancient China and ancient Greece sought and found wise ethical solutions to political problems. He did so by avoiding extremes and cleaving consistently to the middle way, which is also the rational way.

RELIGIOUS ELEMENTS IN CONFU-CIANISM To what extent, if any, do these teachings constitute religion? Are there any religious elements in Confucius's teaching? Or shall we agree with many Chinese scholars who have argued that Confucius's teachings constitute an ethical philosophy but surely not a religion?

As previously noted, if we assume a monotheistic or Judeo-Christian definition of religion, Confucianism is obviously not a religion, but a moral philosophy. Yet in the broader sense of a distinctive system of holy forms which provide orientation for human life, Confucianism comes within the bounds of religion. In western terms, Confucius might be described accurately as a humanistic agnostic. Not God or gods but human beings occupied the center of Confucius's attention. Concerning the shen and the kwei, he bade his followers to honor them but stay aloof.[20] Concerning prayer and afterlife Confucius was agnostic. Asked by his disciples about prayer, he replied cryptically: "My praying has been going on a long while."[21] Asked about life after death, he replied: "Before we are able to do our duty to the living, how can we do it by the spirits of the dead?"[22] Confucius's outlook was summed up precisely in his own aphorism: "To devote oneself earnestly to one's duty to humanity and while respecting the spirits to stay aloof from them may be called wisdom."[23]

Obviously these attitudes do not add up to burning religious zeal. However, at least three religious elements may be detected in Confucius's teachings. First was his love of ritual. His disciple Tzu Kung questioned the ritual sacrifice of sheep, to which Confucius replied, "You love the sheep and I love the ceremony."[24] Lin Yutang has remarked of this aspect of Confucius's teachings that if he had been a Christian, "he would surely have been a high churchman."[25]

A second religious element was Confucius's sense of historical meaning, which located the archetypal good age in the past and sought to return to this idealized past. With different symbols, this glorification of an ideal past has been a recurring attitude in many religions. In the thought of Confucius, the ideal age of the past was the early days of the Chou dynasty. As we have seen, Confucius sought to set the world right by returning to this archaic good time.

Yet the most unmistakably religious element in Confucius's thought was his sense of vocation and mission, his sense of being *called* and *sent*. This attitude is a primary symptom of living religious experience wherever it occurs. In Confucius's case, it was Heaven that called him and sent him forth—or so Confucius believed. Moreover this belief constituted the meaning of his life. Especially during his years of wandering and rejection, this mission sustained him. Hence despite his agnosticism and his scorn of popular religion or superstition, Confucius was in this sense a religious person.

LAO TZU AND CHUANG TZU

Like Confucianism, Taoism originated in the late Chou period. Throughout Chinese history it has been second in importance only to Confucianism, for which it has often served as a foil. Scholars have long argued whether the *Tao te ching* ("Classic of the Way and Its Power") could possibly have been written by Lao tzu, a somewhat shadowy figure who seems to have been an older contemporary of Confucius. While parts of the writing are clearly of later origin (showing the influence of schools and writers who are demonstrably of later times), the weight of scholarly opinion at the present time inclines to Lao tzu (the name means "the Old Master") as a historical figure and the author substantially responsible for the Tao te ching.[26] However, many of the stories which cluster around Lao tzu are easily identifiable as pro-Taoist, anti-Confucian propaganda. Some sociologically minded writers have sought to identify the social class or group responsible for the Tao te ching. For example, Lin Mou-sheng says that the Taoists were "disillusioned intellectuals," in contrast to the successful gentlemen scholars of the Confucian school.[27] Y. L. Fung opines that the Taoists were "hermits."[28]

The Tao te ching is a brief, cryptic poem, usually divided into eighty-one stanzas (though there is a different textual tradition which divides it into sixty-five stanzas). It has been translated into English over forty times and, because of both the generally contextual nature of the Chinese language and the language of the Tao te ching in particular, with widely varying results.

The key term of the Tao te ching is *Tao*, which the previous section of this chapter has identified as a widely recurring term in Chinese language and thought. "Way" or "path" is perhaps the best English rendering of *Tao*, though one translator renders it as "System."[29] We have seen that Confucius used it to characterize the social system and way which he advocated and which he believed to be in accord with Heaven and Earth.

THEMES OF THE TAO TE CHING

The Taoists gave their own highly distinctive mystical and metaphysical interpretation to the idea of Tao. Here we shall list five ideas which recur throughout this remarkable poem.

Nature of the Tao

The most fundamental theme is the nature of the Tao. What then is Tao? The opening lines of the Tao te ching inform us:

> The Tao that can be told of is not the eternal Tao;
> The name that can be named is not the eternal name.[30]

The Tao te ching struggles through many stanzas with the problem of naming the unnameable. The Tao eludes literal designation or naming because it does not fall within the realm to which language primarily refers. However, once this fact is accepted, it is possible by means of metaphor and symbol to find some way to catch the Tao in the human net of words. Several suggestions are made.

The One

One recurring suggestion is to call it "the one" since from the Tao comes one.[31] Another is to designate it by paradox and negation:

> We look at it and do not see it;
>   Its name is The Invisible.
> We listen to it and do not hear it;
>   Its name is The Inaudible.
> We touch it and do not find it;
>   Its name is The Subtle (formless).
> These three cannot be further inquired into,
> And hence merge into one.
> Going up high it is not bright, and coming down low, it is not dark.
> Infinite and boundless, it cannot be given any name;
> It reverts to nothingness.[32]

In addition to the one, these lines show the use of paradox in pointing to the Tao. It is a favorite device, running through the poem.

Symbols

Other symbols for the Tao emerge from study of the Tao te ching, notably water, the female, the uncarved block, the valley, the void, and the infant. All significantly are, in terms of Chinese tradition, yin and not yang. This has led some

Taoist divinity descends from heaven. (Metropolitan Museum of Art, Fletcher Fund, 1938.)

commentators to see a controversy with the dominant Confucianist school, whose terms and images are activist and yang. The Tao te ching says:

> The best (man) is like water.
> Water is good; it benefits all things
>   and does not compete with them.
> It dwells in (lowly) places that all disdain.
> This is why it is so near to Tao.[33]

> The spirit of the valley never dies.
>   It is called the subtle and profound female.
> The gate of the subtle and profound female
>   Is the root of Heaven and Earth.[34]

> Attain complete vacuity.
> Maintain steadfast quietude.
> All things come into being,
> And I see thereby their return.[35]

> He who knows the male (active force) and
>   keeps to the female (the passive force)
> Becomes the ravine of the world.
> He will never depart from eternal virtue,
> But returns to the state of infancy.

He will be proficient in eternal virtue,
And returns to the state of simplicity (uncarved wood).[36]

Anti-Confucianism   Another closely related theme is the overtly anti-Confucian polemic of the Tao te ching. Many stanzas can only be read as deliberate argument against the activist humanitarian ethic of the Confucians. For example, the Tao te ching asserts

Heaven and earth are not humane (jen)
They regard all things as straw dogs.
The sage is not humane.[37]

Even plainer are the following lines:

When the great Tao declined,
The doctrines of humanity (jen) and righteousness (i) arose.
When knowledge and wisdom appeared,
There emerged great hypocrisy.
When the six family relationships are not in harmony
There will be advocacy of filial piety and deep love to children.
When a country is in disorder,
There will be praise of loyal ministers.
Abandon sageliness and discard wisdom;
Then the people will benefit a hundred fold.
Abandon humanity and discard righteousness;
Then the people will return to filial piety and deep love.
. . . .
Abandon skill and discard profit;
Then there will be no thieves or robbers.
However, these three things are ornament (wen) and not adequate.
Therefore let people hold on to these:
    Manifest plainness,
    Embrace simplicity,
    Reduce selfishness,
    Have few desires.[38]

The Natural   In addition to the criticism of Confucianism with its deep involvement in China's pyramidally organized society, the reader can also see in these stanzas the advocacy of a simple, natural way of life. Taoist morality is often termed one of inaction. The Chinese term *wu wei* means "inaction," or "action without action." Many of the texts, taken literally, mean just that. For example, it is said that

Therefore the sage manages affairs without action. . . . [39]

Nevertheless, in context the meaning seems to be one of cooperating with the Tao. Just as a swimmer makes better progress by swimming with the waves than by fighting them, so a person should swim with the wave of Tao. One should thus do what is natural, namely, cooperate with the Tao. The implication is frequently that Confucianism is unnatural.

TAOIST ETHICS Taoist ethics emphasized the way of natural simplicity, and nature's harmony. Like most of the Chou schools it was antimilitarist and had a strong feeling of the evil of war, and also of the coercive processes of government. Taoism was committed to a laissez-faire view of government. "Ruling a big country is like cooking a small fish"; that is to say, too much handling spoils it, asserted the Tao te ching.[40] The ideal social order for Lao tzu was a small rural community away from the urban life and high society so greatly valued by the Confucians.

> Let there be a small country with few people.
> Let there be ten times and a hundred times as many utensils
> But let them not be used.
> Let the people value their lives highly and not migrate far.
> Even if there are ships and carriages, none will ride in them.
> Even if there are arrows and weapons, none will display them.
> . . . .
> Let them relish their food, beautify their clothing, be content with their homes, and delight in their customs.[41]

The contrast with Confucian teaching could hardly be more complete!

CHAUNG TZU'S TEACHINGS The fourth-century wit and mystic Chuang tzu (399–295 BCE) stood in the tradition of Lao tzu, but in several important ways he pushed the Taoist logic onward to new conclusions. Chuang tzu's book combines mystical vision and mordant social criticism. It is the vision of the one which leads to a profound—and comic—sense of the unreality of all else. Or beginning with everyday appearance, Chuang tzu reduced to ridiculous unreality everything which fell short of the One. To western readers this blending of mystical vision and mordant satire—both metaphysical and social—is a most unusual combination. In China, Chuang tzu created a tradition which brought these two elements together, forming a compound of great power and historical significance.

Chuang tzu's book has many passages which express the vision of Tao. The following lines of paradox will suffice for illustration:

> Great Tao has no appellation. Great speech does not say anything. Great humanity is not humane (through any special effort). Great modesty is not yielding. Great courage does not injure. Tao that is displayed is not Tao.... [42]

Human fulfillment lay in ordering one's life according to this pattern.

> He who knows the activities of Nature (*T'ien*, Heaven) and the activities of man is perfect. He who knows the activities of Nature lives according to Nature.... [43]

True to the yin viewpoint of the Taoist tradition, Chuang found the source of things in the abyss of nonbeing.

> In the great beginning, there was non-being. It had neither being nor name. The One originates from it; it has oneness but not yet physical form. When things obtain it and come into existence, that is called virtue (which gives them their in-dividual character). That which is formless is divided [into yin and yang], and from the very beginning going on without interruption is called destiny (*ming*, fate).[44]

It will be noted for Chuang tzu, as for his master Lao tzu, that in these discussions of the Tao or the One, the metaphor of height is conspicuous by its absence. Here is an immanent rather than a transcendent one pervading all things. The Tao is here in our midst, not yonder, elsewhere, or above all things.

It is the vision of this one which generates in Chuang tzu's sharp mind an unremitting sense of the relativity of all things natural and human. If only the One truly *is*, all else is only apparent; its appearances turn out to be mutually contradictory and hence delusory. This led Chuang tzu to his theory of opposites which cancel each other out:

> When there is life there is death, and when there is death there is life. When there is possibility, there is impossibility, and when there is impossibility, there is possibility. Because of the right, there is the wrong, and because of the wrong, there is the right. Therefore the sage does not proceed along these lines but illuminates the matter with Nature.[45]
>
> Pleasure and anger, sorrow and joy, anxiety and regret, fickleness and fear, impulsiveness and extravagance, indulgence and lewdness come to us like music from the hollows or like mushrooms from damp. Day and night they alternate within us but we don't know where they come from....Without them there would not be I. And without me who will experience them? They are right near by. But we don't know who causes them. It seems there is a True Lord who does so, but there is no indication of his existence.[46]

Yet in this curious world of polar opposition and universal relativity each thing seems to find its relative place. So Chuang tzu asked:

> If a man sleeps in a damp place, he will have a pain in his loins and he will dry up and die. Is that true of eels? If a man lives up in a tree, he will be frightened and tremble. Is that true of monkeys? Which of the three knows the right place to live?[47]

Sharp as were his jibes at humankind and society, it was to epistemology that he propounded the ultimately unanswerable question:

> Once I, Chuang Chou, dreamed that I was a butterfly and was happy as a butterfly. I was conscious that I was quite pleased with myself, but I did not know that I was Chou. Suddenly I awoke and there I was, visibly Chou. I do not know whether it was Chou dreaming that he was a butterfly or the butterfly dreaming that it was Chou.[48]

For Confucius and his followers public service was a well-nigh sacred calling. When the messengers of the king came to ask Chuang tzu to become an official advisor, Chuang tzu was fishing. Without looking up, he asked about the fossil tortoise at the royal court. "Is this tortoise better off dead and with its bones venerated or would it be better off alive with its tail dragging in the mud?" The ministers affirmed the latter option, to which Chuang tzu replied, "Then go away and I will drag my tail in the mud!"[49]

To the Confucians and to the Chinese public generally, even more sacred than public service were funeral rites. Chuang tzu subjected them to biting ridicule. When his wife died, his friend Hui Shih came to offer condolence and to his horror found Chuang tzu squatting on the ground, singing, and beating on an earthen bowl. To the visitor's admonition Chuang tzu replied:

> When she died, how could I help being affected? But as I think the matter over, I realize that originally she had no life; and not only no life, she had no form; not only no form, she had no material force (*ch'i*). In the limbo of existence and non-existence, there was transformation and the material force was evolved. The material force...was transformed to become life, and now birth has transformed to become death. This is like the rotation of the four seasons, spring, summer, fall, and winter. Now she lies asleep in the great house (the universe). For me to go about weeping and wailing would be to show my ignorance of destiny. Therefore I desist.[50]

From Lao tzu and Chuang tzu has stemmed a continuing tradition of mingled mysticism and wit.

OTHER CHOU SCHOOLS

While the traditions of Confucius and Lao tzu have predominated in Chinese history, they have by no means been the whole story. The Han historians said there had been six Chou schools. In adition to (1) the Confucianists, or *Ju*, and (2) the Taoists, were (3) the Mohists, (4) the Naturalists, or Yin-Yang school, (5) the Logicians, or school of Names (in Chinese the *Ming chia*), and (6) the Legalists (in Chinese *Fa chia*).

THE MOHISTS The first critic of Confucius was Mo tzu (470–391 BCE), whose criticisms of Concufius stemmed from his own philosophical viewpoint. One of Mo tzu's most characteristic teachings was universal love. Each of us ought to love all people, said Mo tzu, and to love all equally or, as he put it, indiscriminantly. This in turn was based on Mo tzu's belief in the innate goodness of humans, a teaching he shared with all Chou philosophers except the Legalists.

Mo's equalitarian teaching clashed with reigning Confucian view that everyone's love for others must be precisely shaped by social relations. For example, I have an obligation to love my parents more than those of some stranger; and my duty to my ruler differs from my duty to a serf. Confucius's doctrine was that of discriminating love, in contrast to Mo tzu's teaching of equal and indiscriminating love for all people.

Mo declared boldly that for the individual and for society universal love would yield altogether desirable results. Part of this confidence came from his conviction that love naturally "worked" as a basis for human life. As many western students of Mo tzu have said, he was a utilitarian. Yet Mo also believed tht Heaven sanctioned love—and also placed a divine veto on other different and opposing ends or goals of life.

Mo tzu's views of Heaven were sharply critical of Confucius. Where Confucius looked upon Heaven in largely impersonal terms, Mo tzu (alone among the six philosophies) viewed Heaven as personal. Heaven, or God, wills righteousness and also the well-being of the people. People must obey Heaven as they obey the personal will of a human superior, declared Mo. They would also be well advised to heed the oracles by which Heaven's will is made known to us, he added.

In still another way Mo tzu set himself against Confucius. Where Confucius sought to turn back to the ideal goodness of early Chou dynasty, Mo tzu sought to return to the even earlier and simpler times of the Hsia. He outdid Confucius in his choice of the ideal age at the beginning of things.

In view of these features of his thought, it is not surprising that Mo tzu envisaged a simple way of life for his ideal society. Its citizens would be farmers living under a king who did Heaven's will, seeking above all his people's well-being. The good king would seek his people's welfare in literally every department of life, yet nowhere more than in his avoidance of the supreme evil and folly of war. Moreover, the elaborate and expensive rituals of later days would not be present in the ideal times; funerals were to be simple. Mo tzu had harsh words for expensive Confucian funerals.

THE NATURAL-ISTS

The Yin-Yang school was in Chou times little more than a name, a book, and a list of terms. Tsou Yen (305–240 BCE) was identified by Han historians as the founder. It was apparently a school devoted to metaphysics and cosmology which sought to explain things in nature and events in history by their combinations of yin and yang, and also by the five elements or agents: water, fire, wood, metal, and earth. Later, in Han times, this school came to prominence, but before then it is shrouded in obscurity.

THE SCHOOL OF NAMES

The school of Names, or Ming chia, was represented in Chou times by Hui Shih (380–305 BCE) (the friend who visited Chuang tzu at his wife's death), and Kung-sun Lung (b. 380 BCE). These men had no monopoly on the concern with names or words, for this interest was widespread in ancient China. Yet for the school of Names this was the dominant concern, although Hui and Kung-sun frequently disagreed with each other.

What comes down to us from these men are statements of some puzzles, problems, and paradoxes which have fascinated and bewildered students throughout subsequent Chinese history. Hui Shi, for example, propounded the following statement of limiting concepts:

The greatest has nothing beyond itself; it is called the great unit.
The smallest has nothing within itself; it is called the small unit.[51]

Was he thinking of the universal flux of all things in the following:

When the sun is at noon it is setting; when there is life, there is death.[52]

The cosmic orientation of this system of thought is apparent in the following:

Love all things extensively. Heaven and earth form one body.[53]

He also left a budget of debators' paradoxes on which presumably his students sharpened their wits, such as the following:

The pointing of the finger does not reach [a thing]; the reaching never ends.
    A white dog is black.
An orphan colt has never had a mother.
Take a stick one foot long and cut in half every day and you will never exhaust it
    even after ten thousand generations.[54]

Kung-sun Lung occupied himself with the closely related problem of predication. For example, a famous chapter in the Kung-sun Lung book dealt with the question of whether a white horse is a horse. His ideas were developed into a subtle theory of the relation of names (or marks) to the world of things. He seems to have distinguished between what modern western philosophers call *primary* and *secondary* properties.[55]

While the school of Names ceased to exist after Chou times, its achievements were caught up and carried on by other schools and other philosophers.

**THE LEGAL-
ISTS**

Unique among the Chou schools was that known to western students as the Legalists; in Chinese it was called *Fa chia*, which Fung has translated as "men of methods," that is, realistic political methods. It was a school of Machiavellian realism, popular among ancient Chinese rulers and their advisors. Notable among its exponents were Lord Shang (d. 388 BCE), Han Fei tzu (d. 233 BCE), and Li tzu, who was the chief minister of the Ch'in emperor, Shih Huang-ti. The Legalist school was the official school during the Ch'in dynasty, and seems indeed to have had significant influence upon the career of this dynasty. It fell from favor with the fall of the Ch'in. Han Fei tzu was influenced by his teacher Hsün tzu, who was known to history as a heterodox Confucian, but who shared important doctrines with the Legalists. Apparently Han Fei derived from his teacher the notion, rare in ancient Chinese thought, that human nature was not good but evil.

Basically the Legalist school believed in coercive power. Rejecting especially the moral standards of the Confucians and the religious sanctions of the Mohists, the Legalists taught that to be successful, rulers must practice the art of power politics. Their law must be clear and backed by both generous rewards and severe penalties, well known to all. Individual violence, threats, warfare, and regimentation of people must be used by rulers without hesitation when the need arises. The unforgivable crime of rulers is weakness.

Human beings, according to the Legalist theory, are not good or righteous by nature, and hence respond to the hope of reward or the fear of penalty. A human being is, in short, by nature an egotist. The wise ruler knows this, and is able to take this refractory human material and mold it into something resembling a good life. But this good life is the ruler's achievement and not the gift of nature.

Legalism's social ethic envisaged a simple society consisting of farmers, soldiers, and rulers. In particular, the Legalists inveighed against merchants and scholars with their decadent and recalcitrant ways. In the words of Han Fei, they were the vermin of the state. Li tzu practiced this antipathy to scholars who opposed the harsh rule of the Ch'in first emperor. In 215 BCE he issued the order requiring scholars to turn in for destruction all books other than official Ch'in documents. It was a harsh episode in a tyrannical regime. Small wonder that later thinkers looked back upon the Legalists with disapproval amounting to horror.

CONFUCIAN TRADITION IN DEVELOPMENT

Fourteen centuries after they lived, Mencius and Hsün tzu were formally declared by Chu Hsi (1130–1200 CE) to be the "orthodox" champion and the "heterodox" champion respectively. In ancient times they were simply two writers who developed divergent interpretations of the growing Confucian tradition. Mencius, or Meng K'o (371–289 BCE), was roused by the opposition to defend, explain, and amplify the teachings of Confucius. "The words Yang Chu and Mo tzu fill the land," he warned. Yang Chu was a fourth-century hedonist and cynic, and between his extreme and the simple-minded rustic virtue of Mo tzu, Mencius sought to recall his country to the middle way of Confucius.

The life of Mencius bears striking resemblance of that of Confucius. Reared by a devoted and widowed mother, Mencius developed early in life a concern for ritual propriety. He is said even as a child to have played at funeral rituals. Like his master, he sought public office in order, as an advisor to rulers, to reform the government; but like Confucius he failed and wandered from state to state. Like Confucius he was a highly successful schoolmaster. He too retired to his home state, spending his last days in writing and scholarship. He died at the age of eighty-one.

His teachings may be regarded as underscoring and amplifying certain themes and issues of Confucius. He took the idea of human goodness and made it somewhat more explicit and emphatic than did Confucius. The inherently generous and social nature of humans is illustrated by the fact that everyone instinctively runs to help a child who has fallen into a well. Similarly, Mencius asserted, humans are properly remorseful when they have been selfish or cruel.

In interpreting this goodness, he sided in one very important respect with

Confucius against Mo tzu. Where the latter asserted the duty of equal and universal love for all people, Mencius and Confucius argued that love must be discriminating. Its application must be related to the social rank and situation of its recipient. Love guided by reason and related to a well-ordered society is the fulfillment of human life.

In society, the goodness of the people requires the knowledge of a wise ruler if it is to be realized. It is the duty of such rulers to devote themselves to the well-being of their subjects; if they rule to their own advantage, they become thereby evil. This devotion to the well-being of the people is the distinguishing mark of a good and great ruler.

Mencius also spelled out with particular emphasis the evil of war. "War makers are robbers of the people," he said; good rulers are those who maintain the peace. Mencius viewed war as Heaven's punishment against human wrongs and evils. Yet he also taught the right of rebellion against an evil ruler who had apparently lost Heaven's mandate.

A final aspect of Mencius's teaching is often called his *mysticism*. Like Confucius he taught the mandate of Heaven; but here again he pushed the teaching further, saying that in the will of Heaven there is an appointment for everyone and everything. This sense of calling was understood in terms of each person's inner disposition. The virtuous knew their calling, or appointment, by means of inner awareness.

Hsün tzu (298–238 BCE) disagreed with almost all the distinctive views of Mencius. He believed and taught that humans are by nature evil. Therefore, to give expression to our nature is to set loose the forces of chaos and conflict. Rather, our egotistical nature must be trained, guided, and controlled by a strong ruler. Out of such guidance comes whatever goodness humans are capable of. As previously noted, Hsün tzu was the teacher of Han Fei, the Legalist.

Hsün tzu also pushed beyond Confucius in his teaching of the impersonality of Nature or Heaven. The processes of nature, from rainfall to the movement of the stars, take place in ways altogether indifferent to humans and utterly heedless of their prayers, incantations, and sacrifices. Here was a naturalism which was radically critical of popular religion with its prayers, sacrifices, and good and evil spirits. Yet Hsün tzu would not abolish the rites and sacrifices, for they aroused human and useful feelings. They also had an esthetic appeal. Hsün tzu seems never to have asked whether religious ritual could long persist on this basis.

Documents also made their contributions to the developing Confucian tradition, notably the "Great Learning" (*Ta hsüeh*) and the "Doctrine of the Mean" (*Chung yung*). The great Sung scholar, Chu Hsi, selected these two texts along with Confucius's Mencius's "Analects" and Mencius's book to constitute the so-called Four Books which, for six centuries after Chu Hsi until the fall of the Manchu dynasty in 1911 CE, constituted the primer of Chinese education, studied and committed to memory before students began the Five Classics.

The "Great Learning" is a brief essay of somewhat uncertain authorship; its ideas if not its words go back to Confucius, and it stands clearly in the Confucian tradition. It is devoted to the Confucian ideal of self-cultivation or self-realization by means of study, or what the text itself calls the "investigation of things." As the "Great Learning" asserts:

> The extension of knowledge lay in the investigation of things. For only when things are investigated is knowledge extended; only when knowledge is extended are thoughts sincere; only when thoughts are sincere are minds rectified; only when minds are rectified are our persons cultivated; only when our persons are cultivated are our families regulated; only when families are regulated are states well governed; and only when states are well governed is there peace in the world.[56]

"The Mean" (Chung yung) is a brief and anonymous essay in the Confucian tradition. Its key idea is that of "centrality" (*chung*), meaning moderation, balance, and suitableness in the conduct of life. A persistent emphasis of the Chung yung is that in following this ideal, one places oneself in accord with Heaven and Heaven's way.

The second important concept is that of "sincerity" or "truth" (*ch'eng*). This is essential to the full development of human nature. Sincerity is self-completing and self-directing. "Sincerity is the beginning and end of things; without sincerity there is no existence." To cultivate sincerity is to walk in the way of Heaven and Earth which is "broad and deep, transcendental and intelligent, extensive and everlasting."[57]

The Han Establishment of Confucianism

The Ch'in dynasty failed in its bold attempt to unify China. Cruel and high-handed methods carried out by Shih Huang-ti, and rationalized by the official Legalist philosophy, produced an inevitable reaction. After Shih Huang-ti's death in 210 BCE, his ministers strove in vain to continue the dynasty under his weak son. By 206 BCE the Ch'in had disappeared. Out of rebellion and struggle for power emerged Lin Chi, or Kao tzu, founder of the Han dynasty. Except for an interregnum under the usurper Wang Mang, 9–23 CE, the Han dynasty lasted until 220 CE. It was the great imperial, classic age of ancient China.

If we ask why and how the Han emperors succeeded where the Ch'in failed, at least a significant part of the answer lies in their willingness to consolidate power more slowly. In all this, the Confucian philosophy played a significant role as the official philosophy. To be sure, the actual behavior of the Han emperors was sometimes guided by Legalist precepts, but it was rationalized in Confucian terms. The new Han synthesis of philosophies was not pure Confucianism, but a blend of elements of Legalist policies and Taoist metaphysics, as well as ingredients from the Five Agents school and the "Book of Changes."

The central theme of the emergent synthesis was the role of the emperor in his relations on the one hand to the Central Kingdom and its people and on the other to Heaven and Earth. Official views gave to the emperor a position of moral leadership and ritual representation of his people. Yet so far as the day-to-day business of government was concerned, this was assigned to bureaucrats, while the emperor was placed behind a screen of mystery. From this lofty position his office provided sanction for the activities of government.

Ritual sanction was given by the emperor's leadership in ceremonial activities, including notably the sacrifices to Heaven and Earth. A crucial idea in this system was the mandate of Heaven, according to which Heaven's will was manifested in the acts and person of the sovereign. Theoretically, at least, his mandate might be lost by defects and misdeeds on the part of the sovereign. Successful and prosperous rule was widely interpreted as possession of the mandate. More cynical commentators pointed out that the mandate came to rest upon an emperor at the moment when the strength of his sword succeeded in placing him in governmental power.

At a more popular level of thought and feeling, power was rationalized in ancient China by omens, portents, and prodigies, reported and interpreted by court astrologers, philosophers, or oracles. Such omens might be either affirmative or negative, but they were widely believed to declare Heaven's will to the inhabitants of Earth.

Many minds and hands participated in the enterprise of creating and maintaining this official Han Confucian synthesis. The court historians Ssuma Tan and his son Ssuma Ch'ien contributed historical lore concerning the "hundred schools" of Chou times. Men pored over the "Book of Changes" with its trigrams and hexagrams, interpreting not only nature but politics and history in its occult terms. They also added an appendix to the "Book of Changes," which was to prove very important to later ages.

Among the contributors none was more important than Tung Chung-shu, 179?–90? BCE, official court philosopher and counselor to emperors, author of a commentary on the "Spring and Autumn Annals," but most of all synthesizer of Han Confucianism. Tung's own thought seems to have contained important metaphysical ideas from the Five Agents school and also from Taoism. So he interpreted Han politics in terms of their supposed ingredients of wood, fire, earth, metal, and water. Yet all this was held under the dominant Confucian ideas of Heaven, Earth, and Man.

On human nature and education, Tung had his own thoughts, which attempted to synthesize the views of Mencius with those of Hsün tzu. Noting that theorists disagreed on the question of human goodness, Tung developed the idea that good was a term which could not properly be applied to the raw material of human nature. Only by education and political guidance could goodness be achieved. For this reason Heaven ordains both education and politics for the high goal of human fulfillment. As Tung put it, "From Heaven the people receive their potentially good nature, and from the king the education which completes it. It is the duty and function of the king to submit to the will of Heaven, and thus to bring to completion the nature of the people."[58]

As advisor to the emperor, Tung Chung-shu took important steps in the establishment of Confucianism. In 136 BCE he submitted to Emperor Wu the memorial establishing Confucian teaching as the official system of the empire. It read in part: "Your unworthy servant considers that all that is not encompassed by the Six Disciplines and the arts of Confucius should be suppressed and not allowed to continue further, and evil and vain theories stamped out. Only then will unity be achieved, the laws made clear, and the people know what to follow."[59]

Tung followed this move twelve years later, in 124 BCE, with a proposal to found an official Confucian university at the capital. One of the purposes of this university was to supply a trained governmental bureaucracy. By the end of the first century BCE there were 3,000 students in attendance, and in later Han times, the number rose to 30,000. In this way Tung built a bureaucracy well schooled in Confucian philosophy. Tung's work was later to grow into the famous examination system.

In later Han times Confucianism moved further toward its secure establishment by the adoption of official texts of the Confucian classics. Ever since the Ch'in book burning in 214 BCE two sets of texts had existed: New Texts, written in the new script of Ch'in and Han times and doubtless incorporating the views of their newer redactors, and Old Texts, written in the archaic characters of Chou times and claiming to be the pure ancient texts. This situation produced a long-continued scholars' battle between proponents of the Old Texts and the New Texts. It was a battle in which emperors intervened to support one set of views or to repress opposing views. Finally, in 79 CE, in a document called "Discussions in the White Tiger Hall," an official and final recension was achieved. Yet silk scrolls were impermanent things in an impermanent world, and a century later, in 179, by imperial edict, the complete text of the Five Classics and the "Sayings of Confucius" were engraved in stone and set up in a place of honor at the imperial university.[60]

During the Han dynasty the official rites to Confucius began. In 195 BCE Kao tzu, founder of the Han dynasty, performed sacrifices at the tomb of Confucius, though that doughty old warrior was doubtless motivated more by political expediency than by piety. Similar ceremonies at national and prefectural capitals began in 59 CE as part of the Han establishment of Confucianism. During the centuries which followed, the rites to Heaven and Earth and to Confucius provided a unifying cultus for the people of the Central Kingdom. The ceremonies to Confucius became progressively more elaborate. Instrumental music, ceremonial dances, libations of wine, and choral music were progressively added. Confucius himself was given progressively higher titles, first "duke," then "king." Scholars of the Sung dynasty, be it noted, withheld the title "emperor." Ming dynasty scholars reformed and simplified the rites, limiting Confucius to "Master K'ung, the perfectly holy teacher of antiquity." This continued until 1906, when the Manchus in a last desperate effort to stabilize their tottering throne declared Confucius "co-equal with Heaven and Earth." All this was destined to be swept away with the fall of the empire and the coming of the Republic of China in 1911.

While these developments were beginning in high official circles, popular piety also was according a higher and higher position to Confucius in its own way. From Han times onward he was accorded a supernatural birth, and miracle upon miracle was attributed to him. The wonder tales grew with the passage of time.[61] These movements in popular piety in China (as elsewhere in human history) often provoked reactions of skepticism and naturalism among intellectuals. We have already glimpsed the naturalistic views of Hsün tzu at the end of the Chou period. These views were taken up and given mordant expression in later Han times in the writings of Wang Ch'ung (27–97 CE). His *Lun heng*, or "Critical Essays" expressed a single continuous theme, "hatred of fictions and falsehoods."[62] Wang applied his theme to the religious issues of his time. He never tired of pouring scorn on anthropomorphic or personal views of Heaven. "Some foolish men say that Heaven produces silk and grain expressly for man's well-being," but, comments Wang scornfully, this is to "make Heaven a farmer or the mulberry girl of man."[63] Mature and reasonable people are led, rather, to the opposite viewpoint, to a thoroughly naturalistic, impersonal conception of Heaven.

Similarly Wang challenged the popular view that "when men die they become ghosts with consciousness and the power to harm others."[64] All the evidence leads to the opposite conclusion, that when the body dies and decays, consciousness ceases. The popular fear of ghosts is sheer groundless superstition.

Wang also turned his sharp knife upon contemporary scholars who accepted doctrines on their teacher's say-so or because they were ancient. They ought instead to use their critical reason. In similar vein he looked with disdain upon the increasing honor paid to Confucius and his "Analects." Such honor leads to irrational obscurantism. Again, critical reason ought to be one's guide and authority.

NEO-TAOISM

With the fall of the Han dynasty in 220 CE began a period of more than three centuries of disorder and disintegration unprecedented in Chinese history and often referred to as the period of Three Kingdoms (220–280) and Six Dynasties (280–589). During these troubled centuries the Chinese tradition came closer to chaos and complete discontinuity than at any other time in its long history.

Our interest in these historical developments is in their impact upon religion. The rise to prominence of Taoism and the coming of Buddhism to China during this period are not matters of coincidence, but rather must be understood in large measure as responses to this time of troubles. People sought refuge from the storms of their times either in Taoist gardens or in Buddhist monasteries.

Neo-Taoism is a western scholar's designation for the revival of interest in the writings of Lao tzu and Chuang tzu during the third, fourth, and fifth centuries. The fall of the Han dynasty inevitably damaged the prestige of the Confucianism so closely connected with it. Yet it must also be pointed out that many of those who wrote with fresh appreciation of Lao tzu and Chuang tzu during this period also continued to regard themselves as good Confucianists. They found lines from Confucius's teachings to support their Taoist views; notable among such lines was Confucius's remark that "Yen Hui was nearly perfect but often empty."[65] Confucius did not disappear from the scene, but only receded into the background, while the "dark learning" (*hsüan hsüeh*) of Lao tzu and Chuang tzu came into new prominence. Three new accents or emphases were heard in Taoist thought. Y. L. Fung has spoken of rationalists and sentimentalists.[66] With these must be considered a third development, the emergence of a popular religious brand of Taoism.

RATIONALISM

One of the greatest philosophical works of the neo-Taoist period was the "Commentary on the Chuang tzu" attributed to Kuo Hsiang (d. 312 CE). There seems to have been some confusion between Kuo and another figure named Hsiang Hsiu, who lived a generation earlier and held similar views. Whatever the authorship, the result was a distinctive philosophical perspective which came to be known as the Kuo-Hsiang viewpoint, and which consisted of a systematization and development of suggestions made by Chuang tzu and Lao tzu.

The primary tenet of the Kuo-Hsiang viewpoint was that the Tao is "nothing." (*wu*). Lao tzu and Chuang tzu had said this centuries before, meaning probably that the Tao is not any particular thing. The Kuo-Hsiang pushed onward to the view that Nature (*Tien*, Heaven) is simply "the general name for all things."[67] This meant that Nature, or Heaven, is not to be identified with any particular thing, either "here" or "up there." It is simply the scheme of things entire. Since it is literally not any thing, it is *wu*, or emptiness. Yet as the universe it simply and eternally *is*.

Negatively, Kuo-Hsiang argued that there is no creator or lord. Chuang tzu had questioned whether or not such a lord existed; now Kuo-Hsiang answered with a definite negative. There is simply no adequate evidence for the existence of a lord.[68]

The Kuo-Hsiang philosophy was one of flux and had a clear view of the process of change which embraced all things. This process was known as the self-transformation of things, which might be characterized as the way in which each thing comes to be and passes away in the never-ceasing process of becoming. Yet there is a relation between the universe and the flux of things. As Fung has put it, "everything that exists in the universe needs the universe as a whole as a necessary condition of its existence, yet its existence is not directly produced by any other particular thing."[69]

The Kuo-Hsiang viewpoint carried this idea of change into its view of human institutions and morals. Changing customs and morals may justifiably be regarded as the human response to ever-changing circumstances. In the face of the changing human world, Kuo-Hsiang recommended two attitudes, a Taoist simplicity of mind, and an alternation, as circumstances might demand, between activity and passivity (*yu-wei* and *wu-wei*).

The Kuo-Hsiang viewpoint drew out and made explicit still another suggestion of Lao tzu and Chuang tzu, namely, the absolute freedom of the individual. According to this view the individual has the sovereign possibility of withdrawing from social circumstances into his or her own individual and free life.

ROMANTICISM

Other followers of the dark learning were less philosophically inclined. Rather they were men of letters and esthetes. Fung calls them romantics and sentimentalists devoted to *feng liu* (literally "wind and stream"), or nature. They drew upon the Taoist tradition of a "return to nature" as a way of escape from the evils, artificialities, and responsibilities of society. Writers of this school showed a refined and sophisticated hedonism as deliberate and explicit as any in human history. They wrote a famous forgery, the *Lieh tzu* book, attributing their ideas to the shadowy traditional fifth-century BCE figure of Lieh tzu. The famous Yang Chu chapter of this book, translated into English under the title "Yang Chu's Garden of Pleasure," makes the refined and subtle pursuit of pleasure the chief end of human beings, or at least of wise ones.

Similar in outlook was the group called the "Seven Sages of the Bamboo Grove," of the late third and early fourth centuries. In deliberate rejection of Confucian social responsibility they devoted themselves to *ch'ing t'an*, or pure conversation. Pleasure, conviviality, and wit sharpened to a razor's edge were their goals. To their garden of pleasure, or bamboo grove, they withdrew from the turmoil of their times. One member of the group was said to have been followed by a servant with a jug of wine and a spade, the former to refresh him and the latter to bury him if he fell dead. Another story tells about Juan Chi and his nephew Juan Hsien, who with their families were great drinkers and who when they met did not bother to drink out of cups but sat on the floor and drank from a large jar. The story concludes on the following note of naturalism: "And then the Juans drank with the pigs."[70]

Another member of this group was fond of cranes. He was given two young cranes and in order to prevent their flying away clipped their wings. But the clipped cranes seemed despondent, and when their feathers had grown out, the master let them fly away.[71] Still another member of the group, Wang Hui-chih (d.388), opened his window one night on a fresh snowfall whose gleaming whiteness made him think of a distant friend. Immediately he set out to visit the friend though the journey took the whole night. Reaching the friend's house he was about to knock on the door when, on a new impulse, he turned about and returned to his own home.[72]

POPULAR RELIGION

Still a third new development of the Taoist tradition was the emergence of a popular religious movement with its own myth and ritual and much given to magic, shamanry, and similar phenomena. This is only one of many instances in the history of religions in which magic follows mysticism. The reason apparently is that mystics speak in metaphors. They do so necessarily, for this is the only way in which to put into words of the ordinary world their supraworldly message. In the case of Lao tzu and Taoism, the claim to know the eternal Tao was central.

It was only a step from *knowing* the eternal to *becoming*, oneself, eternal or immortal. The Chinese have always had a hankering for elixirs and charms to produce earthly immortality, and Taoism greatly accentuated the trend. It was easy enough for earthly and literal-minded followers of Lao tzu and Chuang tzu to bend their words to this end. The result was that the Tao became a kind of recipe for endless life, which would be guarded and protected apparently forever against all hazards and evils.

These trends gathered momentum during Han times. The emperor Wu Ti, despite his patronage of Confucianism, was much attracted to Taoism and was especially interested in the effort of alchemy to change cinnabar to gold. Chinese alchemy connected "edible gold," or cinnabar, with immortality, a connection that cost some men their lives, since cinnabar is poison. Wu Ti was informed by a court geomancer that if he would perform certain ceremonies to Heaven on a Taoist sacred mountain he would not die. The outcome of this experiment is unknown.

In the first century an enterprising religious leader named Chang Tao-ling founded a secret society devoted to the pursuit of immortality by means of alchemy combined with various techniques of meditation. Since all members of the society had to pay an admission fee of five bushels of rice, his sect came to be called the "Five Bushels of Rice Way" (*Wu Tou Mi Tao*). Under the successive leadership of his son and grandson this organization grew to considerable power. Members said that Chang had discovered the true elixir of immortality and had actually been assumed to heaven on the back of a tiger from the top of the sacred Dragon-Tiger Mountain (Lung-hu in Kiangsi Province). They added that Lao tzu had appeared to him and conferred on him the title "Celestial Teacher." Chang's successors became the line of Taoist "popes," actually chief necromancers living atop Dragon-Tiger Mountain, and in recent centuries doing little but blessing charms and talismans.

The fourth-century scholar Ko Hung wrote a book, *Pao p'o tzu*, devoted to the exposition and defense of the Taoist search for immortality.[73] With ingenious arguments based on the putative immortality of animals such as the crane and turtle, Ko defended the possibility of living forever. He did scholarly research in the extensive lore on this subject in China, including even a volume which explored sexual techniques for achieving endless life.[74] Ko also carried on experiments with magic and alchemy, involving a pill for immortality. Small wonder that his followers told the story that when Ko was eighty-one a friend came to visit him and found only his empty clothes—apparently sufficient proof that he had joined the Taoist immortals!

Popular Taoism also developed an extensive myth and ritual, largely in reaction to the coming of Buddhism to China. Devotion to Buddha appealed to many Chinese people, but it led others to seek for a Chinese figure who might serve a similar function. This process had actually begun in 165 CE when the Han emperor made sacrifices to Lao tzu and built a temple to him. Later, in competition with Buddhism, Lao tzu was accorded virtually divine titles and heavenly associates. Taoist writings were compiled into a canon of holy scripture, and in short, Taoism was launched as a religion. In this process there are clear instances of fabrication of both myth and ritual. On at least three occasions Taoists also gained sufficient power in governmental circles to mount campaigns of harassment or persecution against Buddhism, first in 446, under Emperor T'ai Wu of the northern Wei dynasty, then in 574, under Emperor Wu of the northern Chou dynasty, and most extensively and importantly in 845, under the half-mad Emperor Wu Tsung of the T'ang dynasty.

Meanwhile, as a popular religion Taoism continued to flourish, thriving apparently on felt needs and wishes of the Chinese masses. Many of its gods and godlings have been for centuries a part of the Chinese tradition. There are the "eight immortals," celebrated in legend, pictures, and images. According to Taoist myth these happy folk live in the islands of the blessed, where they are pictured, some sipping wine heated by one of their number while another plays

Contemporary worship at Yuang Tong Temple, Kunming, China. (Ira Kirchenbaum/Stock, Boston.)

the flute. Often pictured alone is the maiden Ho Hsien Ku, who gained immortality through a diet of mother-of-pearl. There is Tsao Shin, the god of the hearth, who is the silent observer in chimney corners and kitchens throughout China. There is also Ch'eng Huang, city god, and innumerable others, gods, spirits, and guardians who claim a place in the Taoist pantheon.

In more recent centuries, popular Taoism has fallen on evil times, and appears to be headed for extinction. This is a topic to which we shall return in the last section of this chapter. However, it is important in this connection to realize that many of the words, ideas, and images of Taoist philosophy and literature found lodgment and new life in Chinese Buddhism, especially Ch'an, or Zen.

CHINESE BUDDHISM

HISTORY

Chinese Buddhist tradition tells the story of the Han emperor Ming Ti (58–75 CE), who saw a vision of a golden man who turned out to be Buddha. On the advice of his counselors, the emperor sent to India for more details and received in return an embassy of Indian monks with Sutras and images. This story, however, has been traced to a forgery of ca. 200 CE.[75] But there is authentic evidence of Buddhism in China even before this time. It traveled from India apparently by way of the trade routes of central Asia. In the second-century literature one begins to see the names of outstanding Buddhist missionaries and translators of Sanskrit texts into Chinese. Notable among such figures was a Parthian prince known to history by his Chinese name, An Shih-kao, who was active at the Chinese capital, Loyang, during the latter half of the second century. Two centuries later, Kumarajiva stands out as translator and missionary and one of the greatest transmitters of Buddhist faith to China. The son of an Indian father and a Kuchan princess, Kumarajiva studied Theravada Buddhism in Kashmir, but was subsequently converted to Mahayana by a reading of Nagarjuna's philosophy. He was seized by an invading Chinese army and carried off to China as a prisoner of war. In the first years of the fifth century he was welcomed to the Chinese capital of Ch'ang'-an, and given the title of "national preceptor," i.e., teacher to the nation. From then until his death in 413, he was active in translation of Indian Mahayana Buddhist documents into Chinese.

Another development was the extensive travel to India by Chinese monks and students of Buddhism. Over the period from the third to the eighth century no less than 200 Chinese students made the perilous journey, many of them to the famous Buddhist university of Nalanda.[76] Two of these men are known by their travel records, namely Fa Hsien, who went to India in 399 by way of central Asia and returned by sea in 414, and Hsüan Tsang, who made the round trip between 629 and 645, by way of central Asia. There were doubtless many others whose records are lost to us, but they returned to China laden with Buddhist texts, images, and ideas.

Buddhism found lodgment in China at this period of Chinese history for many reasons. The fall of the Han dynasty brought a great lowering of prestige to the Confucian teachings, which had been the established faith of the fallen dynasty. The three centuries which followed the fall of the Han were as chaotic and disordered as any period in Chinese history. In such periods people seek shelter from the storms of their times. As already noted, some sought escape in neo-Taoist gardens of pleasure. The rise of neo-Taoism, with its teaching of emancipation of the individual from the social context, was an additional factor favorable to the reception of Buddhism. Taoism provided similarity not only in ideas, but also in words for the difficult task of putting Buddhism's Indian message into the Chinese language.

It would be false to suppose that there was no resistance to the new faith. To many proud citizens of the Central Kingdom, Buddhism was nothing more than an outlandish doctrine of barbarian peoples to the west. They pointed for confirmation to the fact that neither Buddha nor his teaching was mentioned in the Chinese classics, and drew the conclusion that therefore Buddha and his teaching were unworthy of their notice.

One record of the arguments between apologists for Buddhism and Chinese opponents of the new faith is preserved in a document called the *Mou tzu.*[77] It is a valuable record of Chinese charges against Buddhism, and of Buddhist answers to the charges. It noted the argument that Buddhist monasticism and asceticism seemed to conflict with filial piety, for a monk had no family or family ties. His ascetic practices violated his body, which was the gift of his parents. Further his refusal to bow to the ruler seemed clearly subversive and unChinese. Such were the charges, and one by one the *Mou tzu* sought rational answers to them.

The Buddhist missionaries won their argument, at least in the opinion of great numbers of their compatriots who between the fourth and eighth centuries turned to Buddhism. So great were their numbers that in many books of history T'ang China was called *Buddha land*. To the Chinese mind, Buddhism brought a new dimension of transcendence. To the intellectuals it brought an Archimedean point or fulcrum above or beyond the traditional cosmos, or world of nature and society. To the populace it brought good news of a manystoried heaven which might be theirs—not to speak of an equally populated region of hell, as well as Buddhist saviors who would be friends and guides here and hereafter. To many Chinese people Buddhism also brought a more active compassion expressed in works of philanthropy. Conversely, Buddhism was transformed by its encounter with China.[78] The very process of translation, achieved, as we have noted, with the help of Taoist terms, aided in the transformation. To sum up this vast and complicated change, China brought Buddhism down to earth and gave it many new Chinese emphases and accents.

SECTS IN CHINESE BUDDHISM

One feature of Chinese Buddhism which is of considerable historical interest was its fragmentation into sects. Indian Buddhism, to be sure, had produced a

Eleven-headed bodhisattva of T'ang dynasty. (Cleveland Museum of Art, Mr. and Mrs. S. Millikan Collection.)

variety of schools, each arguing the validity of its own teaching. Yet the sectarian divisions of Chinese Buddhism represented a new development. Each Chinese group centered in a particular Indian text which it held and taught as essential truth, and around which it gathered its adherents. These sectarian divisions in Chinese Buddhism are often compared to those of Protestant Christianity. In some ways the analogy is accurate; however, in one respect it is misleading, for Chinese Buddhist sects seldom or never made exclusive claims of the sort so frequent in Protestant Christianity. The Chinese Buddhist groups are also important as background of similar (but by no means identical) groups in Japan.

At least three Hinayana or Theravada sects sprang up in third- and fourth-century China as imports from India. But in the contest for the mind and heart of China, they proved no match for the Mahayana interpretation of Buddhism. In the case of both Theravada and Mahayana groups, the first ones were organized around particular texts and bodies of teaching brought directly from India.

One such early Mahayana group was the *San Lun*, or "Three Treatises," founded by Chi Tsang (549–625 CE). Of the three treatises, two were by Nagarjuna and one by his disciple Aryadeva. When this sect fell into extinction, Nagarjuna's great influence was passed on through others. Another early sect was the *Wei Shih*, or "Consciousness Only" group, founded by the great traveler to India, Hsüan Tsang (596–664), who during his life was one of the leading Buddhists of China. This sect followed the doctrines of the Indian Yogacarya school of Asanga and Vasubandhu. Still a third early Mahayana sect was *Hua Yen*, or "Flower Garland," so called from the name of its favorite Indian Sutra, the Avatamsaka. Its nominal founder was Tu-shun (557–640) but its great master was Fa-tsang (643–712). The influence of these men and groups penetrated Chinese Buddhism and has continued in other sects and traditions.

Three main families of sects have formed the main continuing tradition of Chinese Buddhism: (1) *T'ien t'ai* ("Heavenly Terrace," named for the mountain where its main monastery was located), (2) *Ching-tu* ("Pure Land," named for the pure land of heaven promised to its followers), and (3) *Ch'an* ("Meditation," or dhyana, which is its central teaching).

T'IEN T'AI (HEAVENLY TERRACE)

T'ien t'ai Buddhism was founded by Chih-I (538–597), or Chih-k'ai, as he was sometimes called. He was a war orphan who turned to Buddhist religious practice. Possessed of a subtle and powerful philosophic mind, he was awakened by his teacher, Hui-ssu, to another and different dimension of Buddhism, namely, religious meditation. His synthesis of philosophy and meditation has characterized T'ien t'ai tradition in China and Japan ever since. Its followers have consistently maintained the double emphasis of "eyes of wisdom and legs of practice."[79]

Chih-k'ai's careful study of the Saddharma Pundarika, or "Lotus Sutra," convinced him that it contained the whole of essential Buddhist truth. His main writing was entitled *The Profound Meaning of the Scripture of the Lotus of the Wonderful Law*; his followers have continued to study, expand, and recite this document. Chih-k'ai also taught that Buddha, after he had achieved enlightenment, went successively through five periods of teaching beginning with the "Flower Garland Sutra," second the Hinayana canon, third the major Mahayana Sutras, fourth the Prajnaparamita Sutras, and finally the Saddharma Pundarika.[80] They constituted ascending steps on his road to truth or salvation.

Chih-k'ai's philosophy was a Chinese version of Nagarjuna's philosophy as transmitted by Kumarajiva. As such, his basic teaching might be characterized as cosmic mind defined as universal emptiness. By this was meant what in Chapter 5 was characterized in Nagarjuna as the teaching of "universal relativity." From the absolute point of view, nothing truly is; all things are riddled with contingency, relativity, and internal contradictions. In other passages this was interpreted as a philosophy of universal flux, or as Chih-k'ai put it, as "temporariness."

Yet the world of appearance or phenomena has at least a relative being. In an idealist cosmogony and cosmology, Chih-k'ai derived from emptiness or cosmic mind the ten dharma spheres of the world. In all, these ten spheres comprise the three-stories world of heaven, earth, and hell and their respective inhabitants. However, in other contexts, these levels of appearance or reality were interpreted by Chih-k'ai as a kind of ladder of ascent, beginning at the bottom with the present forms of human experience, the top being that absence of craving and of conditioned, finite reality, which is the supreme goal. The whole system is similar to western ideas of the degrees of being.

CHING-TU (PURE LAND)

A very different type of Buddhist thought and practice was represented by the Ching-tu, or Pure Land, group. Its traditional founder was Hui-yuan, who in the year 402 founded the White Lotus society, composed of 123 monks and laymen united in a vow to be reborn in the pure land or western paradise of Amitabha, or Amida Buddha.[81] Yet the actual work of formulating the doctrine of Pure Land and spreading its message far and wide was done by T'an-luan (476–542). T'an-luan appears to have been seeking health by means of Taoist elixirs when an Indian monk impressed upon him the transitory character of all life and the truth of the Pure Land doctrine. T'an turned to the study of Vasubandhu's commentary on the Sukhavativyaha Sutra with its crucial lines

> Behond the phenomena of yon sphere,
> How they surpass the paths of the three worlds.[82]

and its reference to the prospect of rebirth into that happy land. T'an-luan's *Commentary on Vasubandhu's Essay on Rebirth* shows all distinctive and characteristic traits of Pure Land thought and faith. Humans are sinners, guilty of the gravest violations and evils. Yet by personal relation to the savior Amida, they may be rescued. For this a trusting heart is needed. Also, humans must call upon the name of Amida, repeating this name in fidelity of heart. All who call upon the name of Amida will be reborn in the happy land. In the pure land there will be a pleasant and good life for all. T'an-luan and other converts to Pure Land also pointed out the dire urgency of the human situation, and the need, up to one's dying breath, of confessing faith in Amida Buddha.

**CH'AN
(MEDITATION)**
Perhaps most intensely Chinese of all was Ch'an, or Meditation, Buddhism, traditionally said to have been founded by the Indian monk Bodhidharma in the
late fifth or early sixth century. One estimate puts him in China from 420 to 476,
while another dates his coming to China in 520. He appears to have advocated
meditation, in contrast to both knowledge and good deeds, as the way to enlightenment. Others, too, followed in his tradition with similar teachings, but
Ch'an Buddhism owes its real impetus to the fifth and sixth patriarchs. The fifth
patriarch, Hung-jen, was the leader of Ch'an Buddhism at the time of its split
into northern and southern schools over the issue of sudden enlightenment.
There is current scholarly debate over the interpretation of these crucial
events.[83] According to one account Hung-jen was visited one day by an illiterate
youth from the south who importuned the master to be allowed to stay and
seek the law of the Buddha. The youth's name was Hui-neng; and he stayed on
to work in the monastery kitchen.

One day Hung-jen announced a contest of verses to decide his successor.
A leading contender named Shen-hsiu wrote the following:

> Our body is the tree of Perfect Wisdom,
> And our mind is a bright mirror.
> At all times diligently wipe them,
> So that they will be free of dust.[84]

The fifth patriarch expressed qualified approval of his contribution, but deferred judgment as to succession of leadership. Meanwhile Hui-neng wrote the
following verse:

> The tree of Perfect Wisdom is originally no tree.
> Nor has the bright mirror any frame.
> Buddha-nature is forever clear and pure.
> Where is there any dust?

For good measure he also added the following verse:

> The mind is a tree of Perfect Wisdom.
> The body is the clear mirror.
> The clear mirror is originally clear and pure.
> Where has it been affected by any dust?[85]

His fellow monks were surprised by these verses of Hui-neng, who went back
to pounding rice in the kitchen. The fifth patriarch recognized in Hui-neng his
successor, yet fearing for his safety he called him secretly at night, gave him the
robe and law, making him the sixth patriarch, but sent him away to the south.
So began the split between southern and northern branches of Ch'an Buddhism, the former devoted to sudden enlightenment and the latter to gradual
enlightenment.

Whatever the historicity of these stories, there was a historic split between
northern and southern branches of Ch'an at this time and presumably over this

issue. The northern branch went its own way, but the southern branch stemming from the impetus of Hui-neng developed its own distinctive interpretation of salvation by meditation. The living tradition was continued in the south.

Ch'an (as well as its Japanese progeny, Zen) has been summed up in four traditional maxims:

> A special transmission outside the scriptures;
> No dependence upon words and letters;
> Direct pointing to the soul of man;
> Seeing into one's nature and attainment of Buddhahood.[86]

The first maxim seems to argue for an oral tradition stemming from the Buddha, but apart from the written sources upon which other sects were based. The first two maxims taken together assert a tradition of the inwardness of spirit, independent of literal meanings or ideas. The third maxim might be paraphrased as an intuitive knowing of the self, beyond all intellectual knowledge. The fourth affirms the fruition of this knowledge as the attainment of Buddhahood or the achievement of the awakening or enlightenment which is open to all people and which constitutes humanity's highest fulfillment. Meditation Buddhism has consistently taught that buddhahood or the buddha nature is possible for everyone.

The content of this experience may be described as the union of an individual human mind with ultimate reality in such a way that all craving is overcome, enabling one to see life steadily and see it whole. According to Ch'an and Zen, this experience is not the direct consequence of human seeking or contrivance; it is not under human control. On the other hand, there are no gods to offer supernatural assistance. Humans must seek salvation in their own power. Yet having exerted themselves to the fullest, they must, at the last, relax and permit the experience of enlightenment to happen to them.

One distinctive aspect of Ch'an is the method by which enlightenment it pursued. It consists of disciplined obedience under a master who sets many tasks of labor, study, and devotion. The master may also resort to such extreme measures as shouting or beating. Most distinctive of all, the master may set a *kung-an* (Japanese, *koan*) for the student. This is a particularly puzzling question on which the student must concentrate, seeking an answer or solution. Many koans appear to be paradoxes, reflection upon which serve to jolt the student's mind free from its customary secular ruts and thus prepare the way for enlightenment. Others are thinly veiled metaphors or allegories. In this latter category is the following dialog:

> Question: "Whenever there is any question, one's mind is confused. What is the matter?"
> The Master said: "Kill, kill."[87]

In this context the meaning of *kill* apparently is to overcome or destroy all particular entities along the path to awakening. It is apparently the Zen formulation of the via negativa.

The ontological or metaphysical identity between the worlds of salvation and delusion is the subject of the following koan.

> A monk asked: "How is illusion true?"
> The master answered: "Illusion is originally true."
> The monk asked: "How is illusion manifested?"
> The master answered: "Illusion is manifestation and manifestation is illusion."[88]

Other koans, like the following, seem simply to be enigmatic sayings:

> A monk asked: "How can silence be expressed?"
> The master answered: "I will not express it here."
> The monk said: "Where will you express it?"
> The master said: "Last night at midnight I lost three pennies by my bed."[89]

The koan became a widely used and characteristic teaching device in Ch'an Buddhism. It may be regarded as a distinctive formulation of the recurring religious theme of paradox, whose function is to shake a mind free of its habitual secular world and point it toward awakening. Often the koan was in effect an enacted paradox.

A fourth kind of Buddhism, *Chen yen*, or True Word, arrived late in China. In 712 three missionaries arrived in the capital city, Ch'ang-an, laden with charms, mandalas, and incantations guaranteed to induce the experience of enlightenment. Their background was the kind of tantric Buddhism and Hinduism which we have already seen in India. The new missionaries gained an initial following in the T'ang court, but as it turned out, esoteric Buddhism gained no continuing organized existence in China. Nevertheless many of its practices struck roots in the popular religion and continued in other forms. Also, it soon made its way from China to Japan, where as *Shingon* it has continued in vigorous life to the present.

By the ninth century Buddhism had made its decisive contribution to China. Some aspects of the new faith, like cremation and asceticism, China rejected; other aspects, such as a more active philanthropy and a new philosophic impetus, were accepted. Yet perhaps Buddhism's greatest contribution to the Chinese tradition was the stimulus it provided for the neo-Confucian revival which followed.

NEO-CONFUCIANISM

During the centuries of Buddhist ascendancy in China, Confucianism never disappeared but only receded into the background. From this position in T'ang and Sung times, Confucianism mounted a counteroffensive against Buddhism and neo-Taoism to regain its former position of dominance. To this reassertion of China's classical tradition, the name *neo-Confucianism* has been given. The first stirrings of neo-Confucianism in the T'ang dynasty may be observed in that staunch old classicist, man of letters, and astringent critic of Buddhism, Han Yü

(786–836). In his essay entitled "What Is the True Way?" (*Yüan tao*), Han vigorously attacked both Buddhism and Taoism as unfilial, unsocial, and escapist. Quoting China's ancient classics with approval, Han bade the Chinese to return to the way of their ancestors. He also denounced false and time-serving teachers as unworthy of the classical way of Confucius.

Han concentrated his attack on Buddhism, which was still spreading in the China of his time. His *Memorial on the Bone of Buddha* was a bitter protest to the emperor against the honor which was being shown to a relic of Buddha. Most of all, the emperor should not give aid and comfort by participating in these ceremonies! Rather let him give the order to seize this bone and have it cast into the fire. As for the Buddhists, they are a degenerate and immoral lot, with their ascetic practices and their superstitious ritual around this stinking bone!

In the T'ang, Han Yü was a lonely voice, but in the Sung dynasty, neo-Confucianism became a movement massively influential in both politics and philosophy. In many cases philosophers were advisors to emperors and other

Iron head of Buddha from Sung dynasty. (Metropolitan Museum of Art, Fletcher Fund, 1961.)

governmental officials. Was it not in the Confucian tradition that philosophers should apply their wisdom to the solutions of social and political problems?

Sung neo-Confucianism began with Chou Tun-yi (1017–1073). Chou was much influenced by Taoism. It is said that his philosophic view of the ultimate was given to him in a diagram by a Taoist priest. His ethic of tranquility and "having no desires" shows similar influence. Whatever his sources, Chou's writing expounded a cosmology in which all things proceed from the Great Ultimate (*t'ai chi*). This term and idea may be traced in the Han dynasty "Great Appendix" to the "Book of Changes."[90]

Chou began with the exclamation, "The Non-Ultimate! And also the Great Ultimate."[91] By this he meant apparently the equivalence of nonbeing, or emptiness, and absolute being in a manner which both Taoist and Buddhist philosophy had made familiar. The Great Ultimate became for Chou and his neo-Confucian successors the generating source from which all else proceeded, as well as the goal to which it returned. Specifically, from the great ultimate are derived in succession yin and yang and the five agents—water, fire, wood, metal, and earth; and from the interaction of these forces arise all the myriad things of nature and society. By such a process the Great Ultimate gives birth to the world of everyday experience. The sage is the highest expression of humanity, and by the virtue of sincerity establishes oneness with Heaven and Earth.[92] By *oneness* is meant "having no desire," and having no desire, one is "empty."[93] In such assertions as the last the reader sees Chou's great debt to the Buddhism and Taoism which had come before him.

Shao Yung (1011–1077) continued many of Chou's interests, yet he emerges as a true Confucian, particularly in his view of the sage as the perfect man who with his mind grasps the underlying unity and structure of all being and thus is able to respond rationally to the universe around him in what Shao called the "observation of things." Of crucial importance was Shao's concept of number. Like that of Chou and others, it had esoteric and magical aspects. Yet what is philosophically important was Shao's view that numbers are embedded in the structure of the universe and thus determine reality.

Chang Tsai (1021–1077) produced a philosophy based not on number or principle (*li*) like that of Shao, but upon material force (*ch'i*). This term and idea of material force had had a long history before Chang's time. The Han philosophers had described it as "limpid, colorless substance" which fills the universe and is the raw material of which determinate things are made. Now Chang picked up this idea and used it as the basis of a realistic metaphysics designed to oppose the views of Buddhism and Taoism. According to Chang, out of the never-ceasing flux of ch'i arise all the creatures and realities of the world, including human beings.

Chang's philosophy involved notable formulations of the moral and religious aspects of life. His "Western Inscription" (*Hsi-ming*), so called because it was inscribed on the west wall of his study, is an eloquent synopsis of the whole neo-Confucian view for which he spoke. It is well worth full quotation:

Heaven is my father and earth is my mother, and even such a small creature as I finds an intimate place in their midst.

Therefore that which extends throughout the universe I regard as my body and that which directs the universe I consider as my nature.

All people are my brothers and sisters, and all things are my companions.

The great ruler [the Emperor] is the eldest son of my parents [Heaven and Earth], and the great ministers are his stewards. Respect the aged—this is the way to treat them as elders should be treated. Show affection toward the ophaned and the weak—this is the way to treat them as the young should be treated. The sage identifies his character with that of Heaven and earth, and the virtuous man is the best [among the children of Heaven and Earth]. Even those who are tired, infirm, crippled, or sick, those who have no brothers or children, wives or husbands, are all my brothers who are in distress and have no one to turn to.

When the time comes, to keep himself from harm—this is the care of a son. To rejoice in Heaven and have no anxiety—this is filial piety at its purest.

He who disobeys [the principle of Heaven] violates virtue. He who destroys humanity (jen) is a robber. He who promotes evil lacks [moral] capacity. But he who puts his moral nature into practice and brings his physical existence to complete fulfillment can match [Heaven and Earth].

He who knows the principles of transformation will skillfully carry forward the undertakings [of Heaven and Earth], and he who penetrates spirit to the highest degree with skillfully carry out their will.

Do nothing shameful in the recesses of your own house and thus bring no dishonor to them. Preserve the mind and nourish the nature and thus [serve them] with untiring effort.

The great Yü hated pleasant wine but attended to the protection and support of his parents. Border Warden Yong cared for the young and thus extended his love to his own kind.

Emperor Shun's merit lay in delighting his parents with unceasing effort, and Shen-sheng's reverence was demonstrated when he awaited punishment without making an attempt to escape.

Tseng Ts'an received his body from his parents and reverently kept it intact throughout life, while Po-ch'i vigorously obeyed his father's command.

Wealth, honor, blessing, and benefit are meant for the enrichment of my life, while poverty, humble station, care, and sorrow will be my helpmates to fulfillment.

In life I follow and serve [Heaven and Earth]. In death I will be at peace.[94]

The neo-Confucian movement made notable advances in the work of the two Ch'eng brothers, Ch'eng Yi (1033–1107) and Ch'eng Hao (1032–1085). The father of these two had been a friend of Chou Tun-yi, and they both studied with Chang Tsai. Both of the Ch'eng brothers were neo-Confucian philosophers, yet from their differing interpretations sprang the two significant and diverging directions of this tradition. From Ch'eng Hao came the school of Mind (*Hsin*) which led on to Wang Yang-ming (1472–1529), while from Ch'eng Yi came the school of Reason (*Li*) culminating in Chu Hsi (1130–1200). The latter has been called by Y. L. Fung the school of "Platonic realism."[95] Perhaps it might more appropriately be called the school of "Aristotelian realism."

Ch'eng Yi produced a philosophy based upon the idea of *li*, usually translated as "principle," but strikingly similar to "Platonic idea." All things under Heaven can be understood in terms of their li, or principles, said Ch'eng Yi. "Everything must have its li,"[96] he quoted from the "Book of Odes." What Ch'eng Yi and others called *the investigation of things* consists of discovering, laying bare, and describing these principles which exist within the various structures and processes of the world. This process of inquiry was said not only to explain things, but also to fulfill the mind's life and thus produce self-realization. For Ch'eng Yi and others it came to have moral as well as intellectual significance.

As a further step, all li, said Ch'eng Yi, is ultimately one; in other words, there is one principle underlying and pervading the whole world. As he stated this matter, "You may extend it over the four seas, and it is everywhere true. It is the unchangeable principle that can be 'laid before Heaven and earth' and is 'tested by the experience of the three kings.' "[97]

As a loyal Confucian, Ch'eng Yi held human nature to be originally good. Yet this led to the problem of explaining why some fulfill this potentiality and others do not. Ch'eng Yi explained this in terms of different qualities of their material force, saying that "men endowed with clear material force are wise while those endowed with turbid material force are stupid."[98]

According to Ch'eng Yi the moral fulfillment of human nature took place through the virtue which he called *seriousness*, or *moral cultivation*. Its goal is humanity, or humaneness.[99] Ch'eng went to great pains to distinguish Confucian seriousness from Buddhist tranquility. While there may be superficial similarities, the former has a genuine content while the latter is admittedly empty in nature.

Ch'eng also engaged in sharp polemics on Buddhism and Taoism, which he charged with being against family and humanity. Hence they "can finally be reduced to a pattern of selfishness."[100] Taoism he found downright misleading in its slippery and paradoxical way of speaking. Hence "the Taoists carry with them an element of treachery."[101]

The philosophy that Ch'eng Yi began was brought to its definitive and culminating statement by the great Chu Hsi (1130–1200). Chu's philosophical system began in an assertion of the conjunction of li and ch'i as the form and matter of all things. In every existing thing may be detected li and ch'i. Li has a kind of logical priority; it is the timeless form of things. In the beginning was li, or as Chu Hsi put it, "before Heaven and earth existed, then was certainly only principle."[102] Furthermore, the human mind is a faculty for apprehending and containing li.

All nature was asserted by Chu to be a conjunction of li and ch'i or form and matter. Nature is principle only; but without the material force and solid substance of the universe, principle would have nothing in which to inhere. LIke Ch'eng Yi before him, Chu distinguishes between clear and turbid material force; where there is clarity, li expresses itself freely, but where ch'i is turbid, there obstruction and confusion prevail.

Chu Hsi's fundamental concept was the Supreme Ultimate or *T'ai Chi*, which he interpreted as "the principle of Heaven and earth and the myriad things."[103] The Chinese characters for *T'ai Chi* combine what was originally the sign for the ridgepole of a tent and the sign for pervasiveness. It will not be far off the mark to envisage the universe as a tent with t'ai chi as its ridgepole. As Chu Hsi put it, "The Supreme Ultimate is similar to the top of the house or the zenith of the sky."[104] Chu asserted that while the Supreme Ultimate is one, its manifestations are infinitely many. All things that exist in some sense express the Supreme Ultimate. For this relation Chu used the metaphor of the moon, which is one, but whose light is reflected on the myriad surfaces of the world. The Supreme Ultimate is at once the first and last reality and the highest good, in which all virtues are fulfilled.

Like other Chinese scholars before him, and like intellectuals in many of the world's traditions, Chu Hsi was scornful of anthropomorphic views of Heaven or deity. He shared the reticence and agnosticism of Confucius concerning the shen and kwei of popular religion as well as life after death. Like Confucius he proposed to continue the sacrificial rites for social and esthetic reasons.

Acording to Chu the goal of man was the realization of humanity. He quoted with approval the maxim of Ch'eng Yi, "When man puts impartiality into practice that is humanity," and added that humanity is "the principle originally inherent in man's mind."[105] Out of impartiality and humanity are born altruism and love. So it may be said that Chu Hsi put a metaphysical context around the ethics of Confucius. The result was one of the great philosophic systems of world history.

Chu Hsi was a statesman of note, but he preferred the life of the teacher and scholar. To his White Deer Grotto, students came from all parts of China, imbibing the philosophy which soon became in effect China's official view—challenged but never displaced for the next seven centuries. Chu was a great scholar, whose editions of the classical Confucian texts became the accepted ones. As we have seen it was he who placed the Four Books alongside the Five Classics as required reading for all who would be scholars. It was also he who ruled Hsün tzu to be heterodox and Mencius to be orthodox.

Chu Hsi's philosophy was challenged during his lifetime by the school of Mind, deriving from Ch'eng Yi's older brother, Ch'eng Hao, and Lu Chiu-yüan (1139–1192), or as he was also known, Lu Hsiang-shan. Ch'eng Hao's philosophy expressed many of the same ideas and emphases as that of his younger brother. However, there was one notable difference, namely, a greater emphasis upon the identity of the human mind with the universe and upon the intuitive character of the thinking process by which this identity is achieved and sustained. Chang Tsai had said "that which extends throughout the universe I regard as my body and that which directs the universe I regard as my nature." Ch'eng Hao wrote analogously, "The humane man forms one body with all things comprehensively."[106] By the cultivation of sincerity and seriousness, humans find their place in the scheme of things entire and are thus able to say, "All the operations of the universe are our operations."

What Ch'eng Hao began, Lu Chiu-yüan carried forward. He argued forcefully that humanity is by nature mind, and that mind consists of li. Hence as humans come to see the identity of the li in their minds with the li of the universe, they come to an intuitive sense of oneness with the universe. Lu's philosophy was clearly more subjective and more intuitive than that of Chu Hsi.

The school of Mind received its definitive statement some centuries later in the philosophy of Wang Yang-ming (1472–1529), or Wang Shou-jen, as he is sometimes called. A general and statesman of great distinction and integrity as well as a philosopher, Wang sought in his philosophy to give expression to the principles by which he lived.

Like others before him in the school of Mind, Wang wrote eloquently on the unity of all things. "The great man regards Heaven and earth and the myriad things as one body. He regards the world as one family and the country as one person."[107] This sense of identity is to be realized in filial feeling, not only toward one's own father but toward the fathers of all men, in brotherhood with all, and in attitude of sympathy toward every human being. Indeed, Wang extended this feeling of sympathy beyond the boundary of humanity to include every living being.

The intuitive sense of right and wrong he regarded as "innate knowledge" given to humans by Heaven, and therefore "the original substance of my mind."[108] In this form of knowing, Wang asserted, is the unity of all things, for in all this there is no separation of mind and li. Such dualities come about as a result of selfish desires which breed error. Hence, Wang concluded, "the innate knowledge of my mind is the same as the principle of Heaven."[109]

Perhaps Wang's most distinctive teaching was his doctrine of unity of knowledge and action. When humans know truly, action follows naturally. Conversely "there have never been people who know but do not act."[110] Selfish desires intrude to distort and to separate knowing and doing. Truly to know entails doing, and vice versa. "Knowledge is the beginning of action and action is the completion of knowledge."[111]

RECENT AND CONTEMPORARY ISSUES

Modernity came late and suddenly to China, forced by western gunboats and other armies upon a nation closed off by her Manchu rulers from all outside influence. Great Britain forced open the door in her victorious but inglorious Opium War (1839–1842). Successive privileges of extraterritoriality were forced upon the helpless Chinese nation.

One event of prophetic significance was the Taiping Rebellion (1850–1864) led by Hung Hsui Ch'uan, a South China peasant who had twice failed in the civil service examinations. Coming under the influence of Protestant Christian millennialism, he fabricated a religious-political movement which combined Christian apocalypticism, Confucian ethics, and Chinese peasant revolt against landlordism. The Taipings (this word means "Great Peace") raised the standard of rebellion against the decadent Manchu dynasty and succeeded in conquering large sections of south and central China. The Taipings were finally put down by foreign troops under the English general C. G. ("Chinese") Gordon, and the Manchus were restored to power. However, there is a direct line, politically, from the Taipings to the successful communist revolution of the twentieth century.

Religiously the Taipings were a typically Chinese mixture of elements from different traditions, in this case Christian apocalypticism and indigenous Chinese ideas and images. This combination of religious elements bears striking similarity to the more recent theology of Sun Myung Moon (b. 1920) and his Unification church, founded in Korea in 1954 but currently enjoying popularity in the United States and elsewhere in the West. American young people are attracted by the novel combination of east Asian social ethics and Christian apocalypticism, including a messianic role for Moon himself. However, Chinese or Koreans would find nothing new in this mixture.

There was a brief flare-up of Taoism in the Boxer Rebellion of 1990, for the Boxers, along with other secret societies, were a Taoist sect. The dowager empress was a leader in welding together Chinese nationalism and Taoist voodooism. The Boxers believed that their Taoist charms would protect them from the bullets of foreign devils. There are authentic records of Boxers, firm in this faith, who were shot down and arose and staggered on a few steps before falling again. Such apparently were the powers—and limits—of this faith.

W. T. Chan reports that in 1948–1949 the Taoist center at Dragon-Tiger Mountain and the White Cloud Temple were well kept.[112] Yet at the mountain, the "heavenly teacher" of Taoism, the sixty-third lineal descendant of Chang Ling, had disappeared and was completely forgotten. Under China's Marxist rulers there seems no prospect for Taoism except extinction.

Chinese Buddhism entered the modern world after several centuries of governmental discrimination and anti-Buddhist propaganda. In the present century it has suffered for several decades from what its leaders call *catastrophes*—special taxes, confiscation of property, destruction of temples, and forced secularization of monks and nuns.[113] It cannot be expected that any of these trends has been reversed by Chinese communism.

In the twentieth century there have been some notable efforts at reform and revitalization of Chinese Buddhism. The great Buddhist abbot T'ai-hsü (1889–1947) was indefatigable in his effort to reform and rebuild Chinese Buddhism, seeking to redirect it toward this-worldly, humanistic, and scientific goals. There was concurrently a notable increase in publication and circulation of Buddhist books and periodicals. These people and movements breathed new life into many traditional ideas and organizational structures. Yet their long-time influence in a China ravaged by war and then dominated by communists is, to say the least, problematic. To date, the Marxist rulers of China have given no indication of any attitude other than hostility toward Buddhism or any other traditional religious faith.[114]

The situation, though somewhat more complicated, is not essentially different for China's other major faith, Confucianism. Confucian bureaucrats and philosophers were unable to make any effective response to the coming of western nations, western ideas, and western guns.[115] They were also unable to extricate themselves—or Confucianism—from the downfall of the Manchu dynasty in 1911.

The Manchu, or Ch'ing, dynasty (1644–1911) was toppled by Sun Yat-sen's nationalist revolution of 1911–1912. Efforts which were made to have Confucianism established as a state religion in the new Chinese nation came to naught. The constitution of 1913 asserted that "in the education of citizens the doctrines of Confucius shall be regarded as the basis of moral cultivation." However, the constitution of 1923 said only that "a citizen of the Republic of China shall be free to honor Confucius and to prefer any religion."[116]

Meanwhile the ethical teaching of Confucius—indeed, his whole philosophy—was subjected to an all-embracing critical attack. The New Culture movement which began in 1916 under the leadership of Ch'en Tu-hsui (1879–1942) and Hu Shih (1891–1963) vigorously attacked Confucian ethics, philosophy, and scholarship as hopelessly obsolete and an obstacle to China's progress. Both Ch'en and Hu were forthright partisans of modernity and hence opposed to Confucian traditionalism.[117]

Ch'en was the founder of the Chinese Communist party, though he was later expelled and disowned by the party. He was a lifelong iconoclast. Hu was American-educated, at Cornell and Columbia, and was an adherent of John Dewey's philosophy, which he pitted against Confucius. Through their periodical, *The New Youth*, Ch'en and Hu and their colleagues poured a withering fire upon Confucian ethics, demanding personal freedom from bondage to the family system. Hu initiated what he called a *literary revolution* against stilted and artificial ways of writing and scholarship. He also proposed a mode of thought called *doubting antiquity*.[118] Soon the issues broadened into a debate on the issue of science versus traditional Chinese humanism, with Hu Shih as the protagonist of the modern scientific view. He continued to speak and to write on topics ranging from literature to politics. Hu's social viewpoint was a vigorous advocacy of western constitutional democracy. He was China's ambassador to the United States during World War II. With the rise of Chinese communism Hu became increasingly anticommunistic, and when communism emerged victorious in 1949, Hu fled to Taiwan, where he died in 1963.

When Sun Yat-sen died, the leadership of the nationalist movement and Kuomintang party passed to the more traditional Chiang Kai-shek (1887–1975). In addition to his expulsion of Russian advisors and opposition to Chinese communists, Chiang undertook in 1934 a New Life movement.[119] This was an effort to provide in more traditional terms a new basis for individual and social ethics.

While this program was undoubtedly influenced by Chiang's newly found Christianity, the influence of Confucian ideas and ideals was also clearly present. The content of the new life was declared to be the four traditional Chinese virtues, li (decorum or good form), i (righteousness or duty), lien (integrity or honesty), and ch'ih (sense of shame for what is evil). The whole program was pervaded by the Confucian spirit of self-cultivation.

At the same time that Chiang was launching his popular movement, Y. L. Fung (b. 1895) was constructing his own attempt at modern neo-Confucian philosophy. In the tradition and spirit of Ch'eng Yi and Chu Hsi, Fung sought to construct a new Confucian philosophic synthesis which would make China's tradition and its values available to the twentieth century. The attempt, admittedly ambitious, had some success. However, in 1950 Fung's son denounced him publicly in the manner prescribed by the Chinese Communist party for its members. Fung responded to this denunciation, in effect pleading guilty, renouncing Confucianism and his own life's work in order to embrace Marxism. His subsequent career was as a Marxist philosopher and a hero of Chinese communism.[120]

Meanwhile Mao Tse Tung (1893–1976) pursued his lifelong career in the practice and theory of Marxism. Rising to leadership by his work among peasants in his native Hunan, Mao was one of the leaders of the Long March of the Red Army in 1934. Battling both Japanese invaders and Chiang Kai-shek's Nationalist Army, the communists maintained their existence through World War II, then emerged victorious in 1949. Mao remained chairman of the party until his death in 1976.

He regarded himself as an orthodox Marxist; however, one notable difference from Marx and Lenin is apparent in his writings. Whereas they taught that the industrial working class would, through revolution, bring in the new society, for Mao this messianic role is played by the Chinese peasant class.

While the substance of Mao's teachings is in polar disagreement with Confucius, there are interesting continuities of style. Like Chinese gentlemen from Shang times onward, Mao wrote poetry and did calligraphy. Like Confucius he composed a book, published as *The Teachings of Chairman Mao*, of aphoristic sayings for the guidance of life.

Mao's last years were marked by at least two decisions now widely regarded by the Chinese as mistaken. He inspired and led the Cultural Revolution (1966–1976) which cut China from the world and deprived the nation of essential leadership. Mao also sanctioned and urged massive increase in China's population. His successors have struggled to limit present population to a billion and a quarter.

Mao was followed by a period of openness to the West under Tung Shao ping (b. 1904). However, as these words are written this openness has been replaced by harsh repression of students and others seeking democratization. What the future holds for Chinese Marxism is a question on which the jury is still out.

ISSUES AND QUESTIONS

As students of religion looking at China, past and present, we are confronted by several significant issues. (1) As we have seen, the classical Chinese tradition constitutes a depiction of Man in the cosmos, or as we have argued of cosmic humanism. At many points this Chinese humanism is similar to that of ancient Greece and Rome. More specifically, Confucius's ethics shows striking similarity to Aristotle's. However, this conclusion implies several important questions. Can there be humanism apart from such a cosmic context? Again, recalling the male-dominated character of both Greek and Chinese culture, can there be humanism which includes equally men and women? (2) Chinese Buddhism, while long eclipsed by Confucianism, still directs our attention to the classical interaction of Buddhism and Chinese culture—surely one of the most interesting interactions in human history. One consequence was that the monks' gaze was brought from heaven down to earth, directing Buddhist meditation upon the goods of this world and this life. This change is our key to understanding the Buddhism of China and Japan. Buddhist philosophy, Indian and Chinese, is also essential for our understanding of the metaphysical philosophies of the neo-Confucians, especially Chu Hsi. (3) Taoism, while probably now effectively dead, leaves a legacy in east Asian thought in the concepts of spontaneity and of mystical union with the cosmos. (4) Classical Chinese thought shows a distinctive tradition of critical, skeptical, even antireligious, attitudes in such figures as Hsün tzu, Wang Ch'ung, and others. (5) Chinese Marxism raises a whole new set of issues. First of all, Marxism is essentially a western system based, as we shall argue in later chapters, upon a linear view of history derived from the Bible, in contrast to the cyclic view of Chinese tradition. This may account at least partially for Marxism's attractiveness to the Chinese. Again the concept of Marxism as a tacit or unconscious religion presents a double puzzle to the Chinese. First, there is the question of whether China's central Confucian tradition is religion or philosophy. Second, there is question of a functioning religion whose religious character is not acknowledged by its adherents. Perhaps the simplest assertion is that Chinese Marxism is a value system which functions, in part at least, religiously. Beyond this there is the existential question of just what is the value content of Chinese Marxism. In other words, how shall we evaluate this value system?

NOTES

1. Unpublished remark made in a Claremont graduate school seminar by Chang Chuan-Yüan in 1962.
2. Wing-Tsit Chan (trans.), *A Source Book in Chinese Philosophy*, Princeton, Princeton, N.J., 1963, p. 3.
3. Yu-Lan Fung, *A Short History of Chinese Philosophy*, Macmillan, New York, 1960, pp. 3–4.
4. Edwin O. Reischauer and John K. Fairbank, *A History of East Asian Civilization*, Houghton Mifflin, Boston, 1960, p. 68.

5. James R. Ware, *The Sayings of Confucius*, Mentor Books, New American Library, New York, p. 13.

6. Wing-Tsit Chan, *Religious Trends in Modern China*, Columbia, New York, 1953, pp. 25–26.

7. Confucius, "Analects," VII, 22.

8. Li chi, XI

9. "Analects," XIII, 18.

10. Ibid., II, 7.

11. Li chi, XV.

12. "Analects," XII, 22.

13. Ibid., IV, 2.

14. Ibid., XIV, 36.

15. Ibid., XV, 23.

16. Ibid., XVII, 2.

17. Ibid., IX, 4.

18. Ibid., IV, 8.

19. Ibid., XII, II.

20. Ibid., III, 13.

21. Ibid., VII, 34.

22. Ibid., XI, 11.

23. Ibid., VI, 20.

24. Ibid., III, 17.

25. Lin Yutang, *The Wisdom of Confucius*, Modern Library, New York, 1938, p. 14.

26. Philomene S. Harrison, "Lao Tzu and the Ch'un-Ch'iu Period: An Inquiry into Our Present Knowledge of the Tao Te'Ching," unpublished doctoral dissertation, Claremont, Claremont, Calif., 1963.

27. Lin Mousheng, *Men and Ideas*, John Day, New York, 1943, p. 9.

28. Fung, op. cit., p. 9.

29. Ware, op. cit., vol. 1, p. 2.

30. Chan, *A Source Book in Chinese Philosophy*, p. 139.

31. Ibid., p. 160.

32. Ibid., p. 146.

33. Ibid., p. 143.

34. Ibid., p. 142.

35. Ibid., p. 147.

36. Ibid., p. 154.

37. Ibid., p. 141.

38. Ibid., pp. 148–149.

39. Ibid., p. 140.

40. Ibid., p. 168.

41. Ibid., p. 175.

42. Ibid., p. 186–187.

43. Ibid., p. 191.

44. Ibid., p. 202.

45. Ibid., p. 183.

46. Ibid., p. 181.

47. Ibid., p. 187.

48. Ibid., p. 190.

49. William T. de Bary et al. (eds.), *Sources of the Chinese Tradition*, Columbia, New York, 1960, p. 79.

50. Chan, *A Source Book in Chinese Philosophy*, p. 209.

51. Ibid., p. 233.

52. Ibid.

53. Ibid., p. 234.

54. Ibid., 235.

55. Ibid., 242.
56. de Bary, op. cit., p. 129.
57. Ibid., p. 135.
58. Ibid., p. 183.
59. Ibid., p. 257.
60. Ibid., p. 163.
61. Ibid., pp. 246–247.
62. Ibid., p. 251.
63. Ibid., pp. 251–252.
64. Ibid., p. 253.
65. "Analects," XI, 18.
66. Fung, op. cit., chaps. 19 and 20.
67. de Bary, op. cit., p. 221.
68. Fung, op. cit., p. 221.
69. Ibid., p. 222.
70. Ibid., p. 237
71. Ibid., pp. 236–237.
72. Ibid., p. 235.
73. de Bary, op. cit., pp. 298f.
74. Ibid., p. 301.
75. Kenneth W. Morgan (ed.), *The Path of the Buddha*, Ronald, New York, 1956, p. 184.
76. Reischauer and Fairbank, op. cit., p. 146.
77. de Bary, op. cit., p. 314.
78. H. Nakamura, *The Ways of Thinking of Eastern People*, compiled by Japanese National Commission for UNESCO, Tokyo, 1960.
79. Morgan, op. cit., p. 202.
80. Ibid., p. 200.
81. Ibid., pp. 194–195.
82. de Bary, op. cit., p. 376.
83. Ibid., p. 390.
84. Ibid., p. 391.
85. Ibid.
86. D. T. Suzuki, *Zen Buddhism*, William Barrett (ed.), Anchor Books, Doubleday, Garden City, N.Y., 1956, p. 9.
87. de Bary, op. cit., p. 408.
88. Ibid., p. 405.
89. Ibid., p. 406.
90. Fung, op. cit., p. 513.
91. de Bary, op. cit., p. 513.
92. Ibid., pp. 514f.
93. Ibid., p. 515.
94. de Bary, op. cit., pp. 524–525.
95. Fung, op. cit., chap. 25.
96. de Bary, op. cit., p. 527.
97. Ibid.
98. Ibid., p. 529.
99. Ibid., p. 530.
100. Ibid., p. 533.
101. Ibid.
102. Ibid., p. 540.
103. Ibid., p. 539.
104. Ibid., p. 540.
105. Ibid., p. 556.
106. Ibid., p. 559.

107. Ibid., p. 571.
108. Ibid., p. 576.
109. Ibid., p. 578.
110. Ibid., p. 579.
111. Ibid.
112. Chan, *Religious Trends in Modern China*, p. 152.
113. de Bary, op. cit., chaps. 24 and 26.
114. Chan, *Religious Trends in Modern China*, pp. 118f.
115. Ibid., p. 4.
116. Ibid., p. 8.
117. de Bary, op. cit., pp. 813f.
118. Ibid., p. 844.
119. Ibid., pp. 800f.
120. Chan, *A Source Book in Chinese Philosophy*, pp. 751.

BIBLIOGRAPHY

Chan, W. T.: *Religious Trends in Modern China*, Columbia, New York, 1953.

————: *The Way of Lao Tzu*, Macmillan, New York, 1963.

Chang, C. Y.: *Original Teachings of Ch'an Buddhism*, Random House, New York, 1969.

Chen, K.: *Buddhism in China*, Princeton, Princeton, N.J., 1974.

Creel, H. G.: *Chinese Thought from Confucius to Mao Tze-tung*, University of Chicago, Chicago, 1971.

————: *Confucius and the Chinese Way*, Harper, New York, 1960.

————: *What Is Taoism?* University of Chicago, Chicago, 1982.

Day, C. B.: *The Philosophers of China*, Citadel, New York, 1978.

de Bary, W. T. (ed.): *The Buddhist Tradition*, Random House, New York, 1972.

———— (ed): *Sources of the Chinese Tradition*, Columbia, New York, 1960.

Fung, Y. L.: *A Short History of Chinese Philosophy*, Free Press, New York, 1977.

————: *The Spirit of Chinese Philosophy*, Paul Trench, Trubner, London, 1947.

Girardot, N.: *Myth and Meaning in Early Taoism*, University of California, Berkeley, 1985.

Hughes, E. R.: *Chinese Philosophy in Classical Times*, Dutton, New York, 1960.

I Ching, R. W. Wright (trans.), Routledge, London, 1970.

Jordan, D.: *Gods, Ghosts and Ancestors*, University of California, Berkeley, 1983.

Kaltenmark, Max: *Laotze and Taoism*, Stanford, Stanford, Calif., 1969.

Moore, C. A. (ed.): *The Chinese Mind*, East-West Center Press, Honolulu, 1969.

Morgan, K. (ed.): *The Path of the Buddha*, Ronald, New York, 1956.

Overmeyer, D.: *Folk Buddhist Religion*, Harvard, Cambridge, Mass., 1976.

Reischauer, E., and J. Fairbank: *East Asia: The Great Tradition*, State Mutual Book and Periodical Service, Ltd., New York, 1973.

Takakusu, J.: *Essentials of Buddhist Philosophy*, Orient Book Distributors, Livingston, N.J., 1975.

Thompson, L.: *Chinese Religion*, Wadsworth, Belmont, Calif., 1981.

————: *The Chinese Way in Religion*, Wadsworth, Belmont, Calif., 1973.

Waley, A.: *Three Ways of Thought in Ancient China*, Stanford, Stanford, Calif., 1939.

Wilhelm, H.: *Change*, Princeton, Princeton, N.J., 1960.

Wright, A. (ed.): *Confucianism and Chinese Civilization*, Stanford, Stanford, Calif., 1964.

Yang, C.: *Religion in Chinese Society*, University of California, 3d ed.

9

Japanese Religion

Compared with the long history of China, that of Japan is brief and recent; and it has been much influenced by China. Yet the Japanese have imparted their own distinctive shape to all the materials that have come to their shores from the Asian mainland and more recently from the West. Illustrations of this process of assimilation and transformation range from language and art to virtually every other significant element of Japanese culture. However, there is no more important example than Japanese Buddhism, which is surely as much Japanese as it is Buddhist.

The Japanese and Chinese cultures constitute a study in similarities and differences. For example, China has been accurately called a *culture of affluence* and Japan one of *scarcity*. The vast and fertile river valleys of China contrast sharply with Japanese land, which, while very beautiful, is only 10 percent arable. Again, the soldier has had a low place on the Chinese value system, whereas in Japan he is a principal actor in the drama of history. In both Japan and China, as in other traditions of the first, or cosmic, type throughout the world, nature and society, taken together, constitute the object of ultimate concern. For both China and Japan, furthermore, nature is primarily an esthetic reality to be apprehended by the perceptive eye of the artist. The Japanese have given their own distinctive expression to this theme; as H. Nakamura has put it, the Japanese apprehend the "absolute in the phenomenal world."[1] That is to say, the absolute is not some remote entity beyond this world but is to be envisaged in and through the world of present appearance.

The Japanese tradition has worked with many materials imported from China, as, for instance, the Confucian ethic and emperor worship. However, the end result is something uniquely Japanese. Nakamura has spoken of the unique importance in Japan of the "concrete social nexus," the actual social context of the individual in family, community, and nation.[2] Correlated with this context has been the flexibility and pragmatism of individuals in fitting themselves into the existing situation and living as a part of this concrete social whole. Nakamura speaks of this trait as the Japanese "acceptance of actuality."[3]

Modern Japan alone among Asian societies has succeeded in building and maintaining a highly efficient, advanced industrial society. One of the innumerable consequences of this achievement is a combination, unique on the face of the earth, of the old and the new in Japanese culture. It is a combination that the

Haniwa, or ancient Japanese grave figure of deceased family member. (American Region News Bureau, Japan Au Lenes.)

Japanese appear to accept with a maximum of harmony and a minimum of discord. Nowhere is this Japanese combination of the old and the new more important than in religion.

SHINTO

The customary label for Japan's indigenous religious tradition is Shinto. The name is ironical, for it is Chinese (*shen* means "spirit" or "god"; *tao* means "way"; hence, "way of the gods"). The Japanese rendering of the same expression is *kami no michi*. In a recent book title, Kokyo Ono has proposed "The Kami Way" as an adequate English rendering of *Shinto*.[4] The term *kami* needs explanation, for it is fundamental to Shinto, and it is an elusive term for western students. It surely does not mean "God," and even "god" does not render it adequately. The Greek term *daimon* comes closer, but this word has been largely lost to modern speech and thought. In terms of Chapter 1, *kami* may be rendered as "power" or "holy power." Sometimes this power is somewhat personal—at least personal enough to be invoked or prayed to—but in other situations kami is an object as impersonal as a river, a mountain, or a stone, or it is a pervasive ethos. Perhaps the truth of the matter is that the early Japanese found no necessity to become clear or definite on these issues and so left them vague—to the bewilderment of modern western students of religion. Hence, having sought to characterize kami, we shall leave it untranslated throughout this chapter.

There are many—innumerably many—kami, and the Japanese have never felt the necessity of ordering this thickly populated pantheon beyond the assertion of a functional primacy of *Amaterasu Omikami*. And this, as we shall see, derived largely from the rise to dominance in ancient Japan of the Yamato clan, which worshipped Amaterasu. Speaking generally, the dwelling places of the kami are different aspects of nature or society or some combination of both. Any mysterious, strange, or impressive aspect of the social or natural world is likely to reveal the presence of a kami. But the best summary of this matter is from a celebrated Shinto scholar, Motoori Norinaga (1730–1801 CE)

> I do not yet understand the meaning of the term kami. Speaking in general, however, it may be said that kami signifies, in the first place, the deities of heaven and earth that appear in the ancient records and also the spirits of the shrines where they are worshipped.
>
> It is hardly necessary to say that it includes human beings. It also includes such objects as birds, beasts, trees, plants, seas, mountains, and so forth. In ancient usage, anything whatsoever which was outside the ordinary, which possessed superior power, or which was awe-inspiring, was called kami. Eminence here does not refer merely to the superiority of nobility, goodness, or meritorious deeds. Evil and mysterious things, if they are extraordinary and dreadful, are called kami. It is needless to say that among human beings who are called kami the successive generations of sacred emperors are all included. The fact that emperors are also called "distant kami" is because, from the standpoint of common people, they are far-separated, majestic, and worthy of reverence. In a lesser degree we find, in the present as well as in ancient times, human beings who are kami. Although they may not be accepted throughout the whole country, yet in each province, each village, and each family there are human beings who are kami, each one according to his own proper position. The kami of the divine age were for the most part human beings of that time and, because the people of that time were all kami, it is called the Age of the Gods (kami).[5]

As in the case of all faiths, Shinto has its distinctive myth and ritual. Indeed Shinto is the myth and ritual. It is also the distinctive cluster of values which is the human substance of what is recited in the myth and enacted in the ritual. These values might be summarized in the phrase "the Japanese way of life." As this chapter proceeds we shall seek to unpack this phrase and inspect some of its contents. Meanwhile, it may be remarked that Shinto is the clearest example among humankind's living religions of a type 1 or nature-culture religion.

Shinto also involves the student once more in the recurring question: "What is religion?" More specifically it raises questions about the extension of this concept, for it involves many activities which in other societies would not be conventionally classified as religious. For example, most Americans would not classify community observances such as Memorial Day parades and decoration of military graves or July Fourth gatherings as religious. Neither would they feel that a visit to Washington's home at Mount Vernon or to the Lincoln Memorial were religious exercises. (In passing, it may be noted that recent writers as different in outlook as Will Herberg, Lloyd Warner, and Robert Bellah have spoken of America's new "civil religion" in which in popular myth and ritual the American way of life is celebrated.)[6] In such observances the parallel to Shinto becomes explicit. To this may be added the problems of the word *religion* raised in Chapter 1. Like the Chinese term, the classical Japanese term means "teaching" and only approximates the English word *religion*.

SHINTO MYTH

If one turns to Shinto myth, one may observe significant analogy to American stories of origin and destiny from the landing of the Pilgrims to the legends of Washington, Lincoln, or even more recent heroes. In the case of Shinto, there are no canonical scriptures analogous to the Judeo-Christian Bible; however, there are sacred writings, notably the *Kojiki*, "Record of Ancient Tales," and the *Nihongi* or *Nihon shoki*, "Chronicles of Japan." Precise dates can be assigned to both, the former having been produced in 712 CE and the latter in 720 CE. Both show the influence of Chinese historical writing of the time. Together they contain the main mythological sources of Shinto. Here we shall summarize briefly six of these mythical episodes or themes which have historical and contemporary importance.

COSMOGONIC MYTH   The cosmogony of the Kojiki speaks of the primordial chaos as like an ocean of mud out of which three kami sprang. All three were born apparently without progenitors, and left no posterity. Other kami sprang into being and, in the characteristic manner of kami, became invisible. Among these subsequent kami were Iza Nagi ("the male who invites") and Iza Nami ("the female who invites"), the Japanese versions of the recurring sky father and earth mother. They were ordered by their heavenly colleagues to give birth to the earth. Provided with a spear, they descended to the floating bridge of heaven where they thrust the spear into the brine. As they drew up the spear, the tip formed the island of Onogoro, where they erected a palace and a pillar. Exploring their bodies, they discovered their sexual differences and desired union. Going around the sacred pillar, they embraced, and from their union were born innumerable kami as well as the islands of Japan, mountains, rivers, sea, and finally the fire kami. In this last birth Iza Nami was so badly burnt that she died and withdrew to the nether world.

A well-known student of Japanese religion comments accurately on stories of beginnings that they are not in any precise sense a creation story similar to that in Genesis, where a sovereign Lord calls the world into being out of nothingness.[7] Creation stories of this sort seem limited to the third, or monotheistic, type of religion. But in contrast, these Japanese stories, like many other tales from type 1, or cosmic, religions, simply and artlessly recount the beginnings of the things of nature and culture.

IZA NAGI IN THE UNDERWORLD

A sequel to the cosmogonic myth is the story of Iza Nagi's descent to the underworld in search of his wife. Finding her place, he talked with her, asking her to return to the world. She asked him to wait, meanwhile pleading with him not to look upon her present decomposed state. Disobeying, Iza Nagi lit the endpiece of his comb only to see his wife's hideous, decaying body. In horror at what he saw, he fled, pursued by the ugly forces of the nether world.

What is the meaning of this story, so similar to Mesopotamian, Greek, and other stories of descent to the underworld? Is this a myth of the seasons? Is Holtom right in regarding it as a picture poem depicting a terrific thunderstorm?[8] Or is Ross correct in suggesting a psychological interpretation of the way by which we come to definite consciousness?[9] As is so often true with mythical materials, it seems impossible to make a definite decision of the basis of the document itself. It is possible that several elements are involved.

AMATERASU AND SUSA-NO-O

When Iza Nagi reached the upper world, he paused by the sea in characteristically Japanese fashion to cleanse himself. Ablution and purification are recurring themes in Shinto. In the course of Iza Nagi's ablutions, several kami were born. From the dirt washed from his left eye was born the most important kami of all, Amaterasu. From the dirt washed from his right eye was born the moon kami, Tsukiyomi, while from his nose was born the storm kami, Susa-no-o (or Susa-no-wu). The moon kami is not heard from again in the Kojiki, but the relations between Amaterasu and her brother Susa-no-o are developed in detail. As befits a storm deity, Susa-no-o was violent and capricious, doing great damages to mountains and rivers. Then, according to the Nihongi, he and Amaterasu each produced children, Susa-no-o by chewing up Amaterasu's string of curved jewels, and Amaterasu by chewing up Susa-no-o's sword.

Susa-no-o continued his pranks and depredations, breaking down the divisions of his sister's heavenly rice fields, filling the ditches, and polluting with dung the hall in which she held the feast of the first fruits. His misdeeds achieved a climax when he broke through the roof tiles of her weaving room and threw in a flayed colt. A council of kami, called to deal with the refractory deity, expelled him from heaven to dwell in the region of the Izumo shrine in western Japan.

AMATERASU IN HIDING

Meanwhile the enraged Amaterasu had hidden herself in a rock cave. A myriad of kami sought to entice her out. Their efforts culminated in an erotic dance that provoked roars of laughter and excitement and caused the offended Amaterasu to peer out in curiosity. Thereupon a rope was stretched behind her, beyond which she could not again withdraw.

What is the meaning of these myths? The reader will not be wrong in seeing here the free play of primitive or archaic imagination on perennial themes of nature and society. From the beginning Amaterasu has been a sun goddess. As noted above, she was the deity of the Yamato clan; when this clan won military and political leadership in ancient Japan, their deity assumed primacy as well. Susa-no-o was related in early history to the Izumo shrine. These, and doubtless innumerable other suggestions, are implicit throughout these artless stories.

FOUNDING THE JAPANESE EMPIRE

A politically important myth was the story of Amaterasu's sending of her grandson Ninigi to the earth to rule the islands of Japan. Her charge to him was contained in words which many a patriotic Japanese has learned by heart: "The Luxuriant Land of Reed Plains is a country which our descendants are to inherit. Go, therefore, Our Imperial Grandson, and rule over it! And may Our Imperial lineage continue unbroken and prosperous, coeternal with Heaven and Earth!"[10] Pious tradition reckons these events of the beginning of the Japanese empire to have taken place in 660 BCE, though critical history study lends no support to this or any other date.

ISÉ SHRINE

Of comparable significance was the story of the enshrinement of Amaterasu at Isé, a shrine connected thenceforth with the imperial house. The shrine was built, and in it were placed the three symbols of Amaterasu and the Japanese imperial house: a mirror, jewels, and a sword. Through many centuries of Japanese history, people have made pilgrimages to Isé and there have personally verified this myth. Many more tales, both local and national, might be added, but these are sufficient to make clear the nature of Shinto myth as a celebration of Japanese history and values—in short, of the Japanese way of life.

SHINTO RITUAL

Shinto ritual may be characterized as the enactment in symbolic actions of these same values. Shinto ritual, like the myth, is of diverse origins and combines a wide variety of interests. Elements of animism, fertility worship, worship of ancestors and heroes, and nature worship are only a few of its ingredients. The sun goddess herself combined in her own person many roles. She is the chief deity of Japan and of the imperial house as well as sun goddess.

Shinto rite and myth exhibit an impressive regional diversity. Local shrines and celebrations have always played an important part in Shinto. We have already mentioned two of the most important regional shrines, at Izumo on the west coast and Isé on the inland sea, which achieved nationwide significance.

While Shinto ritual has changed along with all things historical, there have been few if any radical mutations in its long history. Contemporary Shinto ritual thus provides a point of living relations between twentieth-century Japan and its ancient past.

Shrine buildings have been characteristically simple in structure, usually constructed of wood, with whole tree trunks for beams. Traditionally they have

Isé shrine. (Japan National Tourist Organization.)

consisted of a single room, though they are sometimes partitioned. Often ceremonial objects, such as the mirror at Isé, are enshrined within, symbolizing the kami who lives there. But at times the building has served simply as a place where people might go singly or in groups to worship the kami. The most prominent and best-known feature has been the *torii* gateway, which serves as a sign of the shrine. Near the entrance there is running water or a water basin, where the mouth and hands of worshipers may be ceremonially cleansed.

Shinto worship has traditionally consisted of two elements: attendance and offering. The former term refers to all the forms of participation in the ritual, whether procession, dance, or other appropriate ceremony. Offerings in ancient times consisted of such things as first fruits, first catch of fish, or booty of war brought as food for the kami. In modern times the offerings have been food or money. Offerings also include prayers which are punctuated by a clapping of hands in order to attract the kami's attention. Many of the ritual prayers and liturgies preserved from early times show a simple and archaic beauty of language which is characteristic of Shinto.

The festivals of Shinto as well as the values they celebrate are innumerable and diverse, ranging from Kyoto's *Gion* festival, which recalls an eighth-century deliverance from pestilence, to the cycle of the agricultural year. Foods, most notably rice, figure prominently as themes. Among the festivals of national scope is the New Year's celebration, during which millions of Japanese visit the Meiji shrine of Tokyo or other shrines throughout the land.[11]

Among other important observances are the *Nii-name-sai*, or "festival of new food," celebrated November 23 and 24 as a thanksgiving for the harvest, and the *Dai-jo-sai*, or "great food festival," which confirms a new emperor's authority. In the latter, a series of year-long symbolic activities relating to the rice harvest culminate in a ceremonial meal eaten by the new emperor.[12] Again the observer sees in all this a fusion of social and natural values.

Shinto goes back to the prehistoric past of Japan, and in many ways it is not essentially different from other folk religions. What is unusual in Shinto is its persistent vitality. Buddhism pushed it into the background but by no means displaced or destroyed it. Rather, in the background it continued to function as an ethos, or climate of opinion, and even more important, as a climate of feeling and sensibility for the whole Japanese cultural tradition. Also, at significant periods of Japanese history it has thrust its way into the foreground of important structures and events.

BUDDHISM

BUDDHIST BEGINNINGS

Buddhism came to Japan along with written language and other arts of civilized life in approximately the fourth and fifth centuries. Two particular episodes in this process are recounted in the Nihongi. The first occurred in 552 CE, when the king of Paekche in Korea sent to the Japanese court an envoy with an image of Buddha, along with some writings and a hearty recommendation to try the

Shinto shrine at Shimoda, Japan. (Robert Alexander/Photo Researchers.)

new faith. The emperor was delighted, but his court was sharply divided. The new worship began, but a pestilence occurring shortly thereafter was interpreted as being due to the hostility of the national gods; as a consequence the image of Buddha was thrown into a moat and his new temple razed. It was not until 584 that a second start was made. New images and books were sent from Korea. Again forcible measures were taken to suppress Buddhism, but this time to no avail. Learned priests began to arrive from Korea as missionary teachers. Buddhism survived and grew.

Among the most avid students of the new faith was Prince Shotoku (573–621), regent during the reign of Empress Suiko (592–626). As a convert to Buddhism, Shotoku encouraged the building of temples and lectured and wrote commentaries on Buddhist Sutras. His so-called Seventeen-Article Constitution, promulgated in 604, admonished the Japanese people to reverence the three treasures. For, it asserted, "the three treasures, viz., Buddha, the Law, and the Monastic orders, are the final refuge of the four generated beings, and are the supreme objects of faith in all countries."[13] The reader also observes that the influence of Confucian ethical and political ideals as well as Buddhism is apparent throughout Prince Shotoku's constitution.

Evidence of Chinese influence of many sorts, including not only Confucian ethics and Buddhist religion but also the Chinese calendar and the precisely graded Chinese hierarchical system of the royal court, may be observed in Japan from the time of Prince Shotoku onward. Successive embassies to the Asian mainland imported into Japan the T'ang culture of China.

These Chinese influences, and notably the impact of Chinese Buddhism, achieved a climax in the Nara period (710–783). The city of Nara, established as capital in 710, was modeled after the T'ang Chinese capital Ch'ang-an. Travelers from China brought to Nara not only Buddhist Sutras which were currently the focus of Chinese study and meditation, but much else, ranging from the Buddhist custom of cremating the dead (first practiced in Japan on the Buddhist monk Sosho) to new ceremonies for ordaining monks and new methods of road and bridge building and irrigation.

Many notable features of Japanese Buddhism and other aspects of Japanese life and culture date from the Nara period. Among these are the public bath and the Bon festival. The latter celebrates offerings by Buddha's disciple Moggallana, who was effective in releasing his mother from suffering in hell. This ceremony has celebrated the release of persons from netherworldly suffering. It is analogous to Christ's harrowing in hell. From the Nara period comes the great Buddha Vairocana statue, planned in 741 by Emperor Shomu and completed a decade later. This statue, housed in the Todaiji temple, was the central feature of Emperor Shomu's nationwide program of Buddhist temple building.

Japanese Buddhists of the Nara period probably understood little of the subtle philosophy contained in the Sutras which they brought from China. However, they were active in organizing sectarian groups around each new document. In this manner emerged the traditional six Nara sects. Two of these groups never had real or effectual existence in Japan, and none has significant existence today. However, the influence of some of these groups and of their documents has continued to the present in other Buddhist organizations. The six Nara sects were as follows:

1. *Sanron*, or "Three Treatises," was introduced in 625 and was based on the Chinese *San Lun* sect.
2. *Hosso*, or "Consciousness Only," was brought to Japan about 660 and was based on the *Wei Shih* sect of China, whose founder, Hsüan Tsang, had brought its source documents and ideas from India to China in 645.
3. *Kegon* was based upon the *Hua Yen*, or "Flower Garland," sect of China and upon the Avatamsaka Sutra, which was translated into Japanese in 722. The sect has headquarters at Todaiji in Nara and exists as a custodian of antiquities.
4. *Ritsu* was based upon the Vinaya Pitaka and was concerned with problems of obedience such as the ordination, discipline, and morality of monks.
5. and 6. *Jojitsu* and *Kusha* were based on specific Mahayana documents and had no separate historical existence in Japan.

The Nara period also saw the beginning of the continuing process of fusing Buddhist and Shinto forms of religious practice and thought into a single Japanese tradition. For example, the Empress Shotoku, daughter and successor of the Buddhist emperor Shomu and herself a devout Buddhist, declared in a famous statement that she and her people should serve the three treasures (i.e., the Buddha, the Dharma, and the Sangha) with their highest devotion, should next reverence the gods of the shrines of heaven and earth, and should next cherish and love the princes, the ministers, the officials of the hundred departments, and all the people of the land.[14] Buddhism was thus given priority but was incorporated into a structure which also had a Shinto component.

The close relation of church and state in Nara Buddhism, amounting to a virtual Buddhist religious establishment, brought the same abuses which have accompanied established religions elsewhere. As a result the Emperor Kammu resolved in 783 to move his capital in order to escape the influence of the Buddhist clergy. In 794 Heian-kyo, or Kyoto, became the capital. So began the Heian period of Japanese history.

MAIN FORMS OF JAPANESE BUDDHISM

During the Heian period (794–1192) and the Kamakura period (1192–1338), Buddhism in Japan became Japanese Buddhism. That is to say, the religious forms and ideas which had been imported from China during the preceding centuries took root and grew in Japanese soil. It is worth noting that no major new forms of Japanese Buddhism have come into being since the Kamakura period. Both the Heian and the Kamakura were periods of feudalism similar in many ways to the Middle Ages of Europe.

Wooden figure of Buddha from Koryuji Temple. (Japan
National Tourist Organization.)

The early Heian period saw the beginning of the two earliest forms of Japanese Buddhism, *Tendai* and *Shingon*, which have lasted to the present. The founder of Tendai was Saicho (767–822), known to his followers also as Dengyo Daishi; the founder of Shingon was Kukai, whose followers have called him Kobo Daishi (*daishi* means "great teacher"). These two men set sail on the same embassy to China in 804, both seeking further study and illumination as well as sanction for their developing forms of Buddhism. Saicho returned home the following year and Kukai a year later. Each left a lasting mark upon Japanese Buddhism.

As a youth Saicho had separated himself from the Nara sects to spend twelve years in solitary meditation on Mount Hiei. Throughout his life he was devoted to the Lotus Sutra as a source for both study and meditation. He seems to have had the support of Emperor Kammu in going to China to seek sources and sanction for his new Buddhist foundation on Mount Hiei. On his return from China, Saicho was plunged into continuing controversies with the Nara sects and later with Kukai. He apparently did not wish to form a new sect, but he was pushed into it. Saicho had great gifts for organization, devising his own form of ordination for monks and his own rigorous form of monastic rule and discipline. He was strongly nationalistic, recommending his form of Buddhism as a way of building up and sustaining the Japanese nation. His interest in esoteric forms of Buddhism led to disputes with Kukai. The Tendai Buddhism which Saicho founded continues as a living form in Japan today. A contemporary Japanese government source lists 4,665,060 Tendai adherents, divided among twenty groups.[15]

Kukai, who went to China with Saicho, has left a vivid personal record of his tutelage at a monastery of esoteric (in Chinese, *Chen yen*) Buddhism. Returning home in 807 CE with diagrams, documents, and charms (as well as a vast amount of Chinese learning on subjects ranging from calligraphy to bridge building), Kukai founded the Shingon sect. He was a many-sided genius and is revered by the Japanese as an authentic culture hero. His influence on Japanese life has been deep and pervasive.

He was also a wide-ranging student of religion, whose studies embraced the main faiths of both India and China. Out of this study came his idea of these different faiths as stages in the mind's ascent to salvation. According to Kobo Daishi, the ten main steps, in ascending order, were as follows:

1. Unregenerate state of no religion at all
2. Teachings of Confucius and Lao tzu
3. Sankhya and Vaisheshika schools of Indian philosophy
4. Kusha sect
5. Jojitsu sect
6. Hosso sect
7. Sanron sect
8. Tendai sect
9. Kegon sect
10. Shingon sect[16]

Building a monastery on Mount Koya, Kukai set about the propagation of Shingon Buddhism, which found a ready acceptance among the Japanese of his time. Governmental figures list 11,177,524 Shingon members and some 12,000 temples.

In the Heian period esoteric Buddhism spread throughout Japan, pervading both Shingon and Tendai with its mandalas, its charms and magic words, and its secret learning, which was deemed effective to produce salvation, longevity, and immortality. Of the innumerable deities who dwelt within these holy diagrams and holy words, the number was reduced first to thirteen, then to two. These two were Kwannon (whom we have already met in India as Avalokitesvara and in China as Kuan yin) and Fudo. Kwannon is the embodiment of mercy, and Fudo of fearsome retribution.

The closing years of the Heian period saw great disorder and anarchy. During this time, warrior monks of Tendai and Shingon monasteries contended against each other in violent conflict that would doubtless have appalled the founder of Buddhism. This afforded a vivid and grim illustration of the basic Buddhist teaching on the impermanence and misery of all worldly existence. During this time some Japanese Buddhists began to teach the idea of history as a succession of three increasingly evil ages, with the third and worst, the Mappo period, immediately impending.

In this climate of pessimism the establishment of the Kamakura shogunate with its simple but firm objectives provided Buddhism with the basis for new life. Three important new forms of Buddhism emerged in force during the Kamakura period: (1) the Pure Land schools of Amida Buddhism, (2) Nichiren, and (3) Zen.

In the records of the later Heian period, there are stories of Buddhist monks who composed devotional poetry and often went through the streets of Japanese cities and towns singing songs to Amida Buddha, the Japanese rendering of Indian Amitabha. Theirs was a popular movement which was to have great mass appeal among Japan's people. They also marked the emergence in Japanese Buddhism of a pietism similar to Hindu bhakti or Muslim sufism. Among these devotional saints were several notable figures. There was Kuya (903–972), who danced through the city streets calling on the name of Amida, singing songs of his own composition, and inviting others to join in his prayer, *Namu Amida Buddha*. There was Ryonin (1072–1132), who propagated the *Nembutsu* ("Hail Amida Buddha") through liturgical chants and popular songs; and there was also Genshin (942–1017), who wrote a famous volume, *The Essentials of Salvation*, expounding this popular way to salvation which was open to all, laypeople as well as monks, women as well as men. Genshin advocated loving trust in Amida as the power to walk this way. For reinforcement he described the pleasures of the pure land and the contrasting pains of the many Buddhist hells. Genshin also used a newly lifelike and realistic style of painting and sculpture to convey his message to those not able to read.

The greatest of the medieval devotional saints of Amidism were Honen (1133–1212) and his disciple Shinran (1173–1262). They were founders, respectively, of the Jodo and Shin sects. It was Honen who, despite his own intentions, first made a sharp break with other forms of Buddhism. He seems to have experienced a decisive religious conversion as he meditated on Zendo's *Commentary on the Meditation Sutra*. His mind was captured by the passage "whether walking or standing, sitting or lying, only repeat the name of Amida with all your heart. Never cease the practice of it even for a moment. This is the very work which unfailingly issues in salvation, for it is in accordance with the Original vow of that Buddha."[17]

Honen pledged himself to the new way that opened before him, and through his long life he kept this faith. He distinguished between two ways of salvation: one the path of meditation in one's own power (*jiriki*), which he characterized as the difficult path; and the other—the easy path—in the power of another (*tariki*). The latter depended on the mercy of Amida Buddha. It was in effect salvation by grace in contrast to one's own works. According to Honen's way, the human part was the continual confession of faith in Amida

Great Buddha, Kamakura. (Japan National Tourist Organization.)

Buddha by means of the unceasing recital of the Nembutsu. Honen introduced another element into Japanese Buddhist faith and thought, a sense of human depravity. In their helplessness, humans cannot save themselves, Honen asserted, and are therefore dependent upon the grace of Amida.

Honen set about the propagation of the new faith with characteristic vigor, thus making enemies among older Buddhist groups. His books were burned, and he was personally vilified. His success in winning converts led finally to his exile at the age of seventy-three to a remote northern part of Japan. His letter to friends and followers was a noble and courageous document in which he declined to buy clemency by silence and declared his intention to go on preaching in his new home. To his friends and converts he declared, "Mountains and seas may divide us but we are sure of meeting again in that Pure Land."[18]

Among those sent into exile with Honen was his disciple and friend, Shinran, whose offense was that he had violated his monastic vow by taking a wife. He had done so apparently at the suggestion of Honen in order to provide living demonstration that salvation depended not upon works of renunciation but on faith in Amida which transcended any outward circumstance of life. Shinran's followers have adhered to his example of marriage. Shinran believed that marrying and living in the world led his followers to a closer identification with the people whom they sought to help on the way to salvation.

Shinran's theology resembled Honen's in most essential features. He too believed that human nature is sinful and human beings could be saved only by the grace of Amida. He painted sin in even more vivid colors than Honen, and in his exclusive reliance on Amida, he discouraged the worship of other buddhas. Yet in one emphasis he differed from Honen. While Honen had emphasized the recital of the Nembutsu, Shinran focused attention on the inward attitude of faith which properly found expression in this confession. Apart from this inward faith, the words themselves could become a delusive dependence on self, but with this inner attitude of faith even the words might be dispensed with. Shinran's theology was a radical statement of salvation by grace alone. While Shinran made no attempt to organize a new sect around his own faith and creed, his followers inevitably found their way into a new organization, the Shin sect, which together with Honen's Jodo sect constitutes Pure Land or Amida Buddhism. Today some twenty-five Pure Land groups comprise 20,941,532 members.[19]

Jodo and Shin have been characterized by their emphasis on congregational worship, with sermons as a device for instruction. They have also used music and visual arts, especially images of Amida, as helps to worship. Amidist temples are used for weddings and funerals. Their people have been active in the organization of schools, hospitals, and similar social enterprises.

Amida Buddha is one of the great gods of Asia. For popular religion he is a savior to those who heed his call and follow his way, giving both a helping hand through the vicissitudes of mortal life and a guarantee of bliss in the happy land beyond death. For the learned there are Sutras and commentaries to be studied, subtle distinctions to be mastered, as well as arguments with theologians of other ways, such as Zen, which regards Amida's happy land as, at best, a concession to human frailty. Zen theologians have sometimes argued that in Buddhism's many-storied heaven the happy land is one of the lower floors, of which the top is clearly nirvana, where all mortal distinctions are left behind. Amidist theologians will not have it so, arguing back that the personal relation to Amida is the symbol of a reality together as true and ultimate as Zen satori.

The devotional religion of Honen and Shinran in turn elicited a vigorous and violent reaction from Nichiren (1222–1282), founder of the Nichiren, or the sociopolitical sect. Nichiren believed that the devotional piety and other worldliness of Jodo and Shin constituted an immoral diversion of energies needed for the present life, and especially for the common life of Japan. Nichiren was the son of a humble fisherman and was educated at Mount Hiei in the Tendai tradition, which in his time had become more concerned with esoteric Buddhism than with the original teachings of Saicho. Nichiren sought to return to the founder, and was soon forced to leave Mount Hiei. Like Saicho before him, he was convinced of the sufficiency of the Lotus Sutra. It was apparently in meditation on this Sutra that he underwent the decisive religious experience of his life. He changed his name to Nichi-ren (literally "sun lotus") and made the following vow:

Finally, let the celestial beings withdraw their protection, let all perils come upon me, even so will I dedicate my life to this cause....Be it in weal, be it in woe, to desert the Lotus of Truth means to fall to the hells. I will be firm in my Great Vow. Let me face all manner of threats and temptations. Should one say to me, "Thou wouldst abandon the Scripture and expect future bliss through belief in the meditation on Amida; or thy parents shall suffer capital punishment unless thou utterest the name of the Buddha Amida,—such temptation I shall meet unshaken, and shall never be allured by them, unless my principles shall be shattered by a sage's refutation of them. Any other perils shall be the dust before the storm. I will be the Pillar of Japan; I will be the Eyes of Japan; I will be the Great Vessel of Japan. Inviolable shall remain these oaths."[20]

All the energies of his intense personality were now integrated and focused. He resolved to play the role of prophet to his reluctant contemporaries. As we have seen, he denounced Honen and Amidism in unsparing language. He sought also to arouse Japan from its apparent lethargy at the approach of foreign invasion; and he regarded the failure of the Mongol invasion as divine deliverance.

Personalities such as Nichiren often make enemies in high places. For his denunciation of the government he was exiled and twice condemned to death. After the second condemnation, on his way to what he thought was to be the place of execution, he paused before the shrine of Hachiman, whom he regarded as a bodhisattva as well as a Shinto deity, but most of all the special protector of the Japanese nation. There he challenged Hachiman to save him. The execution was set aside, apparently by prearrangement, but Nichiren interpreted it as divine deliverance.[21] Characteristically, Nichiren regarded himself as the "bodhisattva of superb action."[22]

From Nichiren and a tradition of like-minded successors has sprung the sociopolitical or Nichiren sect of Japanese Buddhism. Like its founder and leaders, this group has been characterized by its strong adherence to Japanese patriotism and nationalism. In recent and contemporary times it has generated several significantly nationalistic sects. Today the total number of Nichiren adherents is 31,887,015, divided among some thirty-five groups, the largest total for any main form of Japanese Buddhism.[23]

Also from the Kamakura period comes Zen or Meditation Buddhism. Like other forms of Buddhism, Zen was imported into Japan from China, and in this case on three different occasions: in 1191 by Eisai, the traditional founder of the Rinzai sect; in 1244 by Dogen, who founded Soto; and in 1654 by Ingen, founder of the Obaku school of Zen. Today some thirty-one Zen groups count a total of 10,150,010 members.[24] While by no means the most popular form of Japanese Buddhism, Zen has exerted a deep and pervasive influence on virtually every aspect of Japanese culture. From swordsmanship to flower arrangement, from governmental administration to the tea ceremony, every significant aspect of Japanese culture has known the quickening influence of Zen.

In the opinion of its protagonists, Zen Buddhism, far from being eccentric or esoteric, actually stands in the main line of Buddhist tradition, synthesizing in its outlook ideas and attitudes derived from India, China, and Japan. The defining idea of Zen, meditation, began in India as dhyana and became ch'an in China and zen in Japan; the basic practices of meditation in Zen monasteries testify to this threefold heritage.

Yet none would deny that Zen constitutes a highly distinctive interpretation of the Buddhist tradition. For one thing, it is jiriki in contrast to the tariki view of Amidism. Zen has no savior; each person depends on his or her own power to walk the path to salvation. The nontheistic character of Zen has been of great historical significance. Zen adherents derive it from the Buddha's own teaching and example.

As noted in Chapter 8, Ch'an Buddhism in China brought Indian dhyana, or meditation, down to earth, making its object not a remote transcendental realm but the present, experienced world of nature and society. This cosmic or this-worldly attitude of China made its way to Japan, where it was given even more vivid and forceful expression. In this respect Zen Buddhism offers clear illustration of Nakamura's assertion that Japanese people seek and find "the absolute in the phenomenal world."[25] To this view the Japanese have added their own distinctive accents and their own peculiar intensity of feeling. The result is Zen Buddhism.

The Zen pioneers were Eisai (1141–1215) and Dogen (1200–1253). Eisai made two trips to China, for study and training in Ch'an as well as other forms of Buddhism. Returning home to Japan, he founded temples for the practice and propagation of Zen, both in Kyoto and in Kamakura. The established Buddhists in the former city were hostile, but in the latter he and his followers gained a ready hearing from the nobles of the new Kamakura shogunate. Eisai did not hesitate to mix Zen with other forms of Buddhism such as Tendai, Shingon, and Pure Land. He also brought tea to Japan, ardently recommending tea drinking as a way to health and long life. His treatise "Drink Tea and Prolong Life" was addressed to a Kamakura shogun whom Eisai sought to win from alcohol to tea. Possibly most important of all, Eisai introduced into his native land the philosophic writings of the great Chinese neo-Confucian master, Chu Hsi. Eisai meditated and studied with the so-called southern school in China and hence emphasized sudden enlightenment.

By contrast Dogen derived his version of Zen from the northern school, with its doctrine of gradual enlightenment. Where Eisai was adaptable, Dogen was uncompromising. Born of noble parents, Dogen was orphaned at the age of seven, his mother's dying wish being that he become a Buddhist monk. Ordained by the chief abbot of the Tendai school, he continued to seek for solutions to the religious and philosophic problems that concerned him. In 1223 he went to China, wandering from monastery to monastery in search of enlightenment. On the point of returning home in disappointment, he achieved enlightenment on hearing the monk Ju-ching declare, "In Zen, body and mind are cast off," or in alternative phrasing, the duality of body and mind is transcended.

Returning home to Japan in 1227, Dogen spent the rest of his life in singleminded service of his interpretation of Buddhism. Living successively at

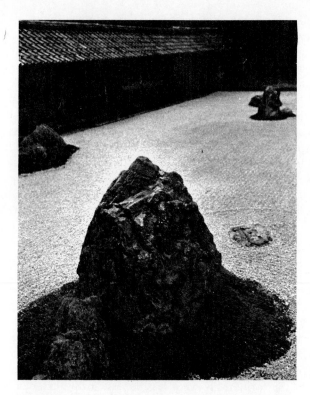

Zen garden of Ryoanji Temple, Kyoto. (Japan National Tourist Organization.)

different temples, he continued to write and to practice his own simple and austere form of meditation. Illness led to his death in 1253. As Dumoulin remarks, Dogen's life was overshadowed by the sorrowful awareness of the transitoriness of all things.

He was also the greatest philosophic mind in Japanese history. His philosophy might be characterized as an unremitting effort to push beyond all dualities of thought and experience to an all-encompassing unity—a unity, we must immediately add, that must be directly experienced in order to be understood. It is called *satori* or *kensho.*

Primary among the dualities of thought for Dogen was the distinction between original enlightenment and acquired enlightenment. The latter is the experience of satori or enlightenment which is sought by Zen Buddhists, while the former is the innate buddha nature, latent in all people and all things. These two are really one, declared Dogen characteristically. Thus the achievement of enlightenment consists of the present realization of the original buddha nature.

Among the further dualities that Dogen sought to embrace and overcome were that between body and mind, which as Ju-ching had declared must be cast off, or transcended; that between the samsara world and the nirvana world, which are the same world seen from different perspectives; and that between practice and enlightenment, both of which in reality are constituted by the one all-important activity of *zazen*, or "meditation." In this last respect Dogen was especially opposed to sudden enlightenment or enlightenment as something apart from meditation.

The Zen tradition has produced many great leaders. Particularly notable was Muso Soseki (1275–1351), known also as Muso Kokushi ("Muso the national master") for his role as advisor to shoguns and other government officials. He was also one of the originators of the Japanese art of landscape gardening.

The period of the Ashikaga shogunate (1333–1568), which followed the Kamakura period, was a time of extensive and intensive cultural creativity for Zen. Zen monks were leading scholars, writers, artists, and political advisors. From this age comes the development of the tea ceremony. Landscape painting was developed by such masters as Sesshu (1420–1500). Drama flowered in the No plays.

To Hakuin (1685–1768) is due credit for the modern revitalization and re-organization of Zen. His *Song of Meditation* is an admirably lucid and characteristic summary of the Zen outlook.

> All beings are primarily Buddhas.
> Like water and ice,
> There is no ice apart from water;
> There are no Buddhas apart from beings.
>
> Not knowing how close the Truth is to them,
> Beings seek for it afar—what a pity!
> It is like those who being in water
> Cry out for water, feeling thirst.
> It is like the rich man's son,
> Who has lost his way among the poor.
>
> The reason why beings transmigrate through the six worlds,
> Is because they are lost in the darkness of ignorance.
> Wandering from darkness to darkness,
> How can they ever be free from birth-and-death?
>
> As Zazen taught in the Mahayana,
> No amount of praise can exhaust its merits.
> The Six Paramitas, beginning with the Giving,
> Observing the Precepts and other good deeds, variously enumerated,
> As Nembutsu, Repentance, and so on—
> All are finally reducible to Zazen.
>
> The merit of even a single sitting in Zazen
> Erases the countless sins accumulated in the past.
> Where then are there the evil paths to misguide us?
> The Pure Land cannot be far away.
>
> Those who even once, in all humility,
> Listen to this Truth.
> Praise it and faithfully follow it,
> Will be endowed with innumerable merits.

But if you turn your eyes within yourselves
And testify to the truth of Self-nature—
The Self-nature that is no-nature,
You will have gone beyond the ken of sophistry.

The gate of the oneness of cause and effect is opened;
The path of non-duality and non-trinity runs straight ahead.
Your form being the form of no-form,
Your going-and-returning takes place nowhere but where you are;
Your thought being the thought of no-thought,
Your singing-and-dancing is none other than the voice of the Dharma.

How Boundless and free is the sky of Samadhi!
How refreshingly bright, the moon of the Fourfold Wisdom!

At this moment what is there that you lack!
Nirvana presents itself before you,
Where you stand is the Land of Purity.
Your person, the body of Buddha.[26]

Throughout its history Zen has placed primary emphasis on the direct experience of satori or enlightenment, which may be understood as the distinctive Zen rendering of the mystical union that we have already met in other interpretations in other faiths and cultures. Zen appeals to the example of the Buddha's experience under the bo tree in India. The whole Zen practice and philosophy point the way to having this experience. From this source the life of Zen flows. Along with teaching (or philosophy) and practice (or meditation), enlightenment is one of Zen's "three pillars."

What are the salient features of satori to those who experience it? The list which follows here has been freely adapted from the writings of D. T. Suzuki, pioneer interpreter of Zen to the modern West.

1. Suzuki speaks of its irrationality (but more precisely stated, the term would be *transrationality*), or its being beyond the rational, factual features of the world of common experience.
2. He lists authoritativeness as a feature, meaning that the experience asserts a sovereign claim over those who have known it, though not over others. Satori is addressed "to whom it may concern."
3. It is an affirmative experience. At least, those who have it testify to its affirmative or ever superaffirmative quality.
4. In similar vein, Suzuki speaks of the exaltation it brings.
5. In contrast to the personal nature of western religious experience, he characterizes Zen as impersonal in quality. Other expositors of Zen have preferred the term *transpersonal*, meaning not "less than personal," but "more than personal."
6. Satori is immediate or intuitive in quality, or in Whitehead's phrase, it occurs in the "mode of presentational immediacy."

Zen monk depicted on scroll painting,
Tokugawa period. (Cleveland Museum of Art,
Norman O. Stone and Ellen A. Stone Fund.)

7. It brings what Suzuki terms a "sense of the beyond." Yet to this we must immediately add that the reference is to the world of present experience in its inclusive totality, and not any supramundane realm or region.

8. To these features must also be added a sense of dependence. While people must walk the path to enlightenment in their own strength, satori is not so much something people do as it is something which happens to them, and it does so in ways independent of human will or volition. Such, at least, is the experience that Zen Buddhists report.

It is an experience which has renewed, reinforced, and redirected the lives of countless Japanese. They have been drawn from the secular world to Zen meditation rooms, and from these monastic halls they have moved back into the common world with new light and power.

During these centuries of Buddhist dominance, Shinto continued its quiet but pervasive influence. We have seen that as early as the Nara period the fusing of Buddhism and Shinto was under way, and during the Heian period, both Shingon and Tendai Buddhism lent themselves extensively to this fusion of faiths. In many instances Shinto and Buddhist rituals took place in the same shrines or temples. There was also a merging of deities. As we have seen, Hachiman, the Shinto war god, became "the great bodhisattva." During the Kamakura period these influences continued and grew in strength. Nichiren Buddhism lent force to Japanese nationalism. The failure of the Mongol invasions in 1274 and 1281 was widely interpreted as divine deliverance by Hachiman and Amaterasu.

One medieval writer and exponent of Shinto worth mentioning is Kitabatake (1293–1354). He wrote a document called *The Records of the Legitimate Succession of the Divine Sovereigns*, in which he did not hesitate to deify his native land. Kitabatake wrote: "Japan is the divine country. The heavenly ancestor it was who first laid its foundations, and the Sun Goddess left her descendants to reign over it forever and ever. This is true only of our country, and nothing similar may be found in foreign lands. That is why it is called the divine country."[27] This growing ethnocentrism, while in no way different from that of many other lands and peoples, was destined in time to come to bring about developments which would doubtless have surprised and shocked its author, who also wrote elaborate explanations and expositions of the three imperial symbols at Isé, the sword, mirror, and jewels.

TOKUGAWA DEVELOPMENTS

The Tokugawa period of Japanese history (1603–1868) consists of two and a half centuries lying between the unification of Japan and the opening of the nation to the West and to modernity. It was an age of national integration, but also of isolation from the outside world. The Tokugawa period was ushered in by three tough-minded military men, Nobunagu, Hideyoski, and Ieyasu, who broke the divisive power of feudalism and forcibly united the Japanese nation in a manner strikingly similar to that of the early modern European kings such as Henry VIII of England. One notable aspect of this unification was the persecution and suppression of Christians. Saint Francis Xavier had arrived in Japan as a missionary in 1542, and before the end of the sixteenth century there was a large and flourishing Christian community. However, to the Tokugawa shoguns these Christians seemed a threat to national unity. There was sporadic persecution, culminating in a revolt of Christians in Kuyushi in 1637. It ended with a massacre of Christians and the closing of the Japanese nation to all outsiders. A few Christians (or *kirishitans*, as the Japanese called them) went underground and maintained an underground existence until the coming of relative religious freedom in the nineteenth century.

Tokugawa shoguns with the ideas of fixed order, like King Canute, sought to hold back all change. Yet beneath the static surface, important changes of many kinds continued to take place, preparing the way for modern Japan. Religiously it was a period when medieval Buddhist otherworldliness, with its goal of emancipation from all worldly bonds, gave way to more secular value systems. Western historians of Japan list four Tokugawa schools or types of ethical and religious thought.

NEO-CONFUCIANISM

The Tokugawa rulers turned for religious and moral guidance not to Buddhism but to the neo-Confucianism of Chu Hsi. As had so often been true in the past, this was a philosophy and code imported from China; but also as usual, the Japanese put their own stamp on what they imported. Tokugawa neo-Confucianism began with a Buddhist monk, Seika (1561–1616), who forsook his Buddhist orders to become a lay philosopher. His disciple and successor, Hayashi Razan (1583–1657), was an advisor and counselor of Ieyasu, the first Tokugawa shogun. He was also one of the architects of the Tokugawa social system. It was his achievement to establish Chu Hsi's neo-Confucian philosophy as the orthodox system of Tokugawa Japan. In 1691 Hayashi's grandson became the first hereditary president of the Confucian University at Edo (or Tokyo). The Japanese followers of Chu Hsi professed to accept his philosophy as a whole. Some of them even practiced Chu Hsi's "investigation of things," with scientific concern for nature and for medical lore. However, the primary emphasis was upon the great Chinese master's ethical philosophy, which performed for them two very important functions, namely, legitimatizing the existing political and social order and providing the individual with moral orientation within Tokugawa society.

While Chu Hsi's version of neo-Confucianism assumed the role of the official philosophy, the philosophic system of Wang Yang-ming (in Japanese, *Oyomei*) also attracted many individual students and followers. The Japanese found particularly attractive Wang's emphasis on intuition and his teaching of the unity of thought and action.

ANCIENT LEARNING

A third group constituted themselves as the school of Ancient Learning, rejecting both forms of neo-Confucianism and going back to Confucius himself. Chu Hsi's vast metaphysical system left them cold, but they were attracted to Confucius's ethic. Especially notable in the school of Ancient Learning was Yamaga Soko (1622–1685), in whose thought and life Confucian ethics joined forces with Japanese feudalism to produce *Bushido*, or the "way of the fighting knight." (The word is from *bukyo*, meaning "the warrior's creed," and *shido*, "the way of the *samurai*, or feudal retainer.")[28] Yamaga was a man of fiercely independent mind, in continual trouble with officials for his unorthodox opinions. His rejection of Chu Hsi in favor of Confucius led to his exile in a remote region of Japan for the last twenty years of his life. There he wrote not only his autobiography, but *The True Facts Concerning the Central Kingdom*, seeking to show Japan and not China to be the true center of all culture, and Japan's imperial line of rulers to be in effect divine. He expounded the lofty mission of the samurai as a dedicated servant of his lord, with the divine emperor at the top of a graded pyramid of lordship. Yamaga was motivated by burning loyalty to Japan and its emperors.

Bushido, as it emerged in the thought and life of Yamaga and others, provided a code and way of life for the samurai of Tokugawa Japan. The "way of the fighting knight," originating in a fusion of Confucian ethics and Japanese feudalism, was in many ways similar to the medieval European code of chivalry, although it differed in its complete absence of romantic love. Unlike his European counterpart, the Japanese knight was not motivated by romantic dreams of his lady.

As popularized, practiced and celebrated, Bushido may be summarized in five main tenets:

1. Loyalty: The knight is bound in personal loyalty to his lord and is thus related to the feudal pyramid of loyalty, at the apex of which stands that supreme lord, the Japanese emperor.
2. Courage: As a soldier the samurai must be brave, rejoicing to sacrifice his life for his lord.
3. Honor: Again as a soldier, the knight cherishes his self-esteem. He regards it as a sacred duty to revenge affronts to his honor. He also prefers death to dishonor. From this last tenet of Bushido derives the duty of ritual suicide. (The popular term *harakiri*, or "belly slitting," has in the West displaced the formal traditional designation of *seppuku*.)
4. Politeness: This generally respected virtue of Japan comes to mean for the knight not only courtesy but also a reticence which scorns any public show of feeling.
5. Benevolence: The knight is devoted to righteousness and justice and must ever stand against evildoers and evildoing.

As will be seen in the next section of this chapter, Bushido was destined for further development and application in modern Japan.

Better than by summary of its tenets, the spirit of Bushido is shown in the popular tale of the forty-seven *ronin*. Based upon an actual happening which took place in 1702, the story soon became a popular tale celebrating the virtues of the brave and loyal knight.[29] A certain lord, goaded beyond endurance, drew his sword and wounded a shogunal officer within the Edo castle. Since to draw one's sword within the castle grounds was tantamount to treason, this lord was required to commit suicide, and his land was confiscated. His samurai thus became *ronin*, "men without a master." However, forty-seven of them vowed vengeance. Knowing that they would be under suspicion, they scattered, some of them abandoning their families and even pretending to sink into lives of debauchery. Their ruse worked; a less strict watch was kept at the enemy castle. Finally one snowy night when half the castle guard had been sent away, they came together and stormed the castle, capturing the enemy of their dead lord. The leader of the ronin respectfully addressed the captive noble, stating their identity and their mission of revenge, and asking him to perform ritual suicide. The enemy lord sat trembling in cowardice, unable to comply. The leader of the ronin leaped upon him and cut off his head with the same sword with which the lord of the ronin had killed himself. Then the ronin went as a group to the grave of their dead lord and offered to him the washed head of the enemy. After this the ronin waited quietly until required by the government to commit suicide. All Japan sang their praises, and ever since they have been the peerless exemplars of Bushido.

NATIONAL LEARNING

Still a fourth important religious development of the Tokugawa period was the school of National Learning, or as it is known to western students, the Shinto revival. This was in essence a strongly anti-Confucian and anti-Chinese appeal to indigenous and traditional Japanese sources of thought and allegiance. Scholars of the school of National Learning pored through Japan's ancient and classical documents, seeking an authentically Japanese path of faith and life. The movement may be said to have begun with Kado Azumamero (1669), sponsor of the school of National Learning. Kado's own studies began the process of Shinto revival which his distinguished successors carried forward.

During the eighteenth and nineteenth centuries, three men stood out as the leaders and makers of the Shinto revival: Kamo Mabushi (1697–1769), Motoori Noringa (1730–1801), and Hirata Atsutane (1776–1848). Kamo sought in Japan's ancient poetry for the true national style and spirit. He also attacked both Confucianism and Chinese influence, though ironically his attack was expressed largely in Taoist terms. The Taoist way of nature became in his writings the way of the divine age or the age of the gods in ancient Japan. Kamo also attacked the Chinese language as a cumbersome vehicle of expression, inferior in every way to Japanese.

Motoori Noringa spent more than thirty years of his life on a *Commentary on the Kojiki*, which he sought to exalt as a national scripture. By massive yet perceptive literary scholarship, Motoori sought to make clear to his contemporaries the simple feeling of wonder or awe in prehistoric Shinto and its innumerable kami. Indeed, Shinto faith consists of this feeling! "Man living in such a strange and wondrous universe, wonders not about its mysteries but only about the wonders of the Divine Age, saying there is no reason for them. If this is not senseless, what is?"[30] Motoori argued that the Japanese myths of beginning constituted the source of the true way, which had been handed down in Japan through the divinely descended line of emperors, but was only partially and imperfectly present elsewhere in the world. He found a central place in his theology for the sun goddess, Amaterasu. He also studied and wrote critical interpretations of the *Tale of Genji* as a sensitive depiction of *mono no aware*, or the "sadness of things."[31]

The most strongly nationalistic scholar of the Shinto revival was Hirata Atsutane, who asserted the supremacy of Shinto over all faiths and the Japanese over all other peoples.

> People all over [the] world refer to Japan as the Land of the Gods, and call us the descendants of the gods. Indeed it is exactly as they say: our country as a special mark of favor from the heavenly gods was begotten by them, and there is thus so immense a difference between Japan and all other countries of the world as to defy comparison. . . . Japanese differ completely from and are superior to the peoples of China, India, Russia, Holland, Siam, Cambodia and all other countries of the world, and for us to have called our country the Land of the Gods was not mere vainglory.[32]

Also in disagreement with Motoori, he taught life after death. Hirata's Japanese pride was modified by an admiration for "Dutch learning," which was the modern science brought to Japan by Dutch traders. Yet he taught that the real source of this, as of medicine, was the Japanese gods who in the beginning had given these gifts to humankind.

The intense and growing sentiment of nationality on which the Shinto revival was based and to which in turn it contributed is a widely recurring human phenomenon; indeed, there are striking parallels in American history and in the history of European peoples at approximately the same historical period. One of the differences in nationalism in Japan was its explicitly religious character. Modern and contemporary history was to witness some unique and grim expressions for the Japanese form of this recurrent phenomenon.

MODERN AND CONTEMPORARY ISSUES

The modern world came late and suddenly to Japan. In 1853 Commodore Perry appeared in Tokyo Bay with letters from President Fillmore asking for trade and the opening of ports where American ships might buy supplies. Having delivered his message, he sailed away to China. When he returned in 1854 with more ships and men, the shogun was helpless to do anything but accede to his request. This episode aroused in Japan a lively debate in which three parties emerged: anti-West, pro-West, and compromisers.

The decline of the shogunate and the death of the antiforeign emperor Komei in 1867 brought a crisis which was resolved in December of that year with the abolition of the shogunate and the accession to the throne of the boy emperor Meiji. Under the new leadership, the Japanese nation undertook a comprehensive process of modernization. The only real question soon became one of the terms along which modernization should take place. Would it be under the guidance of pro-western liberals, who would replace the Japanese tradition with the secular, scientific, and liberal spirit of the modern West? Or would it be under the leadership of staunch samurai, who would use western instrumentalities for the support and maintenance of traditional Japanese values? The nation's destiny for the next century was to lie in the answers Japanese leaders and people gave to these questions. All aspects of both Buddhism and Shinto were also to be involved.

The effective agents of the Meiji restoration were young samurai idealists for whom Shinto was a living and powerful value system. So it was that the new emperor's statements were punctuated with appeals to the kami and to Japanese tradition. In the early 1870s the emperor's advisors sought to make Shinto an established national faith. In the early years of the Meiji restoration, it was given official status through a governmental department. There was much hostility to Buddhism as a foreign ideology, and there was even sporadic anti-Buddhist violence. However, this attempt at establishment and unification proved abortive; by 1875 the government had shifted its position to the modern idea of the freedom and equality of all religions, which found later official formulation in the constitution of 1889.

However, the western liberal facade was somewhat deceptive, for in effect what the Shintoists in the government did was to make a threefold division into (1) shrine Shinto, (2) sect Shinto, and (3) domestic Shinto, and to assert that while sect and domestic Shinto were religious in character, shrine Shinto consisted of nonreligious patriotic allegiance and ritual. In effect, Shintoists were provided with a convenient screen of nonreligion behind which they could operate freely to influence governmental policy and popular attitudes.

This "solution" to the Meiji religious problem is significant in several ways. It is an admirable illustration of the problematic character of the word *religion* (or its Japanese translation, *shukyo*). Also it illustrates the fact that ultimate concern remains ultimate, whatever the conventional label. The loyalty to Japan and its emperor so jealously cherished and propagated by the traditionalists was pushed past all limits and became ultimate in character. The modern role of the Japanese emperor affords perhaps the most effective illustration in modern history of the divine ruler, which has been noted as a recurring feature of nature-culture religions.

Shrine Shinto, once taken under government sponsorship, soon became state Shinto. Approximately 110,000 shrines and their 16,000 priests received governmental support—and along with it they came under governmental control. They ranged from the large and nationally important shrines like Isé, Izumo, and the Meiji shrine in Tokyo, to the many village shrines throughout Japan. The traditional ethnic Japanese values, many of them nonpolitical, which had found natural expression in shrine Shinto were now twisted into forms and necessities of nationalist and militarist propaganda. While the natural ethnocentrism of the Japanese tradition provided a basis in popular credibility, it must be also added that the exploitation of this tradition by the modern militarist party was something new in Japanese history.

This use of the Shinto value system extended beyond the shrines to embrace all aspects of the culture. The Imperial Rescript on Education in 1890 was an intimation of things to come:

> Our Imperial Ancestors have founded Our Empire on a basis broad and ever-lasting and have deeply and firmly implanted virtue; Our subjects ever united in loyalty and filial piety have from generation to generation illustrated the beauty thereof. This is the glory of the fundamental character of Our Empire and herein also lies the source of Our Education. Ye, Our Subjects, be filial to your parents, affectionate to your brothers and sisters; as husbands and wives be harmonious; as friends be true; bear yourselves in modesty and moderation; extend your benevolence to all; pursue learning and cultivate arts, and thereby develop intellectual faculties and perfect moral powers; furthermore, advance public good and promote common interests; always respect the Constitution and observe the laws; should emergency arise, offer yourselves courageously to the State; and thus guard and maintain the prosperity of Our Imperial Throne coeval with heaven and earth. So shall ye not only be Our good and faithful subjects, but render illustrious the best traditions of your forefathers.
>
> The Way here set forth is indeed the teaching bequeathed by Our Imperial Ancestors to be observed alike by the Descendants and the subjects, infallible for all ages and true in all places. It is Our wish to lay it to heart in all reverence in common with you, Our Subjects, that we may all attain to the same virtue.[33]

This document itself also took on a well-nigh holy quality. Shrines repeated its words, all schools had copies, and at the annual ceremonial readings of it, hearers bowed reverently.

In the popular culture, this religiously inspired and sanctioned nationalism grew with the years and decades. Successful wars against China in 1894–1895 and Russia in 1904–1905 imparted to it an increasing plausibility. Books like Sakurai's *Human Bullets*[34] were in effect religious tracts which served to disseminate and stimulate the popular nationalism. The constitution of 1889 began with the fateful assertions, "The Empire of Japan shall be reigned over and governed by a line of Emperors unbroken for ages eternal. . . . The Emperor is sacred and inviolable."[35] What was even more ominous, in this constitution the military leaders were made directly responsible to the emperor and not to parliament.

To be sure, secular liberal voices were by no means absent in Japan during this period, but they fought a losing battle against the rising tide of nationalism.

Political leaders like Baron Shidehara counseled secular and free politics at home and peace with the world.[36] Ironically, the international situation in the first half of the twentieth century strengthened the position of the militarists, notably through Japan's frustrations as the result of World War I and the coming of world depression in the 1930s. At home the rise of an overtly revolutionary Japanese nationalism in such groups as the Amur Society, devoted to assassination of political opponents and to the mission of holy Japan in the Far East and the world, pushed events inexorably toward World War II.[37]

In the years before and during World War II, it was inevitable that state Shinto would identify itself with the national cause. The military defeat of 1945, which hit all aspects of Japanese life with seismic force, brought fundamental changes in Shinto. In December 1945, the American occupation authorities handed down a directive requiring "abolition of governmental support, perpetuation, control, and dissemination of State Shinto."[38] On January 1, 1946, the emperor issued a famous rescript officially renouncing divinity. It read in part:

> We stand by the people and we wish always to share with them in their moments of joys and sorrows. The ties between us and our people have always stood for mutual trust and affection. They do not depend upon mere legends and myths. They are not predicated on the false assumption that the Emperor is divine and that the Japanese people are superior to other races and fated to rule the world. . . .[39]

The years since this historic statement have demonstrated the truth of these assertions. The "de-divinized" emperor continues as a religious as well as a political leader, and, though shorn of militaristic nationalism, as a powerful symbol of Japanese values.

During the first years of the postwar period, the newly disestablished shrine Shinto suffered a sharp decline, but in recent years the annual number of visitors to Isé and other such places has approached the prewar totals. In conscious emulation of American models, the denationalized shrines have organized into an Association of Shinto Shrines whose membership now exceeds 80,000 local shrines and some 61,000,000 members. Shrines are supported and attended by individuals. Religious freedom is guaranteed by the constitution of 1947. The Kokugakuin University exists to provide education for Shinto priests and scholarly study of the faith. The new start is promising, but what the future holds for shrine Shinto only time can tell.

Sect Shinto, officially denominated as religious in the Meiji "solution," has continued to the present to manifest considerable vitality. During the Meiji period some thirteen new sects began. Some are now only a memory, and others had little real existence even from the first. Three of the thirteen are mountain sects, two devoted to worship at Mount Fuji and a third located at Mount Mitake in central Japan. Of those which still survive, the *Tenri, Kurozumi,* and *Konko* sects will serve as a sample of their range and variety. All of them are a blend of elements from Japan's diverse religious tradition, brought together in new ways by the mind and experience of the religious founder or leader.

Tenri kyo (literally, the "Heavenly Reason" sect) was founded by an illiterate farmer's wife named Miki Nakayama (1798–1887), who appears to have been a religious genius. The movement she founded survived government persecution in the World War II period and today reports 1,993,217 members in Japan and an ever-growing number of overseas converts to its active missionary program. In 1837, on the occasion of the miraculous healing of her husband (her son, according to other accounts), she began to receive divine revelations. She devoted herself to religious work, preaching the gospel she had received and gathering a large following around her.

Her faith was based upon the divine parents (*Tsuki-hi*, literally "moon-sun") who seek the well-being of their earthly children. Miki Nakayama placed great emphasis on faith and faith healing. Her followers have emulated her example in teaching and practicing faith healing, though it must immediately be added that this same practice has been a feature of many if not most of the new Japanese religious movements.

Tenri kyo's tenets include a doctrine of creation which is acted out in liturgical dance. The headquarters of Tenri kyo's worldwide activities is the city of Tenri near Nara, which is also the location of its growing university. In recent decades Tenri kyo has sought to divest itself of traditional Shinto features, making the claim to be a separate and distinct religion. Adherents point to its world mission as evidence of this new identity.

Kurozumi kyo was founded by a man known by many names, the last being Munetada (1780–1850). He was a deeply devout man who believed himself the recipient of several revelations of deity; his life was crucially and suddenly changed when, during what he thought was a mortal illness, he was performing his daily worship of Amaterasu. He experienced a feeling of unity with all being, which he interpreted as the grace of Amaterasu. The experience apparently healed his body as well as his spirit. Becoming a devotee of Amaterasu, he went around Japan preaching, performing faith healing, and gathering a following. After his death he was officially designated by the Japanese government as kami, or divine. During the Meiji period the Kurozumi sect grew rapidly, but membership has now leveled off at a reported 407,590 members.

Konko kyo was founded by Kawati Bunjiro (1814–1883), a poor farmer in a tax-ridden region of Japan, who in 1859 received a revelation from God, the divine parent, calling him to seek the salvation of all people. By the time of the founder's death at the age of sixty-nine, the movement had grown to several hundred thousand. A recent census figure lists some 500,000 members. Adherents maintain their faith in the divine parent and practice faith healing. They are also active in education and social science.

The years since the end of World War II have added a newer and vastly longer list of names to Japan's new religions. Some lists of these new phenomena run to hundreds or even thousands of items. All are complicated by the insoluble problems of what is to be counted as an old religion and what as a new religion. Many of these movements are in effect novel formulations of traditional religious patterns. Many more are too transitory to be termed organizations, religious or otherwise. All of them have emerged out of what one observer has termed the "religious ferment" of contemporary Japan.[40] This ferment is the product of tradition and novelty, or the old and the new, in contemporary Japan. The people of this deeply traditional culture have been thrust forcibly and violently into an age of change bewildering in its extent and significance. One response to this situation—and a characteristically Japanese response it is—has been the emergence of new religions which claim to provide effective guidance in this new and puzzling situation.

Notable among these new religions both for its amazing size and rate of growth and for its militant, even belligerent teaching is *Soka Gakkai*, or to use the more traditional label which is often preferred by the group itself, *Nichiren Shoshu*. Beginning in 1930 as a lay movement of Nichiren Buddhism, it was founded by Makiguchi (1871–1943), who was a Tokyo elementary school principal. Conversions were few for the first years. Makiguchi and his followers refused to worship Amaterasu, as was currently required of all Japanese, and they went to prison for their faith. Makiguchi died in prison during World War II and thus became a martyr. His movement came to new life in the postwar years under the leadership of Toda Josei. Soka Gakkai currently claims some 16 million adherents and a rapid and continuing growth. Its manifestations range from the *gohonzon*, or mandala, of Nichiren, and the chant *Namu Myoho Rengi Kyo*, to faith healing and militant missionary activity. Soka Gakkai's militancy has also been directed to politics, and it has elected a dozen or so members to the Diet on a platform of strong nationalism. Soka Gakkai has a new headquarters located characteristically on the slopes of Mount Fuji. More traditional exponents of Nichiren have not hesitated to disparage Soka Gakkai as a false form of Buddhism.

Among other offshoots of Nichiren are *Reiyukai* (Association of Friends of the Spirit) and *Rissho Koseikai* (Society Establishing Righteousness and Harmony), each of which claims between three and four million adherents. Both of these groups practice a kind of group counseling called *hoza*. Both are involved in forms of faith healing. *Reiyukai* is notable for its conservative social outlook, including advocacy of ancestor worship. It supports the *Yasukuni* shrine in Tokyo devoted to Japanese war dead, and it campaigns politically for repeal of Article 9 in the Japanese Constitution, which forbids war as national policy. *Rissho Koseikai*'s concerns range from study of the *Lotus Sutra* to advocacy of world peace.

Another cluster of new religions consists of those which have splintered away from *Omoto* or *Omoto kyo*, "the Teaching of Great Origin." The original Omoto group was founded in Meiji times and has lasted through severe persecution for its pacifist views. Among the half-dozen splinter forms of Omoto, perhaps the most novel is *PL Kyodan*. *PL* stands for "perfect liberty," and its adherents state with pride that the title reflects the resolution of contemporary Japan to have a modernized faith. Among the striking features are a large and excellent golf course adjacent to its national headquarters near Osaka, which has given rise to the appellation the "golf religion," and a creed of twenty-one affirmations beginning with "life is art" and ending with "live in perfect liberty." PL Kyodan claims a total of 600,000 adherents.

Among the other new religions is *Tensho Kotai Jingo kyo*, or *Odoru Shukyo* as it is popularly known, the latter term meaning the "Dancing Religion." This appellation stems from the practice by the founder, Kitamura Sayo, of dancing and singing ecstatically as she preached. This remarkable personality was clearly the focal center of the religious movement she founded in 1945 and led until her death in 1969. She claimed to heal disease as well as to impart new life to her followers. Her missionary travels brought her to Hawaii and to the continental United States. The Dancing Religion claims over 100,000 members and a continuing and rapid rate of growth. While its teaching bears striking parallels to Christian doctrine, the founder understood herself to be the embodiment of a Shinto deity. She was succeeded in leadership of this religion by her granddaughter.

A different kind of religious concern is contained in the Buddhist philosophy of Kitara Nishida (1875–1945) and his followers, who wear the label of the Kyoto School. Nishida's thought centered in fresh philosophic expression of Zen Buddhism. He was professor of philosophy at the Kyoto Imperial University from 1910 until his retirement in 1928. He brought together the Buddhist tradition with modern western philosophers such as Henri Bergson, William James, and the German Neo-Kantians, focusing upon the concept of experience, with a Buddhist reference to subjective factors which distort the self's view of things, Nishida sought "to know things just as they are." Instrumental in this project is the Buddhist Dharma which Nishida called a mirror faithfully reflecting things exactly as they are. Presupposed in this characteristically Zen view of the world is the Buddhist vision of a meaningful totality. Nishida's students and disciples of the Kyoto School continue this mission of interpreting the Buddhist vision to contemporary Japan and the world.

Meanwhile Shinto and Buddhism continue to maintain institutional existence in present-day Japan. Beyond the countless Shinto shrines and Buddhist temples which dot the Japanese landscape, both Shinto and Buddhism continue to be practiced in many homes. There is a *kamidana*, literally a god shelf, around which family devotion takes place. In other cases there is a *butsudana* or Buddhist altar. Indeed some Japanese homes have both! Yet it must also be added that these and indeed all the phenomena of Japanese religion are enveloped in a pervasive secularity, not unlike that of the West, which renders all religion problematic. What the future may hold is impossible at present to discern. Yet as the future unfolds the Japanese continue to want and to have the best of both worlds, that of their traditional past and that of their secular present.

Issues and questions

As we look back over this chapter, what issues emerge for reflection and discussion? First of all, Shinto presents students of religion with a clear-cut exam-

Guest paying his respects at
butsudana, family Buddhist altar.
(Robert A. Isaacs/Photo
Researchers.)

ple, explicit and neatly packaged, of what we called in Chapter 1 cosmic religion. Furthermore Shinto continues in vigorous life. The question is why this
persistent vitality when so many type 1 religions have grown old and died.

Second, nowhere in the world is Buddhism more open than in Japan to
critical study and to thoughtful dialog with other faiths. While various forms of
Buddhism face real problems in maintaining their existences, the picture of Japanese Buddhism is one of relative health. Third, no feature of Japanese culture
is more important or striking than its sharp, sensitive eye for beauty alike in
nature and art. Traditional Japanese art in painting, sculpture, architecture, literature, and music has been religious in inception and spirit. Conversely the
religions of Japan have sought and found expression in the arts. Nowhere is
there more significant interfusion of art and religion than in Japan. This relation
is important alike for our understanding of Japanese religion, and also of the
general relation of religion to art.

Fourth, as we have noted, contemporary Japanese culture is enveloped in a pervasive secularity similar to that of the West. In this contemporary attitude, either here or there, there is little or no overt hostility to religion. Yet the challenge to any and all forms of religion is clearly present. For western students of religion, present-day Japan presents a unique opportunity to study this phenomenon with at least a small degree of detachment.

Another closely related aspect of the critical study of Japanese religion consists in our repeated assertion in this book that the human content of religion is a cluster of significant values which gives meaning to human life, individual and social. Again here, Japan presents us with an excellent laboratory in which to test this thesis. This is true whether our focus is upon Japan's old religions or her new religions, or indeed upon the phenomena which some observers have called Japan's current "crisis of values."

NOTES

1. H. Nakamura, *The Ways of Thinking of Eastern Peoples*, compiled by Japanese National Commission for UNESCO, Tokyo, 1960, p. 527.
2. Ibid., p. 438.
3. Ibid., p. 527.
4. Sokyo Ono, *Shinto: The Kami Way*, Tuttle, Rutland, Vt., 1963.
5. Quoted from William T. de Bary (ed.), *Sources of the Japanese Tradition*, Columbia, New York, 1958, pp. 23–24.
6. See inter alia Will Herberg, *Protestant, Catholic, Jew*, Anchor Books, Doubleday, Garden City, N.Y., 1960; W. Lloyd Warner, *American Life: Dream and Reality*, University of Chicago Press, Chicago, 1953.
7. Floyd Ross, *Shinto: The Way of Japan*, Beacon Press, Boston, 1965.
8. Daniel C. Holtom, *The National Faith of Japan: A Study in Modern Shinto*, Dutton, New York, 1938, p. 106.
9. Ross, op. cit., p. 23.
10. Ibid., p. 28.
11. Ibid., p. 75.
12. Ibid., pp. 79f.
13. de Bary, op. cit., p. 50.
14. Ibid., p. 268.
15. I. Hori (ed.), *Japanese Religion*, Kodansha, Tokyo, 1972, p. 289.
16. Kenneth W. Morgan (ed.), *The Path of the Buddha*, Ronald, New York, 1956, p. 329.
17. Clarence H. Hamilton (ed.), *Buddhism: A Religion of Infinite Compassion*, Liberal Arts, New York, 1952, p. 140.
18. de Bary, op. cit., p. 207.
19. Hori, op. cit., pp. 239f.
20. Hamilton, op. cit., p. 145.
21. de Bary, op. cit., pp. 221 and 226.
22. Ibid., p. 220.
23. Hori, op. cit., pp. 239f.
24. Ibid.
25. Nakamura, op. cit., p. 527.
26. Quoted from the *Blaisdell Institute Journal*, vol. 2, no. 2, June 1968.
27. de Bary, op. cit., p. 274.

28. Ibid., pp. 351–352.
29. Edwin O. Reischauer and John K. Fairbank, *A History of East Asian Civilization*, Houghton Mifflin, Boston, 1960, pp. 620–621.
30. de Bary, op. cit., p. 509.
31. Ibid., p. 526.
32. Ibid., p. 544.
33. Ibid., pp. 646–647.
34. T. Sakurai, *Human Bullets*, Teibi, Tokyo, 1912.
35. Ross, op. cit., pp. 138–139.
36. de Bary, op. cit., pp. 753f.
37. Ibid., pp. 761f.
38. Ross, op. cit., p. 152.
39. Ibid., p. 155.
40. Raymond Hammer, *Japan's Religious Ferment*, Oxford University Press, Fair Lawn, N.J., 1962.

BIBLIOGRAPHY

Abe, Masao: *Zen and Western Thought*, University of Hawaii, Honolulu, 1985.
Andrews, A.: *The Teachings Essential for Rebirth*, Sophia, Tokyo, 1973.
Anesaki, M.: *History of Japanese Religion*, Tuttle, Rutland, Vt., 1963.
Aston, W. G.: *Shinto, The Way of the Gods*, Krishna Press, New York, 1974.
Benedict, R.: *Chrysanthemum and the Sword*, Houghton Mifflin, Boston, 1989.
Bloom, Alfred: *Shinran's Gospel of Pure Grace*, University of Arizona, Tucson, 1965.
Bunce, W.: *Religions in Japan*, Tuttle, Rutland, Vt., 1981.
Chang, C. Y.: *Original Teachings of Ch'an Buddhism*, Random House, New York, 1969.
de Bary, W. T. (ed.): *Sources of the Japanese Tradition*, Columbia, New York, 1958.
Du Moulin, H. (ed.): *Buddhism in the Modern World*, New York, Macmillan, 1976.
———: *Zen Buddhism—A History*, Macmillan, New York, 1988.
Earhart, H. B.: *Japanese Religion: Unity and Diversity*, Wadsworth, Belmont, Calif., 1982.
———: *Religion in the Japanese Experience*, Wadsworth, Belmont, Calif., 1974.
Hamilton, C. (ed.): *Buddhism: A Religion of Infinite Compassion*, Liberal Arts, New York, 1952.
Hisamatsu, S., *Zen and the Fine Arts*, Kodansha International, New York and Tokyo, 1974.
Holtorn, D.: *Modern Japan and Shinto Nationalism*, University of Chicago, Chicago, 1943.
Ichiro, H. (ed.): *Japanese Religion*, Kodansha, Tokyo, 1972.
Ingram, P.: *The Dharma of Faith*, University Press of America, Washington, D.C., 1977.
Kim, H. J.: *Dogen Kigen—Mystic Realist*, University of Arizona, Tucson, 1987.
Kitagawa, J.: *Religion in Japanese History*, Columbia, New York, 1966.
The Kojiki, B. Chamberlain (trans.), Tuttle, Rutland, Vt., 1982.
McFarland, H. N.: *Rush Hour of the Gods*, Macmillan, New York, 1967.
Morgan, K. (ed.): *The Path of the Buddha*, Ronald, New York, 1956.
Ono, S.: *Shinto: The Kami Way*, Tuttle, Rutland, Vt., 1962.
Prebisch, C.: *American Buddhism*, Wadsworth, Belmont, Calif., 1979.
Ross, F.: *Shinto: The Way of Japan*, Greenwood Press, Westport, Conn., 1983.
The Sacred Scriptures of Japan, P. Wheeler (trans.), Abelard-Schuman, New York, 1952.
Sansom, G.: *Japan: A Short Cultural History*, Stanford University, Stanford, Calif., 1952.
Shibiyama, Z.: *A Flower Does Not Talk*, Tuttle, Rutland, Vt., 1970.

Soothill, W.: *The Lotus of the Wonderful Law*, Humanities Press, Atlantic Highlands, N.J., 1987.

Suzuki, D.: *Manual of Zen Buddhism*, Grove Press, New York, 1960.

———: *Zen Buddhism*, Doubleday, Garden City, N.Y., 1953.

Thomsen, H.: *The New Religions of Japan*, Tuttle, Rutland, Vt., 1963.

Warner, L.: *The Enduring Art of Japan*, Grove Press, New York, 1988.

Watts, A.: *The Way of Zen*, Random House, New York, 1974.

Woodward, W.: *The Allied Occupation of Japan and Japanese Religions*, Brill, Leiden, Netherlands, 1972.

10

Zoroastrianism

The Parsees of India, numbering slightly over 100,000 and currently diminishing in numbers, and the few thousand Bodin of Iran, are the sole surviving adherents of Zoroastrianism. Current reports from Iran indicate that the Iranian revolution of Ayatola Khomeini is engaged in liquidating the Bodin (called Gabars by the Muslims). Hence Zoroastrianism appears to be a dying religion.

Small and dying though it may be, Zoroastrianism makes a strong claim on the student's attention. First, it is, as we shall soon see, our first clear illustration of a religion of the third or monotheistic type. Second, it is the inheritor of a great tradition. Its founder, Zoroaster, or in more accurate translation, Zarathustra, was one of the great figures of the Axis Age of the seventh and sixth centuries BCE. From that time until the coming of Islam in the seventh century of the Common Era, Zoroastrianism was the faith of the vast Iranian or Persian empire. From this Middle Eastern base it reached out in many directions to influence other faiths and other peoples. Both Judaism and Christianity show Zoroastrian influences in the figure of Satan and in the hosts of angels surrounding both God and Satan. Zoroastrian gods, symbols, and cults made their way into the ancient Greco-Roman world—Mithras being only the best known of many deities of Iranian origin. The cult of Manichaeism, which was one of the rivals of early Christianity and one of the influences on the thought of Saint Augustine, was apparently a heretical Zoroastrian sect.

As we shall soon see, the religious environment of ancient Iran was remarkably similar to that of neighboring vedic India. However, the emergence of the prophet Zoroaster and, with him, a faith of the third or historical type, represents a direction different from that of India. Indeed, the independent emergence of this type of faith in ancient Iran constitutes a fact which claims our attention and challenges our understanding.

Like Judaism, Christianity, and Islam, Zoroastrianism is a religion of a book—a fact of paramount importance historically and theologically. Even a cursory reading of the Zoroastrian Bible, called the *Avesta*, makes it clear that the reader is in a different religious world from southern or eastern Asia. This book speaks of the one God whose sovereign will is that all people should serve him—and serve no other gods. In other words, with the possible exception of Sikhism, Zoroastrianism is the first example in our study of monotheism, or in the classification of Chapter 1 a religion of the third type. Other examples of the type—Judaism, Christianity, and Islam—will follow in subsequent chapters.

In addition to the predominant metaphorical image of sovereignty or kingship for deity, the reader notes in the Avesta the frequently recurring image of hearing. God speaks, and human beings hear and act. The predominance of the metaphor of hearing over that of seeing may be said to define a religion of revelation. Revelation implies that humans do not have within their own minds and selves the meaning of life, and that therefore God must disclose it to them. Hence God speaks, disclosing himself and his will to humankind; the role of humans is to hear and do the will of God. From this it is only a step to writing down in a sacred book the content of what is heard; and this book becomes the guide for all life.

In this monotheistic understanding of religious experience, humans are related to God in terms of obedience or disobedience to the divine will, and these terms may be taken respectively as the basic definitions of faith and sin. In all this there is an active or volitional element which contrasts sharply with the contemplative or esthetic quality of the religions of south Asia and east Asia. Most of the latter regard volition as something to be transcended in both god and humans. In monotheism, the end of life is the active doing of the will of God rather than the achievement of any passive state of contemplation. This leads to a strong moral and social emphasis in the monotheistic faiths.

Zoroaster presents himself to us as a prophet, a man who out of deep conviction is called by God to speak to humankind. Again, the metaphor of vocation, or calling, is important to prophetic religion, and we shall encounter it in Judaism, Christianity, and Islam as well as Zoroastrianism. Here it is sufficient to point to the contrast between the prophet and other archetypal religious models such as the Hindu sadhu or sannyasin, the Buddhist monk, and the Confucian sage.

Zoroaster's faith emerged in the midst of an ancient Iranian religion which, insofar as scholarly reconstruction is possible, appears to be remarkably similar to vedic Indian religion. If this is true, the diverging religious developments in India and Iran constitute one of the most remarkable contrasts in humankind's religious history. The mountains which separate India and Iran have been the great divide separating religions of the second and third types.

Zoroastrianism confronts the student with many other tantalizing and sometimes frustrating questions. For example, later Zoroastrianism presents the clearest example in the history of religions of moral and cosmic dualism. Other faiths show tendencies in this direction, but no other has pushed this dualism to the extreme conclusion of later Zoroastrianism. Thus the question arises: In what terms is the student to understand this dualism and its relation to Zoroastrian monotheism? What, in other words, are the relations between the good Ahura Mazda and the evil Angra Mainyu?

A different kind of issue is raised by the historical sources of Zoroastrianism, which are fragmentary and often speak with discordant voices. As a consequence, scholarly attempts at reconstruction are, to say the least, limited. A summary list of the main parts of the Avesta and other Zoroastrian sources is essential for the exposition which will follow. The oldest and most reliable parts of the Avesta are the *Gathas*, or hymns of Zoroaster. These hymns or poems are usually attributed to the prophet himself, and together they constitute the core of the *Yasna*, or main liturgy. In addition to the Yasna, the Avesta contains four other main subdivisions: a shorter liturgy called the *Visp-rat* or "Vispered; the *Yashts*, which are hymns or invocations; the *Khurda Avesta*, or "little Avesta," which is a series of hymns addressed to many deities; and, finally, the *Videvdat* (often rendered *Venididad*), or "law against demons," which is concerned largely with problems of ritual purity.[1]

In addition to the Avesta, there are other texts and archeological remains, including a notable series of inscriptions from the great Achaemenid kings such as Darius and Xerxes, which throw light on Zoroastrianism during their times. From a much later date, roughly the third through the ninth centuries CE, comes a series of texts in the Pahlavi language, consisting mostly of translations and commentaries on earlier documents. These primary sources are supplemented by comments of historians, notably Herodotus.

There is a popular Zoroastrian tradition that the original Avesta was written in golden ink on ox hides, and that this, as well as other treasures of the faith, was destroyed by Alexander the Greek in the sack of Persepolis in 330 BCE. However, there is no present evidence to substantiate this tradition.

IRANIAN RELIGION BEFORE ZOROASTER

Whatever is to be known of Iranian religion before Zoroaster must be reconstructed from references to it in the *Gathas*, and it is unfortunately true that this evidence is both meager and conflicting. For example, the *Gathas* contains Zoroaster's attack on animal sacrifice and the *haoma* ritual, yet the Yasna gives place to these rituals.[2] Yet in some other respects a reasonably clear and coherent picture is forthcoming.

It is the picture of a religion of nature and culture strikingly similar to that of vedic India. Even the names of the peoples are similar, for apparently the word *Iran*, like *Aryan*, means "noble" and has a similar etymology. The vedic and Iranian languages are closely akin to each other. In both societies a great number of deities represented a variety of natural and social forces and objects. Two kinds of deities are referred to in both traditions: *daevas* (Indian *devas*) and *ahuras* (Indian *asuras*). It is interesting to observe in this connection that in the course of Zoroaster's prophetic criticism of this tradition, he came to regard the daevas as veritable principles of evil, while among the noted ahuras he selected one, *Ahura Mazda*, as his one supreme and true God. As noted in Chapters 3 and 6, India took the different path of seeing a single principle manifested in and through all the innumerable deities.

Among the pre-Zoroastrian daevas was *Intar*, who like his Indian relative

Indra was a dragon slayer and rain god. Prominent among the daevas was *Mithra* (vedic *Mitra*), god of war and of the sun's light, who elicited from followers the qualities of loyalty and faithfulness. Under many names and guises Mithra was destined for a long and varied life, extending from Iran westward to the Roman empire. There was *Asta*, or *Arta*, principle of order, analogous to the vedic *Rita*. There was *Vayu*, the wind, known by the same name to the Indians. There was also *Yima*, the first man to die and henceforth king of the underworld, known to the Indians as *Yama*. Corresponding to the Indian *Pitaras*, or "fathers," were the Iranian *Fravashi*, ancestors or ancestral principles.

Similar to the Indian *soma* was the Iranian *haoma*; both were potent drinks capable of inducing religious exaltation. Hence both were used as sacrificial libations, and both were sometimes deified. For these ancient Iranians, as for their Indian cousins, sacrifice was a central feature of religion. For them too the fire of the sacrifice was of sacred significance. Unlike the vedic Indians, they had no deity of the fire, but in the course of time the sacrificial fire itself was destined to become the supreme sacred symbol.

Reading between the lines of the Yasna, the student may infer that the Iran of the seventh and sixth centuries BCE was a society of cattlemen, cattle breeders, and farmers. Again, the similarity to vedic India is apparent. These Iranian cattlemen seem to have lived under continual threat from marauding nomads, whom they did not hesitate to identify as the embodiment of evil. Like other societies of the time, this one was highly conservative. The traditional bonds which it placed on individuals might well seem restrictive to an outstanding individual person. Furthermore, beneath the surface of this traditional society, important changes were stirring. They needed the catalytic force of a great personality to bring them to overt reality.

The prophet's life

Into this ancient traditional faith and society, Zoroaster was born. There is the widest disagreement concerning the dates of his life. One estimate places him at 1500 BCE, another at 3000 BCE, and still another at 6000 BCE.[3] The traditional Zoroastrian estimate, endorsed by most western scholars, 628–551 BCE, accords better with existing evidence than any alternative.[4] The crucial clue is the tradition which dates the founder "258 years before Alexander," that is, before Alexander's sack of Persepolis in 330 BCE. This would be 588 BCE, presumably the date of Zoroaster's conversion of King Vishtaspa, which was the turning point of the prophet's career. If this is correct, Zoroaster was a contemporary not only of Buddha, Confucius, and Lao tzu, but of the prophets of Israel and others of the Axis Age around the world. It may be pointed out that if this chronology is correct, Zoroaster's life followed that of the Hebrew Moses by some 600 years.

Zoroastrian tradition has painted a highly stylized portrait of its founder. He received the sacred thread, symbolic of religious coming of age, at fifteen.

He was, it is said, a youth dutiful to his parents and of a compassionate nature. Yet at the age of twenty he left his parents and the wife they had chosen for him to wander forth into the world alone in search of answers to his religious questionings. One source, admittedly late, asserts that he kept a seven-year silence, living in a cave during this entire time.

At the age of thirty he appears to have undergone a decisive and transforming religious experience, receiving the first of a series of revelations which made him the prophet of Ahura Mazda. Standing beside the Daiti River, he was approached by the angel Vohu Manah ("good thought"), who appeared as a colossal figure nine times human size, commanding Zoroaster to lay aside his body and come up into the presence of the heavenly court. There God himself instructed the prophet in the content of the new faith which he was to disseminate. This crucial religious experience is intimated in at least three of the Gathas. In 31:8 Zoroaster sets forth his experience:

> Through the mind, O Wise One, have I known thee as the first and the last,
> As the father of the Good Mind,
> When I perceived thee with mind eyes as the true creator of Righteousness,
> As the Lord in the deeds of existence;[5]

Again he writes in 45:8f:

> —For I have now beheld this with mine eye,
> Knowing the Wise Lord by the Righteousness of his Good Spirit,[6]

In more detail, he declares in 43:7:

> As the holy one I recognized thee, O Wise Lord,
> When he came to me as Good Mind and asked me:
> "Who are thou, whose art thou? Shall I appoint by a sign
> The days when inquiry shall be made about thy living possessions and
> thyself?"
> I made answer to him: "I am Zarathustra, first,
> A true enemy to the wicked with all my might,
> But a powerful support for the righteous,
> So that I may attain the future blessings of the absolute Dominion
> By praising and singing thee O Wise One."[7]

Over the next ten years Zoroaster participated in a series of seven such "conferences," as he called them, with Ahura Mazda or with members of Ahura Mazda's heavenly court such as Vohu Manah and other important angels. Tradition says that with the seventh such conference the revelation was complete. During this time he also began to teach and preach the new faith he had been receiving. Results were at first painfully meager and slow; after ten years he won his first convert, who was also his cousin. In his discouragement he was visited by the evil spirit, Angra Mainyu, who bade him give up his new work and return to the old gods of his people. Like Buddha and Christ, Zoroaster was tempted, but like them he won out.

At the age of forty he began a two-year effort to win to the faith King Vishtaspa. The story here seems heavily overlaid with tradition, yet apparently there is a kernel of historical fact. Vishtaspa, a native prince, dwelt somewhere in eastern Iran surrounded by evil priests and courtiers. Zoroaster's attempts were frustrated by the priests' magic and their influence over the king. As a consequence of these malign forces, the prophet landed in prison. However, after two years of failure, virtue triumphed; tradition says that Zoroaster's miraculous cure of the king's favorite black horse, reinforced by the support of the king's consort, won the day. King Vishtaspa was converted to Zoroaster's faith, bringing with him his entire household and royal court.

Tradition says that the next twenty years were spent in the vigorous and fruitful propagation of the new faith throughout Iran. Two holy wars against the villainous Turanians were fought and won. According to one account (written a thousand years after the supposed event), Zoroaster perished during the second war. The prophet, then seventy-seven years old, was surprised by an invading soldier and met a martyr's death as he officiated before the fire altar. All that can safely be said historically is that during the course of Zoroaster's life, the new faith struck roots into the soil of Iran and began to live and grow. The rest is tradition and folklore.

Despite its meagerness, the evidence is sufficient to show that the life and teachings of Zoroaster represent a historical breakthrough from the first, or nature-culture, type of religion to the third, or historical, type, contrasting with the breakthrough in India from the first to the second, or monistic, type. It also accords with existing evidence to say that this ancient Iranian breakthrough to historical monotheism occurred independently of that which took place in ancient Israel. There were incidental contacts between Iran and Israel, but their traditions originated independently of each other.

THE PROPHET'S MESSAGE

DIVINE REVELATION

The heart of Zoroaster's message was faith in one God, Ahura Mazda, who had revealed his will to the prophet and, through the prophet, to humankind. Zoroaster took his stand firmly on the revelation which had been given him, confident that God himself had disclosed to him the faith which he held. This conviction and vocation defined his role as a prophet, or spokesman for God. This fresh revelation was doubtless related to the newly developing world to which Zoroaster addressed himself. Furthermore, if this faith was of divine origin, alternative diverging faiths had to be accounted false and evil. Zoroaster did not shrink from denouncing them as such. Here again the student notes in Zoroastrianism a distinctive feature of historical or monotheistic religion, namely, the clear, sharp line drawn between true and false religion. It is a line almost absent from faiths of the first two types.

THE ONE GOD

The one God whom he proclaimed was named Ahura Mazda (variously translated as "wise lord" and "lord of light"). Despite the difference in name, Ahura Mazda bears striking similarity to the vedic Indian deity Varuna. The Gathas leave us no doubt that Zoroaster regarded Ahura Mazda as the one sovereign Lord of all creation. Ahura Mazda's will defines the norm for human life, and indeed for all creation. Lordship also meant creatorship; the Gathas tell the story of divine creation in which Ahura Mazda calls the world into being in the beginning. Like his biblical contemporary, Deutero-Isaiah, Zoroaster asked rhetorically:

> Who set the Earth in its place below, and the sky of the clouds that it shall not
> fall?
> Who the waters and planets?
> Who yoked the two steeds to wind and clouds?
> Who O Wise One is the creator of the Good Mind?
>
> What artificer made light and darkness?
> What artificer sleep and waking?
> Who made morning, moon, and night?
> To remind the wise man of his task?
>
> Thus I strive to recognize in thee, O Wise One,
> As Holy Spirit, the creator of all things.[8]

But Ahura Mazda is not only creator; it is he who guides each person's life and the whole process of creation to their consummation. Last things as well as first things, judgment day as well as creation, constituted an essential aspect of Zoroaster's historical monotheism.

ANGELS

Zoroaster's monotheism was qualified by a variety of forms which are variously interpreted as angels or messengers, heavenly attendants or servants, divine attributes, or at times simply personifications. One translator calls them simply *entities*. The reader has already made the acquaintance of Vohu Manah ("good thought"), the angelic messenger who conducted Zoroaster to the heavenly court. There were many others as well. There was Spenta Mainyu ("holy spirit"), who sometimes appears as the "presence of God," but sometimes as a separate and distinguishable being. There were the Amesha Spentas ("the immortal holy ones") such as Asha ("right"), Kshathra ("power or dominion"), Haurvatat ("prosperity"), Armaiti ("piety"), and Ameretat ("immortality"), who

Symbol of Ahura Mazda, from doorway of council hall, Persepolis, Iran. (Oriental Institute, University of Chicago.)

seem sometimes to be understood as modes or aspects of God's being, sometimes as forces or beings, sometimes as personifications. Scholars argue inconclusively over their exact status in the mind of Zoroaster, yet it is quite possible that the prophet himself never cleared up this ambiguity. In any case, the student of religion will not be mistaken in seeing here the antecedents of Judeo-Christian and Muslim angelology.

DUALITY OF GOOD AND EVIL

Zoroaster's universe was populated with evil powers as well as good powers. In the Gathas is to be found a persistent and undeniable tendency to see human experience of the world as a conflict between two opposing principles. The basis for this dualism is variously interpreted by different writers. Zaehner, for example, finds a historical and sociological explanation in the struggle between Zoroaster's people and the hostile, marauding nomads.[9] Some interpreters profess to see here a metaphysical dualistic tendency in Zoroaster's thought. However, it is possible to read the Gathas in much the same way as one reads of the struggle of good and evil as depicted in the Judeo-Christian Bible.

Whatever the interpretation, this duality finds repeated expression in the Gathas. For example, Zoroaster says:

> I will speak of the two spirits
> Of whom the holier said unto the destroyer at the beginning of existence:
> "Neither our thoughts nor our doctrines nor our minds' forces,
> Neither our choices nor our words nor our deeds,
> Neither our consciences nor our souls agree."[10]

Even more plainly, Zoroaster declares:

> Now at the beginning the twin spirits have declared their nature,
> The better and the evil,
> In thought and word and deed, and between the two
> The wise ones chose well, not so the foolish.
>
> And when these two spirits came together,
> In the beginning they established life and non-life,
> And that at the last the worst existence should be for the wicked,
> But for the righteous ones the Best Mind.[11]

At times this duality is expressed as the opposition between *Asha* and *Druj*, "truth" and "falsehood." In later times Druj became *Shaitan*, or Satan, the "father of lies." The Gathas are vague on the point of Ahura Mazda's precise relation to evil and the evil spirit, Angra Mainyu, as he came to be called. Did Ahura Mazda create the evil spirit? Or had evil existed from the beginning as an original part of creation? All these suggestions appear, but none clearly, and none is developed in its full implications. However, on one point the Gathas are unequivocally clear; they teach consistently that Ahura Mazda and his truth and goodness will win out in the end.

HISTORIC STRUGGLE BETWEEN GOOD AND EVIL

Deriving from the lordship of Ahura Mazda together with the dualism just noted is Zoroaster's distinctive view of all history as an agelong war between good and evil. There are good and evil persons, just as there are good and evil spirits. The daevas, or evil spirits, have joined themselves with Angra Mainyu to resist Ahura Mazda and his hosts of goodness. In this war humans are urged to join the forces of Ahura Mazda and Vohu Manah against the evil forces of Angra Mainyu. This means to speak the truth, to aid other good people—and violently to resist evil and evil people. It means practical good deeds like tilling the soil, raising grain, irrigating barren ground, being kind to cows and other domestic animals. The archvillains of this drama of good and evil are the Turanian nomads who worship the daevas, slaughter cattle, and destroy the produce of the field. The end of this war is judgment day, when the sovereignty of Ahura Mazda will be fully vindicated. Zoroaster seems to have believed that the struggle of good and evil was an actual and often a desperate fight, yet, paradoxically, at no point did he doubt the final victory of Ahura Mazda.

THE GOOD LIFE

The war between good and evil which runs through the whole world also goes through the heart of each person. Hence, individual decision or commitment is a supremely important issue. Zoroaster held a fundamental and irreducible belief in the human being's freedom of choice. He admonished his contemporaries:

> Hear with your ears that which is the sovereign good.
> With a clear mind look upon the two sides
> Between which each man must choose for himself.[12]

He also emphasized the active life. Humans are called by God not to contemplation, but to active service. Similarly, there is a strong this-worldly, practical, indeed, material emphasis in his moral values, shown in his illustrations of good conduct, which range from telling the truth to cultivating the soil; yet consistent with his practical nature, Zoroaster seems not to have been concerned with the essential or theoretical nature of the good. Truth, righteousness—surely everyone knows what they are! To all this he added a universal reference. His message was addressed to all humankind. As Ahura Mazda was one, so must humanity be!

His practical and moral nature led him also to pare away much of the traditional ritual of his people. God's first requirement of every person is a good life in society with others rather than the correct performance of a ritual. He had harsh words to say about animal sacrifice and other ceremonies of his people. His views on all these matters paralleled those of his contemporaries, the great prophets of Israel. Zoroaster did apparently retain one outward symbol, the fire, as a symbol of truth. This was destined to become the central feature of Zoroastrian worship.

DEATH AND RESURRECTION

For Zoroaster, God's drama of human life moves inevitably toward consummation. The drama of each life will achieve its climax at the Chinvad Bridge, or "bridge of the separator," so called because the righteous successfully pass over it to "second existence" or resurrection, while the evil people topple off to the place of misery.[13] Zoroaster also intimated an analogous consummation for the larger drama of human history, speaking of Ahura Mazda's victory, dominion, and kingdom. However, these hints are not spelled out in any detail in any extant text which may reliably be attributed to Zoroaster. It remained for his later followers to describe judgment day in play-by-play detail.

LATER ZOROASTRIANISM

Turning from the Gathas of Zoroaster to the so-called later Avesta—the Yashts, the Khurda Avesta, and the Pahlavi texts—the reader is immediately aware of being in a different environment. Important changes have taken place in Zoroastrian faith. These religious changes took place against the background of vast historical changes. A generation after Zoroaster, the great Cyrus made his dramatic ascent to power. In 558 BCE he toppled Astyages, the last Median king, bringing Median and Persian kingdoms together in the Medo-Persian empire. Cyrus began the Achaemenid dynasty, which was destined to hold power until the coming of Alexander two centuries later. Cyrus was a Zoroastrian, though not a zealous or intolerant adherent. As an empire builder, he was willing to compromise among religions in order to keep peace among the many groups of his far-flung realm.

Cyrus was followed to the throne by Cambyses (530–522), then by Darius (522–486), and then by Xerxes (486–468). Darius's inscriptions show him to have been a devout Zoroastrian, ruling by the will of Ahura Mazda and seeking the kind of justice and righteousness proclaimed by Zoroaster. The content of Darius's Zoroastrian faith was in most respects similar to that of the prophet himself. In the case of Xerxes, there were several notable developments. One inscription tells of his suppression of the Daeva cult, an act still within the framework of the original Zoroastrian faith. But others tell of widespread animal sacrifice. Xerxes is also said to have lashed the waters of the Hellespont during his attempted invasion of Greece, calling them bitter waters. This was an act some authorities characterize as conflicting with Zoroastrian reverence for water. Additional deities, including notably the god Mithra and the goddess Anahita, make their appearance—or rather, reappearance—in texts of Xerxes' time. Xerxes was followed by Artaxerxes I (468–425), then Artaxerxes II (405–359).

Notable among these changes from Xerxes onward was the rise to prominence of the magi, who were apparently a priestly group of some sort. Authoritative writers have differed sharply on the identity and significance of the magi. Were they a tribe of Median origin, as Herodotus claims, or were they a priestly class or caste? The evidence is not decisive. Were they faithful transmitters of Zoroaster's message or perverters of it? Both views have been put forward. The Gospel of Matthew in the New Testament tells the story of their coming with gifts for the infant Christ. Herodotus recounts other, less laudatory details concerning the magi—that they made "incestuous" marriages, killed many living creatures (apparently animals aligned on the side of the evil Angra Mainyu against Ahura Mazda), and left their dead to be the prey of vultures and dogs. The original meaning of the word *magu* was "gift," implying divine grace dispensed by these priests. However, the association of the magi with Chaldean astrologers served to give their name its historic connection with sorcery and magic.

Whatever the precise identity and significance of the magi, they appear to have been the official priests of Zoroastrianism during the Achaemenid period. As such they were responsible for three new elements in Zoroastrianism: (1)

the exposure of the dead to be devoured by vultures and dogs, (2) the practice of incestuous (or less pejoratively, endogamous) marriages, and (3) the extension of Zoroaster's duality to include the world of animals and of material things, and its hardening to a metaphysical dualism.

Under Darius and Xerxes the historic Persian attacks on Greece were undertaken. It has often been speculated that if the battles of Marathon and Salamis had ended in Persian rather than Greek victory, the religion of Europe might have been Zoroastrianism. Nevertheless, Zoroastrianism continued to be a living force in the Near East for several centuries. As noted above, Alexander the Great sacked the Persian capital, Persepolis, in 330 BCE, bringing the Achaemenid dynasty to an end. Following Alexander's death, his empire was divided among his generals, Persia falling to Seleucus. The Seleucid family, however, proved unequal to the task of holding power throughout their vast regions. In the late second century BCE, the Parthian dynasty rose to power in Persia, driving out the Seleucids; they held the throne until the rise of the Sassanids in the third century of the Common Era.

In 224 CE Ardashir I drove out the last of the Parthian kings and established a dynasty which lasted until the coming of Islam in the middle of the seventh century. The Sassanids were Zoroastrians and made this the established faith of their empire. A twentieth-century Zoroastrian writer speaks of the Sassanid kingdom as a theocracy, with all the weaknesses inherent in the union of political and ecclesiastical power.[14] Non-Zoroastrian religions, notably Judaism, were severely repressed by the Sassanids. During these centuries Zoroastrianism froze into an orthodoxy whose main tenets will be summarized below.

During the Sassanid centuries there were also several dissident and heretical movements of considerable importance. Most influential for western history was Manichaeism, whose founder, the third-century Mani, shows Zoroastrian influence. M. N. Dhalla speaks of Mani as a Zoroastrian heretic, pointing out his basic ethical and cosmic dualism.[15] Yet where Zoroaster regarded the earth and other material things as good, Mani regarded them as the root of all evil. Where Zoroaster sought the regulation of bodily desires, Mani sought their suppression. In opposition to Zoroaster's teaching, Mani practiced and taught celibacy, fasting, and other forms of asceticism.

Another dissenting movement of Sassanid times was Zurvanism. *Zurvan* has been translated as "time" or "boundless time"; the movement called *Zurvanism* apparently originated in a bold philosophic effort to overcome the dualism of good and evil, of Ahura Mazda and Angra Mainyu, by asserting that they both sprang from Zurvan, or the impersonal principle of boundless time.[16] From this principle, all things derive. Zurvanist speculations may well have been influenced by Aristotle's metaphysics, which exerted a continuous and pervasive influence on the Middle Eastern world. Another possible source for Zurvan was the Maitri Upanishad of India, which asserts that time is the father of all.

Zurvan's combination of myth and metaphysics assumed various forms, one of which approximated philosophic materialism in its denial of spiritual and religious realities, and another of which emphasized a doctrine of fatalism. Some Zurvanist writers elaborated a mythology similar to the Gnosticism of the

Zurvan giving birth to Ahura Mazda and Angra Mainyu. (Cincinnati Art Museum.)

Greco-Roman world. While Zurvanism attracted a wide following, including even some Sassanid rulers, in the end it was ruled heretical by Zoroastrian orthodoxy. Its myths and its metaphysical speculations blurred the distinction between good and evil, which orthodox thinkers held to be the foundation of true faith.

During this same period Zoroastrian orthodoxy was assuming its final and definitive forms. In several notable respects it differed from the earlier teachings of the Gathas. Five such differences will be briefly summarized.

EXALTATION OF ZOROASTER

Most important was the religious exaltation of Zoroaster himself. In the Gathas, Zoroaster appears as a man, listening to Ahura Mazda, talking back sometimes, but always declaring Ahura Mazda's will to humankind. In the later writings he is depicted as a supernatural being, a veritable god become man. His coming has been foretold 3,000 years previously! The demons are forewarned and quake in their impending overthrow.[17] Not only Zoroaster's birth but also that of his mother is supernatural. Once born, the infant is attacked by the demons—and is supernaturally protected by the manifold forces of goodness. The prophet himself performs miracle upon miracle. The great miracle of the cure of Vishtaspa's horse is elaborated in detail. Every aspect of the prophet's life is fitted into a framework of popular supernaturalism—a process of which the history of religions affords numerous illustrations.

ANGELS AND DEITIES

While Zoroaster's monotheism did admit of angels and a few other celestial attendants, there were clear and definite limits. In later Zoroastrianism these limits are surpassed by a vast host of gods and godlings and divine messengers.

Many of the old Iranian nature gods against whom Zoroaster fought return in force, though often under different names or with different functions. For example, Vohu Manah assumes the new function of guardian of cattle. Such powers as Asha ("right") and Kshathra ("power") are now deities of fire and metals, respectively. The Amesha Spentas are female archangels or goddesses. The number of angels has greatly increased.

New deities appear on the scene in force. For example, Anahita makes her appearance in Achaemenid times, and is soon recognizable as the mother goddess and fertility goddess, known by many names in different times and places. Haoma, disputed element in the Gathas, returns as a god to whom animal sacrifices are made. Mithra, never absent in Zoroastrian history, rises to new prominence in Achaemenid inscriptions as a god of light and a recorder of truth and faith in humankind. Still later Mithra makes his migration westward to become Mithras of the Greco-Roman world around whom a whole new—and different—religious movement rose and ran its course. In later Zoroastrianism there was a truly vast increase in the celestial population of the universe!

EXTENSION OF DUALISM

There is also a hardening of Zoroaster's dualism of good and evil, together with an analogous increase in demonic population. As already noted, Zoroaster's

Drawing of the goddess Anahita. (New York Public Library, Picture Collection.)

original duality was rooted in human experience of good and evil. In later Zo-roastrian writings it becomes clearly a fixed feature of the universe. As one writer puts it, Angra Mainyu is now a proper noun—the Evil Spirit. So too are his numerous helpers and colleagues. As Ahura Mazda has hosts of angels and supporters, so too does Angra Mainyu. There is Aka Manah ("bad thought"), Andar (successor of Intar, and relative of the vedic Indra), Sauru, Fauru, and the "numberless myriads" of evil spirits, daevas, and others. Druj, "the lie," has now become a female demon.

As Ahura Mazda was active for goodness at creation, so Angra Mainyu was active in pursuit of evil ends. To oppose Ahura Mazda he made the summer heat and the winter cold, human vices and diseases, demons and their evils, and witchcraft, not to speak of such evil creatures as snakes, locusts, and ants. There was an increasing tendency in later Zoroastrianism to extend the cosmic dual-ism throughout the realm of nature, placing all of nature's creatures on the side of either good or evil.

FINAL JUDGMENT

Later Zoroastrianism spelled out in great detail the story of judgment day as ap-plied both to individual human beings and to the world at large. Individual judgment takes place at the Chinvad Bridge. Four days after death, standing be-fore the divine judges, the soul sees its good and evil deeds weighed in the scales. Then it passes over the dreaded bridge. If the soul is wicked, the sharp edge of the bridge stands edgewise and gives no passage, and the soul plunges headlong to hell. If the soul is good, it is met by an amiable apparition (who turns out to be the soul's good deeds), who embraces it, leading it to bliss on the further side. Both the miseries of hell and the bliss of heaven are described in vivid detail.

As to the final judgment of the world, later Zoroastrianism told an equally vivid and detailed story. The last three millennia are to be presided over by three posthumous sons of Zoroaster—Oshetar, Oshetarmah, and most impor-tant of the three, Saoshyans (or in another transliteration, Saoshyant)—who are destined to preside over the final "renovation" of the world. All the dead will then be resurrected, heaven and hell both being emptied of their residents for the impending great assize. In a kind of trial by ordeal, every living soul will have to walk through the river of fire. To the righteous it will seem like warm milk, but to the evil it will bring unspeakable pain as it burns the evil out of them.

In a final battle following this, Ahura Mazda and his angels will conquer Ahriman and his hosts of evil, and consume them in the final fire. Then at last, all the survivors of these tumultuous events will live together in complete fe-licity. In Zoroastrian metaphor, the whole universe will be made new. Even hell will be redeemed, as Ahura Mazda "brings the land of hell back for the enlarge-ment of the world: the renovation arises in the universe by his will, and the world is immortal forever and everlasting."[18] Many readers will note the simi-larity of this apocalyptic drama to those of Judaism, Christianity, and Islam.

Like Mahayana Buddhism, later Zoroastrianism teaches a doctrine of universal salvation. In the end Ahura Mazda's power will be asserted in the salvation of all the inhabitants of the created world. It is impossible to say what relation, if any, this Zoroastrian version of last things had to the contemporaneous apocalyptic visions of Jews and Christians a few hundred miles to the west of Iran. In the absence of concrete evidence, the similarity must be judged as independent responses to similar religious problems.

CEREMONIAL PURIFICATION

In the later version of Zoroastrianism, religion acquired again many of the ceremonies which Zoroaster's prophetic zeal had purged away; and these ceremonies tended to take on a magical significance. More and more they became a kind of defense in the struggle to avoid ceremonial impurity or guilt. In this effort the Videvdat provided *manthras* (note the similarity to Indian *mantras*), or sacred passages of scripture used as incantations or spells to ward off the demons and their evil powers. Libations of haoma were regarded as particularly powerful means of averting uncleanness or impurity. The juice of the sacred plant was pressed and mixed with milk and holy water; then part of it was poured out as a sacrifice and the rest was drunk by the officiating priest.

In religious history contact with a corpse had widely been regarded as defiling, but this feeling of ceremonial impurity developed to a unique degree in later Zoroastrianism. As we have seen, the magi were the first Zoroastrians who

Parsee worship at the fire temple. (Jehangir Gazdar/Woodfin Camp & Associates.)

exposed their dead for vultures to devour, instead of burying them. Apparently they believed that a corpse would defile the earth, which was on the side of Ahura Mazda in the agelong struggle of good and evil. Nor could a corpse be cast into water or burnt on a pyre, for it would pollute the water or fire. The Videvdat prescribed the *dakhmas*, "towers of silence," which became standard features of Zoroastrianism.

CONTEMPORARY ZOROASTRIANS

When Muslim conquerors swept over Iran in the mid-seventh century, the result was disaster and downfall for Zoroastrianism. It fell with the Sassanid kings with whom it was allied. A few adherents remained and resisted conversion to Islam. They called themselves *Zardustrian* (Zoroastrians) and *Boh-dinan* ("followers of the good religion"), but to the Muslims they were Gabars ("infidels"). Some historians of religion have used this label, but to the adherents of this faith it is pejorative. They have continued to call themselves *Zoroastrians*. In time the Muslim masters of Persia saw that the Zoroastrians were "people of a book," and persecution gave way to tolerance. In more modern times tolerance became official Iranian goverment policy.

The Iranian Zoroastrians have clung tenaciously to their faith. Their priests have continued to officiate at the fire temples, and generations of their sons and daughters have been invested with the sacred shirt and sacred cord, symbolizing their coming of age in things religious. They have also preserved their own distinctive marriage and funeral customs and their extensive rituals of purification.

In recent times there has been increased contact with their fellow Zoroastrians, the Parsees of India, and there have been new stirrings of life in their faith, the suggestion being made that, since their ancestors underwent forced conversion to Islam, the present generation might change its customs and accept converts from Islam and other faiths. Estimates vary concerning their numbers, but the total is probably not more than 10,000. Of this number some 2,000 live by trade, while the balance follow the time-honored Zoroastrian occupation of tilling the soil.

Some Zoroastrians fled Muslim persecution, eventually making their way overseas to India, where they landed at Diu in Kathiawar. They received the permission of the local ruler to land, on condition that they not intermarry with high-caste Hindu women and avoid the killing of cows. Tradition says that they erected their first fire temple at Sanjan in Gujarat. It was subsequently moved to Udvada, where it exists today as a popular pilgrimage place for Indian Zoroastrians. The newcomers soon acquired the name *Parsee* (from the name of the Iranian province of Pars, from which *Persia* is also derived), by which they have been known ever since. At least one writer has suggested that not religion but trade inspired the original migration, and it must be added that trade between Iran and India was by no means unusual at the time of their migration.

Many of the descendents of the original migrants found their way to the vicinity of Bombay, where they have lived and prospered ever since. They turned soon to trade and commerce. A sixteenth-century Portuguese document compares their enterprise to that of Europe's Jews. In the seventeenth century a representative of the Parsees participated in Akbar's discussions among the various faiths of India.

The coming of the British provided the Parsees with their great opportunity, for of all Indian groups they proved best able to adapt themselves to European ways. From the beginning a middle-class group with a great respect for education, they proved to be valuable intermediaries between the British and the masses of India. Their activity proved to be highly profitable, and fortunes were made in shipping and shipbuilding, and later in other industries. As a consequence, the small Parsee community came to have an influence far out of proportion to its actual numbers. To its achievements in business and industry, it

Parsee priests before a representation of Zoroaster. (Bruno Barbey/Magnum.)

soon added others in education, philanthropy, and public service. Its charities, applied first to its own members, were soon extended to the wider Indian community. Some of the largest industrial and commercial enterprises of India, such as the Tatas in steel and iron and the Wadias in shipbuilding, are of Parsee ownership.

The Parsee community is ruled by a council, or *panchayat*. In some cities this includes representatives of each family, while in Bombay it consists of 100 elected members, most of whom are laypeople. To the panchayat are assigned the various tasks of leadership and administration, including the dispensing of funds to needy Parsees.

The basic ceremony of the Parsee faith is worship at the fire temple, in which the worshipper brings a piece of sandalwood to the priest, who with appropriate prayer and ritual places it on the fire which he and his colleagues continuously attend. Parsees hasten to point out that the fire is not a deity but a sacred symbol of Ahura Mazda. The priest gives the worshipper a spoonful of ashes to rub on the forehead. Then, following a priestly benediction, the worshipper retires. Entrance into a fire temple is forbidden to non-Zoroastrians. As its worship is closed to outsiders, so also Parseeism does not accept converts. It is thus a hereditary community.

The high point of the Parsee religious year is the New Year's Day festival. On this day the faithful rise early, say their prayers, don their best clothes, and join other Parsees at the fire temple, which is thronged with worshippers. Following prayer and worship at the temple, the rest of the day is spent in merrymaking and celebration with relatives and friends.

The Parsees have divided into three groups over a difference in procedure for dating New Year's Day. One sect holds firmly to the vernal equinox, March 21 of each year, making the necessary changes for leap year and for shifting from a lunar to a solar calendar. The other two follow different systems which result in considerable variation in the time of year on which the New Year's Day falls. Suggestions are currently heard for a compromise solution to these differences.

There is a ritual of initiation for young people in which the boys and girls are invested with the sacred thread and girdle symbolizing full membership in the community. This ceremony is customary between the ages of seven and nine, with the result that often little of its significance is apprehended by the young person involved. There is considerable discussion of this, and of the wider problem of providing meaningful participation by young people. In an age of increasing secularization in India as elsewhere in the world, there are many Parsee young people who lose interest in their faith.

A related problem is that of maintaining an adequate number of qualified priests for the fire temples. The priesthood is hereditary, a fact which drastically restricts the group from among which future priests may be recruited. Parsee laypeople have provided funds for the education of priests as well as for scholarly research into the Parsee tradition, but the problem of religious leadership continues.

Among the other ritual of the Parsees, none is better known than their funerary customs. The dakhmas, or towers of silence, are stone cylinders some 20 feet in height, with a stone floor and platforms around the inside on which corpses are exposed. There are three tiers of platforms, for men, women, and children, respectively. Once a body is deposited, the vultures speedily reduce it to a skeleton whose bones are deposited on the stone floor, where in time they crumble away. In this way the sacred earth is guarded from defilement.

The funeral ceremony is a procession to the tower, which is usually located on an otherwise vacant hilltop. The body is borne by six professional bearers, whose pay is regarded as compensation for the ceremonial impurity involved. As the bearers deposit the corpse within the tower, the company waits outside. After ritual prayers, they disperse and return home. In Indian communities too small to have a dakhma, interment in lead coffins or stone chambers is customary. In

A Tower of Silence in the desert near Zazd, Iran. (Ray Ellis/Photo Researchers.)

Bombay's Malabar Hill, recent contructions of high-rise apartments overlooking the dakhmas has created controversial issues for the Parsees.

A notable feature of the Parsee community during the nineteenth and twentieth centuries has been the rise of a liberal and reforming spirit. This had led to efforts to study their own tradition with the methods and spirit of modern scholarship. The Parsees have had fewer inhibitions against this kind of scholarship than many traditional faiths. Closely allied to these scholarly activities have been calls to go "back to the Gathas" and to infuse the often empty ritual forms with the spirit of the prophet and his writings.

Another important development of recent years has been the increasing contact between Iranian and Indian adherents of Zoroastrianism. A world conference of the faith was held in Teheran in 1960, and another in Bombay in 1964, and others are planned for the future. Zoroastrians not only worship together but seek to plan together for the future.

The Parsee community of today faces the future with a long agenda of difficult if not insoluble problems. The attrition in membership due to the secularizing trend of the surrounding culture is acutely important to a hereditary religious community. Some Parsees raise questions about this aspect of their faith. Others advise more imaginative programs to hold the allegiance of their young people. Meanwhile, the Iranian revolution of Ayatola Khomeini and his followers persecutes the remaining Zoroastrians with the clear intention of destroying this minority.

ISSUES AND QUESTIONS

If, as this chapter's exposition has shown, Zoroastrianism in its initial formulation by Zoroaster is our first clear example of historical monotheism, the question then arises, what happened to it? The title of R. C. Zaehner's book, *The Dawn and Twilight of Zoroastrianism*, forcefully raises this issue. After the dawn, why the early twilight or, indeed, even dark? The historical sources, such as they are, shed little or no light on why this change occurred between what we have called earlier and later Zoroastrianism. Left to speculate, we can only guess that the original insight of Zoroaster was swallowed up and lost in the traditional society of ancient Iran. If we accept this explanation, then let it be added that there exists a historical tendency—of which this is an example—for religions of the second and third type, once they come into existence, to revert, particularly in their popular aspects, to the first or cosmic type.

To this it must be added that accidents of history, influential as they are in all aspects of human experience, have played a particularly important role in Zoroastrian history. We have noted that the Parsees, as they came to be called, first arrived in India as refugees from the Islamic conquest of Iran. They were granted asylum on the promise not to proselytize. They kept this promise through the centuries, and in twentieth-century India it appears to be a death sentence for this religion.

Again, the Parsees became in the course of time a middle-class community in India. During the days of the British rule this gave them an important role as the intermediaries between the British and the Indian masses. But now the British are gone, and so is this social function.

Still another question easier to ask than to answer is the significance of the cosmic dualism of Ahura Mazda and Angra Mainyu in Zoroastrianism. If we look at the initial statement of this duality in the *Gathas* of Zoroaster it does not greatly differ from the moral duality of good and evil in the Judeo-Christian Bible. However, in the case of Zoroastrianism the duality hardened into a metaphysical dualism. We are left to guess the nature of this hardening process. The result in later Zoroastrianism is a fact of religious history. We are left also to speculate more generally upon the conditions which lead to the birth and death of religions in human history.

NOTES

1. Robert Charles Zaehner, *The Dawn and Twilight of Zoroastrianism*, Putnam, New York, 1961, pp. 25f. See also John C. Archer and Carl E. Purinton, *Faiths to Live By*, Ronald, New York, 1958, p. 326.
2. Zaehner, op. cit., pp. 37–38.
3. 6,000 BCE is the estimate of J. M. Ranina in *The Essential Principles of Zoroastrianism*, P. D. Clinoy, Bombay, 1961, p. 3.
4. Zaehner, op. cit., pp. 33f.
5. J. Duchsesne-Guillemin, *The Hymns of Zarathustra*, J. Murray, London, 1952, p. 111.
6. Ibid., p. 95.
7. Ibid., p. 135.
8. Ibid., p. 65–66.
9. Zaehner, op. cit., pp. 32 and 42–43.
10. Duchesne-Guillemin, op. cit., p. 93.
11. Ibid., p. 105.
12. Ibid., p. 103.
13. Ibid., p. 79.
14. M. N. Dhalla, *History of Zoroastrianism*, Oxford University Press, Fair Lawn, N.J., 1983, pp. 318–319.
15. Ibid., pp. 339f.
16. See Zaehner, op. cit., chaps. 9–11.
17. R. O. Ballou, *The Bible of the World*, Viking, New York, 1947, p. 608.
18. Ibid., p. 634.

BIBLIOGRAPHY

Boyce, M. (ed.): *Zoroastrianism*, B & N Imports, Totowas, N.J., 1984.
——: *Zoroastrians*, Routledge, Chapman & Hall, New York, 1986.
Dhalla, M.: *History of Zoroastrianism*, AMS Press, New York, 1977.
——: *Zoroastrian Civilization*, AMS Press, New York, 1977.
——: *Zoroastrian Theology*, AMS Press, New York, 1977.
Duchesne-Guillemin, J.: *The Hymns of Zarathustra*, Beacon Press, Boston, 1963.
——: *Symbols and Values in Zoroastrianims*, Harper & Row, New York, 1966.

————: *The Western Response to Zoroaster*, Greenwood Press, New York, 1973.

Hinnells, J.: *Zoroastrianism and the Parsis*, State Mutual Book and Periodical Service, Ltd., New York, 1985.

Jackson, A. V. W.: *Zoroaster: The Prophet of Ancient Iran*, AMS Press, New York, 1965.

Modi, J. J.: *Religious Cermonies and Customs of the Parsis*, Luzac, London, 1954.

Moulton, J.: *Early Zoroastrianism*, AMS Press, New York, 1980.

————: *The Treasure of the Magi*, AMS Press, New York, 1972.

Pavry, J.: *The Zoroastrian Doctrine of the Future Life*, AMS Press, New York, 1965.

Zaehner, R.: *The Dawn and Twilight of Zoroastrianism*, Putnam, New York, 1965.

————: *The Teaching of the Magi*, Oxford, New York, 1976.

————: *Zurvan: A Zoroastrian Dilemma*, Biblo and Tannen Publishers, Cheshire, Conn., 1973.

The Zend Avesta, J. Darmesteter (trans.), *Sacred Books of the East*, Oxford, London, 1883.

11

Biblical Sources of Monotheism

This chapter will sketch the beginnings of historical monotheism in ancient or biblical Israel against the background of the cosmic or nature-culture religions of the ancient Middle East.[1] On this foundation Chapters 12, 13, and 14 will consider the successive and diverse developments of this key concept in Judaism, Christianity, and Islam.

The concept (and the fact) of historical monotheism must be clearly distinguished from those religions which diverge and differ in opposite ways from previous cosmic religion. On the one side are the many and various forms of polytheism, or the worship and service of many gods, and on the other side are several differing unitary or monistic concepts of deity or transcendence.[2]

Polytheism asserts that human religious experience has irreducibly plural objects. Indeed adherents of such religions sometimes argue that this plurality of religious allegiance is truer to human experience than any unitary allegiance can possibly be. Some polytheistic religions, such as that of Olympian Greece, posit a full pantheon of deities, representing many different social and national concerns, but also assert a single deity, in this case Zeus, as ruler or king over this multiverse throng. Modern scholars append the label monarchical monotheism to such religious systems, and find numerous examples in human history. The Bible formulates the distinction between polytheism and historical monotheism as the difference between god, gods, and the one God.

Historical monotheism differs also from several other religious systems with which it shares the concept of oneness or unity as a feature of deity. These systems range from Chapter 6's Hindu concept of Brahman to Plotinus in later Greco-Roman antiquity and his concept of the One, as noted in Chapter 2. To cite a single crucial difference, the one God of historical monotheism is characterized as sovereign and loving, while these other forms assert that deity or transcendence is above or beyond any such phenomenon as will or volition.

Perhaps the clearest and sharpest difference between these differing religious systems lies in the biblical concept of linear history. In their various reflections upon history, humanity's different religious traditions employ one of two metaphors, namely, a circle and a straight line, asserting that the historical process is either cyclic or linear in character. We have already encountered examples of both types. The Hindu and Buddhist traditions assert history consists of a beginningless and endless series of cycles, while Zoroastrianism assets a linear concept. In this chapter we shall observe the emergence of a linear view in the course of biblical history; and further, as we shall presently argue, the Bible asserts a linear-dramatic view, with the one God as lord of history.

In ancient Israel's earliest known age, their deity, Yahweh, did not observably differ from other tribal or cultural deities of that time and region. However, in the course of this chapter we will see two major movements of Israel's thought. The first was a turning to the past, specifically to Israel's exodus from Egyptian bondage, viewed as a saving act of God. The second and later move, occurring in the age of the great prophets, was a turning to the future. The prophets, believing in the sovereignty or lordship of Yahweh, could see that other lords and nations were presently in charge of the world. Hence they appealed to a future day of the Lord when Yahweh's lordship would be plain for all the world to see. Out of these two moves, to past and to future, emerged Israel's distinctive linear view of history, extending from creation to judgment day or from beginning to end. Once this idea had come to full formulation, it assumed a critical importance not only for religion but, as we shall see, for all aspects of human culture, not least of all for the basic concept of human selfhood as a piece of history or historic destiny.

The breakthrough, or discontinuous change from religion of the first or cosmic type to that of the third or historic type, occurred in the history of biblical Israel, roughly between the time of Moses (ca. 1290 BCE) and the age of the great prophets (ca. 750–550 BCE). Once this change had taken place, interesting contrasts became possible between the two types, as, for example, between the creation story of Genesis and the beginning stories of Egypt and Babylonia, or between the flood story of Genesis and that of the Gilgamesh epic of Babylonia.

Historical monotheism shows other distinctive features, as, for example, the concept of basic religious experience as revelation, or in Paul Tillich's phrase as "revelatory experience." This means that its nature is the disclosure (the word *revelation* carries the etymology of "unveiling") of essential truth from God to human selves or minds.

In all three of the monotheistic religions, namely, Judaism, Christianity, and Islam, this understanding of religious experience as revelatory leads onward to the concept of a holy book as the record of revelation. Other religions have holy or sacred writings variously interpreted, but for the three monotheisms the concept of divine self-disclosure is basic and central. Hence in all three a Book is of central significance, namely, their respective Bibles for Judaism and Christianity and the Qur'an for Islam. Beyond disagreements concerning the identity of the Book, all three of these religions have sometimes also been entangled in obscurantism and disputes in the interpretation of their Book.

Another distinctive feature of historical monotheism is its social and ethical character, as will be seen in the biblical prophets, to be discussed in this chapter. But this virtue too has its corresponding vice. This is the vice of fanaticism, often culminating in the supreme destructiveness of holy war. Holy wars have been fought in the name of many religions and ideologies. However, the three monotheistic religions have the dubious distinction, at one time or another, of explicitly teaching holy war. It must also immediately be added that all three of these traditions also contain moral resources for coping with this evil.

ANCIENT ISRAEL SEEN AGAINST ITS ENVIRONMENT

The Hebrews were relative latecomers to the ancient Near East. Mesopotamia had known settled, civilized life for approximately two millennia when Abraham left Ur of the Chaldees (ca. 1950 BCE). If Moses and the exodus of the Israelites (ca. 1290 BCE) are taken as the beginning of Hebrew history, they still must be seen against a long background of almost three millennia of Egyptian and Mesopotamian history. The land of Palestine, or Canaan, which became the Hebrew homeland, had known civilized life for thousands of years before the Hebrews arrived.

In modern times, all three of these areas, Egypt, Syria, and Mesopotamia, have been the scene of extensive and intensive archeological study, as a result of which students of religion are now able as never before to see ancient Israel against its environment. The student can, for example, lay the biblical creation story alongside the Babylonian creation story (the Enuma Elish), noting similarities and influences of the older Babylonian story on the biblical story, but also noting even more fundamental differences of viewpoint and outlook in these two stories.[3] Similar comparisons can be made between the flood stories contained in the Babylonian Gilgamesh epic and the biblical story in the Book of Genesis.[4]

The biblical story of Israel's escape from Egyptian bondage in the Book of Exodus is told as the conflict of two kings, Israel's Lord against the pharaoh, the god-king of Egypt, ending in triumph of the Lord and the drowning of the pharaoh and his army. The context of this dramatic conflict is the pharaoh's well-ordered world with its priests and temples, its deities and subjects. There is significant Egyptian influence of many sorts on Israel; but even more important is their fundamental difference of outlook; it is the difference, in Eliade's phrase, between "cosmos and history."[5] The Egyptians held a cosmic outlook, or what our study terms a type 1, nature-culture religion; the Hebrews achieved a historical monotheistic faith.

The Hebrew epic of the Lord and his people must also be seen against the Canaanite or Syrian background of the Ugaritic epic of Baal and Anath, recently unearthed at Ras Shamra.[6] While the Lord of Israel bears some similarity to the divine heroes of this epic, the differences are vastly more important. Israel's Lord has no divine friends or enemies but exists alone in solitary glory. Baal, Anath, and their kindred are deities of nature and culture, while Israel's God is envisaged as lord of history—at first Israel's history, then humankind's history.

ANCIENT ISRAEL'S DIVINE-HUMAN DRAMA

The first books of the Old Testament tell the story of ancient Israel's history, interpreted as the Lord's dealings with the people he has called to his service. Israel's history is also set in the wide framework of world history. The resulting narrative has sometimes been called the *Hebrew epic*, for there are genuinely epic dimensions in this ancient narrative.[7] One well-known student of comparative literature has compared and contrasted the epic style of Genesis with that of Homer's *Iliad* and *Odyssey*.[8] Yet the spirit and viewpoint of this narrative of ancient Israel and its God are so clearly dramatic that to call it a *drama* seems more appropriate than to call it an *epic*.

For many centuries both Jewish and Christian traditions maintained that Moses wrote the five books of the Torah, or Pentateuch. However, modern biblical study, while recognizing a Mosaic tradition, has demonstrated clearly that many pens, many voices, and many minds living and working over long periods of time had a share in the authorship and editing of the first five books of the Bible. Beginning with songs and tales of the patriarchs sung by ancient rhapsodists, the books of the Torah gradually incorporated other parts of the present narrative, law codes, religious confessions, and the like.[9] Scholarly opinions and theories differ on details, but most contemporary scholars agree on four main strands of narrative: (1) Yahwist, ca. 950 BCE, (2) Elohist, ca. 750 BCE, (3) Deuteronomist, ca. 650 BCE, and (4) Priestly, 550 BCE.[10] Woven together by successive generations of editors, they came in time to constitute the present Pentateuch, or Torah. While there are many variations in style, outlook, and historical circumstances, they all reflect the unity of a common tradition, constituting together in the view of their authors the dramatic narrative of God's dealings and covenant with his people Israel.

The first book of Moses is a book of beginnings, or literally of "genesis." It begins (Chapters 1–11) with what has been called a *cosmic preface*, in which the history of Israel is fitted into the larger picture of God's dealings with humankind and indeed with all creation. The divine-human drama begins with the divine creation of human beings and the world. The two creation stories (Genesis 1:1–2:3 and 2:4–3:24) are attributed by most scholars respectively to the P (Priestly) and J (Yahwist or Jahwist) authors. They differ from each other both in religious viewpoint and in factual detail, yet taken together in their overall unity, they also differ profoundly from other stories of beginnings. The Bible's first words are "In the beginning God..." The Genesis "Preface" moves onward from the creation and fall to the flood story, which though clearly influenced by the Babylonian flood story differs from it as monotheism differs from polytheism. From the J writer, a social pessimist, have come also the stories of the fall, of Cain and Abel, and of the tower of Babel.[11]

Genesis 12–50 tells the story of the patriarchs Abraham, Isaac, Jacob, and Jacob's twelve sons. While this narrative has the unity of a common heritage, it also shows an irreducible plurality, consisting as it does of many plots, characters, and viewpoints. At least some of these stories seem to be tales from the pre-Hebrew past of Canaan, reworked to fit into the present biblical narrative.[12]

Adam and Eve. Painting by Albrecht Dürer. (Metropolitan Museum of Art, Fletcher Fund, 1919.)

Early Hebrew narrators attributed the origin of their own nation as well as that of neighboring peoples to a figure named Abraham who in early days had emigrated from the Mesopotamian city of Ur northwestward to Harran in Syria and from thence south to Palestine. While Abraham appears before us as a shadowy figure, modern archeology bears out the tradition of a westward migration into Palestine, assigning a date of ca. 1950 BCE for Abraham.[13]

Hebrew narrators told tales of Abraham, of his life as a nomad in Palestine, of his descent to Egypt, of his generosity to his nephew, Lot, and many more episodes as well. Lot is depicted unflatteringly as the father, by incestuous union with his two daughters, of the neighboring Ammonites and Moabites. Abraham's son by Hagar, Ishmael, is identified as the ancestor of the Arabs. The Hebrew line of succession went through Isaac, the somewhat undistinguished son of Abraham and Sarah, to Isaac's more notable heir, Jacob, or Israel. Hebrew nationalism told how Jacob supplanted his twin brother, Esau, who was the progenitor of the Edomites. According to tradition Jacob's twelve sons were the ancestors of the twelve tribes of Israel. So indeed Genesis is a book of beginnings—Hebrew beginnings and those of other, neighboring peoples. It is also a story of two covenants of God, first with Noah and then with Abraham. The covenant with Noah carried God's assurance to sustain all creation, and the covenant with Abraham gave to all of Abraham's descendants the land of Canaan.

The perceptive reader will see in these stories the style which some students of religion have termed *Biblical realism*.[14] There is little or no glorification of a hero, as in Greek epics, but the plain-spoken narrative of plain people, in all their strength and weakness, all their good and evil, in short, in all their poignant humanity. Under the guidance of one of Jacob's sons, Joseph, the Hebrews found their way to Egypt. The Joseph stories are notable for their unity, for their literary excellence, and for their distinctive view of a providence which guided Joseph's life to fulfillment and success.

The patriarchal stories show forms of life and social organization similar to those of nomadic groups throughout the world. For these people, life was a never-ending search for grasslands for the flocks of cattle, sheep, and goats upon which life depended. Battles were fought over pasturage and ever-scarce water. The primary social group was the larger family under the authority of the father, who was at once priest, judge, and king. His authority in ancient Israel was somewhat limited by a council of elders. Polygamy was generally practiced, and the status of women, while not as inferior as in some societies, was clearly subordinate to that of men. The tribe was a closely knit, interdependent group in which each worked for all. While life was cheap outside the tribe, within the tribe there was a deep respect for personality.[15]

The religious customs of these nomads included a reverent respect for natural objects such as springs, stones, wells, trees, and hills, within which *els*, or deities, were thought to dwell. Yet such polydemonism was not the whole story of religion even at this early date. Some chiefs like Abraham conceived themselves to be in personal relation to deity, like sons before a father. In the worship of the patriarchs there was also a strong element of choice and a consequent sense of personal destiny. Here was the seed from which later religious developments were to grow.

While the full truth concerning Moses is obscured beneath many layers of tradition, it is still possible to discern a few salient historical facts. Perhaps the oldest account of the rescue from Egyptian bondage is contained in the following passage, often called the *Pentateuch in miniature*:

> A wandering Aramean was my father; and he went down into Egypt and sojourned there, few in number; and there he became a nation, great, mighty, and populous. And the Egyptians treated us harshly, and afflicted us, and laid upon us hard bondage. Then we cried to the Lord the God of our fathers, and the Lord heard our voice, and saw our affliction, our toil, and our oppression; and the Lord brought us out of Egypt with a mighty hand and an outstretched arm, with great terror, with signs and wonders; and he brought us into this place and gave us this land, a land flowing with milk and honey.[16]

The Exodus version of the story as well as the account in Deuteronomy expands this tightly compressed account of Israelite history. The Book of Exodus begins with Israel in bondage in Egypt to a pharaoh who "knew not Joseph." The historical evidence for the date of these events does not speak with a single voice, though the end of the fourteenth century is preferred today by most scholars, with the date of ca. 1290 BCE for the exodus.[17]

The deliverer, Moses, was born to Hebrew parents during this time of harsh oppression. Hidden from pharaoh's harsh decree by his parents, he was discovered and adopted by the pharaoh's daughter, and given all the advantages

The infant Moses discovered by the pharaoh's daughter in the bullrushes. Anonymous artist. (Photographic Archive of the Jewish Theological Seminary of America, New York.)

of an Egyptian education. As a young man Moses broke forcibly with his Egyptian environment by murdering an Egyptian slave master. Fleeing to the Sinai Peninsula, he found refuge with the nomadic tribe of Midianites. He lived as a shepherd and married Zipporah, daughter of the chief Jethro (or Reuel, as he is called by one Exodus writer).

Then one day an event of crucial importance took place. On the slopes of Mount Sinai the Lord Yahweh appeared to Moses through a burning bush, commanding him to go down to Egypt to lead his people from slavery to freedom, and promising to lead them to a good future in the land of Canaan. While many of the details of the experience are obscured under several strata of tradition, clearly the narrative points to a direct encounter with God which changed the course of Moses' life and also of Hebrew history. God revealed himself to Moses by setting him this task of great moral and historic significance, promising a great destiny to Moses and his people.

There is a clear difference between J and E (Elohist) strands of this Exodus narrative concerning the beginning of Israel's worship of the Lord. E holds that the worship actually began at the time of Moses. In a crucial passage the Lord says to Moses:

I am the Lord. I appeared to Abraham, to Isaac, and to Jacob, as God Almighty, but by my name the Lord I did not make myself known to them.[18]

It is significant in this connection to note that the divine name YHWH in Hebrew is translated into English as "Lord," while the Hebrew *Elohim* is rendered as "God." The Elohist writer calls deity *Elohim* or *God* throughout the Genesis period, and believes the worship of Yahweh began with Moses. Against this Elohist view, the J writer argues that Israel had "called on the name of Jahweh since the days of Enosh the son of Seth."[19] Whichever is correct, it was through the events of the exodus and on Sinai that the Lord, or Yahweh, decisively manifested himself to his people. This was the climax of the divine-human drama as the Old Testament authors construed it.

Accompanied by his brother Aaron, Moses returned to Egypt to plead for the release of the enslaved Israelites. From this point onward, the story becomes a contest between two deities, the Lord against pharaoh, the god-king of Egypt. Each of these deities performed mighty works or miracles, but the plagues which Moses and Aaron called down from the Lord upon Egypt moved onward to fatal climax in the death of the Egyptian firstborn. Only then Pharaoh desperately commanded Moses and his people to leave Egypt. But as they left, he changed his mind and pursued the fleeing Israelites, only to be overwhelmed by the Lord at the Red Sea.

The later conjoining of the celebration of this deliverance with a spring agricultural festival (such at least is the view of many scholars) provided ancient Israel as well as later Judaism with its best-known and most distinctive holy day, Passover. Thus Passover was given a historical meaning in the celebration of deliverance from Egypt.

Rescued and guided by their God and led by Moses, the Hebrews made their way in a space of three lunar months to the foot of Mount Sinai. The traditional location of this mountain is the south-central part of the Sinai Peninsula, and despite some scholarly controversy, this is still the most probable site. The Exodus and Deuteronomy narratives tell the story of the covenant between Israel and the Lord. While again the details of the event are obscured beneath many layers of tradition, the crucially important features are clear enough. Through these events, the Hebrew faith and nation were called into being. Ever afterward Israel looked back to Sinai as the covenant in which the Lord chose Israel, placing it under command and promise, and in which, reciprocally, Israel freely chose the Lord. Thus commitment and vocation were placed at the heart of Israel's religious experience. Further, the terms of Israel's service of its God consisted of a code for social conduct; in other words, God's primary requirement of humans was the ethical requirement of a good life in society with one's fellow human beings.

This ethical character of Mosaic religion is epitomized in the Ten Commandments, which are surely among the most famous codes in religious history. Attention may be called to two different versions of the Ten Commandments (Exodus 20 and Deuteronomy 5) with their great differences, and also to the fact that the first occurs in the larger context of what is usually called the *Book of the Covenant* (Exodus 20–23). The latter is a detailed code of social legislation and doubtless is ancient Israel's earliest written law code. In its present form it reflects an agricultural way of life and hence must be placed historically during Israel's early habitation in Palestine. Nevertheless the tendency of recent scholarship has been to push its origins back to a period close to Moses.[20]

Among its specific provisions, the Book of the Covenant recognized slavery; the lot of the Hebrew slave was easier than that of the foreigner, and male slaves fared better than females.[21] Women, while subordinate to men, were by no means without rights. The *lex talionis*, or "law of equal vengeance," restrained violence against persons in this age before public law officers.[22] Property rights in animals and land were carefully defined. Throughout this code there was a strong sense of social responsibility. It is particularly noteworthy that some of the laws were stated in categorical rather than hypothetical fashion, "Thou shalt..." rather than "If...then...," thus expressing the clear note of absoluteness in Israel's service of its God. At least one recent writer has contrasted this absolutism and personalism of the Mosaic code with the secularized, qualified, and somewhat impersonal tone of the Mesopotamian Code of Hammurabi.[23]

Israelites worshipping the golden calf in the wilderness. Silk tapestry. (Photographic Archive of the Jewish Theological Seminary of America, New York.)

Some of the provisions of the Book of the Covenant dealt with cultic or religious duties. The Lord was to be sought and found in the Ark of the Covenant, a box traditionally supposed to contain the tablets of the Torah, which was placed in the tent of meeting.[24] Feast days and probably animal sacrifice were prescribed. Most fundamental was Israel's exclusive service and worship of the Lord; the first commandment was "no other gods before me." As has often been pointed out, this commandment presupposes the existence of other deities, and the Books of Exodus and Deuteronomy make this assumption explicitly clear. However, the important point was that Israel was categorically commanded to *serve* no other deity. Consistent with this relation the Lord was conceived as an absolute sovereign who of his own free will kept covenant with Israel. Hence also in this manner his sovereignty was qualified by his love; Israel was God's son whom he loved and chose for a great destiny. Moreover this God who was Lord was also the creator; the famous words "I am who I am" should in the opinion of some scholars be translated "I am he who causes to be," or "he causes to be what comes into existence."[25]

After the giving of the Torah, Israel appears to have wandered nomadically for a generation in the wilderness south of Palestine. There was an initial and unsuccessful attempt to invade Palestine, this and other events of the period being recounted in the biblical Book of Numbers. During this time, Israel lived as a nomadic tribe in the region of Kadesh Barnea. The biblical estimate of forty years for this period fits with modern scholarship, for there is evidence that by ca. 1250 BCE Israel had begun to move into Canaan.[26]

Two contrasting biblical accounts of the conquest of Canaan are contained in the Books of Joshua and Judges. The former describes a brief military invasion under the leadership of Joshua, who was Moses' immediate successor. It was a campaign which ended in complete Hebrew victory and the subjugation of previous inhabitants and division of territory among the traditional twelve tribes. The other account, in the Book of Judges, describes a long, slow, and fitful process of infiltration, crowned with success only two centuries later under the monarchical leadership of Saul and David.

There is doubtless some basis in fact for the account of Joshua's campaigns and the Shechem assembly at which the covenant was renewed and the land divided among the twelve tribes.[27] However, there is good reason to believe that these campaigns were local and Joshua's success temporary. Stories of total victory were the figments of later editors' imaginations.

The Book of Judges, which sketches the history of Israel's first two centuries in Palestine, was written, or at least edited, by a later writer with a different and highly distinctive viewpoint. He recognized Israel's long, hard, and fitful struggle for Canaan, but in this struggle he related good fortune to fidelity to the Lord and misfortune to infidelity. Behind this interpretation historians can discern the two-century period when Israel was locked in mortal combat with other peoples for domination of the land. At one time the Moabites achieved the mastery, and Israel rebelled against them. At another time the Hebrews, under Deborah and Barak, threw off the yoke of the Canaanites under Sisera. This

Moses holding the Ten
Commandments. Eighteenth-century
German wood sculpture.
(Photographic Archive of the Jewish
Theological Seminary of America,
New York. Frank J. Darmstaedter.)

battle is described in the "Ode of Deborah," which is not only a great poem, but also, as one of the most ancient documents in the Bible, an important historical source.[28] At another time Gideon arose as a leader, driving off bands of marauding Midianites.

It was an age of only minimal unity among the Hebrews, who as a result fell victim to other, better-organized peoples. It was also a time of religious conflict and transition. The Hebrews came into Palestine as a close-knit nomadic community, firm in their faith in the Lord. However, they found other religious customs in the new country. Notably they encountered worship of local civic and agricultural deities called *baals* (the word *baal* in Hebrew means "lord," "husband," and "owner"). There were innumerable local baals who functioned as fertility deities of the land and were frequently wed to fertility goddesses called *asherah*. There was also a high god, or baal, celebrated in Ugaritic epic, who manifested himself in storms. It is probable that this latter was the baal whom Elijah opposed at Mount Carmel in mid-ninth century BCE.[29]

The problem confronting the Hebrews was the relation of their God, the Lord, to these new deities. Should they abandon the Lord for these new deities? Did the Lord rule the new country as he ruled the desert? Should they try to blend worship of the Lord and of the baals? It took many centuries to hammer out definitive answers to these and similar questions.

The last and most formidable opponents of the Hebrews for mastery of the land were the Philistines, who were refugees from the disaster which had overtaken Crete, and who made their way across Asia Minor and down the coast of Syria to the borders of Egypt. Repelled there, they settled on the seacoast of Palestine early in the thirteenth century BCE. Ironically, they gave their name to the country, *Palestine* being a corrupted form of *Philistine*. Organized into city-states and well armed, the Philistines subjugated the Hebrews and made themselves virtual masters of the land.[30]

In this dire extremity, the Hebrew people demanded a king who could provide effective military and political leadership. To this proposal there appears to have been continuing opposition from the group in Israel which rejected a king as a competitor with the Lord for Israel's allegiance. This group asserted that only the Lord was really the king of Israel. One of the two source narratives of Saul's tragic reign appears to have been written by such an author, who did not hesitate to write his antimonarchical prejudices into history.[31]

The Bible gives two accounts of Saul's accession to the throne. According to one he was anointed by the seer and priest of Shiloh, Samuel; according to the other, he was selected by lot in a popular assembly of Israel's people.[32] Once in power, he showed initiative in raising an army and driving off the Ammonites from the city of Jabesh in Gilead. Turning his attention to the Philistines, Saul again had initial success, largely because of the daring and imagination of his son, Jonathan, who surprised and defeated the Philistine garrison at Michmash.

Yet Saul could not, or at least did not, follow up his first successes. He alienated Samuel, who turned his support to another aspirant for the throne,

David. Saul was plagued by a recurring mood of melancholy (called by the biblical historian an "evil spirit from the Lord") which robbed him of his resolution and rendered him pathologically jealous of David. After much delay, the Philistines struck at the battle of Mount Gilboa. The Hebrews were routed, both Saul and Jonathan taking their own lives to avoid capture.[33] Saul's reign lasted from 1020 to 1000 BCE.

Saul's death left an open field for David, who during Saul's lifetime had carefully refrained from seeking the throne. He seems to have regarded King Saul as a sacred person, God's anointed king of Israel. When Saul died, David became king of his native Judea for seven years, while Saul's son, Ishbaal, grasped the opportunity to become king of a united nation. His reign (ca. 1000–961 BCE) was the golden age of ancient Israel.

David moved quickly and decisively against Israel's enemies, the Philistines first, then the Ammonites, Moabites, and Edomites. In each case he won a decisive victory. The boundaries of the Israelite nation were extended farther than ever before or ever after. At home, stable government and a prosperous economy, aided by tribute from subjugated peoples, provided unparalleled good times.

David's reign was also marked by a flowering of art and culture. The king was a poet and musician, as well as an enthusiastic supporter of Yahweh. Hebrew language assumed its classical form; and the first redaction of Israel's national epic, that of the J writer or Yahwist, came into being. Little wonder that David's reign became known to later generations as Israel's golden age.

David's personal and family life was not as successful as his public career. An illicit affair with Bathsheba led to his plotting and killing her husband Uriah.[34] This sordid story is told with full realism by the biblican historian, who also informs us of the denunciation of David by David's friend, the prophet Nathan. Here the prophet assumed the role of critic of royal injustice; it was a momentous precedent.

David's family was seldom harmonious. One son, Amnon, raped his half sister Tamar, and for this act was killed by Tamar's brother, Absalom, who was in turn ostracized from the court. Absalom subsequently rose in rebellion against his father. After coming perilously close to success, the rebellion was put down by David's military men, and much to David's sorrow, Absalom was killed.[35]

David's old age was marred by court intrigue and struggle for succession to the throne. The chief contenders were Adonijah and Solomon. The latter, with the help of his mother, Bathsheba, succeeded in gaining the support of David. Upon his accession to the throne, he proceeded to a bloody purge of his rival and his rival's followers.[36]

Solomon, lacking both his father's military ability and his democratic sensibilities, set up his court like an oriental despot.[37] In addition to his famous temple, Solomon's extensive public building enterprises included a palace for himself, another for his favorite wife, the princess of Egypt, a hall of judgment, and many more. He built a navy with a Red Sea base, and carried on overseas commerce, which featured such luxury commodities as ivory, apes, and peacocks. His extensive household included 300 wives and 600 concubines as well as a vast retinue of courtiers, all supported by public taxation. Apparently Solomon's reputation as a wise judge was not based upon a social conscience. It is not surprising that there were repeated rumblings of rebellion during his reign.

Solomon's reign lasted from 961 to 922 BCE. When he died, his subjects met in popular assembly at Shechem to petition for redress of grievances. Meeting complete rebuff from Solomon's son, Rehoboam, the ten northern tribes did not hesitate to secede from the dynasty of David and set up their own government at Shechem (922 BCE). Their first king and leader was Jeroboam I, a former official of and then a rebel against Solomon. This division of the kingdom disastrously split the nation. The southern tribes of Judah and Benjamin remained true to the Davidic dynasty and held the capital city of Jerusalem, while the rebellious ten tribes held most of the nation's territory, wealth, and population. Neither was a genuinely viable unit without the other.

The half century which followed the division was marked by intermittent border warfare, and also extreme instability in the northern kingdom. King followed king in rapid and violent succession until the rise of Omri. A military man who seized the throne in 876 BCE, he built Samaria as capital city and established a secure and prosperous kingdom. Omri's foreign relations with Syria to the north were cemented by the marriage of his son Ahab to the Phoenician princess Jezebel.[38]

Ahab succeeded to his father's throne in 869 BCE and reigned for nineteen years. The most notable event of his reign was the protracted struggle of the Yahwist party under Elijah against Jezebel and her attempt to introduce into Israel the worship of the Tyrian baal Melkart. Jezebel was not only a forceful person, but an enthusiastic devotee of Melkart. Elijah saw the issue of Melkart versus Yahweh in uncompromising terms: Israel could serve Melkart or the Lord but not both. The worship of the Lord was connected in Elijah's mind with both national independence and social justice. When the poor man Naboth was framed and killed by Jezebel in order that she might seize his land, Elijah rose to superb heights as champion of social justice. Elijah's opposition to Jezebel and Melkart came to a climax at the trial on Mount Carmel, where he stood alone in defiance of Jezebel's 400 prophets of Baal.[39]

These and other stories of Elijah were written down not long after his death, probably by a follower. They show a figure second only to Moses among the great men of Israel. Later generations made him the symbol of prophecy as Moses was the symbol of the Torah. Elijah's prophetic career was the foundation for the work of the great prophets of the eighth and seventh centuries.

After Elijah, the northern kingdom, Israel, continued for another century and then, falling victim to Assyrian invastion in 721 BCE, disappeared from the pages of history. The people were carried into captivity never to return, thus becoming the ten lost tribes. The tiny southern kingdom of Judah continued a tortured existence until 586 BCE, when Nebuchadnezzar captured Jerusalem and

Model of Solomon's temple. (The Bettmann Archive.)

carried its people into captivity, decisively ending the national existence of the ancient Israelite people.

Apparently the divine-human drama of ancient Israel's life had come to a tragic conclusion. Yet the miracle was that this was not the end. The story of Israel did not terminate with the end of its national existence. In the historical period to which this discussion has now come, the eighth to the sixth centuries BCE, the focus of interest shifts from national politics to another subject of paramount importance, the rise of prophetic religion.

PROPHETIC RELIGION

What is a prophet? Many would answer immediately and without hesitation that a prophet is a divinely certified forecaster of the future. This understanding of prophecy has support in many religious traditions, from Greece and Rome to India and China. Oracles and oracular speakers are familiar figures in the world's religions. It has some basis in the ancient Hebrew tradition of the Bible, as illustrated by the stories of Balaam, and of Saul's search for his father's lost donkeys.[40]

The Greek word *Prophetes* has the double meaning of "foretelling" and "forthtelling," but the Hebrew word for "prophet," *nabu* (plural *nebiim*), means unequivocally to "speak for." The latter etymology accords with the historic fact that the prophets of Israel believed themselves called to speak for the Lord to Israel, and, in the case of some later prophets, to humankind. The evidence for this interpretation of prophecy will be given as exposition unfolds. To be sure, the prophets of Israel did at times predict; and sometimes their predictions came true, sometimes not. However, the heart of their enterprise lay not in predicting the future, but in declaring God's will to his recalcitrant human children.

Since the biblical prophets were possessed by an immediately and powerfully perceived vocation to speak for God, they have been likened to the mystic who also has an immediate, or direct, awareness of the divine. However, the Hebrew prophet contrasts sharply with the mystic in the prophet's fundamental emphasis on volition and action and hence upon specific moral and social aspects of religion. Where the mystic finds communion or union with God in some transcendent realm, the prophet encounters God in everyday moral and social relations. Holding the standard of God's will as the criterion, the prophet is led to a radical criticism of every aspect of human life and culture. For Israel's prophets, the ethical criticism of religion—as of all human culture—became a definite aspect of religion.

The *prophetic principle*, as it may be called, may thus be defined as the achievement of a point above all human life and culture from which all of life is held under radical criticism. The one God of monotheism has many meanings and implications, which will be developed as our study proceeds. However, the prophetic understanding, involving a viewpoint from which prophetic criticism is undertaken, may be treated as basic. Many of the further meanings and implications of the one God will be noted in future chapters as implications drawn from this premise.

The origins of prophecy in the Bible go far back in history. Later ages looked back to Moses as the archetypal prophet, and as has been argued, the idea of ethical religion is traceable to him. Later, during Israel's first centuries in Palestine, bands of Yahweh enthusiasts wandered the countryside prophesying ecstatically, singing, dancing, working themselves into ecstatic states. Saul is said to have identified himself with one such band.[41] It is possible that Deborah was such a prophet.[42]

Biblical prophecy began to take on a new dimension of ethical and social criticism in such figures as Nathan in David's time and Ahijah in Solomon's.[43] It is important historically to note that this idea of a religiously inspired criticism of political power in ancient Israel is unique in the ancient Middle East, if not in the religions of the whole world. Its importance for western politics as well as religion can scarcely be overestimated.

Prophecy assumed a new importance in the great Elijah of the ninth century. As we have already noted, he was the champion of both social justice and national independence. Moreover, he pushed the Yahwist criticism of baal worship a long step further, in his assumption that Yahweh was lord not only of history but of such natural phenomena as the weather.[44] His mordant ridicule of Baal Melkart and Melkart's priests was a step toward the conclusion of the essential unreality of the baals, and toward the corresponding conclusion that Yahweh was the absolute lord of all reality.

A century after Elijah, the writing prophets (so called because their words and lives now form books of the Judeo-Christian Bible) burst upon the scene, and they managed to hold the center for at least two centuries. These prophets, beginning with Amos and continuing until Ezekiel and Deutero-Isaiah, would not have called themselves innovators; rather, they professed to recall their people to the traditional Mosaic heritage.[45] Yet the manner in which they performed this prophetic task did in fact transform Hebrew religion. It may be said that the prophets *historicized, ethicized, spiritualized,* and *universalized* Israel's religious heritage. Their historicizing emphasis took the double form of recalling Israel to the Mosaic past and what Martin Buber has called a "turning to the future."[46] The prophets asserted that the Lord who had ruled and guided Israel during the exodus and on Sinai still ruled and would yet vindicate his rule of

Wandering Elijah. Painting by Ben Zion. (Photographic Archive of the Jewish Theological Seminary of America, New York. Frank J. Darmstaedter.)

the world. The importance for the development of biblical religion of this looking to the future toward a time of consummation can hardly be overstated.

Although the prophets inherited the Mosaic tradition of the Ten Commandments and ethical religion, they applied this standard to the life of society in new and radical ways. They were especially critical of the institutional religion of their time. Closely allied with the appeal to an ethical or moral standard for the judgment of all human life was an inward appeal to the motives or intentions which are the source of human actions. Only if the heart be pure, argued the prophets, will action be righteous.

Finally, the prophets universalized Israel's religion. As God is one, so humankind is one human family. Thus the Lord was no longer understood as a Hebrew tribal deity, guiding and protecting his people, but as lord of all peoples and nations. One God, therefore one humankind: such is the logic of prophetic thought. From this point onward in Judeo-Christian history, the student sees a radical tension in thought and faith between universalism and what must be termed *particularism* or *nationalism*.

The historical background of the prophetic movement was the late Indian summer of the Hebrew nation. Jeroboam II (796–746 BCE) occupied the throne of Israel and Uzziah (783–742 BCE), the throne of Judah, when Amos, the first of these prophets, raised his voice. On the surface, prosperity prevailed at home and peace abroad. Yet it was the momentary calm before the whirlwind of doom. As the prophets were quick to point out, the domestic prosperity was based upon the grinding poverty of the poor. Internationally, the Assyrians appeared like a dark and foreboding cloud on the northern horizon. Before the eighth century was over, the northern kingdom, Israel, had disappeared from history, and little Judah was left to another century and a half of existence as a meager pawn on the chessboard of empires and conquests. In the midst of this situation arose the great prophets of the eighth century, Amos, Hosea, Isaiah, and Micah.

AMOS (CA. 750 BCE)

The first of the writing prophets was a farmer and shepherd from the remote Judean village of Tekoa. Making his way to the northern shrine city of Bethel, presumably at the time of a festival, he spoke out publicly against injustice and social evils of Jeroboam II's reign. Challenged by the court chaplain, Amaziah, and told to go back home, Amos replied in burning words his own strong sense of vocation to speak for the Lord: "Then Amos answered Amaziah, 'I am no prophet, nor a prophet's son; but I am a herdsman, and a dresser of sycamore trees, and the Lord took me from following the flock, and the Lord said to me, "Go, prophesy to my people." ' "[47] To this vocation Amos brought both a sharp eye for social realities and a fundamental conviction of ethical religion, that God has written his law of justice and brotherhood into the foundations of society. He also brought a literary style which fitted his message.

In several of his prophetic oracles, Amos seemed to regard God's law of brotherhood as written into the structure of human life in such a way that to break this law is to violate the norms of human life.[48] As a wall not squarely built falls of its own weight, so an unjust society must collapse. The notes of judgment and doom are strong throughout Amos's book. Yet divine judgment is never a capricious action of some celestial judge, but rather a judgment rising from the social structure of life itself. Evil is a violation of the norms of human life. As a destroying nemesis, God tracks down evildoers to the ends of the earth or the depths of the sea.[49]

Amos detailed his charges against his unrighteous compatriots. They have sold "the needy for a pair of shoes" and trampled "the poor into the dust," they have made "the ephah small and the shekel great," have used false weights and other sorts of sharp practice.[50]

For the leisure classes Amos had these words:

> Woe to those who lie upon beds of ivory, and stretch themselves upon their
> couches,
> and eat lambs from the flock, and calves from the midst of the stall;
> who sing idle songs to the sound of the harp, and like David invent for
> themselves instruments of music;
> who drink wine in bowls, and anoint themselves with the finest oils, but are not
> grieved over the ruin of Joseph!
> Therefore they shall now be the first of those to go into exile, and the revelry of
> those who stretch themselves shall pass away.[51]

Yet perhaps worst of all social evils was a ritual religion irrelevant to ethical conduct and characterized by temple prostitution and other similar evils. Amos depicts God as saying:

> I hate, I despise your feasts, and I take no delight in your solemn assemblies.
> Even though you offer me your burnt offerings and cereal offerings, I will not
> accept them,
> and the peace offerings of your fatted beasts I will not look upon.
> Take away from me the noise of your songs; to the melody of your harps I will
> not listen.
> But let justice roll down like waters, and righteousness like an ever-flowing
> stream.[52]

This unsparing denunciation of institutional religion was destined to be repeated by each of Israel's preexilic prophets.

Amos's contemporaries added to their ritual a kind of religious nationalism which found expression in the "day of the Lord." This was interpreted as a future time when God would give the Hebrews victory over all their foes. To this Amos replied ominously:

> Woe to you who desire the day of the Lord!
> Why would you have the day of the Lord?

It is darkness, and not light; as if a man fled from a lion, and a bear met him;
or went into the house and leaned with his hand against the wall, and a serpent
bit him.
Is not the day of the Lord darkness, and not light, and gloom with no brightness
in it?[53]

In dark and foreboding images, Amos foresaw the doom of a nation that had failed in essential justice and brotherhood. Presumably he viewed the Assyrians as the executors of God's judgment upon Israel.

Amos saw with equal clarity not only the divine justice but the universality of God which reduced to zero any favored status for Israel. The first chapter of Amos's book is a series of judgments of doom upon all surrounding peoples— in which presumably Amos's nationalistic compatriots could join by simply ignoring Amos's statement of the ethical character of the judgment. But then—to the bewilderment and surprise of his fellow Israelites—Amos followed with God's judgment of doom upon Israel and upon Judah for the reason that they too had failed miserably in essential morality. God's judgment plays no favorites. "Are you not to me as the Ethiopians?" Amos's Lord asks the people of Israel.[54] Indeed their previous knowledge leaves them even more blameworthy: "You only have I known of all the families of the earth; therefore I will punish you for all your iniquities."[55]

HOSEA (CA. 740 BCE)

A few years after Amos, another prophetic voice, that of Hosea, was raised. Although he was like Amos in his emphasis on the ethical nature of religion, Hosea differed profoundly in other respects. He was a native of the northern kingdom, and his words suggest a priestly background. The first three chapters of his book tell of his tragic marriage and family life. These same three chapters may also be said to constitute Hosea's call to the prophetic office. The biblical text of these chapters is obscure; reconstruction is necessary to make sense of the narrative. An attempted reconstruction of Hosea 1–3 follows in the next paragraphs.

Apparently Hosea had married a wife, Gomer, in mutual good faith. Their three children were given symbolic names with prophetic meanings. The eldest, a son, was named Jezreel, recalling Jehu's bloody rebellion a century earlier on a battlefield of that name. The other two were named, respectively, Lo-ammi, "not my people," and Lo-ruhammah, "she who is unpitied," meaning that the Lord would have no pity in his judgment of Israel. So far, Hosea had not diverged from Amos's grim conclusion concerning God's judgment on Israel.

Only then did Hosea discover that Gomer was unfaithful. The biblical passage intimates that she became a temple prostitute. Hebrew law decreed divorce as the just fate for such a person. Sadly Hosea undertook to put the decree into effect when suddenly as a word from the Lord he felt constrained to love his erring wife through all her wanderings and infidelities and by this love to win her back to himself. By analogy Hosea saw that the Lord loved Israel despite her unfaithfulness and sought to win her back to himself. So it was that Hosea looked beyond justice to forgiving love. So too it was that through the tragic events of his marriage Hosea felt himself called to prophesy to Israel.

Like Amos before him, Hosea believed that Israel would suffer for her manifold sins; but beyond judgment he saw redemption and forgiveness. At least once in Hosea's book the marital metaphor changes and the Lord becomes the forgiving father and Israel the wayward son.[56] No other prophet declared the healing and forgiving love of God in more lyrically beautiful language than Hosea.

Hosea's viewpoint was deeply inward. Where Amos criticized evil deeds, Hosea probed the motives of the heart which found expression in such deeds, concluding that the evil affections of the heart are the source of unrighteous actions. Hosea never tired of pointing out the inconstancy of the human heart, turning from God to trivial things, as the source of evil action. One consequence of all this is idolatry—false worship or false love. Also in Hosea's mind the monarchy was related to idolatry, for a king so easily confused himself with God.

In Hosea's view, the Lord is always near. If Israel persists in infidelity, God declares, "I am your destruction, O Israel, who can help you?"[57] Yet God is also always ready to take back his erring human children.

> So you, by the help of your God, return,
> hold fast to love and justice,
> and wait continually for your God.[58]

Hosea's words were a dirge for the northern kingdom. In 732 BCE the Assyrians took Damascus and overran Israel, placing a puppet king on the throne. In 724 BCE he rebelled, the Assyrians besieged the city of Samaria and after a long and cruel siege, took it in 721 BCE. Following their practice, the Assyrians carried the survivors captive to distant parts of their empire, bringing in foreigners to populate the northern kingdom. So the ten tribes passed from the scene of history.

ISAIAH OF JERUSALEM (CA. 742–690 BCE)

Contemporary with Hosea there arose the mighty figure of Isaiah of Jerusalem. His words may be found in the first thirty-nine chapters of the book of the Bible which bears his name. Yet since the Book of Isaiah contains the writing of at least one and probably many other writers, constituting a kind of miscellaneous file of prophetic writings, it is necessary for the reader to distinguish the utterances of Isaiah of Jerusalem from others. Happily his style and content are sufficiently distinctive to make this possible. One of the first and most notable examples is Isaiah's description (Isaiah 6) of the experience which made him a prophet. In the temple at Jerusalem one day "in the year that King Uzziah died" (742 BCE), he "saw the Lord."[59] The vision produced in the prophet a sense of profound awe before God which gave way first to a sense of sin, then forgiveness, and then to a sense of mission. In response to the divine question, "Whom shall I send and who will go for us?" Isaiah replied, "Here am I, send me."[60] Thus launched upon his prophetic career, Isaiah was statesman, preacher, reformer, and spokesman for God to Israel in the tumultuous decades that followed.

He spoke of God's justice and love as Amos and Hosea before him, but he introduced new notes as well. One such new emphasis was the idea of faith conceived as trust in God. The true source of strength was not arrogant self-trust as the nationalists asserted, nor was it trust in arms or in alliances with this or that nation. Rather it was trust in the Lord, who despite all appearances to the contrary was still the sovereign of history.

In a famous scene (recounted in Chapter 7), Isaiah met Ahaz as the king went out of Jerusalem to secure the city's water supply and fortifications in anticipation of impending siege and war. The prophet bade the king not to fear, warning him, "If you will not believe, surely you shall not be established."[61] In the face of the king's mingled incredulity and evasiveness, Isaiah declared a sign. A child would be born, named Emmanuel (meaning "God with us"), and in the length of time necessary for the child to grow to knowledge of good and evil, the king's enemies would be brought to naught.[62] Yet what Isaiah really sought to impress upon the king was that above all kings and warriors, above all nations and empires, the Lord God rules history.

Ancient manuscript of Isaiah from Qumran caves. (Courtesy of John C. Trever.)

This conviction led to some of Isaiah's profoundest—and strangest—words. Like Amos before him, Isaiah believed that God would judge his own people Israel. And he plainly said that the Lord would use the hated Assyrians as his "battle axe."[63] Yet when the Assyrians actually invaded Judah, and Isaiah could see their arrogant and wanton cruelty at first hand, he cried out in change of mind: "Shall the axe vaunt itself over him who hews with it?"[64] Surely the Lord would cast off so arrogant an instrument of his purpose. Proud self-sufficiency constituted the heart of human evil, whether in Israel or her enemies. Such was Isaiah's conclusion as he looked upon the history of his troubled times.

In a famous poetic vision of the day of the Lord, Isaiah declared that all high and arrogant human things would be brought low, and the Lord only would be exalted. God declares an absolute judgment against all forms of human arrogance.[65]

Yet this was not the prophet's last word. As he scanned the future, he saw doom and judgment in the immediate time ahead. Yet he could look beyond this darkness to a better time to come. Isaiah declared that a faithful remnant would persist throught the testing time to come, to a better future. His son bore the symbolic name Shearjashub, meaning "a remnant shall return."[66] He spoke of Israel as a tree cut down, from whose stump new growth would presently come. God spoke of humans in history not only in judgment but in redemption as well.

Moreover, the divine purpose in history would one day come to fulfillment. Isaiah gave few details, but he alluded to the ideal king who would reign in peace and justice.[67] This golden age of the future would be a time when swords would be beaten into ploughshares and nations would learn war no more.[68] In such vivid images Isaiah probed the ways of God in human history.

MICAH (CA. 725–700 BCE)

Beside the great Isaiah, Micah seems small and his words meager. Yet he had a message from the Lord for the reluctant ears of his contemporaries. He denounced the injustices and evils of the cities. From a small town, Bethlehem, he cried, the ideal king would come.[69] Meanwhile, Samaria and Jerusalem would be left as rubble-heaps on the landscape.[70]

Yet these angry words softened to Micah's classic formula of prophetic religion. Its unmistakable allusion to human sacrifice places it during the reign of King Manasseh, who practiced those barbarous rites. Whether it is from Micah or from a disciple is thus questionable, but in either case it epitomizes the spirit of prophetic religion:

> With what shall I come before the Lord.
> and bow myself before God on high?
> Shall I come before him with burnt offerings, with calves a year old?
> Will the Lord be pleased with thousands of rams, with ten thousands of rivers of oil?

Shall I give my first-born for my transgression, the fruit of my body for the sin of
    my soul?
He has showed you, O man, what is good; and what does the Lord require of you
    but to do justice, and to love kindness, and to walk humbly with your God?[71]

DEUTERONOMY (621 BCE)

The Mican allusion to human sacrifice may well have been a reference to King
Manesseh, 687–642 BCE, for it is known that he participated in human sacrifices,
making his son "pass through fire." Manasseh was an Assyrian vassal who
brought Assyrian deities and rituals into the Jerusalem temple, pushing the altar
of the Lord to one side. Also he persecuted the Yahwist party, forcing them underground.

   During this time of hiding, the prophetic, or Yahwist, party formulated
their own program of reform and held it in readiness for the opportune moment. That moment came when after the brief reign of Manasseh's son, Amon
(642 BCE), his grandson, Josiah, came to the throne (642–609 BCE). In 621 he
ordered long-needed repairs to the temple, during which the high priest reported the finding of a long-lost book of Mosaic law, or Torah. This event, reported in II Kings 22:8–20, is regarded by most modern scholars as the recovery
or discovery of the proposals of the prophetic party as they are embodied in the
biblical Book of Deuteronomy.

   The word *Deuteronomy* means in Greek "second law," that is, the second
redaction of the Mosaic law. The Book of Deuteronomy is cast in the form of
three sermonic addresses by Moses to the Israelites as they were about to enter
Canaan. While clearly the book is in the Mosaic tradition, it is undoubtedly the
work of seventh-century prophetic reformers. Its ideas fit well with what we
know of seventh-century Israel. It was proposed, for example, that the remnants
of foreign cults were to be rooted out and destroyed, local shrines which had
been hotbeds of baal worship were to be closed, and all worship centered in
Jerusalem. To the Deuteronomic reformers the worship of one God clearly implied a single sanctuary. In their insistent emphasis upon social ethics, the
Deuteronomic reformers showed the influence of the great eighth-century
prophets.

   The Deuteronomic law code (Chapters 12–26) evinced a sense of social
responsibility which combined in new ways personal rights and property rights.
Every seventh, or sabbatical, year debts were to be canceled, and Hebrew
slaves, though not foreign slaves, were to be manumitted. A judicial system including right of appeal to a supreme court was provided. A king with limited
powers was recognized. Rules of war, including a generous system of draft de-
ferments and a military chaplaincy, were sketched out. War was holy for the
Deuteronomic reformers, and all prisoners and booty were *cherem*, or devoted
to God.[72] There is no knowledge of the extent to which this Deuteronomic reform code was ever put into actual practice.

   The religious spirit of the Deuteronomists is epitomized in the Shema:

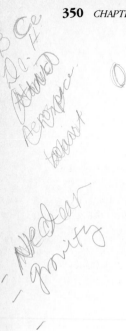

> Hear, O Israel: the Lord our God is one Lord. And you shall love the Lord your God with all your heart, and with all your soul, and with all your might.[73]

There is in Deuteronomy a new emphasis upon the study of God's Torah, as found within the pages of this book. Indeed, precisely here may be said to be the actual beginning of the idea of a sacred scripture; here Judaism was first set upon the way of being a religion of Torah or book. The study and practice of Torah are confidently declared to be the first human duty.[74]

Over and over again the Deuteronomic author exhorts his compatriots to avoid even the suggestion of the worship of false gods. For only so can a good life be achieved and maintained. Indeed these Deuteronomic reformers spelled out with utter consistency of detail the good fortune and prosperity which resulted from the service of the Lord, and the misfortune which they believed would follow the service of false gods. The great eighth-century prophets had argued that justice would bring a good life for Israel, and injustice would spell Israel's undoing. The Deuteronomists went far beyond this to the conclusion that a just God would, as it were, pay off the wages of righteousness and sin regularly and exactly! Some centuries later this view was to elicit the protest of the Book of Job. Later followers of the Deuteronomic dogma who edited some of Israel's historic texts did not hesitate to interpolate this oversimplified view of good and evil into such texts as the Book of Judges.

JEREMIAH (CA. 650–580 BCE)

This great individualist among the prophets was born of a priestly family in the village of Anathoth just north of Jerusalem. The record of his call to the prophetic office makes clear his profound sense of vocation. The Lord is represented as saying to Jeremiah: "Before I formed you in the womb I knew you, and before you were born I consecrated you; I appointed you a prophet to the nations."[75] But it also makes clear Jeremiah's shy and deeply introverted nature and his reluctance to undertake so formidable a career. Yet it was to be his destiny to speak for the Lord to Israel—and to the world—during the tragic years when the Hebrew nation moved to a suicidal end with the destruction of Jerusalem and the exile of its people. During these years, Jeremiah was so consistently pessimistic that the word *jeremiad* has come to mean a doleful prediction of doom.

Jeremiah began to prophesy at the time of the Deuteronomic reform, and it is probable that he collaborated for a time with the Deuteronomists. Yet he broke with these reformers over the issue of a religious and moral code as against an inward faith of the heart. Jeremiah stood consistently for the view that faith is of the heart.

Like Isaiah in the previous century, Jeremiah pondered the ways of God in history. Like Isaiah he believed that individuals and nations were only instruments of the divine purpose which rules history. But Jeremiah drew a conclusion radically different from Isaiah's. Where Isaiah had declared Jerusalem impregnable, defying the invading Assyrians, Jeremiah consistently believed and taught that Jerusalem must fall to the Chaldean king, Nebuchadnezzar.[76] For Jeremiah, to trust in Jerusalem as if it were God would constitute a false and idolatrous faith. Reasoning thus, Jeremiah came to see God working in human hearts beyond any national boundaries. After the first fall of Jerusalem in 597 BCE, Jeremiah, still in Jerusalem, wrote a letter to Jewish exiles in Babylonia telling them to settle down in their new homes and worship God there.[77] For worship, far from being tied to a particular place, was for Jeremiah an inward relation of the heart to God. At home in Jerusalem, Jeremiah continued to oppose the popular religious nationalism of the time and to counsel complete compliance with the Chaldean conquerors—attitudes that led to charges of treason and to attempts on his life.

As events moved to their fateful conclusion, Jeremiah was led to formulate his own distinctive view of the good time coming. During the time when the Chaldeans besieged Jerusalem for a second and final capture, Jeremiah's cousin, Hanamel, offered to sell him land, it being the tradition to offer land first to a relative in order to keep the family inheritance intact. Ordinarily, no one would buy land in a doomed nation. But strangely Jeremiah reversed his previous pessimism and bought the land, saying, "For thus says the Lord of Hosts, the God of Israel: Houses and fields and vineyards shall again be bought in this land."[78]

From this act he moved onward to depict the great good age to come, describing it as a time of a new covenant between God and Israel:

> Behold, the days are coming, says the Lord, when I will make a new convenant with the house of Israel and the house of Judah, not like the covenant which I made with their fathers when I took them by the hand to bring them out of the land of Egypt, my covenant which they broke, though I was their husband, says the Lord. But this is the covenant which I will make with the house of Israel after those days, says the Lord: I will put my law within them, and I will write it upon their hearts; and I will be their God, and they shall be my people. And no longer shall each man teach his neighbor and each his brother saying, "Know the Lord," for they shall all know me, from the least of them to the greatest, says the Lord; for I will forgive their iniquities, and will remember their sin no more.[79]

This passage was destined to have a momentous influence on the minds of both Jews and Christians.

Jeremiah's view of religion was also characterized by a new dimension of individualism. Beyond all communal and corporate aspects, religion was the communion of the individual soul with God. In his prayers Jeremiah poured out his own inner feelings to God.[80] From this stemmed a new sense of moral responsibility of the individual person which also characterized Jeremiah's interpretation of ethics.[81]

When Nebuchadnezzar captured Jerusalem in 586 BCE, he left Jeremiah among the small band of survivors in the ruined city. As previously, Jeremiah sought to reconcile his fellows to their tragic plight. But they would have none of him or his ideas. They assassinated the Babylonian governor and fled to Egypt, kidnapping Jeremiah and taking him along. Our last view of the great prophet is from Egypt as he tells his captors that even there they would not be safe from the avenging hand of the king of Babylon.[82]

EZEKIEL (CA. 625–570 BCE)

Among the captives led into Babylonian exile in 597 BCE was a young priest named Ezekiel, who was to become the religious leader of the little community of exiles which settled on the River Chebar in Babylonia. His own book calls him a "watchman in the house of Israel."[83] His call to the prophetic office is dated precisely, the fifth day of the fourth month of the fifth year of Jehoiachin's exile (593 BCE),[84] and is characterized by fervor and detail, undoubtedly reflecting not only Chaldean art forms, but Ezekiel's own highly vivid and highly visual imagination. It also reflects his intense conviction of the transcendent glory of God before whom all human things are dust, ashes, and filth.

Ezekiel's prophecies can be divided sharply into those which preceded and those which followed the second and final fall of Jerusalem in 586 BCE. The former constituted Ezekiel's own distinctive interpretation of prophetic religion in its denunciation of injustice and of false worship which apparently continued among the people left in Jerusalem. God would bring such people and things to a well-deserved doom, declared Ezekiel in prophetic anger.[85]

However, the fall of Jerusalem transformed Ezekiel into the prophet of the future restoration of Israel.[86] The exile would soon end, he declared, and then the exiles would return home. Judah—and Israel—would be restored, the city of Jerusalem would be rebuilt, there would be a new temple presided over by a new and purified priesthood. In loving detail and in many vivid images, Ezekiel depicted the good time soon to come. He has been called "a priest in a prophet's mantle." Surely his affirmation of ritual religion marked a radical change in prophetic thought. It also marked the direction which postexilic Judaism was destined in fact to take. Torah, sabbath observance, priestly ritual, rabbinate, synagogue—all these features of developing Judaism were present at least in germ in Ezekiel's fertile mind. Small wonder that he is often called *the father of Judaism*.[87]

Ezekiel's vision of the future was notable for still another reason. Its vivid and often bizarre images foreshadowed a new kind of prophetic utterance, which in the course of time developed into *apocalypse*, that is, a vision of the hidden future; a form of faith and writing of great importance alike to later Judaism and early Christianity.

DEUTERO-ISAIAH (CA. 550 BCE)

To the great anonymous prophet of the Babylonian exile, scholars have given the name Deutero-Isaiah, since his writings are to be found in the Book of

Isaiah (Chapters 40–55). They are easily distinguishable from the writings of Isaiah of Jerusalem by differences of style, content, and historical context. Nothing is known of this anonymous prophet and poet beyond his writings. Yet these are sufficient to characterize him as one of the great rhapsodic poets of the world's literature, as well as a mind through which prophetic faith had its culminating expression. He was a monotheist who scoffed at other "gods" and saw all history, with its rise and fall of peoples and empires, as an expression of the power of the one God.[88] Even Cyrus, the rising Persian monarch who was soon to conquer Babylon, was a servant of this universal Lord.

The prospect of Babylon's fall inspired Deutero-Isaiah with hope for his people Israel. For surely Cyrus would permit them to return to Jerusalem.

> Comfort, comfort my people, says your God.
> Speak tenderly to Jerusalem, and cry to her
> that her warfare is ended, that her iniquity is pardoned,
> that she has received from the Lord's hand double for all her sins.[89]

No biblical writer had a more universal outlook, yet none was a more intensely loyal Jew. Between these allegiances there was a profound tension. If the Lord was sovereign of all the earth, was he in any special sense the God of Israel? And if he was the God of Israel, why had he permitted Israel to suffer so much at the hands of the nations? These questions burned their way into his mind; and his answer presents one of the profoundest conceptions of biblical religion, namely, the figure of the "suffering servant," or the "servant of the Lord."

In Deutero-Isaiah's writings is to be found a series of poems (42:1–4, 49:1–6, 50:4–5, 52:13–53:12) which deal with a figure called the *servant of the Lord.* Whom did the prophet mean? Christians have traditionally read these poems as a prediction of the Christ; and Jews have seen in them a depiction of Israel's role in history. To the prophet who wrote them these poems seem to have depicted either the nation Israel or a creative minority within Israel. The important issue of the poems is the servant's vocation, which is, by means of willing endurance of suffering at the hands of the nations, to carry the knowledge of God to all the earth. This was at once an answer to the relation of Israel to universal humanity and to the question of Israel's suffering. In the last of the servant poems, the nations speak of the servant:

> But he was wounded for our transgressions, he was bruised for our iniquities;
> upon him was the chastisement that made us whole, and with his stripes we are
> healed.
> All we like sheep have gone astray; we have turned every one to his own way;
> and the Lord has laid on him the iniquity of us all.[90]

By the servant's willing endurance of suffering the nations are won to the knowledge of God and goodness. Here indeed is an interpretation of Israel's vocation and mission which is fully consistent with the one universal God. In the prophet's words, Israel is to be a light to the nations.

POSTEXILIC JUDAISM

The great watershed of Old Testament history was the Babylonian exile, which extended from 586 BCE to the capture of Babylon by Cyrus in 539 BCE. In 538 BCE a small party of the Jewish people in Babylonia set out with the permission and blessing of Cyrus to repopulate and rebuild Jerusalem and Judah. It was an expedition fully consistent with Cyrus's generous policies with subject peoples.

The religious forms which emerged in the postexilic period exhibited both similarities to and differences from the preexilic tradition of Moses and the prophets. The same conception of God as lord and creator—the God of Abraham, of Moses, and of the prophets—continued to be Israel's Lord. But there were significant differences. Recovering from the critical attacks of the prophets of the eighth and seventh centuries, ritual religion reasserted itself once more. The temple with its priests and sacrifices stood at the center of society. Such features of Judaism as Torah, sabbath, the rabbinate, and synagogue, which had been foreshadowed in the writings of Ezekiel, began to assume their historic shape during the postexilic period.

During the approximately four centuries from the end of the exile to the end of the biblical period, the little land of Judah was a subject province successively of Persian and Greek empires, and then, after a century of independence under the Maccabees (164–63 BCE), of the Roman empire. During this period, Israel's religious life became the central fact of its existence. Four main patterns of religion assumed definite form during this time, (1) priestly and legal Judaism, (2) devotional Judaism, (3) wisdom literature and piety, and (4) apocalypse. We shall consider them in turn.

PRIESTLY AND LEGAL JUDAISM

The first few decades of the community of Jews who returned to Jerusalem are obscure, but apparently their life was wretchedly hard, bearing little resemblance to the bright dreams of Ezekiel and Deutero-Isaiah. However, in 520 BCE, two prophets, Haggai and Zechariah, arose to say that the Jews had fared ill because they had not rebuilt the temple. Under the leadership of these two men, the project of a new temple to replace the one destroyed in 586 BCE went forward with zeal, and in 516 BCE the new temple was dedicated. It was a modest building, but it was school, law court, and general community center as well as house of worship; for its must be added that the energies which in a free people might be expressed in politics here went into one or another aspect of religion.

The priests of the temple were not only leaders in ritual but scholars and lawyers as well. Under their leadership the Torah was completed, and the priestly stamp was placed upon the whole document. One of their best and most distinctive products was the creation story of Genesis 1, with its view of creation in six days, and of the Lord's resting on the sabbath. Sabbath observance was so important that these scholar-priests did not hesitate to write it into the structure of the universe!

These priestly editors also possessed a highly distinctive view of four epochs of history, each related to a significant aspect of priestly religion and each expressed in a distinctive covenant. The first age, that of creation, centered on the sabbath, the second in Noah and the prohibition of the eating of blood, the third in Abraham and the institution of circumcision, and the fourth climactically in Moses, the exodus and the Passover, and the giving of the Torah on Sinai. Despite this somewhat artificial scheme, these writers did possess a view of universal history and of the God who speaks through the ages of history.

Sacrifice was all-important to these priestly minds, and preoccupation with the kinds and forms of sacrificial ritual in all its intricate detail was spelled out in the biblical Book of Leviticus. The high point of the religious year was Yom Kippur, the day of atonement, when the high priest entered the "holy of holies" to intercede for the people.[91] Here as elsewhere the priests sought to make the people ritually holy and acceptable to the Lord.

Another project of the priestly leaders of Judaism was first the canonization and then the interpretation of the Torah. We have seen the origin of the five books of the Torah, and the beginning of the idea of sacred scripture in Deuteronomy. Under the great scribe Ezra, about the year 400 BCE, the Torah was officially designated as the sacred norm of Israel's life. In a ceremony described in Nehemiah 8–10, Ezra led in the public ceremony of reading the Torah, with the people responding by accepting it as the God-given standard for all their life.

To the Torah were added in the course of the following centuries the Prophets and the Writings, these three categories comprising the whole Bible of Judaism. Of the three parts, the Torah has always held first place. Once it was accepted as God's decisive and final word to Israel, two further developments began to take place: it began to be celebrated devotionally, and it began to be interpreted by scribes and rabbis. The interpretation led in the course of several centuries to that vast body of interpretation of Torah called the *Talmud*. The devotional attitudes and practices toward the Torah itself will be discussed below.

DEVOTIONAL JUDAISM

While the dominant pattern of postexilic Judaism was the priestly-legal tradition just described, this was by no means the whole of Judaism. Closely related and ancillary to the dominant pattern was the devotional religion which found its main expression in the Book of Psalms. The Book of Psalms is sometimes called the *hymnbook* of the postexillic temple, and in fact many (though by no means all) of its psalms were written for musical rendition in the temple in Jerusalem.

Parts of the Book of Psalms—or Book of Praises, to use the Hebrew title—antedate the temple, and others show no connection with it. All, however, are religious poems bearing some relation to Israel's faith and to Israel's Lord. There is a great variety in this vast collection. Some of the psalms are great poems; others are doggerel. The religious and ethical level likewise varies; Psalm 109 is a cry for vengeance, while Psalm 51 is a prayer for forgiveness.

Pervading the whole collection is a spirit which may appropriately be termed devotional Judaism. It is a union of prayer and poetry, in which the prayer of human hearts finds expression in the powerful images of poetry. So one psalmist cried out,

> As a hart longs for flowing streams,
> So longs my soul for thee, O God.[92]

So also the Torah itself became the object of devotional expression as in the lines,

> The Torah of the Lord is perfect, reviving the soul;
> The testimony of the Lord is sure, making wise the simple;
> The precepts of the Lord are right, rejoicing the heart.[93]

Amid changing scenes and shifting fortunes, in triumph and despair, Israel's heart clung to its God, and its poetry celebrated this supreme fact.

WISDOM LITERATURE AND PIETY

Bearing little relation to the priests and scribes were the sages who created the type of writing often termed *wisdom literature*. This was a literary type produced by many ancient Near Eastern peoples. Of the many specimens of this type in Israel, three found their way into the Old Testament, namely, Proverbs, Job, and Ecclesiastes. The sages who wrote wisdom literature spoke as elders who had seen much of the world and who out of their cosmopolitan viewpoint and mature experience offered counsel to younger men. The wisdom they offered was neither the heroic faith of prophets nor the legal prescriptions of scribes. At worst it was a pedestrian morality, and at best a cosmopolitan insight into the ways of the world. Seldom did these sages speak as Jews; they usually spoke simply as men possessing wisdom. They concerned themselves with such issues as success and failure, wealth and wisdom, life and death.

A persistent theme of their writings was the relation of virtue to good fortune. The orthodox and complacent authors of the biblical Book of Proverbs were sure that if a person was virtuous, good fortune would automatically follow. Conversely, they held misfortune to be the invariable result of some sin or misdeed. In this they continued the tradition of the Deuteronomists, celebrating a God who regularly paid off the wages of sin and righteousness, and of people who were sublimely content with these wages.

Other more perceptive writers challenged this complacent optimism. Among them was the unknown author of Job, who asked: If God be good, why should the good have such a bad time of it, and the wicked have such a good time of it? His answer took form in the drama of the righteous man, Job, who is made the object of a wager between God and Satan.[94] Beset by every sort of evil, as a crowning affliction Job is visited by three friends who expound the orthodox line of thought that it is for some secret sin that Job suffers; or it is as a discipline from God that evil comes to him.

The Book of Job consists of a prologue setting the scene just described and three cycles of argument between Job on the one hand and his "friends" on the other. Job stubbornly maintains his innocence, resisting the friends' arguments. In search of an answer to his question, he is led even to defy God.[95] Yet he gets no adequate answer. At the end, God appears to him giving him no answer, but rather the assurance and strength of fellowship with which he may surmount his troubles.[96]

While the author of Job clung by a thin thread to the traditional faith in God, other writers of wisdom literature were not so traditional. Among these skeptical spirits was the author of Ecclesiastes, who looked at the hard facts of evil and death and concluded that the Almighty had no concern with humankind. Blind chance rules human life, and death brings extinction, he concluded: "Vanity of vanities! All is vanity."[97]

APOCALYPSE

Another and different pattern of postexilic Jewish faith was apocalypse. The term *apocalypse*, from the Greek word meaning "to unveil," means the uncovering or revelation of a hidden future. We have noted the origin of this form of thought and faith in Ezekiel and Deutero-Isaiah. Only one fully developed example of apocalypse found its way into the Jewish Bible, namely, the Book of Daniel; but there are apocalyptic passages which have been interpolated into other biblical books (e.g., Isaiah 24–26), and there are many such documents which did not get into the Bible. For many centuries this apocalyptic literature was regarded as a vast enigma, but modern biblical study has found the key and unlocked its meaning. This key is that an apocalypse is an interpretation in bizarre symbols of the time in which it was written. It was a tract for its own times.

Apocalypse grew out of prophetic thought on the problems of history. But whereas the prophet was content to see God at work in the normal processes of history, the apocalyptic seer saw all history building up to a supreme climax in the near future. This climax was presaged by an ascending series of evils, and a veritable climax of evil would be reached in the near future. Then, according to the apocalyptic seer, God would intervene, bringing to an end the present evil age and ushering in the great good age of the future. This apocalypse was a desperate way of saying amid bad times that God still ruled history. It was a cry of mingled faith and despair of people who saw no earthly way out of their troubles.

Applying these principles of interpretation to the Book of Daniel, we must note that it was written during the Maccabean revolt against the Greek tyrant named Antiochus IV in the year 164 BCE. Before this time Alexander the Great had displaced Persian hegemony of the Near Eastern world. With Alexander's death in 322 BCE, his empire had been divided among his generals, Seleucus receiving Syria and bequeathing it to his descendants. The Greeks were always more or less ardent missionaries for their language and culture. Hence there was a continuing pressure on the Jews to substitute Homer for Moses and the Greek gymnasium and theater for temple and synagogue. Yet until Antiochus IV, the Greeks were too wise to force their ways down the recalcitrant throats of the Jews.

Antiochus IV followed a different policy. In 168 BCE he forbade the practice of the Torah and the daily sacrifices in the temple, going so far as to set up an altar to Zeus in the Jerusalem temple and to sacrifice on it a pig. This deliberate outraging of Jewish feelings brought revolt under the leadership of Mattathias Maccabee and his five sons, one of whom, Judah, proved to be a military genius.

In cryptic symbols, the Book of Daniel bade the Hebrew patriots to stand fast against Greek tyranny. Thus, for example, the lion's den of Daniel (Chapter 6) and the fiery furnace (Chapter 3) represent the situation of the Jewish people during the Maccabean War. Other symbols such as the colossus with the feet of clay refer to the succession of empires—Chaldean, Medo-Persian, and Greek—between the time of the traditional Daniel and the Maccabean uprising.[98] The heart of Daniel's apocalyptic teaching is that the climax of history is at hand, and that soon the great good age of the future will dawn, in which the Hebrew people will live in peace, brotherhood, and world dominion.

The Book of Daniel is also notable for the first clear statement of the doctrine of the resurrection of the dead. Through most of the Old Testament period, the Hebrew people had no clear idea of human destiny beyond the grave except the idea of *Sheol,* which was a place of shadows much like the Greek Hades, to which both the good and the evil people went. Basically, religion was for the biblical Hebrews a way of understanding human life and living in the present world.

However, the Maccabean revolt raised the agonizing question of whether those soldiers who fell in battle against the tyrant might not have a share in the great age of fulfillment which lay ahead. The answer given in the twelfth chapter of Daniel is that the dead will rise, the righteous to a good life and the evil (i.e., the defectors and collaborators) to their appropriate punishment.

In the centuries immediately following this initial statement, the idea of resurrection underwent considerable development. Basically, resurrection was a way of asserting the sovereignty of God over end as well as beginning, over last things as well as first things. Survival of death was expressed through the idea of the resurrection rather than immortality of the soul for the reason that Hebrew thought had always construed the human being as an integral unity of body and spirit.

The Maccabean rebels were sufficiently successful by the middle of the year 164 BCE to liberate most of Jerusalem and rededicate the temple, though intermittent fighting continued for several years. The Jewish festival of Hanukkah still celebrates the rededication of the temple. An independent Jewish nation under the rule of Maccabean family was set up in Palestine. Amid varying fortunes, it lasted until 63 BCE, when Palestine became a Roman province. The Maccabean age was marked at first by a great flowering of culture, prosperity, and religion. But increasingly it was marred by civil war, so that when the Roman general Pompey appeared in the Near East, both the Pharisee and the Sudducee parties in the struggle appealed to him to bring peace to their troubled land. It was a request he gladly heeded, making Palestine a Roman province.

By now, Israel had come to the end of the biblical period. The canon of the Jewish Bible was fixed by a rabbinical council at Jarnnia in 90 CE. The foundations of biblical monotheism had been laid. Yet this was by no means the end of Israel's path. It was more like a new beginning. However, the unfinished story can better be told in new contexts. Chapter 12 will trace Judaism's way, and Chapter 13 will discuss the beginnings of Christianity. For both Jews and Christians, the persons and events of this chapter are an integral part of the divine-human drama of the one God's relation to Israel and to the world.

ISSUES AND QUESTIONS

We have noted biblical Israel's two movements of thought, first to the past in the narrative of the exodus from Egypt and the giving of the Torah on Mt. Sinai, and second to the future Day of the Lord, the result being a linear view of history extending from creation to judgment day. The later centuries of the biblical period saw also the emergence of another concept, namely, the Messiah (the Hebrew word means "the Anointed One" and the word *Christos* is its Greek translation), whose divinely given mission is to bring in the new age. Thus emerged a concept of the dramatic center of the historic process. In the next chapter we shall trace this concept through Jewish history and in Chapter 12 we shall see its significance to Jesus of Nazareth and the rise of Christianity.

This chapter has also observed the widening of Israel's faith from nation or tribe to universal humanity. "One God, therefore one humanity" was the reasoning of Israel's prophets. Through most of human history the vision of one humanity has remained a distant hope and aspiration, but now in our twentieth century, it is actually becoming a historical fact under the rubric, "one humanity or none." Closely related to this concept of one humankind is the concept of a universal religion, namely, a religion which includes the vision of one humankind, in contrast to those religions which are limited to particular nations, tribes, or people. A corollary of universal humanity is the general concept of the human self, above or beyond any and all particular tribal memberships.

Judaism and Christianity are by no means the only universal religions. We have already seen Buddhism's contrasting path to this same goal, and we will presently observe Islam's still different journey to this destination. Whatever the path, this concept is a great achievement and in our time a precious human resource.

So too is the concept of monotheism, or one God. Its relation to one humankind or humanity is plain for all to see. However, it also has implications for individual human selves and our need for the unification or integration of our human experience. Here a clear distinction must be made between *inclusive unification*, or as is sometimes said, the integration of selfhood, in contrast to what we may call *exclusive unification*, which seeks to maintain the unity itself by walling out threatening forces—a process sometimes called neurosis.

A third cluster of issues centers in ancient Israel's concept of its special vocation and mission or, in popular phrase, of itself as God's "chosen people." We shall return to this issue in the next chapter. Here it must suffice to note that Israel wrestled with this concept over many centuries and produced two sharply contrasting interpretations, the first narrowly nationalistic or ethnocentric and the second universally human. The first posited God's special favor for Israel with the consequence of other persons and peoples as outsiders, not fully human.

We have already seen the centrality of the concept of God's covenants with Israel. Especially we have seen the defining significance of the Mosaic covenant. Of this covenant especially two interpretations were expressed and developed in the Bible. One was a narrow religious nationalism, but a second, articulated by the prophet known to us as Deutero-Isaiah, declared Israel's vocation and mission to be "a light to the nations" or, in other words, to declare to the world that God is one, and God's requirement of human beings is a good life in society with fellow human beings. It requires only observation of history to see that this proclamation of ethical monotheism has in fact been the mission of Israel in history. In this precise sense Israel has been "a light to the nations." We shall return to this issue in the next chapter, seeing the Jewish people struggling through the centuries with this central issue.

NOTES

1. George E. Wright, *The Old Testament Against Its Environment*, Alec Allenson, Chicago, 1950.
2. H. Richard Niebuhr, *Radical Monotheism and Western Culture*, Harper, New York, 1943.
3. See inter alia I. Mendelsohn (ed.), *Religions of the Ancient Near East*, Liberal Arts, New York, 1955, pp. 47f.
4. Ibid., pp. 47f.
5. Mircea Eliade, *Cosmos and History*, Harper Torchbooks, Harper, New York, 1959.
6. I. Mendelsohn, op. cit., pp. 233f.
7. M. E. Lyman, *The Christian Epic*, Scribner, New York, 1936.
8. E. Auerbach, *Mimesis*, Anchor Books, Doubleday, Garden City, N.Y., 1957, chaps. 1 and 2.
9. J. Bewer, *The Literature of the Old Testament*, Columbia, New York, 1922, chaps. 1–3.
10. Be Anderson, *Understanding the Old Testament*, Prentice-Hall, Englewood Cliffs, N.J., 1957, chaps. 6, 10, and 14.
11. Ibid., p. 164.
12. Ibid., pp. 173f.
13. W. F. Albright, *From the Stone Age to Christianity*, Johns Hopkins, Baltimore, 1946, pp. 179–180.

14. Auerbach, op. cit., chap. 1.
15. W. Oesterley and T. H. Robinson, *A History of Israel*, Clarendon Press, Oxford, 1932. See especially chaps. 6, 7, and 10.
16. Deuteronomy 26:5–10.
17. Albright, op. cit., p. 194.
18. Exodus 6:2–3.
19. Genesis 4:26.
20. See inter alia the view of Y. Kaufman in L. Schwarz, *Great Ages and Ideas of the Jewish People*, Modern Library, New York, 1956, chap. 1.
21. Exodus 21:1–11.
22. Exodus 21:23–25.
23. W. Eichrodt, *Man in the Old Testament*, Regency, Chicago, 1951.
24. Exodus 34.
25. Exodus 3:14.
26. Albright, op. cit., p. 194.
27. M. Buber, *The Prophetic Faith*, Macmillan, New York, 1949, p. 13.
28. Judges 5:1–31.
29. I Kings 18:30–40.
30. I Samuel 1–10.
31. See inter alia I Samuel 12–13, as well as a more ancient statement of this viewpoint in Jotham's parable in Judges 9:7–15.
32. I Samuel 9.
33. I Samuel 31.
34. II Samuel 11.
35. II Samuel 13–19.
36. I Kings 1–2.
37. I Kings 1–11.
38. I Kings 16.
39. I Kings 18.
40. For Balaam, see Numbers 22–23.
41. I Samuel 10.
42. Judges 5.
43. II Samuel 11, I Kings 12.
44. I Kings 17.
45. R. B. Y. Scott, *The Relevance of the Prophets*, Macmillan, New York, 1944.
46. Buber, op. cit., pp. 96f.
47. Amos 7:14–15.
48. Amos 7:7.
49. Amos 9:1–4.
50. Amos 2:6–7, 8:5.
51. Amos 6:4–7.
52. Amos 5:21–24.
53. Amos 5:18–20.
54. Amos 9:7.
55. Amos 3:2.
56. Hosea 11:1–4.
57. Hosea 13:9.
58. Hosea 12:6.
59. Isaiah 6:1.
60. Isaiah 6:8–9.
61. Isaiah 7:9.
62. Isaiah 7:10–17.
63. Isaiah 10:5–10.
64. Isaiah 10:15.

65. Isaiah 2:6–22.
66. Isaiah 7:3.
67. Isaiah 9.
68. Isaiah 2:2–4.
69. Micah 5:2.
70. Micah 3:12.
71. Micah 6:6–8.
72. Deuteronomy 21.
73. Deuteronomy 6:4—5.
74. Deuteronomy 6:20–25.
75. Jeremiah 1:5.
76. See inter alia Jeremiah 19–21.
77. Jeremiah 29.
78. Jeremiah 32:15.
79. Jeremiah 31:31–34.
80. Jeremiah's prayers are to be found in several passages between chaps. 10 and 20.
81. Jeremiah 31:29–30.
82. Jeremiah 44.
83. Ezekiel 3:17.
84. Ezekiel 1:1–2.
85. Ezekiel 6–23.
86. Ezekiel 33:21.
87. Ezekiel 34–48.
88. Isaiah 44:9–20.
89. Isaiah 40:1–2.
90. Isaiah 53:1–6.
91. Leviticus 16.
92. Psalms 42:1–2.
93. Psalms 19:7–8. I have substituted the word *Torah* for *Law* in the RSV translation.
94. Job 1–2.
95. Job 31.
96. Job 38–42.
97. Ecclesiastes 1:2.
98. Daniel 2, 7, 8.

B*IBLIOGRAPHY*

Albright, W. F.: *Archeology of Palestine*, Peter Smith, Magnolia, Mass., 1971.

Anderson, B.: *Understanding the Old Testament*, Prentice-Hall, Englewood Cliffs, N.J., 1986.

Bright, J.: *A History of Israel*, Westminster Press, Philadelphia, 1981.

Cross, F., *Canaanite Myth and Hebrew Epic*, Harvard, Cambridge, Mass., 1973.

de Vaux, R.: *Ancient Israel*, McGraw-Hill, New York, 1961.

Fohrer, G.: *History of the Israelite Religion*, Abingdon Press, Nashville, Tenn., 1972.

Gottwald, N.: *The Hebrew Bible: A Socio-Literary Introduction*, Fortress Press, Philadelphia, 1985.

Kaufman, Y: *The Religion of Israel*, Schocken, New York, 1972.

Miller, J., and J. Hayes: *A History of Ancient Israel and Judah*, Westminster John Knox, Louisville, Ky., 1986.

Noth, M.: *The History of Israel*, Harper & Row, New York, 1960.

Pederson, J., *Israel: Its Life and Culture*, 2 vols., Oxford, London, 1926–1940.

Pritchard, J. B.: *The Ancient Near East*, 2 vols., Princeton, Princeton, N.J., 1958–1976.

———: *The Ancient Near East in Pictures with Supplement*, Princeton, Princeton, N.J., 1969.

Rendtorff, R.: *The Old Testament: An Introduction*, Fortress Press, Philadelphia, 1986.

Sanders, J.: *Torah and Canon*, Fortress Press, Philadelphia, 1972.

Stone, M.: *Scriptures, Sects and Visions: A Profile of Judaism from Ezra to the Jewish Revolts*, Fortress Press, Philadelphia, 1980.

Vermes, G.: *The Dead Sea Scrolls in English*, JSOT Press, Sheffield, England, 1987.

———: *The Dead Sea Scrolls: Scrolls in Perspective*, Fortress Press, Philadelphia, 1977.

Von Rad, G.: *The Message of the Prophets*, Harper & Row, New York, 1972.

———: *Moses*, Association Press, New York, 1960.

———: *Old Testament Theology*, Harper & Row, New York, 1962–1965.

Westermann, C.: *Elements of Old Testament Theology*, John Knox Press, Atlanta, Ga., 1982.

12

Judaism

Judaism is frequently neglected in courses or studies in the world's religions, attention moving directly from the more widely familiar forms of Christianity to the more distant faiths of south and east Asia. However, Judaism claims our attention for several good reasons.

While it shares with Islam and Christianity faith in the one God, Judaism approaches God in terms which contrast sharply with the other monotheistic religions. In a summary word, while Christianity approaches the one God through faith in Christ, then interprets Christ through creeds and theologies, Judaism approaches the same God by doing or practicing the Torah, then interprets this practice through the Talmud.

Strictly speaking, Judaism is the faith or religious center of the historic Jewish community or people; and conversely the Jewish people constitute the cultural community in which Judaic faith is deployed. In some ways this relation between faith and culture illustrates the general patterns described in Chapter 1. However, there is one feature which makes the Jewish experience unique. It is that the Jewish people have constituted, through nineteen centuries of dispersion, or diaspora, a minority within larger non-Jewish cultures, often struggling to maintain Jewish identity and existence.

It is a remarkable fact that in the face of frequently overwhelming odds they have succeeded in continuing to exist. Napoleon is reported once to have asked Talleyrand, "Give me a good reason to believe in God." Talleyrand replied, "The Jews, my lord, the Jews!" He was, of course, alluding to the tenacious will to live of the Jewish people, implying that it is rooted in the object of their religious faith.

Closely related to this faith is the Jewish conviction of being God's "chosen people." We have alluded to the biblical foundation of this conviction in the last chapter, and we shall observe it in the course of this chapter.

Like Christianity and Islam, Judaism is a historical religion, and is so in at least two different meanings of the word. First, it is based upon a historical event. In the case of Judaism the event is the exodus from Egypt and the giving of the Torah at Mt. Sinai, interpreted as God's covenant with Israel.

But Judaism is historical in a second sense, namely, its inclusion of what the last chapter called a linear or linear-dramatic view of the historical process. In this chapter we will see the way in which the Jewish people and their leaders

practicing the Torah

have wrestled with this aspect of their faith and existence. In the first century CE, the rabbinical leaders of Judaism rejected the messianic claims of Jesus, and deferred the concept of the messiah to the distant future. However, in virtually every century of the past nineteen, messianic aspirants and claims have arisen. Often the rabbis, concerned with the stability and unity of the community, have put down or opposed these claims. We shall presently observe modern Zionism as a radical secularization of the traditional messianic concept and claim.

This chapter being largely historical, there is an important terminological difference which must be at least indicated in passing. Some historians, notably Jewish historians, assert a continuity from ancient Israelite beginnings to the fully developed forms of *Judaism*, using this word to cover the entire history.[1] Others employ a different terminology, speaking of ancient Israel from Abraham and Moses to the Babylonian exile as *classical Hebraism*, and of *Judaism* as emerging after the Babylonian exile.[2]

In any case, such basic institutions of Judaism as the synagogue and rabbinate apparently originated during Israel's exile in Babylonia. At least, they were very much in existence in the centuries following the exile. To the immediate postexilic age also belongs the canonizing of the Torah under the auspices of the scribe Ezra (ca. 450 BCE).[3] In Chapter 11 the Maccabean period of Jewish history was sketched in relation to the biblical Book of Daniel. The festival of Hanukkah still celebrates the rededication of the Jerusalem temple in 164 BCE after the victory of the Maccabees over Antiochus IV. This victory was followed by a century of independent national existence, often regarded as the golden age of ancient Jewish faith and culture. The century of independence (164–153 BCE) was ended with the coming of the Roman general Pompey. From this time until the end of Israel's habitation in 135 BCE Palestine or Israel was Roman territory.

During the closing biblical centuries, Judaism took form as the faith of the Jewish community. It is indeed this community and tradition of people from that day to this which accounts for Judaism's continued existence. The various features of this faith may be understood as aspects of the ongoing life of this people. The Torah may accurately be interpreted as the "constitution" of this community, in the American political sense of the word. This chapter will seek to sketch the history of Judaism, in the words of a well-known book title, as the story of "great ages and ideas of the Jewish people."[4]

JUDAISM IN THE ANCIENT WORLD

Historically one of the most important developments of ancient Judaism was the *dispersion*, the agelong process whereby many of Israel's people came to be scattered over the world. The process of dispersion began in 586 BCE with the fall of Jerusalem and the Babylonian exile. With the Persian victory over Babylonia in 539 BCE some Jews returned home to Judea. Others, however, remained in Babylonia, forming a Jewish community within Babylonian society.

The process of dispersion was greatly increased two centuries later by Alexander's conquests. Soon there was a large and important Jewish community in Alexandria; and there were similar communities in Antioch, Rome, and almost all the larger cities of the Greco-Roman world.

In the first century, Philo wrote that in Alexandria two of the five areas of the city were almost exclusively Jewish. These Jews of the dispersion, living as they did among Gentile people and ways, were much affected by their environment. Compared with their Palestinian compatriots, they tended to be less strict in interpreting and observing the Torah. Yet the wonder is that they maintained any loyalty at all to Judaism. Actually they maintained their synagogues, paid the tax to support the temple in Jerusalem, respected the decisions of the council, or *Sanhedrin*, and also aspired at least once during a lifetime to make a pilgrimage to Jerusalem. Their refusal to be assimilated completely in Hellenistic culture often gained the hostility of non-Jews and sporadically lit the fires of anti-Semitism.

The ancient dispersion left two enduring achievements, the Septuagint and the philosophy of Philo. Alexandrian Jewish scholars translated the Hebrew Bible into Greek as the Septuagint (often referred to as "LXX"; the term arises from the pious legend that seventy scholars, working independently, produce identical translations). They are said to have been appointed by Ptolemy II, who wished a copy of the Bible for his Alexandrian library. The translation may be dated to the third century BCE. It is important for its instruction of Jewish learning and literature to the Greek world, and conversely for bringing the Bible to many Jews in the only language they knew. Intended to meet the educational and liturgical needs of the dispersion, the Septuagint elicited the disapproval of conservative Palestinian rabbis for its Hellenistic influences and its free renderings of the Hebrew text. The Septuagint is equally important for the early history of Christianity. Not only was it the Old Testament known and used in the Christian community of New Testament times, but as Ralph Marcus points out, without the familiarity with biblical ideas and history diffused in the Greco-Roman world by the Septuagint, Christianity would probably have been unintelligible.[5]

The other great achievement of the ancient dispersion was the life and writings of Philo Judaeus (20–50 CE).[6] Little is reliably known of Philo's life beyond the fact that he was a philosopher-statesman and one of the most honored and learned members of the Jewish community of Alexandria. Apparently he was a leader among his people, for he led an embassy to Rome in 39 CE to plead the religious rights of the Jews before the emperor Caligula; and among his writings is *Against Flaccus*, which protests the anti-Semitic violence of Flaccus, Roman procurator of Egypt.

A product of Hellenistic Greek education and culture, Philo was especially a lover of Plato. However, he was also a loyal Jew who believed that God had spoken decisively to his people in the Torah and through the prophets. To such a mind there seemed great similarity between Plato and Moses. Philo believed and argued that the same God spoke through Greek philosophy and Jewish religion. By means of the method of allegorizing, widely popular in the ancient world, Philo was able to eliminate some of the crudities and anthropomorphisms of the Bible and to exhibit an underlying compatibility between his Greek and Hebrew sources.

For Philo, God was one and spiritual in character. These assertions set the pattern for almost two millennia of theological speculation in Judaism, Christianity, and Islam. They also defined a major tradition of thought in western philosophy. For Philo, this view of deity combined biblical monotheism and Plato's monism. The student is confronted here with one more illustration of attempts to combine aspects of two types of religious outlook, for monism is a feature of what our typology terms a faith of the second type, while monotheism is a feature of the third type. Philo also pushed onward in logical consistency to assert that God is absolute spirit utterly transcending all human limitation and definition. People may say that God is—indeed *supremely* is—but to say *what* he is would impute an altogether undivine limitation to deity. This view of deity as the nameless and transcendent one, so appealing to mystics in all ages and faiths, may be traced from Philo to many other individuals and groups throughout subsequent Jewish and Christian history.

One problem which resulted from this conception for Philo as a Jew was the relation of God to matter. He "solved" it by interpolating between God and matter a series of intermediaries or powers somewhat similar in nature to Platonic ideas. All these principles or *logoi* derive from the *Logos*, or "divine reason," which for Philo was the chief instrument of God's creative activity as well as the rational structure of the universe. This idea of the Logos spread beyond Philo, becoming one of the most pervasive features of Hellenistic philosophy and religion. It was appropriated by Christianity in the preface of the Gospel of John, and found expression in the whole theological tradition stemming from John, which asserted that the Logos, or divine word, was incarnated in Christ.

Ethically, Philo believed, the highest good of life consisted in emancipating the good spirit of each person from the trammels of evil flesh. Yet he also derived much from the spirit of active righteousness and justice to be found in the pages of the Torah and prophets of Israel. Here as elsewhere Philo sought to blend Greek and Hebraic elements. It was for this reason, too, that the conservative rabbis of Palestine had so little use for Philo. Hence his immediate influence was stronger upon Christianity than upon Judaism.

It must be added that Philo's allegorical method of exegesis opened for Jew and Christian alike a way for seeing many levels of mysterious meaning beyond the plain sense of the text of the Bible. Few people of the ancient Greco-Roman world had more pervasive influence on the subsequent religious development of the west than Philo of Alexandria.

The ancient Hellenistic dispersion, though traditionally neglected by historians of religion, has been the subject of extensive recent scholarly work.[7] The results are important for knowledge of both Judaism and the whole western tradition. At this time in its history, Judaism was active in seeking Gentile converts. In the midst of the popular polytheism and the lax morality of the Greco-

Roman world, Judaism's ethical monotheism was attractive to many Gentiles. Many of these people who shrank back from full conversion to Judaism became what Jews of the time called *God fearers*. That is, they adhered to belief in the one God and to the moral aspects of the Torah. It was among these God fearers that Christianity first took root in the Gentile world.

The Hellenistic world was, as Saint Paul expressed it, one of "gods many and lords many."[8] Thus Judaism was one of the many competitors for human allegiance. Most of these faiths which found their way to the urban centers of the Hellenistic world had originated with some one of the innumerable peoples bordering this world, where they had functioned as ethnic faiths, or what Chapter 1 termed religions of the first type. In their new urban environment, their priests and first members were recruited from migrants from the home region. Many of these faiths engaged in missionary activities, with the result that groups of adherents and sympathizers spread out from the center in concentric circles.[9] These social forms, while illustrated by Hellenistic Judaism, were by no means limited to it. They were to prove significant for the meaning of institutional religions in the West.

Hellenistic Judaism retained a remarkable loyalty to the land of Israel as the spiritual home of Jewish people. Jews of the dispersion paid their annual half-shekel contribution to the Jerusalem temple. They sought to make a pilgrimage to Jerusalem, if possible for the Passover celebration. Some arranged to be buried in Israel. In these loyalties and customs historic Zionism was prefigured.[10]

Meanwhile other developments were taking place in Israeli Judaism. From 63 BCE until the fall of Jerusalem in 70 CE (or until the final destruction under Hadrian in 135 CE), Palestine was under Roman rule, and this political fact was of the greatest importance to Jewish faith and culture. Rome's method of ruling Palestine varied during this period. First the Romans sought to rule through an ethnarch, Antipater the Idumean, or Edomite (63–44 BCE), and then through his son, Herod the Great (44–4 BCE). When Herod died, his kingdom was divided among his three sons: Archelaus, who received Judea; Herod Antipas, who received Samaria and Galilee; and Philip, whose lands lay to the north and east of Galilee. Archelaus soon proved so inept that he was displaced by a series of career military governors or procurators, the most famous of whom was Pontius Pilate.

Whatever the system of rule, Rome's demands on the Jews as on other subject peoples were simple and blunt, namely, peace and taxes. In Israel there were continual rumblings of revolt, triggered largely by the fervent and often political messianism of first-century Judaism. Many Jews conceived the messiah as a divinely sent military leader who would deliver the Lord's people from their Roman yoke. On at least three occasions there were large-scale revolts, in 6 CE in Galilee, again in 66 CE, and still a third time in 132 CE. All three times the Romans put down rebellion with bloody cruelty, finally bringing to a virtual end Jewish life in Israel and leading to what is known as the *great dispersion*, which extended from 70 CE (or in some reckonings 135 CE) until the modern founding of Israel in 1948. (Recent and current Jewish historical scholarship has qualified this traditional judgment, pointing to continuing Jewish habitation of Israel, particularly in outlying regions.)

Amid its varieties of belief and practice, Judaism showed some underlying unities. Most basic was the Bible, to which Jews looked as a record of God's covenant with Israel. To be a Jew meant to be a child of the Mosaic covenant, and back of this, of the Abrahamic covenant. Until its destruction in 70 CE, there was also the Jerusalem temple, with its priests and its impressive ritual, which served as a kind of beacon to Jews of the dispersion as well as those of Israel. There was also the Sanhedrin, or supreme council of seventy-one members under the chairmanship of the high priest.

The destruction of the temple by the Romans produced fundamental changes in Judaism. Now the central institution was no longer the temple, but the synagogue, and the leaders of Judaism were not priests but rabbis. A rabbi is a teacher, and the worship of the synagogue consists not in priestly ritual and sacrifice, but in the reading and interpretation of the Torah. From the rabbinical interpretation of the Torah has come the sermon in both Judaism and Christianity. In Judaism this kind of interpretation of the Torah was called *midrash,* meaning "inquiry"—that is, inquiry into the meaning of Torah. The shift in the center of Judaism was not abrupt, for in many ways the center had probably already changed from temple to synagogue by 70 CE; but it was destined to be of historic importance. From being a priestly or sacerdotal religion, Judaism became a faith centered in a community of laypersons led by teachers, whose basic form of devotion was—and is—study of the Torah.

Among the many parties and groups of Palestinian Judaism, the most important were the Pharisees and Sadducees.[11] The latter were the religious liberals of their day, advocating a tolerant and accommodating attitude toward both Roman and Greek culture. Thus they enjoyed the favor of Israel's foreign masters. Socially they were the wealthy, urban, priestly families. Odd as it seems at first glance, their attitude toward scripture was one of literalism; however, for this there was an important reason. By drawing a sharp line of literal interpretation, they could exclude from biblical authority much of human experience not mentioned by scripture; and in such fields they were free to believe and act as they pleased. In opposition to the Pharisees, they rejected many religious innovations such as belief in angels, apocalypse, and resurrection of the dead. Prosperous in this life, they had little interest in a future life determined by a divine judgment.

Closely related politically to the Sudduccees was the smaller party of the Herodians, who wished to return the rule of Judea from Roman procurators to the family of Herod. Since the Herod family had never been very popular among Jews, the Herodians were neither a large nor an influential group.

The Pharisees claimed to be the spiritual descendants of the Maccabean rebels. The name *Pharisee* probably meant "separatist," that is, one whose piety led to separation from an evil world. The Pharisees were people of staunch faith who sought to apply the Torah to all aspects and occasions of life. Taking their stand upon the living spirit of the Torah rather than its strict letter, they accepted such innovations as angels, resurrection, and apocalypse. Morally, the Pharisees were rigorous and at times inflexible, legalistic, and exclusive. They have been compared to the Puritans of Protestant Christianity. They were deeply religious people with whom lay the future of Judaism. The popular Christian estimate of the Pharisees as hypocrites and moral monsters is wide of the mark.[12]

If not the largest party in first-century Judaism, certainly among the most influential were the Zealots, who may be characterized in modern terms as colonial nationalists. Joining together under the motto "No king but the Lord, no tax but the temple, and no friend but a Zealot," they refused compromise and collaboration with Rome, and rose intermittently in violent revolt. It was the Zealots who spearheaded the revolts of 6 CE, of 66–70 CE, and of 132–135 CE. Their conception of the messiah was a heaven-sent general and king who would throw out the hated Romans and set up the messianic kingdom in Judea and Jerusalem.[13]

Unlike the Zealots, the Essenes rejected active, military means for bringing the kingdom of God. Rather, they sought to escape from the present evil world and wait passively for God to bring in his kingdom. Hence they gathered in monastic communities, living under a strict religious discipline including rigid vegetarianism, celibacy, and strict sabbath observance. They wore white garments and practiced frequent ablution rites, as well as community of property and pacifism, waiting quietly until God should bring in his kingdom.[14]

While the Essenes have long been known to students of the Bible, the recent discoveries of ancient scrolls at Qumran on the shore of the Dead Sea have greatly increased interest in this sect. The first scrolls came to light in a cave on the northwest shore of the Dead Sea in 1947. Then followed the discovery of many other scrolls, and extensive digging in this area.[15] Neither the archeology nor the evaluation is as yet complete, but the discoveries point uniformly to an Essene-like community at Qumran on the shore of the Dead Sea from the second century BCE to 68 CE, when apparently Vespasian's Roman armies wiped the community out. The scrolls constituted the library of this community.[16] Some contain hymns of worship, similar to biblical psalms; another records this community's rigorous discipline; still others tell of a mysterious "righteous teacher" who has been persecuted by an evil priest, but who will return in future triumph. The scrolls shed valuable light on Judaism and also, by implication, on Christianity, pointing to greater variety in Judaism than had previously been supposed and to significant parallels in Judaism to Christian beliefs and practices.

In their different ways, the Pharisees, the Zealots, the Essenes, and doubtless other groups as well, professed belief in the coming messiah and the kingdom of God. All these groups held what we have called a *linear-dramatic* view of history according to which a great climax of good and evil was impending. As the present evil age became progressively worse, at the crucial moment God would send his messiah to bring in a great age of fulfillment, which was the

Masada, the Judean desert fortress where Romans defeated a Zealot army, 73 CE. (Courtesy of John C. Trevor.)

messianic or divine kingdom.[17] People differed widely in their views of the messiah's coming and the nature of his kingdom. From the Zealots, who expected a military king on horseback, to the Pharisees, who said that God would send the messiah in his own supernatural way, messianic beliefs extended along a wide spectrum. Similarly too, people argued about the nature of the coming kingdom of God. Few, however, doubted its nearness or its urgency.

The climate of fervent messianic expectation which characterized first-century Judaism is highly important for the understanding of both Judaism and Christianity. In the latter case, it was to form the environment in which Jesus of Nazareth and his followers lived and thought. Its influence on Jesus' thought about the kingdom of God and his own messianic vocation will be considered in Chapter 13.

For Judaism, this fervent messianic expectation contributed largely to the unsuccessful risings against Rome. It was natural that after the disastrous defeats of 70 and 132 CE there should be a reaction against messianism in all its forms. It came largely in the form of an emphasis by the rabbis on the study and practice of the Torah. This aspect of Judaism, which had been important from the time of Ezra, now assumed central significance. The rabbis turned away from messianism, which had brought their people to the brink of destruction, and concentrated attention upon the practice and study of the Torah. Thus, as we have noted, the practice of the Torah became a central feature of Jewish faith and the role of the Torah became comparable in significance to the role of

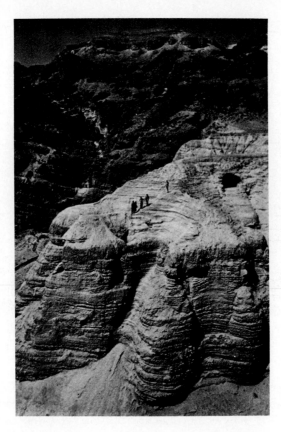

Entrance to caves 4 and 5 at Qumran. (Courtesy of William Brownlee.)

Christ in the Christian faith. Judaism and Christianity may thus be contrasted in these terms. Once more, these two faiths have in common the one God of biblical monotheism; Christians approach this God through faith in Christ and Jews by "doing the Torah." Out of the tradition of study and interpretation of the Torah in Judaism emerged the Talmud.

The word *talmud* means "learning," and it refers to the interpretation of the Torah. Once the Torah had been canonized, the next question concerned its meaning, particularly as people sought to apply its teachings to all the innumerable occasions of daily life. For example, the Torah prescribed rest and no work for the sabbath. Very well, what precisely constitutes work? When does the sabbath begin and end? These and innumerable similar questions demanded answers in order that the Torah might be lived out. So it was that the scribes and rabbis began the agelong process of interpretation. It was a process of thinking not unlike the system of case law which characterizes Anglo-Saxon jurisprudence. For several centuries it was an entirely oral tradition. Then gradually it was reduced to writing, and the fifty-five tracts of the Talmud were the result.

A man with Torah. Painting by Marc Chagall. (Photographic Archive of the Jewish Theological Seminary of America, New York. Frank J. Darmstaedter.)

148 Tannaim

In this centuries-long process, several stages may be noted. First were the oral teachings of the rabbis, the *tannaim,* often in pairs of opposites—as, for example, the teachings of Hillel and Shammai of the first century BCE. There were many other such pairs, making 148 tannaim in all. In 69 CE, while Roman armies laid siege to Jerusalem, Rabbi Johannan ben Zakkai escaped to the Judean coastal town of Jabneh and founded a *beth din* ("house of studies"). He was soon joined by Rabbi Gamaliel, who became leader of this academy, which became the intellectual center of Judaism for the next sixty years. At Jabneh, the canon of the Jewish Bible was fixed, the codification of the oral tradition of the *Mishnah* was begun. Hillel's decisions were given preference over Shammai's, and the process of interpretation continued. The famous Rabbi Akiba lived at Jabneh, before the war against Hadrian (132–135 CE), in which he was martyred.

The academy at Jabneh was a casualty of this war. Extremely repressive measures were put into force by Rome. The mere reading of the Torah became a capital offense. The survivors of this last war against Rome gathered their scrolls together and fled to the extreme north to the Galilean town of Usha, where, despite persecution, they worked on. As repression lessened, the Galilean schools flourished, led first by Rabbi Meir, then by Rabbi Judah, often called *Judah the prince.* Under his leadership the codification of the Mishnah was brought to completion. The word *mishnah* means "study" and refers to that portion of the Talmud which was brought to completion at this time, ca. 200 CE. Composed of the opinions of the tannaim, it was arranged under six main categories: (1) "Seeds," containing mainly agricultural laws; (2) "Feasts," containing rules of observance of holidays; (3) "Women," containing rules of marriage, divorce, and inheritance; (4) "Damages," which had to do with civil and criminal law; (5) "Sacred Things," which had to do with sacrifices and rituals of the temple; and (6) "Purity," dealing with ritual cleanness and uncleanliness. Completed at the end of the second century, the Mishnah spanned nearly six centuries of Jewish life and thought. During the next two centuries, to the Mishnah was added the *Gemara*, or "supplementary learning." Together they formed the complete Talmud. Parallel forms of study had been going on in both Israel and Babylonia, producing, respectively, the Jerusalem and the Babylonian Talmud. The former was complete by the early fifth century, and the latter by 500 CE. The latter is the more important and better known; indeed, for most purposes it *is* the Talmud. By the Middle Ages even Israeli Jews accepted the Babylonian Talmud as their normative code.

The Talmud was the crowning achievement of the ancient Jewish community. It was the product of what has been termed *talmudic society*, the distinctive form of community which grew up in later antiquity under rabbinical leadership and found expression in rabbinical piety and scholarship.[18] The Talmud itself is a record of rabbinical discussion and argument. Its text might be considered as minutes of this meeting, which took place over eight centuries. Its decisions became the normative code of talmudic society.

Talmudic society grew up in Israel (outside Jerusalem, which was forbidden by Rome to Jews) and in other regions of the eastern Mediterranean world. It owed its existence to Roman toleration.[19] The leaders and heroes of this community within the wider Greco-Roman society were rabbis. Its main institutions were synagogue and academy, or *yeshivah*. The latter was a house of rabbinical studies, and the former was not only a house of worship but school, law court, and social center. The synagogue schools carried forward the Jewish tradition of education of children.

The Torah has been the constitution of the Jewish community—as it has traditionally been treated, the divinely given constitution. In these terms, the Talmud may be likened to the American tradition of constitutional law. The simile is particularly useful in the light of the Anglo-Saxon tradition of case law, for the talmudic method was also a "case" method.

In this connection a further contrast with Christianity presents itself. During the period when the Talmud was taking shape, the church fathers of Christianity were producing creeds and theology as interpretations and explanations of their faith in Christ. Each of these forms, creed and theology on the one hand and Talmud on the other, seeks in its different way to explain, interpret, and defend the primary approach to God which stands at the center of both of these biblical, monotheistic faiths.

In addition to the legal or normative aspect of the Talmud, which is called *halakah* (from the Hebrew verb *halaka*, meaning "to talk"), which has been discussed, a word must be added concerning *aggada* or *haggadah*, the narrative

אשר לא ירשיגל
תבמ־לבות אשר בשמנ

Page from a haggadah showing a seder. (Photographic Archive of the Jewish Theological Seminary of America, New York. Frank J. Darmstaedter.)

aspects of the Talmud. These two aspects lie alongside each other with no attempt at logical systematization.

The Talmud is a puzzling document, especially to modern minds, for here law and legend, wisdom and superstitions, old wives' tales and exalted visions lie side by side. The mixture of styles and themes is doubtless the result of the oral tradition of living conversation and argument which lies behind the written text. The Talmud may be regarded as the precipitation into writing of many centuries of talk. Its traditional authority to Judaism has been second only to the Torah which it has sought to interpret. Cursed, misunderstood, and burnt by the hostile, it has been to the Jewish people a light and guide to their path. Aside from its central religious and moral significance, it has stirred Jewish imagination, stimulating literature and other arts through many centuries.

*J*UDAISM IN THE MEDIEVAL PERIOD

Despite occasional harassment due to Jewish refusal to participate in the rites to Caesar, and despite the cruel repression of the Palestinian rebellions, the Romans generally treated the Jews tolerantly. Many Romans maintained a scornful attitude toward sects and superstitions from remote parts of their empire, but their general attitude was one of cosmopolitan toleration. However, the decline of Roman power and the rise of Christianity in the late ancient and early medieval periods proved to be another and a sadder story for the Jews.

Worshiping a Jewish Messiah and sharing large sections of its Bible, Christianity came into the world as a movement within Judaism. The earliest Christians regarded their faith as a fulfillment of Judaism and sought to convert Jews to the new beliefs. However, the Jews resisted conversion, and relations between Christians and Jews gradually hardened into hostility. Christians charged that the Jews had rejected Christ and indeed had killed him. In the course of time, the two religions grew further and further apart. Christianity made itself at home in the Greco-Roman world. From the late first century onward, it became a religion of Gentiles. At the time when Judaism was creating the Talmud, Christianity was fashioning a very different kind of structure, namely, dogma and theology. The rabbis of Judaism scornfully rejected these Christian accommodations to Greek modes of thought and culture.

After the year 312, when Constantine made Christianity the official religion of his empire, the lot of Jews progressively worsened. Increasingly, anti-Semitism became a dark blot upon a civilization which called itself *Christian*. As Christian Europe became more and more intolerant, the Jews looked east-

Early medieval Jewish gravestone from Syria. (Metropolitan Museum of Art. Purchase Funds from various donors, 1902.)

ward, in the direction of Babylonia. During the fourth and fifth centuries CE, the Jewish community of Babylonia became the center of Judaism. As the previous section noted, it was the Babylonian community which produced the definitive Talmud. The Parthian rulers, who were tolerant, were succeeded in the third century by the Sassanids, whose Zoroastrian faith led them to persecute other faiths, denying Jews the right to burial (lest they pollute the earth) as well as the traditional sabbath lights. But despite persecution, the Babylonian Jewish community grew and prospered, providing the foundation for what was to become the Judeo-Islamic age.[20]

Islam burst upon the world in the seventh century with the inspired visions of an Arab camel caravan leader named Muhammad, who became for his followers the Prophet. Muhammad's attitudes toward Jews and Judaism underwent change from initial toleration to pillage and persecution. However, the attitudes of his followers changed in the opposite direction within the first century of Muslim development. In the eighth and ninth centuries, at a time when Christian Europe harried and persecuted its Jews, the Muslim civilization of Baghdad offered to Judaism a large measure of freedom. In the Muslim world, Jews along with Christians were forbidden to bear arms or own Muslim slaves and were compelled to pay a poll tax, but beyond this they generally fared well. There were occasional times of intolerance and persecution, as when the fierce Almohades overran Spain in the twelfth century. However, the general rule of Muslim-Arab civilization from Babylonia to Spain was a freedom and toleration which permitted the Jewish people to build the new forms of faith and culture of the Judeo-Islamic age. As a consequence, the center of Jewish life remained within the Muslim world throughout the medieval period, and Christian Europe remained for the Jews peripheral.

The "great fusion" of elements which produced the new culture began with the widespread use by Jews of the Arabic language.[21] Maimonides and others reproached themselves for writing in Arabic rather than Hebrew, calling Arabic the *servant* and Hebrew the *mistress*, but the practice continued and increased.[22] Hebrew was reserved for religious use and for poetry.

While Babylonia with its large Jewish community and its two distinguished academies at Sura and Pumbedita remained the dominating center of Jewish life during most of the medieval period, there were other notable centers as far west as Cordova, Spain, where also there was a great flowering of faith and culture. What was even more important, there was widespread circulation of people, documents, and ideas throughout this far-flung world. Maimonides, for example, was born in Spain, spent a greater part of his life in Egypt, and died in Israel. The institutional forms of the previous age—rabbinate, synagogue, and academy—continued. Babylonia added the office of exilarch, or leader of the Jewish community in exile or dispersion.

A notable feature of the earlier centuries of the Islamic age was a heightened interest in the Bible, stimulated no doubt by the fact that Islam was also a religion of a book, the Qur'an. A great tradition of biblical study and interpretation arose during these centuries. This biblical interest led to the notable eighth-century movement called *Karaism*. Karaism is traditionally said to have begun ca. 750, when Anan ben David was refused the post of exilarch despite the fact that he was of a leading family and was next in line for this post. The ground for his rejection was his reputation for unorthodox views. He retaliated by organizing a faction which seceded from the main body of the Jewish community. The label *Karaite* (meaning "reader") which was later applied to this movement referred to Anan ben David's conviction that each person had a basic responsibility to guide his or her own life by reading the Bible. The deeper protest of this movement was against the growing authority of the Talmud and the ponderous rabbis who interpreted it. Back to the Bible, said the Karaites, and every man for himself! The Karaites took their Bibles literally and seriously. They abolished the sabbath lights (whose origin was talmudic rather than biblical), they ate no meat but venison, and they opposed physicians and medicine (for the Bible said, 'It is the Lord which healeth thee"). The Karaite movement increased and spread widely, its effect being felt from Persia to Egypt, to Russia and Poland, and as late as 1500.[23] But probably the most important result of the Karaite protest was the response of scholastic philosophy. Karaism had asked challenging questions. What answer would orthodoxy give?

The answer was that distinctive form of philosophic defense and justification of a traditional faith called *Scholasticism*. Both Islam and Christianity also produced notable versions of scholasticism, which will be sketched in Chapters 14 and 15, respectively. In all three cases, Scholasticism made use of the philosophical heritage of Greece, which continued alive and strong throughout the Arab world.

Through most of its history Judaism has not been notably philosophical or theological in outlook. Jewish scholars have tended to be historians and linguists rather than theologians and philosophers. For ordinary people Judaism has been more something to *do* than something to *believe*. However, philosophical questions now began to be asked. How can God be omnipotent? How did the Devil come into existence? Can faith be rationally proved or disproved? To answer these questions, Jewish scholars used philosophic categories, Greek in origin and spirit and preserved by the Muslim-Arab civilization of the times. While the views of individual scholars differed, the common aim of Jewish scholastic philosophers was the rational exposition and defense of faith. For them as for the scholastic philosophers of Islam and Christianity, the fundamental question was the relation of faith (or revelation) to reason.

The traditional founder of Jewish scholasticism was Saadia ben Joseph (882–942). Born in Egypt and given a Greek and Muslim education as well as a Jewish education, he gained a wide reputation as head of the Sura Academy in Babylonia. He was a vigorous opponent of the Karaites and defender of tradition. He translated the Bible into Arabic and was notable for his biblical exposition. Above all he was a rational spirit who sought to reconcile biblical revelation to reason. He argued the rationality of belief in the being and oneness of God, of the commandments of the Torah, and of the messianic age. Like many another rational theologian, Saadia held firmly to a belief in personal freedom.

What Saadia put in motion, others carried forward in Babylonia, and throughout the Arab world, notably in Spain. In and around the Academy of Cordova, founded in the tenth century, there was a great flowering of philosophy, biblical scholarship, and other forms of study and writing. The Jewish community of Spain produced such notable figures as ibn-Gabirol (1021–1058), Judah Halevi (1085–1140), and ibn-Ezra (1092–1167). Gabirol was a poet and mystic whose book *The Fountain of Life* expounded a Neoplatonic philosophy and whose devotion to God found expression in poetry. Halevi too was a man of letters devoted to the inner life, as well as a philosopher. His book *Kuzari* consists of dialogs between the Khazar king in search of a true religion and a Jewish teacher who expounds Judaism to him.

The most important as well as the most famous figure of Spanish Jewry and indeed of all medieval Judaism was Moses ben Maimon, or Maimonides (1130–1204). Born in Cordova, he was educated in the arts and sciences as well as in Jewish studies. Driven from Cordova by the threat of persecution by the Almohades, he and his family wandered to Israel, North Africa, and Egypt. In Egypt Maimonides rose to the position of personal physician of the Muslim ruler Saladin. However, his deepest interest lay not in the medical sciences and arts but in philosophy and theology. He was a learned man in an age when to be learned meant to embrace all knowledge in a single comprehensive system. He commented at length on the Torah and Talmud. Turning from Bible and tradition to philosophy, Maimonides produced the famous *Guide for the Perplexed*.[24] Maimonides was at once a devout Jew and a rational philosopher. Furthermore he believed that faith and reason were facets of a single harmonious reality.

The *Guide for the Perplexed* stands as a justification of traditional Jewish belief by means of philosophy in the Greek tradition. Maimonides also said that his book was not for the common reader but only for the student trained in logic and the sciences of the time. In the tradition of Aristotle's *Metaphysics*, the existence of God was proved by inferences from motion and causation. Thus God was understood as the First Cause and Unmoved Mover existing in pure actuality, prior to all finite or phenomenal reality.

Yet the cosmology of the *Guide* is more Platonic than Aristotelean. Thus finite minds and tongues can speak only negatively of God, declaring *that* God is, but only *what* God is *not*. Affirmative assertions would endanger the supreme unity of the divine.

Maimonides's cosmology viewed the universe as a series of concentric circles, the outermost of which and the nearest to God is active intellect. It is by means of this power that humans come to knowledge. The human soul is characterized by reason, and its rational capacities and achievements are evidence for its eternal nature.

Maimonides provided rational explanations for most of the phenomena of Jewish faith, such as miracles, and the traditional food laws, which he viewed as conducive to health. The anthropomorphisms of the biblical God, he treated as metaphors to assist the human mind. Maimonides's rationalism drew critical responses from others who were more concerned with the possession of faith than with its rational justification. These critical attacks beginning in Maimonides's lifetime have continued in Judaism ever since.

The main features of Maimonides's faith are often summed up in a concise statement contained in his commentary on the Mishnah, often referred to as "Maimonides's thirteen principles" and as near to a creed as any statement Judaism has ever produced. These thirteen affirmations are: (1) the existence of God the creator, (2) the unity of God, (3) his spiritual nature, (4) that he is first and last, (5) prayer to God, (6) prophecy, (7) Moses as the chief prophet, (8) the Torah, (9) that the Torah will never be superseded, (10) that God knows the thoughts of all humans, (11) that God rewards and punishes, (12) that the messiah will come, (13) that the dead will be resurrected.[25]

Not all the medieval Jewish community agreed with Maimonides's view that religion could be expressed and explained adequately in the categories of rational philosophy. Many found mysticism, with its appeal to immediate experience of God, a more attractive path. The record of their seeking and finding is to be found in the *Kabbala*. The word *kabbala* means "tradition," and in this case it refers to an esoteric tradition of mysticism of which the Kabbalists believed themselves the inheritors and which they claimed went back to the Bible. Modern scholars regard the Kabbala as medieval in origin. The mystical seers of the Kabbala wrote commentaries on the Torah and other parts of the Bible, many of them claiming to come from the first or second centuries.

The common postulate was that the Bible and other ancient documents have an inner meaning as well as their plain sense, which was accessible to esoteric inquiries. For example, the ten Hebrew numbers (*sephiroth*) are also letters of the alphabet, and applied to the proper names of the Bible they yield a luxuriant number mysticism in which from the one God proceeds a vast plurality of emanations. When the messiah comes, he will be identifiable by his mysterious symbol, number, and name.

The most famous book of the Kabbala was the *Zohar*,[26] which means "radiance" or "splendor." Many theories of origin have been proposed, but it is now generally believed to have been written in Spain about 1285 by Moses de Leon.[27] The book purports to be an early Aramaic translation of biblical passages and specifically claims that the Bible is not to be taken literally, an assumption which led in the course of time to wholesale allegorizing. Like other mystical documents, the Zohar finds mysterious meanings in biblical names, often in the letters of the names.

The ideas of the Kabbala were drawn for the most part from ancient Gnostic or Neoplatonic sources. These sources held God to be the absolute or boundless (in Hebrew, *en-soph*) of whom no definite or determinate predicates may be affirmed. Between God and the world is placed a series of emanations, at the world end of which are human beings. Humans in the Kabbalist view are microcosms who reproduce in themselves the macrocosm, or world. Human beings are simultaneously animal, moral, and spiritual in nature, and as spiritual can rise to oneness with God. The Kabbalists saw in all natural and human things a wide range of symbols pointing to the higher, spiritual world.

The Kabbala flowed into the continuing stream of Jewish mysticism, making its contribution to this ongoing reality. As Gershom Scholem has demonstrated in *Major Trends in Jewish Mysticism*,[28] no century in Jewish history has lacked mystics who have sought and found immediate oneness with Israel's God. Their path to this goal has been plotted by uniquely Jewish symbols. These symbols include God, the Torah, and the main characters and events of the Bible, all woven together into what the modern reader discovers as a fantastic new fabric of mystical speculation. Undoubtedly some of the colorful threads of this fabric were added by ancient Jewish Gnostics of the Hellenistic world. Whatever its diverse origins, Kabbalism constitutes a major tradition of mystical religion and speculation, and is today studied as such.

At times this Jewish mystical tradition expresses what was termed *mysticism of communion* in Chapter 1, that is to say, immediate communion with Israel's God. However, at other times the viewpoint slips over to mysticism of absorption in God, or of *ontological union*. This latter attitude raises fundamental questions for Judaism as for Christianity. Monotheism draws a clear, sharp line between God and humans, while this form of mysticism asserts their full identity. It is difficult for the student of religion to construe this relation as anything other than a head-on collision. For their part, the medieval Jewish mystics, whether exponents of ontological union or of communion, were expressing varying degrees of impatience with the ponderous scholarship of the rabbis and seeking in their various ways more immediate access to God.

The Zohar continued to be read and studied, particularly after the expulsion of the Jews from Spain. It has stimulated prayer and spirituality, but it has also encouraged magical superstitions (as mystical documents so often do) as well as a succession of messianic candidates. Kabbalism was particularly popular in the sixteenth and seventeenth centuries, outstanding practitioners being Isaac Luria (1534–1572) and his disciple Hayim Vitale, who found cosmic explanations for Israel's historic exile as well as similar explanations and hope for a future return and redemption.

The most recent flowering of Jewish mysticism occurred chronologically within modern times, though in spirit it was altogether within the continuing tradition of the Kabbala. Its home was east European, or Ashkenazic, Jewry. It is called *Hasidism* (the word *hesed*, plural *hasidim*, means 'pious one"), but is not to be confused with the ancient Hasidic movement of the Maccabees. Poland and Russia were the source regions of modern Hasidism. The founder was an itinerant teacher, preacher, and faith healer, known variously as Israel ben Eliezer, Israel of Moldavia, and (to his followers) Baal Shem Tob ('master of the good name"). Born ca. 1700 in Bukovina, he showed no inclination toward talmudic study, being content to wander the hills, finding God in nature. After an unsuccessful first marriage, he lived happily with a second wife. But he was destined for other things. The spirit of God was with him; he began to teach, gathering followers about him and instructing them, and sending them out to teach others. This informal process continued until his death in 1760.

His religious movement had the double aspect of a revolt against the iron-clad authority and the massive scholarship of the Talmud and its learned rabbis and also a spontaneous revival of mystical religion. Against the ponderous learning of the rabbis, Baal Shem Tob pitted the immediate and joyful experience of his glad heart. Never has mysticism been so affirmative in its tone. Since God is in all things, goodness also is in all things and all people. There was no ascetic world denial in this teaching. The pervading attitude was a spontaneous and generous love for all God's world. Informally and aphoristically the Baal Shem Tob taught that God dwells in all things in nature and in all humans. Prayer was conceived and practiced not as petition but rather as a cleaving continually to God in communion and fellowship. By the power of prayer, however, miracles and exorcisms might be wrought—so at least taught the Baal Shem Tob and his followers.

The new movement evoked the violent opposition of orthodoxy. Elijah of Vilna, leader of east European Jewry, excommunicated the Hasidim and forbade all contact with them. This move led directly to the separate organizing of the Hasidic movement, whose leaders set up their own synagogues and ordained their own rabbis, called the *zaddikim* ("righteous ones"). In later times, the zaddikim tended to magic and other abuses of the master's teaching. While there is no record that Baal Shem Tob indulged in messianic visions or prophecy, some later Hasidic seers added this accent to their message.

Hasidism soon grew to be a movement of several hundred thousand, and has continued to maintain a following in Poland, Russia, Israel, and as a result of immigration, the United States. Its mysticism irrigated the parched soil of talmudic scholarship and brought spontaneous emotion back into Judaism. Its simple pietism came alive in untutored hearts for whom rabbinic study was remote and strange. Both chronologically and in outlook it showed striking similarity to Protestant pietism and to such Protestant mysticism as that of the Society of Friends. Its permanent contribution to Jewish faith and thought, and more widely to the faith and thought of the world, has been communicated through the religious philosophy of Martin Buber,[29] which is based on Hasidism.

It is interesting to compare Hasidic mysticism with that of Kabbala, from which it sprang. Both forms found expression within the Jewish community and in symbols drawn from Jewish tradition. Yet while the Kabbala involved an alternation between the mysticism of communion with God and that of complete absorption in God, Hasidism was clearly on the side of communion. Its immediacy was that of people impatient with the ponderous learning of the rabbis, who found communion with God an immediate or direct possibility. They did not seek ontological absorption in the religious object. Whatever the reasons for this difference, its results have been of the greatest importance. Hasidic mysticism stands as one of the clearest examples in human history of the mysticism of communion with God.

Meanwhile, as mystics dreamed, philosophers speculated, and scholars pored over their scrolls, the living heart of Judaism continued to be the Jewish people and their common life, centering as ever in home and synagogue. As the Christian civilization of Europe assumed its distinctive forms, the Jews increasingly became objects of hostility and persecution. Because they resisted conversion and assimilation, they remained a small, visible, and defenseless minority, ideally constituted to serve as scapegoats for the ills of society. All this was theologically rationalized. Were not the Jews "Christ killers"? Pope Gregory VII forbade Christians to employ Jews in any capacity. In 1215, the Fourth Lateran Council ordered the Jew badge to be worn at all times by Jews as a symbol of shame. Jews were forbidden to hold real property, a circumstance which (along with a prohibition to Christians against charging interest) forced Jews into moneylending or banking. Some were able to make a virtue out of necessity, prospering greatly in this occupation.

The Jews were frequently subject to capricious violence, especially during the Christian Easter week. The Crusades, for example, developed into massacres of the infidels at home—the Jews. When the "black death" swept Europe in the fourteenth century, the Jews were suspected of causing it and were massacred in untold numbers. Rumors were circulated of Jewish rites in which the blood of Christian children was drunk, and of Jewish malice in poisoning wells. The Talmud was the object of the grossest misunderstanding; in Paris, it was publicly tried and burned for heresy!

Perhaps the most vivid symbol of hostility and discrimination against the Jews was the ghetto, a prescribed section of a city, usually crowded and unhealthy, where Jews were segregated. In some cities, such as Rome, the ghetto went back to early medieval times; by the sixteenth century, it was a standard feature of Europe's growing cities. Jews were prohibited from living elsewhere and were locked within the ghetto walls at nightfall. Gathering behind these walls, they developed their own community of faith and life, as they were literally walled off from the common culture of Europe, to the double misfortune of both Judaism and medieval Europe. Finally, as the nations of Europe felt the first stirrings of nationalism, one after another expelled the Jews. France expelled them in 1254, England in 1290, Germany in 1298, and Spain in 1492. The harried Jews took refuge in Poland and Russia and in the Muslim world.

During these centuries of Israel's wandering among the nations, seers and scholars continued to ponder ancient traditions and historic destiny. The mysticism of the Kabbala was for many Jews a source of light. Messianic movements continued sporadically to attract the allegiance of some Jews. The expulsion from Spain, leading as it did to the mingling of Spanish, or Sephardic, Jews with those of the Ashkenazic, or east European, Jewry, was a source of new ideas and movements. In the following century the Kabbalist, Isaac Luria, mentioned earlier, announced himself the forerunner of the messiah. The writings of his follower Hayim Vitale spread Luria's teachings throughout Europe. One notable embodiment of these diverse influences was Shabbathai Zevi (1626–1676), who proclaimed himself messiah and attracted a large following. After a varied life, he plunged his followers into disenchantment by embracing Islam. His was the most recent wave of messianism in Jewish history to achieve a large popular following.

During the medieval period in Europe, Jewish faith and life maintained their vitality behind the ghetto walls. It was not easy to be a Jew in the Middle Ages; yet forced within the narrow confines of the ghetto, the currents of faith and culture ran deep. The modern peril of extinction by assimilation did not then exist. Moneylending and pawnbroking were traditional Jewish occupations, though they seldom were full-time activities. Many Jews plied related trades such as working with precious metals or jewels. Others were weavers, dyers, silk manufacturers, or metalworkers. It is said that the Jewish quarter in Sicily and Sardinia was discernible from a distance by the sound of continual hammering.[30] The majority of Europe's Jews lived in poverty and followed the humblest forms of work throughout the Middle Ages.

While there was continuing danger of hostility and attack, it would be an overstatement to present the medieval picture as one of unrelieved persecution. In some regions Jews enjoyed special legal status and protection; and as S. Baron has written, the lot of the Jews was far less cruel than that of the serfs who constituted the majority of Europe's population.[31]

Within the Jewish community the traditional forms of religious observance, though antedating the Middle Ages in origin, came to completion during this time. No holidays in the religious year have been added since the Middle Ages. There was a high level of education, for as has been well said, Judaism viewed "study as a mode of worship."[32] There was no professional rabbinate, this office being filled by those who could meet its intellectual and religious standards and who practiced it as an avocation. Much of religious observance was based in the home. Medieval Judaism held a strong family tradition. Standards of sexual morality were high, and there was general respect for women. This family tradition persists to the present day.

JUDAISM IN THE MODERN WORLD

Emancipation from the ghetto and to full human freedom and equality came late and in reluctant steps to Europe's Jews. The Reformation brought little or no change for the better. With few exceptions, Protestants proved to be as intolerant as Roman Catholics. Martin Luther in his early years wrote favorably concerning the Jews, but when they resisted conversion, he lashed out in bitter and violent prejudice. The modicum of tolerance which Jews enjoyed in seventeenth-century Holland and England were exceptions to the continuing system of separation and discrimination.

The seeds of change were present in the Enlightenment, with its ideas of universal liberty, equality, and fraternity. But it took time for these generous ideals to bear fruit in specific social structures and actions. The application of the ideals of the Enlightenment to the Jews was by no means easy or self-evident, as Voltaire's anti-Jewish attitudes illustrate. Others, however, such as Lessing, were more consistent in their doctrines of religious freedom and toleration. Lessing's play *Nathan the Wise* was a parable of religious toleration. The relation of this play to Lessing's friend and colleague Moses Mendelssohn has long been a subject of controversy; but Lessing's friendship and influence on the life of Mendelssohn were beyond doubt.

Moses Mendelssohn was an outstanding example of Jews who during this age were beginning to break out of the ghetto and into the full life of European civilization. Mendelssohn was born in 1729, the son of a scribe; he was a frail, hunchbacked child, but an eager and outstanding student. In 1743 he went to Berlin, where he became a successful silk merchant, and by avocation a distinguished scholar. Meeting Lessing, and coming into contact with the new ideas of the age, Mendelssohn participated eagerly. His rise to fame was climaxed by the removal of the customary Jewish disabilities. His writing included a dialog on immortality written in Platonic style, entitled the *Phädon*, a translation of the Torah into German, and a volume entitled *Jerusalem*, in which he pleaded the cause of Jewish emancipation. More than anyone else, Mendelssohn led Judaism away from the closed community of medieval Europe toward the open, free, and religiously pluralistic society of modernity.

Despite Mendelssohn and others like him, the old laws and old customs gave way with painful slowness. The French Revolution was a crucial chapter in this story. In 1789, the Declaration of Rights of Man made all men, including Jews, equal before the law. Successive laws in 1790 and 1791 applied its principles specifically to Jews. Despite opposition in the years which followed, these principles spread to other European lands. Napoleon consolidated many of the gains of the Revolution. No special friend of the Jews and not above anti-Semitic attitudes, Napoleon nevertheless found it advantageous to mobilize the Jews of France behind his regime. A gathering called an *Assembly of Jewish Notables* in 1806 pledged loyalty to Napoleon. It was followed by Napoleon's revival of the ancient Sanhedrin. However, the historically important fact was that wherever Napoleon's armies marched, ghetto walls fell.

The fall of Napoleon and the Congress of Vienna brought to Europe a decade of reaction during which statesmen strove to set the clock of history back to pre-revolutionary times. This decade of reaction brought with it eruptions of anti-Jewish activities in many lands, notably Germany. Then and throughout the nineteenth century the Jews sought to defend and to expand their new, hard-won gains. They joined and they read—and wrote—liberal philosophies. Nineteenth-century democracy gradually brought to Jews full admission to the life of European society. It also left a socially liberal stamp on the outlook of the Jewish community, which persists to the present.

The degree of emancipation varied widely in different western nations. These variations were directly proportional to the degree of democracy claimed or achieved by particular nations. But emancipation also varied inversely with nationalism, which in many lands was accompanied by conscious anti-Semitism. Thus emancipation was probably most complete in Great Britain and North

America. It was notably less complete in Germany, in both theory and practice. In Russia and the Balkan countries, which were largely untouched by democracy, Jewish emancipation was virtually nonexistent. Russia continued a system of consistent discrimination and separation, marked by repeated pogroms during the nineteenth century. As late as 1903, the notorious forgery called *The Protocols of the Elders of Zion* was produced by an anti-Semitic monk, with encouragement by Czar Nicholas II. In other lands, the free participation of Jews in the life of society seemed to stimulate anti-Semitism. In France the Dreyfus affair ran its sordid course from 1894 to 1906.

The impact of modernity was felt within Judaism in new views of worship and observance. During the centuries when Judaism was in effect a closed society, it was easy to maintain traditional ways of faith and life. Now, with Jews freely associating with non-Jews, this task became much more difficult. Indeed, it became increasingly inevitable that the modern world should have its impact upon traditional Jewish forms of observance and worship. It is possible to place the new emerging forms of Jewish observance and worship along a continuum representing the spectrum of responses to modernity. As these forms have taken shape in America, they range from Orthodoxy on one end of the spectrum through Conservative Judaism in the center to Reform on the other end. If the institutional forms are not identical in Europe and other parts of the world, many of the same realities have nonetheless emerged.

Reform Judaism began in Germany in groups like the Frankfurt Society of the Friends of Reform, which in 1843 issued a controversial declaration of principles: "*First*, we recognize the possibility of unlimited development in the Mosaic religion. *Second*, the collection of controversies and prescriptions commonly designated by the name Talmud possesses for us no authority. . . *Third*, a Messiah who is to lead back the Israelites to the land of Palestine is neither expected nor desired by us; we know no fatherland but that to which we belong by birth or citizenship."[33] This statement evoked violent hostility from more traditionally minded Jews who saw in it a surrender to modern secularity. Abraham Geiger (1810–1874), who emerged as the leader of Reform Judaism in Germany, had to wage a long fight to assume his position as rabbi of Breslau, and when finally he became chief rabbi, conservatives withdrew and formed their own congregation.

In the United States similar divisions arose, with the significant difference that the institutional forms of American Judaism arose directly from successive waves of immigration during the nineteenth century. There had been a few Jews in America from early colonial days, but immigration greatly increased their numbers in the 1840s and 1850s. Among the first immigrants were German Jews imbued with the spirit of Reform Judaism, and anxious to spread its message in America. Most notable among these newcomers was Rabbi Isaac Meyer Wise (1819–1900), often called *the architect of American Reform Judaism*. Rabbi of congregations in Albany and Cincinnati, Wise was also responsible for the founding of the Union of American Hebrew Congregations (1873), the

Hebrew Union College (1875) for the education of American rabbis, and the Central Conference of American Rabbis (1899).

American Reform Jews sought to formulate their credo in statements made at a conference of rabbis at Pittsburgh in 1885 and somewhat less radically at Columbus, Ohio, in 1937. The latter statement, called *The Guiding Principles of Reform Judaism*, asserts Judaism to be "the historical religious experience of the Jewish people." The heart of Judaism is asserted to be "the doctrine of the One living God who rules the world through law and love," while the human being is asserted to be "created in the divine image. His spirit is immortal." Religion and ethics are said to constitute an indissoluble unity, and Jews are bidden to seek peace, the abolition of poverty, and similar social and ethical goals. The Torah is asserted to be the source of Jewish faith and life, though it is added that each age must adapt its teachings to new occasions and new needs. The Talmud is not mentioned. The synagogue, religious observance, and religious education are urged upon the faithful in a spirit which seeks to be at the same time liberal and loyal to tradition.[34]

In the latter half of the nineteenth century, several important American Jewish leaders drew back from what they regarded as the excesses of Reform Judaism. They founded Conservative Judaism. Among them was Sabato Morais, a leading Philadelphia rabbi before he became founder and first president of Jewish Theological Seminary in New York in 1886. However, the achievement of placing Conservative Judaism on a firm footing must be ascribed above all to Morais's successor as president of Jewish Theological Seminary, Solomon

A photograph from the early 1900s of American Jews celebrating the Feast of the Tabernacle. (The Bettmann Archive.)

Schechter. A distinguished scholar and a deeply devout Jew, Schechter became president of Jewish Theological Seminary in 1901, there consolidating what Morais and others had begun. Congregations of Conservative Judaism are joined in the United Synagogue of America, and its rabbis are members of the Rabbinical Assembly. While Conservative Jews do not adhere to tradition with the full rigor of Orthodoxy, they appear significantly more traditional than Reform Jews.

A significant recent development of Conservative Judaism has been the rise of Mordecai Kaplan's movement called *Reconstructionism.* Kaplan has combined a liberal and naturalistic philosophy of religion or theology with a traditional view of Jewish culture and ways of worship and observance.[35] In 1918 Kaplan founded a synagogue center in New York, bringing together into one organization worship, education, recreation, and many other aspects of social life. In 1935 a magazine called *The Reconstructionist* was started to give expression to these views; and in 1945 the Reconstructionist Foundation issued a revised prayer book. While the new prayer book was less radical than the Reform prayer book, it led to Kaplan's excommunication by the Union of Orthodox Rabbis.

Historically Orthodoxy was the last of the three to assume definite shape in the United States. In the closing decades of the nineteenth century, the source regions of immigration to America shifted from northern and western to eastern and southern Europe. This change brought to American shores waves of Jewish immigrants from Poland and Russia. The Judaism which they brought with them assumed definite form in the United States as Orthodoxy. In 1896 the first American yeshiva, or academy, the Isaac Elchanan Yeshiva, was founded in New York for the education of Orthodox rabbis. Two years later, the Union of Orthodox Jewish Congregations was founded. In 1928 the Elchanan Yeshiva became Yeshiva College, and in 1945 Yeshiva University. It has continued to be the intellectual center of Jewish Orthodoxy in the United States.

American Judaism has grown, according to current figures, to a total of slightly less than 6 million adherents. They are divided approximately as follows: 29 percent Reform, 34 percent Conservative, 2 percent Reconstructionist, 9 percent Orthodox, and 26 percent who list themselves as "other" or "just Jewish." Probably the most significant development of twentieth-century American Judaism is its changed status in American society. Through most of American history Judaism along with Catholicism was a permitted minority in a dominantly Protestant society. The waves of nineteenth-century immigration brought vast numbers of Jews and Catholics to the United States, changing the religious balance of society. These shifts coincided with secularizing tendencies which loosened Protestantism's grip on the society. As a result of these and other developments, the United States became in the twentieth century the land of three faiths: Protestants, Catholicism, and Judaism.[36] This has meant a great enhancement of status for Judaism, as one of the three "religions of democracy."[37] While the smallest, it is by no means the least influential.

While Judaism was putting down roots and growing impressively in America, things were not going so well in Europe. Nineteenth-century Europe brought not only emancipation but also an ominous growth of anti-Semitism. Such ideas, endemic in the European mind from medieval times, grew to alarming proportions in the nineteenth century and became epidemic with the rise of Hitlerism in the twentieth. Hitler and his followers were avowedly anti-Semitic from the beginning, and so it was no surprise that when Hitler's regime came to power in 1933, it passed immediately a series of harsh laws against Jews. Jews were deprived of German citizenship and subjected to progressively intolerable measures, culminating in the extermination camps of World War II in which it is estimated that approximately 6,500,000, or over half of Europe's Jews, perished.

Among the significant Jewish responses to anti-Semitism and more generally to the storms of twentieth-century history has been a vigorous and resurgent emphasis upon the historic tradition and community of Judaism, a response which has been illustrated by many of Judaism's leaders and thinkers. One of the first expressions of this attitude was the life and thought of Franz Rosenzweig (1886–1928). As a youth he studied Hegel and at one point was close to conversion to Christianity. However, as a German soldier in World War I, he returned in mind and heart to the faith of his Jewish tradition. The record of his return is contained in his book *The Star of Redemption*, which was written on postcards sent home to his family from the war front. In the years after the war, Rosenzweig devoted himself to the cause of Jewish education. In 1922 he was stricken with paralysis, but he continued his studies and other work until his death six years later. With Martin Buber he worked at a new German translation of the Jewish Bible. His letters and other writings have communicated to innumerable people his vivid and intensively Jewish personality. In many important respects, the historic epoch of Judaism which began with Moses Mendelssohn ended with Franz Rosenzweig.[38]

Another Jewish response to anti-Semitism has been the contemporary resurgence of Zionism. Throughout the centuries of the great dispersion, many Jews have cherished the dream of returning to their homeland, Israel. In every century some individuals have done so. In the nineteenth century, liberal nationalism reinforced this biblical ideal. Moses Hess wrote a book entitled *Rome and Jerusalem* in which he proclaimed Zionism as a cultural ideal for Jews. Others suggested Israel as a solution for some of the agonizing problems of Europe's Jews. Zionism of a frankly political sort had its origin in the life and work of Theodor Herzl, who was born in Budapest in 1860. By turns a lawyer and journalist, and in early life without apparent feeling for his people, Herzl was wakened to Zionism by the spread of anti-Semitism. In 1896, he wrote a book entitled *The Jewish State*, and the following year he organized a Zionist Congress in Basel, Switzerland.

Herzl spent the rest of his life in apparently fruitless negotiations with European governments. Whereas rulers remained indifferent, many rabbis, Reformed and Orthodox, actively opposed his program. Herzl was succeeded in Zionist leadership by Chaim Weizmann, a British chemist, through whose efforts in 1917 the Balfour Declaration was secured. It committed the British gov-

Photograph of David Ben-Gurion, with a portrait of Theodor Herzl behind him. (Robert Capa/Magnum.)

ernment to "look with favor upon the establishment in Palestine of a national home for the Jewish people."[39] During the 1920s, the work of Zionism went forward despite obstacles. Jewish immigration to Palestine steadily increased; funds were raised, and the Jewish Agency, organized in 1929, gave the movement a central organization.

The rise of Hiterlism and the coming of World War II increased the tempo of immigration to Palestine, and with it the opposition of Arab states. In 1939, under pressure from the Arab states and facing the imminent prospect of world war, Britain abandoned the Balfour Declaration.

In the years immediately following World War II, the victorious allied powers, especially the United States and Great Britain, did little or nothing to solve the desperate problems of Europe's Jews. Meanwhile Jewish immigration to Palestine reached a veritable flood tide.

Tension between Jews and Arabs increased correspondingly. Arabs refused to cooperate with the United Nations Special Committee on Palestine. This committee recommended partition, and this recommendation was accepted by the United Nations General Assembly late in 1947. In 1948, as Great Britain prepared to withdraw from Palestine, war broke out between Jews and Arabs. On May 14, 1948, as the British departed, the state of Israel was proclaimed. It was immediately attacked by Arab states. By January 1949, when armistice agreements were finally reached, the outlines of a nation, recognized diplomatically by all major powers and proved in war, had clearly emerged. Chaim Weizmann was the first president and David Ben-Gurion the first prime minister.

During its first half century the nation state of Israel has maintained its existence and coped with an unceasing agenda of internal and external problems. Living in the veritable cockpit of the Middle East, Israel's citizen army has fought no less than five wars. After 1948–1949, the most successful was the Six-Day War of 1967 which wrested the Golan Heights from Syria, the West Bank from Jordan, and the Gaza Strip from Egypt.

The Law of Return offered immediate Israeli citizenship to any Jew wishing to return to Israel. But the thorny question persists: Who is a Jew? Talmudic law declares a Jew to be anyone born to a Jewish mother or converted by an approved rabbi, which in Israel has meant an Orthodox rabbi. The constitution of Israel combines religious freedom with the establishment of Orthodox Judaism. This has resulted in a situation where 10 to 15 percent are practicing Orthodox Jews, and the balance of the population appears wholly secular in outlook.

Israel has had the support, financial and religious, of the American Jewish community. It has also enjoyed substantial financial and military support, as foreign aid, from the United States government. However, the hostility of the surrounding Arab nations, overwhelmingly Islamic in orientation, has not abated. Since late in 1987 the *Intifada,* or "rising," of the Palestinian people of the occupied areas of Golan, West Bank, and Gaza has plagued the Israeli government. Yet for Jews of all religious orientation, ranging from orthodox to total secularity, the emergence of the nation state of Israel is a historic event of the greatest importance. It has notably enhanced the vigor and morale of Judaism.

Meanwhile, in other parts of the diaspora and in the United States, a new generation of writers and scholars continued to probe the questions of Jewish existence. Most notable among the writers has been Elie Wiesel, a survivor of Dachau. His novels, while passionately Jewish, nevertheless raise urgent and radical basic questions for traditional forms of faith. Notable among philosophers has been Emil Fackenheim. Centers for study of the Holocaust have arisen to pursue issues of historic fact and also of tragic religious symbolism.

JEWISH RELIGIOUS OBSERVANCE

Judaism is a concrete way of life involving practice in a manner which is distinctive in the history of human faiths. "Doing Torah" is a recognized phrase for

Jewish practice or observance. This practice has both moral and ritual aspects. What follows here is a belief summary of the main forms of ritual, which in varying degrees constitute the core of Jewish observance.[40]

SABBATH

Observance of the seventh day as a holy day dates from the earliest biblical period of which there is any reliable knowledge. The Hebrews apparently took it over, along with the seven-day week, from the Babylonians. But here as elsewhere, the Hebrews transformed what they borrowed, for the Babylonian sabbath was a demon's day, while that of Israel was a day of holy rest for people and animals, ordained by the one God. Sabbath observance has varied in its requirements but has traditionally involved rest, and no work, from the time the first stars appear on Friday until the same hour on Saturday.[41] In observing Jewish homes, it begins with the lighting of the sabbath candles by the mother, accompanied by a traditional prayer. Often the house has been cleaned on the previous day in preparation for the sabbath. On Friday evening there is the sabbath-eve service at the synagogue, and at home a meal with the father blessing the wine and pouring the *kiddush* cup for the family and reading the scripture portion for the day. On the sabbath day, Orthodox families go together to the synagogue, though in strictly Orthodox synagogues the women and girls must sit apart in the gallery of women.

DIETARY LAWS

Rooted in the Torah and elaborated in the Talmud, the dietary laws are observed with varying degrees of strictness. In addition to the prohibition against eating pork and other animals which do not "part the hoof and chew the cud,"[42] talmudic law requires the slaughter of meat by specially certified Jewish officials. Another law forbids the mixing of meat and milk dishes (this is based upon the biblical commandment against seething a kid in its mother's milk),[43] a prohibition which in some households necessitates two complete sets of dishes and pots and pans, and in others as many as four sets, two more being needed for Passover week. The historical origin of the food laws is seldom probed by the faithful Jew, for whom it is enough to know that they are a part of God's Torah and a way of identifying oneself with the Jewish people.

CIRCUMCISION

Circumcision has been called the *single sacrament* of Judaism, symbolizing God's covenant with Israel and the individual's membership in that covenant community. The traditional ceremony takes place when the boy is eight days old, and it may take place either at home or at a hospital. Friends are often invited to this festive occasion. A godfather holds the child while a synagogue official performs the operation. Then the father offers a traditional prayer and announces the child's name. There is an analogous ceremony for girls in which the father offers prayer, asking divine blessing, and announces the child's name.

BAR MITZVAH

Bar mitzvah literally means "son of the commandment," and it designates the coming-of-age ceremony for Jewish boys. According to Orthodox tradition, it occurs on the sabbath following a boy's thirteenth birthday and is a time of celebration and of receiving gifts. Among the gifts are a *talith*, or prayer shawl, and a *tephillin*, or a small box containing the words of the Shema (Deuteronomy 6:4–6). In accordance with Deuteronomic teaching, those words are bound on the forehead and over the left arm. The highlight of the synagogue ceremony is a reading from the Torah by the bar mitzvah boy, often followed by an address by him. Reform synagogues also often have an analogous *bath mitzvah* ritual for girls.

SYNAGOGUE

The synagogue itself epitomizes Judaism and the Jewish people, for it is a place of worship but also a school, law court, and town hall. Traditionally, a synagogue may be constituted by ten men; and ten men are traditionally necessary for any service of worship. The synagogue is organized under a layman who is president, and no synagogue has any authority over another.

The central symbolic object in the synagogue is the Ark of the Covenant, behind whose curtains are the scrolls of the Torah. Above the Ark is the eternal light. On the curtain of the Ark is inscribed the six-pointed star of David, and beside it are often pictured two lions. Daily prayers at the synagogue vary widely according to local custom.

HOLY DAYS AND FESTIVALS

The Jewish religious year begins with *Rosh Hashanah*, or New Year, which comes in late September or early October and is a time of both celebration and pious reflection. The first ten days of the new year are ten days of penitence, the tenth being *Yom Kippur*, or Day of Atonement. It is a time of private and public prayer for forgiveness.

Later in the autumn is *Succoth*, or the Feast of the Booths, when many Jews live in cornstalk huts to commemorate Israel's time in the wilderness. It is also a time of thanksgiving, celebrating the fruitfulness of nature, during which homes and synagogues are decorated with fruits and fall flowers. Following the week-long celebration of Succoth comes *Simchat Torah* (rejoicing the Torah).

The annual cycle of Torah readings is completed with the end of Deuteronomy, and the Scroll is rewound to the beginning of Genesis. Congregations celebrate the Torah in joy in this festival.

Coinciding with the winter solstice, and coming close to Christmas, is *Hanukkah*, or Feast of Lights, which celebrates the cleansing of the temple at Jerusalem at the time of the Maccabean revolt. Hanukkah is largely a family festival. For eight days a *menorah*, or candalabrum, is placed in the window, and one additional candle is lighted each night. Often the youngest child is given the privilege of lighting the Hanukkah candles. Gifts and greeting cards are exchanged among friends, and there is extensive merrymaking. In contemporary America Hanukkah has come to be widely celebrated as the Jewish equivalent of Christmas.

There is similar gaiety at *Purim*, which comes in late winter and celebrates the deliverance of Israel by Esther from its ancient persecutor Haman. The biblical Book of Esther is read in the synagogue at this season. The climax of the religious year is *Pesach*, or Passover, which comes in the spring, often at approximately the same time as Easter. It celebrates Israel's deliverance from Egypt, though it has incorporated vernal rituals celebrating such events as the birth of lambs and the sprouting of grain. There are special prayers and services at the synagogue, but the central celebration is the *seder*, or family meal, for which extensive preparations are made. The house is cleaned, Passover dishes and silver are prepared, new clothes are bought, and absent relatives return home. The central feature of the seder is the recital by the father of the story of Israel's deliverance from Egyptian bondage. When this story is completed a festive meal is served, and there is much singing and general merrymaking.

Fifty days after the Passover is *Shebuoth*, or Pentecost. Originally it was the festival of the barley harvest in Israel, but in the course of time it came also to celebrate the giving of the Torah on Mount Sinai. The Jewish religious year provides concrete expression for Judaism's historic emphasis on doing, or action. These ritual observances, taken as a whole, also serve as a vehicle for the expression and communication of the value system which constitutes the content of Judaism.

ISSUES AND QUESTIONS

A first issue turns upon a clear difference between Judaism and Christianity. As we have noted, while Christianity has maintained what is often called orthodoxy, namely, accepted standards of belief, by contrast Judaism maintains what has been called *orthopraxy*, that is, accepted standards of practice or action. This includes both ritual and moral action. As a consequence of this emphasis upon action, Judaism has often shown a much wider range of belief, and freedom of belief, than either Christianity or Islam.

A second issue consists of Judaism's response to modern secularizing tendencies. It is a fact of western history that from the Renaissance to the present, or the very recent past, the story of the West has been one of ever-increasing secularity in virtually all aspects of culture. By "secular" is meant attitudes which

Above: Hannukah painting (Photographic Archive of
the Jewish Theological Seminary of America, New
York. Frank J. Darmstaedter.) Below: Purim
embroidery. (Photographic Archive of the Jewish
Theological Seminary of America, New York. Frank
J. Darmstaedter.)

are not antireligious, but simply nonreligious. Some opponents of traditional religion are active enemies; by contrast the secular person asserts that religion does not greatly matter, then simply walks away. While such tendencies occur in many times and places in world history, they have had a pervasive importance in the modern West, approximately 1500–1900 CE.

This secularizing trend has had a significant impact upon all religions of the time and place; and Judaism has been no exception to this rule. However, the impact upon Judaism has been unique. Many individual Jewish people feeling the force of secularizing tendencies have had little or no interest in Judaic faith.

Yet many of these same people have retained a strong attachment to the Jewish community. For them Jewishness is not a religious but a cultural fact. Whether the Jewish community can hold together without a commitment to its Judaic center is a question which only the future can answer.

A third issue of central significance to Judaism is the concept of Israel's election and vocation, or, in popular parlance, of the Jews as God's "chosen people." We have already noted the biblical sources of this concept, and of its two biblical formulations, one of narrow religious nationalism and the other of Israel's role as the instrument of divine purpose in world history.

The struggle between these two equal and opposite concepts still goes on. In our present global age we offer here two observations. First, Jewish nationalism seems in many ways as problematic as other forms of nationalism. Second, the historic role of Israel's prophets and of Judaism in our human concepts of one God and one humanity are precious and needed resources in our age of global decisions.

A closely related issue is Judaism's agelong wrestle with the concept of history and historical character (as well as the monotheistic character) of the faith. We have noted both the recurrence of messianic figures and claims in Jewish history and also the opposing tendency of deferring such claims to the distant future with present focus on devotion and study directed to the Torah.

We have proposed in this connection a hypothesis that twentieth-century Zionism is in reality a highly secularized form of the traditional messianic idea and attitude. If this be true, it is also pertinent to add that currently observable attitudes both in Israel and in the diaspora cut across many lines of orthodoxy and secularity, and also of nationalism and universalism.

Finally, let us note the importance to Judaism and to the Jewish people of the United States. Approximately half of the Jews of the world live here. Upon the American diaspora falls a responsibility of leadership in present and future Judaism.

NOTES

1. See inter alia Salo W. Baron, *A Social and Religious History of the Jews*, Columbia, New York, 1952. For the same viewpoint, see also Leo W. Schwarz (eds.), *Great Ages and Ideas of the Jewish People*, Random House, New York, 1956.
2. This viewpoint is followed by inter alia William F. Albright, *From the Stone Age to Christianity*, Anchor Books, Doubleday, Garden City, N.Y., 1957.

3. Ibid., p. 266.
4. Schwarz, op. cit.
5. Ralph Marcus, "The Hellenistic Age," in Schwarz, op. cit., p. 138.
6. For Philo's life see Erwin R. Goodenough, *An Introduction to Philo Judaeus*, Blackwell, Oxford, 1962; Harry A. Wolfson, *Philo: Foundations of Religious Philosophy in Judaism, Christianity, and Islam*, Harvard, Cambridge, Mass., 1947.
7. See inter alia the chapter on this subject by Ralph Marcus in Schwarz, op. cit.
8. I Corinthians 8:5.
9. Schwarz, op. cit., pp. 135f.
10. Louis Finkelstein, *The Pharisees*, Jewish Publication Society of America, Philadelphia, 1938. See also Schwarz, op. cit., pp. 108–111.
11. Finkelstein, op. cit., pp. 9–11.
12. See Josephus, *The Jewish War and the Jewish Antiquities*, Harvard, Cambridge, Mass., 1956. See also Louis Finkelstein (ed.), *The Jews: Their History, Culture and Religion*, Harper, New York, 1961.
13. Millar Burrows, *The Dead Sea Scrolls*, Viking, New York, 1955, pp. 227–245; see also Millar Burrows, *More Light on the Dead Sea Scrolls*, Viking, New York, 1958, pp. 136–142.
15.. Ibid., p. 112.
16.. Gerson D. Cohen, "The Talmudic Age," in Schwarz, op. cit., pp. 143–145.
17. Ibid., p. 155.
18. Abraham S. Halkin, "The Judeo-Islamic Age," in Schwarz, op. cit., pp. 215f.
19. Ibid., p. 215.
20. Ibid., pp. 218–221.
21. Ibid., p. 227.
22. Ibid., pp. 215f.
23.. See A. Sachar, *A History of the Jews*, Knopf, New York, 1940, p. 164.
24. Moses ben Maimon, *The Guide for the Perplexed*, University of Chicago Press, Chicago, 1963.
25. Joseph H. Hertz, *The Authorized Daily Prayerbook*, Bloch, New York, 1948, pp. 248f.
26. Gershom E. Scholem (ed.), *Zohar, the Book of Splendor*, Schocken Books, New York, 1963.
27. Ibid. See also Gershom E. Scholem, *Major Trends in Jewish Mysticism*, Schocken Books, New York, 1963.
28. Ibid.
29. Martin Buber, *Tales from the Hasidim*, Schocken Books, New York, 1948.
30. Cecil Roth,"The European Age," in Schwarz, op. cit., p. 297.
31. Salo W. Baron, "The Modern Age," in Schwarz, op. cit., p. 317.
32. Schwarz, op. cit., p. 283.
33. George F. Moore, *History of Religions*, vol. 2, Scribner, New York, 1948, p. 103.
34. Isaac E. Marcuson, *Central Conference of American Rabbis*, vol. 47, Jewish Publication Society, Philadelphia, 1938, pp. 97f.
35. Mordecai M. Kaplan, *Judaism as a Civilization*, Macmillan, New York, 1935.
36. Will Herberg, *Protestant, Catholic, Jew*, Anchor Books, Doubleday, Garden City, N.Y. 1960.
37. Louis Finkelstein et al., *Religions of Democracy*, Devin-Adair, New York, 1941, p. iii.
38. See inter alia Glatzer, N. (ed.), *Rosenzweig: His Life and Thought*, Schocken Books, New York, 1962.
39. Sachar, op. cit., p. 367.
40. See inter alia S. Agnon, *Days of Awe*, Schocken Books, New York, 1948; T. Gaster, *Festivals of the Jewish Year*, Apollo, New York, 1961.
41. See inter alia A. Heschel, *The Sabbath*, Farrar, Straus & Giroux, New York, 1951.
42. Deuteronomy 14:6; Leviticus 11:3.
43. Exodus 23:19.

BIBLIOGRAPHY

Agnon, S.: *Days of Awe*, Schocken Books, New York, 1965.
Baron, S.: *A Social and Religious History of the Jews*, 18 vols., Columbia, New York, 1952–1973.

Browne, L. (ed.): *The Wisdom of the Jewish People*, Aronson, Northvale, N.J., 1988.

Buber, M.: *I and Thou*, Scribner, New York, 1970.

———: *Tales of the Hasidim*,Schocken Books, New York, 1961.

Cohen, A. A.: *The Natural and Supernatural Jew*, Behrman, West Orange, N.J., 1979.

Davidowicz, L.: *A Holocaust Reader*, Behrman, West Orange, N.J., 1976.

Finkelstein, L. (ed.): *The Jews: Their History, Culture and Religion*, Harper, New York, 1961.

Gaster, T.: *Festivals of the Jewish Year*, Peter Smith, New York, 1962.

Herberg, W.: *Judaism and Modern Man*, Atheneum, New York, 1970.

———: *Protestant, Catholic, Jew*, University of Chicago, Chicago, 1983.

Kaplan, M.: *Judaism as a Civilization*, Jewish Publications Society of America, Philadelphia, 1981.

———: *The Meaning of God in Modern Jewish Religion*, Reconstructionist Press, New York, 1975.

Lacks, R.: *Women and Judaism*, Doubleday, New York, 1980.

Moore, G.: *Judaism*, Harvard, Cambridge, Mass., 1930.

Neusner, J.: *American Judaism, Adventure in Modernity*, Prentice-Hall, Englewood Cliffs, N.J., 1972.

———: *Foundations of Judaism*, Fortress, Philadelphia, 1988.

———: *Invitation to the Talmud*, Harper & Row, New York, 1984.

Sachar, A.: *A History of the Jews*, Knopf, New York, 1967.

Sachar, H.: *A History of Israel from the Rise of Zionism to Our Time*, Jewish Publications Society of America, Philadelphia, 1979.

Sandmel, S.: *We Jews and Jesus*, Oxford, New York, 1965.

Scholem, G.: *Major Trends in Jewish Mysticism*, Schocken Books, New York, 1961.

——— (ed.): *Zohar, the Book of Splendor*, Schocken Books, New York, 1963.

Schwarz, L. (ed.): *Great Ages and Ideas of the Jewish People*, Modern Library, New York, 1956.

Steinberg, M.: *Basic Judaism*, Harcourt, Brace Jovanovich, New York, 1965.

Trepp, L.: *Judaism: Development and Life*, Wadsworth, Belmont, Calif., 1982.

———: *The Complete Book of Jewish Observance*, Behrman House–Summit Books, New York, 1980.

13

Jesus and Early Christianity

THE NEW TESTAMENT AS SEEN AGAINST ITS ENVIRONMENT

Like the other two monotheistic religions the history of Christianity is marked by an agelong encounter with the monotheistic character, and also the historic character of its faith. We have noted the recurring and plausible tendency of human religious experience toward plural allegiance or polytheism. How many and how various are the gods—and the value-systems—which bid for human allegiance! In sharpest contrast to all of these tendencies stands the inclusive unification of human experience under the one God and in one humanity.

Similarly the historical character of faith in the one God has occasioned a continuing struggle with the nonhistorical character of both cosmic and acosmic understandings of human existence. While we shall find these issues recurring throughout our study, they also occur in concentrated form in the present chapter.

The New Testament, which contains the story of Christian beginnings, must be understood initially in the context of first-century Judaism, and also more broadly against the background of the whole ancient Greco-Roman world.[1]

As we shall soon see, Christianity began as a religious movement in first-century Palestinian Judaism. Its founder lived and thought within this context. The basic concepts and images of Jesus and of the early Christian movement were thoroughly Hebraic or biblical in character. It is also important to add that Christianity maintained this Hebraic or biblical heritage against systems and movements of the Hellenistic world, such as gnosticism, which would deny or attenuate this Hebraic quality.

However, early Christianity differed from Judaism not only in its allegiance to Christ but also in its openness to the common Greco-Roman environment.[2] By the end of the first century CE, Christianity was dominantly a gentile religion, expressing itself in the Greek (and later, Latin) language. It also appropriated and used much of Greek philosophy, particularly in the Platonic and Stoic traditions, for the exposition and defense of its faith.

Rome's initial contribution to early Christianity was a world of peace and order in which to operate, even though Roman power was destined to turn violently upon the new religion several times in its first three centuries. Rome built the roads and maintained the order which enabled Paul and other Christian missionaries to go about their far-flung travels. Even more basically Rome contributed an image of a universal community of peace and order, which reinforced the biblical image of God's universal kingdom.

Once it had made its way into the mainstream of the ancient Mediterranean world, Christianity was involved in the lively competition of faiths and philosophies of the age. In the space of three or four centuries it won out in that competition, becoming the official religion of the Roman empire. As we shall see, this presented new problems.

For example, it set the stage for what was to come, namely, the role of Christianity in the new culture or civilization called the West, even then in gestation in the ruins of Greco-Roman antiquity. As we shall see in subsequent chapters, Christianity contributed a vital and indispensable Hebraic ingredient. Reinhold Niebuhr once spoke sapiently of the West as a house with four pillars, namely, the mind of Greece, the law of Rome, the energy of the Teutonic tribes, and the conscience of the Hebrew prophets.

The convergence of Hebraic and Hellenic concepts and motifs in the formative age of Christianity produced another consequence in the course of western history, namely, the ideal value called humanism. We shall see this word and concept assume many changing meanings in successive ages. Here we note the Greek component as the concept of the human self as rational subject, and the Hebraic ingredient as this same self as a child of God and hence of intrinsic value. It included also the ethical nature of human life and the deep inwardness which opened human life to transcendence or God. All of these components converged to create a concept of human worth and fulfillment in many varied forms of excellence. We shall see the humanistic ideal assume new shapes and forms in each successive age of the West, and also even more widely in world history.

LIFE OF JESUS

Except for a few verbal shreds in classical and Jewish writings, the sole source of knowledge of the life and teachings of Jesus is the New Testament, and more particularly the four Gospels. While there has always been some study of the Gospels, the fully free and critical study of these documents is a modern achievement; it is a fact that during the past century or so the four Gospels have been as intensively and extensively studied as any writings in the world. The results of this study will be assumed in the following account of the life of Jesus. The first three Gospels—Matthew, Mark, and Luke—taken together show a common outline for the life and teachings of Jesus, in contrast to the Gospel of John, which differs radically in order and outlook.[3] Of the first three (called *synoptic*

Gospels since they "view together" the life and teachings of Jesus) the questions have been asked: "Who wrote them, when, where, and under what circumstances?" These questions may be taken as a definition of the synoptic problem.[4]

The answer seems to be that immediately after the life of Jesus there was a period of oral tradition or transmission. Probably the first written source was a hypothetical document to which modern scholars have given the name Q (the German word *Quelle* means "source"). According to scholarly hypothesis, Q consisted mainly of selections of Jesus' teachings, probably topically arranged and used for instructional purposes within the Christian community. Some such document was probably in existence by ten or twenty years after Jesus' death, that is, by 40 or 50 CE.

It is well known that many more than four accounts of Jesus' life gained currency in the early Christian movement. Of these, the three synoptics eventually won out, gaining places in the New Testament. Of the three synoptics, Mark is clearly the oldest and is usually dated ca. 70 CE. Matthew and Luke were written ca. 95. Both Matthew and Luke combined Mark with Q, though in independent and different ways. The three synoptics differ from each other in style, viewpoint, and many details, though they agree in essentials such as their overall view of Jesus' life and teachings.

The fourth Gospel, written around the turn of the second century and traditionally attributed to the disciple John, differs radically in its portrait of Jesus and in the order of events in Jesus' life. Taking up the widely prevalent Greek idea of the Logos, John interprets Jesus as the incarnate Logos or Word of God.

The following sketch of Jesus' life and teaching will follow the synoptic order and viewpoint as constituting our earliest and probably most reliable portrait of Jesus. True, it is not a photograph but a portrait, which in many details reflects the painter's interpretations and prejudices as well as it does the objective features of the man who sat for the portrait. Yet there is solid critical basis for accepting as historically reliable the main features of the synoptic portrait. The synoptic portrait of Jesus' life will be sketched by means of six main topics: (1) nativity stories, (2) baptism and temptation, (3) Galilean teaching, (4) confession of Messiahship, (5) journey to Jerusalem, (6) last days and death.

NATIVITY STORIES

Mark, the earliest Gospel, contains no nativity story, opening its narrative with the beginning of Jesus' public career. Likewise, the apostle Paul makes no reference to a supernatural birth of Christ, referring to Jesus simply as born of a woman and of the Davidic line.[5] The Matthew and Luke stories are the sole New Testament references to the virgin birth of Christ. It is also noteworthy that in place of a birth story, the fourth Gospel offers a philosophic preface interpreting Christ as the incarnate Word, or Logos. Furthermore, a careful reading will show that the Matthew and Luke accounts differ sharply from each other in specific details. At most points these differing accounts do not clash but are simply independent of each other.

For many readers the value of these stories lies not in literal veracity but in the estimate and interpretation of Jesus which they express. Here was one at whose birth wise men came from far lands with gifts and homage, shepherds knelt, angels sang, and Herod trembled on his uneasy throne. Furthermore, for this unique son there must be a unique mother upon whom devotion might focus. Hence too, in the course of time, Mary became the chief of Christian saints.

By sifting the available historical evidence, many scholars conclude that Jesus was the son of Joseph and Mary and that his home was Nazareth in Galilee. The name *Jesus* is a Hellenized form of the Hebrew name *Joshua* or *Yeshua*, meaning "the Lord saves." Since the New Testament writers seem unanimous in the view that he was born under Herod the Great, his birth date cannot be placed later than 4 BCE. (Several centuries later when dates came to be reckoned from the birth of Jesus, an error was made in calculating the base year, 1 CE; hence paradoxically Jesus was born a few years BCE!)

Of Jesus' childhood in Nazareth very little is known. The Gospels refer to six other children, four brothers and two sisters. Joseph is spoken of as a carpenter, and it was the Jewish tradition for the eldest son to learn his father's trade. Since references to Joseph cease during Jesus' childhood, it has been inferred by some scholars that he died during this time. While the Gospels contain no specific references, one may fairly assume that Jesus had the education customary for a first-century Galilean Jewish boy. This inference is strengthened by Jesus' own teachings, including his references to the Hebrew scriptures, especially Deuteronomy and Isaiah.

BAPTISM AND TEMPTATION

Luke dates the beginning of John the Baptist's public career in the fifteenth year of Tiberius Caesar (29–30 CE), thus providing a peg on which to hang the chronology of Jesus' life.[6] John was an apocalyptic preacher of the impending kingdom of God, or messianic age. To many of his hearers he must have seemed a prophet born out of season (since the period of officially recognized prophecy had closed several centuries previously). He was a striking figure, dressed in haircloth and leather belt and eating locusts and wild honey. His way of life as well as his words asserted his rejection of civilized society as contrary to God's will. He termed the leaders of synagogue and community a brood of vipers, and he warned his hearers to flee from the wrath to come. He taught his followers a radical social morality: a man with two coats should give to him who had none; soldiers should abstain from extortion and from wanton violence; tax collectors should take only their due.[7] John denounced Herod Antipas for living with his brother's wife—a criticism which cost him first imprisonment, then death. Ritually John taught and practiced baptism as an anticipatory cleansing in

Head of the Virgin. Drawing by Leonardo da Vinci. (Metropolitan Museum of Art, Dick Fund, 1951.)

preparation for the coming kingdom. The similarity of John's message to the teaching of the Essenes of Qumran and the Dead Sea Scrolls has frequently been pointed out.[8]

The relation of Jesus to John the Baptist raises many questions. Beyond the fact that John baptized Jesus, the Gospels differ on some details and are silent on others. Did John recognize Jesus as the Messiah? Did Jesus actually become a disciple of John? Why did Jesus seek baptism by John? These and similar questions have been asked again and again for centuries, and no final answers are forthcoming.

The Gospel writers agree in relating the baptism to Jesus' sense of vocation. Mark says that Jesus saw the heavens open and the spirit of God descend like a dove upon him, and he heard the voice of God saying to him, "Thou art my beloved Son; with thee I am well pleased."[9] The dove was a familiar Jewish symbol for the divine presence, and these words are from the Old Testament. The scene is clearly intended as one in which the Spirit of God came upon Jesus, giving him his vocation, or mission, leading him to his unique destiny.

Journey of the Magi. Painting by the fifteenth-century Italian artist Sassatta. (Metropolitan Museum of Art, bequest of Maitland F. Grigg, 1943.)

The parallel passages in Matthew and Luke are more objective than Mark, stating not that Jesus saw the dove descend, but that the dove descended.

The synoptic Gospels follow the baptism with stories of temptations. Mark simply asserts that Jesus was tempted by Satan, but Luke and Matthew describe three temptations: (1) to turn stones to bread, (2) to throw himself from the temple pinnacle and emerge unharmed, and (3) to worship Satan in order to achieve world empire. It is interesting to note that each of the temptations is couched in Old Testament language, and that Jesus' replies are in effect counterquotations of scripture. Underneath these stories lie the real issues with which Jesus was apparently struggling. Should he gather a following by performing sensational miracles? Would his appeal be primarily economic—to bid his followers to live by bread alone? Should his movement be based on the political and military messianism so common in first-century Galilee? Each of these questions drew a negative reply as Jesus pondered his mission.

TEACHING IN GALILEE

According to Mark's Gospel, Jesus first appeared publicly in Galilee, declaring "The time is fulfilled, and the kingdom of God is at hand."[10] These words have been so overlaid with centuries of traditional piety that it is difficult to recover their first century CE meaning. In this study we have pointed (1) to the Bible's linear-dramatic view of history, and (2) to the popularity of apocalypse in first-century Judaism. In this context Jesus' kingdom of God must be viewed as his distinctive formulation of these thought forms.

The synoptic Gospels disagree on the place of Jesus' first public teaching, Matthew and Mark placing it in Capernaum on the north shore of the Sea of Galilee, and Luke in Jesus' home town of Nazareth.[11] In all three Gospels these towns as well as such others as Chorazim and Bethsaida are frequently mentioned. Apparently Jesus made his way from town to town, preaching in synagogues, in open fields, and on at least one occasion on the shore of the Sea of Galilee. The theme of his preaching was the imminent coming of the kingdom of God and the conditions for citizenship in the kingdom. In addition to preaching, he is reported to have healed the sick, to have performed exorcisms, and to have done many other "mighty works." At first he traveled about alone, but soon he gathered to himself twelve intimate followers, or disciples. At one

Head of Christ. Painting by Rembrandt. (Metropolitan Museum of Art, IMM. and Mrs. Isaac D. Fletcher Collection, bequest of Isaac D. Fletcher, 1917.)

point, having instructed the twelve, he sent them out by twos to spread his message throughout Galilee. From the beginning of his public career, there were rumblings of hostility from the leaders of Judaism.

Many questions arise concerning this period of public teaching in Galilee. How long did it last? Guesses have ranged from six months to two years. Even more important, why, when this mission was proceeding successfully, did Jesus abruptly break it off and wander alone with his disciples to Tyre and Sidon and to the region of Caesarea Philippi?[12] One possible answer is that Herod Antipas, who had recently killed John the Baptist, now threatened Jesus' life. Another is that Jesus could see increasingly how Galilee, hotbed of the Zealot party with its violent and radical political messianism, misunderstood him and his teachings. Whatever the reason, this period of wandering to the north effectively ended Jesus' public career in Galilee. And what is more important, in the region of Caesarea Philippi a momentous dialog took place between Jesus and his disciples.

CONFESSION OF MESSIAHSHIP

All three of the Synoptic Gospels record the scene in which as they walked along the road near Caesarea Philippi, Jesus asked the disciples, "Who do men

Christ Preaching. Etching by Rembrandt. (Metropolitan Museum of Art, bequest of Mrs. H. O. Havemeyer, 1929.)

say that I the Son of Man am?"[13] The reply was that some thought he was Elijah, there being a popular legend that Elijah would return just before the messiah. Others thought that he was John the Baptist—come back to life after his murder. "But who do you say that I am?" persisted Jesus. To this Peter, speaking for himself and the others, responded, "You are the Christ the Son of the living God."

This conversation must be understood against the background of first-century Judaism's ardent messianic expectation. Messianic claims were frequent and various; they were often treated as blasphemous by the Jewish leaders and as subversive agitation by the Romans. Under these circumstances, it was natural for Jesus to enjoin upon his disciples the strictest secrecy.[14]

According to the synoptics this was the first time Jesus spoke specifically and directly of the messiahship. Previous to this time, crowds had shouted messianic titles at him, but he had not responded either affirmatively or negatively. Now he spoke, though only privately, within the band of disciples, elliptically, eliciting Peter's confession rather than making a definite assertion. Later, at the end of his life, standing before the Sanhedrin, Jesus was to make his only public statement on this subject in reply to the high priest's question.[15]

The title *Christ* (or *Christos*) is the Greek translation of the Hebrew *messiah*, which means "anointed one." The idea of the messiah, which developed in later Judaism, was that God would send a divinely appointed king who would bring in the kingdom of God. As previously noted, there were many first-century views of the messiah, among the most popular of which was the military-political interpretation held by the Zealots.

The subject of Jesus' messiahship has been discussed in recent New Testament study, and it is generally accepted that Jesus, as the New Testament pictures him, could have little or nothing to do with most popular first-century views of messiahship. Some scholars draw the conclusion that Jesus never made messianic claims, though such claims were ascribed to Jesus by the early Christian church.[16] Other scholars claim that Jesus did in fact make such claims, but that the force of these claims in the historical context of the first century was to assert a novel, indeed radical, reinterpretation of the nature of the messiahship.[17]

The question of Jesus' messianic claim is of crucial significance to Christianity, for Christianity is by definition the religion of those who believe Jesus to be the Christ. Later, other terms came to be used as synonyms for this original title, such as Lord, Savior, Word, and Son of God; but they were attempts to find adequate Gentile, Greek synonyms for the original Hebrew title of messiah. Christianity began with the apostolic confession of Jesus as the Christ, or Messiah.

The transfiguration was presumably a sequel to the confession at Caesarea Philippi.[18] According to all three synoptic Gospels, Jesus took Peter, James, and John to a high mountain, where in a vision they saw Moses, Elijah, and Jesus together. Moses symbolized the Torah; Elijah symbolized the prophets; and Jesus was here understood as the Messiah, who brought both Torah and prophets to fulfillment.

PASSION AND DEATH

Following the confession and transfiguration, Jesus returned briefly and secretly to Galilee, then "set his face steadfastly" to go to Jerusalem.[19] Here Luke differs materially from Mark and Matthew in reporting the length and route of the journey; Luke's story also differs structurally from the other two synoptic Gospels in the inclusion at this point of a large block of narrative and teaching not included in Matthew and Mark.[20] Yet all three Gospels agree that Jesus was apparently making his way to the capital city with full knowledge of the dangers involved. He seemed to be timing his arrival to coincide with the Passover festival, when Jerusalem would be thronged with pilgrims from all parts of the Mediterranean world.

Why did Jesus resolve to make this last perilous journey? Traditional Christianity has often invested Jesus with supernatural foreknowledge, and has viewed the journey to Jerusalem as conscious preparation for his sacrificial death. This appears clearly to be the viewpoint of the fourth Gospel, though not of the synoptics. It is belied by Jesus' response to the events of the last days as they unfolded in the synoptic accounts. Some scholars, including Albert Schweitzer, have argued that Jesus expected a miraculous deliverance by God at Jerusalem which would vindicate him and his kingdom.[21] Perhaps the most adequate view of the matter is that Jesus was a man utterly dedicated to God who went to Jerusalem in simple trust and obedience to the will of God as he understood it.

He entered the city on the back of a donkey, on a day which has since been celebrated in Christianity as Palm Sunday. The popular demonstration of his followers had messianic implications, and his choice of a donkey may be understood as his further attempt to transform the messianic concept from a warlike, military idea to one of peace. Once in the city, Jesus went to the temple and threw out the money changers and vendors of sacrificial animals—an act clearly presupposing messianic authority, and also one which crystallized the opposition into a conspiracy to take his life.[22]

During his week in Jerusalem, Jesus lodged with friends in Bethany, over the Mount of Olives to the east. He came into the city each day to teach on the porches of the temple, arguing his teachings with fellow rabbis, answering questions and setting forth his views like other rabbinical teachers. At least one modern writer on the life of Jesus has concluded that Jesus taught thus for a matter of several weeks in Jerusalem, then withdrew to nearby wilderness and returned to the capital city in time for the Passover week.[23] This view can be supported from the fourth Gospel, but there is little or no basis for it in the synoptics.

On Thursday of the last week, Jesus' disciples arranged for a room in which he might eat the traditional Passover meal with them, within the city of Jerusalem, as Jewish custom required. According to the account in all the Gospels, he reinterpreted this meal to symbolize his own body and blood through which he believed God was making a new covenant with humankind. How much of this scene is historic fact and how much is later Christian interpretation is impossible to say with any precision or certainty.

After the meal, Jesus and the disciples made their way back to Bethany, and Jesus paused for prayer in the Garden of Gethsemane on the slopes of the Mount of Olives. There a mob, sent by leaders of the Sanhedrin and led by the traitor Judas, took him prisoner. He was taken to the home of the high priest, Caiaphas, where an illegal session of the Sanhedrin was convened to try him. The charge was blasphemy, that is, making messianic claims and threatening the destruction of the temple. When perjured witnesses failed to agree, Caiaphas asked Jesus directly if he claimed to be the Messiah. Jesus' cryptic but apparently affirmative reply was his only public statement of a messianic claim, and it was sufficient in the view of Caiaphas and his colleagues to convict Jesus of blasphemy, an offense which in Jewish law carried the death penalty.[24]

To carry out the death penalty required the permission of the Roman authorities. Hence, the next morning, Jesus was taken before the Roman procurator, Pontius Pilate, where the charge was not blasphemy—which would not greatly impress Pilate—but rather sedition—a matter to which Rome and its agents were extremely sensitive. Pilate's role in the trial and condemnation of Jesus is by no means clear, but at least he gave the necessary official order for the carrying out of the death penalty by the cruel method of crucifixion. So, it was thought, ended the life of one who was said to claim to be "king of the Jews."[25]

TEACHINGS OF JESUS

Jesus' primary teaching was the kingdom of God, or as Matthew put it, the kingdom of heaven. In first-century Judaism, this term referred to the historic age of fulfillment which was believed to be immediately at hand, the messianic age to which all Israel looked forward. Jesus' kingdom of God must be regarded as his particular and distinctive interpretation of this widely shared idea.

The idea of this reign of God over all the world has been a part of biblical religion from earliest Old Testament days. If God were the ruler of all, then the world was properly his realm. But, as Israel's prophets pointed out, God's rule was not now apparent; rather, other kings seemed to be effectively in charge of the world's destiny. Hence the prophets appealed to a future age when God's whole will would be done over all the world. Such was the origin of the kingdom of God.[26]

Jesus appeared to have differed from his Jewish contemporaries as to some basic features of the kingdom, notably, the individual requirements for citizenship in the kingdom, its universality, and the basically ethical nature of citizenship in the kingdom. He was in complete opposition to the popular political nationalistic view of the kingdom. In Jesus' view each individual by humble repentence made his or her way into the kingdom, whose membership included people of every race and nation. The requirements of citizenship as

Jesus set them forth in the sermon on the mount were fundamentally moral in nature.

While Jesus' kingdom of God was essentially a universal human brotherhood, there is no basis in his teachings for identifying the kingdom with any particular kind of society or social organization. When Jesus spoke of the kingdom of God he was not envisaging democracy, socialism, or any other ism. Rather he was dealing with a radically different sort of problem, namely, the state of the human world in which God's whole will would be done.

There is no basis in the historical record for any separation of religion from ethics in Jesus' teaching; rather, they are two aspects of a single reality, religion being the inner allegiance of the human heart, and morality or ethics, the conduct which sprang from this source.

The primary religious reality, according to Jesus, was the one God, conceived as lord and creator of all that exists, and as supreme object of human devotion. Jesus never argued the existence of God; but taking this for granted, his primary problem was the relation of human beings to God. It was Jesus' view that the whole reason for the existence of humankind—its purpose on earth—is to do the will of God.

The content of the divine will for human life can be summed up in the single word *love*. Jesus used this word to mean a spontaneous, wholehearted, and complete affirmation of the selfhood of others. Contrary to much current opinion, this teaching is not unique to Jesus or to the New Testament. Several of the Old Testament books had taught God's love for humans and their love for God, notably Deuteronomy, Hosea, Isaiah, and Jeremiah.[27] It must also be kept in mind that for Jesus, the concept of love had an austerity which it lacks in much modern sentimental usage. To him, love included justice and judgment as well as mercy. In the first century *father* meant an authority figure far more than in the twentieth. With these qualifications, it is accurate to summarize Jesus' God as sovereign love. It is a sovereignty which is now hidden, but which will be manifested fully in the coming of the kingdom.

As noted above, religion and morality were for Jesus two aspects of a single integral reality. The basic moral commandments had an absolute or unqualified character based upon a divine "Thou shalt…," and the commandments were all summed up in the single supreme commandment: "Thou shalt love they neighbor as thyself."[28] Jesus had much to say about the unconditional quality of love, and the tensions which it set up with the everyday loyalties of human existence such as family, state, economic order, and the like. Far from being ascetic, he regarded these normal goods as parts of God's creation, yet he argued that all creation must be placed under the supreme goal of the kingdom of God and its perfect goodness, which above all, he admonished his followers to seek.[29]

The content of Jesus' faith and ethic is expressed in his own summary of the Torah and the Prophets: You shall love the Lord your God with all your heart, and with all your soul and mind and strength, and your neighbor as yourself.[30] This famous statement is a double quotation by Jesus of (1) Deuteronomy 6:4–5 and (2) Leviticus 19:18. Asked by a heckler to quote the greatest commandment in the Torah, he did precisely that with greatest accuracy. The basic moral virtue is love conceived as respect for, and affirmation of, personality as made in the divine image.

Yet neighbor-love, so conceived, was for Jesus something more inward than any precise legal code. It was an attitude of the heart; and from the heart, Jesus reminded his hearers, proceed the attitudes that govern actions.[31] Moreover, it was an attitude whose universality extended beyond all barriers of race and class to the limits of humanity. It was precisely this universality which was the subject of such teachings as the parable of the good Samaritan.[32]

In contrast to the good as love, evil for Jesus was an ever-present self-centeredness which sets humans against God and their neighbors. Sometimes it is manifested as trust in one's possessions as with the Rich Fool,[33] sometimes as the pride of the Pharisees who "trusted in themselves and despised the others."[34]

Jesus' demands, both religious and moral, while not ascetic, were rigorous, indeed so rigorous that few have claimed to fulfill them completely. Yet in the context of his teachings and life, one could see that what Jesus sought to do was to depict ultimate human perfection. The practical problem of ethics which followed from this was how this perfection was to be related to all the changing scenes and situations of human life. It was a problem destined to concern the Christian church age after age.

Another significant issue was the relation of Jesus' faith and ethic to Judaism and to the whole Hebraic heritage of the Old Testament. For one thing, Jesus' teachings were more inward and more internationalist or universal than most first-century interpretations of the Torah. He stood against code morality and against the prevalent nationalism of his time. Yet in both respects, Jesus stood squarely on the classical tradition of Torah and the Prophets. Indeed Jesus seems to have regarded his teaching as the fulfillment of the Torah and Prophets.[35]

THE NEW TESTAMENT CHRISTIAN COMMUNITY

THE RESURRECTION OF CHRIST

The primary religious premise for the New Testament Christian community was the resurrection of Christ. At the crucifixion, Jesus' followers forsook him and fled. One may imagine that they also left Jerusalem for their native Galilee, there in disillusionment to resume the occupations they had left to follow the man of Nazareth. Yet the strange fact is that only a few weeks later these same people were back in Jerusalem with an utterly changed attitude. They were the servants of a living faith which within a century was to make its impact felt from one end of the Roman empire to the other, and which in the next four centuries would turn that empire upside down.

What accounts for the revolutionary change? The answer which traditional Christianity has given to this question is the resurrection of Christ—an event which convinced the followers of Jesus that he was not dead but alive—more living and more powerful than in the days of his flesh. Hence, the resurrection might be defined as that event which certified to the Christian community the living spirit of Christ as an ever-present reality.

Precisely what occurred at the resurrection is another question to which the New Testament Christians gave more than one answer, and none without its serious problems. One answer was the story in all four Gospels of the empty tomb, the surprised visitors on the first day of the week, the appearances of the risen Christ, and finally his ascension on a cloud to heaven. Yet from the beginning there were difficulties in this interpretation of an objective physical resurrection, and an ascension of the same sort. Where, for example, did the body go, when Christ ascended to heaven?

It is also a fact that other interpretations were held. In the early 50s, two decades before the earliest synoptic Gospel, the apostle Paul wrote to the Corinthian church:

> For I delivered to you as of first importance what I also received, that Christ died for our sins in accordance with the scriptures, that he was buried, that he was raised on the third day in accordance with the scriptures, and that he appeared to Cephas, then to the twelve. Then he appeared to more than five hundred brethren at one time, most of whom are still alive, though some have fallen asleep.
> Then he appeared to James, then to all the apostles. Last of all, as to one untimely born, he appeared also to me.[36]

One notes that the primary emphasis is placed here upon the risen Christ, and that no mention is made of an empty tomb. Most important of all, one also notes that Paul includes among the resurrection appearances his own experience on the Damascus road, an experience that took place long after the presumed ascension, and that Paul explicitly denies the physical nature of the resurrection: "flesh and blood cannot inherit the Kingdom of God."[37] Paul was a Jew for whom the concept of personality required some sort of embodiment. In the later verses of the chapter quoted above, he speculates about different kinds of bodies, here and hereafter, concluding that in the resurrection all will have bodies, though of a different sort from our present bodies. Later, in II Corinthians, Paul makes a different suggestion concerning life in the resurrection; apparently his searching mind continued to look for an adequate view of this difficult and mysterious matter.[38]

THE EARLY JERUSALEM COMMUNITY

Pentecost marked the beginning of the Christian movement and community, which consisted initially of the small group of Jesus' followers who carried on religious propaganda in Jerusalem. An event of greatest importance to this group occurred on the Jewish Feast of Pentecost in the same year that Jesus died, that is, ca. 31–33 CE. As the Book of Acts tells the story, the Christians were gathered in their upstairs meeting room when the Holy Spirit descended upon them with the supernatural accompaniments of wind, fire, and ecstatic utterance, or "speaking with tongues."[39]

Impelled to speak, Peter made a public address at the end of which, according to the Book of Acts, 3,000 converts were made to the new faith.[40] Pentecost was for Judaism the festival which commemorated the giving of the Torah on Mount Sinai, and according to rabbinic tradition it had been given in the seventy languages of humankind. The Christian story was thus a deliberate parallel, describing the giving of the new and universal faith in what were described as different foreign languages.

"Speaking with tongues" was a frequent phenomenon in the New Testament Christian church, as may be noted from the letters of Paul.[41] The author of the Book of Acts, writing at the end of the first century, appears to be seeking to explain the beginning of this practice; and he does so by tracing it to Pentecost and regarding it as a process of speaking in foreign tongues. Actually, a more realistic view is that it consisted of ecstatic babbling, under the stress of strong emotion. As Paul viewed this matter, speaking with tongues belonged with prophecy, visions, healings, and other preternormal phenomena, as a result of the enlargement of human power which accompanied religious revival. Yet Paul was also sensible enough to suggest that the value of all such experiences lay in their ethical and spiritual quality.

In the view of the Book of Acts, the Christian movement began in Jerusalem. The members of this earliest Christian community were good Jews in all respects except one. They went to the temple, observed the Torah, studied the Bible; but they believed that the messiah expected by all good Jews had actually come in Jesus. To their contemporaries they must have appeared as one more harebrained sect. What made them appear even more eccentric was their firm conviction that Jesus had been raised from the dead, that he was spiritually present in the community of believers, and that he would soon return to earth in power to rule over God's kingdom.[42]

This little group celebrated its faith in worship which in many ways resembled the synagogue service. There was reading of the Jewish Bible and exposition of the text accompanied by prayer to God. But all was interpreted as pointing to Christ. And there was a love feast, patterned after the last supper, celebrating Jesus' memory, his spiritual presence, and his expected return. This reenactment of the Last Supper grew at length into the Roman Catholic mass and the Protestant service of holy communion.

Leadership of the community was by the disciples of Christ, now called *apostles*. (An *apostle* was technically defined in the early Christian community as one who had seen the resurrected Christ.) Members practiced a community of property, according to which they sold their possessions and placed the money in a common treasury which provided for the needs of all. They also shared their meals at common tables. These practices led to abuses, as the story of Ananias and Sapphira illustrates.[43]

From the beginning the Christians were ardent missionaries. After Peter's speech at Pentecost, they carried on ceaseless activity designed to secure conversions, which activity they interpreted as their obedience to the will of Christ. However, it soon brought them into conflict with government. The authorities of Jerusalem wavered between the toleration recommended by Gamaliel and occasionally severe repression.[44] This raised an issue destined later to draw Christianity into fundamental conflict with Rome. Ordered by Jewish authorities to desist from religious propaganda, Peter and John replied, "We must obey God rather than man."[45] This conclusion was regarded by the Christians as a necessary implication of the first commandment.

Another kind of conflict was also quick to emerge in the Jerusalem church. Apparently some members began to take liberties in their observance of the Torah. Differences of opinion were reported over the daily distribution of food between members of the Christian community who were Palestinian Jews and others who were Hellenistic Jews.[46] The former were Jews who had always lived in Palestine, and the latter, those who had lived abroad in the Gentile world and then returned to Palestine. The Palestinian Jews were consistently more rigorous in their observance of the Torah.

To meet this issue, Acts reports, the office of deacon was devised. Yet it is significant that all those selected had Greek names; apparently they represented the Hellenistic group within the Christian community. It is also significant that their leader, Stephen, was soon actively engaged not only in deacon's duties, but also in teaching and preaching. He was soon in trouble with civil authorities, the charges against him being that he was disloyal to temple and Torah. As a result of these charges Stephen was lynched by an angry Jewish mob, thus becoming the first Christian martyr.[47]

This episode has significance as the beginning of the separation between Christianity and Judaism. What began with Stephen had its completion only much later when Christianity had dispensed completely with observance of the Torah and had become a Gentile religion. Other events pointing in this direction followed Stephen's death; for example, Peter in obedience to a vision deliberately breached kosher food laws and also baptized a Gentile.[48] In reaction to such events, a conservative, or Jewish-Christian, party emerged in the Jerusalem church, composed of those who asserted that in order to become a Christian one had first to become a Jew, taking up the full burden of the Torah. Thus arose the issue which was to engage Christianity crucially for a generation and on which the apostle Paul was to say the decisive word two decades later.

PAUL AS MISSIONARY

The apostle Paul's name is associated with the rise of Gentile Christianity. *Gentile* Christianity did not originate with Paul, since the churches of Antioch, Alexandria, and Rome were all founded by other apostles before Paul's rise to leadership. The Book of Acts introduces Paul as the young man who held the coats of those who stoned Stephen. He had only recently come to Jerusalem from his home city of Tarsus for rabbinical study with Gamaliel. His parents were Pharisaic Jews, and his father was a Roman citizen. Paul had learned the tentmaker's trade and had received a traditional Jewish education; from the fact that Tarsus was a center of Stoic philosophy and Greek mystery religions, we may infer for him some familiarity with these phenomena. His own writings confirm this supposition. It must be supposed that on his arrival in Jerusalem his attitude toward the Torah was that of any intensely loyal Pharisaic Jew. Hence it was natural for him to persecute Stephen and other Christians as renegade Jews.

Yet for Paul, as for so many, intense allegiance seems to have concealed inner conflicts. As Acts tells the story, it was on a mission to harass Christians in Damascus that Paul's conversion took place.[49] Paul's own writings agree with the Acts account in interpreting the experience as the appearance to Paul of the resurrected Christ, who said, "Paul, Paul, why do you persecute me?" Paul's response was, "Who are you, Lord?" The reply was, "I am Jesus whom you are persecuting." As Paul said many years later, he was "not disobedient to the heavenly vision."[50] At the time he was led blind into the city of Damascus, where his conversion became known.

According to Paul's own writings, he spent the next three years in Arabia, presumably in seclusion, reintegrating his shattered life and gaining perspective on what had happened to him.[51] Then he journeyed to Jerusalem for consultation with Peter and other leaders of the Jerusalem church. Following this, he settled down for fourteen years of labor in Tarsus and Antioch, presumably first as leader of the Tarsus church and then as Barnabas's assistant at Antioch. The New Testament gives no direct knowledge of these years, yet one must conclude that Paul's distinctive views on the relation of Christianity to Judaism were taking shape in these cities where Jews and Gentiles met and mingled in the Christian church.

Acts and Paul's own letters do provide more detailed knowledge of Paul's later years and missionary journeys. The thirteenth and fourteenth chapters of Acts tell of the first missionary trip undertaken by Paul and Barnabas, at the command of the Antioch church, which took them first to Cyprus, then to cities of south-central Asia Minor. John and Mark accompanied Paul and Barnabas to Cyprus, but then returned home. Paul and Barnabas, however, continued their journey to the mainland of Asia Minor, where they visited successively the cities of Perga, Antioch in Pisidia, Iconium, Lystra, and Derbe.[52] In each city the apostles preached and taught at the synagogue, winning converts who formed the nucleus of a Christian church.

Before venturing further afield, Paul made a journey to Jerusalem in 49 or 50 for the purpose of settling the growing dispute between him and the Jewish Christians of Jerusalem. At this meeting, often called the *Council of Jerusalem*, the question to be decided was whether in order to become a Christian a person had first to become a Jew, observing the Torah. The Jerusalem church answered this question with an unyielding affirmative, but Paul had increasingly believed and taught that anyone who had personal faith in Christ could jettison the Torah. According to Acts and to Paul's own account in the letter to the Galatians, the result of the council was an uneasy compromise permitting Paul to work among Gentiles and the Jerusalem party among Jews.[53] The compromise soon broke down in misunderstanding, and Paul spent the rest of his life propagating his version of Christian faith among Jew and Gentile alike.

Soon after the council, Paul returned to Antioch, then set out across Syria and Asia Minor for Europe. In Troas occurred the celebrated vision of the man from Macedonia saying, "Come over, help us."[54] From Troas, Paul crossed to Philippi in Greece and made his way successively to Berea, Thessalonika, Athens, and Corinth. Paul did not succeed in founding a Christian church in Athens; however, in Corinth he stayed for over two years, founding a thriving if turbulent Christian community. From Corinth he made his way to Esphesus, where he worked for three years, probably from 54 to 57. During these years his break with Judaism became definite and final. It was from Ephesus that he wrote the letter to the Galatians, presumably to the south Galatian cities visited on his first missionary journey. From his years at Ephesus, too, may be dated his stormy correspondence with the Corinthian church. At this time or shortly thereafter, he wrote the letter to the Romans.

Paul made one more journey to Jerusalem, apparently to bring relief funds to the famine-stricken Jerusalem church. Roman soldiers saved him from lynching at the hands of an angry mob of Jewish extremists who accused him of violating essential parts of the Torah and teaching others to do so. He was held in protective custody, at first in Jerusalem, then in Caesarea, which was the Roman port for Palestine. Despairing of receiving a fair hearing for his case after two years or more, he appealed to Caesar. The Book of Acts does not tell the outcome of his trial, but a widely held tradition asserts that Paul perished as a martyr (ca. 60–64), possibly in Nero's persecution of Christians.

PAULINE THEOLOGY

Of equal significance with Paul's work as a missionary and leader of the Christian movement were his bold new patterns of thought. More than any other figure, Paul was the father of Christian theology. Not theoretical or systematic, Paul's thinking was the plain and personal response of his mind to the events in which he played an important part. In simplest terms, Paul was a Jew who found the Messiah in Jesus. The phrases "Jesus is Christ" and "Jesus is Lord" run like a refrain through Paul's writings. To be sure, his thought showed significant influence from Greek mystery religions and Greek philosophy, but the core of it remained thoroughly Hebraic. His God was the God of his Jewish fathers, namely, the sovereign Lord who created and ruled the universe, who had spoken to humanity through Moses and the prophets but who had now, according to Paul, spoken a new and decisive word in Jesus Christ.

For Paul, Christianity was thus a new covenant, a new revelation of God to humanity. As the old covenant centered in the giving of the Torah to Moses at

Mount Sinai, so the new covenant centered in Jesus Christ. Paul devoted much thought and many words to the interpretation of Christ. Frequently he used the term *Lord* (the Greek term *Kyrios*, meaning "Lord," had the basic meaning of a higher being possessing authority), saying, "Jesus is Lord." But going beyond this, Paul came at length to think of Christ as a pre-existent divine figure who had condescended to take on human form, who in his death struggled victoriously with cosmic forces of evil, and who now reigned with God in heavenly places.[55] By a kind of personal faith and trust amounting, according to some statements, to an identification with Christ, his human followers might win a similar victory over sin and death in their own lives.

This Pauline gospel of a dying and rising savior bore unmistakable similarity to many of the Greek and Roman mystery cults which had similar stories and saviors. Paul's description of the eucharist as a Christian mystery lent further support to this view. But there were notable differences as well. Paul's story of the dying and rising God was not fiction but history, to which many Christians could testify as witnesses. Further, neither Paul nor any other Christian leader separated the theme of mystical union with Christ from ethical life. A person who was "in Christ" was expected to show the fruits of faith in ethical life.[56] According to Paul, one apprehends or lays hold upon Christ by means of faith. By faith he did not mean propositional belief or creedal assent, but rather a turning of the heart in trust and allegiance to God in Christ. In Paul's mind, faith and works stood in polar opposition. By means of works humans sought to earn God's favor, to scale heaven in their own human power. Paul argued that the Torah, or Jewish law, called on humans to do exactly this.[57] Realizing the impossibility of this, a person in helplessness turns humbly to God to receive the grace that cannot possibly be earned or deserved. This crucial human act of saying a humble, receptive "yes" to God is what Paul meant by faith.

Paul taught that from grace apprehended by faith sprang freedom.[58] Freedom for Paul meant initially and primarily freedom from the Torah and its demands. In former times, the Torah had been a custodian or schoolmaster to Christ, but now that Christ had come, the Torah is null and void. More positively, freedom was for Paul the spirit-given power to live as "sons of God," as God calls humans. Morality, Paul taught, was not a condition of faith, but its fruit. As the fruit of the tree is to its roots, so is ethics to faith. This metaphor, used repeatedly by Jesus, was also Paul's view of this matter. Moral qualities, he said many times, were fruits of the spirit.[59] For Paul and for Christ, the content of ethics is neighbor-love. Paul frequently characterized this love simply and eloquently by pointing to the figure of Christ as its great paradigm.

THE FOURTH GOSPEL

Paul's importance in the New Testament Christian movement was second only to that of Christ; yet his view of the new faith was by no means the only one in the New Testament community. Of particular importance for its contrast to Paul was the view of the anonymous fourth Gospel. It is traditionally attributed to the disciple John, but modern biblical study has shown this to be highly improbable. Writing around the year 100 CE, probably in the city of Ephesus, its author appears thoroughly familiar with the language and thought of current Greek philosophy and religion. He avails himself of many of the terms and ideas of current Greek thought.[60]

Jesus was interpreted as the incarnate Word, or Logos, of God. The term *logos*, meaning "word," "thought," "rational discussion," had been common in philosophic reflection from the sixth-century BCE figure of Heraclitus. It had been given new and distinctive meaning in the first century by such thinkers as Philo Judaeus of Alexandria, who interpreted the Logos as a cosmic intermediary between God and humans, active in all creation. In effect, for Philo the Logos designated that aspect of deity which is active in all creative acitivity. The word *logos* was to attain widespread use in the next century in Gnostic philosophies. *Gnosticism* is a modern scholar's word for a religious and philosophical movement widely popular in the Greco-Roman world which envisaged the world as divided into matter and spirit and which sought by secret *gnosis*, or "knowledge," to save humans from matter and bring them to the spiritual world. It was this widely prevalent idea which the Fourth Gospel appropriated and used for the interpretation of Jesus. It asserted in effect that the basic meaning and structure of the universe was incarnated in Jesus' life.

Two motives may be observed in this novel interpretation of Christ. Clearly the author was adapting his language to that of the Hellenistic people to whom he was speaking. However, in this language he was attempting to speak his own message. His language, in short, was Gnostic (or protognostic), but the content of what he sought to say, namely, that the divine Logos had become human flesh, was utterly antignostic. It was fundamentally Hebraic.

The author's portrait of Jesus as incarnate Logos took liberties with widely accepted facts and diverged widely from the synoptic portrait of Christ's life. Jesus was interpreted as a pre-existent, divine figure, descended from heaven, who moved mysteriously through human life, speaking in oracles and ever-conscious of his impending sacrificial death. The fourth Gospel was destined to have widespread influence on the interpretation of Christian faith. Its view of Christ as the incarnate Word became the foundation of Christian orthodoxy in creed and theology. This book has also been a veritable fountainhead of Christian mysticism.

VARIATIONS ON A COMMON THEME

Paul and John were not the only theologians of the New Testament community. Other diverging interpretations of Christ and God were not slow to appear. For example, the synoptic Gospels have been treated as primary historical sources for the life of Jesus; yet in their time they also represented a distinctive theological view. The second coming of Christ having failed to occur, Christians began to concentrate attention on his first coming; and it was in this connection that they wrote these Gospels. Theologically the synoptics were distinctive for their emphasis on the human life of Jesus.

Others, however, clung tenaciously to the idea of a second coming, or *parousia*, of Christ. In times of persecution, their views took on added relevance. So it was that during the first empire-wide persecution of Christians, under Domitian in 95–96, the Book of Revelation made its appearance. Its bizarre and vivid images, which followed the stylized patterns of apocalyptic writing and speaking, have proved a veritable gold mine of images for Christian poets and visionaries of subsequent times. In terms of its religious teaching Revelation, like Daniel in the Old Testament, was a tract for bad times, assuring that in bad times as in good, God still reigns, asserting his dominion through Christ. Revelation pictures Christ as a military commander descending from heaven on a white horse and with flaming sword to defeat antichrist and bring in God's kingdom.[61]

There were still other varieties of faith and thought in the New Testament, such as the letter of James, with its eminently practical, moral emphases and its polemic against a faith that does not result in works, and the letter to the Hebrews, with its interpretation of Christ in terms of the Old Testament sacrificial ritual and its exhortation to remain faithful under stress and persecution.[62] There were two letters of Peter, each with its own distinctive variations on the common New Testament themes of God in Christ.

CHRISTIANITY IN THE ANCIENT WORLD, 100–500 CE

CHURCH AND EMPIRE

By 100 CE, Christianity had found its way throughout the Greco-Roman world and had undergone persecution by Nero and Domitian. For many Romans, the Christian movement was only one more of the "oriental superstitions" which had recently flooded the empire with bizarre rites and irrational beliefs. The Romans would have been glad to let the matter rest at the point, for they were tolerant people. However, there were persistent and ugly rumors about the Christians. One was that they worshipped a king other than Caesar. Often, too, the Christians refused to perform the rites to Caesar—rites which most Romans regarded as no more religious than the modern flag salute. Many Christians refused military service and public office. Christians often incurred the charge of atheism for their scornful attitude toward the old gods. There were also ugly rumors of cannibalism at Christian worship.[63]

The Christians were willing, as they put it, to call the empire *good*, but not to call it *God*, or divine, that is, to find the whole meaning of human existence in the empire. To do so would in effect deify Roman values or the Roman way of life, which for the Christians would be a violation of the first commandment.

The conflict of Christ and Caesar extended over three centuries and ended with Christianity as the official religion of Constantine's empire. While the conflict at times involved systematic campaigns throughout the empire, at other times it was a matter of sporadic local outbreaks of public prejudice against the new and strange faith. In 64 CE, Nero burnt Christians in Rome, but there is no evidence that his persecution extended beyond the capital city. In 95, Domitian attempted a more systematic action throughout the empire. Trajan (98–117) is known for his letter to Pliny the Younger advising what both men must have regarded as a mild and lenient course against the Christian nuisance. Christians were not to be hunted out, and if they were willing to sacrifice, they were to be acquitted. Only if they persisted in their refusal to perform the prescribed rites were they to be punished.[64]

Two emperors who followed Trajan—Hadrian (117–138) and Antoninus Pius (138–161)—followed a similar policy. Marcus Aurelius (161–180) initiated a sharper period of persecution. There was also a continuing tradition of local

Catacomb of Saint Callisto, Rome, Italy. (Scala/Art Resource.)

mob violence against Christians. However, it was not until Decius's edict in 250 that a systematic persecution aiming at complete destruction of Christianity was undertaken. Decius's object was to reassert the worship of the old gods who had made the empire great, and in effect to reassert the unity of Rome against this new, subversive force. There were many martyrdoms, and also many who renounced Christian faith under pressure. It was for Christianity a fearful time of trial, lasting, with intermissions, from 250 to 259. Christian assemblies were forbidden, churches and cemeteries confiscated, and church officials banished or executed. Yet the Christian movement emerged from the struggle stronger than ever.

The struggle of the empire against Christianity was resumed in earnest by the soldier-emperor Diocletian (284–311). Viewing with growing alarm the close-knit organization of the church, Diocletian acted in 303 and 304 with a series of edicts which destroyed churches, confiscated sacred books, and forced all suspected Christians to sacrifice to the emperor. Again, as with Decius, there were many martyrs and many who "lapsed." The severity of the persecution varied widely among the local officials who carried out the edicts. But again, persecution actually strengthened what it sought to destroy.

Diocletian's retirement in 311 CE was followed immediately by an edict by Constantine and Licinius granting the church actual toleration. Meanwhile, among the four contestants for the imperial throne, Constantine took decisive action. Before the battle of the Malvian Bridge, north of Rome, in 312, he believed that he saw in a dream the name of Christ with the words "By this sign you will conquer." Hastily painting the monogram *XP* (*Christ reigns*) on his helmet, he won his battle. Believing that the Christian God had given him the victory, from this time onward he was in all practical respects a Christian, though he delayed his own baptism until his deathbed. The edict of Milan in 313 gave Christianity full equality with other religions. In edicts which followed, the Christian church was given an increasingly preferred position, until in 319 heathen or non-Christian sacrifices were forbidden.

The new position of Christianity was a milestone in history. Christians might now serve their God openly, without fear of persecution. But now, and for the next thousand years, there was equal and opposite peril of being an established faith. Now that it was legal and fashionable to be a Christian, all the perils of compromise and nominal allegiance presented themselves. As the issue is sometimes stated, the question is whether, at the time of Constantine, church conquered empire, or the opposite.

EARLY CHRISTIAN THEOLOGIES

The section of this chapter on the New Testament has noted the beginnings of the unceasing activity of stating, interpreting, and defending Christian faith. In the historical period now under consideration, roughly from 100 to 500 CE, two main problems emerged: (1) What is the relation of Christian faith to its alternatives? (2) What is the nature of Christian faith? The answers to these two questions were inextricably bound up with each other.

One type of answer was given by the *Apologists*. As Christian faith came increasingly under Roman criticism, it was natural that explanations and defenses should be undertaken. They appeared in a form of writing called *apologia* (not an apology) for Christianity. Since the writers were for the most part converted pagan philosophers, notably Stoics and Platonists, they tended to construe Christianity as true philosophy. Having searched elsewhere in vain for an adequate philosophy, they found Christianity adequate or true.

Among this group of Christian philosophers were such men as Quadratus and later Aristides, both of Athens, Melito, Bishop of Sardis, the unknown author of the Epistle to Diognetus, and most notable of all, Justin Martyr. Justin, who was martyred ca. 165 CE, was born in the Palestinian city of Schechem and spent his adult life wandering among the philosophic isms of his age. He was by turns an adherent and teacher of Stoicism, Aristotelianism, Pythagoreanism, and Platonism. In his apology he describes the way in which, while he was a Platonist, his attention was directed to the Hebrew prophets and their message.[65]

Justin was a morally minded man for whom the righteous nature of the biblical God was attractive. He regarded as grossly immoral the doctrine that God was neutral between good and evil. The new life to which humans are called by Christ is a life of love for God and for one's fellow beings, said Justin. Judaism had much of this ethical spirit but was encumbered by its vast legalism. Christianity is superior in having the figure and teachings of Jesus Christ, who moreover had come in fulfillment of Old Testament prophecy.

Justin made effective and extensive use of the Logos in his interpretation of Christ. In effect, the Logos is that aspect of the divine nature by which humans are guided to think rationally and live rationally and righteously. By this power, Justin argued, both the philosophers of Greece and the prophets of Israel lived and taught; any rational being, even though professing atheism, lives by this power.[66] While universal in scope, the Logos is incarnate uniquely in Christ. So it is that Christ's coming enables humans to banish ignorance and sin and to achieve a new heart and mind. Human freedom and responsibility and reason were thus primary aspects of Justin's theology. It was Christianity which gave those qualities their highest expression.

One of the most influential and distinctive interpretations of the Christian faith emerged from the catechetical school of Alexandria. Among the most famous educational institutions of the early church, this school grew up in close connection with Alexandria's famous museum and university. It participated fully in the Platonic thought which was the dominant philosophy of Alexandria. Founded by a converted Stoic named Pantaenus, and carried on successively by Clement (150–220) and Origen (185–251), this school became famous throughout the ancient world and made a lasting impact on Christian theology. Clement taught two sources of truth, scripture and reason, with one divine Logos inspiring and guiding both. In Christ the Logos is uniquely active, making him the supreme teacher of human minds as well as the high priest of their souls.

Clement gave the highest place to the Christian intellectual, or as he said, the Christian *Gnostic*. To be sure, the simple Christian might save his or her soul by faith, but better and higher than this was the state of the Christian intellectual who went on from faith to wisdom and for whom salvation consisted in correct knowledge of God. Clement and his successors employed an allegorical interpretation of scripture as a means of finding faith's higher, hidden meanings within the pages of the Bible.

Origen was Clement's student, but a man of enormously greater boldness and capacity of mind than his teacher. While Origen was an avid student of the Bible, he was also a philosopher and theologian who used the Platonic heritage for the interpretation of Christian faith.[67] One of Origen's many achievements was an original and distinctive interpretation of the Christ as Logos. The problem of the interpretation of Christ had been a thorny one from the beginning of Christianity. If God is one, how is Christ related to him? If Christ be regarded as the Logos, does this involve two gods? These and other questions arose in the minds of philosophically minded Christians. Origen met these issues by teaching that the Logos was begotten of God eternally and not created. Both Logos and God were divine and indeed were embraced within a single divine unity. Hence worship might properly be given to the Logos as an aspect of God. However, Origen's usage of words was by no means consistent, and he left a legacy of theological questions which the church was to struggle over for several centuries.

Origen's cosmology divided the world Platonically into spiritual and material realms, and he frequently seemed to imply that spirit was good and matter evil. Humans on earth were good insofar as they were spiritual; but they were also imprisoned in matter. In addition to human beings, Origen taught that the universe was populated by many rational spirits who had immediate and unceasing communion with God. Salvation for Origen was the restoration of humans to a realm of pure spirit; and he taught that this restoration would extend to all people. Hell, or to speak more precisely purgatory, was a consequence of wrong choices, and in the end it will be emptied, and all will be saved. At the end God will indeed be all in all.[68]

A different and opposite kind of theology was illustrated by Tertullian of Carthage (150–222). By profession a lawyer, he brought many of the ideas of Roman law into his interpretation of Christian faith. The first church father to write in Latin rather than Greek, he commanded a terse, epigrammatic style and has often been called the *father of Latin theology*. Tertullian was intense and rigorous in spirit, and his theology expressed his personality. He viewed Christ as God's great paradox, surpassing and confounding the highest philosophical wisdom. Such attitudes led Tertullian to a low estimate of human reason and philosophy. "What is there in common between Athens and Jerusalem? What between the Academy and the Church?" he asked scornfully.[69] It is a fact, however, that Tertullian's own writings borrowed more than he knew from Stoic philosophy.

Tertullian possessed an intense sense of sin and so was led to reflect upon the nature of sin and grace. Grace is conferred, Tertullian declared, through the sacraments of the church. Out of his lawyer's experience he suggested that just as three persons (*personae*) might share title to property (*substantio*) so in the godhead there were three persons and one substance. Later trinitarian theology was destined to follow his lead. Tertullian's austere puritanical nature led him away from orthodox Christianity to the Montanist heresy, yet Latin theology bore the indelible marks of his thought. He has been the archetypal model of many since his time who have sought to understand faith and reason, religion and philosophy, as polar opposites.

HERESY AND ORTHODOXY

As Christianity made its way in the Greco-Roman world, it was inevitable that many varieties of theological interpretation should develop, some of them clearly incompatible with each other, and some viewed, rightly or wrongly, as distortions of the faith. Out of such tendencies grew the idea of heresy and its opposite, orthodoxy. It is significant to note that these ideas were clearly related to the theoretical or theological orientation of early Christianity. Judaism, developing its distinctive forms in this same period and region, had little or no sense of orthodox belief or creed, largely because it placed primary emphasis on doing or practice rather than on belief.

Modern students of religion are likely to deplore the very ideas of heresy and orthodoxy as constituting an enterprise in totalitarian thought control. They will be right about important aspects of the early Christian attitude, but they will also miss an especially important issue. The enterprise of formulating and maintaining correct belief was important in a hostile world, if the new religion was to survive at all. If it was to maintain itself as a distinctive faith, Christianity must possess what modern people might term a *party line*.

The earliest Christian confessions, dating from New Testament times and used as baptismal formulas, were simple statements such as "Jesus is Lord." By the middle of the second century the simple formula had grown to a series of fixed questions and answers, having many of the phrases of the Apostles' Creed, though the final formulation of the Apostles' Creed cannot be traced to a date earlier than the eighth century.[70]

Many of the issues expressed or implied in the Apostles' Creed are those of the second-century struggle of Christianity with Gnosticism and, more particularly, with the teachings of Marcion in the Roman church. As we have previously observed, *gnosticism* is a modern scholar's word for a cluster of philosophic and religious tendencies of the later Greco-Roman world. Something like Gnosticism has already been noted as the Hellenistic context of the fourth Gospel. In general, the Gnostics maintained a dualist cosmology in which the world was bifurcated into a realm of spirit, or mind, which was esteemed both good and real, and a realm of matter, or flesh, believed to be evil or unreal or both. The realm of spirit was believed to be populated by large numbers of beings, over all of whom ruled a remote, unknowable, transcendent deity. For Gnostics, human personality was regarded as a good spirit imprisoned in an evil body, and salvation was thought to consist of rescuing the spirit from its prison. This might be done by imparting esoteric knowledge (gnosis), which each Gnostic teacher and school claimed to possess. Gnosticism also often involved an ascetic morality; since flesh is evil, it must be mortified or suppressed.

While many Gnostics had no connection with either Christianity or Judaism, some of them sought to infiltrate these monotheistic religions with their teachings. For Christian Gnostics an important belief was that Christ was the divine Logos, the chief intermediary between God and humans. However, in the Gnostic viewpoint it was unthinkable that the Logos should take on evil and delusory human flesh. There the Gnostics characteristically denied this incarnation.[71] The human life of Christ was apparent but not real, asserted the Christian Gnostics. Christ hovered over mortal life, never really participating in birth, suffering, and death. Some Gnostics such as Marcion of Rome also denied that the God of creation is the true Lord and God of all. Rather this Jewish God who dubiously created the material world is a minor denizen of the spiritual realm.

The Christian church set itself against these Gnostic views in such affirmations of the Apostles' Creed as "God the Father Almighty, creator of heaven and earth."[72] By implication this was an affirmation of the goodness of all God's creation, material as well as spiritual. Similar affirmations concerning Jesus' birth, suffering, and death were directed against the Gnostic denial of the incarnation. So too, the assertion in the Apostles' Creed of the resurrection of the dead affirmed the salvation of the whole human being and not simply the discarnate spirit. It is thus significant to see that against this ancient heresy, the church affirmed the humanity of Christ and the goodness and reality of material things.

A radically different kind of heresy arose in the second century—a kind which has recurred many times since in Christian history. The second-century version was called *Montanism*, after its leader, Montanus, who prior to his conversion to Christianity had been a priest of Cybele, the great mother goddess of the ancient Near Eastern world. Montanus declared himself to be the vehicle through whom the Holy Spirit spoke. His was ecstatic utterance of a sort familiar in the New Testament "speaking in tongues." He also proclaimed that the present evil age was soon to end and that the New Jerusalem would soon be set up in his native town of Pepuza in Phrygia. His followers disposed of their worldly possessions and responsibilities and journeyed to Pepuza to await the return of Christ in glory. Montanism taught an austere morality. Food and clothing were kept simple, and Christians were required to abstain from worldly amusements. In a time when the church had begun its agelong compromise with the world, this moral rigor had a genuine appeal to sensitive spirits. In an age when formalism had displaced personal conviction, Montanist ideas of the Spirit appealed. Even the great Tertullian was led away into this heresy.[73]

The church acted to condemn Montanism, though a small Montanist following lasted on for many centuries. Meanwhile another kind of issue came increasingly to the center of the stage. Previous sections of this chapter have observed the Johannine idea of Christ as the incarnate Word of God as it continued and developed, especially among such Alexandrine fathers as Origen. Controversies of many sorts arose concerning the relation of Christ to God and to humans. A particularly sharp conflict arose in early fourth-century Alexandria over the views of Arius, who in seeking to preserve the monotheism of Christianity taught that Christ, while firstborn of all creation and God's agent in the creation, was nonetheless a created being. As he worked out his ideas, Arius was forced to the conclusion that Christ was neither truly divine nor truly human, but a third substance inserted between God and human beings.

These conclusions seemed particularly unsatisfactory to Arius's bishop, Alexander, and to the bishop's secretary, Athanasius. The controversy gathered momentum and spread, until Constantine was led to convene a general council of the church in order to restore peace among the quarreling Christians. The council met at Nicaea in May 325; it has often been regarded as the most important council in Christian history. There were three main parties, including a small group of supporters of Alexander and Athanasius and a large middle group with no strong convictions either way and more interested in harmony than in theology.[74]

After rejecting a formulation of Arius, the council proceeded to an amended form of a compromise creed offered by Bishop Eusebius of Caesarea. Among the insertions were phrases like "begotten not made" and 'of one essence with the Father" (*homoousion*), which were clearly anti-Arian in both intention and significance. The council was led in the end to affirm belief

> ...in one Lord Jesus Christ, the only-begotten Son of God, Begotten of the Father before all the ages, Light of Light, true God of true God, begotten not made, of one substance with the Father, through whom all things were made; who for us men and for our salvation came down from heaven and was incarnate of the Holy Spirit and the Virgin Mary, and became man...[75]

Explicitly condemned by the Council of Nicaea were those (Arians) who said of Christ, "There was a time when he was not," or "He came into existence from what was not," or "The son of God is of a different substance from the Father." Thus Christ was definitively declared to be both God and man, both divine and human—a view which has prevailed in traditional Christianity ever since.

Once this result was generally accepted, a further question arose: "How could this be so? How are the divine and human elements related to each other in Christ?" Again there were many answers, much conflict. For example, Apollinarius (d. 392) taught that the divine Logos took the place of a human mind in Christ. Seeking to avoid a double personality, Apollinarius did less than justice to Christ's human nature. Theodore of Moposuesta argued that the union of two natures in Christ was one of moral attitude rather than metaphysical substance. Following this view, Theodore's student and disciple, Nestorius, denied that Mary was the mother of God (*theotokos*), since from her was born only the human nature of Christ.

After apparently interminable arguments and anathemas, the church at the Council of Chalcedon (451) declared for two natures of Christ, divine and human, perfectly blended (the document does not say how!) in one person:

> ...one and the same Christ, Son, Lord, Only-begotten, recognized in two natures without confusion, without change, without division, without separation; the distinction of natures being in no way annulled by the union, but rather the characteristics of each nature being preserved and coming together to form one person and subsistence, not as parted or separated into two persons, but one and the same Son and Only-begotten God the Word, Lord Jesus Christ....[76]

So it was that the Christian church formulated its faith. It is a long distance from the New Testament formula "Jesus is Lord" to Nicaea and Chalcedon, yet the reader can see that Christians walked this road in order to guard the central conviction concerning Christ from misinterpretations which they believed endangered or undercut it. It is possible to understand the concerns of the creed makers, even though many modern people do not share their formulations or sympathize with their attitudes and anathemas.

DEVELOPMENT OF EPISCOPAL AUTHORITY

The church of New Testament times was highly informal in both organization and worship. The apostles were leaders in worship and administration; in both aspects of the church's life this leadership was charismatically exercised. However, with the passage of time, all this changed. Resident bishops claiming authority by apostolic succession supplanted charismatic leaders, and worship moved in the direction of formality. As has been recently said: "About 50, he was of the church who had received baptism and the Holy Spirit and called Jesus, Lord; about 180 he who acknowledged the rule of faith, the New Testament canon and the authority of bishops."[77]

At first, usage varied widely in different regions as to selection of bishops and the nature of their office. However, as time passed, there was greater uniformity in the office and also greater concentration of power. A clear line was drawn between clergy and laity; the ministry came to be not only a full-time occupation, but a vocation set apart by special ordination and committed to a different and higher standard of moral life. The hierarchical organization of the church developed step by step.

One step of greatest importance was the theology and practice of Cyprian, Bishop of Carthage during the Decian persecution. During the initial phases of this persecution, some Christians lapsed from the faith, performing the rites to

Caesar and renouncing Christianity in order to avoid torture and death. When the terror had passed, many of these people sought reentry into the church. A crucial question was who had the authority to receive them back. In some cases presbyters had done so. Cyprian attacked this practice and maintained that only a bishop possessed this authority. As he dealt with this practical issue, his whole view of the church as centering in the authority of bishops took its distinctive shape. In his view, the episcopal authority is unitary in nature, but is exercised independently by each bishop, all bishops being united by the Holy Spirit. This principle implied the equality of all bishops as well as a harmonious order among them. It also clearly implied subjection to the bishop's authority as the mark of a true Christian. "He can no longer have God for his father who has not the Church for his mother," argued Cyprian, adding significantly "if anyone could escape who was outside the Ark of Noah, then he may also escape who shall be outside the Church."[78] So began the doctrine that salvation is impossible outside the church. Cyprian went so far as to argue that since heretics have no genuine part in the church, heretical martyrs would gain no salvation.

Cyprian qualified his view of the equal authority of all bishops by speaking of Rome as "the chief church whence episcopal unity takes its source."[79] Others had said similar things, and still others pushed the primacy of Rome still further, until at length the bishop of Rome emerged in theory and practice as the primate of all Christendom. The authority and prestige of the Roman church had always been great, for Rome was the capital of the world; also, according to tradition the Roman church had been founded by Peter, to whom Christ had given the keys of heaven and hell. The authority of the Roman church was enhanced by its successful stand against the heresy of Marcionism. At the end of the second century, Victor, bishop of Rome, excommunicated protesting churches of Asia Minor in a dispute over the proper date of Easter.[80] Thus Rome's power continued to grow.

It grew even more rapidly as the empire declined, leaving a vacuum of leadership which was filled by powerful bishops of Rome, such as the fifth-century popes Innocent I (402–417) and Leo I (440–461). Innocent specifically claimed authority over all Christendom. Leo not only repeated and reinforced these claims by his elaboration of the primacy of Peter among the apostles and the Petrine succession of the popes; he also acted for the people of Rome in dealing with Huns and Vandals who invaded the city. It was Pope Gelasius (492–496) who wrote to the eastern emperor, "there are...two by whom principally this world is ruled: the sacred authority of the pontiffs and the royal power."[81]

WORSHIP AND SACRAMENTS

Christian worship and devotional practices, as well as church organization, underwent similar development in the direction of formalism. A central feature was an increasing formalism in the celebration of the eucharist. From the charismatic, spirit-filled celebration of New Testament times, both practice and theory assumed ever-increasing formalism. The eucharist was to be celebrated only by properly ordained priests, and participation was preceded by a period of catechetical instruction and was limited to members of the church. Increasingly, people believed and asserted that the bread and wine were the body and blood of Christ, which would impart eternal life. The eucharist was increasingly regarded as a reenactment of Christ's sacrifice on the cross. It became the central and crucial act of Christian worship.

Worship also consisted of Bible reading, prayers, hymns, and a discourse, or sermon. It was customarily held on Sunday, but also on other days as well. The great event of the year was Easter, celebrating Christ's resurrection. The forty days of Lent leading up to Easter, and even more the days of the week immediately preceding, commemorated Christ's suffering and death. Easter, by contrast, was a time of rejoicing. Prayers for the dead and the veneration of martyrs were an increasingly important theme of Christian worship.

Second only to the eucharist in importance was the sacrament of baptism. Pre-Christian in origin, it was taken over by the church and adapted to Christian uses. Originally immersion was the general practice, but gradually it was supplanted by sprinkling or pouring. It was administered to converts and to young Christians as they came of age, though as time passed, infant baptism became more and more the common practice. Baptism was believed to cleanse the soul from original sin and to symbolize the soul's entrance into the church as the body of Christ.

The problem of the forgiveness of sins was a persistent issue. Confession was made, at first publicly to the congregation, then later privately to a priest. With the increasing authority of the clergy came the power of the priest to grant absolution. This development was accompanied by prescribed lists of sins and prescribed practices of penance.

MONASTICISM

With the spread and popularization of Christianity came many new problems involving moral and religious compromise with the world. The problem of compromise was a primary motivation for the monastic movement. Rigorous and ascetic practices had been aspects of Christianity from the beginning. As time passed, sensitive Christians sought with varying degrees of consistency to renounce the world altogether. Saint Anthony (b. 250 CE), often regarded as the originator of Christian monasticism, lived for many years as an ascetic in his own Egyptian village before taking up a hermit's life in the desert. Pachomius (b. 292) introduced a significant change by gathering groups of hermits together into communities; ten of these communities existed at the time of his death.

The normative rule of monasticism in the west was created by Benedict of Nursia (b. 480 CE).[82] It was notable for its combination of rigor and common sense. Benedict's monks were among the first in the West to affirm the dignity of labor. They were important also for their intellectual pursuits. Their three-fold discipline of work, study, and prayer placed Benedictine monasticism among the primary formative impulses of western civilization.

EARLY CHRISTIANITY IN TRANSITION

By the end of the fifth century after Christ, the decline of Rome was a fact too plain for denial. By this time, too, the foundations of the Christian church had been firmly laid; and the historical edifice erected on these foundations, if not complete, had put up many of its main structures. Out of the ruins of Greco-Roman antiquity emerged a new culture or civilization called the *West*, in which Christianity was destined to play a central role. This story will be related in subsequent chapters, notably Chapters 15 and 16.

One figure who will claim out attention in Chapter 15 demands at least mention at this point. Saint Augustine (354–430 CE) was bishop, pastor, and mystic, but above all a theologian and philosopher whose systematic thought gave synoptic expression to Christian faith and life. As we shall see in Chapter 15, Augustine's thought looked forward to the long medieval period of Christianity and, indeed, to the whole course of the West; but here it is important to note that it also provided a remarkable synoptic summary for what had gone before.

Augustine had wandered among the faiths and philosophies of his time before coming to orthodox Christianity, and his thought shows these influences, notably that of Platonism. In his theology, Plato and Plotinus are fused with the Bible in a new unity. Augustine's theology drew together the previous church fathers, correcting some ideas, rejecting others, and uniting all in a comprehensive system. His view of human life found autobiographical expression in the *Confessions*; and in the *City of God* he gave philosophical expression for the first time to a linear-dramatic view of history. We shall return to Augustine and his philosophical theology in Chapter 15.

EASTERN ORTHODOX CHRISTIANITY

Almost from the beginning of Christianity there was an observable cleavage between east and west. It was as though an invisible line had been drawn through a map of the Christian world, extending from Europe in the north through the Adriatic Sea, across the Mediterranean Sea to Africa in the south. To the west of this line lay Spain, Gaul, and Italy, centering on the western capital, Rome; east of it lay the Balkan Peninsula, Asia Minor, and the Middle East, with the eastern capital, Constantinople. The Christianity of the west tended to be active, pragmatic, and legal, while that of the east tended to be contemplative, mystical, and passive. As centuries passed, east and west drifted further apart. Their differences widened and deepened until two forms of Christianity emerged as historic facts.

From the first, some eastern bishops resisted the claims to primacy of the bishop of Rome. In the east the pope's pronouncements were often ignored and sometimes openly flouted. At length, the papal claims, so central to western, or Roman Catholic, Christianity, came in the east to be regarded as schismatic. These trends were reinforced by events of secular history. As the western empire sank into decline, the papacy was thrust into the vacuum of power, wielding both political and religious leadership for the people of Rome and Italy. In the east there was no such decline, the imperial structure being revived and maintained by such able rulers as Justinian (527–565 CE). The Byzantine emperors of Constantinople held the church in close embrace, thus in effect creating the intimate and dependent relation of church to state which was to become characteristic of Eastern Orthodoxy.

One of the first results of this relation was a new compound of faith and culture often called *Byzantine civilization*. This new synthesis had significant features, ranging from the law code of Justinian to the new style of architecture brilliantly illustrated by Justinian's new church, Hagia Sophia ("holy wisdom"). It was also poignantly expressed in the mosaic art which adorned the walls of Hagia Sophia and other churches. Byzantine civilization provided the cultural context for the development of Eastern Orthodox Christianity.

Another notable difference between east and west lay in their responses to the ecumenical councils of the church. Beginning with the Council of Nicaea in 325 and extending through seven such meetings to the Second Council of Nicaea in 767, they were regarded in the east as primary and authoritative sources of doctrine or teaching. While the west respected the councils, it dared to disagree with or even to ignore some of them.

The coming of the Muslims in the seventh and eighth centuries posed serious problems, military, political, and religious, for all Christendom. However, these problems were more urgent in the east than in the west. Constantinople or Byzantium itself was placed under Muslim siege many times before its final fall to the Muslims in 1453 CE. As Muslims captured extensive regions inhabited by Eastern Orthodox Christians, these people became minority groups within Muslim culture, a fact that greatly affected the nature of their Christian faith.

The alienation between east and west was widened and deepened during the seventh and eighth centuries by controversies over the *filioque* clause in the creed and the use of icons in Christian churches. The former problem was created by the insertion, in the west, of *filioque*, "…and the Son…," in the creed, asserting thereby that the Holy Spirit proceeds from the Father "and the Son." Eastern Christians, while not necessarily opposed to this interpretation, nevertheless regarded the insertion as improper. The iconoclastic controversy was aroused by a decree of the eastern emperor, Leo III, in 726, banning the use of icons, both pictures and images, in Christian churches. Leo's motive was apparently to purify the church of pagan elements which had crept in, but he stirred up violent opposition in both regions of the empire. In the east he and his successors were able to force compliance, though at times military power was required. In the west, resistance to the iconoclastic decree was more general and more successful. The pope excommunicated iconoclasts. The issue continued in one form or another for a century or more. The Second Council of Nicaea expounded what came to be the accepted eastern position on icons, that they might be used and honored as visible respresentations of the invisible power and reality of God. Yet from this time onward the eastern church limited itself to two-dimensional pictures, or *ikons* as they came to be called. Meanwhile both two- and three-dimensional art forms continued in the west.

In the east, ikons or pictures of Christ and the Virgin Mary and other saints became a highly significant and characteristic form of both art and religious veneration in church and home. Expressions of veneration range from kissing to genuflexion. Miracles have centered in famous ikons. Theologians have added that these material forms testify to the spiritualization of matter in the Christian community.

The definitive break between east and west came in 1054 CE over the issue of the rights of Roman Catholic Christians in Constantinople. The patriarch closed Roman Catholic churches in that city. Papal messengers responded with a bull of excommunication from the pope, deposited on the high altar of Hagia Sophia. The patriarch replied in kind with a decree anathematizing the pope, and the breach was final. A first step toward rapprochement was taken in 1963 when Pope Paul VI met and embraced the patriarch of Constantinople.

Meanwhile, geographically the eastern and western churches continued to move farther apart. While western Christianity moved northward and westward

Interior of Hagia Sophia, Istanbul, Turkey. (F. B. Grunzweig/Photo Researchers.)

into France, Germany, and Great Britain, eastern Christianity pushed into Russia. So it was that in 1453 CE, when Constantinople, the second Rome, fell before the Muslims, the capital of eastern Christianity was moved to Moscow, which called itself the *third Rome*.

The divergent ways of faith which emerged in east and west present a bewildering pattern of similarities and differences. Four main contrasts may be briefly observed.

1. As noted above, the eastern church was bound to government in relations both close and dependent. As will be seen in Chapters 15 and 16, on Roman Catholicism and Protestantism, the relation of church to state in the west was neither as close nor as dependent as in the east. In western Christendom, many people over many centuries fought with swords and with ideas to maintain the independence of the church. One result has been a tradition in the west of religious criticism of society, which is significantly less evident in the east.

2. Related to these issues have been different views in east and west concerning the nature of the church. In the east there is no pope or supreme ruler over all the church; rather each of the fourteen or more national churches is self-ruled, or *autocephalous*. A kind of big brotherhood, or informal primacy, has at times been exercised by the patriarchs of Constantinople or of Moscow. However, no power except that of influence over the whole eastern church resides in these offices.

   Eastern Orthodoxy agrees with Roman Catholicism and Protestantism in calling the church the body of Christ. Of these three the first two, but not the third, hold the church to possess a divinely given infallibility. However, Eastern Orthodoxy differs from Rome in having no organ of infallibility. Since infallibility exists in the church in general, it has little effective meaning. Eastern Orthodox churches claim to be holy, apostolic, and catholic Christianity; they also believe that both Roman Catholicism and Protestantism have deviated from these divinely given norms.

   Eastern Orthodox teaching regarding the church differs notably from that of the west in emphasis. It regards the church as a divine mystery which is the central fact of human history and whose eventual, or eschatological, aim is the full divinization of the man. At the center of the church is the mysterious God-man, Jesus Christ. The church communicates his divine life to its members through the sacraments. Like Roman Catholicism, Eastern Orthodoxy celebrates seven sacraments. However, its list differs, for it includes anointing, or chrismation, and places the Roman sacrament of confirmation under baptism. For both Eastern Orthodoxy and Roman Catholicism the central sacrament is the eucharist. Yet there are notable differences of interpretation. For Eastern Orthodoxy, the eucharist is the celebration of the incarnation of God in Christ. It is thus by implication an anticipation of the eventual divinization of man.

3. Another notable difference between east and west is the virtual absence in the former of any continuing tradition of ongoing theological discussion and

thinking. By contrast, the west continued for many centuries to argue and discuss theological problems. Eastern Orthodox theology was summed up in the system of John of Damascus, who lived in the first half of the eighth century. His book *The Fountain of Knowledge* gave definitive expression to the Christianized Neoplatonism which had long been popular in the east. After John of Damascus there was intellectual stagnation. The creative energies of eastern Christianity turned from theological reflection to liturgical practice.

4. East and west present contrasting patterns of monasticism and asceticism. Both inherited from ancient Christianity the tradition of spiritual asceticism and rejection of the world sketched earlier in this chapter. Yet in the west, men like Benedict of Nursia gave to monasticism an active and social direction, with the result that monks were among the formative influences on nascent western civilization. Monasticism in the east was by contrast more individualist, more contemplative, and more otherworldly. Even in centers of monasticism like Mount Athos in Greece, monks pursued their upward paths alone. In eastern as in western Christianity monks remained important figures, but they were not so much active agents as pilgrims of eternity reminding other human beings of their eternal destiny.

Modern times have brought new problems and fiery trials to eastern Christianity. In the twentieth century the coming of Marxian communism has frequently resulted in severe repression and persecution of the church. In Russia, new currents of religious thought and feeling during the nineteenth century did little to alter the massively conservative posture of the Russian church and its close relation to the decadent czarist government. These attitudes only served to verify for the communists their view of religion as the opiate of the people. Hence it was not surprising that the first decades of Marxian rule in Russia should be years of harsh repression of the church. The record was similar in lands adjacent to Russia. However, since World War II, many of these restrictions have been removed, and Russian Christians are permitted to practice their faith. In 1961 the Russian Orthodox church joined the World Council of Churches, reporting that it had 30,000 priests, 73 bishops, and 40 million adherents.

At present there are some fourteen independent, autocephalous Eastern Orthodox churches, extending from Moscow to Czechoslovakia, and from Lithuania to Jerusalem. To these are joined several smaller kindred groups from places as distant as Finland, Japan, the United States, Canada, and Australia. It is estimated that the total number of eastern Christians is approximately 180 million. Increasingly these groups are leaving their former isolation for new contacts with other Christians and other religious groups.

ISSUES AND QUESTIONS

As we have seen in this chapter, the Christian religion began as a very small movement in first-century Judaism. From this minuscule beginning, it grew and spread, finding its way throughout the Roman empire. Subsequent chapters will trace its further spread to all of Europe, and thereafter to all parts of the world. Today there are approximately 1 billion Christians in the world.

With growth came also ever-increasing diversity. Yet within its many and various forms, the common element in Christianity, ancient and modern, has been its confession of faith in Jesus as the Christ. We have noted that the first such confession by Jesus' disciples was precisely in Jesus as the Messiah or Christ. We have also noted that the first Gentile paraphrase for this original confession was in Jesus as lord and savior. From this, it was a further step to expound and argue the faith in the philosophic-theological language of the time.

This chapter has noted two crises in the historical developments of early Christianity. The first crisis occurred when Gentile Christians raised the question of whether in order to be a Christian one had first to take upon himself or herself what Judaism called "the burden of the Torah," i.e., full Jewish observance. We have seen the decisive answer given by the Apostle Paul, namely, that if a person had faith in Christ, then the Torah became altogether unnecessary.

The importance of this decision can scarcely be overestimated. For if the opposite answer had been given, Christianity would have lived and died as a small movement in first-century Judaism, having little or no attraction for Gentile people. As it turned out, the ethical monotheism of the Hebraic and Jewish tradition as expressed in Christianity attracted and held an ever-increasing following.

A second crisis, of equal importance but more protracted that the first, occurred when Christianity made its way into the mainstream of the Greco-Roman world. In this wider environment, would the new religion retain its Hebraic or biblical character, or would it be lost in the cosmopolitan culture of the age?

Such a crisis emerged in clear form in the second-century struggle of Christianity with gnosticism and marcionism. If the decision had gone with Marcion and the gnostics, the biblical concept of the world as God's good creation would have been lost in acosmic speculation. Subsequent forms of this same crisis may be observed in the creedal and theological controversies of the next several centuries.

Another, different kind of issue emerged from these controversies in the correlated concepts of orthodoxy and heresy, or in alternative formulation in the concept of dogma and dogmatism. The etymology of this term, and its literal meaning, is "received teaching." However, in the context of early Christianity it acquired the meaning of beliefs irrationally acquired and held by ecclesiastical authority. The losers in theological controversy and conflict were declared heretics, and accordingly were ostracized and anathematized. It is small comfort to note that such attitudes and actions were common in this as in many other traditional cultures, or that such "dogmatic" attitudes grow readily out of the depth of conviction which is an integral element of religious experience. Here indeed is a problematic issue which will be with us throughout our study.

A happier and more affirmative issue grew in early Christianity out of its double legacy of Hebraism and Hellenism. As we have seen from the latter derived such essential tenets as the rational human self and indeed correlatively the rational structure of the world. As we have seen, from the former came the concept of the same self as a child of God and hence of intrinsic value. Coming together in early Christianity these two legacies defined what we have called humanism. With different emphases and formulation humanism has defined a conception of human excellence or worth of great importance throughout western history, and indeed in world history. We shall follow this value as our study proceeds.

A final issue turns upon Christianity's wrestle with the historical monotheism of its faith. We have noted Jesus' Kingdom of God as his formulation of the Bible's linear-dramatic view of history. We have also noted the New Testament's conception of the second coming of Christ as the consummation of history. Almost lost in the acosmic speculations of the Greco-Roman world, the historical character of Christian faith erupted in Montanism, but gained more adequate expression in Augustine's *City of God*. Also Augustine's conception of the human self in the *Confessions* is distinctive as a piece of history or historic destiny.

We have noted the danger of Christianity's historical character being lost in acosmic speculation, which incidentally was common in the later Hellenistic world. However, an equal and opposite peril was that the Bible's concept of linear-dramatic history could be lost in the popular culture of the Hellenistic world.

Against this second loss Christianity asserted what was called its ecumenical character. This word, *oikumene*, meant the entire inhabited world. This image and concept kept the new religion open to an ever-increasing world until in later ages it became global in meaning.

NOTES

1. Floyd V. Filson, *The New Testament against Its Environment*, SCM Press, London, 1956.
2. Samuel Angus, *Religious Quests of the Graeco-Roman World*, Scribner, New York, 1929.
3. See inter alia Ernest F. Scott, *The Literature of the New Testament*, Columbia, New York, 1932, p. 21; Eric Titus, *Essentials to New Testament Study*, Ronald, New York, 1958, p. 28.
4. Scott, op. cit., pp. 21–32.
5. Romans 1:3; Galatians 4:4.
6. Luke 3:1.
7. Luke 3:10–18.
8. See inter alia Theodor H. Gaster, *The Dead Sea Scriptures*, Doubleday, Garden City, N.Y., 1956, p. 12.
9. Mark 1:11.
10. Mark 1:15.
11. Luke 4:16.
12. Mark 8:27f.
13. Matthew 16:31f; Mark 8:27f. Luke 9:18f.
14. Matthew 16:21.
15. Matthew 26:64.
16. See inter alia John Knox, *The Man Christ Jesus*, Willett, Clark & Company, Chicago, 1942, pp. 28f; and John Knox, *Christ, the Lord*, Willett, Clark, 1945, p. 36n.
17. John Wick Bowman, *The Intention of Jesus*, Westminster Press, Philadelphia, 1943, pp. 159ff.
18. Matthew 17:1f; Mark 9:2; Luke 9:28f.

19. Luke 9:51.
20. Luke 9:37–18:31.
21. See Albert Schweitzer, *The Quest of the Historical Jesus*, A & C. Black, London, 1938, pp. 7–11.
22. Matthew 21:12f.
23. Vincent Taylor, *The Life and Ministry of Our Lord Jesus*, Macmillan, New York, 1955, pp. 179–182.
24. Mark 14:64.
25. Mark 15:26.
26. Martin Buber, *The Prophetic Faith*, Macmillan, New York, 1949, pp. 96ff.
27. See inter alia Deuteronomy 6; Jeremiah 31; Hosea 11.
28. Leviticus 19:18.
29. Matthew 6:33.
30. Mark 12:28–31.
31. Matthew 5:17f.
32. Luke 10:30–37.
33. Luke 12:42–48.
34. Luke 18:9.
35. Matthew 5:17.
36. I Corinthians 15:3–8.
37. I Corinthians 15:50.
38. II Corinthians 5:1–6.
39. Acts 2:4f.
40. Acts 2:41.
41. I Corinthians 13:1 and 14:2.
42. Acts 1:4.
43. Acts 5:1–11.
44. Acts 5:34.
45. Acts 4:19.
46. Acts 7.
47. Acts 10.
48. Acts 9.1–10.
49. Acts 26:19.
50. Galatians 1:17.
51. Acts 13:13f.
52. Acts 15; Galatians 2.
53. Acts 16:9.
54. Philippians 2:6–11.
55. Galatians 5 and 6.
56. Romans 2 and 3.
57. Galatians 5:1f.
58. Galatians 5:22.
59. John 1:1f.
60. Revelations 19:11f.
61. Hebrews f:1f.
62. Pliny's letter to Trajan regarding Christians in Bithynia, in Henry B. Bettenson, *Documents of the Christian Church*, Oxford University Press, Fair Lawn, N.J., 1947, pp. 5–17.
63. Ibid., p. 7.
64. Justin's "Apology" in ibid., p. 8f.
65. Ibid., p. 8.
66. Charles Bigg, *The Christian Platonists of Alexandria*, Oxford University Press, London, 1913, p. 276.
67. Williston Walker, *A History of the Christian Church*, Scribner, New York, 1954, p. 76.
68. Bettenson, op. cit., p. 9f.
69. Walker, op. cit., p. 59.

70. Bettenson, op. cit., p. 51.
71. John H. Leith (ed.), *Creeds of the Churches*, Doubleday, Garden City, N.Y., 1963, p. 24.
72. Walker, op. cit., p. 56.
73. Ibid., p. 108.
74. Bettenson, op. cit., p. 37.
75. Ibid., pp. 72–73.
76. Walker, op. cit., p. 57.
77. Ibid., p. 67.
78. Ibid.,
79. Ibid., p. 62.
80. Ibid., p. 124.
81. Ibid., p. 127.
82. Ibid., pp. 164–180.

BIBLIOGRAPHY

Atiya, A.: *History of Eastern Christianity*, University of Notre Dame, Notre Dame, Ind., 1967.

Ayer, J.: *A Source Book of the Ancient Church*, AMS Press, New York, 1970.

Bettenson, H.: *Documents of the Christian Church*, Oxford, New York, 1970.

Bornkamm, G.: *Jesus of Nazareth*, Harper & Row, New York, 1975.

Bultmann, R.: *Primitive Christianity*, Fortress, Philadelphia, 1980.

———: *Theology of the New Testament*, Scribner, New York, 1951.

Chadwick, H. (ed.): *Alexandrian Christianity*, Westminster Press, Philadelphia, 1954.

Cochrane, C.: *Christianity and Classical Culture*, Oxford, London, 1957.

Davies, J. G.: *The Early Christian Church*, Doubleday, New York, 1967.

Eusebius: *A History of the Christian Church from Christ to Constantine*, G. Williamson (trans.), Penguin, New York, 1981.

Ferm, R.: *Readings in the History of Christian Thought*, Holt, New York, 1964.

Frankforter, A. D.: *A History of the Christian Movement*, Nelson-Hall, Chicago, 1978.

Frend, W.: *The Rise of Christianity*, Fortress, Philadelphia, 1984.

Gonzalez, J.: *A History of Christian Thought*, Abingdon Press, Nashville, Tenn., 1970–1975.

Goodspeed, E.: *A History of Early Christian Literature*, rev. by R. Grant, University of Chicago, Chicago, 1966.

Grant, R.: *Early Christianity and Society*, Harper & Row, New York, 1977.

———: *The Formation of the New Testament*, Harper & Row, New York, 1965.

Klausner, J.: *From Jesus to Paul*, Menorah, New York, 1978.

Knox, J.: *Jesus: Lord and Christ*, Harper, New York, 1958.

Latourette, K.: *A History of Christianity*, Harper & Row, New York, 1975.

Lossky, V.: *The Mystical Theology of the Eastern Church*, St. Vladimir's Seminary Press, Crestwood, N.Y., 1976.

McGiffert, A.: *A History of Christian Thought*, Scribner, New York, 1933.

Nock, A.: *Conversion*, University Press of America, Lanham, Md., 1988.

———: *Early Gentile Christianity*, Harper & Row, New York, 1964.

Pelikan, J.: *The Christian Tradition*, University of Chicago, Chicago, 1971–1986.

Price, J.: *Interpreting the New Testament*, Holt, Rinehart and Winston, New York, 1971.

Richardson, C.: *The Church through the Centuries*, AMS Press, New York, 1988.

Tyson, J.: *The New Testament and Early Christianity*, Macmillan, New York, 1984.

Von Campenhausen, H.: *The Formation of the Christian Bible*, Fortress, Philadelphia, 1972.

Walker, W., et al.: *A History of the Christian Church*, Scribner, New York, 1985.

Zernov, N.: *Eastern Christendom*, Weidenfeld and Nicolson, London, 1961.

14

Islam

This chapter on Islam may at first appear to interrupt our account of the Jewish and Christian faiths in the western world. However, history first made this interruption. That is to say, in the seventh and eighth centuries CE, Islam burst upon the world, including Christian Europe as well as the Middle East and central Asia. If western history textbooks accord meager and grudging acknowledgement to this large historic fact, this is only additional evidence for parochialism and bias on the part of western historians and western peoples.[1]

The classification of Islam among the world's faiths, and hence the placing of this chapter, constitute a problem with no easy solution. Clearly Islam is a monotheistic religion, and is also of Middle Eastern origin. But it is equally a fact that Islamic peoples are scattered over the world in utter disregard of typological considerations. There is an Islamic zone extending along the equator from Morocco in North Africa through the Arab states of the Middle East, to Iran, Pakistan, and India, then onward to Indonesia and the Philippines. However, outside of this zone are an estimated 50 to 70 million Muslims in China and central Asia, some 30 million in black Africa, and some 3 to 5 million in the western world. The recent and current rise of the Nation of Islam in North America (sometimes called the Black Muslims) having now some 3 million adherents, constitutes a significant religious movement. Whatever else it may or may not be, Islam is a world religion and demands attention as such.[2]

Islam makes many other forceful claims upon our attention. Surely one of the strongest is that throughout its history to the present moment, Islam has suffered what can only be called a "bad press" in the western world. In addition to this are many significant contemporary issues which in one way or another involve Islam. These range from oil supply and Zionism to what the popular press calls "Islamic fundamentalism."[3]

Islam claims to be monotheistic, often adding the charge that Christianity has compromised or nullified its claim to monotheism through its doctrines of incarnation and trinity.[4] For itself, Islam guards its monotheism with the doctrine of *shirk* as the unforgivable sin. The literal meaning of shirk is "association," that is, the association of anything in the created world with God as creator and lord. Hence shirk means taking some aspect of the created world and giving it the worship and service properly directed to the one God; in other words, shirk is idolatry.

439

Islam also specifically rejects the title Muhammadanism and insists upon the name Islam. While Muslims regard their prophet and founder as the ideal human being, they deny any imputation of divinity for Muhammad as inconsistent with monotheism. The word Islam is from the Arabic root, *slm*, meaning to be in peace, or to be an integral whole. From this root, the word Islam means to surrender to God, and thus to be an integral whole. A Muslim is a person who joyfully makes this surrender.

As we have repeatedly noted, all three monotheistic religions are religions of revelation, and of a book. For Islam the book is the *Qur'an*, and in orthodox tradition, the original Qur'an is asserted to be on tablets of gold in heaven, with the earthly Arabic book as a divinely certified copy. At times this devotion to the Qur'an has involved Islam in problems of literalism and legalism comparable to those of Christianity and Judaism. We also note that equally with the other two monotheistic religions, Islam has at times both taught and practiced holy war.

Arabian Source Region

Like all religions, Islam has been significantly influenced by its social and historical context. Indeed, like other monotheistic faiths—and unlike such faiths as Buddhism—Islam has affirmed and not denied or annulled the particular geographical and historical facts that lie at its base.

A glance at the map of the Arabian peninsula shows several inhabited and civilized regions surrounding the desert quarter. At the end of the sixth century these regions were roughly as follows. To the east lay Iraq, and beyond it the powerful Iranian empire under the Sassanid dynasty. The Iranians controlled the trade routes to central Asia and China. To the west lay Syria and Asia Minor, which were parts of the Byzantine empire. Across the Red Sea from Mecca was Abyssinia, which was generally friendly to Byzantium. At the southwest corner of Arabia lay Yemen, often under Iranian influence.

The Arabs of the region of Mecca were thus caught between the two great powers of Byzantium and Iran. Mecca also lay on the economic crossroads, along the caravan routes between east and west. As a consequence, its people prospered in commerce and finance. Mecca was a flourishing, enterprising center of trade. It was also a religious center for extensive regions of Arabia, possessing as it did the large cube-shaped temple called the *Ka'ba* with the famous Black Stone set in the southeast corner. Pilgrims came from afar on *hajj*, or pilgrimage, to circumambulate the temple, to kiss the Black Stone, and to worship the many icons within the temple. So important to Mecca was this custom that tribal wars and raids were suspended for four months of pilgrimage each year.

Pilgrims could also visit the well *Zemzem*, which popular tradition said had originated with Ishmael, son of Abraham and Hagar. Arabs believe themselves to be the sons of Ishmael, who, when he and his mother were driven out by Sarah, had come to Mecca. One story had it that as his mother frantically searched for water, little Ishmael lay on the ground and kicked. Where his heel struck, there the water of Zemzem sprang up. This well, which had been filled with rubble for centuries, was relocated and dug out by Muhammad's grandfather. Pilgrims also could run with shaking shoulders between two nearby hills as Hagar had done; and they could throw stones down a gorge at evil spirits and their chief, Satan.

The wider pattern of Arab religion was a mosaic of diverse beliefs and practices. Many in the Arabian region were at least nominally Christian, and there were also Jewish communities from Asia Minor to Yemen and to Iraq. For many Arab peoples there was a distant supreme being named *Allah*. The term *Allah* means not "a god" but "the God." For popular piety there were other deities closer at hand and more influential in human behavior. At Mecca there were three goddesses, sometimes considered daughters of Allah: al-Lat, a mother goddess; al-Manat, a female deity of fate; and al-Uzzah, of the morning star. There were also innumerable fairies, jinn, and ghouls who inhabited innumerable objects of nature and society. Fairies were generally favorable to humans, jinn were capricious, and ghouls were consistently malignant. All this constituted an animism (and animatism) in which the world was alive with all kinds of spirits and powers.

THE PROPHET'S LIFE

Into the Arabian scene Muhammad was born, according to Muslim historians on April 20, 571.[5] The name means "highly praised." His father had died before Muhammad's birth, and his mother died six years later. He was taken into the family of his grandfather, Abd al-Muttalib, and on his grandfather's death three years later into the family of his uncle, Abu Talib, who became his lifelong friend and supporter.

Muslim tradition tells many stories of the Prophet's piety, sensitivity, and integrity. Apparently well founded is the report of the name *al-Amin*, meaning "the true and reliable one," which his friends gave him.[6] As a youth he was a shepherd and camel driver, making trips to Yemen and to Syria. Also as a young man he participated in tribal councils and affairs.

On the recommendation of his uncle, Abu Talib, he went to work for a rich widow named Khadijah, managing caravans for her. So well did he perform his duties and so great was their mutual attraction that when he was twenty-five he married Khadijah, who was fifteen years his elder. The marriage was eminently successful. During Khadijah's lifetime the Prophet took no other wives, and even after her death he spoke so well of her that his other wives became jealous. She bore him five children—two sons and three daughters, of whom only one daughter, Fatima, survived infancy. The Prophet was a devoted husband and father.

During the years of his marriage to Khadijah, his religious interests were maturing. Beneath the surface were developing those forces which burst forth in his call to be the Prophet. Apparently his faith in the one God deepened, and with it his repulsion at idolatry and his sense of an impending judgment day. It was a period of increasing spiritual stress. What influence, if any, came from Christian or Jewish sources is beyond reliable knowledge. For several years he retired for a month to Mount Hira for solitary meditation—the practice which lies behind Muslim celebration of Ramadan. During this time he was sustained and stimulated by Khadijah.

Then in February 610, on what Muslims call the "night of power and glory," the angel Gabriel, chief messenger of Allah, appeared, confronting him with an awe-inspiring summons. As recorded in the Qur'an, the voice said:

> Read: In the name of thy Lord who createth,
> Createth man from a clot.
> Read: And thy Lord is the Most Bounteous
> Who teacheth by the pen,
> Teacheth man that which he knew not.[7]

So was given the first fragment of the Qur'an. The angel disappeared, leaving Muhammad in deep distress. Then outside the cave he heard the same voice assuring him, "O Muhammad, Thou art Allah's messenger...."[8] The experience had a shattering impact. Muhammad hastened home to tell Khadijah of his experience—and of his fear that he had been duped by demons or that he had gone mad. She reassured him. Then, according to tradition, they both went to her elderly cousin, Warakah, who was familiar with Jewish and Christian scriptures. When they told him of Muhammad's encounter with Gabriel, he affirmed his belief, saying, "Doubtless it is the beginning of prophecy, and there shall come upon him the Great Law like as it came upon Moses."[9]

And, as so often in the history of religions, it is doubtless impossible here decisively to separate fact from traditional interpretation. Yet one may safely assume a time of anguished questioning, then of reintegration and redirection, as Muhammad took to himself the full force and significance of his experience and came to recognize himself as what the voice had called him, namely, the Prophet (*nabi*) and apostle (*rasul*) of Allah.

Other messages from God followed, though slowly at first. In obedience to the divine voice which had put him under orders, the Prophet began to preach, proclaiming the message he had received. During the first years, results were meager. A few converts were made, but only a few. First was his wife Khadijah, then his cousin, Abu Talib's son Ali, then his servant and adopted son Zaid, then his friend Abu Bekr.

As for the people of Mecca, at first they laughed—a people have so often laughed at those who come with a message from God. Surely this dreamer with his dire warnings of impending judgment was a madman! They smiled and turned away.

But scornful laughter turned to hostility as they saw in the Prophet's public words a threat to the popular religion and the profitable pilgrimage trade. His uncompromising monotheism with its austere moral demands was deeply dis-

Muhammad and the Angel Gabriel. (University of Edinburgh, Arabic and Persian mss., no. 20, f. 45 b.)

turbing to people of the world. Hostility took the form of persecution. Hoodlums broke up his public meetings. His followers became the victims of discrimination and attack. On at least two occasions during this Meccan period the Prophet sent small groups of followers abroad to Abyssinia to escape persecution. At home the Prophet's tribe, the Hashimites, were forcibly confined to a single section of the city. Only the courageous stand of Abu Talib prevented more aggressive action against the Prophet and his followers.

Meanwhile revelations continued to come. They have found their way into the Qur'an and are identified by modern scholars of Islam as revealed at Mecca. Many of them have a strong sense of social justice, and all are pervaded with a foreboding sense of doom and judgment. Here is a sample of *suras*, or sections of the Qur'an, received by the Prophet in Mecca.

When the sun is overthrown,
And when the stars fall,
And when the hills are moved,
And when the camels big with young are abandoned,
And when the wild beasts are herded together,
And when the seas rise,
And when souls are reunited,
And when the girl child that was buried alive is asked
For what sin she was slain…
(Then) every soul will know what it hath made ready.[10]

Every soul is a pledge for its own deeds;
Save those who will stand on the right hand.
In gardens they will ask one another

Concerning the guilty:
What hath brought you to this burning?
They will answer: We were not of those who prayed
Nor did we feed the wretched.[11]

Nay, I swear by this city—
And thou art an indweller of this city—
And the begetter and that which he begat,
We verily have created man in an atmosphere:
Thinketh he that none hath power over him?
And he saith: I have destroyed vast wealth:
Thinketh he that none beholdeth him?
Did We not assign unto him two eyes
And a tongue and two lips,
And guide him to the parting of the mountain ways?
But he hath not attempted the Ascent—
Ah, what will convey unto thee what the Ascent is!—
It is to free a slave,
And to feed in the day of hunger
An orphan near of kin,
Or some poor wretch in misery,
And to be of those who believe and exhort one another to perserverance and
    exhort one another to pity.
Their place will be on the right hand.
But those who disbelieve Our revelations, their place will be on the left hand.
Fire will be an awning over them.[12]

In obedience to the divine voice the Prophet continued to preach and teach. The year 619 CE was a low point in his life. Abu Talib died, and shortly thereafter, Khadijah. Small wonder that Muhammad afterward called it "the year of suffering." During this year he took another wife, Sawdah, widow of a follower who had just returned from the Abyssinian migration.

During this same year he was also visited by a delegation of six men from Yathrib, a city some 250 miles to the northwest. Their city needed new leadership; perhaps Muhammad would come to take charge. A delegation of twelve returned the following year and took an oath to abstain from all polytheism and vices and to observe the strict discipline required of the Prophet's followers. A Meccan follower returned to Yathrib with them, and the following year, the first year before the *hijra*, a larger delegation, seventy-five men, came from Yathrib to swear allegiance and confess their faith—and to urge the Prophet to come to their city.

Muslim tradition tells of a change in the Prophet's tactics. Until now he had relied upon teaching and preaching to put his message into effect. Now he began to plan in terms of political and even military action. Tradition also tells of a last desperate attempt of his enemies to prevent his leaving Mecca. However, he was warned of a plot to assassinate him, and he hid out with a few friends in a cave on Mount Thaur. When his enemies had passed, he and Abu Bekr and a few other followers mounted camels and made the *hijra* ("withdrawal") to Yathrib, customarily a journey of eleven days and 250 miles, in only eight days. Thus occurred the crucial event of Muslim history. *Anno Hegira* 1, A.H. 1 (622 CE), marked the beginning of the Muslim year, from which dates are still reckoned. The way of Islam was launched upon the world.

The problems in Yathrib were vast and uncharted, but the Prophet moved decisively and with a unique kind of authority which combined religious and ethical leadership with political and social leadership. He and his followers created in Yathrib (now renamed *Medina*, "the city") a new state and a new social order which is still regarded as the archetypal model for Muslims everywhere. Records of the Muslim community of Medina in Qur'an and tradition have been studied by Muslims throughout their history as the model for all Muslims and all people to emulate.

While the Prophet was accorded an authority well-nigh absolute, Muslim writers point out that he acted only upon careful consultation and in full cooperation with others.[13] He proceeded first to reorganize, literally to re-form, or reshape, the religious practices of the city. He erected a house of worship, the first mosque, and worked out a cultus and institution which would be pleasing to Allah. Weekly services on Friday, prayer five times daily, the call to prayer from the mosque roof, prostration during prayer, alms for the poor—these and other arrangements followed in order. At first the direction in which one faced while praying (*qibla*) was toward Jerusalem, for the Prophet had both understanding and respect for Jewish or biblical tradition, thinking of his movement as a fulfillment of it. He was first puzzled then incensed when the Jewish community of Medina scorned him. He broke with them openly, ordering the direction of prayer to be toward Mecca.

The Prophet's great gifts of leadership were soon turned outward to foreign relations. He made many prudent treaties of alliance with neighboring

The Hijra. (University of Edinburgh, Arabic and Persian mss. no. 20.)

peoples and also organized an army for Medina. Muslim writers point out the essentially defensive character of these moves, adding quotations from the Qur'an deprecating war and violence.[14]

However this may be, Medina and its Prophet were soon deeply involved in military activities. They began casually, as typical raids on passing caravans, particularly those of Mecca. However, operations soon escalated. At the battle of Badr in 624 the Prophet led a band of 300 who put to flight a larger Meccan force and seized much booty. The following year the Muslim army of Medina turned back a superior retaliatory force of Meccans. The Meccans returned in 627, and Muhammad countered successfully with trench defenses, a new tactic in Arab warfare. Consolidating Medina with surrounding tribes, the Prophet now moved from a position of strength to make a ten-year truce with Mecca. When the truce broke down, the Prophet marched against Mecca, winning over token opposition. His conquest was complete when, in 630 at the battle of Hunayn, his army decisively defeated a coalition of tribes hostile to both Medina and Mecca.

One of his first acts was to go to worship in the Ka'ba. After circumambulating the temple and honoring the Black Stone, he ordered the destruction of the many images within and the obliteration from its walls of paintings of Abraham and others. But the Prophet proved to be a magnanimous conqueror. His previous enemies were pardoned, and the Meccan pilgrimage was opened to all who would accept Islam. Pagan tribes within the city were given a grace period of four months to accept the new faith. If they refused they would thereafter be subject to attack as threats to Islam. This new principle of jihad was qualified in the case of Jews and Christians. Since they were also people of a book, they had the option of retaining their faith if they submitted to Muslim government and paid a special tax. Muhammad continued to believe that Jews and Christians were not idolaters, but members of the tradition which was being completed in his own revelations.

Muhammad was now well on the way to his goal of the unification of all Arab peoples. In the last ten years of his life he personally led no less than twenty-seven military campaigns and planned thirty-eight others. In A.H. 9 (631 CE) he personally led a campaign against Byzantine forces at Tabouk which seemed about to attack his Muslim forces. Other such attacks were being planned when the Prophet succumbed to mortal illness.

In A.H. 10 (632 CE) he made his last pilgrimage to Mecca. On Mount Arafat he gave a farewell discourse to his followers, warning them as ever of the impending last judgment and admonishing them to hold to the beliefs and duties incumbent upon all Muslims, concluding with the words: "O ye men! hearken unto my words and take ye them to heart! Know ye that every Moslem is a brother to every other Moslem, and that ye are now one brotherhood"[15]

It was Abu Bekr who bore to the gathering the stunning news of the Prophet's death. Bluntly he declared: "O people! Lo! as for him who used to worship Muhammad, Muhammad is dead. But as for him who used to worship Allah, Allah is alive and dieth not."[16]

وقا اصحابك اوزرينه كم ها ايها الذين امنوا اصبروا

انقه الله علي ... نه حضرت رماك صلي الله علي

اصحابك وسنته الله تعا لنك فو لنا وقودي كادكن

The Qur'an as revealed to
Muhammad during a battle.
(Art Resource.)

ISLAMIC DOCTRINE

*doctrine — heart
duty — done*

The teachings of the Prophet—or as he and his followers would hasten to correct us, the teachings revealed by Allah to the Prophet—comprise the 114 suras
of the Qur'an. If to this be added the authenticated *hadiths*, or traditions, the *hadiths*
student has all the primary sources of the Muslim faith. It is a characteristically
simple and forthright credo. The faithful Muslim responds to God by saying, in
effect, "I hear and do." Muslim doctrine is what is heard, and Muslim duty is
what is to be done.

The absolutely fundamental beliefs are remarkably few and simple. They
comprise, in one traditional formulation, belief in the unity of God, belief in the
prophetic mission of Muhammad, and belief in the impending judgment day for
all human beings.[17]

Any exposition of Muslim doctrine must begin—and end—with the one
God, Allah, majestic, holy, transcendent, absolutely unique. He alone is absolute

sovereign of the universe, and to him alone must be given absolute allegiance and service. As previously noted, the word *Islam* means "submission," that is, submission to Allah. Not only does he rule all that exists, but he created the universe in the beginning, calling it into being out of nothingness, and he will bring it to the awful consummation of judgment day. Truly Allah is Lord of beginning and end.

As noted above, for Islam the unforgivable sin is shirk, or association of anything creaturely with the unique and transcendent glory of Allah. Islam is monotheism that is as pure—and as extreme—as any monotheism in history.

Of this one God, humans can speak only by negation and metaphor. From our creaturely viewpoint, we can say what God is not, thereby illustrating what many faiths have termed the *via negativa*. Thus it may be asserted that Allah does not partake of any creaturely limitation. By metaphor or analogy, human tongues may say a few things about Allah. Muslim piety has elaborated the "ninety-nine beautiful names."[18] Of these, clearly the most frequent is "the merciful," or "the compassionate." Each sura of the Qur'an begins with the words "In the Name of Allah, the Beneficent, the Merciful."[19] To secular readers of the Qur'an, Allah often seems stern and harsh rather than compassionate. Nowhere does this stern demeanor appear more clearly than in the pictures of judgment day and its consequences, heaven and hell. Yet even here, followers of the Prophet assure us that Allah's compassion is manifested in warning of the wrath to come.

The Qur'an's descriptions of judgment and of heaven and hell are vivid and concrete, as the following samples show:

When the heavens shall be rent asunder,
And when the stars shall be dispersed,
And when the seas shall be commingled,
And when the graves shall be upturned,
A soul will know what it has sent forward and kept back.
O man, what has led thee away from the generous Lord?
Who created thee and formed thee and shaped thee rightly,
Building thee up in such forms as He willed?
Nay, indeed, but ye count the judgment as something false,
Yet over you, indeed, are guardians,
Noble ones, those who write.
They know what ye do.
Verily, the righteous [shall be] in delight,
While the wicked assuredly [will be] in Jahim [a name for Hell],
And they may not be absent therefrom.
What will teach thee what the Day of Judgment is?
It is a Day when no soul will avail aught for another
    soul, but the matter on that Day will be with Allah.[20]

When that which must inevitably come has come,
[And] as to its coming there is no falsity,
[A coming which will cause] abasing [for some and for others] exalting.

When the earth will be shaken a shaking,
And the mountains will be pounded a pounding,
So that they become as scattered dust,
Then ye will be three groups.
The Companions of the Right Hand, what are the Companions of the Right
    Hand?
And the Companions of the Left Hand, what are the Companions of the Left
    Hand?
And those who have precedence, those who have precedence,
They are those who are brought near
In gardens of delight,
Quite a number from the former generations,
And a few from the latter,
On couches inlaid [with jewels]
On which they will recline facing one another,
While around them circle immortal celestial youths (*wildan*)
With goblets and ewers and a cup from a flowing spring,
From which they will suffer no headache nor will they become intoxicated.
Also with such fruits as they may choose,
And such flesh of fowl as they may desire.
And large-eyed celestial damsels (*huris*)
Like unto hidden pearls,
A reward for what they have been doing.[21]

The mercy of Allah is also shown in his sending messengers or prophets to humankind. The Qur'an mentions some twenty-eight prophets, of whom eighteen are Jewish, three Christian, and four Arabian. One, incidentally, is Alexander the Great. Five prophetic predecessors of Muhammad are accorded special homage: Adam, Noah, Abraham, Moses, and Jesus. Concerning Jesus, the Qur'an affirms his virgin birth but teaches that his crucifixion and resurrection were apparent rather than real. It repeats some of his moral teachings but says nothing concerning his lordship or divinity, which for Muslims would constitute shirk—violation of monotheism. According to Muslim views, to Jesus was given a portion of the truth more completely to be revealed to Muhammad; therefore Christians are in Muslim eyes heretics who cling to partial truth when the full truth is available.

Muhammad is in this succession "the seal of the prophets," the final decisive prophet after whom no more will come. He is God's decisive messenger to whom the oracles of the Qur'an were vouchsafed. Muslim piety has also cast him in the role of the ideal human being, who went through all the stages of life and all its varied roles, leaving a model for all humanity to emulate. It would violate Muslim monotheism to claim more than this.

In addition to prophets, the Qur'an teaches the existence of other incidental but by no means unimportant messengers from God, namely, angels. It was the angel Gabriel who addressed Muhammad on the night of power and glory. But Gabriel is only one of the heavenly court of angels. While angels are superhuman, they are creatures whose function, like that of other creatures, is to

A depiction of hell. (Biblioteque Nationale, Paris.)

serve and praise the one God. They also serve such functions as recording human actions, witnessing for or against humans at judgment day, and guarding the gates of hell. *Shaitin* or *Iblis* is a fallen angel, having rebelled against Allah, thus becoming his adversary.

In addition to angels, according to the Qur'an, are numerous *jinn*. Some jinn are believers and some are infidels. All jinn are asserted to be made of fire, while angels are made of light.

Allah makes known his will to humanity in the Qur'an. The word *qur'an* means "recital" or "reading," that is, of Allah's words, given to the Prophet, which in its written form becomes *kitab*, or "scripture." Muslims point to the fact that as he was receiving these messages from God, the Prophet was in a state of divine inspiration which included such accompaniments as physical exaltation, changes of weight and state, and not least of all his own testimony that the words were not his but God's. Many of the Prophet's own words have been preserved in hadiths, to be discussed later. Islam has taught that the words of the true Qur'an are "uncreated" or divine words. Of this the earthly Arabic book is only a supernaturally certified, earthly copy.

All this is true despite the miscellaneous character of the Qur'an, where lofty speculations or somber reflections on the last judgment lie side by side with directions on how to enter a house or other equally homely details. To the secular reader these features reflect details of the Prophet's biography and es-

Page from the Qur'an. (Metropolitan Museum of Art, Rodgers Fund, 1942.)

pecially his particular religious experience. This particularity of detail has never deflected Muslims from their traditional view of the Qur'an as Allah's word to humankind and the Prophet as the divinely appointed though entirely human vehicle of this communication.

The power and style of the Qur'an are marks of classical Arabic literature at its best. These features are often adduced by Muslim scholars as evidence of its unique inspiration: only God could create anything so uniquely good. Only recently have some Muslims sanctioned the translation of the Qur'an into other languages, and even so it is held to be the "meaning" which is thus rendered, rather than the text which is translated.[22]

As for the process by which the Qur'an was committed to writing, the Prophet's hearers memorized many passages as they heard them, thus becoming "Qur'an bearers." Many of them wrote down what they heard on pieces of parchment, wood, leather, or whatever was available. Tradition has counted up twenty-nine such recorders in Medina and a smaller number in Mecca. During the first years a process of oral transmission took place, but as death took more and more of the Qur'an bearers, the need for a written record became apparent. Under the second caliph, Umar, the Qur'an was put into writing. Only passages certified by two witnesses were accepted.[23]

Modern critical scholarship has not proceeded far in the study of the

Qur'an. Different suras have been identified as early or late, and as given in Mecca or Medina, and some developments in the Prophet's thought have been noted. The Meccan suras tend to be shorter, more rhythmic, and poetic, and to deal with fundamental aspects of Muslim faith. The Medinian suras are generally longer and tend to deal with specific issues and problems of the first Muslim community. Some suras cannot be placed with any degree of precision.

ISLAMIC DUTY

Turning from doctrine to duty, the student encounters the so-called five pillars of Islam: (1) confession, (2) prayer, (3) fasting, (4) almsgiving, and (5) pilgrimage. They will be described in order.

The first pillar, confession, is the lifelong obligation laid upon all Muslims to confess their faith, or bear their witness to the faith. This customarily consists of a recital of the *shahada: la ilaha illa'llah muhammadun rasulu'llah*—"There is no god but God [Allah], and Muhammad is his Prophet [or apostle]." These words are omnipresent in the Muslim world, and it is often asserted that simply to repeat them is to convert to Islam. However, orthodox theologians insist that to be effective six conditions must be met: they must be (1) repeated aloud, (2) perfectly understood, (3) believed in the heart, (4) professed till death, (5) recited correctly, and (6) recited without hesitation.[24]

The second pillar is prayer, which is the daily enactment in word and deed of the Muslim's living relation to Allah. In communities where there is a mosque, which is primarily a house of prayer, the call comes from the *muezzin* atop the minaret, yet solitary Muslims must fulfill this duty without such visual and auditory reminders.

Daily prayer occurs five times: at dawn, noon, midafternoon, evening, and night. Liturgical prayer (*salat*) is preceded by ritual purification; and the customary use of prayer rugs is an effort to secure purity of place. In a state of purity the Muslim faces the Ka'ba, the sacred shrine of Mecca, and performs the prescribed prayers, prostrations, and recitation of quranic passages. Besides the five prescribed daily prayers, many devout Muslims observe additional daily periods of prayer, some individual and some at the mosque.

Friday is the day of public prayer at the mosque, though it must be added that unlike the Jewish sabbath or Christian Sunday, Friday has never been a "day of rest" in Muslim lands. The service is customarily held at noon or at sunset in the mosque's paved courtyard, under the leadership of the *imam*. The faithful assemble at the call from the minaret, remove their shoes, perform ablutions, and sit quietly while a reader (*qari*) recites passages of the Qur'an. When the imam appears, he may preach a sermon. However, he is basically not a priest or clergyman but rather a leader of prayer, and his chief function is to lead the congregation in this form of worship. As he repeats the ritual words with bowing and prostration, the congregation follows his actions. Mosques are marked with a niche indicating the direction (qibla) of the sacred shrine of Mecca. Attached to the mosque may also be teachers, or *ulama*, who are learned in the

Qur'an and Muslim tradition. They are men of great importance in Islam; and the great Muslim universities are related to the faith by this means.

In addition to daily and Friday prayers, Islam prescribes prayers for all occasions of life, such as births, weddings, and funerals. Like many other faiths, its ideal is to hallow all areas of life.

The third pillar is fasting during the sacred month of Ramadan, in commemoration of the Prophet's call and practice. This obligation is considered binding upon all Muslims and consists of abstaining from food, drink, and sex from a time in the morning when a white thread may be distinguished from a black one until the time in the evening when they can no longer be distinguished. The essentially nonascetic character of Islam is emphasized by the relaxation of these prohibitions and the general rejoicing and festivity which take place at night. In the lunar calendar of Islam, the holy month may come at different times of the solar year, and its occurrence during the hot months of summer renders the discipline stringent indeed.

The fourth pillar is almsgiving (*zakat*), which is an obligation like the biblical tithe on the individual person to contribute a fixed portion of income to such good causes as the relief of the poor or the freeing of slaves. The amount is normally one-fortieth of one's annual income. In early times the zakat was a tax levied on the faithful, but now it is a purely personal and private obligation.

Linked to almsgiving in most formulations of Muslim faith is the wider principle of social responsibility and social welfare which it illustrates. The tra-

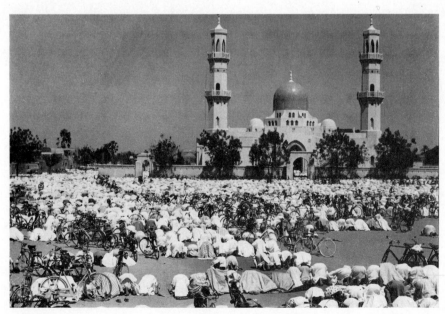

Friday noon prayer at the Kano mosque in Nigeria. (Marc and Evelyne Bernheim/Woodfin Camp & Associates.)

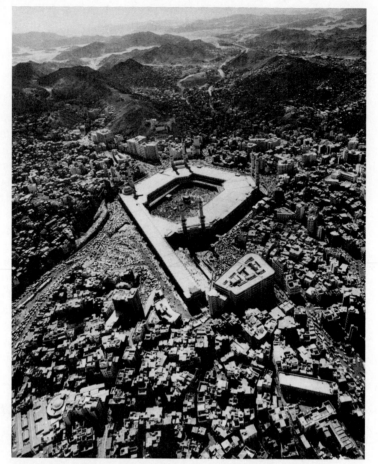

Great Mosque of Mecca, aerial view. (Mohamed Amin/Camera Pix-Keystone.)

ditional operation of zakat has led to the broader idea of law (*shari'a*) as the constitutive principle of the Muslim community. To these moral and social principles we shall return presently.

The fifth pillar of the faith is pilgrimage (hajj). At least once during his lifetime the Muslim should make a pilgrimage to the sacred mosque at Mecca, during the twelfth month of the lunar year, called *shu'l-Hijja*. Groups of the faithful gather from all parts of the Muslim world at Jidda, the seaport of Mecca, chanting, "Here we come, O Allah, here we come...." From this point onward they are in a state of *ihram*, or "dedication," requiring seamless white robes and prohibitions on sex, cutting of hair or nails, etc. Traditionally the 40-mile journey to sacred Mecca has been by camel caravan, but now buses are available. Once in Mecca, the first act is the *tawaf*, which consists of seven counterclockwise circumambulations of the Ka'ba with pauses of obeisance to the Black

Stone. Next is the *say*, seven trips back and forth between the hills *Saafa* and *Marwah*, now enclosed in a long corridor within the Great Mosque. Then pilgrims drink and splash water from the well Zemzem.

The climax of the pilgrimage is the journey on the eighth day of the sacred month to the village of Mina some 4 miles east of Mecca, then the next day onward another 6 miles to Mount Arafat for "the standing," a half-day's ritual of prayer, meditation, and sermon near the site of the Prophet's final sermon. At sundown they return to Muzdahfah on the road back to Mecca for the night. Then follow three days at Mina, where everyone stones three pillars representing the devil and participates in animal sacrifice. Before leaving Mecca for home, pilgrims again circle the Ka'ba.

The significance of pilgrimage in maintaining the vitality and unity of Islam is incalculable. On his return home the pilgrim is called by the coveted title *hajji*. He will be much in demand as a speaker to describe his experience. The numbers of pilgrims continue unabated from all parts of the Muslim world. In one recent year Saudi Arabia had 250,000 pilgrims and the Malays some 300,000. Some recent estimates place the total annual number of pilgrims at 2 to 3 million.

Closely related to the five pillars are a variety of other obligations which are either often or always regarded as binding on the Muslim conscience. For example, a distinguished student of Islam remarks that for at least one extreme Muslim sect, the Kharijites, the holy war is regarded as a sixth pillar.[25] The holy war is repeatedly enjoined by the Qur'an, as, for example, in the following passage:

> Fight in the way of Allah against those who fight against you, but begin not
>> hostilities. Lo! Allah loveth not aggressors.
> And stay them wherever ye find them, and drive them out of the places whence
>> they drove you out, for persecution is worse than slaughter . . .
> But if they desist, when lo! Allah is Forgiving, Merciful.
> And fight then until persecution is no more and religion is for Allah . . . [26]

In contrast to Kharijite literalism, many modern Muslims interpret the jihad in sublimated or metaphorical fashion as striving for the Muslim cause or "fighting the good fight" in a metaphorical rather than literal sense.

Muslims generally have observed the quranic prohibitions against alcohol, pork, and gambling. In this connection Islam has been referred to as the most successful total abstinence society in history. As is well known, polygamous marriage is permitted by the Qur'an, which puts the matter thus:

> Give unto orphans their wealth. Exchange not the good for the bad (in your management thereof) nor absorb their wealth into your own wealth. Lo! that would be a great sin.
> And if ye fear that ye will not deal fairly by the orphans, marry of the women, who seem good to you, two or three or four; and if ye fear that ye cannot do justice

(to so many) then one (only) or (the captives) that your right hands possess. Thus it is more likely that ye will not do injustice.[27]

If the Prophet's teachings concerning the ethics of sex and family be interpreted in historical context, they will be understood as a prophetic defense of the cause of women and children. "Two or three or four" wives meant in this historical context "not more than four." The Prophet was a defender of the rights of such defenseless persons as women, children, and orphans.

As readers make their way through the pages of the Qur'an, they detect considerable similarity between the ethics of the Prophet of Islam and the ethics of the biblical prophets of ancient Israel. In both cases, allegiance to the one God carries the primary obligation of living a just or righteous life in society with one's fellows; injustice is a sin against God.

In Islam, these moral values are given a definite structure and a wide application to politics, economics, and other basic aspects of society through the shari'a (law), to be described in the next section. In Islam as in other faiths, moral ideals undergo qualification and compromise as they are applied to the wider areas of society. In the modern world a process of attrition of traditional morality has gone on in Islam as in other faiths. Nevertheless Islam offers eloquent illustration of the fact that monotheistic religion has fundamental and inescapable moral and social implications.

ISLAM EXPANDS RAPIDLY

The Prophet's sudden death posed the problem of a successor (*caliph*). There were three groups from which a caliph might be chosen: (1) companions of the Prophet, (2) the Prophet's family, and (3) the Prophet's tribe, the Quraysh, or its subdivision, the Ummayads. The companions acted first, placing the caliphate Muhammad's longtime friend and associate, Abu Bekr. He moved with decisiveness to bring remaining Arab tribes into line. He also ordered the gathering of the miscellaneous suras of the Qur'an. During his short reign (632–634), he continued the Prophet's organization of an army and preparation for an assault on the outside world. Abu Bekr lived in patriarchal simplicity, receiving no stipend and transacting all state business in the courtyard of the Prophet's mosque at Medina.

Abu Bekr died in 634 and was succeeded by another companion, Umar (634–644), who ruled until his assassination by the poisoned dagger of a Christian slave. Like his predecessor, he was simple and frugal and also a devout and austerely righteous person. Under his direction the expansion of Islam began in earnest. He sent the great Khalid ibn-al-Walid, called *the sword of Allah*, against Damascus, the capital of Syria, in 634.[28] After a forced camel march from Iraq, Khalid and his fighting men appeared before the gates of Damascus. The city of Damascus fell (in 635) after a siege of six months. Other Syrian cities and towns then fell. The decisive battle for Syria was fought at the Yarmak River on August

20, 636, a fiercely hot summer's day on which the soldiers of the Prophet routed the Byzantine army. Jerusalem fell in 639 and the seaport town Caesarea was betrayed by a Jewish defector in 640.

Egypt was conquered next (639–640), and Muslim armies continued their push across North Africa. By 710 they were knocking at the gates of Spain, and in 732, having conquered Spain, they were finally checked at Tours in central France. On the north-central front, Arab armies marched as far as the gates of Constantinople, which they placed under year-long siege (716–717).[29] Meanwhile still other Arab armies pushed eastward, conquering Iraq, then toppling the decadent Sassanid rulers of Iran (640–649) and bringing Islam to the borders of India. During this time Umar was succeeded by Uthman, who ruled from 644 to 656. Uthman was a companion but also an Ummayad; and he appointed so many Ummayads that serious opposition arose, in the midst of which he too fell victim to assassination.

He was succeeded by the Prophet's son-in-law and cousin, Ali, who was the first caliph of the Prophet's family—a fact portentously significant in Muslim history, as will be seen in the section of this chapter on the Shi'ites, who are Muslim sects claiming that the first three caliphs were usurpers. Ali fell victim in 660 to a poisoned dagger wielded by an extremist follower who disapproved of Ali's leniency to his foe Muawiyah. His assassin was a Kharijite, one of a group whose

Bagdad, eighth and ninth centuries. (The Bettmann Archive.)

violence and fanaticism the student will have frequent occasion to observe in Muslim history.

The vastness and the speed of the Muslim conquests are difficult even to comprehend, let alone explain. Within a single century's time the Muslims ruled an empire two or three times the size of the Roman empire. No single cause suffices to explain so large a fact of history. In part this vast conquest is to be attributed to Muslim faith. The warriors of the Prophet believed themselves to be the servants of Allah, and they further believed that if they died in battle they would go straight to paradise. If they survived they could keep four-fifths of their booty—often wealth beyond the wildest dreams of avarice for these Arabian nomads. The military genius of the Arab generals, their mastery of new techniques such as camel cavalry, plus the frequent ineptitude of their opposition, constituted an important contributing cause. Whatever the combination of causes, the result was a century of conquest unparalleled in history before or since.

It is important to bear in mind that Islam is a universal religion which has interacted with many cultures. Among these is what is often termed *Arab civilization*[30]—though historians from other parts of the Muslim world hasten to challenge any suggestion that *Arab* and *Muslim* are equivalent terms. Actually, even the so-called Arab civilization was a synthesis of many elements fused into a unity by Muslim faith and presided over by Arab rulers. Here is occasion to observe once more what our study has shown many times in human history, the interaction of faith and culture to form a significant compound.

Arab civilization had its first stable center in the Ummayad caliphate founded by Muawiyah and located in Damascus. It lasted for almost a century, from 660 to 750,[31] then was overthrown by the Abbasids (from the Prophet's uncle, named al-Abbas), who moved the caliphate to Baghdad. There, in the "glory that was Baghdad," flowered an affluent and civilized culture.[32] Situated at the crossroads of the world, between east and west, Baghdad could draw upon the cultural legacies of both. Under such leaders as Harun al-Rashid (786–809) and al-Mamun (813–833), Baghdad became the center of the civilized world.

MUSLIM FORMS AND INSTITUTIONS TAKE SHAPE

We have already characterized some of the basic forms of Muslim faith and culture, such as the Qur'an, the Prophethood of Muhammad, and the caliphate. Now we must see the way in which further forms took definitive shape during the early centuries of Muslim history. The list includes forms of thought and feeling, and also social forms. While there are some similarities, there are also many differences from the forms of the other two main monotheistic religions, Judaism and Christianity. We shall describe briefly: (1) *hadiths*, or traditions, (2) *shari'a*, or Muslim law, (3) *fiqh*, or the four main systems of legal interpretation,

(4) *kharija*, or the Kharijites, (5) *Shi'a*, or Shi'ites, (6) the *Sunna*, or "Tradition," sect, (7) *Sufis*, or Muslim mystics, and (8) Muslim philosophy.

HADITHS

While Islam has resolutely refused to deify the Prophet, his teachings, by precept and practice, have always carried the highest authority. Many of the precepts are contained in the Qur'an and hence are regarded not as Muhammad's but as the revealed will of Allah. However, the Qur'an does not cover every human situation. Further, many of the Prophet's contemporaries recalled words or deeds of the Prophet or his close companions which could serve as models for belief or behavior. Many such hadiths (the word means "narrative") were undoubtedly accurate recollections, but as time passed and their numbers grew, many hadiths appeared which were either plainly spurious or suspiciously slanted for or against this or that partisan viewpoint. As a Muslim writer has said, "It is remarkable to note the facility with which even men of undoubted piety did not hesitate to attribute to the Prophet sayings made up by themselves to promote sectarian interests."[33] One imaginative Muslim confessed to outright fabrication of some 4,000 hadiths!

The need for critical sifting led to the rise of a science for testing the veracity of hadiths. The method of testing was to establish a chain of reliable attestors by which a hadith could be traced back to the Prophet or a companion; and on this basis hadiths were judged "sound," "good," or "weak." It was vital to Islam to have reliable hadiths as a basis of Muslim law as well as of personal devotion and morality. Out of this process of critical inquiry emerged several collections of hadiths, of which the best known and most authoritative were those of al-Bukari (d. 870) and al-Muslim (d. 875). The former was an Iranian Muslim who traveled throughout the Near East gathering a vast number of hadiths (some said 600,000!) and sifting them to some 7,300 reliable ones. Eliminating repetition, al-Bukari reduced this number to 2,700. His collection of hadiths has commanded an authority in Islam second only to the Qur'an.

SHARI'A

Muslim law, or shari'a, arose out of the essential nature of Islam. If Allah has revealed his will for humankind, then the eternal destiny of every person consists in hearing and doing the divine will. Such is the austere logic of Muslim monotheism. However, it is equally important that all aspects of human life, corporate as well as individual, be brought into relation to the divine will. It is at precisely this point that Muslim law emerges as a way of relating the divine words of the Qur'an to all the varied circumstances of human society. This is, incidentally, a problem which has emerged analogously in other monotheistic religions. Talmudic law in Judaism, canon law in Roman Catholic Christianity, and scriptural law or norms in Calvinistic Christianity arose to solve similar problems.

FIQH

Four systems of jurisprudence (fiqh) have arisen in Islam, differing in methods, in the degree of liberality or rigor in interpretation of Qur'an for changing circumstances, and in their respective understanding and combination of four aspects of interpretation. These are (1) dependence on Qur'an, (2) dependence on hadiths, (3) reasoning by analogy (*qiyas*), and (4) consensus (*ijma*) of the Muslim community. The most liberal school, the *Hanifite*, was founded by Abu Hanifah (d. 767), an Iranian who lived and taught in Iraq and whose teachings were recorded by followers. His interpretations began with the Qur'an, taking little notice of hadiths and relying heavily on analogy and current consensus. For example, if no quranic teachings were available for a situation, or if an apparent conflict arose, this type of interpretation dealt with it by analogical reasoning from different parts of the Qur'an or by consulting current consensus. The Hanifite interpretation still prevails in Iraq, Iran, India, Pakistan, and central Asia.

The second school, the *Malikite*, was founded in Medina by Malik ibn-Anas (d. 795) and based its interpretation upon Qur'an and hadiths taken together. Where problems arose, Malik consulted Muslim opinion. In particularly difficult problems, he resorted to analogy or even appealed to the principle of public advantage. This school of interpretation is followed in North Africa, in parts of Egypt, and in eastern Arabia.

The *Shafiite* school of interpretation was founded by al-Shafii of Egypt (d. 820), who preferred hadiths to Qur'an when differences arose, for the reason that the hadiths reflect Muslim opinion during developing periods. Yet Shafiite interpretation rejects consensus in all forms as unwarranted speculation. The Shafiite principles of interpretation have been followed in Lower Egypt, east Africa, south Arabia, Palestine, south India, and Indonesia.

The most strictly conservative school of legal interpretation, the *Hanbalite*, was founded by Ibn Hanbal (d. 855), a student of al Shafii who reacted strongly against the liberality—and laxity, as he saw it—of the Baghdad of his times. Hence he rejected all but a strictly literal interpretation of Qur'an and hadiths. For his uncompromising attitudes he was scourged and imprisoned. His followers, notably in Saudi Arabia, have continued his austere attitudes and principles.

KHARIJA

It has already been noted that Ali was assassinated by a disgruntled Kharijite follower. Who were the Kharijites? The Arabic work *kharija* means "to withdraw," and it refers to a fiercely partisan sect of early Islam which practiced and justified the killing of others whom they believed to be unfaithful to Muslim teaching.[34] They justified this practice by their beliefs concerning the community of believers. Members had to justify by their deeds and beliefs their membership in the community. Those who failed were expelled and, in accordance with Arab tradition, outsiders might be killed forthwith—without the guilt of murder on any who carried out the deed. As might be guessed, there were many degrees of infidelity, according to this harsh and exclusive creed. Could a Kharijite, for example, sell his daughter in marriage to a non-Kharijite? Under what circumstances, if at all, could a Kharijite live peacefully under non-Kharijite rulers? We shall see other instances of this extreme attitude in the history of Islam.

SHI'A

We have already noted the Shi'ites as the Muslim sects which asserted Ali as the first true caliph, with the implication that his three predecessors were spurious. The word *shi'a* means "follower," i.e., of Ali. In some parts of the Shi'ite world, the first three caliphs are still formally execrated or cursed every week at the mosque. The Shi'a regard Muhammad as Prophet, and Ali as imam, or divinely appointed leader and model for the faithful. The divinely ordained imamate of Ali is justified by a Shi'ite hadith which represents the Prophet as saying just before his death: "I shall soon be called back to heaven; I leave you two important bequests, the *Koran* and my family."[35] Needless to say, non-Shi'ite Muslims reject the authenticity of this hadith.

Secular historians point to the origin of the Shi'a not in theology or faith, but in history and society. When Muawiyah (archvillain for the Shi'ites) moved the caliphate from Kufa in Iraq to Damascus in Syria, he aroused the opposition of the Arabs of Iraq. The Shi'ite name served as a rallying point for many different causes and traditions whose common element was opposition to the Sunna, or majority party. To this was added in the course of time the distinctive feature of the Shi'a belief in a divinely sent imam or leader of the Muslim community. Indeed, the imam came to be regarded as the authoritative source of Muslim doctrine. There has been, however, a considerable disagreement about the identity of some in the succession of twelve imams. The Shi'a have been riven by sectarian divisions, often of an extreme and violent kind. Usually the resulting sects have gathered about particular imams.

All Shi'ite sects accept Ali as the first imam and his two sons, al-Hasan (d. 669) and al-Husain (d. 680) as the second and third, respectively. Actually, al-Hasan was led by Muawiyah to resign his imamship for a pension—a fact not often recognized by Shi'ites. His younger brother, al-Husain, was not so easily diverted; both he and his young son died in the battle of Kerbala (680) against Muawiyah's successor, Yaze'd. The martyr's death of al-Husain is an event annually commemorated in the Shi'ite world by ten days of lamentation and a passion play depicting the suffering and death of the third imam.

Al-Husain's son, Ali Zain al-Abidin (d. 713), was the fourth imam. One of his two sons was Muhammad al-Bakir (d. 731), through whom according to most Shi'ites the succession continued. However, the sect of Zaidites reject him, accepting his brother Zaid as the true fifth imam. Known as *Fivers*, the Zaidites continue in small numbers in Yemen and in the past have existed from Morocco to Tabaristan. The succession of Muhammad al-Bakir proceeded through his son, Ja'far al-Sadik (d. 765), who in turn had two sons, the older Ismail (d. 760) and the younger Musa al-Kasir (d. 797). Ismail would legitmately have followed his father, as seventh in the line, but he was set aside for drunkenness, a clear and serious violation of Muslim law. His followers have consistently denied the allegation, and when Ismail died five years before his father, they said he was not dead, but hidden, and would come again as the *mahdi*, or "expected one," who would set the world right.

Several important Muslim groups have been Ismailis, or *Seveners*. A ninth-century Persian named Abdullah ibn-Mamum (d. ca. 874), who claimed to be the earthly representative of the hidden imam, built up a secret society devoted to the violent destruction of the Abbasid caliphate. He failed in this ambitious project, but his descendants founded the Fatimid caliphate of Egypt.

A related group of Ismailis, or Seveners, were the Karmatians. Their founder, Hamdan Karmat, had been a disciple of Abdullah. In the ninth century he built up in South Arabia an independent kingdom which extended from Iraq to Yemen. The Karmatians successfully defended themselves against the armies of the Baghdad caliphate. They cut the pilgrimage routes to Mecca and exacted a fee for safe passage. On one daring sortie, they invaded Mecca during the pilgrimage season and carried off the Black Stone, holding it for twenty years and returning it only on the request of their fellow Seveners, the Fatimids of Egypt.

Another, similar group of Ismailis were the Assassins of Alamut, of Persia, founded and led by Hasan Sabah (d. 1124). The Assassins (the name is taken from *hashish*, name of the narcotic which they took in order to induce states of religious exaltation) made the practice of killing a fine art. As practitioners of this dreaded and bloody art, the Assassins were feared throughout the Middle East. Working his way into his victim's confidence, the Assassin would strike him down with a poisoned dagger on some public occasion. He was undeterred by the fact that he too was immediately killed, for he believed that he would go directly to paradise. The Iranian stronghold which was the home of the Assassins was visited and described by Marco Polo on his way to China.

Another offshoot of the Ismailis, or Seveners, are the Druze of Lebanon. Their origin may be traced to the sixth Fatimid Caliph of Egypt, al Hakim (985–1021) and to a teacher of that time, Ismail al Darazi, from whom the name Druze is derived. They broke with traditional Muslim teaching by asserting that al Hakim was an incarnation of deity. They added their own esoteric interpretation of the Qur'an and other sources. While demanding truth within their group, they sanctioned dissimulation (*taqiyah*) or lying to outsiders. In the course of time they separated from Islam and also became a closed sect, forbidden to speak of their religion to outsiders. Today they number between three and four hundred thousand members, mainly in Lebanon, Syria, and Israel.

In contrast to the Ismailis, or Seveners, the majority of Shi'ites accept the whole succession of twelve imams, thus acquiring the designation of *Twelvers*. The twelfth imam, Muhammad al-Muntazar (d. 878), is reputed by Shi'ites not to have died but to have withdrawn into a cave in Samarra up the river from Baghdad. Believers assert that he is not dead, but hiding, and that he will return as the mahdi to set the world right and prepare for the last judgment. In Iran, where some 7 million Twelvers live, the shahs have since the sixteenth century often asserted themselves to be earthly representatives of the hidden imam. More recently the Ayatollah Khomeini has explicitly asserted this claim.

In addition to these main sects, the Shi'a have produced other, smaller and less important groups. Loyalty to their imams has often been deep and stubborn, even to the point of sanctioning dissimulation (*taqiyah*), which in times of persecution has permitted outward conformity to, and inner dissent from, Sunna doctrine. Shi'ite theology has sanctioned allegorical interpretation of the Qur'an, which has sometimes opened the way to a wide variety of esoteric teachings which Sunnis reject. Shi'ite theology has denied the eternal or divine nature of the Qur'an and has asserted freedom of the human will. As we shall see in the next section, this directly disagrees with Sunni doctrine and agrees with that of their enemies, the Mutazilites. Shi'ite doctrine also shares in the tradition of Muslim mysticism called *Sufism*.

SUNNA

The word *sunna* means "tradition," and it refers to the distinctive theology which emerged in the course of two centuries of argument and controversy and gained general acceptance throughout non-Shi'ite Islam. Theological controversy and parties arose early in the Muslim world. For example, an early group called the *Murjites* rose to contest the extreme attitudes of the Kharijites—opposing the Kharijite view that unfaithful Muslims could be summarily killed. The Murjites argued for "delayed judgment," that is, the view that Allah alone knows who is a faithful Muslim, and that Allah will make this judgment on the last day. Hence the issue should be left in his hands! Another party, called *Qadarites*, opposed absolute predestination with the view that human beings are free and responsible.

Still another party of very considerable influence and significance was the *Mutazilites*. Their cardinal doctrines were the unity and justice of Allah, on the one hand, and human freedom and responsibility, on the other. They also insisted upon rational method for the study of things religious, probably influenced by the heritage of Greek thought which permeated the Near Eastern world.[36]

The major premise of the Mutazilites was their insistence upon the absolute unity and justice of Allah. A combination of religious and rational factors led them to this view. From it they drew conclusions which were highly controversial. True, they insisted that no final or absolute position be taken interpreting the justice of Allah. However, in the Mutazilite insistence that Allah is just, opponents saw a compulsion over Allah. They argued that if justice were required of Allah, he would in that case not be absolutely free, as all good Muslims know him to be.

Mutazilites argued against literal anthropomorphic descriptions of Allah, as, for example, having human features or sitting on a throne. They asserted that no attributes external to Allah, as they stated the matter, may be allowed to conflict with his absolute unity. Hence the concrete imagery of the Qur'an concerning Allah (and concerning heaven and hell, too) must be taken figuratively rather than literally.

From the absolute unity of God they argued against the popular notion of the Qur'an as uncreated and eternal. Truly this would deify the Qur'an and thus conflict with the absolute unity of the one God. Rather, insisted the Mutazilites, the Qur'an is this side of the line which separates creation from the creator. Mutazilite theologians in the court of Caliph al-Mamun influenced him in 827 to proclaim the created character of the Qur'an as established doctrine, purging from public life anyone who held contrary views.

Among those who stood out against this official view was Ibn Hanbal of the Hambalite school of shari'a. Chained, scourged, and thrown into prison, he continued to expouse the eternal and uncreated Qur'an. However, the man who turned the tide against the Mutazilites was one of their own number, al-Ashari (d. 935 CE). After many years of study and practice of the rational method of the Mutazilites, at the age of forty he had an intense religious experience or conversion which turned him to polar opposition. He asserted that revelation, not reason, is the source of religious truth, though he still used rational methods for the exposition and defense of divine revelation.

Al-Ashari asserted the absolute uniqueness and the absolute sovereignty of Allah. Since he causes all events, it is he who causes humans to think as the Qur'an bids them do. He conceded that human beings acquired from Allah a certain limited autonomy—al-Ashari called this "acquisition"—and so attained a measure of both freedom and responsibility. Yet he did not shrink from asserting Allah as the cause of evil as well as good.

As for the Qur'an, Ashari asserted that the true Qur'an is eternal in heaven, and that the earthly book is a divinely certified copy. Wrestling with the teaching of the Qur'an concerning the anthropomorphic attributes of Allah, Ashari rejected the Mutazilites' doctrine that these are mere human metaphors, affirming them as part of Allah's inscrutable sovereign will. From al-Ashari's time onward the Sunna was massively conservative in outlook.

MYSTICS AND PHILOSOPHERS

Despite its massive conservatism, it would be grossly inaccurate to suppose that Muslim faith means mainly or solely assent to the traditional credo or that all change and development stopped with al-Ashari. Quite the contrary: the Muslim tradition has continued to generate many sorts of new responses to, and interpretations of, its dominant theme of submission to Allah. Two of these responses, that of the mystic and that of the philosopher-theologian, plus some combinations of the two, must now be considered.

In some of its forms, Muslim mysticism has been a way of cultivating immediate communion with Allah, who is not only transcendent, distant, and alone, but according to the mystics' favorite quaranic passage also "nearer than one's jugular vein." But in other, bolder forms, Muslim mysticism can be regarded as nothing less than a frontal challenge to Muslim monotheism. Some mystics in their journey to God move past direct communion with God to forms of absorption which pass roughly over the line fixed between creator and creation, or between the one Lord and his dominion. So it is that some mystics have involved themselves in the unforgivable sin of shirk.

Islam has also produced a great tradition of philosopher-theologians who have in devotion to freedom sought rational grounds for belief. Al-Ashari might command the faithful to "believe without question," but some bold spirits have refused to accept so anti-intellectual a view of Allah's requirement of his human children.

In the case of both mystics and philosophers, the Greek tradition of thought from Plato and Aristotle to Plotinus was a strong contributory cause, though often it is difficult to discern its precise role. In turn, Muslim mystics and philosophers have had important influence on other traditions, notably Judaism and Christianity.

Mysticism began early in Muslim history. Within the first century, ascetics who practiced celibacy and fasting resigned themselves to the care of Allah and concentrated their minds on the "ninety-nine beautiful names of Allah."[37] The term *sufi*, literally "wool wearer," probably refers to the coarse wool garment which was worn as an ascetic exercise. That these Muslim ascetics and mystics were influenced by Christians of the same bent is very probable, though the lines of influence are hard to trace in detail. Gibb is undoubtedly correct in interpreting Sufism as a popular religious movement aimed at countering the intellectualism of lawyers and theologians.[38] Such indeed has been mysticism's historic function in Islam as well as in other religious traditions. However, there is a further element of protest in Sufism. Against the austere and transcendent monotheism of the Tradition, mystics placed the immediacy of God's presence in their hearts—in the words of the Qur'an, "nearer than one's jugular vein."

In addition to innumerable anonymous pilgrims on the path to truth, as Muslim mystics like to characterize themselves, this way has produced some great individuals who have left records of their pilgrimages and explorations. Among the earliest was a woman saint, Rabi'a al-Adaurya (d. 801), in whom the mystical theme of the love of God found expression in such lines as the following:

> I love Thee with two loves, love of my happiness,
> And perfect love, to love Thee as is Thy due.
> My selfish love is that I do naught
> But think on Thee, excluding all beside;
> But that purest love, which is Thy due,
> Is that the veils which hide Thee fall, and I gaze on Thee,

No praise to me either this or that,
Nay, Thine the praise for both that love and this.[39]

A development of the greatest significance was taken by Abu Yasid al Bistami (d. 815), who taught *fana*, or the annihilation of individual human consciousness during the mystical experience. Proclaiming the identity of soul and God, he cried out, "How great is my majesty!" Some students of mysticism have suggested that he was influenced by Indian mysticism.

Another mystic, Harith al-Muhasibi of Basrah (d. 857), described the stages on his path to truth. They began traditionally enough with repentance, renunciation, poverty, and the like, and continued through trust or faith in God. However, what was most notable was the culmination of the mystical journey in a state called *illumination*, consisting of an ineffable experience of light and love in which human individuality seemed lost or absorbed in its divine object.

The orthodox culmination of the Sufi tradition was the thought of al-Ghazzali, who in life and thought fused Sufism and tradition. Al-Ghazzali was born in Iran but lived and taught in Baghdad. His life story and life work show similarity as well as contrast with his great predecessor al-Ashari. Al-Ashari had been a Mutazilite and made his way by logical method to traditionalism; al-Ghazzali was an Asharite theologian whose creative contribution was to establish theology on the basis of personal mystical experience.[40]

Al-Ghazzali was born in Persia in 1058 and educated in both law (of the Shafiite tradition) and Asharite theology.[41] His reputation for learning and brilliance led to his appointment at the newly founded University of Baghdad. A period of spiritual struggle and crisis led him first through skepticism and then onward to Sufi mysticism. Apparently he found the intellectualism of the theologians sterile and dead. But he also found in mystical experience a way of breathing life into its dry bones.

Becoming a simple Sufi, al-Ghazzali left the university, journeying to Syria for meditation and prayer among Sufi communities. After two years he celebrated his return to faith by making the pilgrimage to Mecca. Then he returned home. For a time he taught again at the university. He began again to write, completing his monumental volume, *The Revivification of the Religious Sciences*. He died at the age of fifty-three in the year 1111.

Al-Ghazzali's achievement consisted in his reaffirmation of Muslim orthodoxy by infusing it with the vitality of Sufi mysticism. Taken alone, the intellectual approach to God was flat and stale. One of al-Ghazzali's books was *The Inconsistency of the Philosophers*, a work in which the author pointed out many alleged inner contradictions of the rational systems and speculations of philosophy. From this impasse al-Ghazzali—and his philosophy—were rescued by the mystic daily communion with God. The core of faith, al-Ghazzali believed, was to turn one's heart in contrition to God, and by Sufi disciplines to maintain this continuing communion with the divine source of all truth and goodness. From this religious experience also sprang al-Ghazzali's great philosophical synthesis, which Muslim thinkers ever since have taken as their definitive formulation.

Other Muslim mystics were not so sympathetic to tradition. Particularly notable was al-Hallaj (d. 922), who pressed beyond communion and illumination to complete absorption in God, and was scourged and killed for his public declaration, "I am the Truth," which was understood by his Muslim hearers as equating himself with Allah who alone is truth. In the writings of al-Hallaj, the reader finds a record of direct communion with Allah rising at length to union in which no duality is experienced or claimed. Al-Hallaj frequently used the metaphor of love for this relation, crying out, "I am He whom I love and He whom I love is I."[42]

Similar reports of the climactic experience of mysticism are given in the writings of ibn-Arabi (d. 1240). He writes:

> Just as he who dies the death of the body, loses all his attributes, both those worthy of praise and those to be condemned, come to an end, and in all the man's states what is Divine comes to take the place of what was mortal. Thus, instead of his own essence, there is the essence of God and in place of his own qualities, there are the attributes of God. He who knows himself sees his whole existence to be the Divine existence, but does not realise that any change has taken place in his own nature or qualities. For when you know yourself, your "I-ness" vanishes and you know that you and God are one and the same.[43]

Ibn-Arabi also boldly drew out conclusions that must have seemed to his Muslim friends a complete denial of the faith:

> There was a time when I blamed my companion if his religion did not resemble mine.
> Now, however, my heart accepts every form: it is pasture ground for gazelles, a cloister for monks,
> A temple for idols and a *Ka'bah* for the pilgrim, thy tables of the Torah and the sacred books of the Koran.
> Love alone is my religion, and wherever their beasts of burden go there is my religion and my faith.[44]

Many of these notes found similar expression in the songs of the Persian mystical poet Jalal al-Din Rumi (d. 1273), who was also the founder of the *Maulawi* (also called *Mevlevi*) order of dervishes. Using the love of friends as his metaphor, he sang of mystical union in these words:

> When the rose is dead and the garden ravaged, where shall we find the perfume of the rose? In rose-water.
> Inasmuch as God comes not into sight, the prophets are His vicars.
> Do not mistake me! 'Tis wrong to think that the vicar and He Whom the vicar represents are two.

> To the form-worshipper they are two; when you have escaped from
> consciousness of form, they are One.
> Whilst you regard the form, you are seeing double: look, not at the eyes, but at
> the light which flows from them.
> You cannot distinguish the lights of ten lamps burning together, so long as your
> face is set towards this light alone.
> In things spiritual there is no partition, no number, no individuals.
> How sweet is the oneness of the Friend with His friends! Catch the spirit and
> clasp it to your bosom.
> Mortify rebellious form till it wastes away: unearth the treasure of Unity!
> Simple were we and all one essence: we were knotless and pure as water.
> When that goodly Light took shape, it became many, like shadows cast by a
> battlement.
> Demolish the dark battlement, and all difference will vanish from amidst this
> multitude.[45]

Words such as these could be taken as little less than a frontal challenge to Muslim monotheism, and there have been many austere orthodox followers of the Prophet who have taken them as precisely that. Yet it is also a fact of Muslim history that others, to use a favorite metaphor of mystics, have drunk at this fountain, refreshed their thirsting souls, and then continued their way along Islam's straight path.

Mystics have often been individualists, defying communal restrictions. Yet inevitably, too, they gather into communities and formulate rules and ways for their common life. So it has been with the Sufis. They have gathered into communities, sometimes in cities but sometimes too in solitary deserts. Usually the communities or orders bear the impression of some striking, attractive person who gathered other men around him. Usually they have begged for food, hence they are called *dervishes* (from the Persian *darwash*, "one who comes to the door"). Often they have used music and dancing to induce mystic exaltation. Local orders and communities of Sufis too numerous and too various in their practices for description here have sprung up in all parts of the Muslim world. Three orders of dervishes must serve here as illustrations of the range and variety of these orders:

1. The *Kadirites* were founded by Abd al-Kadar (d. 1166) in Baghdad. Loosely organized, devoted to philanthropy and piety, and generally shunning extremism, the Kadirites have spread over the Muslim world from Algeria to Java.
2. The *Rifa'ites* were founded by Ahmad al-Rifa'i (d. 1182) and have gained for themselves the designation of Howling Dervishes. In addition to howling, they have been given to such extremes as firewalking and playing with serpents, as well as many form of self-mortification.
3. The *Maulawites*, or Whirling Dervishes, were founded by the Persian poet Jalal al-Din Rumi (d. 1273), who passed on to his followers the use of music and dancing to induce mystical ecstasy.[46]

The history of Sufism has not been free of bizarre aberrations, magic, and superstition. Sufi reverence for saints has also drawn violent reactions from traditionalist reformers. At its best, however, Sufism has produced many good works and renewed piety.

As in other religious traditions, so also in Islam questions addressed to tradition or to mysticism served to generate philosophy. Al-Ghazzali's great theological synthesis has been mentioned. He was a theologian in the precise sense of thinking and studying within Muslim tradition and authority. Other Muslim thinkers, both before and after al-Ghazzali, were less deferential to tradition. They studied and reasoned in ways independent of religious authority and tradition. In a word they were philosophers.

Islamic philosophy began in the attempt of Arab scholars to reclaim the classical Greek philosophic heritage. It is, indeed, to these Muslim scholar-philosophers from al-Kindi to Averroes that the West owes the preservation of Greek philosophy and its transmission through Jewish and Christian Scholastics to the modern world.

The founder of Muslim philosophy was al-Kindi (800–870), tutor to the son of the caliph of Baghdad, who was also the owner of a large library of Greek science and philosophy and friend of Mutazilite theologians, and himself a Neoplatonist. One significant feature of the philosophy of al-Kindi and his successors was the assertion of the literal creation of the world by God at a moment in time. This idea seemed to these philosophers a necessary implication of Muslim monotheism.

In al-Farabi (875–950), Islamic philosophy achieved maturity. His system was a blend of Aristotle, Plato, and Plotinus. At the center was first being or absolute one, which was taken as equivalent to God. He also taught that philosophy and not theology was the highest knowledge, and that the highest goal is to develop and realize one's rational powers.

Whirling Dervishes, who use music and dance to induce mystical ecstasy. (Ira Friedlander/ Woodfin Camp & Associates.)

Abu ali ibn Sina (980–1037), known to the west as Avicenna, was a Persian physician, advisor to rulers, student of Greek philosophy, but most of all, the greatest and most original classical Islamic philosopher. He made and argued the distinction, all-important for subsequent religious philosophy, between necessary being and contingent being. He also argued that in God essence and existence are conjoined, while in contingent beings they are separated. Avicenna sought to translate monotheistic faith into the language of Scholastic philosophy.

The last great Muslim philosopher was Ibn Rushd (1126–1198), or as he is known in the west, Averroes. He was chief judge in Seville and Cordova, Spain, and wrote on Malikite jurisprudence. He responded to al-Ghazzali's *Inconsistency of the Philosophers* with a polemical tract entitled *The Inconsistency of the Inconsistency*, which sought to show the capacity of human reason to attain knowledge of the world, including the things of faith. Averroes was convinced that philosophy and religion are both true and may therefore be harmonized with each other. After Averroes, no philosopher of comparable stature emerged in Islam. Historians have no fully adequate explanation for this lack, but the fact is clear.

ISLAM EXPANDS FURTHER IN AFRICA AND ASIA

Following the incredibly rapid and vast outward thrust of the first century or two, Islam continued to expand in both Africa and Asia. We must now sketch this development.

Stopped at Tours in France in 732CE, Islam rebounded into southern France and Spain. Spain remained wholly or partly Muslim until 1492. Meanwhile the push into Africa continued. From the north African base achieved during the first century, Islam pushed southward. Along the eastern coast it followed merchants and mariners as far south as Zanzibar. In central Africa Islam followed the Nile southward, then penetrated to the regions of the modern states of Chad and Niger. In the west, Ghana was captured by Almoravid armies in 1076. The rulers of Mali in the fourteenth century CE decreed Islam as the established religion. From both eastern and western bases, Islam pushed onward in central Africa.

Meanwhile, in Asia, Muslim expansion followed the central trade routes eastward as far as China. Muslims claims that Said ibn abi Waqqas, a companion of the Prophet, made the long journey to China by sea in 651 CE. However, this may be, Islam arrived in China in force during the first two centuries, over the land trade routes which link China with Europe. Muslim fortunes in China have ebbed and flowed with the passing centuries and dynasties. A high point was reached during the Yu'an or Mongol dynasty (1260–1368), when it was said that eight of twelve Chinese regional governors were followers of the Prophet. The following Ming dynasty was a time of acclimating or the sinification of Islam. The last Chinese dynasty, the Ch'ing or Manchu (1644–1911), was by contrast anti-Muslim. There is little reliable knowledge as to how Islam fares in contemporary China. Indeed, statistics vary widely concerning the number of Muslims in China.

A particularly significant event in Islam's Asian expansion was the conversion of steppe peoples of central Asia, notably several groups, first the Turks, then the Mongols, who in turn became the carriers of the faith to other peoples.

The steppe peoples took Islam in their own terms, finding congenial this simple, straightforward faith with its teachings concerning the jihad, or holy war, waged by *ghazis*, or holy warriors. It is also notable that most of the steppe peoples opted for the Sunni form of Islam. And, in the case of both Turks and Mongols, some groups turned westward, conquering and subjugating previously Muslim lands. Most notable historically was the Ottoman conquest of Asia Minor or modern Turkey.

From central Asia, Islam made its way south into the Indian subcontinent. In 999 Mahmud of Ghaznin (the modern nation of Afghanistan) began a series of raids into northwest India which resulted in a Ghaznid dynasty over that region. A century later the Ghaznids were displaced by another Turkish invader, the Ghorids, who were also Muslims. The Ghorids and their successors achieved dominance in northern Indian with a capital at Delhi, from which Islam spread to most of India.

The most recent Muslim invaders of India were the Moghuls, whose first leader, Babur, secured an Indian foothold in the battle of Panipat in 1526. The Moghul dynasty ruled north India until the eighteenth century.

It is not surprising that Islam, carried thus to India by invading armies, long remained to a great degree the faith of these alien invaders and rulers. Only very slowly did it put down roots into the Indian soil. The relations between Islam and Hinduism were not satisfactory to either faith. Nor indeed have satisfactory relations been achieved at any subsequent time. Islam and Hinduism remain at an impasse in twentieth-century India. For Islam, only conversion could be a satisfactory conclusion, and Hindu India has remained unconverted. For Hinduism, assimilation of the new faith would have been satisfactory, but Islam has remained unassimilated. What has occurred has been aptly characterized as "apartheid" between these two faiths, modified only by peripheral meeting and mingling at the level of popular religion.[47]

As it has developed historically, Islam in India has not differed in fundamentals from Islam elsewhere in the world in belief or practice. One notable characteristic has been the development of an especially strong tradition of Sufism. To this it must be added that despite the mutal alienation of Islam and Hinduism, the ordinary people of India have sometimes been unable to distinguish the Muslim Sufi from the Hindu devotee of bhakti.

The Moghuls were Muslims of varying degrees of devotion and orthodoxy. The greatest of the Moghul rulers, Akbar (1555–1605), was notable not only as an enlightened emperor but as an avid student of India's and the world's religions. As a boy in Kabul, Afghanistan, he had been instructed in the teachings of Persian Muslim mystics. He married a Hindu Rajput princess and recoiled from

A Muslim pilgrim to Mecca meets a Brahman on the road. Sixteenth-century Indian miniature. (Metropolitan Museum of Art. Alexander Smith Cochran. 1913.)

the religious policies of repression and persecution followed by his predecessors. His interest in the many faiths of his far-flung empire led to a notable series of discussions among exponents of the Muslim Sunna and Shi'a, Jainism, Sikhism, Hinduism, Parseeism, and Christianity. The result of these discussions was the proclamation by Akbar in 1582 of his own syncretistic "Divine Faith." While it did not outlive its founder, it stands as a monument to his breadth of mind, his tolerance, and his insatiable curiosity. The reader may recall that Sikhism grew out of the same historical situation which elicited Akbar's concern. It may also be added that Sikhism succeeded where Akbar's Divine Faith failed, probably largely because it was the faith of a real community and tradition of people.

Akbar's son Jahangir (1605–1627) shared none of his father's breadth of mind. He returned to an official policy of intolerance and repression of non-Muslim faiths, which was passed on in turn to his son Shah Jahan (1627–1658)—the builder of the Taj Mahal—and his grandson Aurangzeb (1658–1707).

As the Moghul empire sank into decline, the European nations arrived in force in India. The first arrivals had been the Portuguese, who seized Goa in 1510. They were followed within a century by the British and French, who battled for the domination of India, the British achieving victory by the middle of the eighteenth century. As noted in Chapter 6, with the West came modernity with all its manifold challenges to India's traditional culture. The story of its challenge to Indian Islam will be sketched in the next section of this chapter.

Meanwhile one important premodern Indian Muslim, Shah Walli-ullah of Delhi (1703–1762), must at least be mentioned. He lived among the crumbling ruins of the Moghul empire and sought the reform of Indian Islam.[48] Combining in his own life a steadfast loyalty to the Sunna with ardent Sufi practice, he advocated a reconstruction of Muslim faith. His writings were aimed against the inner distortion and deterioration of Islam and against its loss of influence in Indian society. Muslim reformers and builders of the next two centuries built on the foundations he laid.[49]

The onward march of Islam in Asia did not stop in India. In southeast Asia it pushed into Indonesia and the Philippines. Marco Polo's thirteenth-century travel reports tell of a Muslim community in Sumatra.[50] A Chinese traveler two centuries later described Java as Muslim. In the absence of reliable historical records, we can conclude only that between the thirteenth and sixteenth centuries Islam expanded its beachhead and conquered the islands of Indonesia. From this base it pushed on to the island of Mindanao of the Philippines, whose Muslim faith gained for the people the name of *Moros*.

Turning to another part of the world, we note that Iran had been Muslim since its conquest in the 640s. In the thirteenth century it was overrun by Mongol khans, who were, in turn, converted to the faith. A particularly significant development began in 1499 when Ismail Safavid, a fanatical Shi'ite leader, gathered a military force and conquered Tabriz. In 1500 he was crowned shah of Iran, beginning the Safavid dynasty which ruled Iran throughout the six-

The Taj Mahal, Agra, India, a masterpiece of Moghul architecture. (Courtesy of Leonard Dart.)

teenth century and effectively turned the country to Shi'ite faith. Iran remains to this day the principal Shi'ite nation. Recent statistics show Iran 93 percent Shi'ite and neighboring Iraq 50 percent.

ISLAM CONFRONTS THE MODERN WORLD

The coming of modernity has posed multiple problems for Islam. Islam's massively conservative tradition has often reacted instinctively in antimodern ways. Often modernity has been carried by Christian peoples, making it doubly unpalatable to Muslims. From the Arab world to Indonesia, Islam has often made common cause with colonial nationalism against what is often termed *western imperialism*. For these reasons and others, Islam has not found it easy to adjust to the modern world.

Many of these attitudes found early expression in the militantly antimodern Wahhabi movement of Arabia. The founder, ibn-Abd al-Wahhab (1703–1783), has been called a *Muslim Puritan*. Austere, rigorous, and simple in his faith, he protested alike against inner corruption of the faith, such as he observed in popular forms of Sufism, and against compromise with the world. The slogans of the Wahhabi movement were "Back to the Qur'an," and "Back to the pure Sunna." Yet this return was both narrow and militantly intolerant. Aligning themselves with the kings of Saudi Arabia, they broke out of central Arabia and were finally contained only by the combined military forces of Turkey and Egypt after more than a half-century of fighting.

The Wahhabi movement has left a continuing legacy in Saudi Arabia. In 1924, when the deposed Ottoman caliph ceded Mecca and Medina to Saudi Arabia, the Wahhabis in their iconoclastic zeal turned the birthplace of the Prophet into a resting place for camels and demolished the grave markers of the Prophet and his companions. This extremism finds expression in Saudi Arabia's continuing adherence to the Hanbalite school of interpretation of shari'a. Wahhabi extremism is generally repudiated elsewhere in the Muslim and Arab worlds, though it has stimulated other efforts at reform in many parts of the Muslim world, and it has doubtless stimulated Arab nationalism.

In more recent times, the Arab world has been characterized as the locus of "Islamic crisis."[51] By this is meant the widely held view of Arab peoples that their whole way of life is being attacked, chiefly by the West. In this complex attitude there are strands of feeling as old as the crusades of medieval Europe, but there are also events of history as new as the founding of the state of Israel. Arab peoples and their leaders have responded defensively, and a part of their defense is a close identification of Islam with the Arab cause. This is an identification which non-Arab Muslims often find questionable. Yet it is a combination which often adds a religious dimension to Arab nationalism. It also has generated a vigorous and varied apologetic defense of Islam in books, pamphlets, and journals, and such universities as Al Azhar.

Among popular organizations, the *Ikwan al Muslimum*, or Muslim Brotherhood, has played a role of political activism in the United Arab Republic, though it is necessary to add that its policies have sometimes lacked realism and have promoted violence. Less extreme, and less influential, are such other organizations as the Association of Muslim Youth.

In Turkey and Turkish areas, the problems for Islam are utterly different from those in the Arab world. In 1924 the so-called Young Turks under Kemal Ataturk overthrew the Ottoman empire, abolished the caliphate, and established a new government on a secular and constitutional basis. Church and state were separated, the shari'a was supplanted by secular law, and many new laws on matters ranging from education to marriage, divorce, and the status of women achieved drastic modernization.

Turkish Muslims insist, however, that these changes have in no sense constituted a desertion of Islam, but rather have led to a Muslim reformation.[52] They point out that Islam, separated from state support and state encumbrances, continues to live a vigorous life in Turkey. In towns and cities, mosques continue to thrive, and scholars expound the faith in ways compatible with modern life. Concerning the validity of these claims, only the future can decide.

Islam in India has in modern times generated its own unique issues and problems. Much that has happened in the nineteenth and twentieth centuries has been based, as we have seen, on the life and thought of Shah Walli-ullah. Likewise of great importance, not only to Indian Islam but to the whole Muslim world, is Jamal ad-Din al-Afghani (1839–1897). In his life and teachings he was both Sunni and Sufi, and characteristically he founded the pan-Islamic Khilifat (or Caliphate) movement, designed to draw together all Muslim peoples in mutual defense against European domination and to meet the challenge of the modern world. Afghani's influence extended throughout the Muslim world.

Nineteenth-century India produced a notable Muslim modernist in Sayyid Ahmad Khan (1817–1898), whose lifelong purpose was to demonstrate the compatibility of Islam with the new world that was dawning upon India. He remained faithful to the British during the 1857 mutiny and thereby gained British favor. In 1875 he founded the Muslim University of Aligarh. In journals, pamphlets, and books he proclaimed the compatibility of Islam and its Qur'an with modern science, education, and life.

In this tradition also stood Muhammad Iqbal (1873–1938), poet and philosopher, often called the *father of Pakistan*. Born to pious Muslim parents in the Punjab and educated in Europe as well as India, Iqbal combined ideas and attitudes drawn from Sufism with the philosophies of Nietzsche and Bergson. In addition to his volume *The Reconstruction of Religious Thought in Islam*,[53] which is a classic of Muslim liberalism, he soon became well known for his poetry, which gave eloquent expression to Sufi devotion.

Through the writings of both Sayyid Ahmad Khan and Muhammad Iqbal is to be seen a growing fear of India's Hindu majority. This note of anxious concern grew as the Indian Congress grew in influence and became more extreme in attitudes. Indian nationalism in many of its forms became increasingly Hindu. The reaction was an equally increasing Muslim nationalism.

Out of these attitudes the All-India Muslim League was founded in 1906. At a 1930 meeting of this organization, Iqbal declared for a separate Muslim state in northwest India. The name *Pakistan* was coined by a Muslim student at Cambridge University, Chandri Rahmat Ali, with *P* standing for Punjab, *a* for Afghaniz, *k* for Kashmir, *s* for Sind, and *tan* for Baluchistan. The synthetic word also has the meaning "land of the pure."[54] Rahmat Ali's first manifesto was issued in 1933, and by the late years of the same decade it was being seriously discussed by Indian politicians. In 1947 Pakistan came into existence as a Muslim state whose sovereign power was asserted to derive straight from Allah. It must immediately be added that along with certain other states, such as England, with established religions, Pakistan also has freedom of religion.

Widespread rioting and massacres accompanied the partition of India and founding of Pakistan; and the legacy of hostility continues to the present day. Within Pakistan there are some 66 million Muslims. They are divided between a conservative and a liberal party on issues having to do with the relation of Islam to the body politic. As has usually been true of religious establishments, Pakistan has raised fundamental issues concerning compromises between the ideal and the existing situation. Whether Islam has been strengthened or weakened by this emergence of an Indian Muslim state is still an open question. In 1971 the revolt of East Pakistan, with help from India, led to the formation of Bangladesh as an independent nation. West Pakistan, now the whole nation, has an estimated Muslim population of 65 million people.

One result of partition in India for Islam is that the Muslim minority is proportionally much smaller than in the old India, and anti-Muslim feeling on the part of Hindus has greatly increased. Indian Muslims also confront the issue of participating politically in a non-Muslim and professedly secular state. Culturally they seek to preserve their own ways, ranging from their Urdu language to their Muslim faith. As one sympathetic writer describes their situation, they are in India what the Muslim community is in the total world, an "important minority."[55]

ISSUES AND QUESTIONS

We have seen that the problem of modernity versus tradition recurs in many of the world's religions. In the case of Islam western students often ask, Why is Islam so conservative, indeed so stubbornly traditional? No single answer suffices for such a many-faceted question. A partial answer turns upon the relation of faith to culture. Islam has often been the religion of very traditional, even antimodern cultures, and has appropriated these attitudes to itself. Another partial answer turns upon the coming of modernity in the West, and the rise of an empire-colony relation of the West to nonwestern peoples. The consequence often is an antiwestern and antimodern attitude on the part of third world peoples and nations. Once we begin to disentangle these clusters of relations, at least some partial understanding of this issue may follow.

A second cluster of issues and questions centers in Islam as one of three monotheistic faiths. We have noted that like Judaism and Christianity Islam shares faith in the one God with the concept of revelatory experience and a sacred book and indeed even the vice of holy war. We bring up these common characteristics again in order to remark that Islam exhibits these traits in marked or outstanding ways. In its own words, it is "monotheism pure and simple," often charging that other faiths blur this monotheistic quality. Whatever the truth or falsity of such charges, these common qualities of monotheistic faith do enable Christians and Jews better to understand the genius of Islam.

Islam's particularly vivid and forceful assertion of monotheism can also shed light on another aspect of Islam, namely, its strong and persistent mystical tradition. We have noted some of the important figures and documents of this tradition, especially the figure of al Hallaj for whom the mysticism of communion became the mysticism of ontological union.

How shall we understand the strength and persistence of the Sufi tradition? Several explanations have been proposed. Here we suggest another, namely, that this mysticism is nothing less than a protest against the rigors of Islamic monotheism. Monotheism finds God in what we have called the revelatory experience. The mystic by definition, and by contrast, finds God or transcendence in the sheer immediacy of his own experience, needing no sacred book, no prophet, to justify what is thus immediately given.

If all this is true for the mysticism of communion, practiced by most of the

Islamic mystics, it is doubly true of al Hallaj, who passed beyond communion to full union with God, thus incurring the charge of blasphemy, or *shirk*, and receiving the death penalty. It is also interesting to note two other Sufi figures, Ibn Arabi, who escaped the fate of al Hallaj through a sympathetic ruler, and Jalalal din Rumi, who ever so carefully walked the line between communion and union, writing great poetry in the process.

Still another persistent question for Islam is not its nature as monotheism but what we have called the Bible's linear-dramatic view of history, which is closely linked to monotheism. What happened to history in Islamic experience? The question is a fair but difficult one. One answer is that the Prophet and many of his followers have been so intensely concerned with their own individual judgment by God that little attention is left over for the larger movement of history toward consummation. Another response—and a factual response—to our question is that Islam has not altogether avoided the issues of history and its consummation. For example, Ibn Kaldun (1332–1406) reflected upon world history in his al Mukkadimah. Also Islam has known its *Mahdis* and their expectation of a new age.

A final issue turns upon the Muslim population of the world. Estimates range literally from 800 million to 1 billion. Between these extremes the *Encyclopaedia Britannica Yearbook* and the *World Almanac* agree upon a current figure of 860,338,300.

NOTES

1. One recent valume is a notable exception: W. McNeill, *The Rise of the West*, University of Chicago Press, Chicago, 1963.
2. Kenneth Morgan (ed.), *Islam—The Straight Path*, Ronald, New York, 1958, p. 84.
3.. Arnold Toynbee, *Civilization on Trial*, Oxford University Press, Fair Lawn, N.J., 1948, pp. 184f.
4. See inter alia H. A. R. Gibb, *Mohammedanism*, Mentor Books, New American Library, New York, 1955.
5. Morgan, op. cit., p. 6.
6. Ibid., p. 7.
7. Wur'an XCVI, 1–5, in *The Meaning of the Glorious Koran*, Mohammed Marmaduke Pickthall (trans.), Mentor Books, New American Library, New York, 1953, p. 445.
8. Ibid., p. x.
9. Sir William Muir, *Life of Mahomet*, Smith Elder, London, 1878, p. 132.
10. Qur'an LXXXI, 1–14, in *The Meaning of the Glorious Koran*, p. 431.
11. Qur'an LXXIV, 38–44, in ibid., p. 421.
12. Qur'an XC, in ibid., pp. 440f.
13. Moran, op. cit., p. 13.
14. Ibid., p. 14.
15. Philip K. Hitti, *The Arabs*, Regnery, Chicago, 1956, p. 40.
16. *The Meaning of the Glorious Koran*, p. xxvii.
17. J. Hutchison and J. Martin, *Ways of Faith*, rev. ed., Ronald, New York, 1960, p. 295.
18. Arthur Jeffrey (ed.), *Islam: Muhammad and His Religion*, Liberal Arts, New York, 1958, p. 93.
19. See inter alia Qur'an I, in *The Meaning of the Glorious Koran*, p. 31.
20. Jeffrey, op. cit., pp. 138f.
21. Ibid., p. 140.

22. *The Meaning of the Glorious Koran.* This title derives from the pious Islamic belief that the Qur'an is in Arabic and cannot be translated.
23. Morgan, op. cit., p. 22.
24. Jeffrey, op. cit., p. 155.
25. Hitti, op. cit., p. 54.
26. Qur'an II, 190–3, in *The Meaning of the Glorious Koran*, p. 50.
27. Qur'an IV, 2, 3, in ibid., p. 79.
28. Hitti, op. cit., p. 65.
29. Ibid., p. 81.
30. Ibid., p. 72.
31. Historians disagree on this date, H. A. R. Gibb says 762 CE. See his *Mohammedanism*, p. 15.
32. Hitti, op. cit., pp. 105f.
33. Morgan, op. cit., p. 59.
34. Ibid., p. 53.
35. Quoted in S. Archer and C. Purinton, *Faiths Men Live By*, Ronald, New York, 1958, p. 483.
36. See inter alia Gibb, op. cit., pp. 88f.; Shafk Ghorbal, in Morgan, op. cit., pp. 57f.
37. Jeffrey, op. cit., p. 93.
38. Gibb, op. cit., p. 100.
39. Quoted in Gibb, op. cit., p. 103 (attributed to R. Nicholson, *Literary History of the Arabs*, p. 234).
40. Gibb, op. cit., pp. 108–109.
41. P. K. Hitti, *History of the Arabs*, Macmillan, New York, 1937, p. 45.
42. Arnold and Guillaume, *The Legacy of Islam*, Clarendon Press, Oxford, 1931, p. 218, as quoted in J. B. Noss, *Man's Religions*, 2d ed., Macmillan, New York, 1956, p. 723.
43. W. T. Stace, *The Teachings of the Mystics*, Mentor Books, New American Library, New York, 1960, p. 212.
44. Stace, op. cit., pp. 213–214.
45. I. Goldziher, *Mohammed and Islam*, Yale, New Haven, Conn., 1917, p. 183, as quoted in J. B. Noss, op. cit., p. 724.
46. *Encyclopaedia Britannica*, vol. 12, p. 161.
47. W. T. de Bary (ed.), *Sources of the Indian Tradition*, Columbia, New York, 1958, p. 370.
48. W. C. Smith, *Islam in Modern History*, Mentor Books, New American Library, New York, 1959, p. 51. See also de Bary, op. cit., p. 455.
49. Morgan, op. cit., p. 344.
50. Ibid., pp. 375f.
51. Smith, op. cit., pp. 97f.
52. Morgan, op. cit., p. 285.
53. de Bary, op. cit., pp. 747f.
54. Ibid., p. 827.
55. Smith, op. cit., p. 292.

BIBLIOGRAPHY

Andrae, T.: *Mohammed*, Ayer Co., Salem, N.H., 1986.
Arberry, A.: *The Doctrine of the Sufis*, Cambridge, London, 1977.
———: *Sufism*, Allen & Unwin, Boston, Mass., 1979.
Bosworth, C.: *The Islamic Dynasties*, Edinburgh, Edinburgh, 1967.
Coulson, N.: *A History of Islamic Law*, Edinburgh, Edinburgh, 1964.
Cragg, K.: *The House of Islam*, Wadsworth, Belmont, Calif., 1988.
———: *Counsels in Contemporary Islam*, Edinburgh, Edinburgh, 1965.
Denny, F.: *An Introduction to Islam*, Macmillan, New York, 1985.
Embree, A., and S. Hay (eds.): *Sources of the Indian Tradition*, Columbia, New York, 1988.

Enayat, Hamid: *Modern Islamic Political Thought*, University of Texas, Austin, Tex., 1982.

Esposito, J. (ed.): *Islam in Asia*, Oxford, New York, 1987.

———— (ed.): *Voices of Resurgent Islam*, Oxford, New York, 1983.

————: *Women in Muslim Family Law*, Syracuse University, New York, 1982.

Gibb, H.: *Modern Trends in Islam*, University of chicago, Chicago, 1947.

————: *Mohammedanism*, Oxford, New York, 1962.

Guillaume, A. (trans.): *The Life of Muhammad: A Translation of Ishaq's Sirat Rasul Allah*, Oxford, London, 1967.

Hitti, P.: *History of the Arabs*, St. Martin's Press, New York, 1970.

Hodgson, M.: *The Venture of Islam*, University of Chicago, Chicago, 1974.

Iqbal, M.: *Reconstruction of Religious Thought in Islam*, Oxford, London, 1962.

Kritzeck, J. (ed.): *Anthology of Islamic Literature*, New American Library, New York, 1975.

Nasr, H.: *Ideals and Realities of Islam*, Allen & Unwin, London, 1985.

————: *Islamic Art and Spirituality*, State University of New York, Albany, 1987.

Pickthall, M. (trans.): *The Meaning of the Glorious Koran*, New American Library, New York, 1984.

Rahman, F.: *Islam*, University of chicago, Chicago, 1979.

————: *Islam and Modernity*, University of chicago, Chicago, 1982.

————: *Major Themes of the Qur'an*, Bibliotheca Islamica, Minneapolis, Minn., 1980.

Savory, R.: *Introduction to Islamic Civilization*, Cambridge, Cambridge, 1976.

Schimmel, A.: *And Muhammad Is His Messenger*, University of North Carolina, Chapel Hill, 1985.

————: *Mystical Dimensions of Islam*, University of North Carolina, Chapel Hill, 1975.

Smith, W. C.: *Islam in Modern Hisstory*, Princeton University, Princeton, 1957.

Von Grunebaum, G.: *Islam*, Greenwood, Westport, Conn., 1982.

Watt, W. M.: *Islamic Fundamentalism and Modernity*, Routledge, Chapman & Hall, New York, 1988.

————: *Islamic Philosophy and Theology*, Edinburgh, Edinburgh, 1988.

————: *Muhammad: Prophet and Statesman*, Oxford, London, 1961.

15

Roman Catholicism and the Middle Ages

At the end of Chapter 13 we left Christianity, newly emerged from the catacombs, as the established religion of Constantine's empire. During the same period it was dividing into Eastern Orthodoxy and western or Roman Catholicism, though the formal break between these two did not come until centuries later in 1054 CE. Now we return to Catholic Christianity as the formative faith of the new civilization which historians call the West or Europe.

It is clearly impossible to date the birth of a civilization or culture as one dates the birth of an individual human being. Yet it accords with prevailing usage of historians to say that somewhere between 500 and 1000 CE a new civilization took shape in the ruins of the ancient Greco-Roman world. While no civilization on earth has undergone changes and transformations more vast than those of the 1,500 years of western history, there has nonetheless been a continuing cultural tradition.[1]

This chapter and Chapters 16 and 17 will deal with some of the varied relations between Christianity and the West. In this chapter our concern will be with what Christopher Dawson has termed "religion and the rise of western culture."[2] The medieval synthesis had an all-important religious center, the Catholic faith, in its emphasis on creating, sustaining, and guiding a culture. In contrast, as Chapter 16 will point out, is the Protestant emphasis on the criticism of culture. Taken together these two emphases define one of the sharpest contrasts between Catholicism and Protestantism.

It is important to note that the defining forms of Roman Catholic Christianity both antedate and have long outlived their medieval context. They came into being in the ancient Greco-Roman world many centuries before the Middle Ages. Today the Middle Ages are long dead, but the Roman Catholic sacramental system culminating in the mass, and the Catholic pyramid of authority rising to the pope at the apex, are still living religious forms in every corner of the earth.

Of the approximately 1,500 years of western history, the first 1,000 are embraced by the terms *medieval* or *Middle Ages* and the most recent 500 years by the *modern age*. Between these two ages there is a significant and decisive difference of religious attitude and orientation. Medieval people sought for the source of life's meaning, in spatial metaphor, above or beyond the world of human experience rather than within it. In sharpest contrast, the dominant attitude of modern people is to seek the meaning within this human world. Paul Tillich once characterized this modern attitude as "self-sufficient finitude." In a word, the contrasting attitudes are those of transcendence and immanence. Medieval people lived within a system of authority which claimed a transcendent source. Again, the medieval mind showed an affinity for mysticism, defined as an immediate apprehension of spiritual realities in contrast to the empirical attitude of modern people.[3] As discussion proceeds through this chapter and Chapters 16 and 17, readers will wish not only to test these contrasts, but also to make their own lists of contrasts between medieval and modern traits.

AUGUSTINE'S LIFE AND THOUGHT

Nowhere is the historic transition from Greco-Roman antiquity to the nascent civilization of the West more clearly visible than in the life and thought of Saint Augustine (354–430). On the one hand, he looked back in retrospect and summary to ancient Christianity and to its Greco-Roman context; on the other hand, his main ideas and attitudes looked forward to the age to come, that is, to the Middle Ages, and in some notable respects beyond them to the whole western tradition down to the present day. Augustine was one of the founders of the West. Through his life and thought ran many of the lines of tradition connecting the Greco-Roman past with the ages yet to come.

Augustine's life is recorded in his *Confessions*, which has the form of a dialog between Augustine and God. It was the first autobiography in the western tradition, if not in all history. It was also the first of a long series of similar autobiographical works. In the presence of his God, Augustine discovered his human self, in all its intense and discordant passions and in all its inner depths.

Augustine was born in Tagaste, Numidia, in North Africa, the son of a devout Christian mother and a pagan father. After education in his home city and at Carthage, he began a career as a wandering rhetorist, teaching successively in Carthage, Rome, and Milan. At the same time he rejected as childish his mother's Christianity and began a period of spiritual wandering among the faiths and philosophies of the time. His first excursion was into the dualistic system called *Manichaeism*. Disenchanted by the inability of its leading exponent, Faustus, to answer his questions, Augustine shifted to the skepticism of the New Academy.[4] From skepticism Augustine moved on to Neoplatonism, a philosophy of which he later remarked, "There I read, In the beginning was the Word, but not the Word was made flesh."[5] His time of wandering was also a time of deep personal unrest in which he was torn between asceticism and worldliness. His own agonized prayer was "Lord, give me chastity but not yet."[6]

Augustine's complex life found a new center and new meaning with his conversion to Catholic Christianity in 386. He was baptized and received into the Catholic church by Bishop Ambrose of Milan. Already an admirer of the monastic ideal, he withdrew to seclusion for meditation and dialog with sympathetic friends. Then, accompanied by his mother, Monica, he began the journey back to his native North Africa, where he planned to start a monastery. Monica died at the Italian seaport of Ostia after a dramatic conversation between mother and son culminating in mystical illumination.[7]

Augustine spent the remainder of his life in the service of the Christian church, first as monastic leader, then as priest, then for thirty-five years as bishop of Hippo. He preached, he shepherded his flock, and he wrote voluminously, producing the first great Christian philosophical synthesis. He died in 430 as the Vandals beseiged the city of Hippo.

Augustine's vast body of writings reveal a many-sided genius who addressed himself to all the main problems of Christian faith, and whose interpretations were to determine the course of western thought for a millennium. His earliest Christian writings were concerned with the problems of faith's relation to reason, and of the truth of faith, which were destined to become the defining problems for medieval Scholasticism and for the whole tradition of Christian thought. Augustine's position was that faith had primacy but was fully subject to rational criticism. "I believe in order to know," said Augustine, meaning that the activity of knowing has its own foundations of faith. Indeed, the very activity of doubting presupposes faith, having its own premises or assumptions, argued Augustine, anticipating Descartes by 1,000 years. In the new context of faith, human reason had its own distinctive role, that of understanding faith.

Augustine was churchman as well as philosopher, and in the course of defining the church against those who would split it apart, he gave expression to views which are still normative for Roman Catholicism. The Donatists were a North African sect who maintained that the validity of the Christian sacraments was dependent upon the moral character of the officiating clergyman. This moral rigor stemmed from the previous century's persecution under Decius in which some of the clergy as well as laypeople had defected. Augustine saw in these views not only schism which would shatter the unity of the church, but a perilous subjectivism. On the Donatist basis, how would Christians ever be sure that the sacraments they received were valid? In opposition, he argued that the sacraments of the Catholic church were independent of the character of the priest who administers them. In bold objectivity the Catholic church was asserted to be the "ark of salvation" whose sacraments alone can effectively guarantee eternal life. Augustine also did not hesitate to invoke the help of civil government in repressing the Donatists—a fateful precedent.

While Catholic Christianity accepted Augustine's view of the church and rejected (or seriously revised) his view of humanity and sin, precisely the opposite was true of Reformation Protestantism, which rejected his view of the church and accepted wholeheartedly the great bishop of Hippo's grim view of human nature. Augustine's ideas of humanity were worked out in conflict with Pelagius, a high-minded monk who was repelled by widespread laxity, particularly among the monks of his day, and who sought to achieve higher moral standards by teaching human freedom and responsibility. In sharpest opposition,

Augustine replied with his teaching of total human depravity and the consequent total dependence of humans on God's grace. This view was autobiographical; Augustine believed out of his own tortured experience that God has given him the unmerited gift of faith. He asserted more generally that ever since the fall of Adam, humans are so far sunk in evil that, except for God's grace, perdition is their just and inevitable end. God extends his grace to those whom he predestines to receive it and his stern justice to the rest of humanity. Thus arose the austere doctrine of double predestination—of some people to heaven and others to hell.

In many ways Augustine's most important single work was *The City of God*, which he began in 410 as a response to charges that Christianity was responsible for the barbarian sack of Rome. The book, completed in 426, showed Augustine's view of history as the dramatic interaction of the City of God and the city of this world, each of which is constituted by its own distinctive form of love, the city of this world by self-love and the City of God by the love of God and one's neighbor. This was the first western philosophy of history. The Middle Ages were destined to interpret the relations of church and empire in terms of Augustine's two cities. Even more fundamental throughout the whole course of western history has been Augustine's view of human beings as actors in a kind of divine-human drama, of which God is both author and producer-director. The curtain went up on this drama at creation, the climax is achieved in the coming of Christ, and the final curtain will fall at judgment day. The plot may be understood as God's relation to his erring human children. Each person's destiny consists in finding his or her proper role in the divine-human drama and playing it out with fidelity. Augustine's linear-dramatic view of history was conservative, particularly in its approach to authority. However, once stated, this view was susceptible of other, sometimes radical interpretations, as we shall see in this and subsequent chapters.

Even in the "dark ages" (ca. 500–1000 CE) millennialism persisted, testifying in its way to the Bible's linear-dramatic view of history. Indeed as the year 1000 CE approached, millennial movements erupted with special force.

THE MONASTIC ORDERS

The beginnings of Christian asceticism and monasticism as well as their distinctive formulation in Eastern Orthodoxy were noted in Chapter 13. In broadest perspective the Christian styles of asceticism and monasticism must be understood as distinctive variations on themes which recur throughout the world's religions. In many faiths people have been led to deny and mortify the flesh, devote themselves to celibacy and fasting, and with varying degrees of consistency reject or flee the common life of the secular world.

In the medieval West, monasticism was to become a basic institution of society. Many people in successive generations took monastic vows, rejecting the world. Yet, ironically, these monks helped powerfully, often in ways beyond their knowing, to build the new culture of Europe. During the Middle Ages they helped to maintain and guide its life.

In a notable essay, Lynn White has sought to interpret medieval Christianity as a succession of three great waves of reformation. He writes:

> The history of the Western Church since apostolic times has centered about three great crises: the Monastic Reformation, the medieval Reformation, and the Protestant Reformation. The early Middle Ages were dominated by the results of the first, the eleventh to thirteenth centuries by the accomplishment of the second, the later Middle Ages by preliminary symptoms of the third. Each of these three reformations marked a vigorous reaction of the christian yearning for spiritual perfection to its changing environment and resulted in mutual adaption between Christianity and the dominant social and intellectual forms. While none of these movements can be properly understood without reference to its general historical context, nevertheless, no purely secular economic or sociological interpretation of them is adequate. In each case the initiative towards change came from within the Church itself, arising out of deep spiritual discontent and concern lest the purity of religious life be sullied by worldly influences. Consequently, each of these reformations was essentially ascetic although, since each was dominated by a quite dif-

Medieval monks at work on manuscripts. (Pierpont Morgan Library, New York.)

ferent view of religious perfection, each produced its characteristic type of ascetic in the monk, the friar, and the Puritan respectively.[8]

The first reformation was organized and led by Benedict of Nursia (ca 470–ca. 547). As a student in Rome he was repelled by the evils of the time and fled as a hermit to a cave in nearby mountains. As the fame of his holiness spread, he reluctantly became head of a monastery. About 529 he founded the mother monastery of the Benedictine order on Monte Cassino and formulated its famous rule, which was destined to be model the for all subsequent western monasticism.

Benedict's rule showed his insight into human nature and his genius for organization as well as his dedication to monasticism. It contained wise provisions for all the multifarious aspects of the monastic community, from its daily worship to the daily rations of food and drink and the interpersonal relations of the monks. The great achievement of the Benedictine rule was to make the ascetic aspiration for spiritual perfection a socially constructive and useful instrument for the service of the church and incidentally of western civilization.[9]

Benedict's threefold rule of daily work, study, and prayer was characteristic. Monks did much of the hard work necessary to lay the foundations of a new civilization. What was even more far-reaching was that in this new context, manual labor was no longer slavish or servile (as it had been in the Greco-Roman world), but rather acquired new dignity as a way of serving God. Study too was a form of obedience to God. In the studies and libraries of monasteries, the classical heritage of Greece and Rome was preserved through the Dark Ages, to quicken and guide subsequent ages of the European tradition. The worship and devotion of the monks was a spring from which the life of Christendom was periodically renewed.

The Benedictine rule spread northward, first to England and Germany, then to France. Its monks were the missionaries and pioneers who brought these lands into the Christian fold and laid the foundations for the new civilization.

Yet with passing generations, ardor cooled and had to be periodically revived. Monasticism, which was a protest against worldliness, found the world reasserting itself within the cloister. The sociopolitical organization of the new civilization was feudal, and increasingly the church was caught in the web of feudalism. In the next section of this chapter a few of the chains of this bondage will be described. Here we note that it was a new wave of monastic protest and reform which freed the church from these feudal bonds.

The reform movement began in 910, when Duke William of Aquitaine founded a small abbey at Cluny, populating it with monks from the pure Benedictine tradition and placing the new house under direct papal authority. The time was ripe for change; the new order spread rapidly, becoming the Cluniac movement, and had at one point almost a thousand houses scattered over France, Germany, Switzerland, and Italy. The Cluniac movement brought to the medieval church a new vitality and also a new freedom from feudal domination. It was a Cluniac monk who as Pope Gregory VII brought the emperor to his knees at Canossa in 1077 CE. From Cluniac cloisters the leaven of a new faith was spread abroad into the life of Christendom.

In its turn, however, the world reasserted itself in Cluniac cowl and cloister. But again the worldliness elicited protest and reform. This time the source was a new monastery founded at Citeaux, near Dijon, in 1098. Its discipline was strict, its way of life austere. But its devotion was strong, and like Cluny before it, the Cistercian movement brought a new spirit into monasticism, and hence into church and world.

In great measure the success of the Cistercian movement was due to the influence of a single man, Bernard, Cistercian abbot at Clairvaux. Born of knightly ancestry in 1090, he entered the monastery at Citeaux in 1112. Bernard was indefatigable as preacher and church leader. Impeccably orthodox, he was the sworn enemy of heretics and schismatics. A man of undeniable integrity, his piety was guided and moved by mystical vision, which will be described later in this chapter.

The second great wave of monastic reform which broke over Europe, called by White the "medieval reformation," showed significant differences of form.[10] It found expression not in cloistered monks who forsook the world, but in friars who in obedience to their orders went out into the burgeoning cities and universities of thirteenth-century Europe to teach and to serve the people. The two most important new orders were the Dominicans and the Franciscans.

The Dominican order was founded by Dominic, a devout Spaniard (1170–1221), who on a trip through southern France was appalled at the contempt shown to Catholic Christainity by a widespread movement of heresy and schism whose members were called the Albigensian Cathari. Dominic sought to do something to win these people back to the church. The outcome was the Order of Preachers, popularly known as the Dominicans, founded in 1215 and given the official sanction of the church the following year. The Dominicans emulated the Franciscans in adopting the rule of mendicancy; its members should beg even for daily bread. The new order was organized into provinces with elected officials, thus combining authority with representative government.[11]

The new movement spread rapidly to all European nations and particularly to university centers. Some of the greatest figures in medieval faith and thought were Dominicans, among them being Albert the Great and Thomas Aquinas, who were Scholastic philosophers, Tauler and Eckhart, who were mystics, and Savonarola, the preacher. Ironically, it was the intellectual quality and integrity of the Dominicans which led to their selection as inquistitors, servants of the Holy Office of the Inquisition.

Equally influential in the thirteenth century were the Franciscans. Their founder, Giovanni Bernadone, or Francis, as he came to be called, was born in 1182, the son of a cloth merchant of Assisi in Italy. To the dismay of his sober father, the young Francis lived a gay life. The circumstances of his conversion are obscure, though illness and military service are said to have played a part in turning his mind from the pleasure and business of the world to the love of Christ.

Hearing what he believed to be a command of God to restore the fallen house of God, Francis sold cloth from his father's shop to rebuild the church of Saint Damian near Assisi. His outraged parent took Francis to the bishop to be disinherited. Francis responded by saying that henceforth he had no father but the Father in heaven. His conversion took place in 1206 or 1207.

The following year, on hearing Christ's command of poverty (through a reading of Matthew 10:7–14), Francis took a vow of mendicancy, and more broadly, of imitation of Christ's love and service to humanity. He drew a group of friends about him in allegiance to this vow. Two by two, members of the group went about the countryside, singing, aiding peasants in their work, caring for sick and needy people, and praising God. The movement spread, and more extensive journeys were undertaken. Drawn by the example of Francis' life, more and more people came into his group. His own travels widened, and in 1219 he journeyed to Egypt, where he preached before the sultan.

Unlike Dominic, Francis was not an effective organizer, and it remained for others to give structure to the movement he founded. A revised rule for society was approved by the pope in 1223.[12] Meanwhile Francis withdrew increasingly from the world, spending his time in prayer and singing. He died in 1226, and was proclaimed a saint two years later.

The structure of his order was similar to that of the Dominicans. Similarly too, the Franciscans came soon to have widespread and profound influence. But the nature of the influence differed. Whereas the Dominicans were teachers and philosophers, the Franciscans devoted themselves to works of service and mercy in Europe's cities. The influence of the Franciscans was greatly increased by their third order, or tertiaries, that is, lay supporters who took some but not all of the vows and who provided support and carried on teaching activity.

From its founder the Franciscan movement received a legacy of significant feeling and imagination. Francis had made the first Christmas crèche, and he celebrated his devotion to Christ in song, picture, and story. He was far ahead of his time in romantic feeling for nature. The stories of his preaching to the birds are entirely consistent with what is known of his life and thought. These and similar impulses lived on in his movement, and through his movement found their way into the mainstream of western life.

Particularly pertinent to our present study were the visions of future history of radical Franciscans. A Cistercian, Joachim of Fiore (d. 1204), proclaimed three ages of history, the age of the Father, namely, biblical Israel, the age of the Son, or historical Catholicism, and the future age of the Holy Spirit. Franciscan "spirituals" gave these radical ideas wide circulation. The monastic orders effected successive transformations and revitalizations in medieval Europe, but their significance was not limited to this. Once in existence, they were available for new tasks and new functions which the church might set for them. In days to come these tasks were to be ever-changing and worldwide.

Saint Francis in Ecstasy. Painting by Bellini. (Frick Collection, New York.)

AUGUSTINE'S TWO CITIES: MEDIEVAL CHURCH AND EMPIRE

While Augustine never gave precise details on the relation of the two cities, the Middle Ages did not hesitate to interpret the City of God and the city of this world respectively as church and empire. In the medieval interpretation each was a society complete in itself, with respective systems of authority rising to the pope and the emperor.

The beginnings and development of the papacy were sketched in Chapter 13. During the Middle Ages the papacy achieved its greatest power and prestige. In the very early medieval period, as the Roman empire crumbled and barbarian invaders overran Europe and the Byzantine emperor became more and more remote and unrelated to the west, there were periods when temporal authority lapsed into anarchy. At these times the bishop of Rome was virtually the only center of stability for wide areas of Italy. The result was a steady rise in the pope's power.

In the eighth century there appeared a document called the *Donation of Constantine*, purporting to be a deed of gift in which Constantine, in gratitude to Pope Silvester for curing him of leprosy, gave him not only the primacy of the Catholic church but also the city of Rome and somewhat ill-defined environing regions.[13] The truth and authority of this document went unquestioned until the fifteenth century, when the Renaissance scholar Lorenzo Valla demonstrated its falsity. Meanwhile, by the ninth century the papal states had become a well-established political fact.

Papal power increased in numerous other ways. Gifts of land, the basic form of wealth in feudal society, were numerous. Christian missionaries sent by Rome won new lands to Christianity from Ireland and Scotland to Germany, thus widely extending papal authority.

Christmas day of the year 800 saw the symbolic origin of the Holy Roman Empire. Charlemagne had conquered wide regions of France, Germany, and Italy. He was in Italy to protect the pope and subdue dissident nobles, and as he knelt in prayer in St. Peter's on Christmas day, the grateful Pope Leo III placed upon his head the Roman imperial crown. To many people in Rome and throughout the West, it was the restoration of the imperial power which had been Rome's. To Charlemagne it seemed a fulfillment of Augustine's City of God.

Yet it must be added that for the two centuries following this event, the church was drawn even further into the network of feudal society. Lacking the power to act for itself, it became increasingly one element among others in European feudalism. Church offices were bought and sold, a practice called *simony*, and bishops were appointed by temporal rulers. The pope himself was uniformly subordinated to the emperor.

It was by the Cluniac reform party that the church forcibly broke these shackles and asserted its independence, and indeed its domination. The Cluniac monk Hildebrand became pope as Gregory VII in 1073, with an avowed program of reform and reassertion of the church's power and, as he saw it, integrity.

The right of investiture, that is, appointment of bishops, was the crucial issue. The emperor, Henry IV, appointed a bishop of Milan without Gregory's knowledge or assent. The pope responded by excommunicating Henry and absolving his subjects from their allegiance. In 1077 Henry, surrounded by rising political troubles, made the dramatic move of coming to the north Italian castle of Canossa, where the pope was lodged, and standing barefoot in the snow as a penitent on three successive days until Gregory released him from excommunication.

This dramatic event of 1077 stands as a symbol of papal power over the emperor. However, the outcome of the dispute was a compromise in which the supremacy of the pope in spiritual matters and of the emperor in temporal matters was recognized. In effect a bishop must be approved by both pope and emperor.

The Hildebrandian ideal of the pope's universal supremacy was destined to come close to full realization in Innocent III (1193–1216), whose words and deeds made him the most powerful man in Europe. He forced King Philip of

France to put away a wife considered unlawful by the church. In a quarrel with John of England over the appointment of the Archbishop of Canterbury, he placed John under excommunication, took his kingdom from him, and gave it back to him as a feudal grant on Innocent's terms. Other measures failing, he proclaimed a military crusade against the Cathari of southern France, which the French king gladly carried out. Within the church, Innocent was also supreme. All disagreement among the higher clergy were subject to his final decision. He called the Fourth Lateran Council in 1215 and required it to do his bidding. Truly his reign was the high-water mark of the medieval papacy. Innocent himself put the issue in these words:

> The Creator of the universe set up two great luminaries in the firmament of heaven; the greater light to rule the day, the lesser light to rule the night. In the same way for the firmament of the universal Church, which is spoken of as heaven, he appointed two great dignities; the greater to bear rule over souls (these being, as it were, days), the lesser to bear rule over bodies (these being, as it were, nights). These dignities are the pontifical authority and the royal power. Furthermore, the moon derives her light from the sun, and is in truth inferior to the sun in both size and quality, in position as well as effect. In the same way the royal power derives its dignity from the pontifical authority; and the more closely it cleaves to the sphere of that authority the less is the light with which it is adorned; the further it is removed, the more it increases in splendor.[14]

A century later Boniface VIII (1294–1303) stated the spiritual authority of the pope in equally clear terms.

> We are obliged by the faith to believe and hold—and we do firmly believe and sincerely confess—that there is one Holy Catholic and Apostolic Church, and that outside this Church there is neither salvation nor remission of sins....In which Church there is one Lord, one faith, one baptism....
>
> For this authority, although given to a man and exercised by a man, is not human, but rather divine, given at God's mouth to Peter and established on a rock for him and his successors in Him whom he confessed, the Lord saying to Peter himself, "Whatsoever thou shalt bind," etc. Whoever therefore resists this power thus ordained of God, resists the ordinance of God....Furthermore we declare, state, define and pronounce that it is altogether necessary to salvation for every human creature to be subject to the Roman pontiff.[15]

Yet it is a fact that even as Boniface spoke these bold words, new forces such as nationalism were swirling about the church. Some of these issues will be sketched in a later section of this chapter. Meanwhile it must be noted that the absolute spiritual authority of the Roman pontiff thus achieved in the Middle Ages became a permanent part of the Roman Catholic Christianity. However, what this supreme authority might mean and how it was to be interpreted and reinterpreted were destined to be continuing questions in ages to come. Indeed, no question is more pertinent to twentieth-century

Roman Catholicism than what is and is not involved in the pope's supreme spiritual authority.

Two further aspects of the medieval church's temporal power must at least be mentioned. These are the Inquisition and the Crusades. As to the Holy Office of the Inquisition, it grew up in the thirteenth century during and after the suppression of the Cathari, as a device for ferreting out heretical and schismatic ideas. As already noted, its officials were mainly Dominicans—an order formed with a very different aim. The Inquisition constituted in effect a secret court in which defendants had no right to confront their accusers or examine evidence against them and where they were subject to torture. While the physical punishment of those convicted was committed to temporal government, responsibility lay clearly with the church. The confiscation of the convict's property as spoils to be shared by lay authorities doubtless further fed the fires of persecution. The Inquisition was a highly successful instrument for stamping out or at least repressing dissent. At least, it was successful for the duration of the Middle Ages.[16]

The Crusades were a series of military expeditions against the Muslim Middle East, numbering at least six, with many other expeditions too small for enumeration, the whole series occurring between 1095 and 1291. In 1095 Pope Urban II proclaimed the First Crusade at the Synod of Clermont in France, and in 1291 the last of Latin holdings in Palestine was retaken by the Muslims. Between these two dates, the six major Crusades set out from Christian Europe to rescue the Holy Land from the infidel hands of Islam, ostensibly so that Christian pilgrims might have free access to the Holy Land. Actually many kinds of motives contributed to the Crusades, ranging from religious idealism to the love of adventure, to the desire for economic gain, loot, and pillage. Many sorts of people, from warrior saints to dashing kings or common criminals, participated. Many sorts of results followed from these expeditions, most of them unexpected. One consequence was the legacy of ill-will between Christianity and Islam, as was noted in Chapter 14, which persists to the present day. However, another result was increasing contacts between Europe and the Middle East ranging from trade to exchange of learning. Also, the Crusades make indelibly clear to the student of humankind's religions that Christianity no less than Islam sometimes practices holy war.

LIFE AND WORSHIP IN THE CITY OF GOD

From earliest days, Catholic Christianity has taken with utmost seriousness the nature and significance of the church. St. Paul, writing in the New Testament, called it the *body of Christ*,[17] and Cyprian, third-century bishop of Carthage, termed the church the *ark of salvation*, outside of which there was no salvation. To these metaphors were added the Augustinian view of the church as the City of God.

Citizenship in the heavenly city has been, and still is, construed as extended to the faithful of all places and times, past, present, and future. From Augustine's time onward, it was customary to speak of the church on earth as the *church militant*, the church in purgatory (a doctrine mentioned by early church fathers and elaborated in medieval times) was called the *church suffering*, and the church in heaven was called the *church triumphant*.

The structure of authority within the City of God might be likened to a pyramid the base of which is the ordinary citizens, the Christian laity. At successively higher levels stand clergy and bishops, and at the apex the pope at Rome. As noted in the preceding section, membership in the Roman Catholic church has from medieval times involved submission to the supreme spiritual authority of the Pope.

Life on earth is construed by Roman Catholic Christianity as a preparation for blessedness hereafter. Hence the faithful Catholic perseveres to the end in the hope of the beatific vision in heaven. The chief function of the Roman Catholic church is that of an authoritative, unerring guide through earthly life to heavenly blessedness. For salvation, membership in the Catholic church is a necessary condition, though as will be seen, more modern interpretations have substantially qualified this requirement by reinterpretation of both words, *membership* and *church*. However, medieval Catholics did not shrink from more literal interpretations. For example, Dante placed Socrates, Plato, Aristotle, and Virgil as righteous pagans in the first circle of hell. Other less righteous pagans together with heretics and schismatics were located in lower and less comfortable regions.

Within the official community of the faithful, authoritative guidance begins with clear definitions of sin and salvation. Sin for Roman Catholics as for Protestant Christians is defined as any violation of God's will or law, and salvation is God's free gift through Christ to man, to be appropriated by human faith. The basic difference between these views lies in the Roman Catholic view that the church acting through her priests has the sole authority to absolve people from sin, and more affirmatively to communicate to them the sacraments which are essential to sustain the human soul in grace and prepare it effectively for bliss hereafter. Many features of this view of sin and salvation are premedieval, going back to the earliest Christian church or to the Bible. Yet the full elaboration of this architectonic system as well as its full practice was the achievement of medieval Christianity.

Only a few salient features of the Roman Catholic road map to heaven and hell can be mentioned here. For example, the church has distinguished between venial and mortal sin from an early historical period onward. Venial sins, less serious violations of God's will, come to be viewed as not depriving the soul of sanctifying grace and therefore susceptible of remission by prayer and good works. Mortal sin, which was defined as a serious breach committed with full awareness, came to be construed as depriving the soul of its supernatural life of grace. Therefore, the church has taught that human beings who die in mortal sin go not to purgatory or heaven, but to hell. Attention must be called to the conditional nature of this assertion. *If* a person dies in mortal sin, *then* he goes to hell. However, it is the view of many knowledgeable Catholic theologians that no human knowledge, not even the Pope's, is sufficient for the knower to assert with absolute certainty that anyone has in fact died in mortal sin. Only God knows for sure concerning this matter.

THE SEVEN SACRAMENTS

The seven sacraments are the indispensable guideposts along life's way, or in more illuminating metaphor, they are signs or symbolic vehicles through which God's grace is effectively communicated to human beings, and conversely they are given both light and power for salvation, here and hereafter. All seven were *premedieval* in origin, yet the full delineation and interpretation of the sacramental system was one of the great achievements of medieval Catholicism. The seven sacraments are (1) baptism, (2) confirmation, (3) penance, (4) marriage, (5) holy orders, (6) last anointing, and climactically (7) the eucharist or mass.

BAPTISM   Baptism is both logically and biographically the first of the sacraments. It consists of the symbolic act of pouring water upon a person, while stating that it is done in obedience to divine command and in the name of Father, Son, and Holy Spirit. Its effect is spiritual regeneration and inclusion in the community of the faithful, so that in time the person may proceed in order to the other sacraments. The service of baptism is customarily also a christening in which the child receives his or her Christian name.

Roman Catholic Christianity recognizes the validity of non-Catholic baptism of several sorts. Under extreme circumstances, such as impending death, some person other than a clergyman may perform the ceremony. Under certain circumstances the church accepts the baptism of desire, that is, the intention of the person or his or her parents to have the sacrament, or even the baptism of blood, in which unbaptized persons who give their lives for Christ and the church are received into the heavenly city.

CONFIRMA-   Confirmation is the sacrament by which the church confers spiritual adulthood.
TION   It is usually preceded by a period of instruction in the nature of Roman Catholic faith. The symbolic action consists of the laying on of hands and anointing with holy oil by the bishop as he says the words of confirmation. While not necessary for salvation, it is considered an important step in an individual's growth in grace.

PENANCE   Penance is the sacrament in which God through a priest absolves a person from sin. Four elements are deemed essential: confession, contrition, absolution, and satisfaction. That is to say, the person must confess his or her sins fully and in good faith to a priest who is the confessor. The priest on hearing the confession has authority from God to grant absolution, remitting the eternal punishment which is the just penalty of mortal sin, and remitting also, in part or wholly the "temporal punishment" of sin, which is to say, penal time in purgatory.

This last aspect of penance involves the widely misunderstood Roman Catholic doctrine of indulgence. It is, of course, not permission to commit sin, nor is it payment in advance for future sin. Rather it is a substitution of specified acts such as prayers or other devotions for the temporal consequences of sin. The church's right to extend indulgences depends in turn upon the idea of the treasury of merit, which is a special fund of goodness accumulated by saints (who have had more than enough for their salvation) and now at the disposal of the whole church to be dispensed under papal authority.

MARRIAGE   Marriage is a sacrament performed by two baptized persons who commit themselves to each other in permanent monogamous matrimony. The officiating priest is regarded as a witness: the contracting parties actually perform this sacrament. In extreme circumstances the sacrament can be performed with no priest present. Not only is marriage a permanent union of two souls like the union of Christ and the church, but it is the means by which new souls are brought into the world and—it is hoped—prepared for the heavenly city. Therefore, the Roman Catholic church has always taken a very serious view of marriage. No divorce is permitted (though under carefully defined circumstances annulment is possible), and the duties of the married estate are carefully and fully set forth by Christian morality.

ORDINATION   Holy orders, or ordination, is the sacrament by which priests are consecrated to the ministry of the church. The laying of the bishop's hands on the head of the candidate, with appropriate prayer and solemn ritual, places the priest in the apostolic succession, which goes back through Peter to Christ. The priest is empowered to perform the sacraments and stands under the authority of his bishop and ultimately of the pope.

LAST ANOINTING   Last anointing is the sacrament by which the soul is prepared for death and the life hereafter. It consists of anointing the body with holy oil, accompanied by prayer. Usually too, if possible, it is accompanied by a last confession and a last communion, or *viaticum*. Under special conditions such as warfare, a person other than a priest of the Roman Catholic church may offer to the dying some of the comforts of this sacrament, hearing the prayers of the dying and assuring them of the faith of the church.

MASS   The eucharist, or mass, is the central and climactic sacrament of the church. The word *mass* is English for *missa* and is apparently derived from the words of dismissal at the end of the mass, *Ite, missa est*. The official name of the sacrament, *eucharist*, is derived from the Greek word for "giving thanks," which points to the central theme of the eucharist, human thanksgiving to God for the salvation which his grace has freely given in Christ. The eucharist incorporates a great many elements of worship, such as confession, contrition, and adoration and praise, but the climax is the common reenactment by the priest and people of Christ's saving sacrifice on the cross for the sins of the world.

Vatican II has effected the revolutionary change of vernacular instead of Latin as the language of the mass. It has also greatly emphasized the congregational element of celebration by the church as the "people of God" in which priest and laity each play a part in a common act of worship offered to God.

The vestments of the celebrant symbolize aspects of priestly preparation and function. Colors of some of the priests' vestments change according to the season of the Christian year or for special occasions, such as a nuptial or requiem mass. Central in this eucharist is the altar, sacred to a particular saint and containing relics of that saint.

The eucharist has a dramatic structure rising from the initial greeting and prayer through the Kyrie ("Lord have mercy…"), Gloria, Collects or prayers for the day, Epistle, Gospel, and Homily to the words of consecration which constitute the climax of the mysterious divine-human drama. The celebrant holds up the wafer and then the wine, saying "This is my body…" and "This is my blood.…At this moment the wafer and wine become the body and blood of Christ offered as a holy sacrifice to God for the sins of the world. So Christ's sacrifice is reenacted whenever and wherever the mass is said.[18]

The traditional theological theory by which this Christian mystery is explained is called *transubstantiation*, and it was officially proclaimed a doctrine of the Roman Catholic church at the Fourth Lateran Council in 1215. It was formally explicated by Thomas Aquinas as a change not in external properties and accidents of the bread and wine (e.g., their color, taste, etc.) but in their inner substance (their "breadness" and "wineness").[19]

The dramatic climax of the mass leads on to the communion of priest and congregation and thence to concluding prayers and benediction. Twentieth-century changes do not obscure either the ancient origin of this rite in Christ's last supper with his disciples or its universal or catholic character. Truly the eucharist continues as the living center of Christian worship and faith for the world's more than 700 million Roman Catholic Christians!

Scholasticism: Faith Seeks Understanding

The term *scholasticism* is often used negatively to mean a type of thought which is preoccupied with insignificant details (such as how many angels can dance on the head of a pin!) or which subordinates reason to ecclesiastical authority. While at times Scholasticism has deserved this negative valuation, it is in historic fact a much larger and more significant phenomenon than these modern prejudices indicate. As we have seen in previous chapters, *scholasticism* may quite properly be defined as the use of philosophy for the exposition and defense of religious faith. In this sense we have met it twice already, in Judaism and Islam. Both of these occurrences had significant historical influence on medieval Christian Scholasticism. Indeed, it does not require undue stretching of this word's meaning to see illustrations of it in the classic philosophies of India and

China. Wherever it occurs, *Scholasticism* may be defined as faith seeking under-standing, first self-understanding then understanding of the world.

Augustine is frequently called the *father of Christian Scholasticism*. While he had historical influence, Scholasticism actually came into being many centu-ries later. From the age of Charlemagne, schools played an ever-increasing part in Christianity. From them emerged the medieval universities. Out of the dis-cussions of the medieval Schoolmen emerged Scholastic philosophy, or theol-ogy. It looked back upon a heritage of Greek philosophy and biblical religion and sought to synthesize them into a single whole—and in the process pro-duced something new.

Here we cannot do more than hint at the great magnitude and range of medieval Christian Scholasticism, pointing to a few major thinkers and their handling of important recurring problems. One such issue was the relation of faith to reason. Closely related was that of faith's object, or God: and Scholasti-cism found a close relation between the nature of God and that of humans. Taken together these constitute a cluster of issues never far from the center of Scholastic thought.

Among earlier Scholastics none was more influential or characteristic than Anselm of Canterbury (1033–1109). An Italian by birth who was for many years abbot of the monastery of LaBec in Normandy and who ended his life as arch-bishop of Canterbury, he illustrates the international character of the move-ment. Anselm's approach to philosophy is epitomized in his dictum *fides quaerens intellectum*, "faith seeking understanding." By this he asserted his thought on the basis of faith, but sought philosophically to understand its nature and implications. Philosophy in this interpretation is faith's effort at self-understanding. Paraphrasing Augustine, Anselm declared *Credo ut intelligam*, "I believe in order to understand." In this manner, he sought a middle way be-tween the extremes of uncritical belief and faithless reason.

His approach may be illustrated by his famous ontological argument for the existence of God. Anselm had already written a treatise expounding the cos-mological argument, that is, arguing from the world to God. But, dissatisfied, he sought a better, surer way, and in the ontological argument he believed that he had achieved it.[20]

This argument began from the idea of God as perfect being, a being greater than which is inconceivable to humans. Now the object of this perfect or greatest idea either exists or does not exist. But if we take the second option, we violate the assumption that this idea is greatest or perfect. If to the idea we add existence, we get a result greater than the idea without existence. Therefore we must assume the greatest idea to include the existence of its object. There-fore God exists. So reasoned Anselm!

His position was immediately attacked by a monk named Gaunilon. In an effort at reduction to absurdity, Gaunilon applied this same line of thought to the idea and existence of a perfect island. However, Anselm responded by lim-iting his argument to the single idea of absolute perfection, that is, to the rad-ically unique God of monotheism. Only to this idea does the argument apply.

Since its formulation, the ontological argument has been argued and reargued, accepted and rejected, down to the present moment.

Anselm applied his thought to the theological problem of atonement in a book entitled *Cur Deus Homo* ("Why God Man?").[21] His answer was that God properly demanded satisfaction for human sin, meaning a satisfying of offended honor such as might characterize a feudal noble. Now a being who was simply human could not offer satisfaction, nor could satisfaction be achieved by the sacrifice of a being who was simply deity. Hence only one who was both God and human could achieve the desired result. Anselm's answer was less important than the question he raised—how to understand the sacrificial death of Christ.

Anselm was also deeply concerned with another issue of Scholastic philosophy, the nature of universals, of general ideas or concepts. One party in this dispute, the realists, asserted with Plato that ideas have a reality apart from their basis in sense experience, but the opposing party, the nominalists, asserted that only the objects of sense are real, ideas being simply shorthand expressions for recurring sense experiences. The issue was important to medieval thinkers for the reason that many significant religious objects such as God and the church partook of the same sort of supersensible reality as Platonic ideas. Anselm ranged himself squarely on the side of realism.

An intermediate position on this continuing issue was taken by the best-known Scholastic figure of the next century, Abelard (1079–1142). A searching spirit, but by no means an irreligious man, Abelard attracted a large following as teacher and lecturer. Like many another academic, he had a penchant for criticism. His work *Sic et non* quoted contrary passages from the church fathers on many great doctrines, with no attempt to harmonize them. His view of the atonement differed from Anselm's idea of satisfaction; Abelard argued that Christ's death represents the highest expression of God's love for humanity, and its efficacy in salvation derives from that fact.

Abelard's bold views brought him into conflict with the strictly orthodox Saint Bernard of Clairvaux, who after years of trying, secured Abelard's condemnation as a heretic. This, combined with his personal life, which included the famous love affair with Héloise, made Abelard's life a turbulent one.

Scholasticism achieved its greatest heights in the thought of St. Thomas Aquinas (1225–1274). His career must be seen against the background of new issues of the thirteenth century as well as against the earlier developments of Scholasticism, which have just been sketched. By this time new Aristotelian ideas were seeping into Christendom from Muslim Spain, largely through the writings of Ibn Rushd, known also by his Latin name, Averroes, whose thought we noted in Chapter 14. Previous medieval thinkers had possessed only part of Aristotle's thought; but Averroes, who was himself a bold speculative mind as well as a scholar on the writings of Aristotle, expounded such Aristotelian ideas as the eternity of the world and the mortality of the human soul. These and other, similar ideas were eagerly seized upon by skeptical thinkers in Christian Europe as grist for their mill, with the result that the reading of Aristotle was proscribed at many European universities. For example, the bishop of Paris thrice banned the reading of Aristotle by students of the university during the first two decades of the thirteenth century.[22]

Into this conflict as a mediator came Thomas. He was born of noble parents in the south Italian town of Aquino and educated at the Benedictine abbey at Monte Cassino. Then, to the consternation of his parents, he joined the new Dominican order and went off to the equally new University of Paris to study with the Dominican master Albert the Great. He followed Albert to Cologne, then back to Paris, where he achieved the license to teach. During his brief life, Thomas taught in Paris, Naples, and Rome. He died in 1274 enroute to the Council of Lyons, where he was to have been advisor to the pope. Of his vast body of writings, the *Summa contra Gentiles* and *Summa Theologica*, the latter unfinished at his death, are characteristic. Many centuries later, in 1879, his work was proclaimed by Pope Leo XIII as the norm for Catholic theological teaching.

The key idea of Thomas's vast and architectonic system of theology is the relation of faith to reason. Much of religion—though not all—is susceptible of rational proof. Using Aristotelian reason on the facts of the natural world, it is possible to demonstrate the existence and unity of God. To be sure, reason comes presently to the limit of its capacity, and then one must continue the spiritual journey by faith, which though it goes beyond reason is never contrary to it.

Aquinas's use of reason and argument is illustrated by his five arguments for the existence of God, which occur in slightly variant forms in both *Summas*. They may be briefly summarized as follows:

1. Motion entails or presupposes an unmoved mover. For Aquinas, motion did not mean simple physical displacement, the mathematical formula *s/t* of modern physical equations, but rather the whole fact of change whereby, beginning with potentiality, the process of development toward a *telos*, or goal, occurs. Like Aristotle, Aquinas conceived the world as a process moving toward fulfillment, the source of this process being the unmoved mover.[23]
2. Thomas also followed Aristotle in an analogous inference from the fact of causation to a first cause. By *cause* Aquinas (and probably Aristotle before him) meant the whole productive agency in terms of which a process is brought into being and takes place. In both of these arguments, from motion and from cause, Aquinas also followed Aristotle in denying the possibility of infinite regression; it was inherently irrational and therefore impossible.
3. Aquinas argued from the fact of contingency to necessary being. Obviously, contingent beings exist; but equally clearly, it is not rationally possible to conceive of a universe in which literally everything is contingent. Rather, contingency presupposes necessity, and necessary being constitutes one aspect of deity.
4. A similar argument in the field of qualities, values, or properties moves from the degrees of perfection to perfect being. The argument presupposes that

St. Thomas Aquinas, by Francesco Traini. Christ is above him, Aristotle and Plato are on his left and right, and Averroes is on the ground before him. (Alinari/Art Resource.)

adjectives, such as *hot* and *cold, red* and *blue, good* and *bad*, designate real entities in the world, and on this basis proceeds to argue for the existence of their comparative and superlative degrees. Common human experience of goods and betters clearly and certainly points to an absolute best, which again is part of what people mean when they say *God*. So, at least, Aquinas taught.

5. In contrast to the preceding formulations of the cosmological argument, that is, the argument from the world to its cause in God, the fifth argument is teleological; that is, it argues from the supposed fact of design to a divine designer who, once more, is an aspect of what people mean by *God*. Design exists, ergo the divine designer exists.

Thomas believed it possible to prove with complete logical certainty the existence of the one God. He also traced the way by which the human mind ascended the path leading from the world to God. It is by way of negation of that which is finite, mortal, and conditioned to the *in*finite, *im*mortal, and *un*-conditioned. This way of negation consists of stripping away the limitations of finitude, literally of placing a negative prefix before all the adjectives designating human limitations. To the way of negation he added the way of analogy; and Thomas's carefully worked out view of analogical speaking is an essential part of his philosophy.[24] It is a way of taking certain carefully defined aspects of human life such as reason and love, and referring them metaphorically to the infinite being of God. Thomas's views of analogy have become a major subject of study and writing among his modern followers.

Yet however carefully or adequately carried out, reasoning comes at length to the end of its road. At that point one continues one's journey by faith, which for Thomas seemed to consist of belief accepted on the reasonable, well-founded authority of mother church. Concerning God, such truths of revelation which go beyond natural reason may be illustrated by the creation of the world by God. God's incarnation in Christ, and his threefold manifestation in the trinity. These and the many other truths of revelation are to be taken on faith and lived out as aspects of the Christian's life and preparation for blessedness hereafter.

There are a few things in heaven, earth, or hell that Thomas's all-encompassing system did not treat. Indeed the idea of a *summa*, that is, an encyclopedic summary of all knowledge of all reality, in heaven above, in the earth beneath, and in the waters under the earth, was inherent in his Scholastic viewpoint. Thomas's all-encompassing philosophical-theological synthesis was by no means the only attempt of this kind in medieval Christianity. Other Scholastic philosophers wrote summas. But in many ways Thomas most nearly succeeded in this ambitious undertaking. After him the medieval synthesis began to crack, then to fall apart, as illustrated in the philosophies of such men as Duns Scotus and William of Ockham.

Many students have observed significant parallels between Scholasticism and another characteristic achievement of the Middle Ages, the gothic style in architecture as embodied in the great medieval cathedrals. The gothic style, which grew out of the romanesque, was distinguished by its pointed arch and soaring height. Never before or since has stone been used in structures whose vertical lines so seemed to defy the laws of gravity. The gothic style of cathedral and cloister has seemed to many students of the Middle Ages to express the religious aspiration of the times. The great gothic cathedrals were also an expression of the communal life of this highly unified society and were a work of common labor and common devotion of the people. Small wonder that these great churches should exhibit the same inclusive architectonic unity and the same devotional spirit which found expression in Scholasticism.

Even as people had labored together to create these vast churches, so also people of all stations knelt together within them in common worship of the one God to whom they were devoted. Humble, unlettered serfs might not understand the subtleties of scholastic philosophy, but their spirit was moved by the soaring arches of the cathedral, by its amazing organization of parts into a coherent whole, or by the breathtaking beauty of its stained glass windows and sculpture.

All Christians were drawn together by the faith celebrated in solemn mystery at the high altar of the cathedral. Like the center which draws all the radii to itself, this altar was the center of medieval society. The faith celebrated here was proclaimed in sermon and other forms of teaching. It was notably expounded in the glass and sculpture and the symbolic shops of the cathedral, which was often termed a *sermon in stone*.

True, ordinary people might differ in their apprehension of the faith from the more learned, yet there were impressive continuities even here. So it was that the cathedral was the focal center of thought and life in medieval Europe, the living center of the medieval synthesis. Today, when this is no longer true, these great churches still stand in the midst of Europe's cities as mute memorials to this once great and significant social fact.

MEDIEVAL CHRISTIAN MYSTICS

Mysticism and mystical attitudes have been observed in several of the religious traditions so far studied; it is not surprising to note their emergence in medieval Christianity. Indeed, all three of Chapter 1's categories of mysticism find illustration in medieval Catholic Christianity. These, the reader will recall, are mysticism (1) as an emphasis on the immediacy of religious experience, (2) as immediate communion with the religious object, and (3) as ontological union or absorption in this object.

Mysticism in the first sense has often been asserted to be a primary feature of the Middle Ages, whether the reality involved be the real presence of Christ in the eucharist, or the presence of the Virgin Mary in devotions offered to her, or of some other saint in some particular holy place. Holy or spiritual things were of immediate and vivid reality to the people of this age. For this reason religion held the central place in their society.

The second and third meanings of mysticism found embodiment in particular persons and traditions of the Middle Ages. Some people sought and found immediate communion with God, but others pressed on to complete absorption.

The tradition of medieval mysticism may be traced to Plotinus and other, similar figures in the ancient world, and notably to an anonymous fifth-century Christian mystical document ascribed to Dionysius the Areopagite. The pseudo-Dionysian treatise spoke of three kinds of knowledge of God, linear, spiral, and circular. The first might be termed *inductive*, the second *dialectic* or philosophical, but in the third, or circular, way thinkers retired within themselves and in their inner life ascended the path to God.[25] Plotinus's goal had been absorption, but his Christian followers remained ambiguous on this important point. Whether the circular path ended in union or communion was seldom clear.

Among the many mystics destined to follow this circular path was the ninth-century Johannes Scotus Erigena, who envisaged God, in a classical mystical metaphor, as a fountain from which all reality bursts forth. Even better known was the twelfth-century Bernard of Clairvaux, for whom mysticism as immediate communion of the soul and God became a way of bringing new vitality into the increasingly sterile dogmatism of his time.[26] In his sermons on the Song of Songs Bernard spoke of Christ as "bridegroom of the soul," and in a variety of vivid ways used the love relation to characterize religious experience, thus permitting mystics to understand their raptures as ideal or heavenly love. Bernard taught that this love had three stages, purgation, illumination, and union, though he was not clear whether union meant communion or absorption.

Other mystics hastened to walk the path which Bernard opened up. Bonaventura (1221–1274), bishop and minister general of the Franciscan order, was the author of a life of Saint Francis and of a mystical tract called *The Journey of the Mind to God*.[27] In this journey he found six stages, beginning with the discovery of traces of God in the common world and moving inward and upward through religious gifts of grace to reflection upon the names of God and the trinity, and thence to a consummation in which all the affections of the human heart pass "on to God."

Bolder, and more clearly an exponent of the third view of mysticism, was the Dominican Meister Eckhart (1260–1327).[28] Eckhart was celebrated both as a popular preacher and a writer in the then new German language. In his view, the goal of the religious life was the absorptive union of human being and God in what he termed the rebirth of Christ within the soul. From this viewpoint, human individuality was something ultimately to be laid aside. Only the rebirth of God in the soul is finally real. Eckhart also taught two aspects of deity, one the traditional Father of Christianity but the second termed it *Deity* (*Gottheit* in German) which was virtually the God above God.

These views seemed to Meister Eckhart to be in accord with orthodox Catholic teaching, but others did not think so. He was accused of heresy and died during the proceedings. The subsequent censure by the church did not lessen Eckhart's influence upon a large and continuing group of followers from his own time to the present.

Other mystics with many different emphases, and in many different regions, arose during the later medieval period. There was the fourteenth-century Catherine of Sienna (1347–1380) and her contemporaries in Germany, Johann Tauler (1300–1361) and Henry Suso (1295–1366), who continued in Eckhart's path. There were the Brethren of the Common Life, whose members practiced a monastic and celibate discipline aiming at a mystical religious life. A notable product by a member of this group was a volume by Thomas à Kempis entitled *The Imitation of Christ*, which may be characterized as a combination of the first two of our three types of mysticism.

While these mystical currents of thought and feeling revitalized Christian life, they also had the effect of loosening allegiance to the church. For if humans could come immediately into God's presence, why take the longer, more laborious route through the church with its seven sacraments and its many obligations? While it was not clearly intended so, mysticism contributed to the dissolution of the medieval synthesis.

For the student of religion, the medieval Christian flowering of mysticism shows lines of relation with mysticism of other times, places, and faiths. A few lines of actual historical relation have been traced to mysticism in Eastern Orthodox Christianity and to Jewish mysticism, and even to Islam. Mystics, it seems, are often careless of the ties that bind them to particular religious groups or organizations.

When comparison is made between Christian mysticism and the great mystical traditions of south and east Asia, both similarities and differences emerge. First, it appears that mystics tend to use the symbols of their own religious tradition. Hence the Christian mystics speak of God and Christ, the Jewish mystics of the Torah, the Hindu mystics of Brahman and perchance of Shiva or Krishna, the Chinese mystics of Tao, and the Buddhist mystics of the buddha nature. However, in these variant formulations, recurrent themes emerge. Of these recurrent themes, none is more important than that of communion versus absorption. The significant fact is that Christian mystics (together with the monotheistic mystics of Judaism and Islam) tend to speak of mystical communion with the one God. When, as in the case of Meister Eckhart, the mystic goes beyond communion to ontological union, theological problems of greatest gravity are raised. Yet what is forbidden or at best problematic in monotheism is the avowed and approved goal of the eastern mystics. Their goal is complete absorption in the religious object. From this transcendent viewpoint a negative valuation is expressed toward the present world with its experience of individuality, personality, and action. One corollary of this difference in goal is the contemplative character of eastern mysticism as against the active social character of western mysticism.

THE BREAKUP OF THE MEDIEVAL SYNTHESIS

The thirteenth century was the great period of the medieval synthesis of faith and culture. During this time Thomas Aquinas thought out and wrote his comprehensive philosophical-theological synthesis. It was the age when papal power and prerogative reached its highest point. People worshiped God in the newly finished cathedral of Chartres and in other brilliant representatives of the new gothic style. Dominicans and Franciscans argued with each other and taught the Catholic faith to people of the growing universities and cities of Europe.

Yet as so often happens with great achievements of human civilization, cracks soon began to appear in this imposing structure. In the fourteenth century these cracks widened and deepened. Within two centuries it became apparent that the medieval synthesis was a thing of the past.[29] It was a time, in the words of the Dutch historian, Huizinga, of the "waning of the Middle Ages.[30]

Among the many contributing factors, one of the most important was growing European nationalism, especially in France and England. King Philip IV "the fair" (1285–1314) of France was drawn into bitter quarrel with Pope Boniface VII (1294–1304) over the issue of the king's right to tax church property. It was during this quarrel that Boniface issued his *Unam Sanctam* (quoted earlier in

Cathedral at Chartres. (French Embassy Press and Information Division, New York.)

Book of Hours of the house of Jeanne d'Evereux. Fourteenth century. (Metropolitan Museum of Art, New York.)

this chapter) which, though it was the high-water mark of papal claims to supremacy over civil power, must be regarded as a monument to an age which was passing away, even at the moment when it was promulgated. For Philip summoned the French Estates-General and called the pope a common criminal, and then dispatched an army which held the pope a prisoner. This episode came to be unforgettably etched on human memory.

Soon afterward Philip persuaded the subservient Pope Clement V (1305–1314) to leave Rome for Avignon in southern France. The seat of the papacy was destined to remain there from 1309 to 1377, during the so-called Babylonian captivity, a time when the popes were French and under the domination of the French king. It was a disaster from which the medieval papacy never recovered.

Nationalism stirred in other lands as well. In England John Wycliffe (1328–1384) protested against papal taxes and prerogatives and attacked the corruption of the church. Arguing that the Bible was the law of the church, he and his followers translated the Bible into English. To give the gospel to the people, Wycliffe began sending his "poor priests" out to the cities and villages of England.

Wycliffe's influence spread to Bohemia, in the writings and activities of John Huss (1373–1415). The church condemned Huss and burnt him at the stake at the Council of Constance, but this martyrdom only caused the fires of Bohemian nationalism to burn more brightly. Once more in human history persecution actually spread what it sought to stamp out.

The inner deterioration and corruption of the church, apparent to every perceptive person, were further illustrated by the so-called Renaissance popes, men who rose to the papal office by intrigue and bribery and who in its exercise were more concerned with the new Renaissance art and with Italian politics than with Christian faith or love of Christ. Of the several examples of this phenomenon during the fourteenth and fifteenth centuries, perhaps the most notable, or notorious, was the Borgia pope Alexander VI (1492–1503), who gained the papal office by bribery and used it to advance the fortunes of his illegitimate children, Lucrezia Borgia (by advantageous marriages) and the murderous Cesare Borgia (by assisting him to carve out a political principality within the states of the Church).

As early as Marsilius of Padua (d. 1342?), the author of *Defensor Pacis*, thoughtful Christians were seeking to call a church council to check the inner corruption as well as the irresponsible power of the papacy. Similar voices were raised ruring the next century or two, but other voices rose to defend papal prerogatives. The contest between them was a drawn battle, with the result that no action was taken. When finally councils were called, the situation had disintegrated too far for reform to be possible. The councils did little or nothing to check the disintegration.

Probably more important than any single person or event in the breakup of the medieval synthesis was the subtle but persistent and pervasive shift of human interest from the next world to this world which took place during the Renaissance. It is impossible to assign exact dates for the beginning of the Renaissance or to give precise definition to its nature or significance. However, the reader sees in persons and documents of the fourteenth century a new interest in the world of nature and society and in Greek and Latin antiquity. Petrarch (1304–1374) was interested in Latin literature, especially Cicero, but was also a poet of great gifts himself. Petrarch's friend and admirer Boccaccio (1313–1375), best known for the earthy tales of his *Decameron*, was also a student of Greek who promoted humanistic studies in Florence and Naples.

The Renaissance came to full flower in the arts of painting, sculpture, and architecture in the Italian cities. In Florence under the Medicis, such scholars as Marsilio Ficino sought to combine Christianity with Platonism, even to the point of celebrating Plato's birthday as well as Christ's. In Rome, John Pico della Mirandola, avid and omnivorous student of literature, language, and history, proposed to debate all comers in defense of human dignity.[31] From Italy the Renaissance spread northward and westward to embrace all Europe.

In most of its manifestations the Renaissance was by no means anti-Christian. There was no conscious break with the Christian tradition. Yet it represented a shift of interest from that of the high Middle Ages. Not God but human life was the new center of interest. Not blessedness hereafter but fulfillment during this life was its message. As there will be occasion to note in Chapter 17, this was a trend destined to increase and develop throughout the modern age. Here we note its function in disrupting (perhaps *undermining* or *eroding* would be a more descriptive verb) the medieval synthesis.

ISSUES AND QUESTIONS

In the popular culture of our time the Middle Ages were "other-worldly" in outlook and the modern age is "this-worldly." As with most such judgments, there is both truth and error in both of these assertions. In Chapter 17 we shall characterize the dominant spirit of the modern age of the West by the attitude of human self-sufficiency. By contrast the spirit of the Middle Ages may be said to have been one of human self-insufficiency or dependence upon God. Yet concerning such large issues, surely we must measure words. For example, the

Christian Platonism of the early Middle Ages does indeed seem other-worldly to the twentieth-century reader. By contrast, the Aristotelean thought of Thomas Aquinas gives notably more substance and significance to the life of this world and of our human selves, particularly in their physical and biological aspects. And indeed as the Middle Ages "waned" in the fourteenth and fifteenth centuries these trends notably increased.

In all of this we may well ask what was happening to the Bible's view of linear-dramatic history. We have noted the persistence of millennial images and thought throughout this period. It is interesting to observe concerning Thomas Aquinas that, while his *Summa Theologica* acknowledges such concepts as judgment day, they are pushed into the indefinite future. Meanwhile such radical thinkers as Joachim of Fiore viewed the historic future with radically new hope and expectation. By the age of the Renaissance such images and reflections had become a major theme. We shall follow these throughout the modern age of the West.

We can also observe a similar emergence for the concept of humanism, as defined in Chapter 13. The theology of Thomas Aquinas, drawing as it did upon both Greek and Hebraic or biblical sources, included as a central element a two-story view of the human self and its fulfillment. On the ground floor as an aspect of natural humanity are the four classical or Aristotelean virtues of justice, fortitude, prudence, and temperance, while on the second floor, available by grace only to Catholic Christians, are the theological virtues of faith, hope, and love. As the Renaissance dawned over Europe these virtues became an integral vision of human excellence and fulfillment. Such works of Renaissance art as Michelangelo's more than life-size David celebrated this vision. The Renaissance vision of human excellence has remained in people's imagination ever since, bidding all observers to higher achievement.

However, the Middle Ages had a dark side as well. The vision of human fulfillment did not extend to those outside of Catholic Christianity; and this list significantly included Jews, Muslims, and, within Christianity, heretics and schismatics. Here the story of intolerance and repression is a dark blot on a culture which called itself Christian.

Yet the Middle Ages, however we assess their achievements and defects, do raise a basic issue for the study of religion, which is still with us today, namely, the relation of faith to culture. In this case it is Christian faith and medieval European culture. However, both terms can be generalized to the relation of any faith to any culture. We shall follow this issue through successive ages of the West, and also note its new dimensions for the global issues of our time.

NOTES

1. Arnold J. Toynbee, *Civilization on Trial*, Oxford University Press, Fair Lawn, N.J.; 1948, p. 15.
2. Christopher Dawson, *Religion and the Rise of Western Culture*, Image Books, Doubleday, 1958.
3. Paul Tillich, *A History of Christian Thought*, unpublished manuscript, n.d.

4. Augustine, *Confessions*, V, 3.
5. Ibid., VII, 9.
6. Ibid., VIII, 7.
7. Ibid., IX, 10.
8. Lynn White, in George Thomas (ed.), *The Vitality of the Christian Tradition*, Harper, New York, 1945, pp. 88–89.
9. Henry Bettenson (ed.), *Documents of the Christian Church*, Oxford University Press, Fair Lawn, N.J., 1947, p. 164.
10. White, in Thomas, op. cit., pp. 88–89.
11. Williston Walker, *A History of the Christian Church*, rev. ed., Scribner, New York, 1959, pp. 232–238.
12. Bettenson, op. cit., p. 181.
13. Ibid., p. 137.
14. Ibid., pp. 157–158.
15. Ibid., pp. 161–163.
16. Ibid., pp. 188–189.
17. I Corinthians 12:27.
18. See any authorized missal or catechetical manual. As to the latter, J. Killgallon and G. Weber, *Life in Christ*, 720 N. Rush Street, Chicago, Ill., is striking for the quality of its writing.
19. Bettenson, op. cit., pp. 199f.
20. Ibid., p. 195.
21. Ibid., p. 196.
22. E. Gilson, *Reason and Revelation in the Middle Ages*, Scribner, New York, 1938.
23. For this and other arguments of Thomas for the existence of God, see A. Pegis (ed.), *Introduction to St. Thomas Aquinas*, Modern Library, New York, 1948, pp. 20–27. See also Jacques Maritain, *Approaches to God*, Harper, New York, 1954.
24. Pegis, op. cit., p. 701.
25. Dionysius the Areopagite, *The Divine Names and Spiritual Theology*, C. E. Rolt (trans.), Macmillan, New York, 1951.
26. Ray Petry (ed.), *Late Medieval Mysticism*, Library of Christian Classics, vol. 13, Westminster Press, Philadelphia, 1957.
27. Bonaventure, *Journey of the Mind to God*, Liberal Arts, New York, 1953.
28. W. Blakney, *Meister Eckhart*, Harper, New York, 1941.
29. Walker, op. cit., chaps. 10–16.
30. J. Huizinga, *The Waning of the Middle Ages*, Longmans Green, New York, 1948.
31. John Pico della Mirandola, *Oration on the Dignity of Man*, Regnery, Chicago, 1956.

BIBLIOGRAPHY

Adam, K.: *The Spirit of Catholicism*, Darby Books, Darby, Pa., 1988.
Augustine: *Confessions*, Doubleday, New York, 1960.
Battenhouse, R. (ed.): *A Companion to the Study of St. Augustine*, Oxford, Fair Lawn, N.J., 1955.
Bettenson, H. (ed.): *Documents of the Christian Church*, Oxford, New York, 1970.
Brown, P.: *Augustine of Hippo*, University of California Press, Berkeley, 1969.
———: *Society and the Holy in Late Antiquity*, University of California, Berkeley, 1982.
Copleston, F.: *Aquinas*, Penguin, New York, 1956.
Dawson, C.: *Religion and the Rise of Western Culture*, AMS Press, New York, 1979.
Fairweather, E. (ed.): *A Scholastic Miscellany: Anselm to Ockham*, Westminster John Knox, Louisville, Ky., 1982.
Ferm, R. (ed.): *Readings in the History of Christian Thought*, Holt, New York, 1964.

Gilson, E.: *God and Philosophy*, Yale, New Haven, Conn., 1959.

————: *Reason and Revelation in the Middle Ages*, Scribner, New York, 1938.

————: *The Spirit of Medieval Philosophy*, Scribner, New York, 1938.

Gonzalez, J.: *A History of Christian Thought*, Abingdon Press, Nashville, Tenn., 1970–1975.

Latourette, K.: *A History of Christianity*, Harper & Row, 1975.

Maritain, J.: *Approaches to God*, Harper, New York, 1953.

————: *Degrees of Knowledge*, Scribner, New York, 1939.

————: *True Humanism*, Greenwood Press, Westport, Conn., 1970.

Martindale, C. C.: *The Faith of the Roman Church*, Sheed, New York, 1950.

Panofsky, E.: *Gothic Architecture and Scholasticism*, New American Library, New York, 1976.

Pegis, A. (ed.): *Basic Writings of St. Thomas Aquinas*, Modern Library, New York, 1948.

————: *Introduction to St. Thomas Aquinas*, Random House, New York, 1965.

Pelikan, J.: *The Christian Tradition*, University of Chicago, Chicago, 1971–1986.

Petry, R. (ed.): *Late Medieval Mysticism*, Westminster John Knox, Louisville, Ky., 1980.

————: *A History of Christianity*, vol. 1, Baker, Grand Rapids, Mich., 1981.

Ruether, R., and E. McLaughlin, *Women of Spirit*: Simon and Schuster, New York, 1979.

Walker, W., et al.: *A History of the Christian Church*, Scribner, New York, 1985.

16

The Reformation and Protestantism

Like most other large historical events, the Protestant Reformation is a many-sided phenomenon, hence difficult to comprehend in its totality. The difficulty is increased by differences and disagreements among historians. Secular historians have generally been content to consider the Reformation along with the Renaissance as an aspect of the whole vast and often violent process of historical change by which the medieval world of church and empire was transformed into the modern world of nation states, middle-class economies and societies, and territorial churches. Roman Catholic historians have traditionally interpreted the Reformation as a story of heresy and schism, while Protestant historians have seen it as the recovery of original Christian truth and virtue. There is doubtless a germ of truth in all these partial approaches, yet none is adequate to the whole reality.

The late H. Richard Niebuhr once made the seminal remark that the Reformation might best be approached as a religious revolution within a social revolution.[1] The latter is, of course, the transformation in Europe's history from medieval to modern world; undoubtedly the Reformation was deeply and inextricably involved in this revolution. This social revolution had many causes, ranging from the burgeoning nationalism of European peoples and the rising importance of the middle classes, to technological advances such as the printing press and geographical discovery and expansion such as the opening up of the Americas to European exploration and colonization. Yet the social revolution even in its widest sense is not the whole story of the Reformation.

The inner religious revolution may be characterized by what Paul Tillich has called the *Protestant principle* in the religious life of sixteenth- and seventeenth-century Europe. Tillich defined the Protestant principle as the conviction that all human things must be held under God's judgment or criticism.[2] Conversely this means that all human things—indeed, all created beings—presuppose a transcendent point of criticism. Furthermore, if human life is to find affirmative relation to God, God must take the initiative. In more traditional terms, salvation of humankind is by faith, which is in turn a gift of divine grace. H. Richard Niebuhr called this outlook *radical monotheism*[3] and asserted that as a corollary human life is placed in a state of "permanent revolution."[4] Hence, as a corollary human life under God is forever being shattered and remade. Such is Tillich's Protestant principle; and, if the reader will recall Chapter 10, it will be apparent that it was the prophetic principle of ancient Israel long before it became the Protestant principle. Whatever the label, this is the viewpoint of never-ceasing criticism of all human things when they are under the transcendent principle of one God.

The Reformation had its own particular applications of this principle, often involving extensive adaptation and compromise with local forms of thought and life. In the history of the Reformation, aspects of the inner religious revolution were inextricably mingled with aspects of the outer or social revolution. The result was the period of western history called the *age of the Reformation*.

This age began when on October 31, 1517, an obscure monk named Martin Luther posted a list of ninety-five theses on the church door (which served as the university bulletin board) at the new German University of Wittenberg, thus inviting public debate. Historical scholarship attests that Luther wrote and circulated his theses for discussion. The age of the Reformation ended on the continent of Europe more than a century later with the Peace of Westphalia in 1648, and in England with the Glorious Revolution of 1688. By this time people who were weary of religious war and fanaticism resolved to tolerate differences—and to turn to other interests. Christianity entered this age structurally as one church. What emerged were five main traditions of Christianity: (1) Lutheranism, (2) Calvinism, (3) Anglicanism, (4) sectarianism, and (5) modern Roman Catholicism.[5] To these, subsequent history added three additional topics essential for the understanding of our present religious situation, namely, (6) the eighteenth-century Enlightenment, (7) Protestant pietism, and (8) the American religious experience. We will consider all of these eight topics briefly in turn in the course of this chapter and the next.

LUTHER AND LUTHERANISM

As noted above, Luther's ninety-five theses were the spark that set the Reformation off with explosive violence—incidentally, somewhat to the surprise of Luther.[6] As in all explosions the causal factors were many and complex; in this case they ranged from low clerical morality and the general need for reform to nascent German nationalism and the rise of humanism. Certainly one causal factor was the personality and mind of Martin Luther.

Luther was born in 1483 in Eisleben, of peasant stock. He had the advantage of a good education, preparing for law at the University of Erfurt. A narrow escape from death in 1505 diverted him from this career and led him to pledge himself to the monastic life. He entered the Augustinian order the same year, and two years later he was ordained a priest. He continued his theological studies, concentrating attention on the Book of Psalms and the Pauline epistles. In 1510–1511 Luther made a momentous trip to Rome for his order, seeing at first hand the need for reform of the church.

However, the deepest problems of these years of his life were inward and anthropological or psychological in nature. Luther felt himself increasingly and desperately cut off from God and hence plunged into despair, from which his rigorous practice of ascetic discipline was powerless to rescue him. Many modern readers see psychopathological states in his recurrent periods of despair. Luther's superior in the Augustinian order, Staupitz, was sympathetic, but to no avail. What did avail was what Luther found in the Bible, namely, the momentous idea that God's free gift of grace, which sinful humans could not in the least earn or deserve, could give back the lost meaning of life. Thus he came to believe that humans were justified not by works but by God's grace, which was appropriated through human faith. Faith for Luther, as for Paul and Augustine before him, was a process of turning away from proud self-centeredness to God; it was humanity's humble but joyful "yes" to God, in answer to God's original "yes" to humanity. This liberating conception took shape in Luther's mind as he pored over the pages of the Bible, and it rendered useless all the elaborate aspects of the Roman Catholic system.

Many of these issues came to a climax when the Dominican monk Johann Tetzel appeared in Germany peddling indulgences with lurid sales techniques in order to raise money for the new Saint Peter's Basilica in Rome. It was Tetzel's appearance just across the river from Wittenberg that elicited Luther's ninety-five theses, many of which dealt specifically with the issues of indulgences and God's forgiveness of human sin.

As noted in Chapter 15, an indulgence was not an ecclesiastical permission to sin, but rather a remission of part or all of the temperoal penalty of sin, which is to say, the sentence in purgatory. Proclamations of indulgences normally stated clearly that the receiver must have made sacramental confession of sin and received absolution from eternal penalty in order to benefit from an indulgence. To grant indulgences was, moreover, a right of the pope, based upon the medieval idea of the treasury of merit. The pope presumably might issue checks on this special account of merit, accumulated by the saints. What the age of the Reformation added to these ideas was the abuse of high-pressure sales techniques. But when Luther protested, he soon found himself increasingly driven to protest against the whole system, in the name of his own personally discovered view of grace as the favor of God to be appropriated by faithful and obedient hearts.

While the ninety-five theses challenged abuses, but not the pope's right to issue indulgences, they did characterize repentance as an inward and continuing attitude of the believer toward God rather than any external act. However, in debate with official spokesmen of the church, notably in 1517 at Leipzig with Johann Eck, Luther maintained the scripture as an authority over the church. In 1520 he was excommunicated, and he remained under this ban for the rest of his life. He responded by a public burning of the papal bull of excommunication in the town square of Wittenberg. In this same year he wrote three of his most important tracts: *On Good Works, On Christian Liberty*, and *On the Babylonian Captivity of the Church*.[7] The following year, 1521, he was sum-

Martin Luther. (New York Public Library, Picture Collection.)

moned to appear before the highest authorities of the Holy Roman Empire at Worms. Tradition says that he was shown his writings and given a chance to recant and that he responded, "Here I stand, I can do not other. So help me God."[8] Whether literally true or not, this accurately expresses Luther's character and position.

As he returned home from the imperial Diet at Worms, Luther was abducted by friendly hands at the command of his ruler, Frederick the Elector of Saxony, and was hidden for several months in the Wartburg castle. He used his time to translate the New Testament into German. It was the core of the epoch-making Luther Bible—a monument of German language and literature as well as of Christian faith and theology.

By 1523 Luther was back in Wittenberg, taking an active role in reforming the church. He offered advice and counsel for bringing the mass into line with his evangelical theology, while resisting more radical change. He also resisted the efforts of colleagues like Carlstadt, who sought to push the change to extreme conclusions. Luther called these radicals *Schwärmerei*, "enthusiasts," and denounced them unsparingly. In return, they regarded him as a halfway reformer.

In 1525 Luther married a former nun, Katherine von Bora. The marriage was arranged in haste, thus evoking Erasmus' jibe that the Reformation which at first seemed a tragedy was really a comedy ending in the wedding of a priest and a nun. Actually Luther's marriage was a completely honorable one and evoked some of the most attractive and winsome aspects of his life and thought, records of which are preserved in his *Tischreden*, or "Table Talk," recorded by theological students who lived with the Luthers.

As the German Reformation developed momentum and direction, it took on increasing political significance. This led Luther to seek to distinguish the gospel from the world of politics, the world of faith and grace from the bloody and ugly world of German politics, withal insisting that Christians involve themselves in the secular world. He was also increasingly unhappy with the never-ceasing quarrels of the reformers. Yet his great contribution had been made in his proclamation of the message of God's grace and human faith. Luther died in 1546 on a visit to Eisleben, the town where he had been born sixty-three years before.

Luther's theology bore a close relation to the volcanic personality and life that give birth to it. He was scornful of the elaborate systematic formulations of scholastic philosophies of the church, based as they were on "that blind pagan Aristotle."[9] His own theology was based not on a system, but on his own intense and undeniable experience, and on the Bible and its messages of God's grace. It began where Luther had begun, with the experience of sin, which Luther regarded as the arrogance of the heart which cuts humans off from God and raises idols in proud self-worship. Luther's view of sin was more extreme and less measured than Roman Catholic doctrine.

Luther disagreed with Catholic thought on the relation of faith to reason and thus on the use which Christian faith should make of philosophy. Luther's own training inclined him to the nominalism of William of Ockham, against the speculative reason of Thomas Aquinas; but at a deeper level Luther opposed all confidence in scholastic philosophy as a rival of faith. Such a use of human reason is depraved and sinful, or in Luther's phrase, a "devil's harlot."[10]

Not reason or philosophy, but faith alone was for Luther the instrumentality by means of which humans approach God, or more properly, the way in which they respond to God's grace. By *faith* Luther did not mean primarily a mystical experience (though he was much influenced by late medieval forms of mysticism), but rather the trustful allegiance and obedience of the human heart. It was Luther's fundamental conviction that God had acted in Christ to reconcile humans to himself. Therefore he spoke of Christ as "God's Word," meaning the divine self-utterance or self-expression to humanity. So it is that anyone who responds with faith in Christ is reconciled to God. It is the work of the Holy Spirit which permits the Christian to find the Word among the words of scripture.

The record of this redemptive activity of God is contained in the Bible, which for this reason assumed in Luther's thought a place of priority over pope and church. It was for Luther the final authority. The Christian has only to read its pages with an honest and seeking mind to find amid its words the Word of God. Luther made a clear and sharp distinction between the words of the Bible and the Word which God speaks through them. Thus he declared the words of

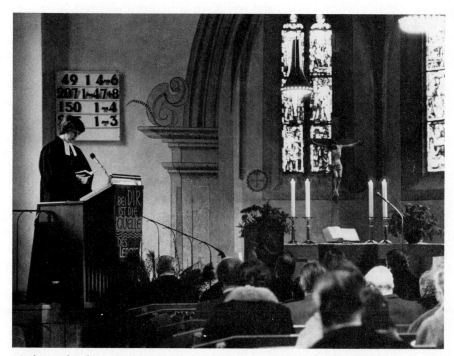

A Lutheran church service, Stuttgart, Germany. (Margot Granitsas/Photo Researchers.)

the Bible to be the cradle of Christ. Luther was clearly not a literalist, as were some others of the reformers and some of his Lutheran followers. Moreover, he did not find the Word of God equally in all parts of the Bible, but regarded Hebrews, James, and Revelation as inferior. James was a "right strawy" epistle, which he would have liked to exclude from the canon of scripture.[11]

The life of faith which follows from God's grace not only makes philosophical speculation trivial and otiose, but is a great leveler. For this truth from God is not the monopoly of priest or theologian, but is everyone's possession. Every Christian is possessed by this truth, and in this service finds freedom, as Luther declared in *On Christian Liberty*. The corollary of justification by faith was the priesthood of all believers, in which everyone was not only his or her own priest but priest to others.

From grace and faith sprang love. Christian love, or charity, was for Luther not a condition of earning God's favor, but rather the by-product in human life of God's grace to or love for humanity. Luther believed that in gratitude to God for his divine love, love welled up spontaneously in the human heart. Few people have described the virtue of love more eloquently than Luther; yet few have been as vividly aware of the tensions of love and hate in the human heart, and of the desperate difficulty in any detailed attempt to apply love to the affairs of the world.

Mention has already been made of the growing duality in Luther's thought of law and gospel, or of the fallen world where group relations are determined by self-will and power, or at best by order backed with force, and the hidden world of God's grace and love which is foreshadowed here on earth in the relations of love in family and church. As Luther himself expressed the matter, he put law on earth and gospel in heaven. As the Reformation developed, Luther assumed an increasingly conservative social and political viewpoint. Drawing back in horror at the prospect of anarchy during the Peasants' Revolt of 1524–1525, Luther wrote *Against the Murderous and Thieving Peasant Bands*. He denounced unsparingly what he regarded as the radical aberrations of other reformers. Nevertheless he continued to view some political action as necessary for the Christian, who must protest social injustice, unjust wars, and so forth. Luther himself remained under imperial ban from 1521 until his death.

The net result of all these tendencies was acceptance, if not by Luther then by the Lutheran tradition, of the duality of church and state, in which the church asks of the state only the liberty to preach the gospel and administer the sacraments. On the other hand, having turned over the problems of social order to the prince or politician, the church refrains from criticism of the existing order, limiting its function to praying for the state and its ruler. Thus denied any social gospel at its beginning, the Lutheran tradition has been one of social acceptance often termed *quietism*. Only when the basic rights of the church are threatened may the church speak out on political or social issues. Nevertheless Lutherans have sometimes spoken and acted in courageous defiance of state power, as was the case in recent history in Nazi Germany and Scandinavia. These events have led to extensive rethinking of the traditional Lutheran social position.

The Reformation in Germany was soon thrust into the troubled waters of interstate politics. By the late 1520s there was a league of Catholic princes and an opposing league of Protestant princes. It was the *protestatio* of the latter group at the Diet of Speier in 1529 which fixed the name *Protestant* upon the Reformation party. Dubious political maneuvering alternated with even more dubious military battles until the Peace of Augsburg in 1555 resolved the struggle on the basis of the formula, *Cujus regio ejus religio,* "Whose the rule, his the religion." Germany was divided only between Catholicism and Lutheranism on the basis of the faith of the rulers of its several states. If people were dissatisfied with the local religion, they might choose to move to another region. The choice was between Catholicism and Lutheranism—but at least this solution brought peace to a people tired of religious strife.

From Germany, the Lutheran form of faith spread to the countries of Scandinavia, where it became the established church. From Scandinavia and Germany it emigrated to North America, where it has continued to exert strong influence among Americans of German and Scandinavian descent.

Lutheran worship as well as theology has continued to bear the stamp of Luther's mind. In marked contrast to some other types of Protestantism, Lutheran worship has maintained a strong liturgical foundation. As to the sacraments, Luther recognized only two of the seven sacraments of Roman Catholicism as biblically based, baptism and the eucharist. In the whole issue of worship it may be said that Luther sought to simplify and purify Roman practice, but that as an intensely devout man he sought forms which would nourish and sustain the Christian spirit. He was particularly fond of music and wrote many hymns both as an expression of his own faith and for use in congregational worship. Choral singing has historically played a significant part in Lutheran worship.

CALVIN AND CALVINISM

As with every other aspect of their life, the cantons of Switzerland proceeded independently with the issues of reforming the church, some maintaining their Roman Catholic faith and others turning to one of the varieties of Protestantism. Leadership among the latter was assumed by the canton of Zürich under the soldier-humanist Huldreich Zwingli. In 1519 Zwingli became priest and pastor of the cathedral at Zürich, a post which he occupied until his death in battle with Roman Catholic cantons in 1531. Zwingli led the people of Zürich in abolishing many Roman Catholic practices and beliefs, and in establishing a biblically based Christian faith whose ultimate authority lay with the Christian community. Progress of the Reformation in German-speaking Switzerland was halted with the defeat of Zürich's army by Catholic opponents in 1531 in the battle of Kappel, in which Zwingli was killed.

In French-speaking Switzerland, events took a different direction. Geneva, be it noted, was at this time an independent republic. During the late 1520s and early 1530s, this city was torn by dissension between Catholic and Protestant parties, due in part to the preaching and activities of the fiery Protestant William Farel. Matters came to a head in 1535–1536 with anti-Catholic and iconoclastic rioting and with the city council torn between Catholic and Protestant parties. By the middle of 1536, Geneva had decided for Protestantism, though probably more for political than religious reasons.

In July 1536, Farel was visited by a young French friend who was en route to visit fellow Protestants in Italy. His name was John Calvin, and Farel persuaded him to stay in Geneva and help with the work of reforming the city. Except for three years, 1538–1541, the rest of Calvin's life was to be identified with Geneva and the Genevan Reformation.

Calvin, born in 1509 of middle-class parents in Noyon, Picardy, had been educated first for a clerical career and then for a legal career. His youthful interests at the universities of Paris and Orleans were those of a serious and brilliant young humanist. His first book, published in 1532, was *Commentary on Seneca's Treatise on Clemency*. Soon afterward, Calvin underwent an experience of "sudden conversion."[12] Nothing is known of this momentous event beyond Calvin's conviction that God spoke to him through the Bible and that God's will must be obeyed. The impact of this experience was to be seen in the whole subsequent life and thought of Calvin. From this time onward his own austere Christian faith had an altogether central place in his life. During the same year, Calvin's friend Nicholas Cop, newly chosen rector of the University of Paris, delivered an inaugural address so Protestant in tone that both Cop and Calvin were forced to flee. There is no basis for the assertion that Calvin wrote the address, though doubtless he sympathized with its sentiments.

Calvin went into hiding in France, then fled to Basel, Switzerland, where in 1536 he published the first edition of his famous *Institutes of the Christian Religion*, destined to grow through many successive editions until the final and definitive edition of 1559. Composed at first as a defense of French Protestantism against groundless charges of the French king, Francis I, the *Institutes* grew into the classical statement of Reformed Protestantism.

Calvin's first position in Geneva was as lecturer on the Bible. A year later he was appointed one of the city's pastors, the only official post he ever held, but one from which he waged a lifelong campaign, against many opponents, to conform the city's life to the will of God. Calvin and Farel moved slowly at first, in 1537 securing passage by the Little Council of Geneva of a measure to excommunicate unworthy people and to impose a catechism and creed on the city. However, the following year the party opposed to Calvin won in the elections, and Calvin and Farel were banished. Calvin spent the next three years with his friend Butzer in Strassburg.

Returning to Geneva after victory in the 1541 elections, Calvin consolidated his position, soon becoming a powerful force in the city. He moved to establish an ideal Christian commonwealth where all life, individual and social, would be conducted according to his own severe interpretation of Christianity. In addi-

John Calvin. (New York Public Library, Picture Collection.)

tion to social and political reforms, Calvin's program regulated individual conduct down to matters of speech, clothes, and manners.

Calvin's record in Geneva was marred by the famous, or infamous, case of Servetus. Servetus, an erratic genius, had written against the trinity in ways similar to modern Unitarians. Condemned to the stake in Roman Catholic Lyons, France, Servetus escaped and, for reasons hard to understand, made his way to Geneva, where his presence was a deliberate political challenge to Calvin and was so interpreted by the opposition party. Calvin accepted the challenge. Servetus was tried, convicted of heresy, and burnt at the stake in 1553. It was an intolerant act in the midst of an intolerant age, though it was also at the time a great political victory for Calvin. Speaking more generally, it stands out partly because so few people were put to death in Geneva—by contrast to the rest of Europe at this time.

Calvin's work at Geneva included many achievements which must be judged affirmatively by any civilized standard. While certainly no democrat in any modern sense, he did sanction the choice of pastors and elders by popular vote of the congregation, thus providing a thin opening wedge for democracy; it is a historic fact that democracy did develop notably in Calvinist lands. An important source was Calvin's system of representative democratic government for the church. Calvin also removed the medieval Catholic ban against interest taking by Christians, thus making possible a great growth of Protestantism among the rising business classes of Geneva and all Europe, though it must immediately be added that this move was hedged about with many qualifications. He also founded the Genevan Academy, which later became the University of Geneva.

Protestants from all parts of Europe, many of them refugees, gathered under Calvin in Geneva, there imbibed his distinctive and vigorous version of Protestantism, and then carried it back home with them. In this way Calvinistic Christianity got its start in France, the Netherlands, Germany, England, and Scotland, and from these bases, in North America. In all these lands the disciples of Calvin were strong personalities, convinced of their election to be fellow workers with God and sure that in the Bible God has given an unerring guide for human faith and life.

In Calvin's native France, Reformed fortunes fluctuated with politics. By the middle of the sixteenth century the Huguenot party, under the able leadership of Admiral Gaspard Coligny, was said to number almost half a million people. Untold numbers of them fell victim to the massacre of Saint Bartholomew's day in 1572. Through the action of the tolerant King Henry IV, they won legal existence in the Edict of Nantes in 1598. Almost a century later Louis XIV felt powerful enough to revoke the edict; as a consequence the Huguenots became a martyr church until the French Revolution. What was even more important, through this intolerant act of Louis XIV, Protestant influence in French life was almost wiped out.

In the Netherlands Calvinism provided courage to resist Spanish tyranny through more than a decade of savage war. Dutch Protestantism was Calvinistic in both belief and church organization. Many influences, including a rising and successful business class, combined to produce in Holland a larger measure of religious toleration than elsewhere in Europe at the time.

Calvinism was taken to Scotland by John Knox, who had served a year and a half as a French galley slave because of youthful Protestant activities. Upon release he found his way to Geneva, where he was pastor to other British refugees and also was one of the translators of the Geneva Bible. Returning to Scotland, he became the chief foe of Mary, Queen of Scots, and main architect of the Calvinistic church of Scotland.

Calvinism found its way to England during the reign of Henry VIII (1509–1547) and flourished during the brief following reign of Edward VI (1547–1553). Violently repressed by Edward's successor, Mary, it emerged again under Elizabeth and her Stuart successors as Puritanism. The Puritan revolution of the seventeenth century will be discussed in a later section of this chapter. From England, Scotland, and Holland, Calvinistic Christianity made the voyage to America, where it entered deeply into the fabric of church and society.

Calvin's thought, as contained in the *Institutes* and his many other writings, constitutes a different and more thoroughgoing type of Protestantism than Luther's. Calvinist worship and church organization were more thoroughly stripped of Roman Catholic features. The pulpit with the open Bible became the center of worship, and the service centered on prayer, scripture, preaching, and congregational singing. Like Luther, Calvin recognized two sacraments, baptism and the Lord's supper; but Calvin went further than Luther in his rejection of such Catholic doctrines as transubstantiation. For him the sacraments were signs of God's promise to humanity. Calvinist churches are ruled by elders elected by the people.

The center of Calvin's interpretation of Christian faith is the will of God revealed in Christ. God rules the world and everything in it. It is he who called the world into being at creation, and he sustains it through every moment of its existence. To finite and sinful human beings, the divine will is inscrutable, and from a human viewpoint, God seems to follow his own mysterious good pleasure. Yet in fact the divine will is holy, righteous, and just. All things are ordained to serve God's glory.

Calvin taught that enough of the divine will is visible by human reason from the order of creation to render humans responsible, yet it is also a fact that human understanding is very greatly dimmed by the depravity of sin. Hence God has taken the trouble to communicate his will in the Bible, which in Calvinistic Christianity constitutes a final authority. Yet Calvin was no literalist about the Bible. He believed that Christ is the Word in the words of scripture, made clear by the Holy Spirit. In Calvinist tradition a literalist view of biblical inspiration was destined to be a continuing issue. In the struggles of Catholics and Protestants, it was perhaps inevitable that the absolute authority of the pope should be countered by the Bible as a "paper pope."

Like Luther, Calvin believed in total human depravity—that is, no part of human nature is exempt from the ravages of sin. This idea of Calvin has been subject to many misunderstandings, especially in modern times. It is traceable to Augustine, to Paul in the New Testament, and even to such figures as Jeremiah in the Old Testament. Even in Calvin's formulation it did not deny or obscure the fact that the natural human being is capable of high achievements in many realms of life. However, since no part of human life is exempt from the self-centeredness and evil of sin, humans are incapable of the crucial religious act of turning to God through their own power. If they are to be saved, God must take the initiative.

Like Luther, Calvin fervently believed that in the Bible, centering in Christ, God has done this. Indeed, salvation is wholly of God, and humans must believe that even their own turning to God is of divine grace rather than of human works. Yet according to Calvin if human beings are not saved by their works, they are saved *to* them. Calvin taught that salvation is fulfilled in righteousness of life. Hence Calvinists were expected to be fruitful in works of righteousness, to show forth their election to salvation by the quality of their lives. In later times Calvin's followers came to believe that righteous character was evidence that a person has been justified, or saved.

Calvin's characteristic emphasis on the divine initiative in salvation led him to the austere doctrine of double predestination, to salvation and to damnation. He taught that God in his inscrutable will has predestined some people to damnation—a fate which divine justice would decree for all—and others to salvation—as an expression of God's unmerited love. Calvin was always careful to point out that predestination is not a doctrine of speculative philosophy but rather an inference from the glory and sovereignty of God.

Reformed Christianity produced a morality of great vigor and of equal rigor. Puritans have been termed "moral athletes."[13] Zealously they strove to make all human life conform to the righteousness of their God. Max Weber has termed Calvinism "this-worldly asceticism."[14] The Calvinist sometimes fell victim to self-righteousness, and sometimes to a hard and loveless legalism in ethics. Nonetheless the popular American picture of Calvinists as humorless fanatics is a crude caricature which does little justice to the humane learning and the catholicity of Calvinism.

As previously suggested, Calvinist Protestantism made an alliance with the rising middle classes.[15] It emphasized the virtues of thrift, hard work, and industry as signs of election, and the vices of laziness and improvidence as signs of perdition. As many writers have pointed out, there has been a close relation between Calvinism and the rise of western capitalism.[16]

Politically Calvinism proved to be the seed plot of modern constitutional government. As previously noted, Calvinism was democratic in its church government. Moreover, Calvinists had the best of reasons for opposing the arbitrary power of rulers. To all forms of political absolutism they said, "God alone is lord of the conscience."[17] The Calvinist view of human sinfulness led many Calvinists to a deep suspicion of all forms of power and hence to the political idea of checks and balances. Calvinist conscience and social responsibility proved to be a good soil in which grew many of the virtues essential to modern democracy.

The english reformation

The English Reformation produced no single great figure such as Luther or Calvin and was even more deeply involved in political and national factors than the German or Swiss Reformation. It was the response of the English people as a whole. English Churchmen often point to its source in an ancient tradition of English Catholic Christianity, allegedly independent of Rome.

The occasion of England's break with Rome was Henry VIII's desire to be legally rid of his wife, Catherine of Aragon, in order that he might marry Anne Boleyn and, he hoped, have a male heir to his throne. Yet beneath these personal events lay many deeper causes. English dissent to Rome was of long standing, going back at least to Wycliffe (d. 1384). English nationalism flexed its muscles in the sixteenth century. The humanism of Erasmus, Colet, and More had a ready hearing in English universities and created a climate of opinion highly critical of the church. The writings of Luther were widely read. Incidentally, Henry VIII wrote a refutation of Luther which gained for him from the grateful pope the appellation "defender of the faith."

Henry, who has been called a tyrant under legal forms, was not a man to be denied. Refused a legal separation by the pope, he resolved to break with Rome. A dutiful Parliament acceded to the king's demands with the Act of Supremacy in 1534. The strongly Calvinist archbishop of Canterbury, Thomas Cranmer, performed the marriage ceremony of Henry and Anne Boleyn. Henry followed up these acts by confiscation of the extensive lands of the monasteries, which he divided among his subservient nobles. However, at this point Henry sought to clamp the lid on the process of reformation. In theology and church government he was no Protestant, and he harried and persecuted those who were.

Henry died in 1547 and was followed by his son, Edward VI, who was a child, and whose Protestant advisors made the most of their opportunity. A *Book of Common Prayer* adapted from many traditional sources was adopted in 1549, and an even more strongly Protestant edition was issued in 1552. More than any other factor the *Book of Common Prayer* has given unity and direction to Anglican Christianity. It combined a Protestant emphasis on the Bible with traditional Catholic forms of liturgy. Typical of the *Book of Common Prayer* was its designation of the eucharist as "the Lord's Supper, or Holy Communion commonly call the Mass." The real presence of Christ in the eucharist was proclaimed, but the Roman Catholic doctrine of transubstantiation was expressly denied. Forty-two Articles of Religion, revising Henry VIII's articles, were passed by Parliament in 1552; they affirmed three orders of clergy—bishops, priests, and deacons—and the Anglican clergy standing in valid apostolic succession.

Edward died in 1553 and was succeeded by his devout Roman Catholic sister Mary, who was intent upon undoing the Protestant mischief, as she saw it. Protestants who under Edward had persecuted Catholics were now burnt at the stake and harried from the land. The persecution was severe but brief, for Mary died in 1558.

England's next queen was Elizabeth, daughter of Henry and Anne Boleyn, and similar to her father in ability, insight, and personal popularity. Her long reign (1558–1604) was one of England's greatest ages. Religiously she sought a middle course between the extremes of Roman Catholicism and Calvinist Protestantism. The Act of Supremacy of 1559 declared the Church of England to stand politically under the crown, the *Book of Common Prayer* to be the standard to public worship, and the episcopate and a revised Thirty-nine Articles of Religion to be the norms of the Church of England. The foundations of Anglican Christianity were laid in these decisions.

While the English Reformation produced no Luther or Calvin, nonetheless the middle way of Anglicanism did find remarkable expression in a single book, Richard Hooker's *Laws of Ecclesiastical Polity*, published in 1594–1597. The author was a graduate of Corpus Christi College, Oxford, and between 1585 and 1591 he was master of the temple, a position which enabled him to preach to the university community. His disappointed rival for the same post, a Puritan named William Travers, spoke from the same pulpit Sunday evenings, thus provoking the quip, "The forenoon sermon spoke Canterbury, the afternoon Geneva."[18]

In 1591 Hooker left the university for a country parish in order to devote himself to writing his *Laws*. In this volume he deliberately sought a middle way between Rome and Geneva. In reaction to Calvinist emphasis on the Bible alone, Hooker based his case on the threefold foundation of the church in scripture, tradition, and reason. While deeply critical of many aspects of Roman Catholicism, he nonetheless refused to reject any idea simply because it was Roman Catholic.

His emphasis on reason found expression in the idea of natural order, or natural law, which had its origin in the mind of God. God has written the idea of natural order into the structure of his creation, or in other words, creation has a rational structure, expressible as natural law. Hooker asserted that the positive enactments of governments or churches were based upon divine and natural laws. The later conception of natural laws or self-evident truths in the thought of men like Locke and Jefferson owed much to Hooker's formulation.

In worship, Hooker's combination of law and tradition led him to vigorous defense of the *Book of Common Prayer* against what he saw as the Puritan desire to thwart all beauty and pleasing forms. Beauty and dignity of worship were worth maintaining, argued Hooker. From his time, Anglicans have placed a higher priority on worship than have most other non-Roman forms of Christianity. For Anglican Christianity the celebration of holy communion according to the *Book of Common Prayer* is the central act of worship and of the church's life.

The Anglican tradition which found expression in Hooker was destined to be tested, tried, and developed in subsequent history, but Anglican history has not strayed far from the formulations of Hooker. From England this form of Christianity spread to the colonies, where it produced the Protestant Episcopal church, to Scotland, where it became the Scottish Episcopal church, and to mission stations in all parts of the world. Anglican Christians find a common center in Canterbury, and their bishops meet in periodic conferences at Lambeth Palace. Yet each national church, indeed each diocese and parish, enjoys a large measure of autonomy. Anglicans frequently regard their church as the bridge between Protestantism and Catholicism. Anglican high churchmen regard themselves as true Catholics, with Roman Catholics and Protestants alike diverging from the true norm. Low and broad churchmen, by contrast, emphasize the Protestant aspect of their tradition.

Queen Elizabeth's pragmatic solution to the religious problem was not destined to go unchallenged. Many of her subjects, dissatisfied with her middle-of-the-road position, sought to push the Reformation further. Their announced intention to purify Christian worship and teaching gained them the name of *Puritans*. Standing on a Calvinist theology and opposing the episcopal form of church government, the Puritans carried on increasing activity throughout Elizabeth's reign. In the next century they played a dominant role in English history.

Elizabeth was followed to the throne by the Stuarts, James I (1603–1625) and Charles I (1625–1643). James struggled throughout his reign with growing religious dissent, and under Charles it broke into open rebellion which cost the king his throne and his head. Under the soldier-statesman Oliver Cromwell, the Puritans made England a commonwealth (1642–1660). Cromwell's own religious views were somewhat to the left of the Puritan majority in Parliament, but politically he favored a national church which would exclude only papists and irreconcilable Anglicans, with a large measure of toleration for dissenting sects such as Baptists and Congregationalists.

The Westminster Assembly, named for its place of meeting, was a notable Puritan gathering of 121 clergymen and 30 laymen called by Parliament in 1643 for advice on religious matters. Excepting a few Episcopalians on one extreme and a few Separatists on the other, the majority were Calvinist in theology and presbyterian in church organization, that is, favoring the rule of the church by elected elders (the Greek word *presbyteros* means "elder") in a representative though centralized democracy. The Westminster Assembly produced the Westminister Confession of Faith, a notable statement of Calvinist Christianity, as well as a longer and shorter catechism and a Director of Worship. All these documents were much influenced by people and ideas from north of the Scottish border. In the Cromwellian period, English Presbyterianism assumed definitive form as the established faith of England. But when the Commonwealth fell in 1660, giving way to the Stuart restoration under Charles II, English Presbyterianism became the faith of a small minority—a position from which it has never recovered. However, during its period of ascendancy it sent many colonists overseas to the colonies, where it grew with the growing nation. In addition to influencing the Presbyterian churches of North America, English Calvinism exercised a strong influence on the theology (though not the church organization) of New England Congregationalism.

The Commonwealth had given way in 1660 to the restoration of Charles II; but the militant Roman Catholicism of Charles's successor, James II, led to the Bloodless Revolution of 1688, which brought the Protestant monarchs William and Mary to the throne. Even more important, it produced the Act of Toleration and Bill of Rights of 1689. England continued to have an established church, but religious toleration and freedom were the law of the land. At first the range of freedom and toleration was narrow, excluding Roman Catholics, Jews, and atheists. Toleration was extended only to dissenting or free churches. Nonetheless a beginning was made for the distinctively modern idea of religious freedom, which once experienced and practiced was to spread, and as people came to understand its meaning, to widen and deepen its meaning.

SECTARIAN PROTESTANTISM—OR THE RADICAL REFORMATION

In addition to the three forms just described, the Reformation produced a fourth, the small sects. Throughout the centuries of Christian history there have been small groups who have arisen to protest the compromises and evils of existing church and society. Indeed, this difference of outlook between church and sect has served as a focus for much fruitful study of Christian history and ethics.[19] According to this view, a church tends to be the religious organization of a whole society—to be, as it were, the society at worship. The church tends therefore to be closely related to the world, thus necessitating compromises and adjustments, but providing religious orientation and guidance for all. In sharpest contrast, sects scorn compromise and adjustment as signifying an alliance with the devil. They have generally insisted that their members join voluntarily; and their customary ceremony of adult baptism has symbolized this feature. Once they have joined the sect, members are rigorously disciplined. In their repudiation of the world of human society, most sects have been pacifist, rejecting as unchristian the evil of war. Some have also rejected private property as evil, others have taken the view of philosophical anarchism, rejecting the institution of government, and still others have even renounced the family as inconsistent with Christian morality.

No century of Christian history has been without its sectarian protests. The Christian movement of the first three centuries has been interpreted as a persecuted sect. Only with Constantine did Christianity take the form of a church. Thereafter, throughout the Middle Ages there were groups such as the Waldensians in twelfth-century Italy, the Albigensians of thirteenth-century France, and the Lollards of fourteenth-century England that illustrated the sectarian pattern. The early Franciscan movement showed some signs of becoming a sect, but the church was wise enough to reach out and draw it back into the fold. It is with this background of agelong sectarian activity in mind that attention is now turned to the sectarian groups which arose during the age of the Reformation.

Characteristically this form of Protestantism produced no single great leader or form of organization, but rather sprang up locally and in great variety in many parts of Europe. Many sectarians held the conviction that Luther and Calvin were only halfway reformers and therefore to be regarded along with Rome as evil. Most of them rejected infant baptism as a meaningless ritual and insisted upon adult or believer's baptism as an expression of an individual's decision to enter the community of believers. From this insistence was derived the label *Anabaptists*, or "rebaptizers."

Groups of Anabaptists sprang up over large areas of Germany, Switzerland, and the Low Countries. Typical was the community which existed for some years in Waldshut, Switzerland, under the leadership of Balthazar Hubmaier. Later the saintly Hubmaier was hounded out of Switzerland to Moravia and thence to Vienna, where he was put to death. In Zurich, Anabaptist leaders were put to death by drowning, in hideous parody of their faith. Generally both Roman Catholic and Protestant leaders cruelly persecuted the Anabaptists. Yet, as often happens, persecution only spread abroad what it sought to destroy.

In addition to believer's baptism, these groups stood for rule of the church by a self-governing congregation, free of control by state and ecclesiastical hierarchy alike. They studied the Bible and sought rigorously to live by its teachings. For the most part, they were quiet, God-fearing people.

For some Anabaptists the Bible led them to politically radical conclusions. Such was the case in the Münster rebellion of 1534–1535. Under the leadership of Melchior Hofman, Jan Matthys, a baker of Haarlem, and Jan Beukelssen, a tailor of Leyden, these sectarians seized control of Münster and set up a new order based largely upon the biblical book of Revelation. Polygamy and community of property were established, and opponents were forcibly repressed. This radical experiment was put down with great cruelty by combined Catholic and Lutheran military forces. The Münster rebellion served to discredit widely such radical sectarian leadership and to divert European Anabaptist groups to peaceful, indeed passive, ways. The leader in this new path was a former priest, Menno Simons, who spent his life as the itinerant leader and guide to communities of sectarians in Germany and the Netherlands. His followers were called *Mennonites*. Many of them emigrated to North America and other regions of the world in search of religious freedom.

Sectarian ideas and activities emerged in England as well as on the European continent during the sixteenth and seventeenth centuries. Some Puritans tended to become more radical as they continued to develop their criticisms of the established church. One such was Robert Browne, who in 1581 founded a church in Norwich, England, dedicated to the radical idea of separation of church from state. His preaching soon landed him in jail. Subsequently he sought refuge in the Netherlands, where his writings argued the case for the autonomy and self-government of the local congregation. Browne is claimed as the father of Congregationalism.

The term *separatist* was applied in England to those who advocated complete separation from the established church and from government control of religion. One such group, under the leadership of John Smyth, fled England for Amsterdam in 1607. There Smyth adopted the practice of adult baptism, and in 1612 his flock returned to London to become the first Baptist Church in England. Throughout the seventeenth century, Baptists suffered severe repression in England, as illustrated by John Bunyan's long life in jail. Roger Williams founded the colony of Rhode Island on Baptist principles, including religious freedom, in 1636. Baptists have generally been characterized by adult baptism, autonomy of the local congregation, and a generally Calvinist theology. Beyond these common features, they have shown enormous variety.

Another separatist group which fled persecution in Scrooby in 1609 found a temporary home in Leyden, Holland, under John Robinson, William Brewster, and William Bradford. But their eyes turned toward the New World, and in 1620 they sent their bolder and more adventurous members across the Atlantic on the *Mayflower* to a place to be called Plymouth, Massachusetts.

As the seventeenth century unfolded, many varieties of sectarian groups flourished in England and on the continent of Europe. So far, attention has been called principally to what have often been termed *millennial* or *apocalyptic* sects, that is, sects which stake their being on the imminent coming of judgment day and the new age. Needless to say, the new age has been conceived in widely different ways. Attention has also been called to the fact that following the Münster debacle, the Mennonites emerged as a *pietist* sect, that is, one which emphasized individual emotive experience of religion on the part of all members without reference to any claims of an impending millennium. Other noteworthy pietist sects were also to emerge.

In addition to apocalytic and pietist types were the mystical sects, illustrated by the Quakers, or Society of Friends, founded and led by George Fox (1624–1681). Fox experienced a mystical conversion in 1648, convincing him that true religion consists not in creed or church but in illumination by the Holy Spirit. He spent his life in obedience to this vision, organizing and propagating a religious society without formal clergy or sacramental worship. True worship consists, said Fox and his followers, in sitting in silence until the divine spirit moves someone to speak. Fox also bequeathed to his followers a strong sense of equality within the whole society and a passion for human brotherhood. From the beginning, Quakers rejected all titles and differences in social rank; they also rejected and opposed both war and slavery. Among the early leaders of the Society of Friends was William Penn (1644–1718), under whom the Pennsylvania colony was founded as a haven for harried Quakers. Since Quakers also believed in religious freedom for all, Pennsylvania soon became a refuge for many religious groups from England and continental Europe. Among American Quaker leaders, John Woolman (1720–1772) was notable for his *Journal* as well as for his opposition to Negro slavery. Quaker zeal for the cause of peace and justice has been rekindled more recently by Rufus Jones (1863–1948), philosopher of mysticism and founder of the American Friends Service Committee. In North America and Europe, and indeed throughout the world, the Quakers have exerted a moral influence out of all proportion to their numbers.

On the continent of Europe during the seventeenth century another notable pietist movement sprang up, in part at least as a response to the sterile intellectualism of orthodox Lutheran and Calvinist theology. In both Lutheran and Calvinist traditions, the vital convictions of earlier days gave way to rigidly correct intellectual beliefs. To all this, *pietism* was an emotional reaction. For pietism, true religion was not assent to a creed but personal, individual, and usually emotional experience of religion. In Germany Philip Spener (1635–1705) and later Hermann Francke (1663–1727) organized small groups of devoted people for Bible study, prayer, and devotions. For the pietist movement, ideas such as sin, salvation, and faith in Christ took on intense and vivid personal reality.

Similar to the pietists were the Moravian Brethren founded by Count Zinzendorf (1700–1760), who was influenced by pietist education. Permitting a group of Moravian Hussites to establish a community on his Saxon estate, he was led to join with them. Under his leadership the Moravian Brethren were founded in 1727. Several communities of Moravians settled among the English colonists of North America. Throughout their history they have been notable in sending missionaries to all parts of the world. Through John Wesley they also exerted a vast influence on the Methodists of England and the United States.

The Methodist revival of eighteenth-century England was begun and led by John Wesley (1703–1791) and his brother, Charles Wesley (1707–1788). The sons of an Anglican clergyman, they attended Oxford, where they were members of a student religious society whose aims were worship and visitation of local jails. This group was known derisively as the "holy club" until someone dubbed them "Methodists" as a scornful characterization of their methodical customs of worship.

Despite his pious habits, John Wesley's religion was destined to be worked out throught a decade of agonized seeking. On shipboard bound for the American colony of Georgia, Wesley was deeply impressed by the personal conviction as well as the calm courage of a group of Moravian Brethren who were also bound for the New World. In Georgia controversy over a woman reduced his usefulness as a priest and missionary, and he sailed for home. In 1738 his religious seeking was answered by a conversion experience at a meeting of an "Anglican society" in Aldersgate Street, London. Wesley recorded in his journal the details of the experience in which he felt his heart "strangely warmed." This experience transformed his life and left its stamp indelibly upon him and the movement he led.

Beginning to preach to the unchurched multitudes of England's growing cities, Wesley soon found himself organizing his converts into religious societies. The Wesleyan movement attracted scant interest in the Church of England, and Wesley, always a devout Anglican, found himself forced, step by step, to found a new sect. A decisive step in this process was his act of ordaining clergymen to carry on the work of Methodism in North America, Anglican ordination being the exclusive prerogative of bishops. Yet once the first step had been taken, Wesley proceeded to ordain other clergymen for the Methodists of Scotland, Newfoundland, and finally England. The Wesleyan movement combined a pietist concern in personal religious experience and conversion with an interest in the people of England's industrial cities and the New World's frontiers. For both of these groups, Methodism offered new hope and salvation.

Still another and different kind of sect is illustrated by the Unitarians. From the first days of the Reformation, there had been intellectual radicals who questioned traditional dogmas as irrational. The doctrine of the trinity drew their heaviest fire. One such person was Michael Servetus, executed by Calvin's Geneva. Faustus Socinus (1539–1604), member of a noble Italian family, was another. Moving from land to land seeking asylum from official intolerance, he found his way successively to Switzerland, Transylvania, and Poland. As a result of his labors, the Polish Brethren church was founded with a unitarian creed. In the centuries which followed, individuals and small groups rose in many parts of Europe to espouse liberal and unitarian ideas. The eighteenth-century Enlightenment gave great impetus to unitarian ideas and societies. In 1773 Theophilus Lindsey withdrew from the Anglican church and organized a Unitarian church in London. Closely associated with him was Joseph Priestley, a dissenting clergyman, also an eminent chemist and the discoverer of oxygen. Priestley spent his last ten years in the United States. Thomas Jefferson is often listed as a Unitarian. In the nineteenth century such Americans as William E. Channing, Ralph Waldo Emerson, and Theodore Parker gave the Unitarian movement an influence far greater than the size of its membership would indicate.

THE ROMAN CATHOLIC REFORMATION AND COUNTER-REFORMATION

It is a fact often overlooked that the process of reformation went on within the Roman Catholic church as well as among those groups which seceded from that church. It is also a fact that as the Protestant forces picked up momentum and seemed in a position to win most of Europe, Roman Catholic forces mounted what in military metaphor may be termed a successful *counteroffensive*, winning back for their church Italy, France, and extensive areas of Germany. Nineteenth-century historians gave the title *Counter-Reformation* to these events.[20] From these events the Roman Catholic church emerged in a massively defensive posture which has defined its characteristic attitude for four centuries. In other words, the Roman Catholic church from the Council of Trent to the Second Vatican Council was almost as much a product of the Reformation as any of the four main types of Protestantism just considered.

Some aspects of the process of revival and reform within the Roman Catholic church, such as the work of Cardinal Ximenes to revive the Spanish church and educate its clergy, antedate by a full generation Luther's breach with Rome. A notable aspect of revival within the Roman church was a number of new orders and organizations—the Theatines, the Regular Clerics of Saint Paul, the Oratory of Divine Love, and many more.[21] Of these new orders, the Society of Jesus, founded by Ignatius Loyola, was the most important and best known.

Loyola was one of the great figures of the age. Born Inigo Lopez de Recalde of a noble Spanish family in 1491, he had a notable career as a soldier. Wounded in battle, he spent his recuperation studying the lives of Christ, Saint Francis, and Saint Dominic. Ideals of chivalry were still alive in Spain, and Ignatius resolved to be a knight of the Blessed Virgin. Hanging up his soldier's armor on her altar he set forth to serve her. As a good soldier and a man of intense faith, he began the rigorous discipline of life which subsequently found expression in his *Spiritual Exercises*. In 1523 he made a pilgrimage to Jerusalem, seeking to be a missionary to Muslims, but was refused by the Franciscans who were in charge of this mission.

Realizing that education would increase his effectiveness, he went to school, advancing rapidly to the university. A born leader, he gathered followers about himself and thus incurred the suspicion of the revived Spanish Inquisition. In 1528 he entered the University of Paris—just as John Calvin was leaving it. Again he gathered a group of like-minded students about himself. In 1534 these companions took a vow to go to Jerusalem to labor for church and humanity or, failing that, to put themselves at the disposition of the pope. The Society of Jesus was finally recognized by Pope Paul III in 1540, and Ignatius was made its first "general," an office he held until his death in 1556.

The Society of Jesus spread rapidly throughout Catholic regions of Europe and was instrumental in reviving Catholicism and holding these regions for the church. Members encouraged frequent confession and communion, and they used their position as confessors to nobles and kings to advance their own intense and sometimes extreme interpretations of Catholic faith and to oppose both Protestantism and defection among Catholics. The Jesuits were active and influential at every level of education. The international character of their order made them particularly effective servants of the church.

Nowhere were Jesuits more active or was their record more glorious than in foreign missions. Within a century of the order's founding there were Jesuit missionaries on every continent on earth, where they preached and taught and made converts for their faith. The Jesuits were also intrepid explorers and travelers. Francis Xavier (1506–1552) reached India by 1542, went on to Japan in 1549, and died in 1552 just as he was entering China. Matteo Ricci reached China in 1581. In North and South America, French and Spanish Jesuits traveled, explored, and observed, founded missions and schools, and ministered to many human needs.

A second main instrument of the Catholic Reformation and Counter-Reformation was the Council of Trent. Ecumenical or universal councils of the church extend in a long tradition back to the Council of Nicaea. Chapter 15 noted the effort of the conciliar party which sought in vain to reform the church by convening a council. Such calls continued to be heard in the sixteenth century in efforts to heal the breach between Catholic and Protestant and restore the lost unity of Christendom. It is ironical that when a council finally met, its function turned out to be not the reconciliation of Catholics and Protestants, but the definition and assertion of the Roman Catholic position against Protestantism. The Council of Trent met in the north Italian city of Trent and had three distinct periods, 1545–1550, 1550–1552 (when German Protestant delegations were admitted), and 1562–1564.

On every disputed point the council took a hard line against Protestant thought and practice.[22] Against the Protestant view of the supremacy of the Bible, the council reasserted the Roman Catholic doctrine of the equal authority of scripture and tradition. It denounced the views of Luther and Calvin on justification by faith alone. In the interpretation of the eucharist, transubstantiation was stoutly maintained. On the issues of penance, purgatory, and indulgences, the Council of Trent conceded nothing. The major conclusions of the council were summarized in the *Tridentine Profession of Faith*, acceptance of which has since been required of all converts to Catholicism.[23]

In keeping with this new militancy of Roman Catholicism, Pope Paul III reorganized the Holy Office of the Inquisition for use in any part of Europe where governmental officials would support or permit it. It proved to be an

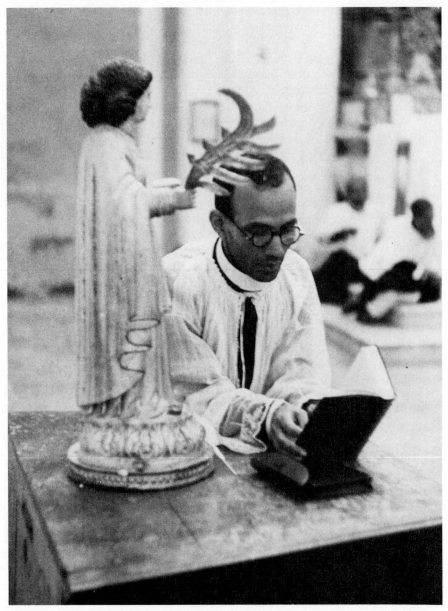

Jesuit at prayer in modern-day India. (Werner Bischoff/Magnum.)

effective device for purging a country of Protestantism. Italy was the first country to be thus cleared. Another instrument of great effectiveness was the Index of Forbidden Books. Beyond their immediate effectiveness at the time, the significance of these and similar measures of Roman Catholicism was to indicate the defensive posture which that church was taking and was destined to maintain throughout the modern centuries of European history.

The nineteenth and early twentieth centuries witnessed a series of events which brought Roman Catholic defensiveness to a climax. In 1846, Pope Pius IX came to the papal throne, supposedly a liberal. However, disenchanted by the revolution of 1848, he turned to policies which were not so much conservative as reactionary. In 1864 he issued the famous *Syllabus of Errors*, which was a list of errors to which the Roman pontiff—and presumably all Christians—must never be reconciled.[24] Lumped together in this list of errors and evils were pantheism, naturalism, absolute rationalism, moderate rationalism, indifferentism and toleration, socialism, biblical societies, and in summary "progress, liberalism, and civilization as lately introduced." Seldom has a great religious body taken so completely negative a view of its environing world.

The climax of Pius IX's pontificate was the Vatican Council of 1869–1870, or as it is now called, *Vatican I*; and the most significant action of this council was the affirmation, by a vote of 533 to 3, of the doctrine of papal infallibility. This doctrine, frequently subject to popular misunderstanding, asserts:

> The Roman Pontiff, when he speaks *ex cathedra* (that is, when—fulfilling the office of Pastor and Teacher of all Christians—on his supreme Apostolical authority, he defines a doctrine concerning faith or morals to be held by the Universal Church), through the divine assistance promised him in blessed Peter, is endowed with that infallibility, with which the Divine Redeemer has willed that His Church—in defining doctrine concerning faith or morals—should be equipped: And therefore, that such definitions of the Roman Pontiff of themselves—and not by virtue of the consent of the Church—are irreformable. If anyone shall presume (which God forbid!) to contradict this our definition; let him be anathema.[25]

Ironically, during the same year, 1870, the Italian army and people under King Victor Emmanuel put a forcible end to the states of the church. Pope Pius IX responded by declaring himself the "prisoner of the Vatican." This issue was settled a half-century later by the Vatican Concordat with Mussolini.

In the same spirit of opposition to modern trends was the encyclical *Pascendi* of Pius X in 1907. Its objective was to destroy Catholic modernism. This was a movement of Roman Catholic biblical scholars, theologians, and philosophers seeking to reconcile Roman Catholicism with modern scientific and critical knowledge. Among Catholic modernist leaders were George Tyrrell in England, Alfred Loisy in France, and Friedrich von Huegel in Germany, the first two of whom were excommunicated. As late as 1950 Pope Pius XII expressed similar sentiments toward modern biblical scholarship in the encyclical *Humani Generis*.

All these events serve to underscore the revolutionary significance of the Second Vatican Council of 1963–1965. For in a summary word, with Vatican II the Roman Catholic church changed the direction it had maintained since the Council of Trent. The attitude of resistance and opposition to the modern world

St. Peter's Basilica and piazza, Rome. (Keystone Press Agency.)

was replaced at Vatican II by one of engagement with that world in all its manifold aspects. Previous to Vatican II the relation of Roman Catholicism to other forms of Christianity was one of rigid separatism. From Vatican II onward these ways appear clearly convergent.

RELIGION IN THE UNITED STATES

While Roman Catholicism might stand in resistance to the modern world, such a position was hardly possible for Protestantism, which lacks any organ of central authority such as the papacy. Furthermore, Protestantism has always placed great emphasis upon freedom as an inherent part of faith. As a result of these features, Protestantism has interacted significantly with many aspects of the modern mind and world, sometimes rather indiscriminately taking to itself the latest colors and fashions of this world to produce what has been termed *culture Protestantism*. At the other extreme have been Protestant forms of well-nigh total rejection of the world of modern culture in what is often called *fundamentalism*, and in some forms of sectarianism. However, at its best, Protestant Christianity has interacted with modern culture to produce significant new forms of religion.

Nowhere has the interaction of Protestant faith and modern culture been more important than in the United States. It is known to every American schoolchild that the English colonization of the New World was carried out largely by Calvinist and sectarian Protestants in search of the religious freedom which was denied them in Europe. This interaction of faith and successive forms of culture has constituted a large portion of American history. One of the first and most ironical chapters in that history deals with the New England establishment, or theocracy. The Puritans responded to their new environment by establishing a tyrannical rule over every aspect of human life. The rule of God through his ministers was extended over church, state, and even people's private lives. Illustrative of this Puritan establishment was the Mather dynasty in Massachusetts, begun with the migration of Richard Mather from England in 1635 and extending to his son, Increase Mather (1639–1723), and his grandson, Cotton Mather (1663–1728). All the Mathers were clergymen and leaders of the community. Increase Mather was president of Harvard College, a position which he was forced to resign in the midst of political dispute. Both Increase and Cotton Mather were authors of several books. Both of them played somewhat dubious roles in the Salem witchcraft trials of 1692. By the later years of Cotton Mather's life, it was apparent to others, if not to him, that he was the spokesman for an age which was rapidly passing away. Secularizing trends were apparent in many aspects of society. In short, the Puritans were becoming Yankees.

Puritanism was soon to give place to other, more indigenous patterns of religion. In this historic transformation the role of leadership passed to Jonathan Edwards (1703–1758). A precocious child who entered Yale College at the age of thirteen, with a philosophic mind of great originality, Edwards be-

St. Mary's Cathedral, San Francisco (Roman Catholic). (Courtesy of John Hutchison.)

came a devoutly religious man. Upon graduation from Yale he went to assist his grandfather, Solomon Stoddard, as pastor of the church in Northampton, Massachusetts. Stoddard had sought to accommodate himself sensibly to the cooling zeal of his parishioners. Edwards, by contrast, attacked their growing self-sufficiency. Out of his sermons from 1731 to 1735 emerged the colonies' first religious revival—and what is even more important, the pattern of revivalism in American religion. Edwards's position eventually forced his resignation at Northampton, which he left for the frontier town of Stockbridge, Massachusetts.

Meanwhile similar events had been taking place in other American colonies, notably with Theodore Frelinghuysen in New Jersey and the Tennents, father and son, in Pennsylvania and New Jersey. Many of the currents of revival converged in the visit to the New World from 1739 to 1741 of the celebrated English preacher and revivalist, George Whitefield. Out of all these events emerged the "great awakening." Not only did this revival result in renewed faith, it had many other fruits in the founding of schools and colleges and in varied humanitarian causes.

The great awakening was followed at the end of the century by the "great revival," or "second great awakening," whose effects were felt especially on the frontier. The revival pattern of religion might be termed a result of the interaction of Protestant faith and frontier society. The frontier was the western edge of this thrust into the wilderness. Frontier society was rough, simple, and mo-

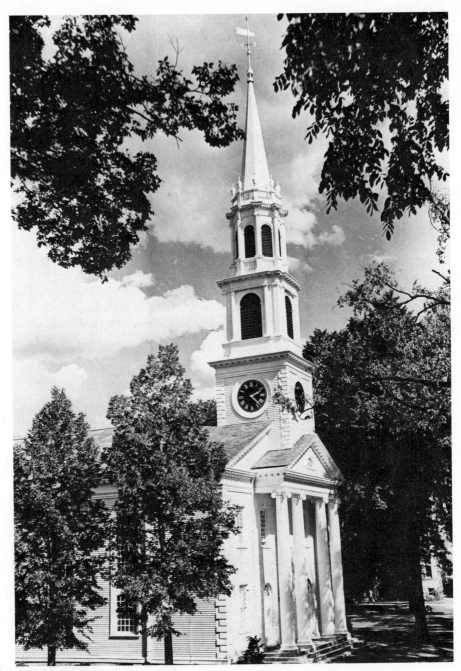

First Congregational Church, Williamstown, Massachusetts. (Courtesy of Henry Flint, Jr.)

bile. To be relevant to these conditions, religion had to partake of these same qualities.

Methodist and Baptist circuit riders went from settlement to settlement, preaching, saving souls, baptizing, marrying, burying the dead—in short, bringing what religion they could to these outposts of civilization. In vast camp meetings people of the American frontier gathered from wide areas to hear sermons exhorting them to make their own acquaintance with religious realities. Traditional Protestant revivalism was charged with high emotional voltage, and behavior frequently became ecstatic. People shouted, jumped, rolled, or even passed into unconsciousness as they "got religion." The pattern of revivalism had a clear and functional relation to American frontier society; today this pattern continues in less clearly functional ways in such figures as Billy Graham.[26]

Another milestone in American religious development was the achievement of religious freedom and toleration. As noted above, the New England Puritans were intolerant, and yet the modern idea of tolerance was born in seventeenth-century England. From England it was exported to the colonies, where it was destined to find more pervasive and radical application than in Europe. Many persons and many factors cooperated to apply and develop this idea. Ideas of Baptists such as Roger Williams and Quakers such as William Penn were supplemented by the more secular and rationalist views of the eighteenth-century Enlightenment as expressed in the thought of Americans

A revival meeting. (New York Public Library, Picture Collection.)

such as Thomas Jefferson, Benjamin Franklin, and Thomas Paine. In many of these persons religious toleration was an integral part of a larger whole, namely, their allegiance to constitutional government.

Even more than as an ideal goal, toleration was demanded as a necessity of American social life. These and other factors all converged to make religious freedom the "lively experiment" of American Christianity.[27] While religious freedom has a "made in America" label, it has in recent times been exported to many other parts of the world.

Another decisive influence on American religion was the nineteenth-century immigration from Europe. Beginning in the 1830s and 1840s this immigration brought to American shores first Roman Catholic and then Jewish immigrants.[28] At first these groups existed as minority groups in a dominantly Protestant culture, sometimes tolerated and sometimes the victims of cruel intolerance. Yet these newcomers were destined to make their impact. For in the twentieth century United States was to develop a threefold religious pluralism. This is a theme to which we shall return in Chapter 18.

The nineteenth century brought also the large-scale urbanization and the industrialization of the United States with all their attendant social problems. These vast new movements elicited many religious responses.[29] The revivalists moved their activities from the frontier to the new cities—with notably diminished results.

Another response was what has often been called the *social gospel*. Reclaiming the heritage of Christianity as a religion addressed to society as well as to individual people, many nineteenth-century American Christians sought Christian solutions for the new problems of society. Their suggestions varied widely, from settlement houses in teeming American cities to industrial YWCAs and YMCAs, to the advocacy of social and political reforms, and even to the suggestion that Christianity entailed a socialist reorganization of society. Among the leaders of the social gospel movement were the pastor Washington Gladden (1836–1918) and the theologian and teacher Walter Rauschenbusch (1861–1918). We shall return in Chapter 18 to this and similar trends as aspects of the contemporary situation in religion.

Amid the diverse forms of Protestantism, it is perhaps significant to note that Protestant emphasis upon freedom has been an important factor in creating this fragmentation. Yet it is important also to understand Protestantism as a form of Christianity. The term *Protestantism* is misleading; rather we should understand *Protestant* as an adjective modifying *Christian*, and the Protestant Christian as sharing many beliefs, attitudes, and practices with other Christians, of Roman Catholicism and Eastern Orthodoxy.

ISSUES AND QUESTIONS

This chapter has noted the beginnings of modern secularizing processes in western culture, and the next chapter will deal with this topic in more detail.

Meanwhile let us simply characterize secular trends or tendencies as nonreligious in quality. We bring this subject up here in order to observe its influence on one aspect of the relation of Protestantism to the environing European and American culture. In the course of time, as this culture has become ever more secular, many concepts and values of Protestant origin have seemed to float freely in the culture, there to be appropriated by any who wished to have them. Thus one need not be a Lutheran to feel the impact of Luther's mind, nor a Presbyterian to be influenced by Calvin, nor a Baptist to feel the force of sectarian Protestantism on his or her mind.

This observation leaves unanswered many important questions about value, such as those of value genesis and value maintenance. However, it does assert the general availability of many concepts and values among the varieties of Protestantism as well as the possibility of new combinations in new historical situations.

As a second issue, this chapter has raised the question of whether there is or can be a Protestant humanism comparable to that which the last chapter delineated in the Roman Catholic tradition. Let us answer by saying that properly speaking the word Protestant is an adjective modifying the substantive or noun Christian. This being the case, there is good reason to assert the humane or humanistic character (or at least the real possibility of such!) of the Christian allegiance in the Protestant as well as the Catholic tradition. We shall return to the topic of humanism again in the next two chapters noting different meanings of the words humane and humanism and also fresh applications to new situations.

Finally let us underscore the way in which Protestant Christianity, lacking any single center of authority or criticism, has often been at the mercy of the diverse winds of doctrine which blow in through modern culture. Thus in some of its many interpretations Protestantism has been little more than a tribal faith of culture, German, American, or other. Yet wherever it has retained a measure of fidelity to the content of the two words of its title, namely, Protestant and Christianity, it has been a religion of the third type, namely, faith in the one God. Among the many meanings of this primary allegiance has been a criticism of the idols of false gods of modernity and a cleaving to the image of the one God, hence one universal humanity.

NOTES

1. I have been unable to locate this assertion in any of his published works. It was a remark made in a meeting of the Society for Theological Discussion in New York City, ca. 1956 or 1957.
2. Paul Tillich, *The Protestant Era*, University of Chicago Press, Chicago, 1948, pp. 161f.
3. H. Richard Niebuhr, *Radical Monotheism and Western Culture*, University of Nebraska Press, Lincoln, 1960, pp. 161f.
4. H. Richard Niebuhr, *The Meaning of Revelation*, Macmillan, New York, 1941, p. 118.
5. See Albert Outler's essay "The Reformation and Classical Protestantism" in George Thomas (ed.), *The Vitality of the Christian Tradition*, Harper, New York, 1945, for a discussion of the Reformation under the first four of these topics. To Outler's list I have added the fifth.

6. H. Bettenson (ed.), *Documents of the Christian Church*, Oxford University Press, Fair Lawn, N.J., 1947, pp. 259f.
7. Ibid., pp. 272f.
8. Ibid., p. 285.
9. Martin Luther, *Works of Martin Luther*, The St. Louis Edition, vol. 2, Concordia, St. Louis, 1956, p. 146.
10. Ibid., vol. 20, p. 232.
11. *Luther's Works*, vol. 35, *Word and Sacrament*, E. Theodore Bachman (ed.), Muhlenberg Press, Philadelphia, 1959, "Prefaces to the New Testament," p. 362.
12. Williston Walker, *A History of the Christian Church*, rev. ed., Scribner, New York, 1959, p. 349.
13. Ralph Barton Perry, *Puritanism and Democracy*, Vanguard, New York, 1944.
14. Max Weber, *The Protestant Ethic*, Talcott Parsons (trans.), G. Allen, London, 1930.
15. Ibid. See also R. H. Tawney, *Religion and the Rise of Capitalism*, Harcourt, Brace & World, New York, 1947.
16. See inter alia Ernst Troeltsch, *The Social Teachings of the Christian Church*, Olive Wyon (trans.), Macmillan, New York, 1931.
17. J. Calvin, *Institutes of the Christian Religion*, vol. 2, John T. MacNeill (ed.), Ford Lewis Battles (trans.), Westminster Press, Philadelphia, 1960, p. 1520.
18. Harry Emerson Fosdick, *Great Voices of the Reformation*, Modern Library, New York, 1954, p. 335.
19. Troeltsch, op. cit.
20. The term *Counter-Reformation* was introduced by Leopold von Ranke, the great nineteenth-century German historian.
21. K. S. Latourette, *A History of Christianity*, Harper, New York, 1953, pp. 855–856.
22. Bettenson, op. cit., p. 381.
23. Ibid., pp. 370–372.
24. Ibid., p. 381.
25. Ibid., p. 383.
26. Franklin Littell, *From State Church to Religious Pluralism*, Anchor Books, Doubleday, Garden City, N.Y., 1962.
27. Sidney Mead, *The Lively Experiment: The Shaping of Christianity in America*, Harper & Row, New York, 1963.
28. Will Herberg, *Protestant, Catholic, Jew*, Anchor Books, Doubleday, Garden City, N.Y., 1960.
29. Ibid., pp. 81–82. See also Mead, op. cit., for a different interpretation of these trends.

BIBLIOGRAPHY

Ahlstrom, S.: *A Religious History of the American People*, Yale, New Haven, Conn., 1972.

Atkinson, J. (ed.): *Luther: Early Theological Works*, Westminster John Knox, Louisville, Ky., 1980.

Bainton, R.: *Here I Stand*, New American Library, New York, 1978.

Bettenson, H. (ed.): *Documents of the Christian Church*, Oxford, New York, 1970.

Brauer, J.: *Protestantism in America*, Westminster John Knox, Louisville, Ky., 1972.

Brown, R.: *The Spirit of Protestantism*, Oxford, New York, 1965.

Calvin, J.: *Institutes of the Christian Religion*, J. T. MacNeil (ed.), F. L. Battles (trans.), Westminster Press, Philadelphia, 1960.

Dillenberger, J., and C. Welch: *Protestant Christianity*, Scribner, New York, 1954.

Ferm, R. (ed.): *Readings in the History of Christian Thought*, Holt, New York, 1964.

Frankforter, A. D.: *A History of the Christian Movement*, Nelson-Hall, Chicago, 1978.

Gaustad, E. (ed.): *A Documentary History of Religion in America*, Eerdmans, Grand Rapids, Mich., 1982–1983.

Gonzalez, J.: *A History of Christian Thought*, Abingdon Press, Nashville, Tenn., 1970–1975.

Herberg, W.: *Judaism and Modern Man*, Atheneum, New York, 1970.

————: *Protestant, Catholic, Jew*, University of Chicago, Chicago, 1983.

Latourette, K.: *A History of Christianity*, Harper & Row, New York, 1975.

Littell, F.: *From State Church to Religious Pluralism*, Anchor Books, Doubleday, Garden City, N.Y., 1962.

MacNeil, J. T.: *The History and Character of Calvinism*, Oxford, London, 1954.

Manschreck, C. (ed.): *A History of Christianity*, vol. 2, Baker, Grand Rapids, Mich., 1981.

Marsden, G.: *Fundamentalism and American Culture*, Oxford, New York, 1980.

Niebuhr, H. R.: *The Kingdom of God in America*, Harper, New York, 1959.

————: *Social Sources of Denominationalism*, New American Library, New York, 1957.

Pauck, W.: *The Heritage of the Reformation*, Free Press, New York, 1961.

———— (ed.): *Luther: Lectures on Romans*, Westminster John Knox, Louisville, Ky., 1977.

Perry, R. B.: *Puritanism and Democracy*, Vanguard, New York, 1944.

Tawney, H.: *Religion and the Rise of Capitalism*, Peter Smith, Magnolia, Mass., 1962.

Tillich, P.: *The Protestant Era*, University of Chicago, Chicago, 1948.

Troeltsch, E.: *The Social Teachings of the Christian Churches*, University of Chicago, Chicago, 1981.

Walker, W., et al.: *A History of the Christian Church*, Scribner, New York, 1985.

Williams, G.: *The Radical Reformation*, Westminster, Philadelphia, 1962.

17

Modern Criticism
of Religion

The modern age is usually dated from the Renaissance and Reformation (ca. 1500 CE) to the present or, as will be argued later in this chapter, to the recent past (ca. 1900 CE). While it was initially a period in the history of the West, in many of its important aspects, modernity has been exported so extensively to the nonwestern world that it has become virtually a worldwide phenomenon.

Like all large historical concepts, modernity is difficult to define with precision. However, the aim of this chapter permits us to bypass such larger issues by limiting our exposition to a few of the main implications of the modern spirit for traditional religions. Initially this impact was upon Judaism and Christianity, but more recently the traditional faiths of South Asia and East Asia have been drawn within the scope of modernity and its critical impact.

The modern age has seen criticism, pervasive and radical, of every aspect of human culture including politics, economics, art, science, philosophy, and religion. This criticism has been so intensive and so extensive that it is no exaggeration to call it the defining feature of modernity. The modern age is the age of criticism. While our present focus is the criticism of traditional religion, this has been an integral part of the general criticism of tradition in all the manifold aspects of culture.

Criticism of religion did not begin with the modern West. Rather it appears as a pervasive and perennial human phenomenon, rooted in the fact that even as a human being is a self needing some faith or value system to guide the course of life, so this same self is a critical mind seeking truth in this as in other regions of experience. Since this double fact is so, it is not surprising to observe the recurrence of criticism in many of the religious traditions studied in this book. Such criticism was notably present in ancient Greece and in classical China, yet the reader will also recall that the heavily sacral tradition of India had its mordant critics in the Carvaka or materialist philosophy. Such critical attitudes and ideas recur throughout human history. Notwithstanding these facts, the criticism of traditional religion which has taken place in the modern age of the West is so vastly more extensive and intensive that it must be judged in effect to be something radically new. Thus, for example, for the first time in human history it has been possible for some critics to assert the total abolition of religion as a desirable and achievable goal. As a result of this modern criticism, people in all parts of the world have been divorced from religious traditions in numbers and to a degree without parallel in previous history.

This modern attitude toward traditional religion involves the convergence of several necessary presuppositions. In a few summary words, these include factors as diverse as the success of modern natural science and scientific technology, the achievements of modern capitalist economics, and of a whole cluster of modern philosophies which dispense with or do without God. These range from the skepticism of strict empiricism to the metaphysical systems of Marx, Nietzsche, and Freud. All of these factors converge upon the conclusion that humankind both can and should live without religion.

Whether in its new, modern form or its recurring historical form, the criticism of tradition raises an important but seldom recognized issue concerning the relation of criticism and the traditional values which it criticizes. A. N. Whitehead has remarked that "if men cannot live on bread alone, still less can they do so on disinfectants."[1] Criticism of tradition may be likened to a disinfectant whose function is to kill harmful bacteria; criticism has for its purpose the destruction of irrational and inhumane aspects of tradition, in religion and all else. These are worthy objects, but they have limits. As Whitehead's aphorism implies, disinfectant cannot serve as food, and criticism does not provide for that affirmation of value which is distinctively the content of faith. Indeed, precisely the opposite appears to be the case; criticism presupposes the existence of the values and faith which are its proper business to appraise and test. With reference to the vast numbers of twentieth-century people who have no relation to any historic faith, the crucial problem, stated in secular terms, is that of value creation and value maintenance. This is an issue to which it will be necessary to return during the course of this chapter and Chapter 18.

ELEMENTS OF MODERNITY

Since the modern spirit did not spring into existence all at once, but rather developed historically over a period of several centuries, it will be illuminating to glance quickly at three main aspects of its development: (1) the Renaissance, (2) the rise of natural science and scientific technology, and (3) the Enlightenment, including its commitment to constitutional government. The cumulative impact of these historical forces will be sufficient to provide us with a working definition of the modern spirit, particularly in its relation to traditional religion.

THE RENAISSANCE

The last chapter approached the Renaissance as a protest against the medieval age of the West. It was primarily a movement of revival or, literally and etymologically, of "rebirth" in European art, literature, and general learning, of the fourteenth, fifteenth, and sixteenth centuries. It began in the city-states of Italy but spread to other parts of Europe; it also spread to embrace more and more aspects of the culture. Since it was a many-sided affair emphasizing freedom and variety, exception may be taken to almost any generalization about it.

The Renaissance was basically Christian in outlook. While it involved tensions with the Christian past at many points and also many new emphases, nevertheless there was no break, either conscious or unconscious, with the tradition. While it deliberately sought to recapture ideas, attitudes, and forms from ancient Greece and Rome, many of its essential ideas were Judeo-Christian in origin and nature. Such, for example, were the idea of the dignity of human nature made in the image of God, the sense of the infinite meaning of the individual human self, and the joyful affirmation of the whole panorama of the world of humanity and nature as God's creation.

Yet it is important to note the new elements and changed emphases of the Renaissance. There was an implied criticism of medieval ideas and attitudes even as early in the Renaissance as Petrarch (1304–1374), divided as he was between his love of poetry and of faith, between this life and eternal life, between love of Laura (to whom he wrote sonnets) and love of God.

The Renaissance criticism of medievalism involved increasingly radical attacks on the ideal of monasticism. Erasmus pilloried the vices and follies of monks; and with vastly less restraint Rabelais pursued this same theme.[2] Such criticism was also directed at medieval scholastic theology, with its flights of overgeneralized speculation and its logic-chopping methods. The intellectual ideal of the Renaissance was not Thomas Aquinas writing his *Summa Theologica*, but Erasmus poring over manuscripts in order to achieve a critical text of the New Testament; or it was Lorenzo Valla exposing the forgery of the *Donation of Constantine*. It was Marsilio Ficino, of the Florentine Academy, adding the study of Plato to that of the Bible and proposing to celebrate the birthday of Plato as well as Christmas.[3]

The most fundamental change of the Renaissance was its shift of interest and attention from God to humanity and from heaven to earth. For some thinkers, such as John Pico della Mirandola (1463–1494) writing his *Oration on the Dignity of Man*, God's chief distinction was to have created human beings who became virtually divine in their own right.[4] Pico and others were particularly scornful of the traditional idea of original sin. Not human sin and God's forgiveness but human possibilities and achievements constituted the faith of the Renaissance. Its central tenet was the boundless and creative freedom of the human self. Erasmus spoke for the Renaissance when he wrote *On Free Will*. The contrast between Renaissance and Reformation became clear when Martin Luther replied with *The Bondage of Will*, asserting a position even more extreme than that of the Roman Catholic church.[5]

The Renaissance developed in detail the implications of its central tenet of belief in humanity. Not preparation for the hereafter, but the enjoyment of the rich goods of the present life is the chief end of human life. The fine arts of painting, sculpture, architecture, and literature became primary human pursuits, and their flowering was both cause and confirmation of the belief in humanity. Not even the papacy was secure against the new faith. Of the so-called Renaissance popes, Julius II commissioned Michelangelo's *Moses* and the Sistine Chapel murals; Leo X, of the Medici family, shared his family's interest in art and also its involvement in Italian politics; and Alexander VI, father of Cesare and Lucrezia Borgia, was a great patron of the arts.

The significance of the Renaissance for subsequent periods of the West lay in its new and distinctive view of humanity, which was, in the defining metaphor of the movement, the human self reborn, or renewed, and hence standing in the presence of an open future with its infinite possibilities beckoning forward.[6] This aspect of the Renaissance is to be seen in its many utopias. In addition to Sir Thomas More's *Utopia*, there were such pictures of the perfect society as Campanello's *City of the Sun* and, in earthier style, Rabelais's *Abbey of Theleme* with its motto, "Do what you will." There was also Giordono Bruno's similar idea of the infinite worlds which opened before the human mind. In these writings there was not yet the idea of actual historical progress, but there was clearly the basic image of human renewal or rebirth. This vision of renewal carried its own seminal implications, including an ever-increasing criticism of the past, from whose fetters human life must be freed in order to fulfill its limitless possibilities. The modern age is the story of the development of these implications in theory and in practice.

The Renaissance also showed another fundamentally modern trait in its increasingly secularized view of human life and society. *Secularization* is a word of many meanings and uses. Perhaps the most basic meaning is "freedom from ecclesiastical control." Thus a school or educational system is secular when it is free from church control. Closely related but not identical to this is the freedom from appeal to religious sanctions, rules, or motivations. In this meaning of the term, the modern West has seen a progressive secularization of such concerns as politics, economics, and art. One by one, these major human concerns have left the medieval household of the faith and, coming of age, have set up housekeeping on their own. Obviously this development is closely related to the modern belief in human autonomy, which is a still further meaning of the term *secularization*. In most general terms of all, secularization may be characterized as any movement of the human mind or life away from the conscious religious center of personality or culture. As such it is a generally observable and recurring trend in many cultures and persons. For example, ancient Greece of the fifth century BCE shows a secularizing trend, as does Tokugawa Japan. In colonial America the movement of New England culture from the seventeenth to the eighteenth century, from Cotton Mather to Benjamin Franklin, is another illustration of a secularizing tendency. Yet the general movement of the modern West from the Renaissance onward is surely the most massive and all-inclusive secularizing movement in all human history. As such, it is one of the defining features of modernity. Modern people are secular in outlook, feeling no need to relate their interests to any religious center. While at times antireligious, their general attitude is more adequately described as nonreligious.

In all its essential traits the Renaissance stands as the spring from which the modern spirit has flowed—in religion as in all else. Yet it must also be asserted once more with equal force that it involved no open break with traditional religion. Rather, it may be asserted that in the Renaissance the paths of modernity and tradition began to diverge. In the following centuries they were destined to move further and further apart.

THE RISE OF NATURAL SCIENCE

Many leaders of the Renaissance, such as Erasmus and Rabelais, were scornful of the nascent natural science of the times, but others such as Leonardo da Vinci were scientists and engineers as well as artists and scholars. There were important lines of relation, both positive and negative, between the Renaissance and the rise of modern natural science; yet the two must be approached as distinguishable historical phenomena.

The new way of thinking which was to become modern natural science developed quietly and gradually in laboratories and studies throughout Europe. Its course was influenced by many interests and many casual conditions, ranging from technological needs to new mathematical speculation. Then suddenly in the seventeenth century—the *century of genius*, as it has been called—science burst upon the world.[7]

In its first impact, particularly as related to religious tradition, the new science took the form of a revolutionary new view of the physical universe. For ordinary people of the Middle Ages the world had been a three-storied affair, with God and heaven above, human beings in the middle, and Satan and his minions in the basement. If Ptolemy's—or Dante's—cosmology involved refinements or revisions in this picture, it did not greatly alter its overall significance. Human life still occupied the center of the stage, solicitously watched over by the divine management of the universe.

This human-centered view of the universe was rudely shattered by the revolutionary discoveries of early modern natural science. Copernicus's volume *Concerning the Revolution of the Celestial Spheres* (1543) placed the sun rather than the earth at the center of things. However, this view remained a mathematical speculation until Galileo developed its implications and tested them with his newly constructed telescope. The clash between the new science and the old theology came into the open when Galileo was summoned before the Holy Office of the Inquisition in 1616 and again in 1633 and was forbidden to teach that the earth revolved about the sun. Galileo's writings as well as those of Kepler and Copernicus were placed on the Index of Forbidden Books—where, incidentally, they remained until 1822, when as one writer put it, "the Sun received the formal sanction of the Papacy to become the centre of the planetary system."[8]

What Copernicus began and Galileo greatly advanced came to brilliant fulfillment—to final completion, it seemed at the time—in Isaac Newton's *Mathe-*

A depiction of Copernican cosmology, with the sun at the center of the universe. (British Museum.)

matical Principles of Natural Philosophy (1687). By means of the law of universal gravitation, Newton construed the universe as a single realm of mathematical order. Here was convincing mathematical proof that the universe is one vast harmoniously ordered mechanism. Few new ideas in human history have had implications greater and more revolutionary than this. While scientists pushed onward from this victory to new problems and new territories to conquer, other people sought during the Age of Reason, or the *Newtonian age* as it was called, to develop the implications of the triumphant new Newtonian or scientific reason for all aspects of human life and society. Earlier, Pascal had spoken for traditional religion concerning the new cosmology when he exclaimed, "The eternal silence of infinite spaces frightens me."[9] Other people had very different reactions and responses.

Meanwhile, natural science moved onward, proving itself to be not simply a body of results—impressive as the Newtonian results might be at the time—but a dynamic and ongoing new method for knowing. As such it was capable of rendering any and all particular results obsolete and of constituting a kind of permanent revolution in human knowledge. The scientific method as it developed showed two aspects, one mathematical and rational, and the other empirical and experimental. Contrary to many popular views of science, the rational aspect had been the first to take shape. For example, Copernicus's heliocentric view of the universe was the product of his deductive, or mathematical, search for a logically simpler view than that of Ptolemy. In a similar spirit Galileo explored nature, seeking illustrations for his conviction that the great book of nature is written, as he put it, in geometric terms.[10] Different sciences and scientists combined the rational and the experimental aspects of science in widely different ways. Yet in the whole historical movement of modern natural science, it has been the interaction of these two aspects of the method that has accounted largely for the enormous power and creativity of science.

From the beginning, science grew out of technological needs and problems, and its answers greatly influenced technological development. As science moved forward, technology continued to force vast changes in society and to remake the face of the earth—sometimes for human welfare, often for apparently opposite results, but always in ways that no human being could ignore. The revolution in science and technology still goes on, at an ever-accelerating pace and with no end in sight. It continues to force changes in every aspect of human life. To many people around the world modernity means scientific technology, whether embodied in automobiles, steel mills, Coca-Cola coolers, or nuclear fission.

In the continuing relation of science to traditional religion and theology, the publication of Charles Darwin's *Origin of Species* (1859) and the coming of evolutionary theory constituted an event in biological sciences of comparable magnitude to the discoveries in physics of Copernicus, Galileo, and Newton. From thinking of themselves as fallen archangels, human beings were rudely called by this new theory to view themselves as apes who had made good—and whether they *had* made good became increasingly problematic. We shall return to this topic in the next section of this chapter.

As theologians, philosophers, and others continued to ponder the implications of science, science itself continued to move onward. Beyond Newton and Laplace lay Einstein; beyond Darwin lay Freud and his explorations of the inner life. Beyond every present achievement lies the future. By renouncing absolute truth and asserting all its results to be provisional and tentative, science has been able to push forward into an ever-open future. This open future of science has been sometimes promise and sometimes threat, but in either case has become in the twentieth century the largest, most momentous fact in the human world.

The clash of science with religion has constituted a major and pervasive theme of modern thought, affording one more illustration of the general theme of modern criticism of tradition and modern rebellion against traditional authority. Most writers have seen the science-religion struggle as a battle of the free and progressive scientific mind against the fetters of prescientific authority.

A. D. White's monumental *A History of the Warfare of Science and Theology in Christendom* envisioned the struggle in precisely these terms.[11] A. N. Whitehead, who wrote of these matters from his own novel viewpoint, remarks that "for over two centuries religion has been on the defensive and on a weak defensive," and concluded that "it will not regain its old power until it can face change in the same spirit as does science."[12] Until then religion's long retreat, step by step as science advances, is likely to continue. Such at least is the dominant modern image of the relation of science to religion and theology, and no candid observer would wish to deny that it contains much important truth.

Only as students of this problem take full account of this truth have they a right to go on to other aspects of the multifaceted relation between science and religion. Yet much current writing on science and religion has proceeded to some of these further aspects. Some writers have called attention to the fact that science originated in the western tradition, which has been infused and informed by the Judeo-Christian tradition. Accordingly they point to significant aspects of the latter tradition which have served—or so it is claimed—as necessary presuppositions of modern science. For example, the Judeo-Christian God transcends the world, thus opening the way to secularization of the world, which is a necessary precondition to scientific understanding and control of the world.[13] Human beings do not scientifically manipulate a world which is "full of gods"; and this phrase may be taken as descriptive not only of ancient Greece but of all nature-culture, or type 1, religions. Attention is also frequently called to the biblical doctrine of creation, with its affirmation of the reality and goodness of the world of nature in contrast to faiths which regard nature as illusory appearance; this contrast expresses the difference between views of the world in religions of the second and third types. Still other writers call attention to the need for moral guidance of science if science is to be used for human welfare rather than illfare. Meanwhile, however these issues may finally be resolved, it is safe to characterize the modern age as the age of science. The creation of modern natural science is surely the most important achievement of the modern age. It remains for the human race to learn to live with its achievement.

THE ENLIGHTENMENT

Reference has already been made to the Age of Reason as an attempt to apply the spirit and method of triumphant Newtonian science to all aspects of human society and life. The people of the eighteenth-century Enlightenment sought rationality in politics, in philosophy, in religion, and in ethics. Not even art escaped the influence of rational form, as the poetry of Pope, the music of Handel and Haydn, and the formal pattern of an eighteenth-century garden all testify. It was a century in which European people devoted themselves to the ideal of universal and harmonious rational order in all human things; and they had few doubts that human reason was sufficient for this ambitious undertaking.

The Enlightenment had varying impact upon different European nations. In England, which had had its social revolution during the previous century, the Enlightenment was a moderating process. In France it was revolutionary, producing Voltaire, Diderot and his Encyclopedia, and the French revolution, with its battle cry of "Liberty, equality, fraternity!" and the goddess Reason replacing traditional Catholicism. In the colonies, it produced such varied figures as Benjamin Franklin, Thomas Pain, and Thomas Jefferson. Both the Declaration of Independence and the Constitution of the United States may be said to express varying moods of the Enlightenment.

In its basic affirmations the Enlightenment continued and extended the faith of the Renaissance in human life, its freedom, and the infinite possibilities that open before it. The new ingredient in the Enlightenment was science, both as rational method and as achievement. Science was also doubtless the primary basis of the Enlightenment's basic belief in human progress, for natural science offers concrete examples of intellectual progress. Science was and still is humankind's clearest example of progressive or cumulative knowledge. From the intellectual progress of science, it was an easy and natural step to human progress. As scientific knowledge increased, so also human happiness and well-being would increase; such at least was the optimistic credo of the eighteenth century. Proclaimed cautiously and moderately by the English, and with lyric enthusiasm by such French writers as Condorcet, the belief in progress expressed well the Enlightenment's confidence in human beings and reason.

As for sources of this belief, many contemporary writers trace it to the Bible and its linear and dramatic view of history. Chapters 11 and 12 noted the biblical sources of this idea, and Chapter 15 sketched Augustine's formulation of it in his *City of God*. This view of history gave expression to millennial and messianic beliefs that have continued to erupt throughout Jewish and Christian history. Belief in progress emerged from belief in the millennium, as Carl Becker has written, when early in the Enlightenment, belief in God became belief in nature, and belief in original sin was transformed into its opposite, belief in human perfectability.[14] As a consequence, the City of God became the City of Man and was relocated somewhere in the human future. To state the matter theologically, progress might be characterized in Augustinian terms as grace, prevenient, immanent, and at least in some formulations, irresistible.

The Enlightenment differs from the Renaissance in two important ways relating to religion, namely, its strong humanitarian ethic and its conscious break with the Christian tradition of theology and faith. As to the former, the Enlightenment held a firm conviction of universal humanity, based no doubt on the Judeo-Christian idea of God's universal kingdom, but expressed more often in rationalist terms than in traditional religious terms. The belief implied a critical attack on all irrational institutions and practices of society. Specific applications of this rule varied widely from person to person, but they included such causes as opposition to absolute monarchy or sometimes more radically to all monarchy, to war, to slavery, and to maltreatment of criminals and the insane. Affirming a cosmopolitan or universal ideal, the Enlightenment was hostile to all forms of provincialism or parochialism, ranging from political nationalism to religious dogmatism.

No other issue was more characteristic of the Enlightenment than its passionate opposition to religious bigotry and intolerance, that is, to all particular forms of religion held on grounds which were deemed irrational or "dogmatic" and which led to actions that violated freedom and humanity. In practice, these convictions of the Enlightenment led to strong advocacy of religious toleration and freedom.

In this cause the people of the Enlightenment found allies among Protestant sects such as the Quakers and the Baptists, who for their own compelling reasons opposed religious establishment and intolerance. As a result of their combined efforts, the traditional patterns gave way in some western nations to systems of freedom and toleration. England had made a start in 1688 with the Act of Toleration, though toleration was limited to non-Anglican Protestants and did not extend to Roman Catholics, Jews, or atheists. While Great Britain subsequently extended toleration and freedom to all its people, it has continued to combine this tradition with an established church.

In the United States the lively experiment of religious freedom has been a central theme in the national tradition. It was rooted in historical origins and has been demanded by practical necessity. Many of the colonists were Protestant sectarians fleeing intolerance and seeking religious freedom. Also, the United States came into being in the eighteenth century under Founding Fathers who were men of the Enlightenment. The idea of religious freedom in the United States owes its origin to an alliance of such religious figures as William Penn and Roger Williams with rationalists such as Jefferson and Franklin.[15] As we have seen, for these men religious freedom and tolerance were part and parcel of the whole wide commitment to constitutional government.

American religious freedom and toleration did not come into being all at once, but gradually, as a step-by-step process. Some American states did not relinquish religious establishments until the 1820s. Furthermore, the meaning of religious freedom was greatly widened and deepened as immigration increased the diversity of the American population during the nineteenth century. In the storms of twentieth-century history, Americans are finding still new meanings and implications in their system of religious freedom and diversity. Thus the lively experiment continues to the present moment.[16] The idea of freedom of religion, developed in the United States, has been widely exported to all parts of the world, with the result that today, however much it may be distorted in practice, religious freedom is widely regarded as a fundamental human right.

It is difficult for Americans born and nurtured in religious freedom and diversity to see how genuinely revolutionary this idea is. With very few notable exceptions, such as King Ashoka's reign in ancient India, the overwhelming practice in human history has been religious uniformity and establishment, with prohibition of dissent. The new position must be seen as one of the great achievements of the modern age.

The Enlightenment not only criticized religious intolerance and bigotry but also mounted a massive attack upon traditional Christian faith and theology. This criticism began during the seventeenth century with the moderate liberalism of people like Lord Herbert of Cherbury, who taught that human reason operating in the manner of Newton could establish such tenets as the existence of one God, his creation and government of the world, and the immortality of the soul. Deists likened the relation of God to the world to that of watchmaker to watch. Revelation might go further than reason and tell human beings more about God. For example, it might certify the biblical miracles and prophecy, but natural reason laid the foundations upon which the edifice of faith and revelation was erected.

In the course of time the rationalists' criticism of traditional religion became more and more radical. First, all supernatural aspects of religion were attacked as superfluous and repugnant to reason; then the argument from watch to watchmaker was subjected to withering critical attack by skeptics such as David Hume.[17] In France the course of eighteenth-century thought moved onward not to the cautious and careful skepticism of Hume, but toward the dogmatic materialism of Holbach and the equally dogmatic rationalism of Diderot or Robespierre. In both cases the critical spirit of the Enlightenment made a clean and conscious break with the Christian tradition. After the eighteenth century, thoughtful westerners might be Christians, but only consciously and by a deliberate effort of mind. Clearly this was something new in western history. Indeed, it was something new in human history. The absence of an Enlightenment in the religious history of India and other oriental cultures marks a fundamental contrast between East and West.

THE RADICAL CENTURY

In some important ways the nineteenth century reacted against the dominant Newtonian rationalism of the eighteenth. Nineteenth-century romanticism was a way of saying that not only science but also art, history, and religion are legitimate concerns which in their distinctive ways illuminate and enrich human life. Not only scientific reason, but also feeling, imagination, and volition are legitimate aspects of human experience. Nature is the object not only of scientific study but of poems, of landscape paintings, and indeed of contemplation.

True as this may be, and important as the romantic reaction was, with specific reference to the issue of this chapter, namely, modern western criticism of traditional religion, the nineteenth century continued and drove deeper the Enlightenment's criticism of traditional religion. So true is this that the nineteenth is clearly the radical century. It is so in the etymological sense of going to the roots of this issue.

The radical impact of nineteenth-century criticism of religion will be outlined here through a few important individuals. Back of most of these radical critics stood the imposing conservative figure of Hegel, whose system of philo-

David Hume. (New York Public Library, Picture Collection.)

sophic idealism dominated much of nineteenth-century thought. Hegel had deserted theological education for a career in philosophy, in which his great achievement was the construction of a comprehensive, all-embracing system of metaphysics. Hegel's philosophy, sometimes called *absolute idealism*, was his ambitious attempt to embrace all reality in a single systematic whole, the key concept of which was mind, or spirit (the usual English translations of the untranslatable German word *Geist*). It is impossible here even to hint at the rich suggestiveness of Hegel's philosophy, except to say that while both nature and self were expressions of mind, it was history which provided its most significant manifestation. Hegel treated history as the progressive unfolding of mind. Hegel's mind resembled the traditional God of Christianity in some significant ways, but differed sharply in others. Also for all its suggestiveness, Hegel's philosophy was also extremely ambiguous in its key terms.

It is therefore not surprising that his students, followers, and interpreters should be divided into two warring camps, the "right," or "old," Hegelians, and the "left," or "young," Hegelians.[18] Hegel's own social outlook was massively conservative; he believed that the Prussian state of his time was the unique embodiment of the world mind or spirit. It is therefore ironical that the left Hegelians should include some of the most revolutionary figures of the nineteenth century. Among the young Hegelians was Ludwig Feuerbach, who greatly influenced the criticism of religion. Like Hegel he began as a Protestant theological student and then rebelled. Going from Heidelberg to Berlin, he came under the influence of Hegel. Feuerbach taught for a short time at Erlangen, but for the greater part of his life he held no academic position. He sought to recast Hegel's philosophy radically in the direction of naturalism and materialism, the view of the world which asserts the sole reality of nature and denies any supernature or transcendence. His most important book, *The Essence of Christianity*, was published in 1841 and translated into English by George Eliot.[19]

While avowedly hostile to traditional Christian theology, Feuerbach regarded himself as a friend of religion, and he regarded his book as a viable reformulation of its living and human essence. In its traditional forms he asserted that religion is both illusory and delusory, that is, both false and misleading. As to the real existence of God or gods, Feuerbach was explicitly atheistic. They do not exist! Only nature exists, said Feuerbach, meaning the material and biological environment together with one's own body and the bodies of other human beings. The gods are "wish-entities" (*Wunschwesen* in German), products of the wishful bent of human imagination. Religion, in short, is a result of wishful thinking or wish fulfillment. This idea was by no means original with Feuerbach. In one form or another, it has emerged in several of the traditions presented in this book. The significance of Feuerbach was to give explicit, full, and systematic expression to this view. From his time onward this explicitly atheistic approach to religion was ready at hand for others to accept, to work at, and to develop further.

One reader of Feuerbach was Karl Marx, who punned that all the young Hegelians had been baptized in Feuerbach (*Feuerbach* means in German "fire-spring"). Karl Marx (1818–1883) was also a left Hegelian, who studied at Berlin in the years after Hegel's death, becoming deeply involved with other left Hegelians. Marx received his doctorate in 1841 but was destined never to occupy an academic position, spending his life rather as a radical newspaper editor, a revolutionary agitator and organizer, and an exiled, poverty-stricken scholar in the British Museum. No one in the twentieth century is ignorant of the worldwide and revolutionary impact of his thought, for it has become the official dogma of the communist movement. It is by this sequence of events that explicit and militant atheism has become the official creed of millions of twentieth-century people.

Marx's religious ideas were decisively influenced by Feuerbach. Following Feuerbach, he asserted that material nature was the sole reality, thus denying any possible existence to any transcendent or spiritual reality. Like Feuerbach he believed deity, or the supernatural, to be a figment of human subjective and wishful imagination. However, Marx went beyond Feuerbach in his analysis of the ways in which religious experience is sociologically formed, conditioned, and used or misused. In Marx's own words, religion is the "opiate of the people."[20] Inherently delusory in nature, religion, like opium, has the function of deadening pain—the social pain of the masses—thus making them less rebellious, more acquiescent to their misery. For Marx, religion, along with education, art, and all culture, is simply and plainly a tool by which the dominant classes of society maintain their domination. It is accordingly not simply delusory but also fundamentally immoral and therefore ought to be completely abolished. That Marx and his followers have deemed this result not only desirable, but also possible and feasible, has been due in part to their confident faith in humanity. Marx regarded his views in this respect as in direct line of succession from the Enlightenment. He concluded that once humans have broken the chains of their social slavery and stepped into the new world of freedom and communism, they will have no further need for the crutch of religion. Incidentally, many of Marx's specific judgments concerning religion are shared by people who are by no means Marxist in social outlook, or in fact to whom this social philosophy is repugnant.

Sigmund Freud (1856–1939) shared Marx's debt to Feuerbach's psychological understanding of religion, but he gave this idea a profoundly different formulation. Freud was the founder of psychoanalysis, which is both a technique for curing mental illness and a general theory of the human self in its total relation to the world. The latter aspect of Freudian teaching has significant similarities to both philosophy and religion. Freud shared Feuerbach's view of reality as limited to nature, denying categorically the reality of anything supernatural or transcendent. To the psychological process which produces and sustains religion, Freud gave his own detailed interpretation. Religion, he argued, is an infantile neurosis in which the image of an almighty and omniscient father is projected onto reality[21]; it is a delusion born of neurotic dependence. Freud shared with Marx the humanistic view that since humans are alone in the world they ought to be content to stand alone. However, Freud was vastly less certain than Marx of the possibility of attaining this goal—at least for most people.

Freud also differed from Marx in his lack of antireligious feeling, and in his genuine though somewhat furtive interest in the subject. He read widely in the anthropology of religion and used mythical terms and symbols in meaningful ways in his psychoanalytic studies. If Marx's attitude was angrily antireligious, Freud's was melancholically nonreligious. One of Freud's early students, Carl Jung, broke with his master on this issue and produced a version of psychoanalytic doctrine of considerable significance to both the practice and the study of traditional religion.[22] As a consequence, the total impact of psychoanalysis has been less hostile to traditional religion than Marxism has been. Indeed, in some versions it has been a device for providing fresh interpretations of traditional religions. However, for Freud and his followers, the conclusion was nonreligious. Mature people will learn to stand upon their own feet and face the tragedy of human existence in their own strength, assert Freud and his followers. This view must be counted as a late aspect of the radical century's criticism of traditional religion.

The impact of Darwin and the theory of evolution was of a different sort from that of Marx or Freud, but in the end was no less radical. Darwin was a dedicated scientist, with no conscious desire to criticize or disturb traditional

Charles Darwin. (New York Public
Library, Picture Collection.)

ideas. Yet, as noted earlier in this chapter, Darwinian evolution collided head-
on with prevailing theological views of human origin and divine creation. The
opening battle in this war took place a year after the publication of the *Origin
of Species*, at the 1860 meeting of the British Association for the Advancement of
Science. There Bishop Wilberforce sought to ridicule Darwin's new account of
the origin of the human species, and was effectively refuted and roundly castigated by Thomas Huxley, who was soon to be known as "Darwin's bulldog." In
the decades which followed, the Genesis versus evolution controversy spread
in both Great Britain and America. In the United States the publication (1910–
1912) of a series of pamphlets called, "The Fundamentals," asserted a literal interpretation of Genesis to be one of the absolutely necessary ingredients of
Christian belief.[23] It also provided a label for an antimodern interpretation of
Christianity. The controversy achieved a mock heroic climax in the Scopes trial
of 1925 in which Clarence Darrow and William Jennings Bryan appeared as at-
torneys at a Dayton, Tennessee, trial of a school biology teacher. In the succeeding years, the controversy receded, only to be revived in the 1970s and
1980s by the so-called Creation Science movement, which asserted the Genesis
story of the Bible as science rather than religion.

    Darwinian evolution had other implications as well. Marx was convinced
that it lent support to Marxian ideas of human social development. Herbert
Spencer argued with equal assurance that laissez-faire capitalism constituted the
application of the Darwinian idea of survival of the fittest to human society, and

Sigmund Freud. (National
Library of Medicine.)

a whole generation of social Darwinists echoed his claim. Spencer also generalized Darwin's idea of biological evolution to a universal law of progress,
which operated as a beneficent cosmic escalator. Spencer did not doubt that the
highest point in this universal progress was nineteenth-century Europe. He
combined his dogma of progress with agnosticism toward the traditional God.

The idea of evolution was given a radically different direction by the German philosopher Friedrich Nietzsche (1844–1900), with his idea of "superman," or "overman" (the German word is *Übermensch*). The son of a Lutheran
pastor, Nietzsche was educated as a classical philologist. He was an angry rebel
against the established values of nineteenth-century middle-class Europe, regarding them as a conspiracy against the vital powers of the creative minority of
human individuals. Nietzsche angrily attributed the hated way of life to Christianity and middle-class rationalism in philosophy. As a consequence his
archvillains were Jesus and Socrates. In relation to the former, Nietzsche boldly
called himself an antichrist.[24] Christianity he castigated as slave morality and as
a rebellion of the weak against the strong. Both Christian love and philosophic
rationalism he viewed as a betrayal of individual creative vitality to the medioc-
rity of the human herd.

Nietzsche's own credo was expressed in the ambiguous and much misunderstood phrase "will to power."[25] What he meant was not the will to dominate
other people, but the will to create, a vitality of the sort that finds embodiment

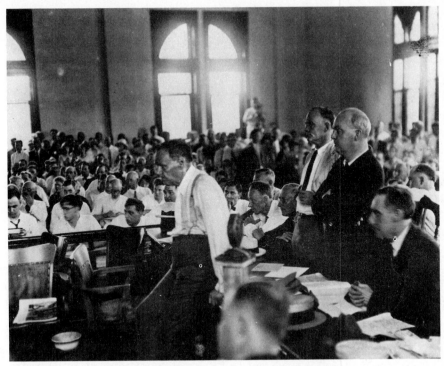

A scene from the trial of John T. Scopes, convicted in 1925 of violating a Tennessee statute forbidding the teaching of evolution in the state's school system. Clarence Darrow is seated on the desk; Scopes is seated behind him. (The Bettmann Archive.)

in a great artist. In terms of these values, Nietzsche called present humanity a disease and lyrically foretold the emergence in the future of overman, or superman.

Nietzsche was militantly anti-Christian. "God is dead," he shouted in *Thus Spake Zarathustra*, meaning the God of traditional Christianity. However, Nietzsche was by no means antireligious. Indeed, he did not hesitate to cast himself in the role of prophet of a future faith. The outlines of this faith are not altogether clear, but it appears to have been a hard Dionysiac vitalism to be espoused by a minority of human beings with whom the future was alleged to lie. In terms of this faith, Nietzsche called for a transvaluation of values.[26] The reader does not need to accept all that Nietzsche had to say in order to see that in his writings the criticism of traditional western religion had reached its most radical point.

SOME MODERN CREDOS

This chapter has advanced the thesis that the modern age and spirit have involved a process of ever more radical criticism of traditional faiths. This criticism has also involved doubt of varying kinds and degrees. Sometimes it has been the purely intellectual doubt of Descartes, employed as a means for establishing his own individual existence: "I doubt, therefore I am."[27] For other thinkers the process of criticism has involved doubt of a more existential and personal quality. For them doubt became a kind of polar opposite to faith.

Some modern people have devoted themselves to criticism and doubt with little apparent need for any more affirmative attitude. Others, however, have felt the need to affirm in words as well as in action the faith which guides their lives. They have felt the need to say *credo* as well as *dubito*. What follows here is a sampling of modern credos selected from the many possibilities for their contemporary interest and pertinence.

THE THOUGHT OF SPINOZA

Baruch (or Benedict) Spinoza (1632–1677) stands as one of the supremely great figures in the history of philosophy, both for the creative power of his thought and for his single-minded personal dedication to the life of thought, or as he put it, to "eternal things." Spinoza was born in Amsterdam, where his Portuguese Jewish family had fled from the Spanish Inquisition. He studied for the rabbinate, but encountering the radical scientific views of his Dutch teacher, Van der Ende, Spinoza developed a philosophy widely rumored to be "heretical," which led to his excommunication in 1656 by the synagogue. He responded by changing his name from the Hebrew *Baruch* to the Latin *Benedict*; in both languages it means "blessed." He was to know the blessedness of dedication to the faith of his own choosing. Earning his living by lens grinding, which aggravated a tubercular condition, he died at the age of forty-five as piously and humanely as he had lived. But Spinoza left in his writings a philosophic and religious vision of the world, breathtaking in its bold originality and brilliant in its clarity.

Spinoza's integral vision had two components: (1) his study of the new, modern scientific view of the world and (2) his traditional Jewish piety. He used traditional religious terms like *God, salvation*, and *immortality*, but he filled them with new content drawn from scientific study. The result was a reinterpretation of traditional Judeo-Christian faith, radical in its criticism of anthropomorphic views of God as well as other self-centered and childish ideas, but also of unquestioned authenticity in its deep spirit of piety and devotion.[28]

Spinoza defined God or nature (*Deus sive Natura*) as infinite substance, or that which alone is capable of self-existence. Maimonides and Aquinas before him had approached deity as ultimate reality or absolute reality, and Spinoza followed in this succession. His boldness lay in his reinterpretation of this old idea. He took as ultimate reality the universe revealed by modern natural science and proposed to treat as supreme reality the object matter of science. True, such a God is not personal, and Spinoza rejected as childish any view of deity as being personal in nature. Nevertheless, he continued to use the traditional religious language for his new views. He would say perhaps that it is no more inaccurate to use personal than impersonal language to point the altogether unique divine object.

Spinoza distinguished between knowledge of God, which is the province of philosophy, and obedience to God, which is the goal of religion. To help attain the latter, the Bible and its traditional language are well suited. Philosophy and religion accordingly supplement each other in the service of God.

Spinoza viewed human beings as the slaves of ignorant craving, and his description of bondage recalls Buddha's description of human misery. Spinoza believed that the path from bondage to freedom lay in the passionate devotion to truth for truth's sake, or as he expressed it, to the "intellectual love of God."[29] This allegiance he believed capable of leading a person out of warring affections and disaffections to the sunlit life of reason in which one dwells amid eternal things. Again in his new terms, Spinoza rejected as childish bondage all popular ideas of life after death. His new view constituted not only immortality in the only defensible meaning of that term, namely, life with a timeless or eternal quality in the present moment, but also freedom, which is the life of rationally determined choices. Such was Spinoza's bold modern credo.

He was modern in many ways other than in his reinterpretation of tradition in the face of new scientific knowledge. His biblical studies anticipated by two centuries the development of the higher criticism of the Bible. He knew no other way of study than by use of the free human intellect. Also, he formulated his own credo of religious toleration as alone consistent with the reason and freedom which were integral aspects of his own philosophy and religion. Truly, Spinoza was a modern saint; and as saints sometimes are, he has been an inspiration to many people since his time.

PROTESTANT LIBERALISM

Another modern credo may be labeled *Protestant liberalism*. Attention has already been called to the attitude of weak defensiveness which has so largely characterized Christianity during the modern period. In Roman Catholicism, decisions of the Council of Trent, enforced by the church's system of authority, may be said to have institutionalized this largely defensive and negative attitude. The Roman Catholic church seemed to be saying a continuing and insistent "no" to all that was modern, liberal, and forward-looking. As noted in Chapter 16, this negative attitude grew until the middle of the nineteenth century, when in the *Syllabus of Errors* (1864) the pope listed the modern trends condemned by the church and forbidden to Catholic Christians. The First Vatican Council of 1869–1870 declared the pope infallible and irreformable when he spoke to the whole church on matters of faith and morals. These attitudes were continued in the papal denunciation of Catholic modernism in 1905. In the light of these persistent attitudes, the new direction of Roman Catholicism under Pope John XXIII (1958–1963) and Pope Paul VI and the Second Vatican Council are of the greatest historic importance. While it is too early to offer detailed appraisal of the new trends, it is not too early to assert that a historic trend of four centuries' duration has been reversed.

Protestant Christianity, having no single central authority and being less shielded from the new developments of modern culture, has been shaped and reshaped by that culture. Protestant responses to the thought and practices of the modern world must be placed along a wide and continuous spectrum ranging from well-nigh total negation to an equally total and uncritical affirmation. During the present century, the fundamentalist movement in American Protestantism will serve as ready illustration of Protestant negativism, with its rejection of Darwinian evolution and, in some formulations, of Copernican astronomy, and with its rigid assertion of biblical inerrancy.

For other Protestants a more affirmative alternative has long been available. By *affirmative* is meant here simply more congenial or congruent to the modern world. Whether this is a good or a bad thing—indeed, what good or bad would mean in this context—is another and a different question which will have to be answered by each reader in the light of his or her own primary valuations. Our task here as elsewhere is to characterize significant historical developments. In this particular case, thoughtful persons have disagreed over the question of whether liberal religion is to be judged good or bad. In any event, in Protestant Christianity there has grown up over the past two centuries a liberal attitude and outlook which seeks to maintain the Protestant faith's relation to the Christian tradition but to make it acceptable and relevant to the modern world.

Protestant liberalism has developed in a great variety of forms which can only be sketched in here. The intellectual foundations of Protestant liberalism were laid by the German philosopher Immanuel Kant (1724–1804) in his *Critique of Practical Reason*.[30] The first of Kant's three great critiques ended as negatively for traditional theology as did the skeptical philosophy of David Hume. However, in the second critique Kant traced a path from moral experience (which for Kant was indubitable and inescapable) to the religious affirmations of God, freedom, and immortality. Kant's own religious faith thus was in effect cautious eighteenth-century rationalism. Yet his great importance was that he reopened the gates of possibility for forms of religious thought and experience which his contemporaries had deemed closed.

Among those who moved on, seeking to develop the new possibilities, was Friedrich Schleiermacher, whose *Addresses on Religion to Its Cultured Despisers* (1799) and *Christian Faith* (1834)[31] are often considered the foundation of modern theology. Schleiermacher began not with God or the Bible, but with religious experience; God entered the picture as the object of religious experience or, as Schleiermacher put it, of religious consciousness. Clearly this was a new approach to an old subject. It was remarkable how much of traditional Christian faith found its way back into Schleiermacher's theology through his new approach and method. What Schleiermacher began, others carried forward in their own ways. Albrecht Ritschl, for example, distinguished between judgments of fact and of value, interpreting faith as derived from or embedded in value judgments.[32] The influence of Ritschl and his student and successor

Wilhelm Herrmann was particularly strong on the American Protestant theology. Both in Europe and in the United States, what emerged from this theological movement was the means for relating the Christian tradition to the modern age.

Other developments within Protestantism served the same objective. The higher criticism of the Bible, that is, the free and critical study of the Bible with a view to answering questions of authorship, began in the eighteenth century and came of age in the nineteenth. Rejected and viewed with alarm at first, it was subsequently accepted and adopted within Protestantism. The free study of other religions—history of religions or comparative study of religions—has undergone a similar development.

Still another aspect of liberal Protestant thought and practice has been its fresh consideration of the ethic of Christianity. Christians had never been completely oblivious of the ethical implications of their faith. In modern times a succession of reforming groups and movements have sought to focus attention on specific problems, ranging from slavery to the excesses of the industrial revolution. As noted in Chapter 16, in the United States after the Civil War there grew up a liberal Protestant movement preaching what its proponents called the *social gospel* and determined to relate the Christian ethic to the whole of society.[33] The movement attracted some of the best minds in American Protestantism; it spread to other parts of the Protestant world, and in the course of development it has become an important aspect of the life and thought of the National and World Councils of Churches. While questioned and ignored in some quarters, and condemned in others, it has undoubtedly given to Protestant thought and faith a fresh approach to the world.

HUMANISM

While liberal Christianity sought to mediate between tradition and modernity, other people believed that the conflict was irreconcilable, and hence they broke with traditional faith. Within the past century many such people have called themselves *humanists*, thus providing another new meaning for this already multivalued word. By use of the term, these modern humanists have sought to assert that, unable in the age of modern science to believe in the traditional Judeo-Christian God, they propose still to believe in humanity.

Humanism in this sense of the word has had several organizational or institutional forms. The French philosopher and sociologist Auguste Comte (1798–1857) organized in Paris a Church of Humanity, in which the "great being" or humanity replaced the traditional God and which taught that altruism would conquer egoism.[34] Comte created for his new faith an elaborate cultus, borrowed largely from Catholicism, with priests and sacraments and even a positivist calendar in which the names of scientists and scholars replaced saints. However, this contrived faith never attracted a following and, as a consequence, did not outlive its founder.

There has been a somewhat different outcome for the Ethical Culture Society, founded in 1876 in New York City by Felix Adler.[35] Adler was a student for the rabbinate who rebelled against what he thought to be Judaism's excessive legalism and turned to philosophy. Accepting the ethical philosophy of Kant, he sought to give it concrete expression in the various areas of society, from family to school, economic order, and state. At the center of society Adler envisaged a religious organization, voluntary in nature, whose leaders would be ethical teachers rather than priests and whose purpose would be to inculcate moral values in its members. Adler's New York Ethical Culture Society grew to over a thousand members, and it spread to other cities of America and Europe. The Ethical Culture movement engages in educational, philanthropic, and social reform activities. Its worship is simple, combining readings from inspirational literature, music, meditation, and addresses on topics of ethical significance. There are no doctrinal requirements for membership.

Similar to Ethical Culture, but specific in its rejection of traditional theism as a religious belief, is the American Humanist Association.[36] Recruited mainly from left-wing Protestants and Jews, its members are held together by common ideas and purposes more than organizational ties. A bimonthly magazine, *The Humanist*, is published, conferences are held, and propaganda is carried on. However, it must be added that this outlook appears distinctly less popular in the second half of the twentieth century than it did in the first half.

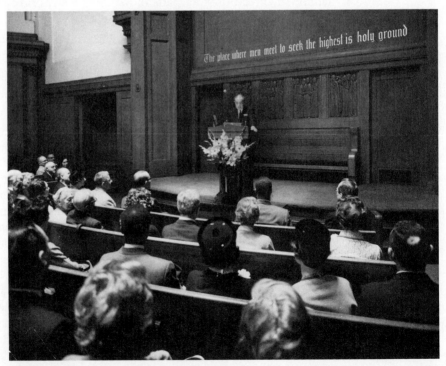

The place where men meet to seek the highest is holy ground

An Ethical Culture Society meeting, New York City. (Courtesy Ethical Culture Society, New York.)

Humanism is not only an organized movement and creed but also the unexpressed outlook of countless modern people. This outlook has its basis in the method and achievements of science. This belief is sometimes consciously expressed but often exists simply as a confident acceptance of the scientific outlook and a willingness to live and act in these terms. Frequently related to this is an allegiance to humanity either explicit or implicit in quality and generating a wide range of social concerns and reforms. Among the attempts to give explicit formulation to humanism are Corliss Lamont's *Humanism as a Philosophy*, John Dewey's *A Common Faith*, and Julian Huxley's *Religion without Revelation*. In wider, more pervasive form, the humanistic outlook has functioned as the climate of opinion of the modern world, thus finding acceptance in countless minds and lives that have never given it conscious articulation. How it will fare in the postmodern future remains a question.

This exposition of liberalism and humanism has been limited to their expression in the Judeo-Christian tradition both because these tendencies have been developed furthest in this tradition and because this tradition probably stands closest to the experience of most readers of this book. Yet the fact is that the spirit of liberal accommodation to modernity and of humanist rebellion against tradition has had increasing application to all of humankind's religions. Increasingly the issues outlined here have relevance to the Asian faiths. The only question is what kinds of responses these faiths will be capable of making to the challenge of modernity.

THE END OF MODERN TIMES?

In recent decades many writers have asserted that the modern age is now past and that humankind has embarked upon a postmodern period. Nicholas Berdyaev wrote *The End of Our Times* in 1933.[37] Some years later and in a somewhat different context Norman Cousins wrote *Modern Man Is Obsolete*. However, others have responded with what Charles Frankel has called "the case for modern man."[38] The issue is evidently controversial, and happily no wholesale judgment is necessary for the purposes of this chapter. Nevertheless, understanding of the contemporary situation in religion requires that we begin to appraise some of the issues involved in the wider situation.

One central fact is that the criticism of tradition which has been so pervasive and fundamental an aspect of the modern spirit seems to have run its course. There are very few uncriticized beliefs or traditions left for critical treatment. To be sure, there is a perennial critical function of reason which must be exercised by every generation and every individual and in every tradition. But criticism in its radical and avowedly modern sense seems to have done its work, at least in the modern West. In the opinion of some observers the acids of modernity have eaten away the fabric of traditional beliefs and acceptances so completely that little or nothing is left.

This appraisal of the contemporary situation has been expressed in various ways. Tillich has spoken of a "cultural void," which might be identified as the empty place in many contemporary minds and hearts where traditional faiths or values used to be. It was this aspect of modernity that led to T. S. Eliot's metaphor of the "wasteland." Writing from a very different perspective, David Riesman has diagnosed the present situation as a shift from tradition-directedness and inner-directedness to other-directedness, or conformity to social context.[39] Having no personal values or faith, the contemporary human being is content simply to conform to the social context. Lonely and naked people huddle together in crowds. Whatever the specific formulation, these various diagnoses all point to a seismic change in the basic attitudes and orientation of contemporary people—in their faith, or value orientation.

This change in attitude may be expressed as the shift away from criticism of tradition and rebellion against authority to a profoundly new kind of issue. The new issue may perhaps be formulated as the question, "Where amid the storms of our times can genuine meaning be found?" Having completed that rebellion against tradition and authority defined as modernity, people now ask a different question: "What is the meaning of life? What shall I live for?" The reader will recall this as one formulation of what in Chapter 1 was termed the *fundamental religious question*. However, the problems of the twentieth century have given it a peculiar urgency and timeliness and significance.

The contemporary search for meaning takes many forms. One of the most significant is the existentialist movement in contemporary philosophy, literature, and theology, for which the question "What is man?" or more personally, "Who am I?" is the common and central feature. Many answers are given, including the specific avowal of no answer, but it is the question which is the significant and common feature of this movement.

It is not possible for any except oracular or prophetic persons to see what forms the future will take. Yet it is significant for whatever future may come to be that our present situation is characterized by a question. This question defines a new opportunity and challenge for humankind's traditional faiths. It was asserted in Chapter 1 that the perennial function of religion has been to provide life orientation, to give a convincing answer to the question, "Why am I alive?" This question is being asked today in new and urgent ways which give relevance to those faiths which are bold and wise enough to adapt their traditional answers to the new situation.

ISSUES AND QUESTIONS

Of the issues raised by this chapter, none is more persistent or more important than the cluster of problems gathered under the rubric of science and religion. As we have indicated, some of these problems such as Genesis versus evolution have effectively been solved, but others persist. How may we use natural science and scientific technology for human welfare and not ill-fare? We have dared to suggest that basic human values which inhere in religious experience may point toward an answer to this question.

Another issue in this cluster is the systematic overvaluation of science; this is sometimes called *scientism*. If we treat modern science not as a highly successful body of human knowledge but as an all-comprehensive value system, we may awake to find ourselves in a state of idolatrous worship of a false god. Yet it is perhaps sufficient to observe in this connection that scientism occurs more often among the philosophic camp followers of science than among practicing scientists.

Another closely related issue raised by this chapter is the pervasive and ever-increasing secularization of modern culture. From the beginning of modern times to the present moment, this trend has increased, and there are no present signs of any diminution. This poses a major challenge to all of humanity's traditional religions. For in many past situations these religions have received favors and perquisites of many kinds from the leaders of society. Not infrequently they have enjoyed the status of being established religions, with both the privileges and the penalties involved in this relation. What seems clear at the present time is that all such relations are literally being dissolved by the acids of modern secularization, and thus may be said to have no future.

The powerful challenge to traditional religions is to live—and live effectively—in this new secular environment. To live effectively means not only to exist but to carry on the religious function of value creation and value maintenance. Religions which are vital and vigorous will accept this challenge. Indeed this challenge is the measure of their vitality.

The pervasive secularization of society has created what we may call a level playing field on which the diverse faiths, philosophies, and value systems may fairly compete for the allegiance of human hearts and minds. We shall return to this issue in the next chapter.

Another issue which must at least be acknowledged here is the full emergence, in the consciousness of the West and of the world, of traditional religions of South Asia and East Asia. As we shall see in the next chapter, this development, from the eighteenth century to the present, greatly increases our awareness of religious diversity, of literally, multiversity.

Finally we must at least take cognizance of the persistence throughout the modern age of trends and tendencies which can only be described as antimodern. Among many such phenomena, none is closer to the center of religious attention than what is sometimes called "worldwide fundamentalism." Among people who feel threatened by one or another aspect of modernity there is a pervasive tendency to return to some premodern aspect of tradition, then to assert it militantly or belligerently, as a defense against present threats. Such phenomena have surfaced not only in Christianity but in Judaism, Hinduism, Islam, Buddhism, Shinto, and perhaps other traditions as well.

It is perhaps small comfort to observe that these movements cannot in the long run prevail. However, they do raise the pertinent question of what aspects of modernity need correction or even rejection and on the other hand what may be accepted as valid or adequate.

NOTES

1. A. N. Whitehead, *Science and the Modern World*, Macmillan, New York, 1927, p. 87.
2. Desiderius Erasmus, *In Praise of Folly*, Reeves and Turner, London, 1876; Francois Rabelais, *Gargantua and Pantagruel*, Jacques Le Clercq, (trans.), Heritage Press, New York, 1942.
3. See John Herman Randall, Jr., *The Making of the Modern Mind*, Houghton Mifflin, Boston, 1940, p. 122.
4. John Pico della Mirandola, *Oration on the Dignity of Man*, Regnery, Chicago, 1956.
5. Desiderius Erasmus and Martin Luther, *Discourse on Free Will*, Ernst F. Winter, (ed. and trans.), Ungar, New York, n.d.
6. This point is developed in detail by Reinhold Niebuhr, *The Nature and Destiny of Man*, vol. 2, Scribner, New York, 1943.
7. Whitehead, op. cit., pp. 57f.
8. W. C. Dampier, *A History of Science*, Cambridge, London, 1942, p. 124.
9. Blaise Pascal, *Pensées* 25:18, as quoted in Ernst Cassirer, *An Essay on the Dignity of Man*, Yale, New Haven, Conn., 1944, p. 14.
10. Quoted from Randall, op. cit., p. 237.
11. See inter alia Andrew Dickson White, *A History of the Warfare of Science and Theology in Christendom*, Braziller, New York, 1955.
12. Whitehead, op. cit., p. 270.
13. See M. Polanyi. *Science, Faith and Society*, University of Chicago Press, Chicago, 1964, and *Personal Knowledge*, University of Chicago Press, Chicago, 1958.
14. Carl Becker, *The Heavenly City of the Eighteenth-Century Philosophers*, Yale, New Haven, Conn., 1932.
15. See Franklin Littell, *From State Church to Religious Pluralism*, Anchor Books, Doubleday, Garden City, N.Y., 1962.
16. See inter alia Sidney Mead, *The Lively Experiment*, Harpter & Row, New York, 1963.
17. David Hume, *Dialogues Concerning Natural Religion*, Social Sciences Publ., New York, 1948.
18. See inter alia Karl Löwith, *From Hegel to Nietzsche*, Holt, New York, 1964.
19. Ludwig Feuerbach, *The Essence of Christianity*, Harper Torchbooks, Harper, New York, 1957.
20. Karl Marx, *Early Writings*, T. B. Bottomore, (trans. and ed.), McGraw-Hill, New York, 1964, p. 44.
21. Sigmund Freud, *The Future of an Illusion*, Anchor Books, Doubleday, N.Y., 1957.
22. For Carl Jung, see inter alia his *Psychology and Religion*, Yale, New Haven, Conn., 1938.
23. See inter alia N. Furniss, *The Fundamentalist Controversy*, Yale, New Haven, 1954.
24. See *The Philosophy of Nietzsche*, Modern Library, New York, n.d.
25. Ibid. See especially "Beyond Good and Evil."
26. *The Philosophy of Nature*. See especially "The Genealogy of Morals."
27. René Descartes, *Meditations and Selections from the Principles*, John Veitch, (trans.), Open Court, La Salle, Ill., 1941.
28. See inter alia his *Treatise on God, Man and His Wellbeing* in *Spinoza Selections,* ed. John Wild, Scribners, New York, 1930.
29. Spinoza, *Ethics* and *On the Improvement of the Understanding*, James Gutman (ed.), Hafner, New York, 1949. See especially Ethics, prop. XXXII–III.
30. J. Kant, *Critique of Practical Reason*. tr. Beck, Bobbs, Merrill, New York, 1956.

31. F. Schleiermacher, *Lectures on Religion to Its Cultured Despisers*, Cambridge, New York, 1988; *The Christian Faith*, tr. Stewart, Clark, Edinburgh, 1976.

32. Albrecht Ritschl, *Christian Doctrine of Justification and Reconciliation*, T. Clark, Edinburgh, 1902.

33. C. Howard Hopkins, *The Rise of the Social Gospel in American Protestantism*, Yale, New Haven, Conn., 1940.

34. Auguste Comte, *Positive Philosophy*, Franklin, 1875–1877; see also J. S. Mill, *Comte and Positivism*. University of Michigan Press, Ann Arbor, 1961.

35. Felix Adler, *An Ethical Philosophy of Life*, Appleton-Century-Crofts, New York, 1918.

36. J. A. C. F. Aure, *Humanism States Its Case*, Beacon Press, Boston, 1933. See also J. Dewey, *A Common Faith*, Yale, New Haven 1934; C. Lamont, *Humanism as a Philosophy*, Philosophical Literary, New York, 1950; J. Huxley, *Religion without Revelation*, Mentor Books, New York, 1957.

37. Nicholas Berdyaev, *The End of Our Time*, Sheed, London, 1933. Norman Cousins, *Modern Man Is Obsolete*, Viking, New York, 1945; Charles Frankel, *The Case for Modern Man,* Harper, New York 1956.

38. Paul Tillich, *The Protestant Era*, University of Chicago Press, Chicago, 1948, pp. 55f.

39. David Riesman, *The Lonely Crowd*, Yale, New Haven, Conn., 1950.

*B*IBLIOGRAPHY

Becker, C.: *The Heavenly City of the Eighteenth Century Philosophers*, Yale, New Haven, Conn., 1932.

Berger, P.: *The Sacred Canopy: Elements of a Sociological Theory of Religion*, Doubleday, New York, 1969.

Bergson, H.: *The Two Sources of Morality and Religion*, University of Notre Dame, Notre Dame, Ind., 1977.

Dampier, W.: *A History of Science*, Cambridge, London, 1965.

Descartes, R.: *Discourse on Method and Other Writings*, Wollaston (ed.), Penguin, New York, 1968.

Feuerbach, L.: *The Essence of Christianity*, Harper, New York, 1957.

Freud, S.: *The Future of an Illusion*, Norton, New York, 1975.

Greene, J.: *The Death of Adam*, Mentor Books, New York, 1961.

Huxley, J.: *Religion without Revelation*, Mentor Books, New York, 1957.

Kant, I.: *Selections*, T. Greene (ed.), Scribner, New York, 1929.

Lamont, C.: *Humanism as a Philosophy*, Ungar, New York, 1982.

Lepp, I.: *Atheism in Our Time*, Macmillan, New York, 1967.

Mackintosh, H.: *Types of Modern Philosophy*, Fontana, London, 1963.

Macquarrie, J.: *Twentieth Century Religious Thought*, Scribner, New York, 1981.

Marx, K.: *Selected Writings*, D. McLellan (ed.), Oxford, New York, 1977.

Niebuhr, R.: *The Nature and Destiny of Man*, Scribner, New York, 1943.

Nietzsche, F.: *The Basic Writings of Nietzsche*, W. Kaufman (ed.), Modern Library, New York, 1968.

Polyani, M.: *Personal Knowledge*, University of Chicago, Chicago, 1958.

———: *Science, Faith and Society*, University of Chicago, Chicago, 1964.

Popper, K.: *The Open Society and Its Enemies*, Princeton, Princeton, NJ, 1966.

Randall, J.: *The Making of the Modern Mind*, Columbia, New York, 1975.

Ruether, R. (ed.): *Religion and Sexism*, Simon & Schuster, New York, 1974.

Schleiermacher, F.: *The Christian Faith*, T & T Clark, Edinburgh, 1976.

————: *On Religion: Speeches to Its Cultured Despisers*, Cambridge, New York, 1988.

Spinoza, B.: *Selections*, J. Wild (ed.), Scribner, New York, 1930.

White, A. A.: *A History of the Warfare of Science and Theology in Christendom*, Peter Smith, Magnolia, Mass., 1978.

Whitehead, A.: *Science and the Modern World*, Free Press, New York, 1967.

18

Traditional Faiths and the Human Future

THE POSTMODERN PROSPECT

At the end of Chapter 17 it was suggested that the modern age is past or passing, and that humanity is now moving into a new period of history which is postmodern. The task of the present chapter is to sketch some of the implications of the new situation both for traditional faiths and for whatever new religions or new value-systems lie ahead.

Many of the fundamental issues of modernity have ceased to be crucial and have been pushed aside by new issues and problems. The central issue of modernity, emancipation from tradition, has largely achieved its goal. Yet this modern emancipation has brought with it consequences unforeseen by the great pioneers of modernity. In degree and numbers unparalleled in previous history, people of every land and tradition have been emancipated from their old allegiances, but in the absence of any effective replacements they have been cut adrift on the sea of existence, their lives guided only by impulse, pleasure, and conformity. Cities around the world number such people by the million. For these people, servile allegiance to tradition is no problem. Indeed, for many there appears to be no felt problem at all. For the more sensitive individuals a new problem has emerged: Where amid the turbulence of our times is any human meaning to be found in existence? As noted in Chapter 17, this change from the modern to the postmodern situation is marked by the shift from the question, "How shall I free myself from servile allegiance to tradition?" to the question, "Where and how shall I find meaning in existence?" In the changed situation, some aspects of the modern age remain as secure achievements while others have become obsolete. Our first task is to take cognizance of the new landscape. This section of the chapter will be concerned with a few important features of the contemporary religious landscape.

FREEDOM AND RESPONSIBILITY

The enduring achievement of modernity has been its emphasis on freedom. True, many people of previous ages have known that human personality is free and responsible, but the modern age has made this fact altogether central and has at least begun the task of its detailed application to all the various aspects of individual and social life. Despite the twentieth-century popularity of totalitarianism, this is an achievement which will not be undone. Having once tasted freedom, *Homo sapiens* is unable to completely forget it. However, it is to be expected that the emphases and accents given to freedom will change with changing times and situations.

Most modern interpretations have emphasized, quite properly in historical terms, the negative aspects of freedom. Freedom has meant, in Erich Fromm's terms, "freedom from."[1] It has been defined as the absence of hindrances to or interferences with the individual, whether these be of political, ecclesiastical, or other origin. People will be free, it has been urged, when they are out of prison and rid of all chains.

Yet one of the first lessons of the postmodern age is that while such negative aspects are necessary, they are by no means sufficient conditions of freedom. Freedom is not only "from" but "to" and "for." It has not only its negative but its positive requirements. It is possible for people to be out of prison and rid of chains, yet to fall short of freedom. Among the many positive requirements of freedom is a principle of allegiance strong enough to hold the human self together in unity and to give it purpose and direction. By a *principle of allegiance* we mean what in other connections we have termed an *ultimate concern*. Another formulation is a basic value-system. The terms are synonymous. However characterized, it is what holds the self together in functioning unity. The perplexing problem is to find some such principle which will perform this function without again reducing the self to bondage. Having suggested that the traditional faiths at their best have performed this function for their adherents, we may now extend the suggestion to say that they may continue to fulfill this function in the present and future.

For some people of the present as of every past age, freedom and its corollary, responsibility, are a burden and a task too great to be borne. Such people will always be looking for some higher power or authority upon which they can unload this burden. Many contemporary cults and movements as well as some traditional religions provide ample illustration for this dehumanizing fact. The last chapter spoke of worldwide fundamentalism. Contemporary religious and political history also shows many movements which are, like the Grand Inquisitor, all too ready to assume this kind of power over other people. Yet this chapter and this book are written on the assumption that to the extent to which persons are willing to shed their freedom and responsibility, to precisely the same extent they divest themselves of their humanity. To say this is not to advocate any one faith or to condemn others, but to set conditions for any faith which a person may hold without sacrificing that central core of freedom which constitutes humanity. Accordingly our primary concern is with forms of faith, actual and possible, which address people in and through and not outside their fundamental freedom. Whether there are or can be such forms of faith is a central issue before thoughtful persons today.

Paul Tillich sought to deal with these issues in his threefold category of heteronomy, autonomy, and theonomy.[2] Heteronomy is the situation, as the etymology of the word suggests, in which an alien norm stands over the self, whether this norm be religious, political, or of some other sort, and reduces the self to slavery or bondage. Since it stands in tyranny over the self, it frequently provokes the rebellion of autonomy. In autonomous situations, there is no authority over the human self; the self provides its own norms or laws. Yet it is a fact of human history that autonomy has frequently been unstable, being little more than a point of transition from one heteronomy to another. Hence Tillich was led on to the category of theonomy, the ideal situation in which there is an equivalence between the commands of God and the aspirations of human selfhood. The term *God* implies a monotheistic faith, yet Tillich's formulation can easily be generalized to cover all religions or value-systems by substituting for *God* the neutral term *religious object* or *object of ultimate valuation*. That such a "theonomous" situation is difficult is undoubtedly true. Yet, it may be added, so are many other good things. But they are possible. Our task here is achieved if we recognize this as one human possibility among others in the contemporary situation.

TACIT RELIGIONS

Another very important feature of the contemporary situation is the rise to power of what Tillich has called the *quasi-religions*, namely, systems of allegiance like communism and Nazism which have some of but not all the traits of religion.[3] Here these systems will be called *tacit religions*, which may be defined as systems of allegiance or valuation which function religiously, in part or in whole, in the lives of their adherents but are not recognized by their adherents as religious. They have also been called *unconscious religions* and *substitute religions*. Whatever the designation, it is important to see that in the contemporary world they constitute some of the strongest rivals to the traditional faiths for human allegiance.

This whole region is fraught with pitfalls and controversies, but it lies so clearly across our path as to be unavoidable. Attention must first be called to the fact that use of the term *religious substitute* or *substitute religion* is descriptive and in no way evaluative. It is meant to imply no judgment as to the good or bad qualities of such phenomena, but only to recognize that there are systems of value and thought which function religiously (as this book has defined and expounded religious functioning) but not recognized as religions by their adherents. Surely it does not require extensive factual observation to verify the existence of such phenomena. While they are by no means limited to communism and extreme nationalism, these two systems probably constitute the most important existing religious substitutes in the contemporary world. They will be considered briefly in turn.

Karl Marx's thought was discussed in Chapter 17 as a part of the radical century's criticism of traditional religion and as marking a historic development in atheism. It will now appear ironic if not contradictory to assert that Marxism constitutes a substitute religion providing a functioning system of life orientation or life valuation for countless millions of people. Indeed, some observers of communism have offered the blunt evaluation that its evil is not atheism but idolatry.[4] What they mean is that behind the facade of atheism stands an absolutism which functions in much the same way that monotheistic religions assert that idolatry functions. It would take us far beyond our present field of study to evaluate this charge fully or adequately. Yet it is an important feature of contemporary religious history that such claims are made.

The assertion of communism's religious significance is by no means novel. Almost five decades ago Middleton Murry called it the world's "one living religion."[5] During the 1930s such writers as William Temple, Reinhold Niebuhr, and Paul Tillich were characterizing communism as an unconscious religion and were attempting to lay bare what they thought to be its false and misleading character.[6] More recently such diagnoses have become widely popular.

Assuming the religious significance of Marxism, it becomes important to ask what kind of religion this is. In many important ways it is a by-product of the Bible and the Judeo-Christian tradition. Many observers have agreed in calling it *Judeo-Christian heresy*. In terms of our typology of religions, Marxism constitutes a clear illustration of the third type. This designation seeks to call attention to the view of historic destiny which in Chapters 11 and 13 was observed in the Bible and in Chapter 15 in Augustine and his *City of God*. Communism is one of the inheritors of this tradition. To call it *heretical* is to assert that it gives distorted expression to the basic ideas involved. For example, both biblical and Marxist myth tell stories of the original perfection and fall of humanity. In contrast to the biblical story, the communist story begins with primitive communism; and the fall occurs when the landlord and soldier combine to subjugate the worker. Evil is characterized by Marxism as acquisitiveness or lust for property rather than arrogant pride or rebellion against God.

Again, Marxism's explicit atheism does not obscure the messianism which centers in Karl Marx. From this, other traits of religion follow in succession. The Communist party functions as a kind of church or sect whose sacred scriptures are the writings of Marx and Lenin and whose leaders function sometimes as priests and sometimes as prophets. Some writers have even commented on the emergence of holy places such as the tomb of Lenin to which the faithful go on pilgrimage. These and other aspects of Marxism provide impressive verification for the thesis of this book that religion as ultimate concern is a perennial and undeniable feature of human life. Deny overt expression to religion and it is not destroyed but rather forced underground, where it finds expression as covert or substitute religion. Truly, humankind is *Homo religiosus*!

Of religious significance comparable to communism is modern nationalism in its various guises, particularly in extreme forms such as German Nazism, Italian fascism, Japanese militarism, and the radical right of the United States. In most modern nations nationalism has functioned as "man's other religion," providing a functioning total value system which people need to render life meaningful.[7]

To readers familiar with recent world history, the religious quality of nationalism will be sufficiently clear in Nazism and fascism. Here are systems of ultimate concern and valuation or of total orientation exhibiting many of the features of traditional religion, ranging from a holy leader surrounded by a context of ritual and myth, to total devotion to the cause on the part of faithful followers. While Nazism and fascism were unconsciously religious, pre-World War II Japanese militarism had direct and conscious continuity with the national religious tradition. In Chapter 9 we noted the distinctive Japanese formulation of the recurring themes of sacred ruler and sacred nation or land and sketched the ways in which these traditional elements were used by Japanese ultranationalists in the period culminating in World War II. The question may be asked: "When does loyalty to the nation become religious in quality?" The answer is: "When a human concern becomes ultimate in the sense described in Chapter 1."

Many Americans who recognize the religious significance of nationalism elsewhere in the world have given little or no thought to its place in their own situation. Asserting the traditional American doctrine of the separation of church and state, they apparently consider this issue disposed of. However, it does not exceed the bounds of factual or historical study to point out that this conclusion is premature. Whatever the official formulation, whenever loyalty to the nation is taken as total or absolute, it may be assumed to have religious significance. Whenever any concern becomes ultimate, it takes on religious significance. That American nationalism functions in this way for many groups of the so-called radical right, some ostensibly secular, others avowedly religious, will be clear upon observing their writings and their behavior. Whatever their conscious religious professions, the American nation is their actual object of ultimate concern. Again it will be well within the bounds of historical study to assert that Uncle Sam functions as their god.

The religious quality of American nationalism is by no means limited to extremist groups, but rather runs like a major thread through the fabric of American tradition. The New England Puritans believed that God had called them to found a new order of life in this new land. The great seal of the United States proclaims a *novum ordo saeculorum*, "a new order of the ages." The tradition of American manifest destiny has frequently assumed the significance of a religious substitute, from Polk to McKinley. Lincoln proclaimed American democracy as the "last great hope" of humankind, and Eisenhower remarked that the United States is a missionary society to the world.[8]

Many of these valuations have found expression in what has recently been called America's *civic religion*. Writers as different as Lloyd Warner and Will Herberg point to the religious significance of American national holidays such as Memorial Day, July Fourth, and Thanksgiving.[9] They also point to the ways in which such ostensibly Christian festivals as Christmas and Easter are invested with ethnic significance. In American churches and synagogues people call upon the biblical God, but the actual value content of their religion invests him with the significance of Uncle Sam, their faith becoming in effect a religion of American values or the American way of life. Robert Bellah gives thoughtful expression to the central American value-system as a "civil religion."[10]

The kind of religion constituted by nationalism is sufficiently clear from what has already been said. It is not, like Marxism, a new form of biblical religion, but is rather a powerful reassertion of religion of the first, or nature-culture, type. In this respect the Japanese experience is illuminating, for it presents the actual historic continuities of such an ethnic tradition. But the value content is similar in other national traditions as well. The ghosts of the divine pharaohs of Egypt, of the Roman Caesars, of the Chinese sons of Heaven, and of countless tribal chiefs walk the earth again in contemporary nationalism. To make the same claim in value terminology, the national values are asserted to constitute the whole meaning of life; beyond the borders of the nation, nothing of any significance exists. Such is the nationalist credo. The historian of religion may note here a clear conflict with all the universal religions, that is, those which address persons as members of the human family. In a day when continued human existence depends upon global solidarity of humanity, such faiths pose a mortally serious practical problem to all who are concerned with the human future.

While communism and nationalism probably constitute the most significant religious substitutes of the contemporary world, the list by no means ends here. Like the ancient Romans, contemporary people have constructed a populous pantheon. This is even true of the academic community, despite its professions of agnosticism. On many university and college campuses are professors and students whose conventional academic agnosticism is belied by an allegiance, which is virtually total and final, to science, to democracy, to American values, to progress, or to humanity. They provide effective illustration of Robin Williams's remark that every community has its functioning religion.[11]

Whatever the readers's evaluation of these substitute religions, their presence in the twentieth century in great numbers and force makes one fact abundantly clear. It is that the human need for religion shows no sign of abating. People still need some faith to guide the course of their lives, to provide them with life orientation. If overt religious forms or symbol systems are denied them, or if these do not speak with light and power, they will cleave to covert religions. Indeed, in the minds of many thoughtful observers, the chief contenders for the allegiance of human hearts, for ultimate commitment and concern today, are not traditional faiths (these are often regarded as polite embellishments of a civilized life) but the quasi-religions, or religious substitutes.

RELIGIONS—NEW AND RENEWED

While the religious substitutes flourish, what of new movements of explicitly religious character? What indeed of the traditional faiths of the world which have been our primary object of study in this book? What ones of the latter show signs of life, and which ones are dead or dying? Let us consider these questions in order.

Perhaps the first observation is to note the veritable plethora of new religious movements which today clamor for popular attention. Sometimes, as with Synanon or Scientology, for example, while claiming religious status, they have few roots in traditional religious forms. Sometimes, like EST, they are drawn from many sources (ranging in the case of EST from Lao tsu to Freud) by a charismatic leader who proclaims an essentially new faith. Sometimes, as in the many forms of drug mysticism, they draw upon sources as varied as the Tibetan Book of the Dead or, as in the case of Carlos Castaneda, Mexican Indian religion.[12] Stanislaus Grof's explorations of LSD, as reported in his book *Realms of the Human Unconscious*, draw heavily upon what our study has labeled *unitive mysticism*.[13]

Previous chapters of our study have noted contemporary movements which spring from traditional sources. Zen Buddhism, Vedanta, and the many brands of Yoga come to mind in this connection. Transcendental Meditation may be characterized as a modernized version of Vedanta philosophy and yogic meditation.[14] The Krishna Consciousness organization, popularly known as the Hare Krishna movement, is a contemporary formulation of Hindu bhakti.[15] The Aurobindo discipleship, both in India and around the world, is a mixture of traditional Vedantism and the modern western philosophy of evolution.

Moving from India to China, we recall that in Chapter 8 we identified the Unification church of Sun Myung Moon as a new blending of elements long known to east Asia, in this case Confucian ethics, Korean folk culture, and Christian millennialism and messianism, the last centered in Moon and his mission. From the Chinese tradition the I Ching is today the source of western phenomena ranging from cookbooks to physical exercise regimens and holistic medicine. Japan has found a ready export market for its new religions, notably Soka Gakkai, but also including phenomena ranging from Zen to Tenri kyo and PL Kyodan.

From Islam have come a variety of forms of Sufi mysticism and discipline. Also from Islam, Bahaism began as an Iranian sect, founded by Mirza Husain Ali Nuri in 1863 in protest against traditional Muslim exclusivism. Called by his followers *Baha Ullah* (which means in Arabic "splendor of Allah") and hailed as Islam's promised one, he died a martyr's death. Today Bahaism has organizations around the world and headquarters in Wilmette, Illinois, and Haifa, Israel. The movement called *Subud* also stems from Sufi mysticism, in this case in combination with Japanese folk elements, including notably ecstatic speech and action. As we noted in Chapter 14 the Nation of Islam in the United States continues to grow and to move closer to traditional Islam.

But what now of the traditional faiths of the world which have been the subject matter of this book? How do they fare in the storms of the twentieth century?

First, let us note briefly two traditional faiths which appear either dead or dying, namely, Taoism and Confucianism. The former has apparently been slowly expiring for several centuries. According to W. T. Chan, the reason is that some centuries ago it simply stopped thinking.[16] It is probably true that the Marxist rulers of China have already interred Taoism's moribund remains. Similarly, Confucius and Confucianism in their massive conservatism appear to have little or no future in Marxist China.

In contrast to these two dead or dying faiths are others which seem very much alive but whose life appears totally identified with a particular group of people. This is true of two Indian minority faiths, the Jains and the Sikhs. They seem to be holding their own, but they also appear limited by the boundaries of their past and present communities.

Another closely related class of religious phenomena is that in which nationalism finds expression in terms of traditional religion, in many cases being the determining factor in present religious development. Examples may be selected at random from the developing nations of Asia and Africa. Southeast Asian Buddhism provides instructive illustrations extending from Sri Lanka to Vietnam. We have previously noted the rise of Soka Gakkai in Japan. Islam lends a religious quality to Arab nationalism in such organizations as the Ikwan or Muslim Brotherhood. In Judaism the net effect of some forms of Zionist extremism is Israeli nationalism. In Hinduism, examples range from Swami Dayananda and the Arya Samaj to the Jana Sangh and numerous other organizations which identify Hindu religion with Indian nationalism. The reader will recall that Tagore and Gandhi disagreed over this issue, and also that Gandhi was assassinated by a fanatical Hindu extremist who believed that Gandhi had conceded too much to India's Muslims.

Mention may also be made at this point of a notable contemporary instance of what may perhaps be termed *denationalization*. The use (or misuse) of shinto by the Japanese militarists of the nineteenth and twentieth centuries was pointed out in Chapter 9, as was the fact that during the American occupation the emperor renounced his divinity and Shinto was disestablished. These latter developments were the crucial events in a process of denationalizing Shinto, transforming it into a relatively nonpolitical religion which provides expression for the Japanese way of life. The transition has been difficult, but statistics indicate an impressive measure of success. There is even a university, Kokugakuin, which is devoted to the scholarly study of this faith and tradition.[17] Here again contemporary Japan affords another instance of significant religious experimentation.

Turning to the larger and historically more important religions, what signs of health and sickness, of vigor or morbidity, does the observer find? Of the world's faiths, Hinduism is perhaps the hardest to observe. Clearly it is under attack by modern and scientific persons and trends. In India's cities caste is being eroded, though in villages it is very far from dead. Many modern-minded Indians point impatiently to the massive conservatism of Hinduism. India's need is not for religion, they argue, but for steel mills, scientific agriculture, and population control. Yet it is also a fact of contemporary history that new life has been breathed into old Hindu ideas during the great century that began with Ram Mohan Roy and ended with Gandhi. The Ramakrishna order (sometimes called the *Vedanta Society*) carries on good works and active Hindu religious propaganda both in India and around the world. Apparently oblivious to modern criticism, most of India's millions continue to be Hindus in their traditional ways.

The picture is equally mixed for Buddhism. Some Buddhist ideas and groups seem moribund. To western students the present state of Chinese Buddhism is obscure, but there are few indications of vitality. The Chinese communists appear to have succeeded in their attempt to liquidate Tibetan Buddhism, forcing the Dalai Lama into a *diaspora*. Opposing such trends is the Buddhist revival in central India, where adherents are reliably estimated to number 3 million people, though critics point to the primarily sociopolitical significance of this form of Buddhism. Southeast Asian Buddhism shows stirrings of new life from Ceylon to Cambodia and Vietnam, though it must be repeated that in every case there is a strong admixture of nationalism. The state of Japanese Buddhism, while controversial, appears on the whole to be one of health. After we make the necessary discounts for western faddism, Zen presents a picture of considerable vigor, both intellectual and religious. The larger and more popular Amidist groups are at least holding their own among the people. There is no lack of new movements attempting to interpret Buddhist tradition in fresh terms to contemporary Japan. There are some signs of an ecumenical spirit in Buddhism which attempts to bridge the gap between Mahayana and Theravada.

Islam's monumentally conservative posture was noted in Chapter 14. In recent times it has generated a great deal of defensive behavior among Muslims, particularly in their dealings with the West. The central contemporary question is whether this massively conservative posture can be changed sufficiently to facilitate genuine adaptation to the contemporary world. There are some signs of adaptive rather than defensive behavior in Islam, from Pakistan to Turkey, and there is vastly greater variety in Islam than is usually supposed by western observers. As has been true before in Muslim history, it may be that Sufism will be the agent of creative change. Yet if the opinion of as sympathetic and perceptive an observer as Wilfred Cantwell Smith is to be accepted, the issue of Islam's future still hangs in the balance at the present moment. In black regions of Africa, Islam prospers as the vehicle of racial equality and justice.

For Judaism the central contemporary facts are what is known as the *Holocaust* and the emergence of the state of Israel, which as we noted in Chapter 12 have stirred both Judaism and the Jewish community to their depths, with the consequence that Judaism is probably more intensively and extensively alive and creative today than it has been for many centuries past. Individual Jews continue to disagree with each other and with tradition in matters religious; and for many, their Jewishness is more a cultural than a religious fact. But for others the religious center of the community has become a matter of fresh concern. Thus Judaism continues as a relatively small religion, and outside of Israel a minority culture, but very much alive and exerting an influence out of all proportion to its numbers.

In Roman Catholic Christianity the overarching fact is Vatican II and its consequences. In Chapter 16 it was asserted that Vatican II marked a historic change of attitude from the defensive and hostile posture which extended from the Council of Trent through Vatican I to a stance of positive encounter with the world. One among many consequences of this fundamental change has been the emergence of new forces and vitalities of diverse sorts. Some of these forces, ranging from theology to the arts, antedated Vatican II; but in the new climate of thought and feeling, they appear both more visible and more influential than before Vatican II. Indeed, some forms of theology as illustrated by Karl Rahner and Hans Kueng substantially helped to create Vatican II. Other currents, such as Latin American liberation theology, owe a large part of their influence to this new climate. In matters ranging from the vernacular mass to theological study and artistic expression, the world's largest single religious organization clearly appears to be moving into a new age. Despite resistance and inertia, the Roman Catholic church today seems to face forward rather than backward. Likewise its lines of relation toward other Christian groups are convergent rather than divergent.

In Protestantism, the ecumenical movement antedated its emergence in Roman Catholicism, and it has assumed somewhat different forms and emphases. Beginning as far back as the first decade of the present century, it sought at first to draw the different Protestant bodies together in common tasks at home and on mission fields. From this it moved onward to press toward unity of creed, institutions, and organizations. Many other streams of influence fed into the ecumenical movement. Among these was a notable revival of theological thought and study, embodied in such individuals as Karl Barth, the Niebuhr brothers, and Paul Tillich. Still another influence was the social gospel, as noted in Chapter 16.

In recent years there have been many moves toward rapprochement between Protestants and Roman Catholics. These have ranged from mutual consultations among theologians to meetings for mutual fellowship and exploration between adherents of the two forms of Christianity or to official and quasi-official representation at each others' ecclesiastical gatherings. What the future holds is not clear, but Protestants and Roman Catholics today appear to be facing toward each other rather than away from each other.

In American Protestantism during the years after World War II (as well as in American Catholicism and Judaism), there was a rate of growth at times twice that of population growth, with the result that religious adherence, church attendance, and almost every other index of participation stood at all-time highs. However, more recently this increase slackened and then ceased altogether. Also it must be recorded that despite the quantity, the quality of this faith has

been widely questioned, for this return to religion has not been accompanied by either any significant increase in knowledge of the faith or any of the significant fruits of genuine religious faith.

Another current phenomenon of American Protestantism has been the emergence of numerous right-wing fundamentalist groups. Usually holding to biblical literalism, claiming to stand alone in the true Protestantism, damning the ecumenical movement, and frequently holding reactionary social and political views, these groups have achieved and hold a considerable following. Apparently they appeal to a felt need of many people in the storms of the twentieth century.

Yet in American Protestantism and, one suspects, elsewhere as well, the greatest single problem of traditional religious faith is not such reactionary movements. Nor is it the antireligious stance of Marxism and other similar ideologies. Rather it is the problem of nominal allegiance. Thus it is not excessive to say that the effectiveness of the traditional religions in the contemporary world will be measured by the degree to which they can close the gap between the concerned minority and the masses of nominal adherents. While it exists around the world, nowhere is this gap more significant than in the contemporary United States.

CONTOURS OF FAITHS TO COME

In the past, ages of radical change have often produced new religions. The coming of civilization brought with it new religious forms and systems from China to Mesopotamia and Greece. The Axis Age of the ancient world brought Confucius, Lao tsu, Buddha, the prophets of Israel, and others. Will the present period of human history, which is surely a crisis as deep and pervasive as any previous one, produce some radically new religion or religious orientation? Or will the human future be one of nonreligion or secular value-systems? The only factual answer that can be made is that there are no signs of such new developments at the present time. Since this is the case, it is reasonable to predict that future faiths will be constituted by some of the shapes and forms of the past, perhaps in new combination. Let us, then, glance backward at our study, asking what are some of these main forms or shapes of human religious experience.

First we note again that it is the paradoxical combination of finitude and freedom in the human situation which generates religion. If like other creatures human beings were simply finite, religious behavior would not emerge. If, on the other hand, human beings were simply free spirits, they would not need religious orientation and guidance. Each of the different faiths we have studied has its own distinctive configuration of these two elements, and we may suppose that future faiths will find new expressions of the human combination of freedom and finitude or dependence.

ULTIMATE VALUATION

In Chapter 1 Paul Tillich's somewhat controversial concept of ultimate concern was proposed as the basic component of religious experience. Since it has been repeatedly referred to in the course of our study, readers have surely begun to form their own conclusions as to its relevance and adequacy. The paraphrase *ultimate valuation* has the advantages of being slightly less volitional than *ultimate concern*, including esthetic as well as moral values, and hence better able to include those religions whose basic stance is esthetic. Yet some such concept will remain as long as the organization of individual life or personality and the organization of social life in culture remain basic human needs. For both personality and culture demand a functioning center. Such values provide not only functioning unity but also orientation and direction along a path of life.

THE QUALITY OF THE SACRED

Holiness or sacredness was identified in Chapter 1 as the unique affective accompaniment of ultimate concern and commitment. Yet as we have been able to observe in the course of our study, the holy or sacred has lived a very problematic life in the history of the world's religions. It has served as a screen to hide the manipulations of the magician, has served as a roadblock in the road of human intelligence, has been a device for enforcing acquiescence in tyranny and injustice. Tyrants, shamans, and diseases have all been interpreted by countless human beings as authentically sacred. Sometimes the division of human society and human experience into two realms, the sacred and the secular, has been a way of putting up "no trespassing" signs over large areas of human experience.

Accordingly it is fair to ask whether there can be expressions of the sacred which successfully avoid these historic pitfalls. Again, only future events can give the actual answer, yet it accords with past experience to assert this possibility. If anything is observably true of the sacred, it is the infinite variety of its expressions. The quality of holiness attaching to voodoo differs from that which inheres in the Zen meditation hall. That which is to be seen in the person of Christ differs qualitatively from that of Buddha or Muhammad. Since this is so, it is at least possible that there may be forms which do not conflict with the sense of reason, justice, and humanity. In one set of symbols or another, humans must make their peace with the universe in which their lot is cast. The holy will be the emotive accompaniment of this ultimate adjustment, as it may be termed. And if this quality be combined with our highest values, the result will be a quality of reverence which does not conflict with, but fulfills, our humanity.

Expressions of the sacred of this sort will involve no conflict with the modern idea of the secularization of society. They would, of course, conflict with the negative dogma of secularism which categorically denies any legitimate existence to the sacred. It may be argued with much justification that a secular society is not hostile to religion, but provides a kind of neutral environment in which different faiths are free to pursue their ways and works. For faiths that are vital and vigorous, such an environment is an opportunity and a challenge. The problem is accordingly not to combat secularization as an evil, but to discover new ways of communicating sacred value in this new historic context. For there is every indication that the agelong drift toward secularization will continue into the future.

It is a view frequently argued in these pages that no form of the holy is experienced as a direct object of human interest. That is, people do not say "Let us have an experience of the holy," or "Let us be reverent." Rather, these emotions occur as by-products of situations of ultimate commitment and concern. Also they occur through the mediation of powerful symbols or symbol system. To the symbols of faith attention must now be turned.

SYMBOLISM

Previous pages of this study have argued that ultimate concern demands and receives expression in powerful and concrete symbols. It was also pointed out in Chapter 17 that the modern age has carried out a radical, devastating criticism of traditional symbols and faiths. The result is that the hold of these symbols and symbol systems upon human minds and heart has been greatly loosened. Tillich has spoken of this contemporary situation as one of "broken symbols," that is, symbols which are recognizable as such and not as literal or scientific truths. The great question is whether in this radically new kind of context, religious symbol systems can maintain their power over their adherents. This question is a genuinely open one. The answer will lie in the actual destiny of the world's traditional faiths. Literally, a dead faith is simply one whose symbols no longer speak with light and power to the minds and hearts of people.

To these observations it is necessary at this point only to add that in the world of the mid-twentieth century a great deal of significant free play and experimentation with symbols is taking place in both religion and the arts. One cannot read a poem by Eliot or Rilke without realizing that authors are actively seeking for fresh symbols which will adequately express what they have to say; and what poets have to say is often strikingly similar to what traditional faiths have said through their symbol systems. This observation, made about poetry and other literature, is equally or even more true of the visual arts of painting, sculpture, and architecture. In all these arts there has been a deliberate abandonment of old symbols as worn out and an exploration in search of new images or symbols. Often this search has seemed revolutionary or nihilistic, as in Picasso's painting and sculpture, in which the ordinary forms of things are twisted and distorted beyond all recognition. Yet the search that underlies these apparently strange pictures and shapes is not nihilistic but genuinely humanistic. Free imaginative play with new forms has been a characteristic of painters like Rouault and Chagall and of architects like Le Corbusier. Often these artists and others like them have worked with traditional religious themes, but even when this is not true their work has an undeniable religious significance. In their various ways contemporary people seek images and symbols by means of which they may communicate the meaningful character of life.

The work of philosophical theologians such as Tillich, Buber, and Suzuki reveals an analogous search and experimentation in the world of ideas for new symbols, or for new interpretations of old symbols which will provide light and power for contemporary minds. Here, in the free play of images in the contemporary mind, the possibility of negative results is always present—as it is in any experiment. Yet also, as in any real experiment, the situation before the experimenter is genuinely open. Clearly the last word has not been spoken. The part of honest and sensitive persons is to find expression as adequately as they can for what they believe to be meaningful and true and to stay in communication with other seekers. In some such terms as these the contemporary experiment with life symbols goes on. The results lie in the lap of future history.

MORAL AND ETHICAL VALUES

Turning our attention to the moral and ethical aspects of ultimate concern or valuation, we note that the contemporary situation seems as fluid as in other aspects. At least a part of the modern criticism of traditional faiths has been moral in its inspiration. Traditional faiths have been criticized because they have violated their own moral values. Teaching justice and love, they have often practiced fanaticism and hate. The details of these criticisms are well known to any thoughtful person, whatever his or her own estimate of them. The commonly accepted conclusions of these criticisms may serve as agenda for the moral features of future faiths.

It has been a feature of most traditional faiths to provide moral values to

Guernica. Mural by Pablo Picasso. (Prado Museum, Madrid.)

Christ Mocked by Soldiers. (Painting by Georges Rouault. Museum of Modern Art, New York, Purchase.)

guide the footsteps of adherents in their active and interpersonal life. The values to which people give allegiance in the experience of faith not only find expression in the symbols of the arts, but they also provide moral guidance. Religion and ethics are thus not two separate and different enterprises but two aspects of basic value experience. Certainly as humanity moves into the unknown future before us, people will need such moral guidance. The only real question is whether the traditional religions will be equal to the task of providing it.

*H*UMANISM AND THE WORLD'S FAITHS

Our study has already come upon at least two distinguishable uses of the multivalued word "humanism," and this section is about to add a third. The first two are respectively the Renaissance concept of human excellence in any and

The Ark Brought to Jerusalem.
Etching by Marc Chagall.
(Museum of Modern Art, New
York, gift of Mr. and Mrs.
Bernard J. Reiss.)

all aspects of cultural life, and the nineteenth-century concept that since the word God is out of date, we should accept Humanity as a substitute.

Our new, third concept of humanism finds its definition in the situation disclosed by our study, that *homo sapiens* is not given its essential nature, namely, humanity, in the way in which other species are given their essential nature as, for example, the dog's caninity, the cow's bovinity, etc. In sharpest contrast, our humanity is not a gift of nature but a dignity to be won—or lost. It has been a central thesis of this book that our humanness, our humanity, is won or lost in the process of active life, in terms of the basic value configuration or system to which we give allegiance. It is a further aspect of this central thesis that each of the world's religious traditions has its own distinctive configuration of values which aims to fulfill or realize our humanity. Thus there is not one humanism; there are several. The task of disclosing these distinctive configurations of value which are the human contents of the world's religions is complicated by the fact that these religions speak a mythopoeic language, a language of expressive symbolic forms. Nonetheless, analysis will make clear the fact that

Le Corbusier's modern church of Notre Dame du Haut, Ronchamps, Alsace. (Courtesy of George Holton.)

among these various value-systems or symbol systems there are both significant similarities and equally significant differences. The basic similarity of each and all of these systems is that they all claim to fulfill or realize our humanity. This assertion constitutes the world's faiths as so many competing humanisms.

Let us try to express these relations among the world's faiths, philosophies, and value-systems by means of a parable. Imagine a circle with one person at the center, and a diverse throng of people spread around its circumference. The person in the middle appears to be talking to him or herself. If we listen carefully, we will be able to hear some muttered questions: Who am I? Why am I here? Why am I alive? or just Why?

The people around the circumference of the circle seem to be calling out their answers to these questions of the person in the middle. Some of these people ignore those around them; some jostle others. There are even quarrels, with curses, charges, and threats, breaking into fighting. A few seem intent to engage others in conversation.

We may identify the person at the center as Everyman of the medieval Christian folk drama. Readers familiar with the contemporary philosophic movement often called Existentialism will recognize its influence on this present formulation, though we hasten to add that ours is more the existentialism of Tillich and Buber than of Heidegger or Sartre. To state the message asserted by our parable in other different terms, let us say that at the human level, life becomes conscious and self-conscious, thus eliciting the existential question, Why am I (or are we) alive? Our thesis is that the central function of the traditional religions, as well as the operative philosophies and secular value-systems, is to provide convincing and illuminating answers to this human question.

Concerning this question and its divers answers, several comments demand to be added. First is that the question itself has very many forms, some of them only partly articulated or conscious. Second, the answers given are not so much discursive or theoretical as practical. This question and these answers are not those of students and teachers in a classroom, but rather are those which are acted out on the playing field of human existence. Third, this whole situation constitutes what the philosopher William James called a forced option. In other words, both question and answer cannot *not* be. The active character of human existence demands or forces question and answer into consciousness, though of course no one answer is demanded or compelled.

At this point some readers will respond that our parable has literally turned the nature of religious faith upside down. Such faith in any or all traditions, they will respond, is not about the human self but is rather about God or transcendence. Indeed, to assert that it is about human life is radically to misunderstand religious experience.

To this we reply that God or transcendence enters religious experience initially as a way of certifying a given answer to the existential question. This answer is not just any answer but that which is given by God or by some other symbolic form for transcendence. The answer itself consists of a way of understanding and living out human existence. Some will reply this last assertion may at first seem to articulate a radical new view of religion. Actually it is no more radical or new than the traditional claim that religions consist of truths to live by.

To this primary claim many religions add important qualifications. For example, Christianity claims not only that God gives us human beings the answer to the question of what or who we are, and how to live, but also gives divine guidance and communion which provides crucial help in living out this relation. As our study has shown, other religions make analogous assertions. Among these many claims are assertions that this or that way is true or adequate, or even more adequate than any of the others.

LET THE BEST FAITH WIN

Glancing backward over the course of human history and prehistory, the student observes many patterns of interreligious relations. Probably the most prevalent pattern over the long course of past history has been mutual isolation and ignorance, interspersed by conflict between peoples and their faiths. Yet these are by no means the only relations. During the Axis Age, the universal religions arose, and with them universal claims. The reader will recall that universal religions are those which, transcending ethnic limits, address their messages in one way or another to all humanity. Most often the universal messages of these religions have taken the form of mission and missionary activity aimed at conversion. Christianity, Judaism, Buddhism, and Islam have all exhibited this pattern of proselytism or conversion from one religion to another.

However, this too is by no means the only way of interreligious relations. History has also shown examples of syncretism or the deliberate mixing of religious traditions. Yet here we must measure words. Wherever people of different religious traditions meet and mingle, there is a mixing and mingling of their religious traditions. Often this mixing of religions is peripheral and not central in character. An example is the peripheral mixing of Christianity with the Platonic tradition of thought and devotion in later Greco-Roman antiquity.

In contrast to such peripheral mixing is that which centrally and intentionally involves the basic images and concepts of two or more different religious traditions. To cite instances of such central mixing, the Moghul emperor Akbar attempted (unsuccessfully, let it be added) such a project in his "Divine Faith." A successful blending of central elements of Islam and Hinduism took place in Sikhism during the same age of Indian history. Other more recent attempts at syncretic mixing have occurred in theosophy and at the Parliament of the Worlds' Religions at the 1893 Chicago World's Fair. The Ramakrishna mission has continued such efforts. A particularly striking proposal for syncretic mixing occurs in Aldous Huxley's later, postskeptical writings, notably *Time Must Have a Stop* and *The Perennial Philosophy*. The Bahai movement in its own way pursues the goal of syncretic mixing. Still other, different ways of interreligious relations continue to occur in the context of modern study of the history of religions.

In sharp contrast to all of these historic ways stands the contemporary proposal for interreligious dialog or, in plain words, for the conversation of faith with faith. To be sure, some such conversation has taken place wherever people of different faiths have met and mingled. To this it must immediately be added that as a consequence of modern means of transportation and communication such meeting of people and faiths is today taking place as never before in history. All that remains is to make this dialog intentional and deliberate.

As this takes place, a few assumptions and preassumptions become explicit. Throughout this study we have noted witness or testimony as a primary form of religious expression and experience. Deeply held convictions seem to demand such expression in one form or another. What is new in interreligious dialog is reciprocal witness or testimony. One party speaks words of witness to the other; then vice versa, the other responds. One of the essential presuppositions of dialog is mutual respect. Closely related is at least enough receptiveness or openness to facilitate mutual comprehension. Such receptiveness may, of course, be dangerous. One may be persuaded or convinced by the other party to the conversation!

The aim of interreligious dialog is mutual understanding, which may or may not lead to agreement. Indeed it may lead to disagreement. In many situations such as activities to promote peace and justice, agreement may lead to common action. However, the possibility of basic disagreement is also always present. In some important respects the world's different faiths, philosophies, and value-systems represent different understandings of human existence and different ways of living out those understandings.

In such circumstances, the conclusion is a competition for human minds and hearts. Let the best faith win! Such a competition will be very different from the competition and conflict of faiths and philosophies in the past. Past competition among religions has been marked by ignorance, acrimony, and conflict, whereas the present context takes place in freedom and deliberately seeks mutual understanding.

It is also important to note that the present competition for human hearts and minds takes place on what may be characterized as the level playing field of secular society. In this new situation, what is meant by "the best faith"? The answer is the most adequate faith, meaning satisfying the widest field of facts encountered in the course of human existence. In religious freedom each one of us will make such judgments of adequacy for ourselves.

A *TIME OF WAITING*

The present postmodern age has been variously characterized as a time of waiting—for God, for Godot, or for whatever surprising new value-systems the future may bring. This chapter has sought to trace a few of the implications of this time of transition for the faiths of humankind.

Some of the readers of these pages are doubtless adherents of one of the world's faiths. Others in equal probability stand apart from all such adherence. Still others will have begun or ended the study as seekers for a faith not yet achieved or clearly articulated. Whatever one's own view, it is well for each person to realize that there are others of eminent intelligence and integrity who disagree with it. It is also well to realize that for all humanity and for all aspects of the human situation, the present is a time of rapid and unprecedented change toward a future so radically open and novel that no one can descry the shape of things to come. In such situations it has been said that we must simply expect the unexpected.

In the things of faith or religion two or three further words may be added. We must face this future with integrity and candor as the only possible basis on which an authentic faith may be erected. Let all persons be what they are seriously led to be, stand where they are seriously led to stand, on whatever convictions form the base of their being. It is well also to face the future with the openness of intellectual and spiritual freedom. Such receptivity is hazardous, for what people take into themselves they become. Yet the opposite attitude of the closed mind and spirit is more than dangerous—it is fatal.

The attitude of combined openness and conviction involves inner tensions which must not be underestimated. Yet many people can testify from personal experience that such tensions can be creative rather than destructive. Recent and current psychology has made much of the viewpoint of the participant-observer, that is, the participant in group activities who simultaneously seeks to observe what takes place in the human interactions involved in the group. Students of religion might well consider the viewpoint of the participant-observer as an approach to faith. They may find here valuable clues for both study and practice.

ISSUES AND QUESTIONS

Since this whole chapter has been devoted to questions and issues concerning the present religious scene, it may seem superfluous to add more issues and questions at the end. Yet it is appropriate to glance back across our whole study, lifting up a few final questions and issues which pertain to the book as a whole.

One such issue, noted in the last section above, has to do with the attitudes of student and participant in religion. By now readers can make their own assessment of this relation. For his part, the author repeats his conviction that those religions which can withstand critical appraisal stand the best chance of continued life. In this sometimes astringent fashion, study can serve the well-being of humanity's faiths.

One all-encompassing issue of great contemporary importance can be put in Arnold Toynbee's concept of "challenge and response." According to Toynbee, history presents challenges to humanity's many civilizations, and only those who successfully meet and cope with these ever-new challenges continue to live and flourish. The whole of Chapters 17 and 18 has dealt with the modern and contemporary challenges to traditional faiths. In a summary word, this challenge to be what traditional faiths have often claimed to be, value-systems by which their adherents live. Their human function is thus the genesis and maintenance of values. Hence, in this context, our last word is the biblical maxim: By their fruits we shall know them.

One contemporary formulation of the function of religion centers in the conception (made widely popular by the late Teilhard de Chardin) of humanization and dehumanization. Religions consist of cluster or configurations of basic value in terms of which human beings win—or lose—their humanity. Thus we humans are persons in the making. In this lifelong process of humanization and its opposite, religious faith plays a central and crucial role.

NOTES

1. Erich Fromm, *Escape from Freedom*, Farrar & Rinehart, New York, 1941, p. 134.
2. Paul Tillich, *The Protestant Era*, James Luther Adams (trans.), University of Chicago Press, Chicago, 1948, pp. xvi and 56–57.
3. Paul Tillich, *Christianity and the Encounter of the World Religions*, Columbia, New York, 1963, pp. 5–6.

4. See inter alia John Bennett, *Christianity and Communism*, Association Press, New York, 1948, pp. 81–82.
5. J. Middleton Murry, *The Necessity of Communism*, Cape, London, 1932.
6. Reinhold Niebuhr, *The Nature and Destiny of Man*, vol. 1, Scribner, New York, 1943; Paul Tillich, *The Religious Situation*, H. Richard Niebuhr (trans.), Meridian Books, New York, 1956. For Temple's writings on this subject, see *The Christian Newsletter* for the 1930s.
7. Edward Shillito, *Nationalism: Man's Other Religion*, Willett, Clark & Co., Chicago, 1933.
8. Will Herberg, *Protestant, Catholic, Jew*, Anchor Books, Doubleday, Garden City, N.Y., 1960, p. 92.
9. Will Herberg, op. cit.; W. Lloyd Warner, *American Life: Dream and Reality*, University of Chicago Press, Chicago, 1953.
10. Robert Bellah, *Beyond Belief*, Harper & Row, New York, 1970, p. 186f.
11. Robin M. Williams, *American Society: A Sociological Interpretation*, Knopf, New York, 1951, p. 312.
12. Carlos Castaneda, *The Teaching of Don Juan*, University of California Press, Berkeley, 1968.
13. Stanislaus Grof, *Realms of the Human Unconscious*, Dutton, New York, 1976.
14. Jacob Needleman, *The New Religions*, Doubleday, Garden City, N.Y., 1970, chap. 5.
15. Ibid., chap. 6.
16. W. T. Chan, *Religious Trends in Modern China*, Columbia, New York, 1953, chap. 4.
17. Floyd Ross, *Shinto: The Way of Japan*, Beacon Press, Boston, 1965.

BIBLIOGRAPHY

Barbour, I.: *Issues in Science and Religion*, Harper & Row, New York, 1965.

Bellah, R. (ed.): *Religion and Human Progress in Asia*, Free Press, New York, 1965.

Berdyaev, N.: *The End of Our Time*, Sheed, New York, 1933.

Brown, R.: *Theology in a New Key: Responding to Liberation Themes*, Westminster John Knox, Louisville, Ky., 1978.

Buber, M.: *Between Man and Man*, Macmillan, New York, 1985.

———: *I and Thou*, Scribner, New York, 1970.

Carmody, J.: *Ecology and Religion*, Paulist Press, Ramsey, NJ, 1983.

Chan, W.: *Religious Trends in Modern China*, Columbia, New York, 1953.

Cobb, J.: *Beyond Dialogue: Toward a Mutual Transformation of Christianity and Buddhism*, Fortress Press, Philadelphia, 1982.

Cox, H.: *Religion in the Secular City*, Simon & Schuster, New York, 1984.

———: *Turning East*, Simon & Schuster, New York, 1977.

Frankel, C.: *The Case for Modern Man*, Books for Libraries Press, Freeport, NY, 1972.

Grof, S.: *Beyond the Brain: Birth, Death, and Transcendence in Psychotherapy*, State University of New York, New York, 1985.

Hammer, R.: *Japan's Religious Ferment*, Greenwood, Westport, Conn., 1985.

Hocking, W.: *Living Religions and a World Faith*, AMS Press, New York, 1976.

Knitter, P.: *No Other Name?*, Orbis, Maryknoll, NY, 1985.

Littell, F.: *From State Church to Religious Pluralism*, Anchor Books, Doubleday, Garden City, NY, 1962.

Marx, K.: *Selected Writings*, D. McLellan (ed.), Oxford, New York, 1977.

Mead, S.: *The Lively Experiment*, L. Feuer (ed.), Harper & Row, New York, 1963.

Needleman, J.: *The New Religions*, Crossroads, New York, 1984.

Niebuhr, R.: *Faith and History*, Scribner, New York, 1949.

———: *Pious and Secular America*, Kelley, New York, 1977.

————: *The Self and the Dramas of History*, University Press of America, Lanham, Md., 1988.

Rahman, F.: *Islam and Modernity*, University of Chicago, Chicago, 1982.

Riesman, D.: *The Lonely Crowd*, Yale, New Haven, Conn., 1952.

Schuon, Frithjof, *The Transcendent Unity of Religions*, Harper & Row, New York, 1975.

Smith, W. C.: *The Meaning and End of Religion*, Harper & Row, New York, 1978.

————: *Towards a World Theology*, Westminster John Knox, Louisville, Ky., 1981.

Suzuki, D.: *Zen Buddhism*, Anchor Books, Garden City, NY, 1956.

Thomsen, H.: *Japan's New Religions*, Tuttle, Rutland, Vt., 1963.

Tillich, P.: *The Courage to Be*, Yale, New Haven, Conn., 1952.

————: *The Future of Religions*, Harper & Row, New York, 1966.

————: *The Protestant Era*, University of Chicago, Chicago, 1957.

————: *Theology of Culture*, Oxford, London, 1959.

Glossary

The key below interprets the symbols which are used in this glossary to designate the various religious traditions with which particular terms are to be identified. The emphasis has been upon relevance rather than exhaustiveness in specifying the path or paths of faith within which a term is commonly encountered. The absence of any symbol whatsoever denotes either that the term is meaningful in most if not all of the major historic religions or that its individual referent is not included among the symbols employed herein. The identifying definitions provide the necessary explanations in either case. The extensive cross references are provided as aids in placing unfamiliar terms into their respective contexts.

Ai: American Indian or Native American
Af: African traditional religion
B: Buddhism
Ch: Christianity
Co: Confucianism, Neo-Confucianism
E: Egyptian religion
F: Folk religion
G: Greek religion
H: Hinduism
I: Islam
Ja: Jainism
Ju: Judaism
M: Mesopotamian religion
Sh: Shinto
Si: Sikhism
T: Taoism, Neo-Taoism
V: The religion of the Vedas
Z: Zoroastrianism

Abhidhamma Pitaka: (B) The "metaphysical Basket" consisting of philosophical treatises, the third section of the Pali canon of scripture (*Tipitaka* q.v.).

abosom: (Af) Spirits or powers, intermediaries between high God and human beings.

adharma: (H) Evil, vice lack of merit; the principle of rest as a constituent of the universe (see *ajiva*), inertia entailing a lack of value, thus, evil.

adhvaryu: (V, H) Altar-building priest.

adi buddha: (B) Primordial buddha nature; see *dharmakaya*.

Adi Granth: (Si) The sacred book of the Sikh faith.

advaita: (H) Nondualism; the monistic school of vedantic philosophy founded by Shankara.

Agni: (V, H) Fire god; sacred fire, of the altar as well as the sun.

agnidh: (V, H) Fire-kindling priest.

agnosticism: Denial of the possibility of knowing (or suspension of judgment concerning) whether there is a transcendent power grounding all finite reality.

ahimsa: (Ja, B, H) Nonviolence; the ethic of noninjury to any and all living beings.

Ahriman: (Z) See *Angra Mainyu*.

Ahura Mazda: (Z) "Wise lord," "lord of light," the one supreme deity who is sovereign over all creation. (For origin of the name see *asuras*.)

ajiva: (Ja) All that is not living (*jiva*, q.v.), comprising space, time, matter, *dharma* (q.v.), and *adharma* (q.v.)

Allah: (I) The one, true, sovereign God; exalted by Muhammad in contradistinction to the polydemonism of earlier Arab religion.

Amaterasu: (Sh) Sun goddess, chief among the pantheon of *kami* (q.v.).

amesha spentas: (Z) Immortal holy ones, modes of divine activity or divine personifications; forerunners of western angelology.

Amitabha (Chinese, Omito; Japanese, Amida): (B) An aspect of universal buddha nature, Buddha's "body of bliss" (*Sambhogakaya*, q.v.); deity of the *sukhavati* heaven (q.v.), widely honored throughout the east as a savior buddha; one of the *dyyani buddhas* (q.v.).

Amma: (Af) Creator god of the Dogon tribe.

anatta: (B) The ultimate unreality of a substantial self or soul; no-ego, no-soul.

anekantavada: (Ja) The many-sidedness of reality; an epistemological doctrine, composed of *nayavada* and *syadvada* (q.v.), which affirms that the world's complexity or multiformity transcends human conceptualizaion of it.

Angra Mainya: (Z) "The evil one"; the chief personification of the spirit of evil in opposition to *Ahura Mazda* (q.v.), engendering an ethical dualism which took on cosmic proportions in later times; known also as *Ahriman*.

anicca: (B) Impermanence, transitoriness, the absence of substantiality in the external world.

animatism: (F) See *manism*.

animism: (F) The primitive belief that everything in nature has a soul (*anima*); the attribution of selfhood to inanimate beings; misplaced personalism. Also, the theory that religion had its origin in such a belief.

anthropomorphism: The attribution of human characteristics to deity.

antinomianism: The practice of seeking salvation in complete freedom from obedience to moral laws, or in deliberate flouting of such laws.

Anu: (M) The god of heaven and erstwhile ruler of the gods.

apocalypse: (Ju, Ch, Z) A vision or revelation of a hidden future, employing bizarre symbolism of its own times, in which present history is seen to be leading up to an impending end.

Apollo: (G) A member of the Olympian pantheon, variously worshiped as a pastoral deity, an archer god, the god of revelation associated with the Delphic oracle, and later a sun god.

Apsu: (M) The primordial god, one of the original divine pair (the other being *Tiamat*, q.v.) from whom all other deities derived.

Aranyakas: (V, H) "Forest books," transitional writings between the *Brahmanas* and *Upanishads* (q.v.); a portion of the vedic tradition.

Artemis: (G) Goddess of wild nature, protector of animals as well as lover of children.

artha: (H) Material prosperity, success; one of the four acceptable aims of human life (*purushartha*, q.v.).

asana: (H) Correct posture and bodily control, the third stage of Yoga discipline.

asat: (V, H) Nonbeing, unreality, chaos; untruth. (See also *sat, satya*.)

Asha: (Z) Truth, the right, in opposition to *Druj* (q.v.); later personified as a deity of fire.

Asherah: (M) Canaanite fertility goddess; consort of *Baal* (q.v.).

Ashramas: (H) Stages of life; particularly in *Jnana marga* (q.v.), the four stages being, successively, that of student, householder, hermit, and ascetic holy man (*sannyasin*, q.v.).

ashvamedha: (V) The horse sacrifice, a late vedic ritual assuring salvation to its accomplisher.

Asta, Arta: (Z) See *Rita*.

asuras (Iranian, ahuras):   (V, Z) In pre-Aryan India, the spirits of natural forces, which came to be regarded in vedic times as evil spirits and by Zoroaster as the opposite. (See also *devas*.)

Atharva Veda: (V, H) The fourth Veda, consisting of magic incantations.

atheism: The denial that there is a transcendent power grounding all finite reality; also, frequently, an attitude functioning as a basis for opposition to particular religious institutions.

Athena: (G) Warrior maiden and, in the Homeric pantheon, goddess of wisdom.

atman: (V, H) Selfhood; absolute or universal self; the foundation of individual subjecthood and therefore the true self; the ultimate as discovered within oneself; the transcendental ego. (See also *brahman-atman*.)

aum, om: (V, H) Mystic syllable, symbolizing the fundamental reality of the universe. Its three letters came to represent the three major Vedas as well as the unity of the three major deities, Brahma, Shiva, and Vishnu. The word is considered to exert mystical power when meditated upon. (B) The threefold body of the Buddha (*trikaya*, q.v.).

autonomy: The situation in which there is no authority over and beyond the human self, which provides its own norms or laws. (See also *heteronomy, theonomy*.)

Avalokitesvara, Lord Avalokita: (B) The Mahayana bodhisattva of great compassion, mercy, and love; known later in feminine form, as *Kuan Yin* in China and as *Kwannon* in Japan.

avatara: (H) "Descent," incarnation, particularly of Vishnu. (B) The coming to human birth of a *bodhisattva* (q.v.).

Avesta: (Z) The sacred scriptures of the Zoroastrian faith, fragmentary and uncohesive in their transmitted state.

avidya: (B, H) Ignorance, consisting in the delusion of the separate existence of the self and a corresponding confusion about the true nature of reality. (See also *vidya*.)

baal: (M) Canaanite fertility deity, often local in scope.

Bardo Thötrol: (B) "Tibetan Book of the Dead," guidebook for transmigrating souls, containing also many of the distinctive values of Tibetan Buddhism.

bar mitzvah: (Ju) Literally, "son of the commandment"; the male coming-of-age ceremony.

belief: Propositional faith; an assent of the intellect to convictions concerning the character of reality.

Bhagavad Gita: (H) "Song of the Lord"; India's most cherished religious document, an epic poem of multiple authorship incorporating a wide variety of philosophical viewpoints; a prime source of *bhakti* (q.v.).

Bhaisaguru: (B) One of the three principal *dhyani buddhas* (q.v.), the buddha of healing.

bhakti: (H) Religious devotion; worshipful adoration of a particular deity as a means of obtaining grace.

bhakti marga: (H) The "way of devotion," one of the three paths to salvation.

bo (or bodhi) tree: (B) "Wisdom tree," the tree under which Guatama was sitting when he attained enlightenment.

bodhisattva: (B) In Theravada, a buddha to be, such as Guatama before his enlightenment and *Maitreya* (q.v.). In Mahayana, a candidate for buddhahood who, on the verge of enlightenment and having attained an almost inexhaustible store of merit, delays entrance into nirvana in order to help suffering humanity.

Bonism: (F) The indigenous folk religion of Tibet before the advent of Buddhism.

bot: (B) Meditation hall in a Theravada monastic complex (*wat*, q.v.)

brahma: (V, H) Prayer; the holy power believed to inhere in the sacrificial prayers of the Brahman priests.

Brahma (masculine): (H) The four-faced creator god in popular Hinduism, a member of the *trimurti* (q.v.).

brahman (neuter): (V, H) Absolute reality, that which is ultimately and supremely real; being as such, being stripped of all its qualifying predicates, hence being in and beyond beings. (See also *brahman-atman*.)

Brahman (or Brahmin): (V, H) A member of the priestly class, at the head of the caste system, which rose to prominence through control of the holy power (*brahma*, q.v.) invoked in the performance of sacrifice and ritual.

brahman-atman: (V, H) The unity of the self with absolute reality, the ultimate lack of distinction between self and not-self; the oneness or absorptive union of the objective and the subjective.

Brahmanas: (V, H) "Priestlies," prose appendixes to the Vedas composed by the Brahmans, containing detailed instruction in the meaning and performance of sacrificial rites.

Brahmanaspati: (V, H) "Lord of the ritual," deification of the power of the sacred prayer word (*brahma*, q.v.) in sacrificial ritual.

Buddha: (B) The "enlightened one" or "awakened one"; originally descriptive of Siddhartha Guatama, founder of Buddhism, but in subsequent developments in Mahayana the term came to encompass a variety and multiplicity of buddha figures which are manifestations of an all-pervading buddha nature underlying the universe. (See *inter alia, trikaya, manushi*

buddhas, dhyani buddhas, bodhisattva.) (H) The ninth avatar of Vishnu.

Bushido: (Sh) "The way of the warrior," a Japanese code of chivalry incorporating Confucian ethics, Japanese feudal traditions, and Zen Buddhist self-discipline. Its classic expression is in the tale of the forty-seven ronin.

butsudana: (B) The "buddha-shelf," an altar often found in private homes in Japan.

caliph: (I) Successor to Muhammad as religious and political leader of the Muslims, though in later times only the latter; any of several successions of such leaders. The last caliphate was ended in 1924 with the overthrow of the Ottoman Empire.

Carvaka: (H) India's indigenous tradition of materialism, heterodox in its rejection of the vedic tradition.

chaitya: (B) Chapel or temple commemorating a holy place and often housing a Buddha relic; a characteristic form of Indian Buddhist art.

Ch'an: (B) "Meditation" (*dhyana*, q.v.); sect of Mahayana in China. (See also *Zen*.)

charisma: An extraordinary power spontaneously emanating from an individual, which thereby invests that person with an influence and authority within the religious community.

Chen yen: (B) "True word," esoteric sect of Mahayana in China, which became *Shingon* in Japan.

ch'eng: (Co) Sincerity, truthfulness.

cheng ming: (Co) "Rectification of names," semantic precision in the use of language as a basis for social order.

chi: (Co) Material force, vital energy pervading all existence; one or two elements generating the universe (the other being *li* q.v.).

chih: (Co) Knowledge, wisdom, insight.

ch'ih: (Co) Conscience; sense of shame for what is evil.

Ching-tu: (B) "Pure Land" sect of Mahayana in China, whose adherents are devoted to *Amitabha* (q.v.).

chinvad bridge: (Z) "Bridge of the separator," upon which the soul's fate is determined after death.

Christ: (Ju, Ch) See *messiah*.

chthonic: (G) A type of deity or divine power that inhabits earth or subterranea.

chün tzu: (Co) "Magnanimous man," the ideal man who embodies all the virtues in their proper combination.

Ch'un ch'iu: (Co, T) "Spring and Autumn Annals," one of the Five Classics of Chinese tradition.

chung: (Co) Moderation, balance, the mean; being in accord with one's true nature, conscientiousness.

Code of Manu: (H) An inportant *dharma shastra* (q.v.).

cosmogony: Theory and lore concerning the origin of the universe.

dagoba: (B) See *stupa*.

daimon, daemon: (G) A secondary divinity ranking between gods and humans; a *godling* (q.v.).

dakhma: (Z) "Tower of silence" where bodies of dead are exposed to birds of prey.

dalai lama: (B) Spiritual leader of Tibetan Buddhism; the present one has been exiled from Tibet since 1959.

Dang: (Af) Important divinity of the Dinka tribe, son of heaven and earth, storm god, ancestor of the Dinkas.

darshana: (H) "Point of view," a system of philosophic thought, sometimes one which is orthodox in its acceptance of the vedic tradition.

day of the Lord: (Ju, Ch) In prophetic literature, the expected decisive intervention of God in history when humanity would be severely judged; in *apocalypse* (q.v.), the last judgment at the end of this evil historical aeon.

Deism: (Ch) A type of natural religion, which is limited to what can be known rationally apart from special revelation.

Demeter: (G) Mother Earth, goddess of fertility.

demiurge: (G) A subordinate deity to whom was ascribed the creation of the material world.

demon: An evil spirit, often dwelling in some element or force of nature and causing misfortune or destruction.

devas (Iranian, daevas): (V, Z) "Shining ones," gods; vedic personifications of beneficent powers of nature, which came to be regarded by Zoroaster as principles of evil, demons. (See also *asuras*.)

Dhammapada: (B) "The way of truth," an important moral treatise within the *Sutta Pitaka* (q.v.) of the Pali scriptures.

dharana: (H) Concentration of attention upon a single object of meditation, the sixth state of Yoga discipline.

dharma (Pali, dhamma): (Ja, B, H) The cosmic moral order of law of righteousness which sustains the universe. This word, not strictly translatable into English, is to be further identified as follows: (Ja) "The good," understood as the principle of motion and accordingly one of the constituents of the universe (see *ajiva*). (B) Truth; the norm; the doctrine of the Buddha; duty; justice. (H) Personal righteousness, virtue, duty, the first of the four ends of human beings (*purushartha*, q.v.).

dharma shastra: (H) A manual for moral guidance teaching the way of *dharma*, a prime example being the *Code of Manu*; such treatises are *smriti* (q.v.).

dharmakaya: (B) The "body of essence," one of the three aspects of the cosmic Buddha (*Trikaya*, q.v.); the primordial buddha nature, known also as *Adi Buddha*; sometimes identified with nirvana.

dhyana: (H, B) Meditation, contemplation. (H) The seventh stage of Yoga discipline. (B) The method of enlightenment in the meditation sects of *Ch'an* and *Zen* (q.v.).

dhyani buddhas: (B) Buddhas of meditation, who have achieved buddhahood as cosmic spirits without human manifestation.

Digambaras: (Ja) The stricter "Skyclad" (unclothed) sect of monks and their lay followers.

Dinka: (Af) Sudanese tribe whose religion was studied by G. Lienhardt in *Divinity and Experience*.

Dionysus:: (G) The god of wine and ecstatic rites around whom a savage mystery cult developed.

docetism: (Ch) The doctrine that the humanity and suffering of Jesus Christ were only apparent and not real; adjudged heretical by the early church.

Druj: (Z) Falsehood, a spirit of evil who in later times became *Satan* (q.v.).

dubkha: (B) Misery, suffering, which is the true nature of existence.

Durga (or Thaga): (H) The fierce patroness of the cult of Thugs, one of the numerous manifestations of *Shakti* (q.v.).

Dyaus Pitar: (V) Father Heaven, comparable to Greek Zeus but suffering an early decline in importance.

Elohim: (Ju, Ch) One of the names by which God was known to early writers of the Old Testament; later identified with *Yahweh* (q.v.).

Enuma Elish: (M) "When on high," the first words of the Babylonian creation story, by which it is known.

Fa chia: (Co) Legalists, the Chou school of political realism in China.

faith: Ultimate or primary valuation, ultimate or unifying concern, embracing the whole of human experience; that life orientation which is determinative of all other allegiances. The expression of this concern in some historic religious community. A set of statements of propositions expounding the content and meaning of this concern (see also *belief*.)

fetish: (F) An inanimate object in which supernatural power, invocable through *magic* (q.v.), is believed to or induced to dwell.

filioque: (Ch) "And from the Son," a phrase inserted in western texts of the Constantinopolitan Creed affirming that the Holy Spirit proceeds from the Father *and* the Son.

fiqh: (I) A system of jurisprudence interpreting the *shari'a* (q.v.).

Fravashi: (Z) Ancestral principles, preexistent external souls of living beings; similarly known in vedic India as *pitaras*.

Gaina Sutra: (Ja) One of the source documents of the Jain faith.

Ganesha: (H) Elephant-headed deity in the Indian popular pantheon.

Garuda: (H) Bird god of popular Indian religion and vehicle of Vishnu.

Gathas: (Z) "Hymns of Zoraster," the oldest part of the *Avesta* (q.v.).

Gemara: (Ju) "Supplementary learning" added to the *Mishnah* (q.v.) to form the *Talmud* (q.v.).

ghost dance: (Ai) Nineteenth-century American Indian movement; members believed that their dance would recall ancestors, restore the past, and bring in a good new age.

Gilgamesh: (M) Semidivine hero of a Babylonian epic structured around the futile quest for immortality.

Gnosticism: (G, Ch) A modern term for a diversified religious-philosophical movement, widespread in the Greco-Roman world, which proclaimed a matter-spirit dualism and a salvation from the former to the latter through secret knowledge (*gnosis*).

godling: A divine spirit or minor deity of considerably restricted dimension, often local in scope.

guna: (H) In *Sankhya* (q.v.), a constituent, quality, or "strand" of matter (*prakriti*, q.v.), of which there are three: *sattva* (intellect, harmony), *rajas* (active power, passion), and *tamas* (inertia, darkness). These three *gunas* in distinctive combination in a human soul (*purusha*, q.v.) define a personality.

gurdwara: (Si) "Gate of the guru," the Sikh temple.

guru: (H) Spiritual teacher. (S) The spiritual and temporal leader of the Sikh community until the termination of the guruship in 1708.

hadith: (I) Tradition, narrative; a recollected saying of Muhammad, of varying authenticity.

haggadah, aggada: (Ju) The nonlegal or narrative traditions incorporated into the *Talmud* (q.v.).

hajj: (I) Pilgrimage to Mecca, the fifth pillar of the faith.

hajji: (I) One who has completed the *hajj* (q.v.).

halakah: (Ju) The legal or normative aspect of the *Talmud* (q.v.).

Hanukkah: (Ju) "Feast of lights," eight-day celebration at the winter solstice commemorating the rededication of the temple during the Maccabean revolt.

Hanuman: (H) The monkey god of Indian popular religion.

haoma: (Z) See *soma*.

Hasidism: (Ju) A mystical and pietistic movement originating in eastern Europe out of the tradition of the *Kabbala* (q.v.).

hegira: (I) The withdrawal of Muhammad from Mecca to Medina in 622, the pivotal occasion which marks the beginning of the Muslim era according to that system of dating.

Hera: (G) Maiden goddess who became the wife of Zeus and patroness of married women.

heteronomy: The situation in which an alien norm or law is imposed upon the self, subjecting the self to bondage. (See also *autonomy, theonomy*.)

Hinayana: (B) The "lesser vehicle" or "small ferryboat." (See *Theravada*.)

holy: The quality of reverence, the emotive accompaniment of ultimate concern and commitment.

homoousion: (Ch) "Of the same essence," a phrase in the Nicene Creed referring to the substantial identity between the Son and the Father in the godhead.

Hosso: (B) See *Yogacarya*.

hotar: (V, H) God-invoking priest.

hsaio: (Co) Filial piety.

hybris: (G) Pride.

hylozoism: The doctrine that all matter has life.

i: (Co) See *yi*.

I ching: (Co, T) "Classic of Changes," a handbook of divination, one of the Five Classics of Chinese tradition.

icon: An image or picture of an object of religious devotion.

idolatry: Devotion to idols or images of deity, regarded as objectionable in monotheistic religions but widely accepted in other types.

ijma: (I) Consensus; agreement by the knowledgeable concerning the validity of a religious opinion.

imam: (I) Leader of prayer in Muslim worship. In *Shi'a*, a divinely appointed successor to Muhammad, comparable to the *caliph* (q.v.) of the *Sunni* (q.v.).

immanence: The doctrine that deity indwells the phenomenal universe. (See also *transcendence*.)

Indra: (V, H) Storm and war god, of major importance in the Vedas but later declining to the status of a minor rain deity.

Indrani: (V, H) Wife of Indra.

isatpragbhara: (Ja) The state of bliss attained by souls beyond the cycle of transmigration; the Jain heaven.

Ishtar: (M) The great mother goddess of the ancient near East, known under a variety of names.

Ismailis: (I) Seveners, Shi'ites who regard Ismail as the seventh imam and authentic successor of Muhammad.

Iza nagi: (Sh) The "male who invites," the sky father among the Japanese *kami* (q.v.).

Iza nami: (Sh) The "female who invites," the earth mother among the *kami* (q.v.), wife of Iza nagi.

Japji: (Si) The traditional morning prayer silently repeated daily by the faithful.

jen: (Co) Human-heartedness, humaneness, concern for humanity; perfect virtue, true humanity, the essential foundation of all moral qualities in the individual.

jihad: (I) "Holy war" waged against non-Muslims.

Jina: (Ja) Conqueror, one of the titles accorded *Mahavira* (q.v.).

jinn: (I) Supernatural spirits of either good or evil. (See also *shaitin*.)

jiriki: (B) In *Jodo* (q.v.), the difficult path to salvation through reliance on one's own human power. (See also *tariki*.)

jijva: (Ja) Life, soul; all that is living, constituting along with *ajiva* (q.v.) the two ultimate, eternal categories of the Jain dualistic universe.

jivan mukti: (H) One who has achieved emancipation

from the burden of *karma-samsara* (q.v.) while still living, through the experience of *samadhi* (q.v.).

Jnana: (H) Saving knowledge, wisdom; comprehension of the all-embracing unity of reality. (See also *vidya*.)

jnana marga: (H) The "way of knowledge," one of the three paths to salvation.

Jodo: (B) A Japanese Pure Land sect founded by Honen, emphasizing human depravity and devotion to Amida through recital of the *Nembutsu* (q.v.).

Ka'ba: (I) "Cube"; the large cube-shaped shrine in Mecca in which the sacred Black Stone is embedded.

Kabbala: (Ju) "Tradition," writings of medieval origin giving expression to an esoteric tradition of mysticism.

kachinas: (Ai) Divinities, ancestral spirits, ceremonial dancers, and image dolls of southwest American Indians.

kalacakra: (Ja, B, H) "Wheel of time," the cosmic symbol of the cyclic character of history.

Kali: (H) Fierce black goddess and consort of Shiva, whose devotees worship her also as the great mother; a particular exemplification of *Shakti* (q.v.).

kama: (H) Love, pleasure, desire, sensuous or sensual fulfillment; one of the four traditional aims of human life (*purushartha*, q.v.); in Indian popular religion, the god of love.

kami: (Sh) Holy power, sometimes personalized; the name given to an innumerable host of entities or phenomena widely ranging from ostensible deities or godlings to mere manifestations of extraordinary or awe-inspiring potency.

kamidana: (Sh) The "god-shelf," an altar in the private home which is the center of worship in domestic Shinto.

kandhas: (B) See *skandhas*.

karma (Pali, kamma): (V, Ja, B, H, Si) The law of the deed, action and its inevitable consequence; the chain of cause and effect which holds a person in bondage to delusion.

karma marga: (H) The "way of works," one of the three paths to salvation.

karma-samsara: (V, Ja, B, H, Si) The fated cycle in which the consequences of human deeds continually result in subsequent incarnations.

karuna: (B) "Feeling with others," compassion, mercy.

kevala, kaivalya: (Ja) A trancelike state of emancipation and perfect knowledge, similar to the Hindu *samadhi* (q.v.).

Khalsa: (Si) The "community of the pure," a strictly disciplined brotherhood whose members bear the name of Singh ("lion").

koan: (B) A riddle or puzzle on which the Zen pupil concentrates as a guide to enlightenment. Known in Ch'an as *kung'an*.

Kojiki: (Sh) "Record of ancient tales," sacred writings dealing with ancient and prehistoric Japan.

Krishna: (H) God-hero of the *Mahabharata* and divine charioteer of Arjuna in the Bhagavad Gita, the eighth avatar of Vishnu and also a god in his own right.

Kshatriya: (V, H) A member of the noble or warrior class, second in rank in the caste system.

Kshitigarbha: (B) The Mahayana bodhisattva who has vowed to deliver all humanity, especially children and the wicked from suffering. Known as *Ti Tsang* in China and as *Jizo* in Japan.

Kuan Yin, Kwannon: (B) See *Avalokitesvara*.

kung'an: See *koan*.

kwei: (T) Evil spirits in Chinese popular religion.

Lakshmi: (H) Wife of Vishnu and giver of good fortune; and exemplification of *Shakti* (q.v.).

lama: (B) "One who is superior," the Tibetan monk.

li: (Co) (1) Good form, propriety, ceremony, decorum, correct order, not only in a human being and society but extending also to the very fabric of the universe. (2) Principle, form, very similar to the Platonic idea, one of two elements which generate the universe (the other being *ch'i*, q.v.). (These are two separate and distinct characters in the Chinese language.)

Li chi: (Co, T) "Record of Rites," the last of the Five Classics of Chinese tradition.

lien:: (Co) Integrity, honesty.

lingam: (V, H) Phallic symbol, particularly prominent in the worship of Shiva.

Logos: (Ju, Ch) Divine word or reason, the chief instrument of God's creative activity regarded in the Christian tradition as having been incarnated in Jesus.

Madhyamika: (B) Central school of Indian Mahayana philosophy, founded by Nagarjuna, which emphasized the ultimate unreality of all appearances and the universality of the void (*shunya*, q.v.).

magi: (Z) The official priesthood in later times, whose origins and precise identity are clouded in mystery.

magic: The endeavor through fixed ritual to bend or control natural phenomena to one's own purposes.

Mahabharata: (H) Epic of over 100,000 stanzas, the world's longest poem, recounting the great war of the bharatas; one of India's chief religious classics (*smriti*, q.v.).

Mahadeva: (H) "The great god," the title accorded *Shiva* (q.v.) by his devotees.

Mahasthama-Prapta: (B) The Mahayana bodhisattva who represents the wisdom and mercy of the Buddha.

Mahavira: (Ja) "Great hero," the name by which Nataputta Vardhamana, the founder of Jainism, is primarily known.

Mahayana: (B) The "great vehicle," "great ferryboat"; the larger, more widespread, more speculative, and less conservative of the major sects; the more inclusive vehicle of salvation. (See also *Theravada*.)

mahdi: (I) The "expected one," the hidden *imam* (q.v.) whose coming will set the world right.

maithuna: (B, H) Sexual intercourse, of a sacramental character in *Tantrism* (q.v.).

Maitreya (Pali, Metteya): (B) The compassionate buddha of the age to come.

maitri (Pali, metta): (B) Loving-kindness, true friendliness, compassion.

mana: (F) Holy power; mysterious, impersonal power indwelling objects, persons, or events, causing them to be regarded as sacred.

mandala: (B, H) A symbolic pictorial representation of the universe, into which gods are sometimes diagrammatically placed.

manism: (F) The theory that religion originated in the perception of *mana* (q.v.) in holy objects; also called *animatism*.

manitu: (Ai) Sacred power or divinity of American Indian peoples. (Also called *orenda*, q.v., and *wakan*.)

Manjusri: (B) The Mahayana bodhisattva of wisdom; the personification of supreme wisdom known in China as *Wen-yu*.

mantra: (V, B, H) A sacred word, verse, or formula mystically embodying a deity or divine power.

manushi buddhas: (B) Figures such as Gautama who have begun from a human base in their attainment of enlightenment and complete buddhahood.

mara: (B, H) Death, sometimes personified as the god of death.

Marduk: (M) Babylonian war god who rose to prominence as creator god and chief deity.

marga: (H) Path, road, way of salvation.

maruts: (V, H) Storm spirits, attendants of *Indra* (q.v.).

maya: (H, Si) Illusion; the delusory appearance of the phenomenal world.

medicine man: (Af, Ai) Religious figure combining oracular prophecy and folk medicine.

messiah: (Ju, Ch) "Anointed one," the divinely appointed ruler who was expected to usher in the kingdom of God on earth; the title accorded Jesus by his followers. Known also, from the Greek, as *Christ*.

michi: (Sh) Path, way.

midrash: (Ju) "Inquiry" into the meaning of the Torah; rabbinical, homiletic interpretation, from which the sermon has been derived.

Ming chia: (Co) The Chou school of Names in ancient China.

Mishnah: (Ju) "Study," the earlier portion of the *Talmud* (q.v.), containing codified collections of laws.

Mithra: (Z, G) Iranian god of war and light, who migrated westward to the Greco-Roman world as *Mithras*, the focus of a widespread mystery cult.

Mohists: Followers of the Chou philosopher Moh tsu, who taught universal love and a personal heaven.

moira: (G) Fate, the impersonal law which controls the destiny of gods as well as humans.

moksha: (V, Ja, B, H) Emancipation; salvation as liberation from the bondage of finitude, the ultimate goal of humanity, which is completely attainable only after death.

monism: The doctrine that all reality is ultimately of a single character, that all is one.

monotheism: (Z, Ju, Ch, I, Si) The doctrine that the transcendent power grounding all finite reality is unitary and personal in character.

mysticism: The doctrine of the achievement of religious experience involving an immediacy of apprehension of the religious object, either in communion or in ontological union and absorption.

myth: Sacred story or narrative which serves as a vehicle for the authoritative expression of central values that provide meaning and direction for human life.

Nandi: (H) Bull god in Indian popular religion and the principle vehicle of Shiva.

nayavada: (Ja) "Viewpoints"; an aspect of the doctrine of man-sidedness (*anekantavada*, q.v.) which affirms that an object of thought may be considered from seven distinct but equally valid points of view.

Nembutsu: (B) "Hail Amida Buddha," the ritual invoking of Buddha's name.

nemesis: (G) Doom, tragic fate, an important element in ancient tragic drama.

neti neti: (V, H) "Not this, not that"; the process of arriving at the true nature of absolute reality by stripping away every qualifying (and therefore, limiting) predicate until one reaches being as such. (See also *via negativa*.)

Nichiren: (B) Japanese sociopolitical sect, characterized by patriotic nationalism combined with Buddhist devotion.

nihilism: Nothingness; the doctrine that nothing exists or is knowable or meaningful.

Nihongi, Nihon Shoki: (Sh) Chronicle of Japan, sacred writings.

nirmanakaya: (B) The "body of manifestation or appearance," the aspect of the cosmic Buddha (*Trikaya*, q.v.) which appears on earth.

nirvana (Pali, nibbana): (B) "Blowing out" of the flame of passion in the cessation of ignorant craving and the attainment of emancipation from finite limitation; the transpersonal state of release from all attributes of phenomenal existence; the supreme goal of human existence.

niyama: (H) Observance of self-culture, the second state of Yoga discipline.

noble eightfold path: (B) The formula of moral and intellectual development leading to enlightenment and emancipation.

Nuer: (Af) African tribe of southern Sudan whose religion is studied by W. Evans-Pritchard in *Nuer Religion*.

nyaya: (H) "Inference"; the orthodox *darshana* (q.v.) of logic semantics.

Olorun: (Af) Creator deity of the Yoruba people.

Om: (V, B, H) See *aum*.

om mani padme hum: (B, H) An extremely potent *mantra* (q.v.) incorporating the sacred syllable (see *aum*), "the jewel" (*mani*) "is in the lotus" (*padme*), and a petition for protection (*hum*).

Omito: (B) See *Amitabha*.

omophagia: (G) A rite of some mystery cults, in which a live animal is torn asunder, its blood drunk, and its flesh eaten by frenzied worshipers.

orenda: (Ai) Spiritual power rendering persons and objects holy or sacred. (Also called *manitu*, q.v., or *wakan*.)

orisa: (Af) Intermediary deities of the Yoruba people.

pagoda: (B) A towerlike structure with a characteristic multiform roof, which may have originated as a *stupa* (q.v.) but which has become important as a center of ritual activity and festival celebrations.

palyopama: (Ja, B, H) A single twelfth-turn of the cosmic wheel of time (*kalacakra*, q.v.).

parinirvana: (B) The full realization of *nirvana* (q.v.), attainable only at the end of earthly existence.

parousia: (Ch) The eschatological second coming of Christ.

Parvati: (H) A consort of Shiva, kind and gracious in demeanor.

path: A cluster of life values which provides humans with convincing and illuminating answers to the fundamental questions of life's meanings.

Persephone: (G) Maiden goddess, daughter of Demeter.

Pesach: (Ju) Passover, vernal festival celebrating Israel's deliverance from Egypt.

Peyote cult: (Ai) American Indian cult centering in sacramental eating of peyote, a hallucenogenic cactus plant.

pharoah: (E) Any of god-kings of ancient Egypt.

Pitaras: (V) "Fathers"; see *Fravashi*.

polytheism: The concept that the powers of gods governing the universe are multiple in number; the practice of being apparently committed to a plurality of ultimate values.

Poseidon: (G) God of the sea and of horses.

Prajapati: (V, H) "Lord of creatures," a creator god in late vedic tradition.

prakriti: (H, Ja) Matter; one of the two basic elements of the universe in *Sankhya* (q.v.), the other being spirit (*purusha*, q.v.).

pranayama: (H) Regulation of the breathing, the fourth state of Yoga discipline.

pratyahara: (H) The freeing of the senses from all objectivity, the fifth stage of Yoga discipline.

Prithivi: (V) Mother Earth, an early goddess linked with *Dyaus Pitar* (q.v.).

prophecy: (Z, Ju, Ch, I) The activity of "speaking for" the one God in monotheistic religions; the "forthtelling" of the divine will by keenly sensitive interpreters of their historic situation, occasionally but not necessarily involving future predictions.

Proto-Shiva: (F) Horned god of pre-Aryan India.

puja: (H) Worship; devotion externally manifested.

Puranas: (H) "Ancient tales," writings which are extremely important for popular piety.

purdah: (I, Si) The veiling and seclusion of women.

Purim: (Ju) Late winter feast associated with the biblical Book of Esther.

purusha: (V) Cosmic person, the soul of the universe. (Ja, B, H) Spirit, mind, the human soul in its essential immateriality. (See also *prakriti, guna*.)

purushartha: (H) The four permissible goals of human life, the traditional ends of human beings. See *artha, dharma, kama, moksha*.

Purva Mimamsa: (H) "Interpretation of the first part [of the Vedas]"; the least philosophical and most conservative of the orthodox *darshanas* (q.v.), characterized by atheism and an emphasis upon the literal validity of the Vedas.

pyramid: (E) Huge square-based stone structures with four triangular sides meeting at a point, built as royal tombs.

Q, Quelle: (Ch) "Source," a hypothetical document containing teachings of Jesus which scholars believe was used in the composition of two of the Gospels, Matthew and Luke.

qari: (I) Reader of the Qur'an at mosque services.

qibla: (I) The direction in which the worshiper faces in prayer (toward Mecca).

Qur'an: (I) The holy book containing the divine revelation to Muhammad, of which the earthly Arabic text is considered to be only a copy of the eternal perfect book in heaven.

rabbi: (Ju) A teacher, expert in the exposition of the Torah.

rajas: (H) One of the *qunas* (q.v.).

Rama: (H) The ideal man, hero of the *Ramayana* (q.v.) and the seventh avatar of Vishnu, sometimes worshiped as a deity in popular religion.

Ramayana: (H) The "adventures of Rama," an epic poem which serves as a major source of popular devotion in Indian religion.

religion: A system of holy forms providing an all-embracing life orientation as a community of *ultimate concern* (q.v.) gathered about a single cluster of concrete symbols.

revelation: (Z, Ju, Ch, I, Si) Divine disclosure of previously unperceived truths, such as the will of God in the meaning of human life.

Rig Veda: (V, H) The earliest and most significant of the Vedas and the oldest source of Aryan religion, comprising a wealth of religious poetry of multiple authorship, dating from the second millenium B.C. though remaining in oral tradition for a number of centuries.

rishi: (V, H) Seer, sage, inspired poet; one of those who were originally responsible for the composition of the Vedas.

Rita: (V) Cosmic order or the deified personification thereof, known similarly in Iran as *Asta* or *Arta.*

ritual: The ceremonial observance of formal symbolic actions relating to some particular occasion or aspect of individual or social life.

Rosh Hashanah: (Ju) The New Year observance in the religious calendar.

Rudra: (V) A storm god who later became *Shiva* (q.v.).

sabbath: (Ju) The seventh day of the week, observed as a holy day of rest.

sacred: The accompanying attribution of that which is valued as of ultimate concern.

sadhu: (H) Holy man, one who has achieved an experience of undifferentiated unity with the absolute. (See also *sannyasin, samadhi, jivan mukti.*)

salvation: The attainment of a wholeness of being in which the vicissitudes of human existence are overcome whether in ultimate fulfillment of one's true personhood, in a transpersonal emancipation from bondage to phenomenality, or in realization of other conceptual models.

Sama Veda: (V, H) The third of the Vedas, consisting of selections from the Rig Veda used in ritual.

samadhi: (Ja, B, H) A trancelike state in which the individual achieves an experience of absorption into ultimate reality while still living; in Yoga, emancipation, the eighth and final stage of self-discipline.

Samantabhadra: (B) The Mahayana bodhisattva of compassion and mercy; known in China as *P'uhien.*

Sambhogakaya: (B) The "body of bliss," one of the three aspects of the cosmic buddha (*Trikaya,* q.v.), known also as *Amitabha* (q.v.).

samsara: (V, Ja, B, H, Si) Transmigration of the human soul through successive rebirths; perpetual reincarnation. (See also *karma-samsara.*)

samurai: (Sh, Co, B) The military or warrior class of Japanese feudalism. (See also *bushido.*)

Sangha: (B) The monastic order founded by the Buddha, continuing to the present day in Theravada and in some other Buddhist groups.

Sanhedrin: (Ju) The council of elders, a rabbinical body with religious jurisdiction in post-exilic Judea.

Sankhya: (H) "Distinction"; the orthodox *darshana* (q.v.) which emphasizes the attainment of salvation through properly distinguishing between spirit and soul (*purusha,* q.v.) and matter (*prakriti,* q.v.).

sannyasin: (H) The fourth state (*ashrama,* q.v.) of life in which the individual experiences *samadhi* (q.v.),

thereby becoming *jivan mukti* (q.v.); consequently, an ascetic holy person similar to the *sadhu* (q.v.).

Sarasvati: (H) Wife of Brahma and patroness of wisdom; a manifestation of *Shakti* (q.v.).

sat: (V, H) Being, the existent, the ordered universe.

Satan: (Z, Ju, Ch, I) Originally, the father of lies (see *Druj*), who migrated from Iran to become identified with the chief spirit and personification of evil in a cosmic framework of moral dualism. (See also *shaitin.*)

sati: (H, Si) The self-immolation of a widow on her husband's funeral pyre.

satori: (B) In *Zen* (q.v.), the immediate experience of enlightenment or awakening, transrational and transpersonal in character.

sattva: (H) One of the *gunas* (q.v.).

satya: (V, H) Truth, the real

satyagraha: (H) "Truth force" of Mohandas Gandhi, known in the west as the doctrine of nonviolent resistance.

Savitar: (V, H) A solar deity who functions as stimulator, generator, vivifier.

Seder: (Ju) Family meal which is the major element in the Passover celebration (*Pesach,* q.v.).

shahada: (I) The fundamental confession, "There is no God but God (Allah), and Muhammad is his prophet," the recital of which constitutes the first pillar of faith.

shaitin: (I) The evil *jinn* (q.v.) whose leader is "the Shaitin," God's adversary and humankind's tempter. (See also *Satan.*)

Shakti: (H, B) "Female power"; the personification of a god's power or energy; the essential mother goddess in all her various exemplifications.

shalako: (Ai) Annual winter dance ceremony of the Zuni people, renewing the life of the community.

shaman: (F) Sorceror priest who endeavors to secure desired results through the practice of *magic* (q.v.).

Shamash: (M) Babylonian sun god, from whom Hammurabi was presumed to have received his famous law code.

Shang-ti: "Lord on high," pre-Chou Chinese designation of Heaven. (See *T'ien.*)

shari'a: (I) The whole body of religious law which is conceived to have authority over all human life, individual and social.

Shebuoth: (Ju) Pentecost, the celebration of the giving of the *Torah* (q.v.) on Mount Sinai.

shen: (T) Good spirits in Chinese popular religion.

Shi'a: (I) "Followers"; the Muslim party whose adherents (*Shi'ites*) are followers of Ali as the divinely appointed first successor (*imam*) to Muhammad. (See also *Sunni.*)

Shih ching: (Co, T) "Classic of Songs" or "Book of Odes," a poetic miscellany which is one of the Five Classics of Chinese tradition.

Shin: (B) A Japanese Pure Land sect founded by Shinran, similar to *jodo* (q.v.) but with a stronger emphasis upon the importance of inward faith.

Shingon: (B) See *Chen yen.*

shirk: (I) "Association" of anything creaturely with the one true God; hence idolatry, the cardinal sin.

Shiva: (V, H) "The auspicious one," the destroyer; a major deity in the popular pantheon and a member of the *trimurti* (q.v.). (See also *Rudra, Mahadeva.*)

shruti: (V, H) "Heard," referring to writings believed to have been divinely revealed to an inspired individual (*rishi*, q.v.); hence, sacred literature distinct from uncanonical writings (*smitri*, q.v.).

shu: (Co) Reciprocity, a moral principle comparable to the golden rule of Christianity.

Shu ching: (Co, T) "Classic of Documents" or "Book of History," a collection of chronicles and the like, one of the Five Classics of Chinese tradition.

Shudra: (V, H) A member of the servant class at the bottom of the cast system, generally non-Aryan in race.

shunya: (B) Void, emptiness; that which is devoid of all distinguishing characteristics and thus has no phenomenal existence; hence, blessedness beyond existence. (See also *Madhyamika.*)

Shvetambaras: (Ja) The less conservative "White-clad" sect of monks and their lay followers, which comprises the majority of the Jain faithful.

sikh: (Si) Disciple, student; specifically, a follower of the way of Nanak.

Sita: (H) The supremely virtuous wife of Rama in the *Ramayana* (q.v.).

skandhas (Pali, kandhas): (B) The five personality components which enter into temporary and non-substantial combination to form an apparent soul or self.

smriti: (V, H) "Remembered," referring to writings which have arisen out of the teachings of ancient sages; hence, religious classics as distinguished from canonical scripture (*shruti*, q.v.) on which they are largely based.

soma (Iranian, haoma): (V, H, Z) A potent drink used as a sacrificial libation because of its tendency to induce visions and feelings of religious exaltation; sometimes deified, as the lord of the drink who is responsible for its intoxicating potency.

Spenta Mainyu: (Z) Holy spirit of *Ahura Mazda* (q.v.), sometimes conceived of as a separate angelic being.

sphinx: (E) Large statue or figure having the body of a lion and the head of a man, ram or ox.

Sthanakvasis: (Ja) An iconoclastic sect of late origin which has rejected ritual and temple worship.

stupa: (B) An earth mound enshrining a relic of the Buddha, sometimes constructed with a *wat* (q.v.), which usually tapers upward gracefully to a pointed pinnacle; known similarly in Ceylon as the *dagoba*. (See also *pagoda*.)

Succoth: "Feast of booths," an autumn celebration commemorating Israel's sojourn in the wilderness.

Sufi: (I) "Wool wearer," the name given to the communities of mystics after the clothing which their ascetic predecessors originally wore.

sukhavati heaven: (B) The pure or happy land, a paradise of the intermediate realm between nirvana and the world, presided over by *Amitabha* (q.v.).

Sun dance: (Ai) Traditional ceremonial dance of plains Indians of United States and Canada, renewing the life of the community.

sunna: (I) The body of orthodox tradition incorporating prophetic teachings outside the Qur'an.

Sunna: (I) The traditionalist party which constitutes the major Muslim way.

sunni: (I) A member of the majority party which adheres to the entirety of the Sunna. (See also *Shi'a.*.)

sura: (I) A section or chapter of the Qur'an, of which there are 114.

Surya: (V, H) The sun or sun god; often linked with *Ushas*, the goddess of the dawn.

Susa-no-o: (Sh) The storm kami and brother of *Amaterasu* (q.v.).

Sutra (Pali, Sutta): (B) A discourse attributed to the Buddha or a disciple which now holds the status of scripture.

Sutta Pitaka: (B) The "basket of discourses," a collection of didactic material which constitutes the second section of the Pali canon of scripture (*Tipitaka*, q.v.).

svarga: (B, H) Heaven; a concept employed, in lieu of nirvana, by both King Ashoka and *Purva Mimanmsa* (q.v.).

swadeshi: (H) Loyalty to one's own land or tradition, a central concept in the thought of Gandhi and his followers.

syadvada: (Ja) "Perhaps," conditional or relative predication; an aspect of the doctrine of many-sidedness (*anekantavada*, q.v.), which affirms that reality expresses itself in multiple forms so that no absolute predication concerning an object of thought is possible (wherefore "perhaps" or "somehow" must be prefixed to every statement).

symbol: A word, object, or event which mediates an experience of the holy by evoking and sustaining a conscious awareness of ultimate concern.

syncretism: The intentional merging of elements from two or more separate traditions or religious movements into a single path of faith.

taboo: (F) That which is forbidden to ordinary use because of the presence of holy power therein.

tadekam: (V) "That one [thing]," the impersonal creative impulse in late cosmogonic speculation, which as primal reality is neither being nor nonbeing and out of which arises the gods as well as all phenomenal reality.

T'ai chi: (Co) The great ultimate, the one supreme ultimate reality which is infinitely manifested throughout the universe.

Talmud: (Ju) "Learning," the multivolume interpretation of the *Torah* (q.v.) put together by rabbinical scholarship of several centuries.

tamas: (H) One of the *gunas* (q.v.).

tannaim: (Ju) Oral rabbinic teachings, often in pairs of opposites, which became codified in the *Mishnah* (q.v.).

tantra: (B, H) Any one of a considerable number of religious texts and ritual manuals of late origin which are the basic treatises for *Tantrism* (q.v.).

Tantrayana: (B) The "vehicle of the tantras," a name for tantric Buddhism (see *Tantrism*).

Tantrism: (B, H) An esoteric religious movement which places particular emphasis upon magical rites and formulas, erotic practices, and mystical experiences as aids to the achievement of salvation.

Tao: (T, Co) Cosmic way or path; the eternal dynamic way of the universe and its preordained rational structure. To tread the Tao is to live in perfect harmony with the cosmic order.

Tao te ching: (T) "Classic of the Way and Its Power," a brief cryptic poem attributed to Lao tsu which functions as the authoritative source for Taoist tradition.

tapas: (Ja, H) Asceticism, practiced as a means of achieving emancipation of the soul from bondage to material things.

tara: (B) Savioress, consort of a deity, comparable to the Hindu *Shakti* (q.v.).

tariki: (B) In *Jodo* (q.v.), the easy path to salvation through relying on the power of another, i.e., dependence on the grace of *Amida* (q.v.). (See also *jiriki*.)

tat tvam asi: (V, H) "That art thou"; the ultimate identity between self and objective reality. (See *brahman-atman*.)

tathata: (B) "Suchness," that *Yogacarya* (q.v.) concept of the absolute, the positive aspect of the void (*shunya*, q.v.); pure undifferentiated being, which alone truly exists and which is the source of the phenomenal world.

Tendai: (B) Japanese sect founded by Saicho, emphasizing the teachings of the Lotus Sutra.

theism: The view of reality which affirms a transcendent power grounding all finite being. (See also *monotheism, monism*.)

theocracy: Government of a people by leaders who claim to rule according to divine authority.

theology: Rational inquiry into matters pertaining to deity and to the relations of deity to humans; the endeavor to achieve critical understanding of the object of the ultimate concern of oneself or of others.

theonomy: The ideal situation in which the normative demands of the object of one's ultimate valuation are identical to the fundamental aspirations of human selfhood. (See also *autonomy, heteronomy*.)

theophany: The visible manifestation of God or a god to a human being, usually in some tangible form.

theotokos: (Ch) "Bearer of God," a title applied to Mary, the mother of Jesus, in the early church.

Theravada: (B) "Way of the elders," the more conservative of the major sects, which insists on the sole authenticity of the Pali canon of the scriptures (*Tipitaka*, q.v.) and claims direct descent from the Buddha. (See also *Mahayana*.)

Thunderbird: (Ai) Divinity of spring and guardian of tribe for several American Indian peoples.

Tiamat: (M) Primeval goddess whose slain body becomes heaven and earth in the cosmogonic myth of the *Enuma Elish* (q.v.).

T'ien: (Co, T) "Heaven" as the source of human destiny and object of natural piety, conceived in terms of impersonal divinity.

T'ien ming: (Co, T) "Mandate of Heaven," the divine sanction under which a Chinese ruler was considered to govern.

T'ien t'ai: (B) "Heavenly Terrace" sect of Mahayana in China, similar to the Japanese *Tendai* (q.v.).

Tipitaka (Sanskrit, Tripitaka): (B) "Three baskets," the Pali canon of scripture which is recognized as authoritative by Theravada and which is partially accepted in its Sanskrit version by most Mahayana sects.

tirthankara: (Ja) "Ford finder," one who discovers a way across the stream of human misery to the far shore of salvation. Tradition mentions twenty-four of them, the last having been *Mahavira* (q.v.).

Torah: (Ju) "The law"; the first five books in the Hebrew canon, comprising the Pentateuch.

totem: (F) An animal or natural object from which a tribe envisages itself to be descended and around which group life is centered.

transcendence: The doctrine that deity stands over against all finite reality as its ground and source. (See also *immanence*.)

transubstantiation: (Ch) The Roman Catholic doctrine of the miraculous transformation of the inner substantial reality of the eucharistic elements into the body and blood of Christ in the priest's performance of the mass.

trickster: (Ai, Af) Recurring divine figure whose role is to play tricks and jokes on human beings, also at times a creator deity.

trikaya: (B) In Mahayana, the "three bodies" of the Buddha, comprising the primordial and ultimate "body of essence" (*Dharmakaya*), from which emanate its heavenly manifestations constituting the "body of bliss" (*Sambhogakaya*), from which in turn has emanated the "body of appearance" (*Nirmanakaya*), which alone has been present in earthly existence. (See also *trimurti, trinity.*)

trimurti: (H) The great triad of Brahma, Shiva, and Vishnu, sometimes regarded as the threefold manifestations of absolute reality (*brahman*, q.v.) or as the universe in its triple role as creator, destroyer, and preserver. (See also *Trikaya, trinity.*)

trinity: (Ch) The doctrine of the threefold character of the godhead as Father, Son, and Holy Spirit, traditionally understood as three eternal and ungenerated manifestations of a single personal reality.

trishna: (B) Ignorant craving; the desire for self-gratification in separateness from one's cosmos, which is the root of human misery (*dubkha*, q.v.).

tushita heaven: (B) A heaven below the level of the buddha realms, from which the preexistent Buddha descended to earth and where the future buddha now resides.

Tvashtar: (V, H) The divine blacksmith.

ulama: (I) Conservative scholars learned in the Qur'an and the Tradition (*Sunna*, q.v.).

ultimate concern: Ultimate or primary valuation, unconditional and unqualified values or loyalties; those all-embracing convictions which give unity and meaning to the life of an individual or of an entire culture.

Uma: (H) Goddess of light and a consort of Shiva.

Upanishads: (V, H) Highly philosophical writings, originally appendices to the *Aranyakas* (q.v.), which complete the body of vedic literature recognized as *shruti* (q.v.).

upaya: "Skillful means," or a way of thinking in *Mahayana* (q.v.) in which the basic ideas of Buddhism are freshly related to changing situations in the world.

Ushas: (V, H) Goddess of the dawn. (See also *Surya.*)

Utnapishtim: (M) Narrator of the Babylonian flood story in the Gilgamesh epic.

Vairocana: (B) A solar deity and manifestation of the primordial nature of the cosmic Buddha (see *Dharmakaya*).

Vaishya: (V, H) A member of the working class of merchants, artisans, and farmers, third in rank in the caste system.

vajapeya: (V) A royal rejuvenation ceremony in late vedic ritual.

Vajrapani: (B) The Mahayana bodhisattva of power.

Vajrayana: (B) The "thunderbolt vehicle," the esoteric sect of tantric Buddhism (see *Tantrism*).

Varuna: (V) Sky god, who became morally important as the source of all righteousness, the revealer of sin, the judge of truth, and the one who rewards and punishes.

Vayu: (V, H) Deity of the wind.

Veda: (V, H) "Knowledge"; the most ancient of India's sacred writings, regarded as divinely revealed to inspired seers (*rishi*, q.v.) and therefore *shruti* (q.v.). The four Vedas proper (*Rig, Yajur, Sama*, and *Atharva*, q.v.) constitute Veda Samhita, whereas the entire corpus includes also the interpretive appendices of the Samhita (the *Brahmanas, Aranyakas*, and *Upanishads*, q.v.).

Vedanta: (H) "End of the Veda"; the most influential and significant of the orthodox *darshanas* (q.v.), which is primarily interested in the doctrines of the Upanishads (which are the culmination of the Vedas); characterized by philosophic idealism and varying degrees of monism. (See also *advaita*)

via negativa: The "way of negation," wherein one endeavors to comprehend the nature of God or absolute reality by discerning what it is not. (See also *neti neti.*)

vidya: (B, H) Knowledge as comprehension of the ultimately real. (See also *avidya, jnana.*)

vibara: (B) Monastery, chapel.

Vijnanavada: (B) See *Yogacara.*

Vinaya Pitaka: (B) The "basket of discipline" consisting of monastic rules, the first section of the Pali canon of scripture (*Tipitaka*, q.v.).

Vishnu: (V, H) The "preserver," and exemplar of divine love, who descends to earth in numerous incarnations (see *avatara*); a member of the *trimurti* (q.v.) among the pantheon of deities.

Vishvakarman: (V, H) "Maker [or doer] of all," an apparent creator deity of later vedic writings.

vision quest: (Ai) Coming-of-age rite of American Indian peoples, in which young people are sent into the wilderness for solitary meditation in quest of a vision of tutelary spirits, which fixes the individual's character and life.

Vohu Manah: (Z) The angel of good thought, through whom Zoroaster received many of his divine revelations.

Vritra: (V) The chief of the demons, slain by Indra in a vedic cosmogonic myth.

wakan: (Ai) See *orenda.*

Wakan taka: (Ai) "Great spirit" as embodiment of *wakan* or holy power.

wat: (B) The characteristic walled cluster of buildings constituting a monastic complex in Theravada lands.

Wei Shih: (B) See *Yogacarya.*

woman power: (Ai) Belief prevalent among many American Indian peoples that women embody numinous or holy power.

Wounded Knee: (Ai) Massacre by United States soldiers of American Indians who wore ghost shirts and believed that the *ghost dance* (q.v.) would protect them from evil.

Wowoka: (Ai) American Indian messianic leader of the nineteenth century.

wu: (T) Nothingness, nonbeing, emptiness, with which the *Tao* (q.v.) is sometimes identified.

wu wei: (T) Nonaction, passivity, "action without action," which constitutes the core of the Taoist ethic.

Yahweh: (Ju, Ch) "Lord"; the English rendition of the Hebrew YHWH by which God was known among the Israelites, particularly after the exodus.

Yajur Veda: (V, H) The second Veda, which contains sacrificial formulas.

Yama: (V, H) Lord of the dead.

yama: (H) Restraint, self-control, the death of desire, the initial stage of Yoga discipline.

yang: (T, Co) The cosmic energy mode which is the active, bright, warm, dry, masculine principle, comprising with *yin* (q.v.) the *Tao* (q.v.).

yantra: (B, H) A geometrical diagram employed in tantric magic rites.

YHWH: (Ju, Ch) See *Yahweh*.

yi, i: (Co) Duty, obligation, righteousness, right relationship; the correct form of social relations as concrete expressions of *jen* and *shu* (q.v.).

yin: (T, Co) The cosmic energy mode which is the passive, dark, cold, wet, feminine principle, comprising with *yang* (q.v.) the Tao.

Yoga: (H) The way of salvation through inner discipline; the specific *darshana* (q.v.) which teaches a rigorous system of self-discipline aimed at developing one's powers of insight in meditation as a means of emancipation, sometimes regarded as the practical counterpart of the philosophy of *Sankhya* (q.v.).

Yogacarya: (B) The "way of union," the Indian Mahayana philosophy of idealism emphasizing an essential or absolute consciousness (*alayavijnana*, q.v.) as being the ultimate character of reality (see *tathata*); known also as *Vijnanavada* ("consciousness only"), which became *Wei Shih* in China and *Hosso* in Japan.

Yom Kippur: (Ju) The day of atonement, the tenth day of the Jewish New Year.

yoni: (V, H) Ring-shaped female sex symbol. (See also *lingam*.)

yu wei: (T) Activity, active doing, the undersirable opposite of *wu wei* (q.v.).

zaddikim: (Ju) The "righteousness ones," the rabbinical leaders of *Hasidism* (q.v.).

zakat: (I) Almsgiving, the fourth pillar of the faith.

zazen: (B) In *Zen* (q.v.), the technique of sitting for long periods in disciplined meditation as a necessary preparation f r *satori* (q.v.).

Zen: (B) "Meditation" (*dhyana*, q.v.) sect of Mahayana in Japan, nontheistic in character and this-worldly in orientation, wherein the truth is sought in the unity of immanent reality.

Zeus: (G) Father Sky; chief of all the deities in the Olympian pantheon.

ziggurat: (M) Pyramidic edifice at the center of a temple compound, symbolizing the earth mountain.

zurvan: (Z) "Boundless time"; in late developments, the impersonal principle of time for which all reality derives.

Index